JOHN BROWN PATON

Photo by Pendry, Nottingham.

J B Paton

[Frontispiece

JOHN BROWN PATON

A BIOGRAPHY

BY HIS SON
JOHN LEWIS PATON

HODDER AND STOUGHTON
LONDON   NEW YORK   TORONTO

Printed in 1914

TO

MY SISTER MARY

My best acknowledgments are due to many relatives and friends who have given me help in many various ways; to the Lord Bishop of Hereford (Dr. Percival), to the late Mr. Andrew Brown Paton, to Mrs. Mary Higgs of Oldham, Miss Emily H. Smith, Miss C. A. Scott, Miss Julie Sutter; to the Rev. David Watson, Rev. J. E. Flower, Sir A. W. Dale, Mr. C. E. Hecht, the late Mr. Jas. Stuart; to old students, especially the Revs. J. W. Dickson of St. Helens; R. Reid of Pendleton; Luke Beaumont of Rock Ferry; Alfred Cooke, A. G. E. Gibson of Middlesbrough; J. H. Fry of Norwich; Robert Jackson of Brighton; W. Robinson of Lytham; John Stevenson of Sutton-in-Ashfield; Thomas Towers, F. W. B. Weeks; to Mr. J. Harrison of Preston Bows; the Revs. James Marchant, J. A. Meeson, J. Radford Thomson, Principal D. L. Ritchie, Mr. A. Mansbridge—also to my senior colleague, Mr. Francis Jones, of the Manchester Grammar School, who made it possible for me to have the necessary leisure for this work.

MANCHESTER GRAMMAR SCHOOL,
    Sept. 1913.

To you, who underneath the weight of years
   Wear the young heart that Hope alone can feed,
   To you, who from the snare of party freed
Christ's will in all our wranglings still can hear,
Who still can see the Gospel vision clear,
   Gleam-follower, you who know the nation's need
   And Churchman of all Churches still must plead
For faith to fight and love to persevere.

To you, knights-errant of the Table Round,
   We come with tidings of our perilous quest
      To hear your voice and see your eyes flash light,
   And though no more your lance is set in rest,
Unfaltering still your lips the call shall sound
   To send us back fresh-hearted to the fight.

H. D. RAWNSLEY.

1910.

CONTENTS

CHAPTER I

BIRTH AND BOYHOOD . . . . . . PAGE 1

CHAPTER II

COLLEGE DAYS 20

CHAPTER III

SHEFFIELD 30

CHAPTER IV

MARRIAGE 53

CHAPTER V

LITERARY WORK 66

CHAPTER VI

THE FOUNDING OF THE INSTITUTE . . . 75

ix

CHAPTER VII

PAGE

THE INSTITUTE AT WORK 95

CHAPTER VIII

PASTORUM PASTOR 115

CHAPTER IX

CIVIC WORK AT NOTTINGHAM. THE OLD CATHOLIC
    MOVEMENT 131

CHAPTER X

THE EXPANSION OF EDUCATION 145

CHAPTER XI

THE INNER MISSION 186

CHAPTER XII

THE BUILDING OF THE EDUCATIONAL BRIDGE . 200

CHAPTER XIII

SOCIAL INSTITUTES AND SOCIAL HOLIDAYS . . 212

CHAPTER XIV

THE LAND PROBLEM 235

CHAPTER XV

PAGE

THE COLONY OF MERCY 246

CHAPTER XVI

NATIONAL HOME READING 270

CHAPTER XVII

THE SUNDAY-SCHOOL 298

CHAPTER XVIII

TO SAVE LIFE 311

CHAPTER XIX

RETIRING FROM THE PRINCIPALSHIP . . . 332

CHAPTER XX

A MINISTER AT LARGE—THE PRAYER UNION . 375

CHAPTER XXI

THE EDUCATION QUESTION 389

CHAPTER XXII

THE INSTITUTE OF SOCIAL SERVICE . . . 404

CHAPTER XXIII

PAGE

THE YOUNG MEN'S BRIGADE OF SERVICE . . 421

CHAPTER XXIV

THE NEW GOSPEL IN SCOTLAND 436

CHAPTER XXV

MINISTERIAL JUBILEE 447

CHAPTER XXVI

CHINA 453

CHAPTER XXVII

THE PROBLEM OF THE CITY POOR . . . 468

CHAPTER XXVIII

THE CHURCH 479

CHAPTER XXIX

TWILIGHT AND EVENING BELL 499

BIBLIOGRAPHY 527

INDEX 531

ILLUSTRATIONS

J. B. Paton . . . . . . *Frontispiece*

PAGE

J. B. Paton, Æt. 30 48

Congregational Institute, Nottingham . . . 80

J. B. Paton, Æt. 40 144

Lingfield : The Farm, and the Colonists at Work . 236

Lingfield : A Group of Colonists, with the House Father and Mother 240

Lingfield : At Work in the Fields . . . 244

Epileptic Colony, Starnthwaite, near Kendal . 264

Mrs. Paton 520

INTRODUCTION

WHEN a new era is about to dawn, God sends his prophets to prepare the way. A new era is dawning in Britain. We are moving towards a new social order based on a new conception of the worth and potentialities of human life, permeated with a new and vital spirit of human brotherhood. The prophets have not been wanting, and among the leaders who bore their part in the increasing purpose of their age, worthy to rank " in high collateral glory " with the great, was John Brown Paton.

The generation in which he was born accepted the social evils of the day as part of the ordained system of things, which must be endured, and could at best be palliated. To him the very existence of those social evils was a challenge to the heart, intellect, and energies of organised Christianity. For Paton to discover the existence of an evil was simply to know that it must be overcome. To sit down under it and accept defeat was to put a limit on Christ's power to save, an insult to the Lord and Giver of life.

It is the distinguishing quality of a great mind that it sees things on a large scale, envisages a problem as a whole, attaches itself to great objects, and plans a campaign before it fights a battle. Paton had the synoptical and strategic mind. Early in life he learned from Immanuel Wichern the idea of the Inner Mission, and all his manifold philanthropic activities were inspired by that central idea.

He had not only the synoptical mind, but the instinct for action. The Church of the middle of the nineteenth century as a whole had lost its daring, its power of attack. Whatever its enterprise in the mission field, it was at home what Abraham Lincoln would have called " a stationary engine." It was content to hold its own against the attacks of science, it fished for men with an angler's rod. Paton showed it how to cast the net with a wide sweep, and take the aggressive by a demonstration of new power in organised works of healing and mercy and social uplift. All his work was constructive, for he held that the way to banish an evil spirit was to find the right spirit which could fill its place, and he always believed that good was stronger than evil. All his work was in the line of a positive synthesis between personal and social salvation; and those who knew him best could see that it was his own inward synthesis taking objective shape. To him the history of the world was the history of a great redemption; that redemption was still in process of evolution; it was man's glory to work it out in co-operation with his Redeemer. It was a redemption of the whole man, body, mind, and spirit; it was a redemption in the world, not out of it. Like the seer on Patmos, he saw the heavenly city descending from heaven, begotten of heaven but realised on earth.

Emerson expresses the desire for " some one to show me how to do what I can do." That is what thousands feel, and that is the question that John Brown Paton set himself to answer. His ultimate vision was of far horizons, but his immediate plan of operations was near and actual. He set himself to stem the wastage of our educational system in the period of adolescence, and the rapid deterioration of character which accompanied it. Evening classes, clubs, social institutes, brigades for boys and girls, intellectual discipline, physical exercise, games and recreation, reading, music, art, every wholesome kind of activity which can combat and replace the demoralising influences of our crowded cities—all found an advocate in him. He awakened people to see the growing peril of rural depopulation, and set himself to learn all he could from Continental nations, and the sporadic efforts of earnest folk in our own country, that he might bring all possible lessons of experience to bear upon the solution of the problem. He felt the tragedy of unemployment and the cold cruelty of the Poor Law. He had a heart for the crippled and epileptic child. From his feeling were born the labour colonies and epileptic homes at Lingfield, Starnthwaite and Marple, where those " who once were men " become men again. He saw how the gifts of reading and leisure were to many a curse rather than a blessing, through lack of some one to show the more excellent way, and the Home Reading Union, the social institutes came into being. He laboured for what he called " applied Christianity "—civic leagues of help which should unite all men and women of good-will in each town to work together for the welfare of the poor and weak, for the relief of poverty, the increase of health and beauty in the city. By such means and many others he sought to work out in practice the great plan of redemption, not alone by converting individual souls and training individual lives, but by providing new and healthy conditions of life for men, by kindling the love of service and the feeling of brotherhood, and inspiring all human law and custom with a definite, normative Christian purpose and motive.

He could not have set all these societies going, and kept them going, unless he had been a wonderful persuader and inspirer of men. No one who met him failed to catch something of his fire. He not only showed men the path to tread and the work for them to do, he made them feel that there was no other life worth living except the life of self-renouncing service. It might be said of him, as was said of Morison, that he was sent of God to lift the shutters of our faith. Said a friend who is himself a leader and a king among men, the Bishop of Hereford, " There is no living man to whom I owe so much." To the casual person who met him in the train he gave the same impression as to the friend of years: " This is a

b

man to whom God is more real and more natural and more certain than anything else in the world."

His perfect combination of the evangelical and the catholic ideal made him perhaps the greatest fusing personality of his time. He refused to see the barriers which other men find insuperable, and, refusing to see them, he walked quietly through them, no man resisting. Probably no Free Churchman had so many intimate friends among the clergy of the Established Church; certainly none had so many fellow-workers. In the larger and diviner ether of the Christ-like life—

Hoarse dogmatisms to his fine note were won.

He was recognised by all as a Bishop of the Universal Church, and those who would have been at a loss to say in *what* they believed, believed in him.

He was a seer of visions, but he was also the most practical of mystics. His work was his joy. "Work and make music," the words which came to Socrates, were constantly on his lips, and may be said to have been the motto of his life. He was one of those in whose categories of being the possible took the upper hand of the actual, and therefore to the end he was always projecting something new and carrying men forward into some hitherto unconceived dispensation of grace and glory. To him the golden year was always at the doors, and lesser men who sat in the shadow knew that the day was at hand

Seeing thy shining forehead lit
With his inspiring prophecy.

In attempting to write the story of his life two difficulties have beset me throughout. It has been difficult to prevent the story from degenerating into a mere series, or even patchwork of philanthropies. For those who look beneath the surface it will not be hard to see that the central and inspiring idea of all is the Inner Mission of the Church. From that root sprang all his philanthropic work, and the affiliations, though not obvious, are never hard to trace.

Again, the very multiplicity of his activities tends to swamp the man himself. No account of what he did, however elaborate, would give anything but a faint idea of what he was to his day and generation. Great as his work was, the man was greater than his work. His highest and happiest achievement, his richest gift to the world, was himself. All human action has a twofold result: one as it affects the outer world for good or ill, the other as it builds up the inward man of the heart in goodness, in strong determination and assured wisdom. It was this " God's light organised " in his high soul, this primal element of joy and hope and faith and love, transfusing his solider qualities, which made John Brown Paton, to all who knew him, a revelation in the flesh. He bore in his face his credentials as an ambassador of Jesus Christ. It was not the great things he accomplished, but the great saint he was, which makes his life-story so well worth the telling. The fibre of it remains inwoven in the work of the world. If the true glory is a light which shines not from others upon ourselves, but from ourselves upon others, then that true glory is his.

SERVIENDUM ET LÆTANDUM

Lay palm and olive on his gentle breast,
   For well his life-long battle day is o'er;
   Victor he goes, unparted evermore
From all he loved and hoped for, to his rest.
Upward he led us to fair Duty's crest;
   Then cried: " Behold, Christ's feet are on before ! "
   And other worlds of service to explore
He went unfaltering on his heavenly quest.

For all his soul on ministry was set,
   And thro' the dust of party, clash of creeds,
      One face shone out to light him to the end,
And those pierced hands last seen on Olivet
   Dowered him with passion for the people's needs,
      And that great love which makes all sorrow friend.

H. D. RAWNSLEY.

CHAPTER I

BIRTH AND BOYHOOD

" Every Scottish man has a pedigree."—LOCKHART.
"True high birth is in the mind, it was never in the flesh."—KING
ALFRED.

THE scene where our story opens is a small country town of
Ayrshire nestling in the pastoral valley of the River Irvine.
The valley has the softly rounded outlines of the red sand-
stone. Its east end is dominated by the helmet-shaped
hill of Loudoun, on the top of which the Romans kindled
their beacon-fires, and the Covenanters in later days kept
watch for Claverhouse and his dragoons. Towards the
west the river flows past the stately castle of the Earls
of Loudoun, and on to the industrial centre of Kilmarnock.
On the south lie the wooded slopes of Lanfine, where the
quarries are. On the opposite side the land slopes upwards to the high, heather-clad moors, where there are no
trees to narrow in the wide horizons of the sky.

The little town of Newmilns has a history that goes
back to days before the time when good King James IV
bestowed on its inhabitants, by the charter of 1490, all
the privileges of self-government, a weekly market, and
a yearly fair. But there are sterner memories of the
" killing times " which stamp themselves on every child's
mind in Newmilns. In the kirkyard he sees the stones
of John Morton and John Gebbie of Feoch, who were
shot by bloody Graham of Claverhouse in 1679, and of
Nisbet of Hardhill, a tough old warrior-saint, harder than
the hill from which he took his name, the man who be-
wailed as a national sin the soft-heartedness that spared
the lives of the prisoners taken at the fight of Drumclog.
Right in the centre of the town stands an old battle-
mented castle. The bare-footed laddies play handball
now against its walls, but the old folks tell of the rough

1

Highland soldiers who were quartered there in King Charles II's time to overawe the Covenanters of the district. They tell of the eight prisoners who were brought in one day from a little country place down the valley, " being taken at a meeting for prayer," how the men of Newmilns attacked the castle and set free the prisoners, and how one of the storming party was shot in the rescue. The manse, half-hidden in its bower of trees below the bridge, keeps fresh the memory of another Scottish worthy, John Nevay, the pastor of Loudoun, who, " in the time of Scotland's purest reformation," went into exile rather than swear the oath of allegiance to King Charles II. John Howie's book, which stands alongside the Bible on the cottage shelf, will tell you the story of his life, and of the letters he wrote from the foreign shore to his old flock ; how he gloried in the honourable testimony they were bearing to the truth and the kingdom of Christ, and added, like a true shepherd of the sheep, such words as these to his letter : " I can do no more but pray for you ; and if I could do that well, I had almost done all that is required." The same manse treasures another memory. This is a story we do not need to search out in books, for the old folk of the village still tell of the divinely gifted ploughboy, with the dark, lustrous eyes, who once stayed there, and left on his dressing-table in the morning, as his parting gift, some of the simplest, sweetest lines he ever wrote.

The inhabitants of the parish in the year 1830 are a strange blend of Davie Deanses and Silas Marners. In the villages are the hand-loom weavers. Their trade is beginning to feel the pressure of the industrial revolution in the large factories. In this world's gear they are poorly sped ; few, if any, earn as much as a pound a week, and they eat the bread of carefulness from day to day. But they are men of shrewd sense, they know the value of books, they are fond of discussion, determined that, so far as in them lies, no economic disadvantage shall rob them of their inheritance in the things of the mind.

They are keen politicians, though as yet they have no vote, and the newspaper which comes down from Glasgow is passed keenly from hand to hand. Political discussion, with keen thrust and counterthrust, and much heckling of orators, is carried on in many a parlour-kitchen, and whenever a group gathers at the street corner or on the green. The leading spirits are keen Chartists, for, like Robert Burns, they have read Tom Paine, and they are not blind to the significance of what Richard Owen is doing among the working folk across the Ayrshire border. The reform of Parliamentary representation, the abolition of Corn Laws, the five points of the Charter are the prominent topics of debate, and the quieter, thoughtful spirits less noisily are turning their minds to the new co-operative movement, and the prospects it holds out of self-help and economic independence. There are strong infidels too—" nullifidians " we call them—very positive in their assertions, and very open in their contempt for the Sabbath and spiritual things, exercising considerable influence among the more intelligent of the younger men.

In the country there is a very different breed of men. Among the small farmers and the farmers' labourers the old Covenanting stock still survives. Many a farmhouse treasures an old musket or a sword that has been used against Claverhouse and his dragoons, or, it may be, a Bible which has borne the sword company at the camp-meeting and on the field of battle. They are a sturdy, God-fearing race, the mainstay of the kirk, who continue patiently in well-doing, too deeply rooted in the habit of faith to be moved by the excitements of social and political unrest.

Such was the little township to which my father, John Brown Paton, was brought as a baby, before he was quite one year old. He was born in the neighbouring town of Galston, on December 17th, 1830. What manner of home it was into which he was born let his own father tell in a letter which he wrote to his eldest son many years later:

" To-morrow you will complete the 33rd, and enter on the 34th year of your life, and I just send a line to wish that it may prove among the most useful and happiest years of your existence. . . . May you be spared to see many a happy return of the 17th December. 'Tis a day which I can never forget—chiefly from the following circumstances, which I believe you never heard before : your mother had for three days been in sore travail, and your two grandmothers, with the midwife, had almost lost hope of either a living mother or a living child, and I had gone into another room to call on Him who has said 'Call on Me in the day of trouble and I will deliver, It was when on my knees so engaged, that the first sound of your voice reached my ears, and my prayer was turned to thanksgiving and praise. It is often said, 'The time of extremity is the time of God's opportunity,' and so have I often found it. He is ever faithful. O! that we could always be faithful to Him."

His father's name, Alexander Paton, takes us up to the moors and back to the " killing times " of the seventeenth century. Alexander Paton's ancestor was one of Scotland's leaders in those days.

On the slopes of the moors, facing the peaks of Arran in the west, lies the farm of Meadowhead. John Paton, of Meadowhead, is one of the Scots Worthies. He went out to help Gustavus Adolphus in his fight for the Protestant faith in Germany, where " for some heroic achievement, at the taking of a certain city, he was advanced to a captain's post." A stout, trusty, God-fearing soul was the captain, such as Scotland needed in those troublous days. He seems to have been the man to whom the countryside looked for a lead when there was any fighting to be done, whether it was the stragglers of the Duke of Hamilton's army who were infesting the peace of the neighbourhood, or whether it was the flag of the Solemn League and Covenant which called to arms. He was there when the Covenanters were beaten by Montrose at Kilsyth ; he was there when, in the same year, Leslie turned the tables on Montrose at Philiphaugh. He took up arms for his king at Worcester when his king fought for his rights, but he drew his sword unhesitatingly against his king when obedience to the earthly monarch meant disobedience to the Heavenly Father. He led his regiment at the battle of Bothwell Brig. After the defeat he was proclaimed a rebel, and "a round sum was offered for his head." For more than four years he lived the life of a hunted thing on the moors, wandering, old man as he was, "in dens and caves of the earth," helped again and again to escape by loyal friends, but being "also a great succourer of those sufferers himself."

At last he was taken and was brought before the Lords of the Justiciary. There was no need of evidence. He acknowledged of his own accord that he commanded a party at Pentland, that he joined with the rebels at Glasgow about eight days before the Bothwell fight, that he led his regiment there against the forces of the king. " Do you not acknowledge authority ? " asked the Council. " I acknowledge all authority according to the word of God," was the answer. The sentence was death, and after eight days he was hung in the Grassmarket under the shadow of the Castle rock which he had helped to defend. His last words show the man. " I was never a great orator, or eloquent of tongue," he says, " though I may say as much to the commendation of God in Christ Jesus as ever a poor sinner had to say." He protested his adherence to the Scriptures, the Covenants, and the whole work of Reformation. " I leave my testimony, as a dying man, against the horrid usurpation of our Lord's prerogative and crown right: I mean that supremacy established by law in these lands, which is a manifest usurpation of His crown, for He is given by the Father to be Head of the Church. As to my persecutors, I forgive all of them ; instigators, reproachers, soldiers, private council, justiciaries, apprehenders, in what they have done to me ; I wish they may seek forgiveness of Him who hath it to give, and would do no more wickedly." And so he died, with pardon on his lips, as a true soldier of Christ. " Of him," says the chronicler, " it might be truly said that he lived a hero and died a martyr." His flag, his Bible, and his sword still remain ; they bear the evidence of the service they have seen, and folk point out that on the short, straight, thrusting blade of the sword there are twenty-eight hacks, one for each year that the persecution lasted.

The mother, Mary Brown, was a native of the town to which the first year of her married life brought her back again. The story of the courting is interesting. The Browns, who lived at Newmilns, were anti-Burghers and worshipped at Galston. The Patons, who lived at Galston, were Burghers and worshipped at Newmilns. Half-way the two families would meet at the Hag Bridge, and at those meetings love grew and ripened. Alexander Brown, her brother, was one of the leading men of the

town. He was among the first to be elected to the office
of Bailie when the Act of 1832 gave some share in the
election to the popular vote. He was known as one of
the most earnest and eloquent upholders of the temperance
cause, one who was ready to do battle with any " nulli-
fidian " in wordy warfare on the town green. The memory
of some of these debates lasted on for many years, and is
not yet extinct. He became afterwards lay minister of
a small Baptist Church in the town. Mary Brown had
much of the finer spirit of her brother. She was a woman
of delicate feeling and gentle tact, with a quick sense for
spiritual things. Her love for her children she showed,
as is the way of Scottish mothers, not in fuss or over-
demonstrativeness of affection, but in careful training in
all good ways. Her great ambition was that they should
grow up into goodness. She was a mother, too, of strong
will and unfailing self-respect, patient and resolute in
adversity, unwearied in industry. Her third brother,
Andrew Morton Brown, migrated to England, entered the
Congregational ministry, settled first at Poole, later at
Cheltenham, and became one of the leaders of English
Nonconformity.

Such was the home into which John Brown Paton was
born as the eldest child. " God's hand was busy at work
for me," he once said, " before I was born."

Alexander Paton had been a hand-loom weaver. Soon
after moving to Newmilns, he was appointed to take charge
of the first co-operative store in the town. The shop
stood in the main street, half-way between the town hall
and parish kirk, and the family lived at first above their
shop, but moved in 1835 to a new-built house, No. 8,
Grey Street, which had a stretch of garden at the back
and a brook that sang its quiet tune at the far end. The
trees which Alexander Paton planted are still growing.

He was a man of keen scientific and mechanical interests.
Any clock or watch belonging to a friend was pretty
sure, if it went wrong, to find its way into his hands. He
was a great reader. The Literary and Philosophical
Society provided him with the use of a library and a
microscope. Later on he became president, and in this
capacity arranged for the new minister of Loudoun, the
Rev. Norman McLeod, to deliver a series of lectures on
Geology, the new science which was furnishing such

formidable weapons for the nullifidians to use against the faith. He was keenly interested in church work, and his well-known integrity and ability earned him the position of office-bearer in the new United Secession Church, when the Burghers and anti-Burghers sank their differences and amalgamated their Churches. In such a home, with its careful husbandry both of time and money, with its steady interest in the things that are more excellent, with its family worship morning and evening, the little boy grew up in the nurture and admonition of the Lord. He was sent to school in the May after his fourth birthday, and Dominie Brown had easy work with him; spelling and grammar seemed to come by nature. He was an expert even in penmanship. Friends of later days will find this hard to credit, but there is evidence which cannot be gainsaid. As eldest of the family, he was his father's constant companion, and to no dominie did he owe any debt of culture or moral influence comparable with that which he owed to his father.

"He is one," he wrote in later days, "with whom life is far less than duty, and with whom gentleness of feeling is inwrought with grand vigour of conscience.

"I bethink me now of hours of sickness when his nursing was gentle as a woman's, when he cared not for sleep himself, and seemed to know no fatigue, that he might attend to me;—and the same to all of us."

There were no "organised games" in those days, but there was the saw-pit, which was a grand place for hide-and-seek; there were shinty and marbles, and there was hand-ball the lads might play up against the old castle wall when the men were not about. In all these games the little lad with flaxen, curly hair, called "Johnnie Pawton," was a leader; he was a sturdy little man, with high spirits and not without a dash of the rogue, and he had a way of getting the other children to submit to him. There were fine rambles through the "policies" of Lanfine, where the woods were free to all, and there were the blackberries and nuts, and many childish treasures. There was the quarry too, and when it was wet, or little limbs grew tired, there was the village "natural" who would tell the children stories if they gave him pins, one story for each pin. In these days of eleemosynary institutions, that figure has disappeared from village life; but in those days the poor "natural" was the daily butt and playmate of the children. There was the old soldier, who cut heather and sold brooms. His head had been touched by the sun. "If I had been Adam," he used to say, "I wouldna' ha' eaten the apple." The children used to call after him, "You've missed a step," and then laugh when he turned round to pick up the step he had missed; but, all the same, he had wonderful stories of foreign countries—no fairy tales, but real, true stories of grim bayonet-charges and galloping horse and cannon, and drums and trumpets. Sometimes mother would send out the lad in the evening to take him a bowl of soup, and it was canny work carrying the dish level up the dark rickety staircase of the old "Ducat" castle where he lived. That was the only luxury the straitened circumstances of the home allowed, the luxury of doing good, and the children had the joy of sharing in it. There was John Conn, who used to collect eggs from the farms and cottages, and send them in to the shop. He was often glad of a bite, and sometimes he needed a bit of nursing. It was to Alexander Paton's house he came in his last illness, and it was in his house he died—the children's first experience of that chill shadow feared of man.

In 1838 his uncle, Morton Brown, who had just settled in his first pastorate at Poole, came to see his parents, and, loving the lad's mother with more than a brother's love, loved the laddie also, and took him off to spend a year with him in Poole, to see new faces and new manners, and to make new friends, for the lad had already the gift of winning the love of every one he met. Here he laid in the most golden memories of his opening years. It was the roseate time of life, the sun had just risen above the horizon, the trailing clouds of glory were flushed with the rich hues of dawn. Here he was "showered upon and drowned with the very nectar of love." Every one made a pet of the young minister's little nephew from the north, and he, being of a warm, sensitive, responsive nature, drank in the sunshine of this new life, so different from the sterner life in the north.

" I have sat in the pulpit," he writes, " when dear old Mr. Durant would have me on his knee until he stood up to preach. . . . I formed dear friendships here, some of which still continue, the threads thereof not snapping, though they have been taken through the darkness of death and now link the immortals to a mortal."

He returned home after a year, and his young, ardent, loving nature felt the chill of the northern skies. He missed the demonstrative affection of the south. Not that the Northern love was less, but the sterner Scottish heart puts restraint even upon its family affection for fear it should rob the Lord of His due. Anyhow, all the boy's hopes of future happiness were pictured henceforth in the bright colours of that year's honeyed enjoyment. He did not moan or pine ; his spirit was too buoyant and active for that. But he shut up his heaven of memories in his heart, and often in silent hours gazed lovingly on the pictures that were hung on the walls of his mind. Henceforth he yearned for the south as his home.

He was sent to the parish school, and studies and schoolmaster were more severe. There was the Shorter Catechism to be got by heart, and there were long chapters of Romans, and there was Latin now, with its declensions, conjugations, and strict grammar laws. Norman McLeod had just been presented to the living of Loudoun, and had brought with him to the manse a younger brother, Donald, who was also entered at the parish school. The genial, forceful, open-hearted personality of the new minister was beginning to make a great difference in the village. Never a man had a happier genius for friendship. He was friendly with the grand folk at the castle, and the good ladies at Lanfine, and he was equally friendly and hearty with the man who was cleaning out the byre, or the weaver who thought that Richard Owen and scientific discovery were knocking the bottom clean out of Old Testament and New Testament alike. He was friendly, too, with the dissenting ministers—Dr. Bruce, of the United Presbyterian Kirk, and Mr. Rogerson, of the neighbouring Darvel. He would give lectures on Geology, and write articles for the learned periodicals ; but he was just as ready to have a crack with the weaver over his evening pipe. In the life of this young Christian minister,

so full of brotherliness and all healthy fun, the young
men of the parish began to get an altogether new conception of what the Christ-life meant; and the new
Sunday School, the Bible Society, the week-day preach-
ings, the prayer-meetings, brought a fresh spirit of vital
godliness into the little town.

Of the school-days only one incident survives. It was
a winter's day, and the frost was so keen that the ice was
forming on the pools of the River Irvine. The schoolmaster had told young Paton and Andrew Smith to go out
and clean their slates. The river flowed hard by the school-
house door, and the boys took their slates and sponges
down to the river-side. Andrew Smith let his slate fall
in, and Johnnie Paton, in trying to rescue it, ventured too
far upon the ice and went through into the deep water.
Before he could be got out he was insensible, and in
future, both he and—let us hope—his schoolmaster also—
were more careful.

The story of his boyhood can best be told in his own
words. It was not often that my father was in a remin-
iscent mood. His eyes were always turned towards the
future, and the Kingdom that was nigh at hand. But he
wrote some notes of the early days for a history of the
Paton family which was compiled by American cousins.

"The first thing I remember," he said, "is the great
interest and pleasure that my uncle William awoke
among the children and young people of his native village, and of Newmilns and Darvel. On his return from
London, where he had lived for some few years, he introduced into the villages, and I may say, throughout the
whole valley, the bright children's songs which were
common in London at that time, but were, I think, almost
unknown in Scotland, such songs as:

"'There is a happy land,
Far, far away'—

and others with the same inspiring note in them. Quite
a new excitement and joy were created in our school
gatherings, and in our homes, by the singing of these
hymns, so new in their catching joyousness. This experience came at a very opportune time, when religious excitement and fervour prevailed in that district, during

what was known as the 'Morisonian Controversy.' That
movement was, in many respects, not only like the
breeze of the morning of a new day, which dispelled the
dark shadows of a severe, and almost fatalistic Calvinism,
and awoke the minds of men to larger and truer conceptions of God's infinite compassion and love for His lost
children, but it also brought about from the fervour and
excitement that pervaded the community, not only in
Kilmarnock, but in the neighbouring villages, a true revival of religion ; and the hymns which my uncle William
introduced to our schools, and to all the children of the
district, harmonised with the more generous and inspiring
notes of the new doctrine of which Dr. Morison was then
the prophet.[1] Among my earliest memories as a boy is
the delight of those Sunday expeditions to Clerk's Lane
Church, when I joined large companies who went on foot,
or in ordinary carts, to Kilmarnock, to hear the earnest
discourses on the greatest religious themes, intermixed
with the singing of new, bright, spiritual songs.

" It is with pleasure that I relate some events in my
father's life, which show the dignity and purity of his
character, his fine and manifold gifts, and the great influence which he exerted, not only over his family, but over
all who knew him. I remember with what respect and
love my uncle William looked up to my father as his
elder brother. My father was engaged in the fields on
the road from Galston to Newmilns, and my uncle told
me how he went, when a little boy, to my father in order
that he might hear him read out of some book which he
always took with him. We know, from our grandfather's
library, and our father's, that the books which were thus
read by the elder boy to the younger were books either
of a fine religious and moral character or books of a
scientific value, because these were the only types of
books which I ever saw in their libraries. The only other
thing that I know of his youthful days was that he was
fond of music, and played in the village band. And I
know that he was able to play more than one instrument
—a gift, which, unhappily, none of his children inherit
from him.

" My first memory as a child should, I think, be stated

[1] The Rev. James Morison was called to Clerk's Lane, Kilmarnock, in
1840.

here, because it shows what was my father's character, and what was the earliest teaching of my parents. Our home in Newmilns was above the home of one who was named 'Merchant Lambie,' because he had, I believe, a small shop. I remember now, my being carried up-stairs in the arms of the eldest daughter of Merchant Lambie, Jean Lambie, in order that I might be placed on the old man's bed, who was near his last hour, that I might repeat to him what he had heard me, as a very little child, repeat when sitting in his chair by the fire-side, namely, the Scotch version of the 23rd Psalm :

> "'The Lord's my Shepherd, I'll not want,
>   He makes me down to lie
> In pastures green. He leadeth me
>   The quiet waters by.'

As I say, that is the first memory of my life, when I was a little under four years old, and it shows what was the religious spirit and teaching of my home and of my parents.

"What I have now to say concerning my father during the early years of my life till I was fourteen years of age, when I left Newmilns in order to go to Cheltenham, may be stated under distinct heads.

"He took an active part in the work of the Church. The Burghers and Anti-Burghers united and formed a United Secession Church. The building of this church took place whilst I was four or five years of age. My father had been appointed a 'manager' of the Church—which is the name given to officers who are now called in Presbyterian churches 'deacons.' He took an active part in the building of the church, and was well qualified to do so, as he had very considerable knowledge of archi-tectural plans and of building. I remember his frequent visits to the place during its building, and the visits of some distinguished visitors, who came to the opening of the church, one or two of whom came to our house to see my father. I remember especially Dr. Ritchie of Edin-burgh, and I seem to see the venerable head and appear-ance of Dr. John Brown, the leading divine of the United Secession Church, and the father of the author of "Horæ Subsecivæ." At that time the minister of the Secession Church in Newmilns was the Rev. John Bruce, afterwards

Dr. Bruce, who was connected by marriage with some of the leading members of the Church. Mrs. Bruce was a daughter of Dr. Ferrier, and he was able thus to secure the attendance of very able men at the opening of this church, which still stands in our native village, and is a well-proportioned, commodious, and beautiful place.

"My father was in full sympathy, as all our relatives were, with the great Morisonian revival, and heartily embraced Dr. Morison's views with regard to the universality of the atonement, and the free offer of the gospel to all. In consequence of my father's sympathy with these views (though he never took the active part that my uncle, Mr. Alexander Brown, took in propagating them, and in forming congregations in Galston and Darvel to uphold them), he was, I know, somewhat of a 'suspect' by the leading officers and the minister of the church, although he was always on friendly terms with them, and was much respected by them. I seem to remember that the baptism of one or two of our family was postponed,[1] if not altogether refused, because of my father's liberal views.

"I remember also, with very vivid distinctness, the great controversies of that time in which I was permitted, even though a boy, to take part, and especially the hour that was spent in the interval of public worship by friends who came from neighbouring villages or country districts, when these were the great themes of discussion.

"My father, along with his more liberal and enlightened views upon the great question of the redeeming work of our Divine Lord, was also led to sympathise with the more democratic form of church life which is held by Independents and Congregationalists. He was probably led to consider the question of church polity, and to favour Independency, from his intimate relations with my dear uncle, Dr. Morton Brown, who was then pastor of an influential church in Poole, and also by his acquaintance with the Rev. Mr. Dickinson, pastor of a Congregational Church in Kilmarnock. In consequence of his sympathy with Independency, when my father and our family went to Glasgow, he became a member of the Congregational Church there, of which Rev. David Russell,

[1] The baptism of the youngest son of the family was postponed until a supply came to take the place of the regular minister.

M.A., son of the famous Dr. Russell of Dundee, was pastor. Of this Church he was an honoured member until he left with our family to live with my brother Andrew in Crosby.

"My father through life was a very earnest temperance worker. The old Scotch habit of drinking whisky on all festive occasions was universal, and there were a great many in these villages smitten with the curse of drunkenness. Against this prevalent usage, and against this terrible sin of drunkenness, my father contended with fervent protest, and was, with my uncle, Dr. Alexander Brown, the leading temperance advocate in our village. He was the president of the Order of Rechabites, and under his influence and direction I was, at a very early age, the president of the junior tent of Rechabites, which, I remember, bore the picturesque title of the 'Blossom Tent.' I can remember, with greatest joy, a summer holiday festivity in connection with our juvenile Rechabite tent. William Bruce, my most intimate boy companion—son of the manse, and second son of Dr. John Bruce—was associated with me as a leading member in our 'Blossom Tent,' and we organised an excursion to Eaglesham, across the moors. We hired carts and took our banners with us and made a great show. The scent of the moorland air and the brightness of the summer sun on that visit to Eaglesham have never left me.

"There is one incident in connection with my father's temperance work which I must specially record, as I learned more from that one incident of the Spirit of Christ, and of the true meaning and nature of redemptive service in the world, than from any other experience of my life, or from any books that I have read. There was a weaver who lived next door to us who was a great drunkard. He was persuaded by my father to sign the pledge; he did so, but found it impossible, he said, after his work was done, to go out and mix with his fellows, and especially to pass the open door of the public-house; the scent of the whisky and the songs of the revellers inside made the temptation too great for him, and he pleaded with my father that he would let some one go with him hand-in-hand, when he went for a little walk, because he thought that then he would be secured against the temptation that beset him. My father asked me thus to walk with him hand-in-hand, and I did so, and was able to save that man, for whom I had much respect, from the peril to which he was exposed. I learned in that way that it is by sympathy and friendly succour that we are able to save men from the evil that tempts them.

" Another incident in my father's temperance work I am also glad to record. Along with another most intelligent and zealous worker in our village, Mr. Nicol Cameron, he set out on what might be called a Temperance Gospel Mission. They went to Strathaven and some other place, speaking in the open air, and wherever they could get an audience. They were thus able to spend a few days in what was a real crusade, and I remember the great pleasure with which we saw them leave us, and the greater pleasure with which we saw them return from their campaign. I believe that the memory of my father's earnest testimony and faithful service as a temperance reformer, along with that of my beloved uncle, Alexander Brown, whose intellectual gifts and speaking ability made him perhaps the foremost temperance reformer in our district, are remembered by the oldest inhabitants of our village to this day.

" I should like to mention my father's interest in general, and especially in scientific, knowledge. He was the president of the Literary and Scientific Society in our village. They had frequent meetings, and had a remarkable collection of scientific apparatus. I have a special recollection of electrical apparatus. During my early youth ' Chambers's Information for the People ' was being introduced, and there was, at that time, a wonderful revival of popular interest in science, occasioned by the cheap literature of a higher kind, dealing with scientific questions. I read with avidity every number of ' Chambers's Information ' as it came out, and also from the school library some of the volumes of an old ' Encyclopædia Britannica.' [1] But my special delight was in some lectures and scientific discussions which were held in connection with the society.

" In connection with this society, it is interesting to note that three men, who became well known afterwards, took an active part in it. Dr. Norman Macleod, whose

---

[1] Other books were Hogg's "Instructor," John Bunyan, Pollock's "Course of Time," Dick's "Astronomy," "Helen of the Glen," "Tales of the Wars."

first charge was in Loudoun parish, and who became very
friendly with my father, gave a delightful course of
lectures in the United Secession Church, under the auspices
of that society, on geology. I remember these with the
greatest delight, and seem still to see the long scroll hung
up, on which the order of the different strata of the earth's
surface was printed in large letters. Mr. Neeson, who
then lived in Kilmarnock, gave one or two lectures to the
society. He was a well-known mathematician, and soon
afterwards left for London, where he became known as
one of the most eminent actuaries of his time. Dr.
Fulton also brought his orrery and described it to the
Literary and Scientific Society in Newmilns. That orrery
was constructed by him with wonderful exactitude in his
little cottage at Fenwick, and was afterwards taken to
London, where it created considerable interest. Another
lecturer on electricity who stayed with us was the Rev.
Mr. Dickinson, the Congregational minister at Kilmarnock.
I have a special recollection of a visit I paid with my
father to his study at Kilmarnock, when he showed me
some most delightful experiments which I have never
forgotten.

"In connection with these scientific and intellectual
interests of our village, I must specially speak of the conversations at our fireside between my father and some
working men of fine character who were our neighbours,
and who were thus associated with my father in these
interests. I recall my father walking with two or three
of these men, who were weavers, on the road leading up
to the manse in which Dr. Bruce lived, and, stopping to
describe the movement of the moon around the earth, and
the nodes of the moon, and drawing with his stick some
lines upon the ground. As if I had only heard it yesterday, I remember one of these men, when my father had
drawn the diagram, shouting out, 'Man, I ha'e it noo.'
It is delightful to think of these pure and noble interests
which filled the minds of the working men in our village,
and of the part which my father took in cultivating these
higher and purer interests and pleasures of life. I have
mixed with many classes since, but I reflect with grateful
satisfaction upon the life of these humble men, who were
poor in this world's substance, but who had a fine range
of intellectual knowledge and sympathy.

" These were the days of the great Chartist Movement, and our village was deeply stirred by it. I do not seem to remember that my father took so great a part in this movement as he did in the other more social and intellectual movements of which I have spoken. On the other hand, there was one great controversy in which he took part—'The Ten Years' Conflict,' as it was called, then began, which led to the disruption of the Established Church of Scotland and the Free Church. A lecturer of the Established Church, named Mr. Lecky, visited our village in order to uphold the establishment and the State control of the Church. This was strongly opposed by numbers in the Secession Church. Mr. Alexander Brown challenged Mr. Lecky to a public discussion, which was first held in the Parish Church, and afterwards, because, I believe, of the crowd that attended, on the Town Green. My father was one of the chairmen. A silver watch was presented to my uncle afterwards for his splendid services in upholding the spiritual independence of the Church of Christ against this rather famous champion of the State Church : the watch is still held and greatly prized by his son, Mr. Andrew Brown.

" These incidents in my father's life, when I was associated with him in my boyhood, are, I believe, worth recording. I ought to add that my father was a man of very considerable and varied gifts. He had considerable gift as a designer, and he was able to prepare the working patterns of the muslins which were woven then on hand-looms by the weavers who formed the chief part of the population of our village. He drew these designs, which required much accuracy in drawing, as from them the pattern was transferred to the Jacquard machine, which was then being introduced instead of the old service of the ' draw-boy,' whom I remember working with each weaver at his loom. He was also engaged frequently in measuring land, and other forms of measuring ; and one of his frequent employments was the cleaning of clocks, and, I think, also of watches. This showed that, along with his intellectual tastes, he had distinctly mechanical gifts, and in this, I believe, he followed in the steps of our grandfather, whom I remember well, and to whom I think that much that I have said about my own father might be applied.

2

" Another trait I will add, and then I have done. My
father was a true gentleman, not only in his manner, but
in his inner thought and feeling ; a man of fine ideal and
of conduct, with a large and beautiful humanity, and at
the same time with a courtesy and gentleness of manner
which never left him. And all this, be it remembered, was,
in a sense, the product of the family inheritance under
the influence of his own father, and of the Christian circle
in which his early life was spent ; but it was also the
result of faithful cultivation of his varied intellectual and
social gifts under the inspiration of a noble religious faith."

At the age of ten John Brown Paton's schooling came to
an end. He had already begun to learn in the school of
actual life by assisting his father in the business of the shop.
Now came the time for leaving home and launching out into
the wider world. A boy was wanted in the printing office
of the ' Kilmarnock Herald,' a weekly paper. Young
Paton applied, and was accepted. His duties included
a certain amount of reporting and sub-editing, so that
the new boy was brought into close contact with the
editor, Mr. Alexander Russel, afterwards famous as
" Russel of the ' Scotsman.' " Here he worked for ten
months, and found time, in addition to his other duties,
to start three Temperance and Debating Societies. The
first one was started in the back room of a certain Dr.
Smith, and it is worth while noting that all of the members, except one, became professional men, ministers,
doctors, or lawyers, and the one exception was a Mr.
Macrae, who became a large manufacturer, and lived at
Hawick.

At the same time he was very busy with his friend,
William Bruce, on a Sunday afternoon class for boys at
Newmilns. There is still an old man at Newmilns who
remembers how he came home and told his mother what
he had heard at the class ; he must have been nearly as
old as his class teacher. All the while that class teacher
was learning Greek and Hebrew from a Mr. Steedham.

Already he had found a purpose in life beyond himself
and felt its urgency ; already he was about His Father's
business.

The determinant factors of his childhood are thus not
hard to discern. There is first the home ; through the

tenderness and purity, the strength and wisdom of his parents, he comes to the knowledge of Him from whom alone all tenderness, purity, strength, and wisdom spring. There are his brothers and sisters, seven in number, whom he has to care for and help. There is the memory of the brave men who were willing to give their lives and defy the whole embattled power of the king rather than do violence to the inward light and the law of conscience. There is the deep-rooted Calvinism of his Scottish ancestry—God the Sovereign, the only source of man's righteousness and salvation, His Will the ground, the dominant and decisive factor of all human life. There is the new message that came through James Morison— the wideness of God's mercy, the universality of His atonement, and of the working of His Spirit. Then there is the controversy which led to the great disruption of 1843, when, under Chalmers, 470 ministers gave up their manse and their living that they might assert the great positive principle of Churchmanship, a principle not based on State, or patronage, or method of government, but on the simple bedrock truth of the New Testament, "Ubi Christus, ibi ecclesia." Among his father's friends these are the great absorbing topics of discussion ; and they are central things, they do not belong to the peripheræ of life.

Then there is the first-hand influence of such forceful and contagious personalities as Norman McLeod, Alexander Russel, James Morison, men who had not only ability, but the deeper insight and oversoul which make genius.

Truly God's hands did not cease to be busy at work for him after he was born.

CHAPTER II

COLLEGE DAYS

" Get ready thy tools, God will find the work."—R. BROWNING.

AFTER spending a year in this apprenticeship to journalism, young Paton once more went south, again at the invitation of his uncle, Dr. Morton Brown, who had now settled in a pastorate at Cheltenham. Young as he was, he was appointed usher in a private school at Gloucester, kept by a Dr. Benham, for it was clear enough to all who knew the lad that his real bent was not journalism, but teaching and learning. What he was like as a schoolmaster no records enable us to say, save that he threw himself into this work with intense vigour and earnestness, that the boys did after their kind and tried how far they might take liberties with the new teacher who was so nearly on their own level of age, also that they did not carry the experiment further than the first attempt. A single incident survives. One evening, while visiting some friends in the city, he expressed a wish to learn how to swim. Mr. March, the head of the household, at once, with the help of the music-stool, showed him the proper movements of the limbs and invited him to join his bathing party on one of the rafts in the river. Mr. March had already taught several lads by passing a band of webbing round the learner's chest and holding him up by means of a mopstick until he had acquired the art. Young Paton was treated in the same way, but, to his teacher's surprise, he struck out at once with all the skill and confidence of a practised swimmer, and shouted to Mr. March that he did not want to be held up any more. Mr. March was surprised to find his help so soon made superfluous, and for years afterwards would refer to the incident as a re-

markable instance of what intelligence, self-possession, and
pluck could accomplish.[1] No wonder that "the young
tutor was a great favourite with all the boys."

At what time he first turned his thoughts to the
ministry it is not possible to say, but they were already
tending in that direction, for while in Gloucester he made
a beginning as a preacher in Southgate Street Independent
Chapel, of which the Rev. Joseph Hyatt was minister.
It was probably here that he preached his first sermon,
and those who heard him had no doubt that it was his
high calling to be a minister of the Word. There was the
same quiet self-confidence in his first attempts at preaching as in his first attempts at swimming. His holidays
were spent at Cheltenham with his uncle. One Saturday, when Dr. Morton Brown seemed hardly fit for duty
on the next day, his nephew of fifteen declared himself
quite ready to take his place.

It was at his uncle's house that he met Professor Henry
Rogers, the brilliant scholar and writer, who had given
up the chair of English at University College, London, to
take up work at the college which had been newly founded
through the generosity of George Storer Mansfield and his
sisters for the training of Independent ministers at Springhill, Birmingham. That meeting decided the choice of
career, and in 1846, before he was sixteen years of age,
the name of John Brown Paton was entered on the roll
of students of Springhill, with a Padmore Scholarship to
help him through his course. Here he settled down to
read for his London matriculation.

For the next seven years he was a student at Springhill.
The conditions were not ideal, for the new buildings were
not yet, and the premises then occupied were divided into
two halves by the road, so that one portion of the little
community, numbering some twenty in all, was largely
cut off from the other. They were also rather uncom-
fortably near to the busy city's central roar. But young
Paton was not one to make trouble over such things ; even
then he had begun to say to himself, if not to others :
"Difficulties are our inspiration to higher effort," and
the story goes that he chose a room which was specially
noisy, so that he might learn the better how to concen-

[1] The story is told by Mr. W. March in "Success by an Inventor,"
p. 32.

trate his mind upon the work in hand, undiverted by
outside distractions.

Among those entering in the same year was Philip C.
Barker, the son of the resident tutor ; the following year
has the names of Robert Ainslie Redford and Robert
William Dale, and in 1848 the only entrant was Edward
William Shalders. All these became fast friends of my
father. There are no friendships of after-life which are
quite so warm, spontaneous, and intimate as between
those who are " bred upon the self-same hill," and live in
daily and hourly contact with each other in the days when
knowledge begins to unroll her ample page and life begins
to open out its larger issues and potentialities. Of the
coming of young Dale into this society my father said :

" I remember the wonder and admiration with which
we greeted him when he first came to us, for even then,
when only seventeen years of age, he had a reputation as
a preacher. A volume of his sermons had already been
published, and one or more papers written by him had
appeared in our denominational magazines. It was delightful, however, to find, when he came, that there was
no touch of vanity or conceit in his spirit or his manner.
There was, indeed, a staidness of deportment, and ma-
turity of thought, which made it difficult to believe that
he was a youth of seventeen years. But then, as ever
after, there was a breezy naturalness and a buoyancy
of temperament which made his companionship most
delightful and invigorating."

Such was the intellect against which he had to measure
his strength, " and we all felt then, what many have felt
since, that it needed a certain courage to meet the onset
of his charge in our college debates." It is in the atmosphere of such fellowship of mind with mind, and all the
informal, unconscious give and take which it involves, that
the most vital element of college education consists. Of
Paton's contribution to that common life, these words of
Mr. Shalders may give some idea :

" He was my senior as a student, though somewhat
younger in years. His amazing industry, tenacious
memory, the grasp of his understanding, Christian en-

thusiasm, and unfailing *bonhomie*, were evident then, and continued with him throughout life."

One incident shows the eagerness of young souls protensive to their future work. Thomas Binney had been delivering the address at the May meetings of 1848, and had taken as his theme, " The Mission of Congregationalists to their Times."

" When the newspaper containing the report of his address arrived, some half-dozen of the students took it out into a field close by and sat through the summer afternoon beneath the trees listening to it as it was read aloud. ' At the close,' Dale says, ' up sprang one of the audience and cried with enthusiasm, " Three cheers for Binney and the young men." I haven't given such hearty cheers for I know not how long.' " [1]

The most distinguished and inspiring of his tutors was Henry Rogers, then in the prime of his manhood, " a consummate thinker and writer," my father says of him. Rogers was professor of mathematics, English language and literature, and mental and moral philosophy. He had already contributed brilliant articles to the " Edinburgh Review " in the days of its greatness, and, in spite of the manifold duties of his chair, was writing at this time for the " British Quarterly " and other periodicals. Henry Rogers was a man of keen critical intellect, brilliant in conversation, and catholic in the sweep of his reading and interest. He had all the grace of Puritanism, without a trace of its exclusiveness and sourness. His essays are forgotten, but his chief work, " The Eclipse of Faith," still gives the image of his mind and thought. As an apologist of the Christian faith, he is said to stand in the succession of Butler, and, as regards his line of argument, this is truly said. Like Butler, he takes up what a scientist twenty years ago has called a " suicidal position," a position, however, to which more recent thought is largely returning, that of resting reason itself upon faith. But, in his manner, Rogers differs as widely from Butler as one writer well can from another. He has not the same momentum of march, but he has what Butler

[1] " Life of R. W. Dale," by his son, p. 49.

lacks, a lively play of fancy, a happiness of allusion and quotation, and a power of putting himself in the position of his adversary and seeing things from his point of view. The conversational form into which he throws his essay gives full play to all his delicate gifts.   The chief religious danger of the time, to his mind, was not Romanism or Tractarianism, but "a subtle and charming form of scepticism, which, while rejecting the history, miracles, and all peculiar doctrines of the New Testament, claims to embody the essence of genuine Christianity." And there is real humour in the way he embodies this de-Christianised Christianity in one of his characters, a thinly veiled disguise of Francis W. Newman, who, "after stripping himself, fragment by fragment, of his early creed, walks through this bleak world in a gossamer gauze of transparent spiritualism which makes you both shiver and blush to look at him."

Though not resident in the college, Henry Rogers was continually in close personal contact with his students, for, not content with his formal lectures, he met some six or seven of his students in his room twice a week, and there, among his books, they would read and discuss the great classics of literature and philosophy. In this associative reading, which was my father's first "reading circle," he learned a method of reading which was far more valuable than the method which is usually called "getting a book up for examination." He learned that a man does not necessarily know a book because he remembers it and can reproduce it ; to know a book one must cross-examine it as Socrates cross-examined a sophist, never accepting half solutions of difficulties as complete, nor allowing obscure corners to remain unexplored because they do not seem important. He learned that the books which yield the most profit are those which make a man think most. He learned also how much keener is the enjoyment of reading when the pleasure is shared with others, and how much deeper and more manifold becomes the meaning of a book when the light of many different minds is brought to bear upon it. When, in later years, Henry Rogers published "The Eclipse of Faith," the Springhill students recognised in the book many of the discussions they had held in the author's study.

It was from Henry Rogers that the students learned

the sense of literary form, the wonderful power of the best words in the best order. It was from him they learned to love such thinkers as Pascal, Plato, Burke, Butler, and Descartes. It was not so much that they read and talked over these particular books freely : the more important lesson was that they formed there the appetite for the things that are more excellent, and that they did not " grow pale at the sacred draughts." Above all, they did not fail to see that, to this master of letters, there was one Book which stood out above all other books in the grandeur of its style and the power of its message, the Book which was of more than human origin.

But the educative forces of college life are not limited to the four walls of the building (which in this case were considerably more than four). It is said that good scholars are bad citizens. But in such a community as Birmingham, with its stirring public life, both civic and political, that would be hardly possible. All the great national questions, the abolition of the Corn Laws, Lord Ashley's efforts to protect the life of women and children working in factories, the demands of the Chartists, and all the hopes and aspirations centring round the Great Exhibition were eagerly canvassed wherever men met together in companies, either great or small, in Birmingham ; and the company was not small when men like Cobden or Bright or Lushington or Edward Miall were billed to speak. The echoes of the larger world of Europe were heard in the Town Hall. Louis Kossuth told them how the young republican movement of Hungary was quenched in blood. Gavazzi, the friar of Bologna, who was forbidden to mention the word " Italia " from the pulpit, told of the struggles of the Italian patriots for a country. Feargus O'Connor voiced the wrongs and miseries of Ireland. J. B. Gough brought with him the message of the great Temperance Movement in America, R. W. Emerson the utterance of her best thought. Emancipation was in the air. Among the down-trodden races of Europe it was a struggle for political emancipation, in America it was the struggle for the emancipation of the slave, and in France Louis Blanc was preaching economic emancipation for the disinherited classes of society. In the Church there was the Tractarian Movement, and the Roman Catholics were bestirring themselves to win back

the English to the fold.   They were stirring times ; merely
to live in them saved a mind from being parochial.   The
life of a great town may not be the most conducive either
to health or to study, but it gives a young man a big
world in which to think and feel.   Here, too, the young
student saw for the first time the results of the industrial
revolution in our great towns—the immense increase in the
production of material wealth which had come through
harnessing the forces of steam and chemical agents to the
purposes of manufacture ; and, side by side with the growth
of wealth, the growth of destitution among the poor, the
sharpening of social contrasts, the gradual widening of
the gulf which separated the poor from the respectable
middle-class folk, and their estrangement from the Church.

In the town there were several religious leaders of
power.   John Angell James, at Carrs Lane, was closely
associated with the college as Chairman of the Board of
Education.   There was George Dawson, a church to
himself, too individual to be held in by the restraining
bonds of any society which he did not himself control ;
but with a strong note of actuality, for all that, in his
teaching.   But Paton's favourite was a man of less pretensions, whose quiet, seraphic spirit was like a health-
bearing breeze from heavenly places.   Robert Alfred
Vaughan was only seven years Paton's senior.   His
temperament and upbringing had been almost as diverse
from his as it is possible to conceive ; possibly it was
for that reason that they were drawn to each other so
strongly, each finding in the other something that was
lacking in himself.   Vaughan was a poet ; at the age of
twenty-one he had published his first volume with the
desire " to face criticism early " ; he was also artistically
gifted, and had thought of art as a profession.   He had
studied in Germany and written on Origen for the " British
Quarterly."   He was at this present time projecting a
series of dramas to illustrate the history of the Church,
but had been diverted to the study of the mystics—a subject never yet presented to the English mind—and was
learning Spanish and Dutch that he might study at first-
hand the authorities needed for carrying out his work.
It was to his chapel in Steelhouse Lane that young Paton's
membership was transferred from Gloucester, and as soon
as he was placed on the preaching list after the expiry of

two years, Ebenezer Chapel was one of the first pulpits which he supplied. Paton has given us, from his own pen, a picture of his friend and his companionship.[1]

"His preaching was distinguished by the abundant and happy use of imagery. Often his sermons were a series of pictures ; but, like his Lord's, his pictures were all brilliant with the light of heaven. Nature and life became transfigured as they were seen to reveal not only the physical but the spiritual laws of God. How often I have heard him—and his expressions yet dwell with me—thrill the heart by a home picture, in which the love of the child, and the yearning care of the parent, were made to typify the divine relations of God's family.

"I cannot portray the private character of my friend ; and if I were to do so, I might be charged with representing an ideal and not a real character. So, at any rate, I should have judged Mr. Vaughan's character, had I merely met with it in a description, and not enjoyed the felicity of knowing it by long and intimate intercourse. As regards intellectual power, his books are a true reflex of that exhaustless memory, genial humour, and brilliant imagination which shone in his conversation, as well as in his writings. But there was a spontaneity and alertness in his turns of thought and naive illustrations, when engaged in conversation, which exceedingly enhanced their effect. There was no satire, because there was no bitterness in his nature, but humour—quaint, fantastic, happy humour, like Paul Richter's, only more elegant— overflowed his table-talk, and imparted to it the richest flavour. Yet, over all his speech and manner there breathed a sacred tenderness, which flowed not from any earthly source, but was the fragrance of a heavenly spirit. The domestic love that shone in his home, and was the bright atmosphere in which his nature bloomed, was exquisitely pure and happy. The fond joyousness, the quiet, playful humour, the soft, brooding, godly care, with which he delighted himself in his children, and bound their hearts to his ; and, especially, the noble grace, the ceaseless courtship with which he won every day more closely to himself her whom he loved to call ' The Angel in the House '—here the innate manhood of Alfred

[1] " Memoir of R. A. Vaughan," by his father, pp. 276–81.

Vaughan beamed upon me, the highest image I had ever
dreamed of—self-forgetting, ever-thoughtful, winning,
helping, hallowing affection. His nature, which was trustful, affectionate, and given to meditation, seemed to be
ground well prepared for the seed of God ; and surely in
it that seed grew and fructified as is rarely seen on earth.
He always appeared to me like the beloved Apostle, whose
head lay confidingly on the breast of Christ, and to whom
were revealed the most glorious visions of the beautiful
future of Christ's Church.

" His religious zeal did not indeed take the form of
intense practical activity. He was persuaded that his
study was the proper sphere of his labour for Christ and
the Church. The delights of religious meditation were
to him infinitely sweet. He loved to bring Christ near
to him, and to live, even as St. John would have done,
with the assurance that his dearest Friend and Brother
was never absent from him. The religious theme which
engrossed our conversation more than any other was the
Brotherhood of Immanuel. To know Him as possessing
the power and wisdom of God, yet as being our Elder
Brother, was the joy of his soul. To grow up into His
likeness was his single desire. And to be with Him, as
now he is, in His Father's home, was his abiding hope."

From Alfred Vaughan he learned the love of poetry
and of natural beauty. It was with the same friend that
he paid his first visit to Germany, and began his study
of the German language and German thought. At this
time, when mental culture was looked upon as dangerous,
especially for women, in many pious circles, Alfred Vaughan
witnessed to the truth that all knowledge, all beauty,
should be pressed into the service of God.

It was during his student days, in one of the vacations,
that he met Sidney Dobell in the streets of Cheltenham,
and was introduced to him. It was in origin, literally,
" a passing acquaintance," but it ripened quickly into
closer attachment. They had " exchanged eyes." The
poet finds himself " betrayed into unwonted prolixity "
in writing to his young friend ; he thanks him for " that
genial, noble-hearted letter of yours," addresses him as
" Caro mio," sends him copies of his books, and writes
intimately about his meaning and his purpose in them.

The young student pours out his soul unreservedly, tells all the story of his life, and what he means to make of it.

"To *live* the doctrine, you say," writes the poet, "there indeed, you have arrived at the great secret of power. Every day shows me more and more that every word of man or of God must be *made flesh* before it can be efficacious to our human nature. Incarnation, corporal epiphany, is the true way to preach in this world. God help you in that brave resolution ' to live '; I can sympathise with it from my heart, for it is my own first aspiration. I have no faith in the poetry of a poet who is not himself a poem."

The friendship, thus begun, lasted until the poet died in 1874.

Paton's work as supply brought him into contact with many Churches and made him many friends. The happiest group of all was at Oswestry. There he was always welcome, and always at home. He was a great favourite in the circle of " Old Chapel " friends. There was something out of the common about the congregation of Old Chapel. There was a local magazine of real literary merit; the editor and the contributors were members of Old Chapel, and one of them, Mr. Shirley Brooks, who afterwards became editor of " Punch," was secretary of the Sunday School. On Monday mornings there were breakfast parties, for in the days before the visitation of the penny post became so frequent and exacting, and before daily newspapers arrived before the coffee, breakfast was still a social function. After breakfast there were walks, and picnics, and fun, rollicking fun galore. " My remembrance of him," says Mr. Woodall, " is of one who always added a ring of cheerfulness to any company into which he came." The mention of Oswestry friends, of Mrs. Thomas, or any of the Minshull family, would always light up my father's face with smiles even till the last.

He finished his college course by winning a double M.A. at London University. He was first in Philosophy, taking the gold medal, and in the same year he was third on the list for the M.A. in Classics. It was the first time in the history of the University that any candidate had passed two M.A. examinations in the same year.

CHAPTER III

SHEFFIELD

" I believed, and therefore did I speak."
" Qualis vocatio, talis successus."

THE harrow of the Industrial Revolution had passed over
Sheffield, as it had passed over Birmingham, only its
effects were more cruelly exemplified in Sheffield. The
growth of industry had been more rapid, for the world's
hunger for steel had been growing steadily since the year
1830, and had been stimulated in the years 1854 and 1855
by the sinister demands of war. The stress of the new
conditions had not fallen, it is true, so heavily upon the
women and children as in the spinning and weaving districts. But for the men and the lads, both in their
factories and in their homes, the conditions of life were
grimy, hideous, depressing. In Sheffield, as elsewhere,
the first effect of machines, invented " to shorten labour,"
was to vastly prolong the hours that men worked ; the
larger scale on which production was organised produced,
at first, conditions which were nothing short of brutalis-
ing. The old skill, the old joy and satisfaction in the
work of one's hands, were no more, and men were herded
in huge factories, where they were mere slaves of the
machine, which went by the name of " the iron man."
Instead of the old country town, with its happy cottage
industries, " not a beggar to be seen, nor an idle person," [1]
there was the factory with its heat, its deafening rattle,
its tall chimney which hung out a black flag over the
town and defiled God's sunlight ; instead of the village
ale-house, there was the gin-palace ; instead of the village
green, the backyard and a blasted cinder-heap ; instead of the maypole, the forge, with its horrid flames
lighting up the darkness ; instead of the cottage with its

[1] D. Defoe, " Tour through Great Britain."

creepers and bit of garden, there were dreary rows of ill-built, blackened, back-to-back houses.

Neither municipal nor church development had kept pace with the rapid growth of Sheffield industries. Though Sheffield had had a corporation since 1843, it had not yet acquired the control of the police, the maintenance of the streets, the management of sanitary arrangements and drainage. Not till 1848 had the borough obtained a Commission of the Peace. Gas and water were supplied by private companies. The streets in the centre of the town were very narrow, over-crowded, irregular; there were no great public buildings to dignify the city, and the civic life, such as it was, was anæmic.

The Churches, just as much as the civic authorities, seemed as yet unconscious of the magnitude or the claims of the problem which confronted them. They showed little power of concerted action. The workmen of the town were beginning to realise that their one chance of betterment lay in combination; Sheffield was the birth-place of trades-unionism. But the Churches were engaged each in their several affairs, working placidly on the old lines. Sixty thousand of the inhabitants never attended a place of worship. Yet hardly any combined attempt was made to face the position thus created until at the begin-ning of 1853 a special committee was appointed by the Congregational Churches to watch for opportunities of church extension. The attention of this committee was directed straightway to the Sunday School which had been started by Queen Street Congregational Church in the thickly populated district of the Wicker. The work had been going on for some thirty years; already in 1835 a new schoolroom had been built, and James Mont-gomery, the poet, had presided over the opening meeting. The proposal of the committee to form a new church at the Wicker was favourably received by Queen Street. The new railway-stations and the building of large fac-tories had led to the upgrowth of a considerable new popu-lation to the north of the River Don, and till recently there had been only one small place of worship for some 10,000 people. Some forty-five members banded themselves to-gether to go out and form the nucleus of the new venture.

" In thus separating themselves from the mother-

church," says the Rev. F. W. B. Weeks (to whom I am
deeply indebted for help in this part of the narrative),
" they were actuated by the very highest feeling of
loyalty to Queen Street and loyalty to Christ.   In no sense
were any of them dissatisfied.   In no spirit of rivalry was
the work commenced, but they ' hived off ' as a perfectly
natural consequence of spiritual prosperity and entered
on work which was necessary, but in every respect sacrificial."

The spirit in which they acted is expressed in the letter
which communicates their determination to the mother-
church :

" We, the undersigned, having in view the extension of
the Redeemer's Kingdom, have agreed to unite ourselves
together as an Independent Christian Church.   Whilst
thus separating ourselves from the community to which
some of us have long been united, and in connection with
which we have pleasing associations, we would wish to
entertain towards the Church at Queen Street, with its
minister and deacons, sentiments of affection and esteem,
and hope to be ready at all times to unite in efforts which
may benefit our denomination or extend the cause of
Christ.   To many of us this step is a trial, yet we believe
that the providence of God is pointing out our duty and
saying to us, ' This is the way, walk ye in it.'   May the
influences of the Holy Spirit be largely shed forth upon
you : may grace, mercy, and peace be multiplied towards
you."

The first act of worship was a Communion Service conducted by the Rev. J. H. Mins, the Queen's Road Pastor,
in which they consecrated themselves to the work and
commended it to their Master.
A site was secured for the new church at the corner of
the Burngreave and Grimesthorpe roads, a point on which
streets converge from every direction.   Plans were prepared by Messrs. Weightman, Hadfield, and Goldie, and
building operations were started without delay.   The
foundation-stone was laid on Easter Tuesday, 1854.
And now began the search for a pastor.   Many ministers were heard, but " none of them appeared in all re-

spects suited to the circumstances of the church. . . . The deacons were then led providentially to solicit the services of the Rev. John Brown Paton, M.A., who had just completed his preparatory course at Springhill College, Birmingham." From the first they seem to have felt that he was the man appointed to lead them. Though he was still untried, his character, his gifts, his burning zeal and exhaustless energy, his personal charm, banished all their hesitancy, and a special church meeting held on August 14th, 1854, sent him a cordial and unanimous invitation to become their pastor " with a prospect of great usefulness." There were other calls which offered more emolument, more chance for private study, and easier conditions of service ; what this call from the Wicker had to offer was more work, more difficulties to overcome, more opportunity for aggressive work. There was something also which appealed to the young student's heart in that band of workers who had gone out as pioneers of the new Church ; they were praying men and women, and round such a centre he saw a great work could be built up. In a word, the necessity of Sheffield was greater, and that decided him. He accepted the call, and on October 8th he preached his first sermon as minister of the Wicker Church. He took as his text St. Matthew xvii. 5 : " And behold a voice out of the cloud, which said, This is my beloved Son, in whom I am well pleased ; hear ye Him." His first work is to hold up his Master in all the glory of His transfiguration.

" We are now looking forward," he said, " if God so will, to a course of self-sacrifice and combined labour, and it is well, before we begin this life of constant toil and perhaps of frequent sorrow, to gaze earnestly on the exceeding loveliness and matchless dignity of Him for whom all labour and sorrow must be endured, for, remember, the glory of the Master will one day be the glory of His servants also, and especially to impress on our hearts those words which should for ever consecrate us to His unfettering service."

They are the words of one who has counted the cost, and makes light of all work and all sacrifice in comparison with the joy which is set before his eyes. They are the

words of one who meant each member of the community
to be his fellow-worker in this high service.   Then follows
a series of sermons on " If any man would come after Me,
let him deny himself, take up his cross daily, and follow
Me."   Doing the will of God, doing good to others, bearing the will of God—these are the duties which are linked
to each other with reciprocal influence.

Through all the sermons, even through those which are
preached over those who have passed away, runs the
note of joy which always goes together with self-devoted
work.   His first birthday at the Wicker falls on a Sunday,
and his text is, " Delight thyself in the Lord, and He shall
give thee the desires of thine heart." [1]

" Man gives his rewards for the labour that is done.
God gives His rewards for the delight we feel in the
labour.   So opposed are man's ways and God's.   Man
rewards for the difficulty ;   the vaster the difficulty the
grander the recompense.   God rewards for the delight
we experience in our labour ;   and the greater, the more
enthusiastic and intense the delight, the more munificent
will be His reward."

He did not fail himself in the great task of happiness.
" Mr. Paton, or, as we familiarly styled him, ' J. B.,' and
sometimes ' Our Young Bishop,' was glowing with hope
and expectancy," says Mr. Gunn, who was a member of
the Church in those days.   " It was an inspiration to be
in his company.   All was brightness and enthusiasm."

In the following July came the Ordination.   The
sermon was preached by the Rev. J. Baldwin Brown, and
the Rev. Professor Barker, the resident tutor of Springhill College, gave the charge.

It was not long before he began " hitting the devil in a
new place," indeed in more new places than one.   There
was an old chapel in Garden Street, which had been closed
for years.   It was on the point of being sold to the Roman
Catholics, but he stepped in and saved the situation.   Five
members of the Wicker [2] were told off to go and relight
the old beacon-fire.   They did not like going, but they

[1] Psalm xxxvii. 4.
[2] Mr. John Fitzgeorge, Mr. Newton, Mr. Outram, Mr. Roberts, and Mr.
G. E. Tucker.

went; and from a small beginning succeeded in raising a strong Church. There were a large number of Welshmen in the iron-works who did not know enough English to follow an English service. A room was secured for them, and services in Welsh were arranged. There were village Churches all round needing help. A band of village preachers was formed, who were ordained as elders for this special work, and the duties were divided out among them. There were fairs and markets, and wherever men were gathered together, there was a chance which was not to be missed for telling them of the good news of Christ. Ministers of the Church of England, and other denominations, worked with him, and their co-operation was one of the happiest features of his Sheffield life. Bishop Moorhouse, who was then Vicar of Sheffield, writes me about some of these experiences :

" Your father and I, with some other ministers and friends, went down on a certain occasion to address the crowd assembled at the Sheffield fair. We mounted on a wagon which had been provided, but had scarcely taken our places, when a number of roughs got under the vehicle and tried to upset us. They were foiled, however, by ecclesiastical ponderosity. I remember very well how instantly your father commanded a friendly attention by his sunny smile and charming manner. He was often interrupted in his address, and I was struck by the happy adroitness with which he replied to the questions which were shot at him. He said to me, as we went away, ' Didn't you feel yourself greatly helped by the interruptions ?—they were like half a dozen new texts, besides showing us what the people wanted.' I know that, as you suppose, your father frequently preached from the trough of a pump in a place called West Bar. Unhappily, I never was present on any of those occasions. But perhaps it may give you some idea of the nature of the task, if I relate to you an incident from my own experience while preaching from the same place. I had been urging upon the people the madness of neglecting the interests of the soul in devotion to bodily pleasures, when a man stopped me by a question. ' You are talking about the soul,' he said; ' I believe that the only soul we have is the brain.' ' Why do you believe that ? ' I asked. ' Well,' he said, ' I read the other day, that a man who had been knocked down in the streets of Paris, and who had suffered a fracture of the skull, was unable to think. They took him, however, to a hospital, and when the brain had been relieved from the pressure of the skull, he could think as well as ever.' Now I might easily have said, ' There are two theories about the brain—the one is that it *is* the mind ; the other is that it is the necessary instrument of the mind. The facts you speak of are just as easily explained on one of these theories as on the other, and therefore you have no business to assume that only one of them can be true.' This, however, would have been too general a statement to produce much effect on such an audience. I said, therefore, ' A sculptor who was fashioning a statue went to his dinner. In his absence mischievous boys bent his chisel out of the perpendicular. He found, on his return, that he could not proceed with his work. As soon, however, as he had straightened his chisel he could proceed as well as ever. Now, would you conclude from that, that it was the chisel that made the statue, and not the sculptor ? Surely it only means that the chisel was the sculptor's necessary instrument.' That showed them what I meant, and for the time satisfied them. I tell you this to show the kind of work your father undertook. I know that he was popular with his scratch audiences of working men, and I am sure that he could deal with their difficulties far better than I could. I am sorry that I can only give you this kind of indirect illustration of your father's work in the streets."

Next to godliness came cleanliness. He headed a movement among working men for the erection of a building in which hot and cold baths could be had at a low price. Club-rooms were built in connection with the baths, and were opened " for free social intercourse, for reading news, and for proper recreation." Another room was set apart as a class-room for the teaching of those elementary principles of science which bore on the trades in which the men were engaged. The best way to fight the public-house, he felt, was not to meet it with a blank negative, for man is by nature social, and his social instinct rightly claims its satisfaction. He saw that the weakness of the temperance cause was on the constructive side. The reason of its failure was that it failed to provide opportunity for social recreation of a higher nature.

Of his intercourse with working men only an incident survives :

" He was returning home late one Saturday evening from Attercliffe," says Mr. A. J. Outram, " and on the way a fight was taking place between two men. ' J. B.,' as we used to call him, interfered to stop it, when some one called out, ' Give it him.' ' Who says that ? ' said the pastor. ' You won't hurt me; I have my Master with me.' "

Meanwhile, the work at the Wicker was growing fast. On July 15th, 1855, the new church was opened and the pastor preached from the great text, " For me to live is Christ."

" As a Church these words may be adopted by us. Our establishment, our hope as a Church, are expressed in the one word Christ. Are we asked, whence cometh our strength ? We reply, ' From Christ.' Are we asked, what is our purpose and our prayer ? The reply is, ' For Christ, to magnify Him, to lift Him up, that the perishing world may behold Him.' . . . Each individual Christian has this special object to fulfil beyond the personal trust and consecration which he offers to Christ, viz., to maintain the honour of Christ among his friends and neighbours, and to diffuse His love so as to win them to the same trust and consecration He has offered, and these objects are magnified in their importance and sublimity as we confess them to be the aim and aspiration of a Christian Church. We unite ourselves by the most solemn pledge, declaring that for us to live is Christ, that in our own communion we shall stir up each other to more absolute dependence on Him, and more increased, self-sacrificing devotion to Him, and that thus, strong in our omnipotent Lord, and devoted to His glory, we shall band together in holy enterprise for the defence of His truth and the extension of His kingdom. The object and glory, the strength of our life as a Church, is Christ."

The vigour of the new pastor and the inspiration of his leadership led his people from strength to strength. The

measure of their joy in the doing the work of the Lord
was the measure of their reward.   On the first anniversary of the opening the new organ was opened free
from debt.   By the year 1860 there were 240 members
in the Church, and the Sunday School was " in an in-
conveniently crowded state " with 389 children (the
boys outnumbering the girls), and a staff of 56
teachers.   There was an evening school for working
men, a Young Men's Association, a Village Preachers'
Society, a Dorcas Society, a Christian Instruction
Society.   Money was raised for home missions, for
Rotherham College, for the infirmary and dispensary, for
New Chapel in Cemetery Road, for the Mission to the
Jews, for the London Missionary Society, for the Silcoates
and Lewisham Sunday Schools, the total amount raised for
all church purposes being £1,045.   More than half of this
sum was given to these outside causes I have enumerated.
There was no debt.   There had been no bazaar.   New
buildings were opened for the Sunday Schools in the
January of the following year, and after a short and
solemn service in the old buildings the whole school
marched in procession to the new, the Bible being carried
at the head of the procession.

No one man, however indefatigable, could have carried
all this work through by his own exertions.   It was done
by the earnest co-operation of all.   " Each of you," says
their pastor (it was his constant message), " each of you
will feel that it is his bounden duty to engage in some
Christian service connected with the Church.   The Church
is not a dormitory for sleepers, but a hive for workers."

One hour each day at least he kept sacred to feed the
secret springs in prayer and Bible study and devotional
communion with his God ;   Friday and Saturday each
week he kept for thought and preparation.   Always, when
the work of the Lord's Day was over, he made it his habit
to render solemn account to his Master.   " I always
spent an hour or more on Sunday evening in my study
for meditation, a review of the past and forecasting of
the future. . . . What a solemn, happy hour it was ! confession of sin, longing after higher effort and aim.   ' Nearer
to Thee, my God, nearer to Thee,' and how thy prayers
were wings to my soul.   I *did* get nearer to my Lord,
clung more firmly and yet humbly to His pierced bosom,

saw more the beauty of His face." The first day of each month he set apart " for self-examination, prayer, and devotional reading." All through the heat and strain of his active life he kept this habit of secluded communion with the source of all power. It was the secret of his unfailing spiritual freshness and strength. The more he mingled with the active world of men and affairs, the more he felt the need of this cloister in the heart. "There is something true," he would say, " in the teaching of the old Gnostics. Directly a project begins to take material shape, the struggle with evil begins. At all sorts of unsuspected turns you get jealousy, misunderstanding, misrepresentation, suspicion—the workings of the Demiurge." When these " unsuspected turns " brought the jarring note, it was in the Chamber of the Presence he tuned his heart again to the joyous music of service. It was there he breathed the " larger ether, the diviner air " which lifted him up above all pettiness, all things sordid and mean.

" Often on a tramp I have felt the light and happy spring when I have been able to lay my knapsack aside for the day. How delightful the liberty ! How strong and clear the play of the unburdened limbs ! Such is the joyous strength and freedom of the Christian who has got faith to live by his prayers, whose provider is God, who cumbers himself with no more than a day's need, assured when the new morning dawns, wherever he may be, the same all-bountiful and gracious God will give him fresh supplies. " In all my search for truth I pray to God that He, by His good Spirit, may help me ; not that He will work instead of me, but in me ; not that He will suspend the activity of my own mind, but that He will, by an unconscious influence, quicken and concentrate and direct all my powers so that my quest may be successful ; and so I pray to Him that in the utterances of my mouth He may guard me, not only against intentional falsehood and wilful error, but against any mistake, any deceitful word which will misrepresent His truth."

It was thus the burden of increasing work was borne, not by him, but by his all-sufficing Master. And as he daily commended to God the cares and needs of his little flock, and the activities that were opening out on every side, so he did not hesitate to throw himself upon the prayers of his people.

"When I contemplate the responsibility of my lot till it seems to gather about me in stupendous folds, and to become almost unbearable in its weight, then do I feel sometimes, with an agony of feeling, the need of your prayers : to save the perishing, to proclaim truth which is in its greatness beyond expression, to know that upon my zeal, faithfulness, unswerving devotion in any measure, the salvation of souls, the spirituality of this Church may depend—such duties, devolving especially upon one man, should call out from you the continual and earnest breathings of your heart on his behalf. Brethren, pray for us."

The great texts provided by the historic events he never neglected. There were such local events as the founding of the Y.M.C.A., there was the day of National Humiliation for India, the American War and the great question of Slavery, followed by the appeal for the sufferers in the Cotton Famine ; there was the Bicentenary of Black Bartholomew's Day, and the celebration of the Ejection of 1662, on which he read a paper at the Bicentenary Conference at Leeds ; there was a sermon on Florence Nightingale, and no one will ever forget the Sunday when he stood up and told his congregation that Prince Albert had passed away, the Queen had lost her Consort, and the country had lost its best friend and noblest helper. There was no gulf of separation between the pulpit and the pew. He had special addresses for business men; for then, as now, men were saying it was not possible to be a Christian in business. "Man's will," he tells them, "rules supreme within himself; no power can master it. Matter may yield to force, the strongest fortress may yield to assault, but man's will remains free." He has three lectures for the freethinkers on "The Credulity of Scepticism," and another address to secularists, meeting and answering their stock arguments against Christianity. He discusses Colenso and Strauss. He has lectures on some early heroes of the Christian Church, St. Bernard the Crusader, St. Polycarp, St. Chrysostom, St. Augustine,

There is one course on St. Paul, and another on his favourite
Epistle to the Ephesians. And the summing up of our
duty to our fellow-men is put in two short sentences :
" Let them be as Christ to you. Be ye as Christ to
them."

The impression he produced, as a man and a preacher,
on a chance meeting with one who was too unpretentious
to set up in any way as a critic, may be gathered from
the following letter :

" I walked up to him and said I was glad to see him in
W. B. once more, as I had not seen him since his student
days. 'But,' said I, 'you know my son, F. R., better than
you know me.' He started with a pleasurable surprise
and spoke some kindly words of you which we and all
who know you endorse as not unfittingly applied, but
which I will not repeat. I was at once struck with his
benign face and manner, wonderfully affectionate, sympathetic nature, overflowing loving-kindness, and all the
human and divine virtues which so strongly appear in
his pulpit utterances. That so brief, but long-to-be-re-
membered interview, was soon over. . . . Mr. Paton has
the very same fault that is complained of in Dr. Parker,
energetic notes and inaudible ones—perfect whispers,
and sometimes dumb show without even the whisper.
Much was lost, and this was regretted on account of the
great fascination in the preacher's voice and manner of
delivery, which can never be forgotten by any one. The
straining to catch every syllable was painful, yet the
strain continued through the two long discourses, and
never before could there be observed such a breathless
stillness, just as if the building had been void. What a
matchless, flexible voice ! the quiet, earnest tones of which
were perfect music, prolonged in some words in his own
peculiar manner, not a note in his grand scale left unused.
Never was such feeling put into words, voice and emotion
being perfectly attuned. How impressive was the intense fervour, the strange, clinging, yearning entreaty
which will stick to memory like unearthly strains of
harmony ! The only similar kind of moving eloquence
which remains in my ears was from the heart of the Baptist minister, Mr. Chown, of London. But that gentleman
did not use, or care about, a gamut, but went on in one

even flow of his own peculiar, charming, entrancing strain; while Mr. Paton was startling with his lightning-flashes, and his speaking gestures were wonderful to behold, his various action was almost ceaseless. But I now feel the folly of running on in this style to one who knows the man and can describe him so much better. I did think to say a word on the remarkably devout spirit of Mr. Paton. The prayers were even more moving than the sermon. They lifted us into the presence of the Eternal. There were pauses in the prayer, frequent pauses, sometimes in the middle of a sentence. He seemed to be looking to God to give him the next word. The sense of God's presence was very near to us in those pauses. Never was such solemnity and humility; he was as one seeing and feeling the invisible."

No mere reproduction of the words he used will give any adequate impression of his preaching. With him, more than with most preachers, the man himself was the sermon. What drew all classes round him, from the highest to the humblest, was the feeling that they were listening to one who had entered into the real life of the people as he had entered into the real presence of his God. In the themes he selected, and in his manner of handling them, there was an intensity of human feeling which vitalised them, and no one listening could help believing that the man who was addressing them was not only a man of God, but a man of large heart, overflowing with human brotherliness, and burning with a passion for the saving of human souls.

" I have almost no personal recollection of him," says one who was a little fellow not yet in his teens in those days, " except his dignity in the pulpit and the breaking out of frequent gracious smiles as he preached."

But it is even more as a Pastor than as a preacher that he is remembered in Sheffield. The work of the Pastor he spoke of as his " happiest office."

" I enjoy no work like this, going from man to man, bidding them be of good cheer—one struggle more, higher and higher, heaven is before us; or passing from the bedroom of one sick and dying to that of another. Death has lost all its hatefulness and fear to me. I have seen no mortal beauty such as glows on the pale but glorified countenance of so many of God's saints when they have neared their home. They seem to catch, as they draw near, far-distant echoes of the music above, and to see, ere they leave us, the splendour of those mansions in our Father's house. When asked where I have seen the greatest happiness on earth, I should say—'Incomparably the greatest on the death-bed.' Oh the hours of enchantment I have spent talking with weary Christians just going home! For there I have learnt something of the very talk of heaven, and I have left them thinking rather I had talked with angels than with men."

One of his flock writes :

" I never met him without receiving a warm greeting, and a look and a word of encouragement. He often visited us. We had a large garden, and he used to time his visits so as to find us in the garden. He revelled in its brightness, and would often join us when we were busy in it. The Bible-classes and the Teachers' meetings were seasons of real instruction and much encouragement. The teachers were led to speak of their own experience, so that the class was a conference on methods of spiritual work."

He was specially happy among his young men.

" I don't know why it is—you must not smile—but I cannot do so much good among young women. I feel I can speak so much more freely and strongly to young men. Consequently, my Church has a larger number of men than women, and is, so far, I should think, a solitary exception in England."

But he had taken a larger field than the Wicker for his parish. He took the initiative not only in restoring old Churches, but in starting new ones, e.g. at Broompark, and he was a leader in the Yorkshire Union.

" I well remember," writes the Rev. Mr. Robertshaw, minister of Stocksbridge, " the speeches Mr. Paton made at the Annual Meetings. For a time they were quite a feature of these meetings. In one speech he would be seeking to revive some old cause; in another, he would startle us by introducing some brand-new scheme of usefulness. So he kept the Union alive and active."

Two little touches are needed to complete the picture. Children were an unfailing source of joy to him. He was always at home with them, and they with him. German philosophy, Arabic, Syriac, and correcting proofs had not choked the springs of the child nature within him.

"We had a garden of about three acres," writes Mr. Arthur Lee, the son of his friend, Mr. Henry Lee, of Manchester. "I was four or five years of age when my father took the place, and soon after your father began to visit us and put us up to flying kites. He showed us how to make them, and on one visit started us on a monster which was flown in due course, a ball of extra strong string being provided. I remember so well your father tying the end of the string to one of the pillars of the verandah on one side of the house when the kite was high up in the air, and showing us how we could send messengers up to it. He gave us great joy, and we always looked forward with pleasure to his visits."

There was another little friend, the daughter of Mr. Henry Bateman, of Clapton, who looked forward to his coming.

"Though I do not think I was more than four years old when he first came to our house," writes Mrs. Fairbairns, "I quite remember feeling he was *my* friend, in a way no other visitor was. We had two staircases in our house, and when he knew I was going up to my nursery, he loved to run up the other way and meet me half-way, snatch me up and carry me the rest of the way up, stopping to have a game with me. He invented lovely stories for my dolls'-house, and we used to play with great vigour—rather to the dismay of my nurse, who thought I got quite out of bounds with such a playmate. We used to have great fun in the garden, where, if alone, I was not allowed to go out of sight of the house. With him I might go anywhere, and we used to play hide-and-seek, and he would lift me on to his shoulder, and let me pick fruit off the trees and feed him. I quite well remember how I hated the ' Eclectic ' ! I didn't know what it was, but I knew I never got a hearing when I heard that word—he was so grave, and not at all my playmate.

" He is wonderfully little altered from my early memories, except for age, and when I saw him last year,[1] and he held out his hands, and kissed me, I could imagine myself five years old, in a pinafore, and with long curls, which always used to amuse him.

" I had a lovely likeness of him hanging in my dolls'-house; but when that was given away I destroyed all the pictures, as I could not bear that they should fall into strangers' hands.

" These very slight recollections serve, I think, to show the manner of man he was when he was twenty-four, fresh from college, and full of honours ; simple, warm-hearted, affectionate, so that even a little child looked on him as her friend, and, now the years have passed, still holds him in the love and esteem which have never faltered for fifty years and more."

But, absorbing as was his work as preacher and pastor, it did not absorb the whole man. His mind never was, and never could have been, parochial. He was wider than his parish. All along he was finding time to forge ahead with his studies, to keep in touch with literature, and to write articles for the press. Time is very elastic in the hands of the man whose will is strong enough to plot out resolutely a time-table for each day. What his daily day was like may be gathered from what he writes to a friend :

" The first hours of the day, from 6—9½, I devote to Oriental studies, Arabic or Syriac, the later 3 hours till 12½ to English, or Greek, or Latin, or French, or German —to the classics of such languages as I am acquainted with. I am engaged with an American friend in preparing an edition of Seneca, the old Latin philosopher. It gets on but slowly.

" At 12½ I dress, and go out to visit my people, spending an hour and a half, and returning to dinner at 2½.

[1] Written in 1906.

I spend the time after dinner dreaming, or reading poetry, or with a newspaper. Then tea at 4, and the evening for work till 10.30.

"From 4 to 5½ was once given up to History and Science, now to the 'Eclectic.' From 6—9¼ to Literature. On Tuesday I ought to write a leader for some London paper,[1] but I have not been fit for it lately. Then there are the reviews I am now engaged on, two on Inspiration, one on China, and one on the Middle Ages.

"Wednesday, of course, is lecture evening, when I must prepare to speak to my people. I always exceedingly enjoy these quieter week-evening services. On Monday evening we have a Prayer-meeting. On Tuesday and Thursday evenings we have an Adult School open, and I am sometimes there, not often. My Young Men's class is a sort of self-acting machine. They meet on a Monday evening, and this winter (1858-9) I have appointed another President, or rather Vice-President, who conducts it when I am not there. Otherwise, one occasional absence on my part would interrupt its work and prosperity. When at home, and at liberty, I am there, of course. It matters nothing what their subject may be. I generally find I can instruct them from my pretty general reading without much special preparation. On Friday evening I begin to prepare for the Sabbath, and on Saturday morning from 9½ to 12½, and afternoon and evening, and all day on the Sabbath, I prepare for the two services; sometimes I have three.

"I am secretary of a new Village Preachers' Society which I formed here. We have 12 stations in connection with it, and 60 preachers, 50 of them laymen, and, of that 50, 24 belong to my Church.

"I am actively engaged on the Committee of the English Chapel Building Society, which is the only general society I work for.

"There are the host of incidental calls of all sorts, and the committee-meetings for Schools, Missionary Societies, etc., in which I take a full share."

But, however carefully his plans were laid, there was always something cropping up to break through the ordered sequence of his day. Calls for public service were

[1] Usually the "Patriot."

numerous ; the diocese of his villages needed much super-vision ; doors of usefulness were continually being opened, and, with every opening of the door, there seemed to come God's call to go in and possess the land in His Name. " I regard myself," he writes, " as a missionary more than anything else."

" Multitudinous engagements absolutely plough through one's own plans. The difference between the college life and the ministerial consists in patching up broken days and making the most of them when holes are knocked in bottom and sides, whereas at college every day was whole.

" Oh these public meetings and committees ! Just for instance. On Monday at 12 I am to be at Don-caster at a committee-meeting. On Tuesday at 12 I meet a committee in the Y.M. Association rooms. On Thursday I am to be at Worksop to speak.

" There you have a picture of my daily life. . . . When tolerably well, my work is a plaything to me. It never wearies me much; but I have not been quite well, though so much better to-day and yesterday. Yet I never, when weary, feel depressed in spirits. Depression I never knew. When weariest most, I am often happiest : a quiet aching sense of calmness creeps over me."

One of his letters gives us a peep into the room which was the central clearing-house of all his various activities :

" Here I am, perched at my desk—a broad, noble, slanting desk : in front of me a row of dictionaries and grammars, mostly of ancient languages. At my right, on the desk, a large copy of Seneca and Cicero and a few other books. In the middle of the room a long table, loaded with books in different rows, each representing a different class of subject and order of work. In the corner a large escritoire ; books again, and a series of small drawers, into which I can pop small papers. And there in the centre am I, squat on my high stool, and dashing away with my pen."

Above the mantelpiece stood out, in bold print, his motto, the three words which embodied his aim in life : Consecration—Concentration—Punctuality.

Work was his delight. He revelled in it. "Work," he says, "is the noblest, reallest thing in the universe, the best worship, the highest delight." Work was carried on at high pressure. The whole of his lecture on St. Augustine and the Latin Church was written out, from start to finish, on the afternoon of the Sunday on which it was delivered. No wonder the handwriting became feverish, and hard even for himself to decipher. "It would weary you," he writes, "to read such a hurry-graph as my sermon is." Yet in these first years of his pastorate there is no sign of flagging. Languor was not in his look. His body was the absolute servant of his iron will.

"How am I?—*i.e.* how is this body of mine, child of the clay. It weareth well:—what with the absorption of other dust, the solid brickwork seems not to crumble, nor the cement to loosen. I eat, drink, sleep—too much betimes, and I think—for I do not often ruminate thereon or ask my clayey companion the question—all goes on rightly. The machinery does not creak to my hearing, and I hear no grumble, so I may presume this Pariah of the Desert who has undertaken to be my slave for the short tent-pilgrimage I make here, considers itself pretty well attended to, and in tolerable condition. . . . I believe few men have a stronger physique than I, else some of my work could not have been done. I have run long, desperate races with men in the prime of health, and have seen them sink while I spurred on to the goal.
"My spirits never flag. Depression I never knew, so kindly tempered are the elements of my constitution and so good has always been my God."

Yet the constant drain was telling on him; he was overdrawing his account, and even the millionaire can play too long at that game. There were signs that his "clayey companion" was beginning to remonstrate. Throat and eyes both gave admonitory signs, and in the last year of his pastorate there was a serious and prolonged period of illness. How this was brought about by the piling up of Pelion upon Ossa, and adding to all his Sheffield work the duties of a London editor and Theological Tutor at Manchester, will be told in a subsequent chapter. Meanwhile there is a pleasanter story to tell.

J. B. PATON, ÆT. 30.

Extracts from Diary

"*Oct.* 13*th*, 1858.—May I be kept ever humble ; no boasting, no self-laudation, either directly or indirectly, but let all be done for Christ's glory ; and let Him be all in all. May I show Him forth, not myself, and oh, may I increasingly throw all my trust on Him—His grace and condescension to save even such as I am—may I feel this more, His atonement, His present aid. Never may I trust on my own strength for a single instant. O Jesus, hold me up, warn me, save me in those moments when I am lost to myself.

.   .   .   .   .

" Every day my prayer and labour should be to know more of Christ. It is a day lost in which this is not done, for to know Him, to have Him, is to have life. This will be done by working with him and for Him, and in His Spirit, at my desk doing my Father's will, and when out visiting and calling—in His Spirit, for thus best I shall know Him.

.   .   .   .   .

" Lord, lead me to marriage if it be Thy will, and sanctify me for it. Bless her whom Thou mayst have chosen for me. Let me be faithful in keeping this journal.

.   .   .   .   .

" *March* 2*nd*, 1860.—Now for my life work. I have felt as if this were to be (so far as my study goes) the building up of argument of Christian evidence on these two grounds :

" I. Its root : growth in Old Scripture, involving all the difficult questions of O.T. inspiration, Jewish economy, etc., etc. Hence study of Hebrew, Aramaic, etc.

" II. Its climatic conditions on its appearance. Show that it could not have been produced from any conditions of human thought extant in the world then—Seneca, Cicero, Epictetus, Greeks. Give résumé of their moral philosophy and of Alexandrian (I propose publishing a series of volumes bearing on this topic).

" In my present preparatory training, Hebrew, Arabic, etc., faithfully studied, and Seneca and Cicero edited, and get fuller grasp of great essential nature of Christianity.

4

For this latter object, write essays on its conditions, and discipline myself in religious philosophy.

.   .   .   .   .

" I have seen to-day the importance of spending Thursday, Friday, and Saturday evenings on Sermons. Now my style is being formed and my character is being fixed, make every effort. Thursday and Friday evenings, and Saturday before 8, if necessary, on morning sermon. Saturday 8—11 evening sermon ; write out last quarter. Spend whole Sabbath in revising, committing, altering sermons. Preaching, my work—the work which my Master has given me to do. Spend strength on it : influence to be gained : souls to be saved. I bless God that He has shown me this. Do it regularly for Him.

" On Sabbath continue preparation ; fervent prayer, especially at night; always spend an hour alone with God in prayer; then to bed.

" Oh, be instant in prayer against great sin, its terror will again encompass me unless, O Jesus, Thou hold me up. Also, against indulgence in morning. Oh, it is a light cross, and I can show my love by it. Let me therefore despise the pleasure. It is for life the habit must be formed. Oh, pray for all, for all and always.

" *January* 1855.—The one safeguard is prayer. 1 hour every day in reading Bible, $5\frac{1}{2}$—6 and 10—$10\frac{1}{2}$; also in making constant prayer. O Jesus, with Thee I am safe, and shall be all the year through.

" In order to aim this year higher in spiritual attainment I have resolved to set apart first day of every month for special prayer and meditation. Remember Jesus' night of prayer and all good men—fast, watch and pray. Let all walks be seasons of self-examination and prayer, especially every Monday morning, when I begin the week ; occasionally omit dinner, therefore fasting and prayer.

" O my God, reveal to me the corruption of my heart, the heinous guilt of my past life ; especially the evil of pride, self-love, vanity, and self-trust. See the paper which shows the two sins to be one ; flesh tries to be master."

Constant references show how strict he was with himself.

" Oh let me live by prayer. I have neglected this, and hence the awful failures of November 25th and December 19th."

General Rules

" Pray—before beginning any period of study, especially at 6.30, 3, and 6 o'clock for pure thoughts and concentration on my Master's work. Also at close of day.

" Before all meals ask to glorify God.

" Before going out, to walks, to visitation, or to parties and meetings, pray to get good, to do good, to enjoy fellowship with Jesus, and thus to glorify God.

" Prayers for myself (a) general, (b) special, as required by circumstances.

" These three in particular: (1) greatest sin, remember words of Christ to look to Him, keeping mind engaged with work and Christ; to be perfectly pure, truth in all things, up in morning; (2) for relatives and friends; (3) for my own people, especially those in whom I may be specially interested.

" General prayer for these objects in evening, 10, and walk at other seasons for blessing and for special object.

" In walks, seek beauty and truth, having fellowship with Jesus. Also exercise voice. Especially cogitate about reading and about material for every composition. If any good thoughts, jot down in note-book and return at 2, put them in book or on paper.

" Spend only one evening a week away from study, and that very seldom. Try to get all four evenings for work.

" Sabbath.—Spend whole day on sermons, with constant prayer for myself to be quickened, etc., and for my people to be profited. Therefore not go out to dinner, nor to supper. Return to pray. Especially pray before leaving house for worship, and in evening spend one hour in retirement in prayer for blessing and self-examination."

To Rev. T. Brine

SHEFFIELD,
May 1st, 1909.

" I thank you for sending me the Jubilee report of the Church. How well I remember seeing for the first time the corner where the church now stands, which was already occupied by builders (?) and the foundations of two houses. I saw at once the value of the site as central to the district, and I, with a certain temerity, at once offered to purchase the site with the foundation-walls that had been already built, and I appealed to some wealthy friends in Sheffield to assist in finding the purchase-money. I remember well how Mr. Hoole also gave me £100 in order to save Garden Street Chapel, which otherwise would have been sold, in order to assist in the erection of the Cemetery Road Church. I am most grateful to think that Garden Street was thus preserved for the great ministry that has been carried on there since, especially at the present time. I need not say, therefore, with what pleasure I would have come to take part in your Jubilee services if it had been at all possible. But it is now nearly two years since I have been able to preach."

CHAPTER IV

MARRIAGE

" Love took up the harp of life and smote upon its chords with might."
—TENNYSON.
" The star of the morning, who has ushered in a happier day for me,
and shall tremulously shine in the sweet dawn of all this lower life."—
JOHN BROWN PATON, to his Wife.

HE had taken a little house in Sheffield in the Burngreave
Road. His elder sister Mary kept house for him, and for
the first four years his younger brothers Alan and James
lived with him and went to school. There were other
family claims upon the eldest son. But when, in 1859,
his younger brothers were ready to go out into the world,
and other claims became less insistent, the channel was
left open for feelings long pent up.

" For years," he says, " I have been schooled in a stern,
sad school of adversity, and it has been well for me that
it has been so, for the discipline of faith and patience and
submission have been wrought in me. Dearer friendships
with the noblest and purest on earth have been my crown
of rejoicing, and the happiness of family love has grown
wider and deeper as one after another of our family has
grown up and decided for Christ; but often, how often,
my heart has yearned and cried through the dark for a
closer, twining sympathy and affection."

At length his prayer was to be answered. He had been
learning to bear the yoke in his youth, and bearing it
joyously, " always thanking God that He put me to no
sore struggle between my heart and my duty." But it
must have been hard for a nature so open, so self-giving,
never to breathe a word to any one of what he was keeping
back repressed in his heart. And all the time the yoke of
family duty was preparing him unawares for a sweeter
yoke, and a yoke-fellow who was to share all his truest,

53

strongest, innermost life and work till life and work in
this world were done. For such a nature as his the individual life must ever have been incomplete and un-
satisfying.   But now life was to be a monologue no more.
For four years he had known Mr. William P. Paton, of
Newton Place, Glasgow, an Eastern merchant, and a
leading deacon in Dr. Wardlaw's Church, who had been
for many years a director of the City Mission, and had
taken a prominent part in the religious and philanthropic
life of the city.   He had been a widower for many years.
His daughter Jessie kept house for him, and a very
hospitable house it was.   Mrs. Beecher Stowe speaks of
the hospitable welcome she found in it on her visit to
Scotland.

Mr. Alexander Paton had moved with his family to
Glasgow in the year 1846, and had joined the Congregational body.   In this way, the two families which bore the
same name, but were not in any way related, had got to
know each other.   There were also other connexions.
Mr. R. Alfred Vaughan and his wife were intimately
acquainted with the Paton family at Newton Place.
Another friend of my father's, Mr. Batchelor, of Sheffield,
had been preaching recently at West George Street Church
as a candidate for the vacant pulpit, and Mr. W. P. Paton,
on behalf of the Church, went over to Sheffield to hear
Mr. Batchelor in his own church, and make inquiries.
While at Sheffield, Mr. W. P. Paton appears to have called
on his namesake as one whom he could ask for confidential information.

It was not long after this call in Sheffield that the
young pastor of the Wicker was repaying the call in
Glasgow.   This call, too, was on a strictly confidential
matter, and had reference to another vacancy at Sheffield
of a much more personal nature.   The wooing was short,
and it was victorious.   When on January 23rd, 1859, he
went up on the night-train from Glasgow to London, the
sound of the wheels was shaping itself into a music which
was new to his heart, and his eyes told of triumph tasted.

Though the wooing was so short, and the decision came so
quickly, his choice had not been ill-considered or rash.

" I heard, before any one knew of my feelings and my
hopes—it was as rapturous music to my soul—my mother

praise you again and again for what you did to Willie
Henderson; how kind and attentive you were to him.
Shall I tell you what you did, for I have it all by heart?
. . . Besides, my mother and father both told me (only
in the course of conversation, without the remotest idea
of the hungry ears that heard them), of your labours on
committees, and your self-denying benevolence. Others,
too, confirmed this glad news. Then, dearest, I was
most observant, or rather, my soul was so awaked, that
each sound was heard, each movement, each look was
seized and treasured. There was so much in just one
word you said : ' We started *exactly* at the ¾ hr. in the
cab '—that was to Hill Head, and there was the faintest
accent on ' exactly,' and I knew it was true—you had been
so thoughtful as to be *exactly* punctual. I saw you did
your work calmly, so quietly it might not be seen to be
done, as if a fairy had crept in and out and done it; but
it was done methodically and well. And oh, the charm
of this—the dear sight of this to me, and I exclaimed :
' That is what I need. I have no such method, no such
calmness; but she will help me. And if my energy may
bear her on, though tenderly, that shall be hers.'

" Then so much else I saw; the simplicity of your dress
matched the guilelessness of your manner ; your hands
lost not their *own* dear worth through being covered with
diamond rings. We spoke of your departed, sainted
brother-in-law, and that face, the mirror of your soul, was
instantly dimmed, and the soft, lustrous dew stole into
your eye, mixed with a sunny light, the light of Hope and
Immortal Love ? Again, and how I reproach myself!
I spoke of the death of my dear young friend, William
Bruce. I saw in an instant the quiver come into your
lips, the trembling sensibilities of a soul that sorely loved
and sorrowed. I had forgot, or I would not have mentioned the cause of my dear William's death; but that
quiver reminded me, and I was so grieved. Forgive me
that transient wound. How much besides ! Did I not
watch your eye as I spoke of the Malagasy martyrs—
standing in the fire of that grand evening sunset as they
did—and your look told me of a sympathy with such a
faith, and a readiness for such a death. Pupil dear, shall
I tell thee more, or is this argument complete to show thee
I was not blindfolded and very rash ? Yes, I must add

one more word. I told my parents, and they, who have heard much of you, said how good God would be if He gave me such a wife. I spoke to my dear friends now with you,[1] and they told me more of you, and all of it, such as I was thirsting to hear.

.   .   .   .   .

"Then, dear, you say, ' Weak, most weak, I must have been thus to have led you on to pour out such holy, lavish love as these treasured letters reveal.' Is there not a want of logic there ? I am so glad I can point out the flaw in your reasoning, for oh ! I do dislike logical, syllogistic women ; and this error is thrice dearer to me than the grandest syllogism. How strong, most strong you have been, I should say, so to lead me. Is it not a very poor compliment to me to say I should have been led by weakness ? No, it is thy strength that compelled me—a strength not thine own, but God-given, for it lay in that nature and sympathy which is His gift, and not thy own. Isn't it wicked in me thus to correct you ? But then, I said I should be your teacher this morning."

To love, to have such a one to love, filled his whole life with throbbing, tremulous joy. The deep springs of his primary affection were unsealed, and the flood of the new passion spread over his whole life and thought and work as the waters cover the sea. It is not possible to quote from the letters he wrote at this time without the feeling of one who intrudes into a sacred place, and yet it is equally impossible to pourtray what he was in himself without giving some indication, at least, of what his wife was to him. From henceforth the two are become one.

"It just flashes on my mind—how different all was before I met you, and how wonderful is the Providence which has knit our very souls' inmost fibres together, for so it seems as if now, love, we lived one life. Thy feelings pulse through this heart as through thine own, and every thought of thine, by some strange harmony, is tuned in such perfect accord with all my thoughts that no longer, love, can I believe in the *duality* of us two.

.   .   .   .   .

[1] Mr. Batchelor and his wife.

" Come, love; all my work says Come, and nerve him for the work which his God and the Church require from him.

" Love, hasten to join the streams of my life with thine, that they may flow together, that our work may be one, that on the river of our commingled life we may upbear and float the ark of God, that, as you say, no eye may discern, no analysis separate the tidal currents of the two streams that have met, embraced with a gurgling kiss, and now flow calmly, grandly on to their ocean rest in eternity."

His letters are sometimes the shortest of notes, sometimes full outpourings of his innermost feelings ; sometimes written in the quiet of the morning hour in his study, sometimes dashed off at a deacon's meeting, or on the platform of a public meeting, or on a chance leaf torn from his pocket-book, as he leans against the staircase waiting at a club. Sometimes he rushes into a friend's house after a long day's visiting, or even into a chemist's shop to get a sheet of note-paper and an envelope, so that the looked-for letter may not be missing next morning on the breakfast-table in Glasgow.

" It has been a glorious gallop ever since I left thee," he writes, after a short mid-week visit he has snatched from his busy life; " but I have won through, somewhat tired.

" Every minute of the day, while harnessed and pulling steadily at my work, my thoughts have been sweetened and sanctified. . . . Thou art His gift to me, and day after day He gives me to drink deeper and more sweetly of the chalice of His love.

" My heart bursts almost with the longing to fly to her. How can I delay ? Were it not that I have a prouder, grander wish than even that of seeing you—and that is to be worthy of thee—I would not stay."

His whole being has come under a new control, its whole current flows in a new channel.

" It seemed as if the hard, dead winter had flown away in my soul, the flow of brooklets, the song of birds, the

thrilling of the young leaves as they burst from their cells
to bask in the soft, warm sun, all the golden tumult of the
happy spring, was in me.

" I have never felt the sweetness of such love before,
though I have often fancied it, longed for it, prayed for it.

" A new pulse beats along my soul, and every beat
carries thy name, thy love, thy soul, with it. It is a
piercing, honeyed, almost agony of joy.

" I can hardly stay my hand. It will write, will only
write ' my own,' ' all my own,' ' my own Jessie,' and I
could fill a letter with these words that fill my soul.

" I look through vistas now—till, alas, these foolish
eyes cannot see—on a *home* and a long *one* life, where
thou art set in the sky which embosoms it."

The joy of the betrothal holds perpetual festival in his
heart. Sweeter and sweeter grow the image and the
name of her he loves, and stronger, day by day, the
mystic claim by which he binds her to his heart. ' Each
day my bride grows so dear that the love of yesterday
seems cold to-day." Out of the abundance of the heart
the mouth speaks.

" My heart feels like the drooping cloud which cannot
soar aloft again to its nest in heaven till it has poured out
a rich flood on the earth. My heart cannot buoy itself
up, or rest in peace till the fulness overwrought find an
utterance.

" I leave my desk, sometimes in the mid-volley of some
long paragraph, to go to that secret drawer where these
golden treasures are lying, and then I read and re-read.
Thou hast found the clue which has led into the inmost
labyrinths of my soul, and there, where never mortal eye
or foot had been before, I see, so soft, the glint of my
dear one's face, I hear the soft patter of her feet, and the
lonely corridors and rooms, dumb for so many years—
hark ! they are musical with a new voice and a ceaseless
song. It is spring throughout all my soul."

With the new gust of feeling there comes new insight
into poetry. " Some of the most beautiful passages,
which once were hieroglyphical to me, are now as plain
as sunshine. There is a new meaning and a new zest in

work." Already he shares it all with her, and all his duty is set to heavenly music. All his work is turned into song. At one time it is a sermon—

" I am sure I never preached a better sermon in my life than I did last night from the text ' He that believeth shall not make haste.' And why ? Because, love, the purity, tenderness, peace and joy of thy soul had descended and nestled in mine. And oh ! my love, I now have a yet dearer aspiration and stronger spur in life; but how I need thee to help me."

Sometimes it is a struggle with a forthcoming number of the " Eclectic Review." Contributors disappoint him, printers are late with the copy, or mislay the last portion of an article.

" The writers have failed me in some cases, and in one or two others have written badly, so that I must doctor or tinker their work up a bit. But I love such a conflict, as it were, with circumstances. It turns every day into a Waterloo; and, you know, we must beat the French.

" So I go, having just given and taken one long, sweet kiss from thy face which I often keep open on my desk here while I mingle strange ejaculations with all my work. I should not wonder finding it in the next ' Eclectic ' all over like the word ' Selah ' in the Psalms, ' Bless her,' ' Jessie dear.' "

He shares his reading with her :

" I have such an eerie, sad, fearful impression hanging on me from reading a bad, though most powerful book— ' Wuthering Heights ' by Ellis Bell (Emily Brontë). I bought it yesterday to relieve the tedium of travelling, and have just finished it—but oh, the dolour, the sad, crushing horror it distils through my soul—worse far than any goblin story, though of the same sort. I feel its miasm clinging to me, and as if it made me unworthy to write to thee.

" 'Twas the fiendish counterfeit of our love in that tale that struck the awful chill through me. A passion theirs was as demons might cherish—yet not strong and true, while so cursed. I wonder where that elf-woman culled her herbs to decoct such a poisonous charm as her tale contains. . . .

"I have read 'The Tremendous Adventures of O'Grahagan '—with regret, because my spiritual life decayed."

Another time it is his pastoral visitation :

"Amid my own joy I have visited the home of the sick and the place of death. I have seen the wife stooping over the face which relaxed from its distortion into the calm rest of death, and heard her sob her Amens, ere he died—while I prayed. Oh, it was a sad, wonderful, terrible scene. He seemed just at last to gain his foothold on the Rock of Ages, from which all day before he had been driven off by the restless surging of alarm. He said so touchingly to me, ' Oh yes, the outcast is received at last ! ' "

Amid all the varying scenes of his life she is always his " helpful, restful one."
There is only one joy that overpowers the joy of the love she has given to him, and that is the joy of pouring out his love for her.

" All the argosy-burden of the wealth of this freighted heart which sailed over life's sea to thee, to pour out all on the shore of thy love.
" 'Tis a happy infatuation has seized me, and all my nature, not only my sensitive feelings, but this calm judgment whose independence I had so sternly guarded now owns thy dear delightful sovereignty. . . . 'Tis the joy of giving thee my love that now, I think, doth overpower that so sacred joy of receiving thy love."

From first to last the love of the wedded life is regarded, not as apart from God's love, but a part of it, and being such it becomes a true sacrament of life. " Not one of thy letters," he writes, " have I read, but it has flowered into prayer. I am less my own now, and, therefore, more of Christ's." And the service of Christ means, not dalliance, but stern and unremitting work.

" And now what an inspiration is mine, my love ! To

raise, honour, bless thee, and, in the enjoyment of thy watchful love, to accept the highest earthly proof of my Father's favour. So in prayer, and in holy, aspiring effort, let us prepare for that eternal sphere in which love, worship, work, may all be one and the same, in brightening, varying change the same.

"Thus may thy spirit and mine be formed, rooted, growing, flowering, fruit-bearing in love. Unutterably my cup overfloweth and my soul yearneth, blessed and crowned in this new brighter diadem, to be more than ever consecrated to my work, to save souls, to turn the wicked from the error of their ways. . . . My love for thee will never be a let or hindrance to holy enterprise, but a sweet and ever-present incentive. . . . Only, O Saviour, make me worthy, pure, a shrine beautiful and sacred for such a soul as hers.

"But it is to my God I must speak out this great joy. Oh, how in our deepest, highest experiences, the un-uttered, unutterable roll of the soul beats itself upon the infinite! How, again and again, I have raised these hands and this inner voice to bless Him for all the mar-vellous past! but most of all for this, his diadem, the priceless joy wherewith He has crowned it all.

"Pray for me that I may be thy pure-minded, strong-bodied, whole-hearted, divine-souled husband. I need some of thy firmness, thy pureness, and much of thy gentleness, and *all* thy method.

"I do entreat thy prayers—that for this month, in the work before me, I may be single in my aim, may be wholly spiritual in thought and feeling, and may be true, unfalteringly true to the Highest.

"I do trust my love to be true to me, not in dalliance but in severe and heroic work. I need thy help especially to assist me in keeping the stern routine of my plan—a plan which is so perfect in its symmetry and so badly broken and impaired by my weakness. . . . I see that a noble future may be wrought out for God. I trust to thee to make me a better workman for my God.

"There is tenacity, enthusiasm, patience, and terrible labour in me, yet accompanied by a strange weakness. I am an iron rod, but with india-rubber jointings. Then fail not in thy brave decisiveness. It makes my soul thrill with ecstasy to see the work so often, so sadly foiled,

done at last, and to thee I shall be indebted. Oh ! Love
rejoices to owe thee the debt. I am not ashamed to be
indebted to thee. I rejoice and glory in it."

But the strain is not always pitched in the solemn key.
He can be playful. He can accept without one trace of
murmuring an adverse decision, if she so wills it ; what
she wills is wise, and he does not question it. He can
discuss the most prosaic details of the measurements of
floors, the size of the drawing-room chiffonier, and which
is the best colour to choose, so that wall-papers and cur-
tains and carpets may blend in a harmonious colour scheme.

" I will be the Principal in the University of my loved
one's heart, and I hereby dismiss all the Professors from
their respective chairs. I am determined to teach every
department—fill every chair myself. It will impose such
an absorbing and therefore happy task on me.

"Dearest scholar, true, fond pupil, thy first lessons
will begin at the early hour of 6, for the first hour of my
day shall be spent with thee. And every hour of the day
afterwards will be registered to go through a long, sublime
curriculum, through which I'll take thee, every day of
every year to come, and there shall be no vacation. How
art thou pleased with thy self-elected Principal ? To-
morrow she shall know more of his Honours' programme.

" Ah, I call myself the Professor, but it is only a poor
trick to hide my eager, humble docility. How is it the
Professor peruses with such care each word of his pupil's
lesson ? He is, I fear, but a humble scholar after all,
and thou art *the* Royal Instructress whose words are life
to him.

" The change that has come over modern cosmic science
has come over me. Once geocentric, with this dust-ball
for its axis, now heliocentric, with the fire-lighted sphere
for its centre, its pillar, and its glory, and these daily
letters, like fresh currents of pulsing tidal force, do send
me whirling in joyous career aye round thee. There,
dearest, to match thy Niagara, and, if thou art drowned
in thy simile, so am I whirled and dizzied and blinded
in mine.

" It is thy home which we are about to furnish. I
know how much of comfort steals into us almost uncon-

sciously by the familiar objects around us ; and, if they be not in a sort of harmony with our taste, a continual insidious pin-pricking goes on : I must leave thee to say what sort of carpets, what coloured paper-hanging, and what sort of furniture we shall have. . . .

" It is just the most important rooms which must be furnished first, the sitting and bedrooms. Or am I to bring thee back to a plastered barracks ?

" I do so admire the old men who could sit at an oaken table on a sanded or scrubbed floor, but had frescoes of Titian or Raphael on the walls. It is the old preference of soul above sense, a picture to teach the eye, mind, heart, above carpets to warm the feet, or glossy tables to dazzle the eye.

" I think a *Home* should be a *School*, and I should like a good specimen of colour and form to be in our ' School-room.' A good religious or moral picture is a grand and perpetual sermon."

They make up their minds to keep the expenses of the plenishing well within the sum they are able to pay in the form of ready cash. There are no debts of the past throwing their dark shadow across the sunshine of the wedding-day, and there are to be no liabilities that tie them for the future. " I would rather live in a deal hut than in debt," he says. " I know thou would'st." The future will bring its own claims with it when the time comes to educate the children. Meanwhile, there is an insurance policy and " a good, lusty library as a break-water " in case of need.

" Love goes on crutches till his rites be done," says Shakespeare. Love in this case was soon promoted from crutches to wings. On September 14th, 1859, they were "no more twain, but one," and sped on their way to the south, stopping in London on their way to see the October number of the " Eclectic " safely in the printer's hands.

The marriage with one so perfectly suited to his tempera-ment, his need, his heart's desire, was the best of all God's gifts to him. And

" God's best gifts put man's best dreams to shame."

Her personality, welded with his, completed the personality of both ; her treasury was rich where his was poor, so

that in the union of the two there was not simply the
addition of one to one, but a new fulness and a new harmony which were not in either separately. " Grace "
was ever one of his great words, and one of his great
qualities : it was she who taught him how to be gracious.
His instinct was for aggression, adventure, conflict : it
was she who brought into the strenuous activities of his
life sweet ordering and arrangement, the quietness and
the confidence which disciplined and husbanded his
strength. His disposition was always to see in a man
what he wished to see, and to believe of him better than
the man deserved ; her intuition of character saw in
men what was actually there, and steadied his judgment.
To him in his outward life came the rough contact with a
hard world, but in the home there always awaited him
gentleness and sheltering peace which saved him from
becoming hard. Hers was the great love which does all
the little things, that are at once too little and too sacred
for the publicity of print ; the love that stands between
a man and all the petty irks of life. She lived for
him, as he lived for his fellow-men. And the love of
both was the love " that in higher love endures," the
love that grows ever stronger, gentler, helpfuller, and
holier to the end.

A more perfect accord of heart and spirit and mutual
helpfulness there could not have been. " I have found
one," he writes to a friend, " whose every thought seems
a glad answer to the highest thought of my mind." Her
nature was strong where his was weak, and yet in fullest
harmony with his faith and his striving. He had been
conscious of need, and she had been to him as an answer
to prayer ; she had come to a heart which had loyally
prepared itself for the new control, and her coming not
only fulfilled the highest aspiration of the past, but consecrated him for the wider responsibilities and more
strenuous work of the future. To her he committed the
wealth of his life and its powers, and, in the giving, there
opened up to him, as never before, the vision of what
life might be. " Already I feel that Christ has been at
the marriage of our spirits," he says, " for all the common
water of my life has been changed into glad, rich, purpling
wine." The letters of the after-time may be shorter, but
the spirit of them is the same all through.

" We are richer than we were then," writes my mother, as the golden wedding draws near, and she looks back to the golden days of the wooing, " richer in trust and love and blessings than we were then, and I can't write what is in my heart for you . . . keep your brain quiet and your heart resting in the love that abideth and in the joy of our Father's peace."

Peace was her wedding gift to him, a gift that was not of this world, that was new every day and yet did not wear away, a peace which was, as Goethe says, " beyond all summits." It was the gift his ardent, urgent nature needed most. It made him calmer yet stronger ; it did not weaken his power, but made its effect gentler.

She had never herself known a mother's love, and it had been part of her lover's joy to give her his own love, if possible, in the fullest measure of devotion, that he might in some degree make up to her this loss. What she was herself, as a mother to her own children, is a thing too sacred for the blazon of the printed page, and she could tell most—her own invalid child who never had the gift of speech and never was far from her mother's side. But she was as a mother to many a one outside her own home who needed sympathy and guidance and love. " I have lost my best friend," said one of her old servants, when I told her the news of my mother's death, and that was all she could say ; her tears told the rest.

CHAPTER V

LITERARY WORK

"I many a time say the writers of newspapers, pamphlets, poems, books, these are the real, working, effective church of a modern country."— THOMAS CARLYLE.

THE young literary aspirant has usually a certain shyness about his début in print, when what he has written first dons the robes of immortality. But Paton's experience on the Kilmarnock newspaper, his association at college with such a fellow-student as R. W. Dale, who published a volume of sermons before he became a student, and his close contact with two real men of letters like Henry Rogers and Robert Alfred Vaughan, had enabled him to get over this print-shyness at an early age, and had turned his thoughts in the direction of writing. It was indeed clear to any thoughtful mind that, with the wide democratisation of printed matter, the Church could not accomplish her mission in the world if she neglected so powerful an instrument for moving the conscience and moulding the opinions of men.

Moreover, the free republic of letters gives a special chance to Nonconformists. There is no doctrinal subscription required of those who enter it ; talent is the only countersign required to pass to the highest seats. Yet—

"Nonconformists," he says, "have been backward. They have written many tracts, but no tractates. Manifestoes from all sections of the Anglican Church—rationalistic, ritualistic, and evangelical—have appeared in volumes of essays ; but within the last five years, I believe I am correct in saying, no volume, whether written by various pens or by one, has appeared from our denomination bearing on the great questions in debate. One consideration gives the greater seriousness to this grave deficiency. Amid the unrest of this age there is a very deep and earnest, and even solemn spirit of inquiry. Men are agitated and perplexed. Educated men, shaken from their old moorings, are seeking passionately to know the truth. In this mood they are only irritated by the smart philippics that are written for popular tracts, or appear as pungent newspaper articles. The grave questions in hand need to be solidly, comprehensively treated, to guide and satisfy a true inquirer."

The opportunity for press-work was not long in coming. Directly after taking his degree he wrote an article on the philosophy of Locke, which favourably impressed the editor of the "Eclectic Review," who found him eager for further service. " I am labouring under an academic plethora," he wrote, " and anxious to blow off steam." The " Eclectic Review " had been founded some fifty years before, to voice the principles of Evangelical Nonconformity and represent its culture and scholarship in the world of letters. To its earlier issues John Foster and Robert Hall had contributed ; but its reputation had not been maintained ; new blood was needed. Like the downtown derelict Church at Garden Street, it needed a resuscitator, and the two college students from Spring Hill, Paton and Dale, undertook the task of resuscitation in 1856. Their joint-partnership is very happily described by Dr. Dale :

" In the course of a year or two, Dr. Paton became responsible editor, and, in some undefined way, I shared the editorship with him. But Dr. Paton was a man of enormous energy, and, as far as editing was concerned, I was very much in the position—I was about to say—of a *sleeping* partner. That description, however, would be singularly inappropriate. For once or twice in the month Dr. Paton used to come to me about 8 or 9 o'clock in the evening, and we discussed subjects and writers till midnight, or till 2 o'clock in the morning, and then he left for his train ; so that, whatever share I had in editing the ' Eclectic ' was rather hostile than friendly to sleep. Dr. Paton had wonderful vigour and buoyancy in those days, and his fertile mind teemed with literary schemes. During Mr. Ryland's editorship I had written many ' short notices,' as well as papers which were dignified

with the name of 'articles,' and the 'short notices'
became still more numerous when Dr. Paton succeeded
him." [1]

This is not the only night journey which figures in the
correspondence of this period. He travels up to London
by night, finds that a promised article has not arrived,
and the printer has lost the concluding portion of another ;
there are proofs to correct, and there is other business to
transact ; he spends the whole day working at fever-heat,
gets to bed at 1 a.m., and spends the following night again
in the train for Sheffield. This is enough to satisfy the
ingenium perfervidum of the most perfervid Scot. But
it was a greater strain than even his unbounded energy
could stand. He was incurring financial risk as well,
and a new arrangement became necessary.

" Hitherto," he writes in May 1859, " not only the
editorial, but the business conduct of the ' Eclectic ' has
devolved largely on me, and it is impossible that I should
in Sheffield here be able to manage the business of such
a concern. I willingly risked my money—as much as I
felt at liberty to risk—in labouring for an enterprise I
deemed so important; but unknown responsibility might
have ruined me."

Accordingly, in 1859, with the help of Mr. Samuel
Morley, Mr. John Crossley, of Halifax, Mr. F. Barnes, and
Mr. Perry, of Chelmsford, the " Review " is put on a new
footing and published by a new firm. Fresh features
are introduced. One of its chief articles is occasionally
signed. The articles are more varied, and have a more
original flavour. They do not to so great an extent as
before take the form of reviews of books. There are
nature-sketches and descriptions of travel. " The aim
is not to don the professor's gown and call the readers
to the class-room, but to take an arm-chair by their own
fireside." In its political articles it advocates a large
extension of the suffrage, the shortening of the duration
of Parliaments, a fair adjustment of proportion between
the number of the representatives and the number of

1 Magazine of Young Men's Bible Class, Carr's Lane, Birmingham.
Number 10. April 1st, 1894.

the electors, and vote by ballot as a protection against bribery and corruption. The education of the people is a prominent subject, but there is strenuous resistance to the centralising tendency of the age " which is precipitating the conduct of our social and individual life into the hands of the Government. A system of national education means waste of public money, it interferes with the natural responsibilities of parents, and leads to diminished virtue among the people." The review stands for self-reliance and self-government. It refuses to take the House of Lords quite seriously. Social questions take a prominent place: " The Drainage of the Metropolis," "Frauds in Food and Medicine," " Degeneration," " Treatment of the Insane," " The Beer Bill (November 1859)," " The Smoke Nuisance," " Life in a Colliery District," are well discussed, with first-hand knowledge and experience.

Science was asserting her claims to the attention of cultured men. It was the time when, to use Charles Kingsley's words, " Darwin was conquering everywhere and rushing in like a flood, by the mere force of truth and fact." But steadily, through this unsettling fermentation of new thought, the " Eclectic " maintains the Omnipotence of Spirit and refuses to believe there is any opposition between science and religion. The religious standpoint is whole-heartedly maintained. A flippant or pretentious attack on the sacred verities of the Christian faith does not escape chastisement. The Review is not " an infant crying for the light." It knows Him on whom it has believed. " The conductors of the 'Eclectic' do not profess to be seeking for the truth on the great questions of theology, but to have found it. If they were still seeking, they would hold their peace, till their search had proved successful."

Among the contributors during these years were Alfred Wills (the founder of the English Alpine Club, afterwards Judge of the Queen's Bench), P. H. Gosse the zoologist, Alexander Smith, the poet, and his friend, Sidney Dobell, Principal Tulloch, Mary Howitt, Miss Anne Manning (the author of " The Household of Sir Thomas More "), and Miss Frederika Bremer, the Swedish novelist and traveller, Walter Thornbury, and Dr. J. Baldwin Brown.

The editor himself has probably some part in every

number. He reviews books of all sorts : grave books like
the memoir of his friend, Robert Alfred Vaughan, sportive
books like Doran's " Monarchs retired from Business,"
German literature and philosophy, novels and poems.
He writes papers on " Our Theological Colleges "
(January 1859), and others on " Inspiration," " The
Sunday Question," Peter Baynes, Dugald Stewart, and
" The Nature of Poetry."   A series of his papers on
Colenso were reprinted from the " Eclectic " with an
appreciative note in a volume entitled, "The Pentateuch,
its Divine Authority Vindicated." Sidney Dobell helps
him in various difficulties at the beginning and puts him
" au fait with the business of literary matters."   " I look
upon you," he says, " as my secretary of state in rebus
Eclecticis."

In October 1861 he read a paper at the Congregational
Union meetings at Birmingham dealing with the religious
interests of the Continent, reviewing the main movements
of religious life in Germany, France, Switzerland, and
Italy, and urging the Union to include among the objects
of its Bi-centenary celebrations the building of a new
Independent Church in Paris—a proposal which was
carried into effect.

At the same time he was writing leading articles for
the " Patriot " on the burning topics of the day. We
hear of them being written after supper, and taken down
to catch the 4 a.m. train from Sheffield up to town. We
hear, too, of his attending debates at the House of Commons when up in town, and turning in to the Patriot
office to snatch some sleep on a pile of newspapers.

But such journalistic work brought him no abiding
satisfaction. It was desultory, and thereby interfered
with that systematic study of Biblical scholarship and
early church history which began to absorb his mind at
this time.   There were, moreover, the inherent drawbacks
of periodical literature. As J. S. Mill points out, it
cannot, like a book, wait for success ; it must either succeed immediately, or not at all ; and for that reason it
is almost forced to profess and inculcate opinions already
held by the public to which it appeals ; it cannot do the
more solid work of rectifying opinion and shaping out new
thought.

Accordingly in 1861 he was already casting abroad for

some one to relieve him of the editorial work for the
" Eclectic," and in 1862 he found him in the Rev. E.
Paxton Hood. He still went on doing journalistic work
for the " Patriot " intermittently till 1866, but this represented merely the by-product of his mind. His serious
efforts were given to more scholarly work for the Quarterlies.

Some of the scattered papers he afterwards put together and published in two volumes entitled, " Criticisms
and Essays."

The articles which at the time attracted most attention
were written in reply to Renan's " Vie de Jésus." These
were published in book form in 1864.[1] He opens with a
general review of the philosophic tendencies of the age
which have produced the book and given it its vogue,
and he shows how, by jettisoning the miraculous, Renan
commits the grossest outrage on that reason and true
historical science which he proposes to save. Christ's
works of power are congruous to the nature of a God
who is love ; the reconstruction of Renan is congruous
neither to reason nor to fact. Renan's attempt to show
how what is supernatural was produced by natural causes,
to eliminate the miracles of mercy and of power is itself
to suggest a miracle which is impossible because it is
immoral. His theory that monotheism is a native growth
of the Semitic mind is shown to be untenable, and equally
untenable is his hypothesis of the formation of the Gospels.
His carelessness in the interpretation of texts is laid bare,
a carelessness amounting to falsification ; his qualification of all his statements with the convenient phrase " à
peu près " is shown to be as sloppy as it is tantalising.
His chain of reasoning reduces him ultimately to the
absurdity of stating, first, that popular opinion regarded
miracle-working as necessarily the distinctive mark of the
Messiah; secondly, that Jesus, who worked no miracles,
was accepted as the Messiah. The brilliance of Renan's
work reveals the more strikingly that what he attempts
is impossible. Since the work of Jesus and the growth of
Christianity are not of man, they must be of God. The
net result, therefore, is that M. Renan's book, so far
from weakening the Christian faith, becomes " one of the
widest and firmest ramparts built in outer defence of the

[1] A Review of the " Vie de Jésus," by M. Renan. (H. Tressidder, Lond.
1864.)

citadel. . . . We repeat that this book is a new and rich
contribution to Christian Apologetics."

In essentials, the attack on Christianity to-day is the
same as it was when this book was published. There is
the same " adulation of Jesus " coupled with the refusal
to believe His witness of Himself. There is the same
pseudo-scientific hesitation in crediting His works of
power. There is the same attempt in the name of science
to eliminate all responsibility of the individual by reduc-
ing all human action to determinism. There is the same
willingness to accept Jesus as a pre-eminent moral teacher
and prophet, the same unwillingness to accept Him as
Son of God and Saviour of the world. Paton's little book
of 160 pages still remains, after fifty years, the best
armoury for meeting these attacks on their own ground and
demonstrating the untenability of their position.

To his Wife

"PARIS,
"September 27th, 1860.

" After breakfast, I started to ' do ' Rouen. The front
of the Cathedral, you know, is supposed to be the finest
piece of Gothic in the world, erected in the fourteenth century, when Gothic art was at its prime, and now, being a
little frayed and eaten with time, its hoary front looks
magnificent, the light greyish colouring giving the best
effect to the rich stony screen, which falls down, light
as network, over the face of the Cathedral.

" . . . We went to the heights above Rouen to see the
Church of St. Marie du Bonsecours, which is very famous
for the glittering gaudiness with which the whole of the
interior is decorated, the pillars, walls, and roof being
all gorgeously covered with blue and gold so as to produce
an overpowering effect, not religiously, but sensuously.
It is one blaze of colour. From the height, too, there is
a fine view of Rouen and of the Seine which flows through
the valley. This scene reminded me of some of the views
from the Rhine, especially from that point opposite
St. Gras, where we climbed one beautiful autumn day
last year. There is one peculiarity in this view which is
very striking. In the broad stream of the Seine there are

islands, all of one shape, though of different sizes, like long canoes or vessels, beautifully clothed with verdure and lying in line down the river.

" . . . Now for exercises in writing and talking. I must work here, for I mean to know French ere I return."

To the Same

"PARIS,
"*Sept. 29th*, 1860.

" I am doing my best to prepare myself for the future now. I see the future, and I do most profoundly wish to prepare for it; but, as my aim is high, the labour will be immense. I am exceedingly glad I came to Paris, for, though I cannot learn the language perfectly in three weeks, I shall lay a foundation for rapid progress. Every scholar must have a correct knowledge of French, and should speak it, as also of German—and this exact know-ledge, within the next year or so, I shall, if God will, acquire. But how much else there is to be done! I wanted to tell you, before I left, that you have had a specimen in the advice received, and in the hubbub of con-flicting opinions about Manchester,[1] of the very different views and principles of life adopted by different men. I think I could almost have predicted what each man would have said, but do not think that these opinions weighed with me. I wanted and waited only to get hold of a clear principle to guide me. Most certainly the greater works remain to be done in Manchester. The positions laid down by Mr. Bachelor are repugnant to me, but the work is not yet finished at Sheffield. The school, the Mission Church, the transposition of Seacroft Chapel in-dicate a present work to be done in Sheffield which must be done, and will be done soon. This consideration alone decided for me. I knew that Duty would show itself, and, when seen, 'tis easy, though hard to follow it.

" What, then, with preaching—and by the way I am studying that subject, here, a little—my own studies for the Church (which must be with me the central, deepest channel of my life) and these external labours—how thronged with fervent thought the coming days will be! But, dear wife, 'tis rest with thee, rest and love, the two words which make heaven, and our home—oh! let it

[1] This refers to a call he had received to a pastorate in Manchester.

be thus—nay, it will be, our heaven on earth, the Lamb
being the Light and the Temple thereof."

To his Wife

"Paris,
"October 8th, 1860.

"I have just been to see the tomb of Napoleon, which
is open only on Monday. 'Tis a grand rotunda, in the
centre of which his tomb is placed, aglare with gold, and
consequently little consonant with the thought of death,
or of a tomb, but lustrous with glory."

CHAPTER VI

THE FOUNDING OF THE INSTITUTE

" He who does the work is not so productively employed as he who multiplies the doers."—SAMUEL MORLEY.

THE work at Sheffield had brought the young pastor into contact with the chief problems of Congregational statesmanship. He saw the moral wastes of the large towns, and the churches standing among them without having any sensible influence on them. They were too self-centred. There was no outgoing. If one stood a few feet away, one saw barely a glimmer of the Gospel light, and felt no glow of the warmth of God's love. There was need of evangelists and of missioners. In the country districts there was the same need. The country villages had once been the stronghold of Independency; but times had changed, and the country churches had to depend for bare maintenance and alimentation on the help of the wealthier Churches in the towns.

The causes of this state of things were manifold, but one obvious cause of the decline was the shortage in the supply of trained ministers. The denominational colleges were supplying barely 50 per cent. of the total number of ministers required year by year, and these trained men were naturally attracted to the towns. The country Churches were left very much to the mercy of untrained men who had the gift of glibness with no adequate knowledge of the Bible they set up to expound, no training in the use of the mother tongue, no grounding in the elements of theology.

The Village Preachers' Association had grappled with the problem of the villages which lay in the neighbourhood of Sheffield, " the circumjovial planets," as Paton used to call them, and a little army of lay preachers had been organised. In the same way the deacons of the Wicker had

75

been set to work at the mission stations in their own immediate neighbourhood, supporting the missioner, working with him in Ragged Schools, beating up the neighbourhood with personal visitation on the Sabbath, holding meetings and classes in the week, running penny banks, and so forth. " The poor people esteem the missionary," he writes, " when he is ably supported by careful friends, and not thrust out as their scapegoat into the wilderness to perish." But the supply of trained missioners was scanty. Their number was largely recruited from other denominations. It was not that the gift or the call was wanting. When God needs work to be done, He supplies the men to do it; but there was no training provided for these men, who had the gift for this work among the people. Consequently, all these experiences were bringing home to Paton's mind the need of a new Training College which should not be merely a replica of the colleges already existing, but prepare men, on a shorter and a less academic curriculum, definitely for evangelistic work both at home and in the colonies, and give a chance of practical training to such men as were called late in life to the work of a minister.

Dr. Joseph Parker, then minister of Cavendish Church, Manchester, had been thinking on the same lines. He had begun by taking a few men of this type to work in his own study under his direction, and out of that little family group had grown up the idea of what he first intended to call " The Operative College"; but this title was discarded when he began to put his idea into practical shape, and he ended by founding the Cavendish Theological College. He had been in communication with Paton while shaping out the idea, and when the college was opened he sent for Paton to help him. Dr. Parker himself took the Sermon Class, the Rev. J. Radford Thomson, M.A., of Heywood, took the bulk of the tuition work; his subjects were English, Greek Testament and Church History. Paton took Theology and Philosophy; the Sermon Class was added after Dr. Parker's resignation. He used to come over on Tuesday, take three classes, and get in essays and papers from the men. He took a night's rest on the couch in the vestry, and taught further classes the next morning, beginning at seven o'clock. " He went at his work full of enthusiasm," says Mr. Radford Thomson, " and he was specially bent on making the men work.

' Now, Thomson,' he would say, ' drag the harrow over the fellows ; give them the gallop.' There was no easy going for any student when he was about, and no mercy for the student who had been idle. Nor shall I ever forget how he encouraged me when I was going in myself for my M.A. I remember the intensity of his look as he stood in Oxford Road and said to me, ' Sink a deep well and let the water spurt up in the face of the examiners.' "

The following extract from reminiscences by the Rev. James Ervine, an old Cavendish student (1911), gives an inside view of the college life.

" Once a week there was a service in the large Church Hall, at which the students had to preach in turn. Many of Dr. Parker's people came in to that service. Two students were always appointed to take notes, and set down anything for criticism in the matter or manner of the speaker. The criticisms were delivered on the following morning at a class presided over by Dr. Paton. No one, when preaching, was allowed to use any MS. beyond a few notes ; the penalty for doing so was to be compelled to preach on the next occasion. I need hardly say it was quite effective. Well, my turn came. I was not quite so miserable as on the first occasion, but in the criticism class next morning I got an unmerciful rating. My theology was criticised, my North of Ireland accent, voice, what I did with my hands, how I stood on my feet, the use I made of my eyes ; grammar, pronunciation, and so many other things, that, had it not been for the great kindness and good-nature of Mr. Paton, who came to my defence, I believe I should have turned out and gone home in despair. I was all upset when I got to my lodgings, debating with myself whether I would ever be any good as a minister. Just then my favourite text came to my aid, ' Is there anything too hard for the Lord ? ' I rose from prayer calmed and encouraged to persevere—and I must say, too, with the feeling that one day I would be a critic, and then ! !

" I look back upon this part of my college life as most important. The training and discipline, the criticisms and castigations were, indeed, a blessing in disguise. All the students were passionately fond of Mr. Paton and Mr. J. Radford Thomson."

That Mr. Ervine's feeling of appreciation towards the tutors was the feeling of all is shown by the address which was presented to the tutors on August 27th, 1863.

" . . . Some of us came to you raw from the counter, the warehouse, and the workshop, and we are fully conscious that your patience must have been great to have borne with us in our faults and failings. Then it was that, in you, we saw the gentleman and the Christian : and that Christian forbearance which you have always exercised has made an impression upon our minds which we believe time will never efface. Never have we been so forcibly impressed with the truth of what the Scotch orator said, viz. ' that men may erect a monument of virtue which the storms of life will never destroy.' And that monument is in writing our names, by kindness alone, on the hearts of those we come in contact with day by day. You, dear Tutors, have erected that monument. Your names are written indelibly on our hearts ; and we trust that as long as memory retains her seat, we shall remember our connection with you with unfeigned gratitude.

" While we express our regret at Mr. Thomson's change, we express our strong wish and are somewhat buoyant with the hope, that our most revered theological Tutor, Mr. Paton, will become the Principal of the new College. There can be only one opinion on this subject, and that is that Mr. Paton is the man for this important office, and we are confident that, if he can see it his duty to take it, he will make it a college inferior to none in the denomination."

Cavendish College had been started as an experiment for a period of three years.   At the end of the period, in 1863, a conference was held at Derby in which many leading men took part to consider whether the experiment should be carried on and under what conditions.   At this Conference Mr. J. W. Sidebottom, of Manchester, presided ; the old colleges were represented by Mr. Barker, and several whose names were even then famous in Nonconformity took part : Rev. G. W. Conder, Rev. Guinness Rogers, Rev. E. J. Hartland, Rev. J. B. Figgis, and Mr. Samuel Morley.   The resolution to continue the work was unanimous.   It was also agreed that it would be wiser not to restart work in

Manchester with Lancashire College so close at hand, but
on a larger scale and in a new centre. The Rev. Henry
Ollard, of London Road Church, Derby, suggested Nottingham as the best strategic point for the new Institute. It
was central, it had strong Congregational Churches, and
gave splendid scope for mission work in the rapid growth
of its population. The proposal thus made was warmly
supported by Mr. Samuel Morley, who employed thousands
of work-people in the town and neighbourhood. Nottingham was accordingly chosen. At a subsequent meeting of
the Executive Committee appointed by the Conference to
carry out the plan a letter was received from the students
of Cavendish College expressing their joy that the college
was not to be discontinued, and respectfully suggesting
that the Theological Tutor of Cavendish should be appointed as Principal of the new college. That the Committee did not regard their action as intrusive is proved by
the fact that they acted on the suggestion. They met
on September 10th, 1863, elected the Rev. Henry
Ollard, F.S.A., as Secretary, and agreed to offer the post
of Principal to the Rev. J. B. Paton, of Sheffield; the
post of English Tutor and Finance Secretary to the Rev.
Frederick Smeeton Williams, of Birkenhead. Both appointments were accepted. The new Principal, in accepting, writes to the Committee :

" I see clearly, and feel greatly, the responsibilities of
the office I assume. But I have waited and sought to
know my Lord's will in making my decision, and I commend myself to His direction, and rely on His strength
in fulfilling the high duties which I believe He commands
me to undertake. My prayer to Him has been, and will
be, that His grace may be to me according to my great
need.
" My recent affliction and retirement from public work
have led me to profound self-examination, which has led
me further before God to define my aims in life and to
concentrate my energies for their attainment. I enter
accordingly on the new sphere of service in the Church of
Christ which you have opened for me, that I may consecrate myself, body and spirit, to its arduous and manifold
labours, and realise in them the full purpose of my life.
These labours will be congenial to my habits and tastes,

and I am grateful for the slight experience of them I have already enjoyed which assisted me in deciding to devote myself wholly to them."

His letter then goes on to map out the work under three headings : (i) his work as Tutor, (ii) his work as Principal, (iii) his relation to the students who have left the Institute, and to the Evangelistic agencies which the Institute may promote or establish throughout the country.   It is clear that he was already taking large views of the work which lay before him.

The acceptance of the new work at Nottingham meant the giving up of the old work at Sheffield.   It was a great wrench to his feelings.   There had been other attempts to allure him to larger, and in some ways more attractive spheres of work, but none of these had been of his own seeking, and the pull of the Wicker had been in every case stronger than any counter-pull from other places.   He had been eminently happy among a people so ready to co-operate, so forward to be doing the will of God.   Sheffield remained his one and only cure, and, though the new call came to him as a mandate from his Master which he could not gainsay, it was in terms of his Sheffield experience that he interpreted to his students the principles and practice of Pastoral Theology ; and the love of Sheffield friends and fellow-workers never weakened in its hold upon his heart. In the retrospect of his first and only pastorate, there was no jarring note.   His letter of farewell is the utterance of a man who acts under the strong constraint of One whom he dare not disobey.

WOODBANK, SHEFFIELD,
Oct. 21st, 1863.

To the Church of Christ worshipping in the Wicker Congregational Church, Sheffield

" DEAR BRETHREN IN CHRIST,
    " I now herewith resign the office of the pastorate among you, which you confided to me, and which I accepted from you, nine years ago.   Your first pastor, entrusted by you, when yet young and inexperienced, with most solemn responsibilities, after striving to fulfil them, in much weakness often, but yet with abiding love towards you, I now replace into your hands the trust you generously

CONGREGATIONAL INSTITUTE, NOTTINGHAM.

gave and sustained in my hands. Amongst you I elected to commence my ministry, though feeling my unfitness for it, foreseeing the arduous work to which I committed myself. It becomes me, first of all, to acknowledge before you the abounding mercy and goodness of my God and Saviour during these early years of my ministry, in this my first and only pastorate. In Him did I put my trust, and He has not put me to shame. I would that I could have done more for the glory of His own great Name, and for the cause of His Church, but for the little that He has enabled and permitted me to do or suffer, for His sake, I render my thanks before you unto Him, and may He forgive the ignorance, and failings, and many transgressions of His servant among you.

" To you also, dearly beloved brethren, I am, and shall ever be, bound by ties of grateful memory and imperishable love. To the dead who welcomed me here, to the living with whom and for whom I have laboured, my heart is knit by associations so sacred and special that I feel they can never be weakened or undone. For your confidence and love I can only give you now—-as I have ever given you—my gratitude and my prayers to God on your behalf. Continue to me your first pastor that confidence and love which have been my solace and strength hitherto, though I be now called to part from you for a while and to labour elsewhere in the service of our Lord.

" The main reason, as I need not inform you, for the decision which is now announced to you has been the consideration of my health. To undertake the manifold duties which the pastorate of this Church in this enormously growing neighbourhood will require the full and tireless activities of a man in robust health. At present, such health is not mine. An invitation has been presented to me opening for me a sphere of duties which I may safely discharge. I have very anxiously desired to learn my Master's will. He has shown it me very clearly. And though my obedience to it requires this sacrifice—the severing of holy bonds with the Church of my first and faithful love—I make it in reverent submission to Him whose alone I am.

" It is an unspeakable joy to me to remember that our union has not been fretted by any discord, and that in many ways God has manifested His favour unto us.

6

" May peace and love, with faith, from God the Father
and our Lord Jesus Christ, remain still and increase among
you.   Stand fast, brethren, in one spirit, with one mind
striving together for the faith of the Gospel.   Continue
in prayer, and watch in the same with thanksgiving.   Walk
in wisdom toward them that are without, redeeming the
time.

" May God speedily bring to you one who shall take up
the honourable, the arduous, the blessed office from which
I now retire.   More worthily and successfully may He
fulfil its many duties.   Sustain him, as you have sustained
me, with your sympathy, co-operation, and prayer, and, oh,
may your Lord and my Lord continue to help this Church
and make it a praise in the neighbourhood.   Let us not
forget each other where our remembrance will be prayer.
Let us ever pray that my God may supply all our need
according to His riches in glory by Christ Jesus, that He
may keep us from falling, and present us faultless before
the presence of His glory with exceeding joy.

" I am,

" Yours in Christ,

" JOHN BROWN PATON."

The founding of the Nottingham Institute marks a
crisis in the history of the denomination.   Congregational
Churches are dependent on voluntary contributions; they
are consequently in danger of existing mainly for those
who are in a position to pay such contributions, and of
neglecting the ministry of those who are too poor to
support a Church and a Minister.   They had not in 1863
any collective organisation capable of grappling with
the two-fold problem of the decaying country Churches on
the one hand, and the needs of the rapidly growing towns
on the other.   Again, a Congregational Church makes
special demands upon its minister, and depends for its
vitality, more than others do, on the qualities, the resources, the zeal and energy of its minister.   The qualifications, both academic and spiritual, of the men turned out
by the existing colleges, were of a high order.   But the
number of such men was insufficient; it was barely enough
to supply the already existing Churches in the towns; it
took no account of the increasing demands of Canada,
Australia, and the English-speaking colonies; it was

making no provision for the hundred new Churches that
were to be established by way of celebrating the Bicentenary of 1662. Nor did the existing colleges prepare
men for the service of the country Churches, nor to serve as
city missionaries, for aggressive work among the poor.
They had no help to give to the man to whom the call to
the ministry came late in life, perhaps after marriage, or
to the man who lacked all higher education, whose zeal
was not according to knowledge ; their curriculum gave
no assistance towards the equipment of the pioneer
preacher who gathered his audience at the street corner,
and spoke from the doorstep or a chair borrowed from a
neighbouring house. And yet, if Congregationalism was
to be saved from becoming the religion merely of the
respectable middle class, if it was to be saved from the
spiritual deadness of those who worship in the comfort
of well-padded pews and never go out into the highways
and byways to preach the Gospel to the poor, it was these
men of poorer educational qualification, men for the most
part of humbler origin, but touched with the live coal
from off the altar, filled with evangelic spirit, knowing
the people because they were themselves of the people,
speaking to the people in words the common people
understand—it was these evangelist pioneers who were
to save it. To all who had the eye to see, to all who
prayed in sincerity " Thy kingdom come," the need was
clear and pressing. The new Congregational Institute
supplied it.

This was no new discovery. Many years before Pestalozzi had said : " No one should be able to mix more
unrestrainedly with the common people, no one with a
heart so open and so warm as the minister. They ought
to be men of the people and ought to be trained as such." [1]
More recently Dr. Enoch Mellor had called attention to
the growth of the large towns as " outstripping with dis-
heartening rapidity all the agencies that are established for
overtaking and vanquishing their ennui, indifference, and
wretchedness." At least one of the older colleges had been
established with the view of providing itinerant village
preachers of the Word, but the general movement towards
higher intellectual efficiency (largely helped by the foundation of the University of London, which threw its degrees

[1] Pestalozzi, "Lienhard u. Gertrud," § 87.

open to Nonconformists)—a movement admirable in itself—had led to the neglect of other duties which could not with safety be left undone.

The root principle of the Congregational Church is to receive no one into the ministry who is not called to this high service. This call of God is evidenced by two signs ; on the part of the man himself an earnest, pure, and abiding desire to engage in one or other of the public services of the Church ; and secondly, on the part of those among whom he labours, manifest tokens of God's favour in the use of these gifts. The consent of the brethren is held to ratify the inward call of the individual, and give him the assurance that his call is of God. This root principle of the Churches is of vital importance because it is a safeguard alike of their purity and doctrine. Those whom God Himself calls and sends are to be employed, and none other. If the Church thus recognises God's call, it is her plain duty to give these men that education and equipment which are necessary for the effective discharge of their particular work. But God's call is not limited to men of one social grade, or of one age. His free Spirit bloweth where it listeth. The system of ministerial training must, therefore, follow the lines laid down by the working of the Spirit ; it must adapt itself to different ages and to varying gifts. Take the man who was sent in early life into business or a trade. His education was probably strictly on com-mercial lines, and scanty at that, and in his life in the office or the workshop he has forgotten all the grammar he ever knew. But God's call comes to him. He joins the fellowship of the Church, he engages in the religious work of the Church. The love for such work grows upon him day by day, and the manifest tokens of success make it clear to himself and to his fellow-workers that God has given him a special gift for ministerial work and the preaching of the Word. But he needs training. It is no training for the ministry to set such a man as this down to grind gerunds, and all the disciplinary drudgery of the schoolboy. He is no longer in his teens ; he has míxed with life ; it may be he is married. His mind is comparatively matured and settled in his habits. True, he lacks the knowledge of Latin accidence and Syntax, but his mind is not, there-fore, untrained ; he has had the training of the school of practical life ; he knows humanity " in its shirt-sleeves,"

and in the light of his experience of men and men's work
he has been mastering his Bible, has ripened his judgment,
and fortified his character. God has work for such men
as these to do ; but it is not the work of Latin construing.

" If the revived earnestness of the Churches raises up
likely men for our pulpits, we cannot submit to have these
men, with the living flame of love glowing in their hearts,
plunged into the vapour-bath or wrapped in the eternal
wet-sheet of a monastic college. When men in business,
awakened by love for souls, have discovered their power
of utterance and have a call from God to preach, what
more ludicrous than to put these men to the most un-
profitable task of gerund-grinding, which has not the
slightest reference to their after work, damps perhaps for
ever their first love, cramps and withers the sinews of
intellectual energy, and chokes or conventionalises their
free, native, urgent power of talk." [1]

What, then, must the training for such a man be, one who
is called of God ? He must know his own language and
prove his aptitude for the work. The English language is
the instrument he must use in commending the Gospel to
his fellow-men. The good workman must know how to
handle his tools. He must practise extempore speaking.
No real live evangelistic work is done when a manuscript
stands between the preacher and his audience. He must
know his Bible ; he cannot know it too intimately. In
these days, when the working classes are so widely infected
with the cavillings of infidelity, he must know something
of the solid mass of evidence which upholds the authority
of the Book of books, and attests the divinity of our
religion. He must understand its meaning, that he may
open it up clearly and bring it home to the minds of common
folk. He must store his memory richly with those great
Bible histories, Bible parables, Bible visions, those " large,
divine, and comfortable words " which are the best garrison
of the human soul. Again, he must know what he believes,
and be able to give a reason to him that asks ; he must
hold, therefore, with the utmost distinctness the main
dogmas of the Christian faith, " which are the master-light

[1] J. B. Paton to Dr. Joseph Parker (undated).

of all seeing, and the mainspring of all power in Christian preaching."

Such, in outline, are the principles upon which the curriculum of the Nottingham Institute was based. Circumstances have changed since these principles were enunciated at the Inaugural meeting by the new Principal. Education has spread ; there is no longer now any need of Mason's " English Grammar." Social problems have become more prominent, and the working man's mind is busy thinking them out. The minister, accordingly, must know something of political economy and the new science of sociology. The curriculum has adapted itself to these new conditions ; it is wider, and it is longer. But the backbone remains the same, and its end in view remains unchanged.

But this is not all ; the training which is given inside the class-room loses all its potency unless it is translated into practice. The student, just as much as any other follower of Christ, must be a doer of the Word, and not a hearer only. One of the reasons for selecting Nottingham as the site of the college was that it afforded such manifold scope for mission work in co-operation with the several Churches of the town. The students were, of course, to be ready to supply vacant pulpits on Sunday in the ordinary settled Churches, but over and above that, each man was to spend six hours every Thursday in visiting among the poor and in mission work, either in the open air or at the preaching station. When a lad of the working-class is educated, too often the tendency is to make him lose touch with those of his own class and " scorn the base degrees by which he did ascend." This danger was not overlooked. The Institute curriculum was devised to educate a man in his class, and not out of it.

" As I have said elsewhere, so I repeat here," said the new Principal at the Inauguration, " concerning those who are to be the ministers of the Gospel to the masses of the people. Their sympathy for, and acquaintance with, the working classes must be quickened and strengthened by every means. To elevate their sympathies away from that circle or region of life in which all their life is to be spent, is fatal. Burning zeal, tender patience, perseverance in watching for souls, tact in trying all methods to win one

soul, a clear, firm grasp of the great central truths of the
Gospel, a mind saturated with Bible words and thoughts,
and a thirsting love for the classes they go forth to seek,
and, with the Lord, to save—these are the qualifications
of the men who will be England's great evangelists."

One of the old students who had been an able-bodied
seaman before the mast put the whole truth of the matter
in the pictorial language of one who has been in touch with
actualities all his life and studious of no books save one :

" Jesus once established a little college, and sailors were
its first students ; the inner circle were sailors to a man
and sailors by profession. And others were not only
fishers of men, but fishers. If Paul was not a sailor, he
was what we should call a sail-maker ; born in a seaport, a
great voyager, shipwrecked three times, and on that
memorable voyage he practically had command of the
ship. . . . The Master's work needs the small craft as well
as the big ocean liner. The aim of the Institute is, speaking
nautically, to take the present latitude and longitude of
the craft, consider his past voyaging, carrying or cargo
capacity, refit him accordingly, and send him on those
voyages for which he is best adapted. Some other colleges
attempt to make small fishing craft into coasters, and
coasters into ocean steamers, and many of our pulpits are
standing witnesses of this folly. I couldn't carry, myself, all the deck-hamper of Latin and Greek and Hebrew.
If you had tried it on me, you would have had me laid up
in dock all the time, or stranded on a lee-shore." [1]

The wisdom of the new venture was soon justified by
results. Before it had passed through the stage of infancy,
it had earned its right to live. The number of applicants
at opening for admission was fifty-eight ; of these thirty-
two were accepted, including several of the old Cavendish
men. The four Congregational Churches of Nottingham
gave to both students and tutors a most cordial welcome.
The Home Missionary Society expressed their great
interest in the Institute and their readiness to aid it by
every means in their power ; they decided to send students

[1] Rev. E. W. Matthews, Secretary of British and Foreign Sailors'
Society, " Chart and Compass," 1885.

to be trained at Nottingham. The Irish Evangelical
Society similarly expressed its confidence, and many
meetings of County Associations and other conferences of
ministers and laity accorded their unanimous support.

Six mission-stations were mapped out at once in the
poorer districts of the town, and the students went out
two and two visiting in the neglected courts of the slums,
speaking wherever they got a chance to speak, and getting
to close quarters with the work. Every Saturday morning,
when they met their Principal in class, they talked over
freely with him and with their fellows the difficulties they
had encountered, the questions which had arisen, the
successes which had cheered them in their work. This
mission work was carried forward into the holidays. In
Cheshire, in Cumberland, in Sussex, in Derbyshire, in
Northamptonshire, in Hampshire, in Dorset, in Durham,
the Brothers Minor were lifting up the fiery cross and
proclaiming the salvation of the Lord. Let one picture
suffice :

" On the approach of your vacation," writes the Rev.
Charles Williams, of Sibbertoft, " I asked that one of your
students might spend some weeks at my house, and do
among the villagers what was entirely beyond my power.
The result was one of joy and gratitude. I have looked
with great interest and delight again and again on a crowd
of all ages gathered about him, as he stood on a chair,
beneath a wide-spreading tree, and with earnest affection
preached repentance towards God and faith in our Lord
Jesus Christ ; and on a large number following him,
perhaps singing as they went, to my house, where a spacious
room and hall were crowded to the door, that these
people—be it remembered, after a long and hard day's
toil—might listen to other exhortations, and engage in
the offering of other prayers. Opportunities were also
secured for a private and personal dealing with the souls of
inquirers, and many were visited at their own homes.

" As our room became too small, a large barn was fitted
up and crowded with men, women, and children. Visitors
—among whom were two well-known brethren in the
ministry—were astonished and greatly pleased with what
they saw and heard. Nothing of the kind had ever
occurred in that village or its neighbourhood. Similar

efforts were made in four other villages, and in some with
remarkable and delightful results. The hearts of many
were fully opened to their new friend—to whom they
found easy access and ready sympathy—and here, be it
particularly observed, is one great element of an evangelist's
success. Many asked to correspond with him, and I have
repeatedly read letters written by horny hands, and in
uncouth-looking words, uttering the sincerity of contrite
hearts, over which I have wept. To every one of these he
promptly and kindly replied. In a word, some seed
previously sown now sprang up ; some of the truly pious
were roused ; some of the wavering became decided for
God ; mourners in Zion were comforted ; some of the
hopeful and of the hardened were won for Christ ; and the
nearest Congregational Church received such additions as,
the pastor declared, formed a new feature in its history.

" A painful bereavement in God's providence compelled
soon after my removal to a distant city. Before my
departure I arranged for a series of Bible readings and
of prayer-meetings to be statedly conducted, under the
guidance of some of the best men in the village ; and for
the continued preaching of the Gospel, chiefly by your
students. The pastor of the nearest Church wrote to me,
saying that he had never preached to a people so desirous
of Divine truth." [1]

A big railway contractor applied for a missionary to
work among his 700 work-people. One of the students
who had himself been a plate-layer on the railway was sent
accordingly, and found at once the field of his life-work
among the navvies.

In the second year there were already fifty students
under training. Two new mission-stations were set up in
Nottingham, and the movement was carried to the " circumjovial planets," the villages lying around the town.
Here, again, one picture must suffice. The village of
Burton Joyce lies about four miles east of Nottingham.
The people were mainly engaged in handloom stocking-
weaving. Their moral and religious condition had for
long been specially distressing to those familiar with it.
Mr. Samuel Milne, a member of Friar Lane Church, who
resided in the village, had long been desirous that some

[1] " Report of the Congregational Institute," 1865, pp. 18, 19.

new and earnest effort should be made for the evangelisation of the people.   Three students were told off to start
the venture.   One afternoon each week was spent in house-
to-house visitation.   The invitations to Sunday afternoon
services were so largely responded to that in six months
a larger room had to be taken, and there were services
morning and evening on Sundays, with a Bible-class,
numbering over fifty members, meeting in the afternoon,
and evening classes both for girls and men during the week,
and a week-night religious service.

" Some of the most striking and wonderful conversions
have taken place," says Mr. Milne.   " Men and women of
great natural force of character, but steeped in sin, clothed
in rags, and their houses the picture of misery and wretchedness—are now transformed, being newly clothed and in
their right minds, their hearts set right with God, and their
homes the abodes of peace and comfort.   One of these
men, who was perhaps the most notoriously wicked man
in the village, is now an earnest and devoted Christian,
his old companions look upon him with amazement, and
the more respectable, who were inclined to doubt, are at
length constrained to admit, as in the case of Saul of
Tarsus, ' Behold, he prayeth.'
" Another man, recently, in publicly reviewing his past
life, referred to the fact that just twelve months ago
he spent 17s. in drink at Burton Feast, and 24s. the week
but one following at Carlton Feast, when he got so drunk
as to be unable to find his way home, and had to be conveyed by his associates.
" This man attended one of our services at the club-
room, was arrested by the preacher dwelling on the word
' Come,' being part of the clause ' whosoever will, let
him come.'   His heart was touched and wounded.   He
went home and tried to pray, but could not ; he attempted
to drown his religious convictions by recourse to in-
toxicating drink ; but the Spirit of God mercifully continued to strive with him, and, after suffering intense
anguish of mind for three or four weeks, he was led to
find peace through believing in Jesus.   He soon commenced family prayer, to the utter bewilderment of the
younger members of his household.   One son had left
home, and, being on the point of returning, was written to

by his sister to the effect that—' you will see such a sight at home as you never saw before '—referring to the practice of kneeling down at the domestic altar." [1]

Such was the pastoral apprenticeship of the Nottingham men, and such were the signs with which God sealed His approval of their work.   On all sides the applications for Nottingham men began to come in beyond the ability of the Institute to supply.

It was soon proved that the prosperity of the new Institute did not in any way injure the older colleges who gave the fuller academic course.   Quite the contrary ; the older colleges were helped by tapping a new source of supply.   Several of the younger men who came to Nottingham showed such promise that, after a year of preparation, Nottingham was able to draft them on to New College, Springhill, Lancashire, Cheshunt, Rotherham, Airedale. The special preparation given to such men entailed a good deal of extra labour to the Nottingham tutors, but it prevented any misunderstanding, or any breach arising between them and the sister institutions, and the names of such men as Dr. John Hunter, Rev. J. Brierley, Rev. W. S. Houghton, Rev. Charles Herbert, Rev. W. H. Towers, Rev. J. Holden, Rev. A. J. Viner, have always reflected lustre on the Institute which first opened its doors to them.   In the first twenty-one years of its existence, it sent over one hundred men in this way to the older colleges, practically all of them men who would have been unable to enter any of them, had not the Institute given them a helping hand.   Such men, going forward to the other colleges, after mixing with the older men at Nottingham, men who had already been at work in the harvest-field of the kingdom, were able to counteract any tendency on the part of the more favoured men to regard the Nottingham men as in any way inferior, whether in point of understanding, or force of character, or spiritual endowment.   The work of preaching the Gospel to the poor is not in any sense (except as regards salary), inferior to that of preaching in the settled pastorates, and God does not stamp as " inferior " men who carry on the most important branch of His work.

The new wine soon began to burst the old skins.   The

[1] " Report of the Congregational Institute," 1865, pp. 17, 18.

private house which was first taken became too small in
the course of the first year. Another building, originally
intended for a boys' school, was taken in Waverley Street
overlooking the Arboretum. But this, too, in turn proved
insufficient. A good site was secured in Forest Road on
what was then the outskirt of the town towards the
north-west. Its position on the top of the sandy hill,
where an old windmill stood, with a stretch of Sherwood's
forest primeval, and the large amphitheatre of the race-
course lying immediately below, was sufficient guarantee
against the recurrence of such health troubles as had
arisen before. The site was paid for by the contributions
of Nottingham friends, and sufficient help was promised
from outside sources to justify the committee in proceeding at once to erect a building.[1] The design submitted
by Mr. R. C. Sutton, a well-known Nottingham architect,
approved itself as at once the most serviceable and the
most artistic. On June 26th, 1867, the stone was laid, and
twelve months later, on June 17th, 1868, the new building
was opened and dedicated.

Each of these occasions gave the Principal a chance of
stating afresh the needs which had called the Institute into
being, and the principles which determined its methods
and its aims :

" Growth, expansion, is not only the sign, but the
necessary condition of life. The young branches and
abounding foliage of this spring and summer, or the
girdling ring of wood that yearly swells and strengthens
the stem, not merely show the life of the tree, but are
the means of maintaining, are the sources that feed and
replenish that life. When the branches are barren, the
heart withers. If no new life is given, the old life dies.
And so it is with every living thing. 'Tis the mystery and
glory of life everywhere. To give, is to get ; to grow
without, is to grow within ; the life that seems to be lost
is found again, and is aggrandised and rejoiced by the
apparent loss. But chiefly does this law rule and shine in
the Church, where the highest life, the eternal life of the
Son of God, abides and manifests itself. A stationary state
of society, in which a perfect balance shall exist betwixt
loss and gain, births and deaths, produce and consumption,

[1] Mr. J. W. Sidebottom, the chairman, contributed £1,000.

may be the envy and the millennial dream of political economists ; but a stationary state can never, in this dispensation, be the desire of the Church. 'Tis, in fact, impossible. A Church or a communion of Churches, must increase or it must decrease. It must continually show its life by new shoots, blossoms, fruits, and thus gather greater fulness of life to itself. If its fertility cease, it immediately shrivels away into death. If it cease to propagate itself—to extend its influence, numbers, labours —by constant effort and sacrifice, that moment it begins to recede, to narrow and weaken itself. In the Christian Church, aggressive warfare is the only mode of internal defence, Hence, then, the desire for fresh and variously adapted mission agencies in our Churches, to widen their influence and increase their number. It is the principle, the holy passion, of Conservatism that gives birth to the desire. That Independency may continue to be what it has been, it must arouse itself to be far more than it has been. If not forward, then backward it must go. For to them that have shall be given, and they shall have more abundance ; but from them that have not, shall be taken away even that they have."

And so the venture of faith had succeeded, and the Institute which had started without a penny of endowment had translated itself after five years into a handsome, well-equipped building of brick and stone.

Extracts from Diary

" In Hull, after hearing Mr. Hilditch's most solemn and impressive and exquisitely written and spoken address, I felt ashamed in having spoken to him and in feeling towards him without that respect which such a man deserved at my hands. Remark how respectfully, simply, naturally Mr. Martin listens to every one, pays respect to each.

" Throughout the whole of these meetings learnt : first, that I have not yet chastened and controlled myself to sufficient calmness—inward, gentlemanly, controlled strength. Second, that I am not yet physically able to endure such meetings. Remain at home much for five years maturing thoughts, cultivating speaking in class and style in writing, acquiring calmness and strength of demeanour in public action, practising greatly the newly discovered lessons in speaking, management of lungs and jaws ; then fit to take useful place in public life.

"Above all, learned at Hull that prayer abiding, and every evening and morning, alone gives conscious happy presence of Jesus and the wisdom and power, the calmness inner and outer, that springs from that communion alone.

"Noticed, when Mr. Martin was here, Nov. 3rd, with me, his great courtesy, yet simple kindness, his willingness to do what he was asked or desired, his many beautiful thoughtfulnesses for others."

A postscript to his wife's letter

"MY DEAR FRIEND,

"This postscript assuredly proves that I am a most obedient husband. For picture the circumstances under which it is written. I am busy in my study, deep among the wreckage of a foundered German Philosophy, seeking to recover a few ingots, when slowly and quietly the door opens, and Jessie glides in, bearing this scandalous half-sheet of paper, and orders me instantly to sit down to pen a postscript to her, and therefore my, friend. I, like Dr. What you call Him ! in Mrs. Stowe's 'Minister's Wooing,' or like any other of my periwigged, black-clothed Brethren of Divinity, meekly obey, and therefore prove myself an obedient husband—while I do most firmly and joyously repeat, Jessie is a darling wife.

"N.B.—Adds my mother, 'The test of a darling wife is getting him out of bed every morning at a quarter to six.' "

CHAPTER VII

THE INSTITUTE AT WORK

"When I look at the urgency of an interest so pressing and practical as this, I scarcely know how to express my utter repugnancy and distaste, when told of the degradation or the danger which lies in the employment of men as functionaries, because they have not had the full university education, or are not able to combat with learned infidelity in sentences of Greek and Hebrew character. The *odi profanum vulgus* of the Egyptian priesthood, who, wrapt in hieroglyphic mystery, forbade the access of all but the initiated to their temples, is not more hateful in my eyes than is that freezing interdict of certain doctors or dignitaries, which, if given way to, would lock up the bread of life from the multitude, and lay obstruction on the free circulation among our streets and lanes of those waters of life which are for the healing of the people."—DR. CHALMERS.

WE have seen the students sallying out two and two, like the knights of the Round Table, carrying with them the good news of deliverance to the captive. We can now turn to look at them as they are gathered under their leader at their new-built Camelot on the Forest-hill.

Nine o'clock in the morning sees them mustering at the Institute from the different houses in which they have been billeted for residence. True they are senior men, but they still have much of the school-boy, and they have plenty to talk about. There are the incidents of their mission work, or their supply work last Sunday, the comparative merits and demerits of their landladies, and their dietary, the newly started football-club which wonders whether it dare challenge the High School. The Principal had been round to some of the lodgings ; the first thing he did was to thrust his walking-stick up the chimney to see if it was stuffed up with newspapers. "I won't have my men working in poisoned air," he said. General Booth, they say, is going to send one of his boys to the college next term. What would he be like ? Would he wear a red jersey ? Would he come out with "Hallelujah" in the middle of the Sermon Class ? Two men here from

95

Mrs. So-and-so's have not got through the work set ; they
were sent for by the Principal last night to help with a
press of correspondence, and had to take down a big pile
of letters and packages to late post at the General Post
Office. This is called "nursing the baby." It struck
the men as a bit hard on them, but the Doctor's myriad-
minded activities need as many secretaries as a Government
Department, and every man at the Institute is ready to
do a good turn ; besides, who would not do good turns all
the time to win a smile and a word of thanks from the
Principal's wife, who was hard at it herself, copying letters
up till the last moment ?

The student who acts as librarian is early on the spot,
and is exchanging new books for old. The senior student
is busy opening the letters marked "Supply," and is
making entries in a big ledger-like folio. Every one has a
friendly word for Mr. George Taylor, the caretaker, who
knows how to take chaff and to give it, and knows every
student who has passed through the Institute. Many are
the messages to "George" which have to be delivered
when the men come home from the holidays.

But the hour has struck, and George has rung the bell.
Every one is in his place. The creak of the anteroom door
is heard, and the Principal comes in. He wears no aca-
demicals : for all his double M.A. and his gold medals,
he is a man and a brother ; he wears no gown, but he
wears the gladness of the morning on his brow. A word of
prayer, sometimes from one of the men and sometimes from
the Principal, opens the class. The subject is Butler's
"Analogy." It is stiff work ; it isn't until you have got
through it three times that you begin to catch the sense
of it, and are able to start the skeleton analysis on which
the Principal insists. No mere abbreviation of the
author's language will do. The Principal will not accept
that. It must be a restatement in a man's own language
of what the author says ; it must be transfused, as the
doctor says, "transfused through the student's mind,"
and thus become vitally interfused with the student's
own associations and currents of thought. "It is your
thought currents," he says, "which feed your mental life,
as your blood feeds the life of your body." Reading for
the Principal is not sauntering through a book, and having
a more or less blurred impression of what it is about. Each

idea has to be clear-cut and firmly grasped. There is no slipshod thinking allowed. The Butler class is a lethal chamber for the skim-the-dish type of mind which is impatient of slow approach, or the showy half-knowledge which talks the more the less it knows.

The Principal does not lecture much. He calls on this man or that to answer his questions, and his questions are such that one has to make quite a well-ordered speech to answer them. To recall the ideas on the spur of the moment, ideas too which are somewhat subtle and remote for ordinary apprehension, to put these ideas in correct language with all the class listening—is no easy task. But it teaches a man to speak. Practically all the teaching is by question and answer based on some difficulty which has arisen in the reading or some question that has been raised in class. The Principal is a tutor rather than a Professor. Instead of saying, "This is truth, and I will tell it you. Your business is to remember it and, when the time comes, put it in the shop-window for examination purposes," he tells but little, and that always in answer to a need felt or expressed. He is a sort of elder brother who has had some special advantage in the search for knowledge, and who is helping on his fellow-seekers. After all, the best teacher is not one who pumps knowledge into a man, but one who enables a man to teach himself. And it is wonderful how quickly the hour goes when minds are all at work in living touch with each other, and grappling with a problem which none can finally solve because it concerns things that are infinite.

For this reason all easified text-books were eschewed at the Institute, books which by carefully ignoring diffi- culties, suggest that they do not exist, books that with a plausible simplicity make it appear as if final and ultimate truth could be shut up under a few tabulated headings. The Principal believed in tackling the great thinkers first-hand. He held very cheap the glib, small-minded theologians who criticise John Calvin without mastering what John Calvin wrote. " They will have to go to school to John Calvin when they get to heaven," he said. " He could have taken a dozen of them in a pinch of snuff." But his reverence for Calvin did not make him a Calvinist. " Calvin allowed logic to rule in his system of theology," he said, " but not in his commentaries."

7

There is one class every week which is more exacting and at the same time more inspiring even than Butler. It is the Sermon Class, which is held upstairs in the Morley Hall. Every student has to prepare a sermon-plan once a fortnight and hand it in to the Principal. Sometimes this is done at home, and sometimes a text is given out in class and a quarter of an hour is allowed for the preparation of the plan—a good practice in the mobilisation of thought. Once each session a student has to preach a sermon before the whole assembled body, a junior and a senior alternately. The rest who listen have to criticise. On the front row sit the grave and reverend seniors ; one of them has to criticise the plan, another the exegesis, another the composition, another the language and phraseology, another the gesture and delivery. To face them is an ordeal sufficient to unnerve the boldest spirit. On such occasions the familiar friend, in whom we trusted, lifts up the heel against us, as though he were destitute of all bowels. And if the fellows let us down lightly, the Principal has a wonderful way of turning our most floriferous efforts inside out, and revealing the emptiness within ; the phrases and similes, which shone so resplendent when we thought of them last night, look very shoddy in that fierce light which beats upon the victim of the Sermon Class. But it is a part of the necessary educational process that a man should be reduced to his lowest terms and equated to nought. It is a good tonic to hear outspoken criticism, not modified by the suppressions imposed by the require- ments of drawing-room society. It acts like the cold- water douche in the morning ; it drives the warmth in- wards ; it takes the swelling out of the head and sends it to the heart. At any rate, old students look back on the Sermon Class as the part of their training which did them most good, and, wherever old students meet, it is the sayings and the incidents of the Sermon Class round which the conversation centres. Great as was the Doctor in every department of college work, he was superlatively great in the Sermon Class.

" Preaching before the Sermon Class, with the Doctor in the chair," writes the Rev. W. Harrop, of Blackburn, " was rarely undertaken by any man with a light and confident heart. Within the compass of my college days it was attempted once, and only once. That day the preacher's tone was wrong. Reverence, humility, awe, were missing, and a sermon without these is but a performance. The Doctor was always solemn; for once he was severe. The usual criticism over, he rose and said : ' Mr. ——, you have rendered one great service to-day, and only one. There are students here for the first time, and you have given them a memorable example of how *not* to do it.' Then, turning to the new men, of whom I was one, he went on, ' Never one of you bring a sermon here like that.' We all felt the justice and the necessity of the words."

" He could be very severe in criticism," writes the Rev. Luke Beaumont, of Rock Ferry. " I have heard him say, after knocking off his glasses and rubbing his nose, looking straight into the face of a student : ' There is one excellent thing about your sermon, Mr. —— ; it is very good indeed. I mean the text ; burn the rest.' But he gave the severe criticism at the outset, and then his noble face would light up, and he would speak words which healed the wound and sent the student back to his work feeling that, by dint of hard study and prayer, he would be a preacher some day. Dr. Paton never smote to kill, except he hit some evil thing. But he did deal hard blows to rouse men, and then in their weakness he gave them of his own abounding strength.

" After a sermon by a very youthful student, when the critics had done their duty, Dr. Paton rose and said, without any introduction, ' Splendid, splendid, splendid ' —then, after a pause—' calf's-meat ' ; and the word described perfectly the young, tender, and mucilaginous production delivered that morning. It was good, but so youthful and tender."

The Rev. Robert Reid, of Pendleton, writes :

" After the appointed critics in the Sermon Class had performed their task (which was usually done with great relish), the Principal took the matter fully in hand and delivered his summing-up. This was the stage which we all anticipated with eager and joyful expectation. It was then that we were regaled, edified, and inspired with those brilliant flashes of insight, of pungent wit, playful sarcasm, biting humour, or wise counsel which, far more than any

mere originality of method (although he had that, too),
gave distinction to the Sermon Class.   One of the doctor's
favourite and chosen instruments for the excision of
disfiguring growths and accretions was the weapon of
ridicule.   None could wield it to greater purpose, or with
such consummate deftness and skill.   By apt, but de-
signedly grotesque, caricature of some stiff and awkward
gesture, or ungainly posture, the offence was rendered so
vivid and so memorable to the guilty student as, usually,
to secure his instant and complete emancipation from the
habit, at least in its more aggravated form.   Ungainliness
of gesture was corrected by a bit of exaggerated mimicry.
If, for instance, a man was guilty of holding one arm
akimbo, and the other arched, with the hand pointing
upwards, the Doctor would strike an attitude and ex-
claim, ' Coffee-pot.'   No one could fail to see either the
striking resemblance in outline to that household utensil,
or the ludicrousness of the figure which the ungainly and
ungraceful preacher had presented when addressing his
hearers.   Every gesture was required to have boldness,
strength, and grace.   Anything cramped, finicking, or
suggestive of weakness was to be rigorously avoided.

"Sometimes a memorable phrase, without any accompanying action, would so emphasise a particular
defect as to make its recurrence an almost impossible thing.
To a man whose intensity appealed to the Doctor (as a
soul on fire never failed to do), but whose delivery lacked
refinement and grace, he remarked : ' Mr. ——'s style of
delivery reminded me of a terrier shaking a rat ! '   This
made the occasion for a memorable appeal to cultivate
' grace ' (a favourite word, to which he always gave a
manifold significance, laying special stress on its connota-
tion of winsomeness and charm)—grace of delivery without
any sacrifice of force or ' passion ' (another favourite word).
The dullest amongst us was made to realise what preaching
meant, and what possibilities it contained.

"Not seldom the critics themselves were subjected to
the Doctor's criticism.   If they failed in severity, he
made it his business to supply the defect ; but if, as
occasionally happened, they were unduly caustic and
destructive in their criticism, the Doctor invariably fixed
on some feature that was worthy of commendation and
lessened the poignancy of the censures that had been

passed by eulogising the meritorious element that had
been overlooked. In the case of a student whose sermon
and delivery had been conspicuously tame and commonplace, lacking in every element of strength and grace,
poor in conception, crude in expression, feeble in delivery—
the critics had been mercilessly severe. Metaphorically
' they hewed Agag in pieces.' It was a matter of curious
speculation to some of us (knowing the principles on which
the Doctor was accustomed to act in such circumstances)
as to what element our Principal could discover which
was worthy of commendation. There seemed to be absolutely nothing on which to lay hold and say, ' Sirs, this
is not to be despised.' The crucial moment was reached,
and the Doctor, as usual, drawing himself up to his full
stature, and passing his fingers through his hair (a characteristic action, especially when something of moment was
to be said), began very deliberately to admit the justice
of the strictures that had been expressed. ' But,' with a
sudden brightening of countenance, ' you know, gentlemen,
Mr. —— has the grand faculty of going on—a wonderful
faculty,' and forthwith he proceeded to enlarge upon the
advantage of being able, without painful pause or confusion, to *keep going* even when some circumstances might
have arisen to interrupt the flow of thought or interfere with
the self-possession of the speaker. As a mere means of
escape from momentary intellectual confusion, or the
awkwardness arising from having lost the next point of
departure in manuscript notes, 'the faculty of going on' was
invaluable. It was the one thing that had been in evidence
during the delivery of the sermon on which no comment
had been made ; for the student possessed a certain
fluency of speech, and had manifested an occasional independence of manuscript, which, escaping all other minds,
had been noted and seized upon by the Doctor as offering
a means of refuge from the utter condemnation that
otherwise would have been merited. I never observed a
finer example of the genius which the Doctor possessed for
discovering remote and dimly discernible virtues amid
what seemed to call for unqualified condemnation.

" I have heard of another instance of a similar kind in
which, after the student (a very earnest fellow, whose early
educational advantages had, however, been very meagre)
had been severely handled by the critics on account of

certain obvious defects in the composition of his sermon,
the Doctor, who had been impressed by the man's earnestness, said : ' Gentlemen, if I had happened to go into some
country church when our brother was preaching, I should
have said " This man is not cultured, but he is sincere." '
And I have no doubt a very eloquent and convincing
exposition followed on the indispensable virtue of sincerity.   That was an element which made instant appeal
to the Doctor's heart.

   " Of a man whose style of delivery was rather jerky,
and who had no command of modulation beyond a certain
periodic violence of expression, the Doctor, in his criticism,
remarked, ' The explosions kept us awake.'   The student
was warned that expressive force is not always energy.

   " Another less merciful criticism, because there was less
to merit mercy, was expressed thus : ' Flat, floundering,
and flabby, and the greatest of these is flabby.'

   " Of a somewhat superficial sermon he said : ' The
preacher did not dig deep enough : there were too few
diamonds and too much surface earth.'

   " One day the sermon had been specially mellifluous.
It was like eating the lotus.   The polished and placid
periods had soothed us with a feeling of inexpressible content.   The Doctor got up, and, drawing one hand slowly
over the other as though he were stroking a kitten—' Palm,'
he said, ' palm—so soothing !   But I don't want soothing,
I want knuckle,' and up went his tight-clenched fist, as
though he were going to knock some one down.

   " Longfellow somewhere says :

> ' Great is the art of beginning,
> Greater the art of ending.'

Dr. Paton never allowed us to forget the importance of both
introduction and conclusion.   If any of his students mar
a sermon by a weak or unsuitable conclusion, it is certainly
not due to any defect in the teaching, very definite and
most emphatic, which he received at the Institute.

   " ' The introduction to a sermon,' he impressed upon us,
' should concentrate the mind on the subject of the dis-
course : prepare the hearers for it, so that they may enter
into it with zest, interest, and delight.   It should be a
" brief stimulant," not of a piece with the body of the
sermon—i.e. not too much like the sermon ; it should lead

up to, but not deal with the main subject. Make good your point in the body of the sermon,' he would say, ' and drive it home in the conclusion. The momentum of one thought should press upon another, and the great momentum should be felt in the conclusion. It should be a gathering up into a focus of all the thoughts that have been expressed; a grappling-time, a wrestling-bout with every soul. Never say " Now, in conclusion "—we ought to know we are on the rapids !

" ' Let your words be short, sharp, piercing, epigrammatic, containing the force of what has been said throughout the sermon. Remember the " sabre-cuts of Saxon speech."

" ' The structure of the sermon should be a vertebrate column. It must have backbone, and every thought in it should grow out of the main columnar theme. There should be statement, exposition, advocacy, enforcement. One thought must lead up to another. There is no tediousness, if there is progress. See to it that the sermon leads to some definite goal. You may stay to pluck a flower or two on the carriage drive, you may let us have a glimpse of some landscape on the way; but you must not let us stroll down any side-avenue, however tempting. You must keep our thoughts fixed eagerly on the house to which you are bringing us, and, above all, you must see us through, you must bring us home.'

" One man's composition was condemned because ' every paragraph was like a granite stone '—there was no organic relation, no growth, sequence, progress. Woe to the man whose sermon was bombastic, weakly rhetorical, lacking in argument, given over to the merely descriptive or emotional, or to noisy declamation. The Doctor wanted passion in his men ; but he wanted (as he was fond of saying) ' solidity and depth ' of passion, begotten of personal soul-experience. ' Unction and argument must never be divorced. Men of this college must have grit and grip in everything. Grip must appear in the structure of your sermons. Marshal your thoughts ; don't leave them straggling about like a disorderly mob. No slipshod endings, end a sentence strong, and express it strongly. True rhetoric is animated conversation.'

" We were to bring the truth we preached into immediate and vital relation to men's lives and make it a

living force. Of one sermon which had little vital power,
the criticism was : ' The great moral truths underlying the
Incarnation, the Atonement, the Resurrection, were not
set forth so as to appeal to the conscience, but were stated
in a fusty, schematic, forensic style. Don't expound these
things as a lawyer expounds a legal system. These things
have life in them. The words of Christ's messenger are
spirit, and they are truth. They must have nothing jejune,
dry, and husky ; they want the full ear of spirituality.'

" Always, too, there was the clarion call for courage and
endurance. The Doctor was merciless to the man who
wanted the ' soft jobs.' ' It is to a cross we are called—
not a cushion. Heroism always means a cross.'

" Some luckless student, in preaching, remarked :
' Kind words and deeds do not require much capital.' I
shall not readily forget how the Doctor caught up the
phrase, and exclaimed, in tones of intense feeling, ' Don't
they ? ' You can understand how, from that starting-
point, he led us to the centre of things.

" Once, when a student had been preaching on the
problem of suffering, the Doctor propounded a question
in terms which set some of us thinking. This was the
question : ' Is there more in the evil of to-day than is
necessary to develop the character to combat it ? '

" The art of ' delivering ' a sermon was one in which we
received memorable instruction. If a man had any
capacity whatsoever for preaching, any, even the least,
instinct for such a ministry, the Doctor would not fail to
reach him and bring out the best that lay in the poorest
and most meanly equipped amongst us. And the idea
instilled into us was, that all the art and device of man
in such a case were to be employed solely and simply to
gain entrance for our message and give to it the effectiveness
for which we longed. ' I don't want to send you out to be
what are called " fine preachers," competing with other
fine preachers from the older institutions. I want *effective*
preachers. Get your message home.'

" While insisting on tenderness and the soul of reverence,
the need for sympathy and for pleading with men, there
was ever a call from the Doctor for what he described as
' The Bugle Note ' in our preaching ; and we caught that
note, so far as our capacities would permit, from his own
speech and spirit. No student will fail to bear his en-

thusiastic testimony to the immense inspirational force
that he felt Dr. Paton to be in every relation, but especially in the Sermon Class, excepting always those
personal interviews in which he communicated something
of his own glowing ardour to our colder souls, and made
us believe with his belief.

" His passionate insistence on a large, noble, and worthy
conception of salvation found frequent expression in the
Sermon Class. ' The *whole man* is saved ; the whole of
life is included in the Christian redemption. The soul
cannot be saved by itself and sent off in a box to
heaven.' "

" It was a well-known feature in Dr. Paton's conduct
of the Sermon Class," writes another old student, " that,
when he noticed a preacher receiving an undue share of
criticism, he took sides with the preacher, and vice versa.
One morning, a student had been dealt with somewhat
severely by his fellows. The last critic added to the load
already received by saying that Mr. —— had done no
more than ' splash in the froth of his own rhetoric.' Dr.
Paton turned on the critic and said, ' Then Mr. —— is to
be heartily congratulated, for many preachers have not
even that to splash about in.'

" On another occasion the preacher had been dealt with
somewhat leniently, but he had one fault which always
came under Dr. Paton's lash. He used to impress on us
the three rules of oratory : ' Stand up ! speak up ! shut
up ! ' and he repeatedly insisted on the second. On the
occasion referred to the preacher failed to speak up, and
the critics allowed the defect to pass without a word. The
Doctor closed the class by saying : ' Mr. —— has failed to
preach this morning ; he did not speak up. In fact, all the
time I have been reminded of a bee buzzing in a bottle.'

" He had a great dislike of the use of hackneyed phrases
in preaching. Once a student preached on ' The Uniqueness
of Christ.' He began one section of his sermon by pointing
out that every other religion or system of philosophy failed
to reach the real seat of trouble and unrest in human life.
' Every one of them fails,' explained the preacher, ' but
Christ, and He touches the spot.' At the close of the
sermon Dr. Paton remarked : ' Gentlemen, I did not spend
my energies to found this institution, and in training men,

that they may go about the world advertising a patent medicine.' "

One student writes :

" When Dr. Paton criticised my first appearance and sermon in class, in the early part of it I felt, without any doubt, that at any rate I had missed my calling, and that I ought to go home, pack my things, and take the return journey.   But, as Dr. Paton proceeded, there was a new tone, a change in speech, that could be felt, a getting together of fragments, the growing unity of good things, and I began to say, ' I think I can preach ' ; later on, as the Doctor closed, ' I can preach.'   Then came the closing prayer, and the one who had been criticised blessed the hand that had smitten him, for he who had destroyed had also restored.   The hallowed feeling Dr. Paton produced at the close of the Sermon Class rests upon his men to-day."

As his conception of his own work was high, so the conception of their life-work which he held up before his students was nothing short of the highest.   He delighted to magnify the office of the minister.   He refused to approve those who, in their reaction against sacerdotal claims, stripped themselves of the title and distinguishing marks which express reverence for the position of those set apart for the Master's special work.   He was himself to the end, as he described himself in his will, " a minister of the Gospel."   The ministry was not merely the inculcation of certain articles of belief, not the mere artistic presentation of the truth, it was the holding up of the Saviour to mankind perishing for the lack of Him ; it was the embodying the life of the Saviour in one's own. A minister's business is to be a minister ; not a ruler, but a servant.   " Never grudge service, never shirk the burden ; count it always an honour to serve."

" Prophets we must be, to declare the Father's love ; and how can we declare it unless our own hearts burn with the same consuming passion ?   Priests we must be, to enter into the Holy of Holies and plead for men ; and how shall our prayers intercede unless our heart bleeds with a sense of the world's sin ?   How shall we bear the transgressions and lift the transgressor unless first we put ourselves beneath the load ? "

It was because he was himself so fully possessed with the ministerial spirit that he was so quick to discern it in others. A young candidate had sat for the Entrance Examination and failed. The committee considered his case, and decided to put him back for three months. He was called into the room to hear the fatal decision.

" You ought not to have given up your situation," said a member of the committee.

" I shall do something," replied the disappointed young man.

" What will you do ? "

" Preach."

That answer, in one flash, showed the man : the very type of man for which the Institute was intended. He was admitted on probation for three months, and at the examinations made good his place, for he was found at the top of the list in some subjects, and not far off the top in any.

That was why his men loved the Doctor ; they saw in him the same great passion for souls which had called them out from the ordinary avocations of the world to be ministers of the Gospel. They knew that he saw what was best in them, and appealed to that. It was this which made the management of the Institute work so smoothly. " I like the Indicative Mood," he said, " I prefer to use it. But, remember, I have the Imperative Mood behind me, and can produce it at any moment." The Imperative Mood would have died of atrophy long since, if it had depended on the Institute.

Relations were very easy and natural where the Imperative Mood was so little in use.

" Where were you last night ? " he said to a student who did not know his Butler.

" In my study, Doctor."

" Had you your studying cap on ? "

" Yes, Doctor—but it didn't fit."

A merry twinkle, and he passed on.

In later years he smoked one cigarette a day after his evening meal.

" I found him once," says Mr. Beaumont, " engaged with

his cigarette. ' Only one a day, Mr. Beaumont,' he said ; ' and they are very cheap.' ''

A few days afterwards there were some pamphlets to distribute, but one pamphlet from the Anti-narcotic League was not in evidence.

" I saw some Anti-tobacco pamphlets," said Mr. Beaumont.

" Ah, Mr. Beaumont knows too much," he said, with uplifted hands and the same merry twinkle of the eye.

When the time came for going out into the ministry, it was from the Principal the students received their marching orders and the last word of benediction.

The Rev. J. W. Dickson, of St. Helen's, writes :

" When I was near the end of my course I was called to the Church at Parton, Cumberland. The Poulton-le-Fylde deacons had told me that there was a desire to invite me as minister, but it could not be done for several weeks. The call from Parton came, and I had to reply. Submitting the question to your father, he called me into ' the study.' Before advising me, he asked my own opinion. I told him I would prefer Poulton, as more adapted to my ability, and so forth. But I thought Parton was most in need of a man. Ten men might be induced to settle at Poulton, to one at Parton. ' That decides the matter,' said your father. ' Always go where you are most needed, and you will never go far wrong.' ''

" The evening before I left Nottingham," writes the Rev. A. G. E. Gibson, of Middlesbrough, " on the conclusion of my course, I went to see Dr. Paton to say good-bye, and to thank him for all his help to me. We had a long talk together in his study, in the course of which he discovered my connection with the Scottish Covenanters, a circumstance which appeared to interest him keenly. At the close he gave me a small copy of ' Scots Worthies ' and wrote in it :

> " ' In memory of his student days.
> With the love of his tutor and friend,
> " ' J. B. P. '

" As he gave it to me, we shook hands, and then, laying his hand on my shoulder, he said : ' Mr. Gibson, you came to me from one seaport ; you are beginning your ministry in another. You will know a little about shipping.' I replied, ' Yes.' ' Then, my brother, you will know what I mean when I say, in your ministry be content to be the propeller. Keep under the water, well under, out of sight,' and (with thrilling emphasis) he added : ' But do the work. I have tried that plan,' said he, ' for over forty years, and I find that it pays.'

"These were his farewell words to me, and they were given with such power that, even after fourteen years, they are as full of inspiration as ever."

The bonds which bound the Nottingham men to their Principal were not severed when they left Nottingham. It was usually he who gave the charge at their ordination, and he was constantly in request for anniversary services or the opening of new buildings. He could not always go, but he never failed to write, and to follow up what he had written with the prayer of intercession.

To an Old Student

" MY DEAR MR. HITCHCOCK,
      " I wish that I could be with you at the ' welcome ' meeting to-morrow, to say to the friends who are now associated with you how pleasant has been our fellowship during the last four years ; how faithfully you have worked as a student and as a mission worker ; how much we esteem you ; and how warmly we commend you to their loving confidence and sympathy.
      " Your life has been, from birth, encompassed with a spiritual atmosphere. Your home has always been a home of prayer. Those nearest to you have watched over you with holy and even passionate longing and entreaty that your ministry should be one of intense and patient ardour, of Christian fidelity and gentleness, and that it be sustained and crowned by God's richest grace. May it be seen in you, so prepared by a spiritual providence for this divine service, what God can do in and by a holy, consecrated man.
                    " Ever yours affectionately,
                              " J. B. PATON."

To a Church Secretary

"*Nov. 10th, 1896.*

" DEAR MR. ANDERTON,

"I wish I could be with you on Thursday in order to express to your friends the confidence and joy with which I commend my friend, Mr. Hitchcock, to their prayerful sympathy and love.

" Mr. Hitchcock has had in a very special manner the blessing of a mother's prayers, and the influences of a home fragrant with the spirit of Christ. These influences have enriched and hallowed his whole nature from his earliest years. He has thus been a Timothy in his early experiences of life, and I am glad that he has now come to you, and I hope he will bring to you as much comfort as Timothy, beloved of Paul, brought to the great Apostle.

" I am very glad, too, that Mr. Hitchcock is not only favoured by working under your guidance, but is being called to labour in a Mission Church. I do hope that he will be, not only a faithful minister himself, and a faithful missioner, but that he will awaken and organise and lead forth all the forces of the Church into mission service, so that your Church may continue to fulfil the great purpose of Christ's Church, namely, the redeeming of men out of the darkness and the death of sin into the eternal light and life of God.

" Mr. Hitchcock has many qualities fitting him for splendid service in this department of the Church. He is a man of strong principle and of definite conviction. At the same time, he has great earnestness of purpose and of feeling. Above all, I know him to be a man of prayer, who seeks the inspiration and the abiding forces of patient love which can come only from communion with our redeeming God and with His Christ.

" May the ordination service be one that will be remembered by Mr. Hitchcock and your Church for many days to come, because of the Pentecostal blessings showered down upon you when you are assembled together for the solemn purpose of dedicating Mr. Hitchcock to the work of the ministry, and of supplicating for him the outpouring of the Spirit of God to seal and sanctify him for his office."

To a Friend

"*Sept. 20th*, 1882.

" My dear Mr. Russel,

" I am glad to hear that you are presiding at the ordination of my friend and late student, Mr. Miller.

" Although I am quite unable to attend the numerous ordinations (that are held every year, and especially at this time of the year) of my students in their first settlements, I had hoped to be able to attend Mr. Miller's.

" I sent him down to Glasgow on what I felt to be a difficult and a responsible undertaking, when the mission church at Hutchesintown was in great straits.   Mr. Miller has worked with great enthusiasm and fidelity in the midst of the difficulties of his position.   And I have greatly rejoiced to hear that these difficulties are being overcome, and that the ordination service will be held to-morrow, amid many bright auguries, and with the happy confidence that, if God continue His blessing, the Mission Church will be established in strength to carry on its aggressive, spiritual work amid the great population in which it is situated.

" It was my earnest wish to express my sympathy with Mr. Miller, and unite with my brethren in publicly recognising him as the pastor of this missionary Church which he has served so well, and in supplicating for him the manifold grace of God in His arduous and noble office.

" I am happy to testify to his Christian consistency and zeal and his affectionateness of disposition, his diligence in study, and his devotion in mission work whilst at Nottingham.   I commend him to the confidence and esteem of my ministerial brethren in Glasgow, and to the prayerful love of the members of his own Church.

" May the ardour of a holy passion for the redemptive work to which he again consecrates himself in the service of to-morrow continually inflame his soul.   And may our God, through Christ, give him holy wisdom and sustaining courage, in the prosecution of His own business."

To the Rev. John Hunter

"*Sept. 20th,* 1882.

" DEAR FRIEND,

"It is with a profound regret that I find myself unable to attend your Recognition Services in Hull.

"The warm affection and regard which I cherished for you as a student have grown during the years in which you have laboured for our blessed Lord as a minister of His Church, and these deepening feelings have been mixed with admiration for the noble work you have been enabled to do, not merely in your pulpit, and in the service of your own Church, but in the wider fields of social and political activity.

"Though unable to unite with my brethren in the public services of to-morrow, I will join with them in fervent prayers to our God and Father that He may clothe you with His grace and power and wisdom and love, that He may make your ministry yet richer in blessing to His Church and the world, and enable you, as the teacher and leader of a united, loyal, and earnest Church, to lift up multitudes to the salvation that is in Christ, unto the praise of His glory."

Sometimes there were occasions of a more personal nature which helped to draw closer the bond of fellowship.

"*Nov. 7th,* 1900.

" DEAR MR. HITCHCOCK,

"I think I gather, from the name you have printed at the corner of the card you kindly sent me, that you have honoured me by giving your little boy my name as part of his Christian name. I shall be very happy to be thus remembered by you, and associated with you and your family in your home life. I remember with great pleasure all I knew of your own home-life, and can only pray that the same influences may distil upon the young life that has been given to you by God. I wish that my life had been more fruitful for good, and I can, therefore, only pray that your dear son may grow to serve my Lord, and to serve Him more faithfully. This is the true life indeed, to know the love of God in Christ, not only to ourselves, but to a fallen world, and to be a fellow-worker with our Lord in the great ministry given to Him in winning this world from sin and death to holiness and life.

" May I thus send congratulation to your dear wife and blessing to your dear boy."

The correspondence with old students grew more and more in volume as their numbers increased to four hundred. It was a tax upon his time, but it was a continual dew of blessing on his heart.

From the Rev. Jas. Grant

" Your letter came to me revealing the kindness of your heart towards one who humbly admits that whatever zeal has dominated his ministry has been the enthusiasm inspired by your own passion towards every cause that pointed to the bettering of man and the sweetening of the conditions which surround the common life of our times.   Again and again I have felt in my work, especially on Tyneside, how Dr. Paton would have accepted the tremendous social problems of Gateshead as a great challenge for spiritual enterprise."

It was a constant joy to his men to report to their old leader, and a constant help to crave his counsel in time of perplexity and embarrassment. They were practically all of them " in the firing line," but they had not learned at Nottingham to be daunted by difficulties. If those who work among the poor have much to depress them in their surroundings, they have also much to encourage them, for the experiences of old Nottingham men prove that it is the minister among the poor who sees most of the fruit of his toil. The " news from the front " was always a joy to the Principal, and as the joy of joys to him was always the joy he could freely share, he was always taking in some old student's letter and reading it to his men before classes began. Nothing did more to bind together the fellowship between past and present. In his reply to such messages the note is always the same : " Courage, pray on, fight on : to him who fights for Christ

8

there is no failure." And again and again the old watchword of the fight is held up afresh.

" You know that the redemptive mission of the Church —the Gospel which we are to preach, and for which this age is earnestly crying out, is, to my mind, much grander and more human and real than some conceive it to be. We need all the fire and spiritual unction of the glorious evangelic faith of our fathers ; for the first fundamental harmony to be restored is that of the soul to God ; but the love that can win the souls of men back to His heart shows itself, as in Christ Himself, in bearing and taking away the diseases and sorrows of men in the present evil world.

" Thus our Gospel is not the sacrifice of this world to the next, or other-worldliness, as Infidel Socialism says. It is the bringing down, in sacrifice and service by the Church of our Lord, of the Grace and Truth, the Harmony and Peace of the eternal world, to this distracted and sinworn world ; so that now here on earth, among sinful men and women, the kingdom of heaven is seen to come. Our prayer, and therefore our mission and our labour, is, that this kingdom may come, here, in the souls of individuals and in the society around us."

CHAPTER VIII

PASTORUM PASTOR

" O broad-armed fisher of the deep,
 Forgive the name I gave ;
The fisher's joy is to destroy,
 Thine office is to save."
St. Andrew. "To the Anchor."

In becoming a teacher Paton did not cease to be a pastor. In Nottingham, as at Sheffield, he was at his happiest and best among young men, and he got the best out of them by giving of his best to them. It was not so much a question of knowledge ; knowledge could be got from books. What he gave his men was what no book can give—the ideal of their work, the whole conception of what it meant and how to go about it. It was no easy life-task which lay before the Nottingham men, and he never sought to minimise its hardship. But he had a wonderful gift of making his men fall in love with hardness, and find their joy in the steep and narrow path that scales the heights. It was not to any aloofness that he owed this influence. He was their comrade in the path that climbed the Hill Difficulty, himself a fellow-climber. They shared with him in all he had to give; and what he gave was endued with such grace in the giving, that it won a man's heart, as well as roused his ambition for higher and holier achievement. It was because he was sharing his life with them in this intimate way, that he had what one of his old students speaks of as " a wonderful way of making you feel he loved you."

In such a matter, the chronicler does best to stand aside, and let those speak who knew him as their teacher.

The Rev. Robert Jackson, of Brighton, was one of the first students at Nottingham. He was a born preacher ; one of the irrepressible type : wherever he could get a tub, he was on the top of it. He had been at the beginning strongly averse to going to college ; he thought he would become bookish, and lose the spontaneity of his nature and his style. He writes :

" I shall never forget Dr. Paton as he used to come smiling from his little room, the first thing in the morning, and, without looking to the right or left, he would walk to the front. Then, taking in at a glance what students were present, he would offer a few words of prayer which seemed to inspire me and lift me up. I never heard a man who made me feel so ashamed of myself, and I determined, by God's help, to be more worthy of the man I loved and revered. I shall never forget his prayers. Even now they make me feel better ; but then, I used to feel sometimes that I should like to march out to be crucified.

" Another very impressive time was when he was appointing the students to their work. His little addresses on these occasions used to fill me with the sense of the greatness and privilege of the work. This is the sort of thing he would say to us : ' Gentlemen, you have a glorious Gospel, a wonderful message to deliver, and you have a wonderful language (the language of Shakespeare and Milton) in which to deliver it.' Then he would give the list : ' Mr. A. goes to Hucknall, Mr. B. goes to Ilkeston, Mr. C. to Bulwell,' and then, as I was a little erratic, and ready to get into trouble for open-air preaching, he would wind up—' Mr. Jackson stays at home, and Gammie stops also to look after him.' The disappointment this was to me was sometimes more than I could bear, and I have been known to burst out : ' Why did you not send me home, Mr. Paton, before you gave such an address ? You just worked me up to the highest pitch of eagerness to preach, and then you tell me I must stay at home, with Gammie to look after me like a watch-dog. It's more than I can bear.'

" I recall our sacramental seasons in college, when Dr. Paton would tell of the dying—yet undying—love of Jesus ; and would make our hearts burn as he told of the sweet tenderness of His great heart.

" Some more personal acts of his naturally touched me deeply. One day I shall never forget. I was poor, and found it a hard task to get through. He came to me and said : ' Jackson, I don't think you are warm enough.'

Then he went upstairs and fetched me two pairs of pantaloons. I cannot think what Mrs. Paton would say when she missed them, but he said : ' There, these will keep you warm ; go and get them on at once.' Another time he said : ' Jackson, you do not take enough care of yourself,' and he took off his beautiful overcoat then and there, and said, ' Wear it.' When I would have spoken, he said, ' I shall soon get another.'

" Dr. Paton had such a great and beautiful influence upon young men as was most wonderful to see. He used to say to me : ' You will go on and on, and kick over all the traces in the universe.' I remember one little incident. I was waiting to go to Curbar, where I was afterwards ordained, and we were walking along a street in Nottingham, and he was urging me to go somewhere I did not want to go. That was the one time I felt he was unkind. At last he said, ' Jackson, you are like a thoroughbred horse ; you will kick yourself to death.'

" Then I went to Curbar, and he came over to my ordination, and he preached from the text, ' We that are strong ought to bear the infirmities of the weak, and not to please ourselves.'

" How many acts of kindness I remember ! One young student had misconducted himself in some way, and had notice to quit. This man came to me and said, ' Jackson, if any one can move him, it will be you. Will you try ? ' ' Yes,' I said, ' I will try.' So I went into the Doctor's private room and said, ' I have come to ask you to dismiss me instead of that young fellow. I shall always get through somehow. Please let me go instead of him. He is far more promising than I.' He replied, ' That will do, Jackson ' ; and he kept us both.

" There was not a kindness under heaven that Dr. Paton would not do for me, and I can speak, too, of his patience with me. He was a strong man, but he had such a loving, gentle heart. Many times he has looked into my face, and I have felt the wonderful power of his love, as it seemed to burn into me. I would not be without these memories for anything, and I do not think we shall be long parted. If I have helped to cheer or comfort one sad heart on my way, I owe it all, under God, to Dr. Paton, and his sweet influence upon my unbalanced nature.

" Professor Williams, too, was a power for goodness.

When I was poorly, he would come in at the close of the class, and take me into his dining-room and give me egg and milk, which his dear wife had prepared for me.

" Then there was Gammie. He was a raw-boned Scotch-man, an out-and-out Calvinist. When he and I had quarrelled, he would say, ' Never mind, dear fellow, come along ' ; and he would carry me on his back up to bed like a child. Dear Dr. Paton, in his kindness of heart, used to say to him, ' Gammie, you give him anything he fancies. Get him a few oysters, or anything he wants, and keep an account of what you spend.' And Gammie used to go trotting out to get me the oysters, or whatever I fancied. These things are sacred to me.

" Gammie gave me a little book in which he wrote : ' Robert Jackson, from his friend, Gammie, whose love for him was wonderful, passing the love of women.' "

The Rev. E. W. Matthews, Secretary of the British and Foreign Sailors' Society, one of the best-known of the Nottingham men, who still has all the bluffness, breeziness, and bonhomie of the sailor, though he wears a black coat, writes :

"When that great American general, Ulysses Simpson Grant, reviewed the British troops at Gibraltar, he said they had victory in their tread. When John Brown Paton walked into the class-room (I can hear it now), he had victory in his tread.   When he mounted his desk-platform, it was with the joy of Spurgeon to his pulpit, and Nelson to his quarter-deck on the eve of battle.

" It was an inspiration to see the animation, the perfect abandon he revealed when dealing with great writers, great thoughts, and great ideals as he held his men. ' There is only one Captain on board this ship,' I heard in my sea-faring days. Men like a man who is captain in fact, as well as in name ; they delight to serve him, follow him, and be made by him. Dr. Paton himself was a captain born. When he lifted up his voice he spake as one having authority, and not as the scribes. He was more than captain, he was Admiral of the Fleet, the Home Fleet, Colonial and Foreign. You will find the captains he has trained on all waters, all animated more or less by that great soul.

" At twelve years of age I went to sea with my father ;
but the Spirit of God moved upon the face of the waters,
and on a never-to-be-forgotten Sunday morning, on board
the floating Bethel in the harbour of Alexandria, Jesus
Christ revisited Egypt.   Seeing the Bethel flag flying, He
walked on the waters, came aboard, and found in the back
seat in the corner a sailor-lad, bowed down in anguish of
spirit, and said, ' It is I, be not afraid.   Thy sins, which are
many, are all forgiven.'   Well, at this time I did not go
up to the apostles at Jerusalem, neither did I confer with
flesh and blood, but began in sailor English to witness
that my Lord had done great things for me.

" But with such experiences, valuable as they were,
where could I be licked into shape, and who was the man
to do it ?   Navigation I had picked up like a ship on fire,
but now another fire possessed me.   How could I navigate
the souls of men ?   A good friend of my family, a Wesleyan
Superintendent, said, ' It's true you have been blessed to
the souls of men, but you woke up too late for any college
training ;   there is no provision made ecclesiastically for
such as you ; but my friend Captain T. will take you as an
officer.'   I had then reached twenty.   The Church seemed
to have made no provision for a sailor ;   yet the sea was
God's school.   All the time opportunities came for ' the
converted sailor,' as he was called, to give his witness of
what he learnt of God upon the sea.   Books were not
neglected, and I picked up from good men and women as I
went along.   Without going into details, an unseen Hand
guided my steps, and a greater than my former counsellor
sent for me.   It was a great day for me when Dr. Paton
introduced this young fellow from the sea to his College
Committee.   I was admitted to the School of the Prophets,
and Dr. Paton himself took me down (with many encouraging words) to a Mrs. Ward, in Southey Street, my
shore cabin.   Looking at the past, I ought indeed to be
specially thankful to those who made the doors wide
enough to take me in.

" The first thing that impressed me about my new
Principal was his largeness of mind and heart.   Not only
was he, as the President of the Church Congress said,
' learned in ancient and modern languages,' he was also
in living sympathy with the great ocean currents of
German and French thought, and he was in persona

touch everywhere with the great practical movements making for righteousness and the Kingdom of God. If you ask me what made him such a wonderful power as a teacher, I should answer, ' It was because he was in living touch with the great world outside the college ; he was a teacher, and something more.'

" I never met a great man yet but who had in him much of the lion and the lamb. Looking out of our college window one afternoon, I saw Dr. Paton going the rounds of his garden, a book in one hand, and with the other wheeling a long, invalid carriage with a much-beloved daughter. So this invalid child, unable to talk or walk, was sent to him, that, while he was lion-hearted, he might carry in his bosom God's wee lamb. So it was with Moses, Paul, Luther, and the rest, and was not the ' Lion of the tribe of Judah ' the ' Lamb of God ' ? How wonderful, how infinitely interlaced in our lives are the manifold ministries and marvellous providences of our God ! That day as I watched the strong man in the garden, tending his weak lamb, sent by God to mellow, soften, and beautify a strong nature which might have been rugged, I won't say harsh, I saw that other side of Dr. Paton's nature, and the unconscious influence, coming through that upper window, came to my heart, as from the garden of God.

" Every leader of men must know his man. It is a priceless gift. It makes me laugh now, as I think how the Doctor divined his various men. Like Joseph of old, he knew his brethren. It is impossible to deal with men in the bunch, or crowd ; one must come near to them, commune with them, in short, individualise. Dr. Paton understood me, my weaknesses and strength, and did not allow the vices to blind him to my possible virtues. As I was descended from the old smugglers, there was a good deal of the salt and restlessness of ocean in my make-up, and it wanted some working and guiding, without too much of the wet blanket. Dr. Paton, in one of his letters to Mr. W. L. Adze about his sailor protégé, said : ' Matthews is a good fellow, but, like a high-spirited steed, he wants reining in. He established the first Templar Lodge in Nottingham, and our Temperance and Templar friends would take him away (to town and country meetings) from his studies.' Dr. Paton knew well his men. One man wants the whip, the fellow on the next form the rein.

" So happy was I under my new captain at Nottingham that the thought of departure never entered my mind. If it did, it was not entertained. Sailor-like, I nestled up to the heart of my teacher, who had become counsellor and friend. But that ancient city of Antwerp, with its historic memories—Flemish, Dutch, Spanish, commercial and spiritual, wanted a chaplain for the British and Foreign Sailors' Society. The call came, and I felt a drawing to the city where William Tyndale found shelter and completed his immortal and eternal work for the English-speaking race ; where Miles Coverdale took up the glorious work, and where John Rogers, the first martyr in Queen Mary's reign, was chaplain.

" My response to the urgent and repeated call was, ' Yes, if my Principal so decides.' Dr. Paton, instead of taking a narrow, parochial view, at once, with his great outlook, took in the situation. He might have said, ' No, we have prepared you for a Congregational Church, to a Congregational Church you must go. We have trained you for evangelistic work, you must go to a village Church, or to a slum district of one of our big English cities.' Instead of which he said, ' You have passed through the sea, God's school, you are a graduate of that big University, your life has led up to it.' The call was such that, though my term at college was not finished yet, I must accept it, and be responsible for supplies. Here again my Principal said, ' I will make it easy for you. Stay another year. I have two or three men who need a change. Antwerp ministry will be an education for them. Accept the offer and I will send the men. You can go in your vacations.'

" That is the way he handled his men. He went up to his mount of vision, looked out upon the sea, and said to his students, previously drawn out of many waters, ' Launch out into the deep ; let down your nets for a draught.' What a joy it was to me, shortly afterwards, to welcome this prophet of Nottingham at Antwerp ! I can see him now. He had been on solitary pilgrimage in parts of Europe by rail and road, and when he turned up, he reminded me of a Livingstone after tramping the desert. He was down at the heels, his clothes were worn, but there was enough light gleaming in the eyes to guide his followers in the dark."

" He always knew when a man was falling short of the best that he had it in him to do," says another, " and a man was shamed by the thought. I was once low down on the list for the weekly examination we had at that time. He did not rate me in front of the class, but he met me one morning in the hall, took me up to where the list was posted, pointed to my name, which was nearer the bottom than the top. ' That's no place for you,' he said, and I saw to it that it never was my place on the list any longer."

He was full of great catchwords which seemed to drive home his lessons like hammer-strokes.

" ' There are three things you must cultivate,' he said to me," says Mr. Enoch Gittings, " and another man would have said, ' There are three things you lack' ; but he knew how to put it. ' There are three things you must cultivate —Precision, decision, and incision.' "
Other sayings were :
" Look up and lift up."
" No life to God save where there is death to sin."
" We cannot give to Him unless we receive from Him."
" Simplicity is not shallowness ; simplicity is getting at the bottom of things."
" Earth is one gate to heaven."
" To be holy is not only to have the health of God ; it is to make it."
" Be methodical—hurry is a waste of time."
" Work and make music." [1]

He had in wonderful measure the gift of tact, which may be defined as great principles applied to small matters, but does not mean that small matters are made disproportionately great.
The Rev. Luke Beaumont, of Rock Ferry, says :

" The students in residence [2] had grievances, and it was decided to represent these to Dr. Paton, one representa-

---

[1] See Plato, "Phædo." What the spirit said to Socrates was one of the great watchwords of Paton's own life.
[2] This was after the death of Mr. F. S. Williams, when the Tutor's residence was turned into a boarding-house.

tive going from each study. The complaints were of a trivial character, but the young men saw them big, and appeared before the Doctor. He reclined on his couch in the midst of piled-up books. The head of the deputation explained, and then Dr. Paton questioned each man :

" ' What is your complaint, Mr. —— ? '

" ' Well, Dr. Paton, the linen has been very badly ironed, and—— '

" ' Ah, you have my deepest sympathy. I suffer often in the same way. Now Mr. ——, what is your complaint ? '

" ' The beds have not been well made recently, Doctor ; they have been very hard, and general—— '

" ' Again, you have my sympathy. Do you know, my bed is sometimes so hard when it is made by strange hands that I can scarcely sleep ? '

" ' Now, Mr. ——, what do you complain about ? '

" Needless to say, there were no more complaints.

" Then he gave us the best address I ever heard on how to manage a Church. We should have much in our ministerial life, he told us, to disturb the even tenor of our way ; things would not always go smoothly. But it would be fatal if we let things get to that stage which crystallised them out into a solemn deputation, a scheduling of grievances, and a public meeting. Better deal with such things privately, and not allow things slight and petty to be magnified into serious and solemn dimensions."

Paton spoke from experience. In all the thousand and one affairs in which he was engaged, there were innumerable little rubs that called for the charity which endureth all things, and is proof against all pin-prickings. His charity never failed. Relations with colleagues were always cordial, and even intimate. With none were they more cordial and intimate than with him who was his friend before the Institute was founded, his first colleague in the Institute work, and his colleague till called home in 1886, after twenty-three years of joint partnership—the Rev. F. Smeeton Williams, a man endowed with rare literary gift and genial kindliness of soul, true and strong in his private friendship, true and strong and fearless in his public work. Mr. Henry Ollard, the first Secretary of the Institute, and later a lecturer in Church History, was another dearly loved colleague. " My Lacordaire " was the name that Mr. Ollard gave him. "Paton," he said on his death-bed in 1875, "my dearest, truest, and best friend, is the repository of my choicest and best thoughts." The same affectionate relationship subsisted between Dr. Paton and his successor in the Principalship, the late Rev. J. A. Mitchell, M.A., and Mr. Mitchell's successor, the Rev. D. L. Ritchie, a man after his own heart, who, with commanding energy and fulness of inspiration, carries on the work of the Institute in a way which was a constant joy to the founder in his declining years. A nature brimming over with affection led him ever to seek the warmth and sympathy of kindly friendship, as a flower turns to the warmth and gladness of the sunlight; and one of the great gifts of mercy for which he gave thanks to his Heavenly Father was the unfailing friendship of his colleagues and of his successors. As colleague after colleague in the course of days passed to his reward, he dedicated himself afresh to the work they had shared so long with him. "That is the meaning of the phrase, 'baptized for the dead,'" he would say. "I am now baptized afresh to do that work more diligently, so that there be no lacking in it."

"These years are over," he said in Addison Street Church at the funeral service of Mr. Williams, "and I stand here bereft of my companion and friend; bereft, too, of all but one of the many friends who began this work with me. But the God of grace who called me to this work abides, and our faith abides. . . . You, who are of younger days, cannot know the energy, the sacred and almost desperate energy, with which we of middle life feel called upon to fill up the few years that remain with work which shall be more abounding, so that our own service shall be faithfully rendered, and that no loss shall come to the great cause of our redeeming Lord and the interests of our fellow-men from the passing away of one of those who have laboured with us."

A letter to a colleague.

" DEAR FRIEND,
    " As to your letter, there is much in it which I appreciate very cordially—also something in it which I have not found it easy to comprehend. As tutors, we have

to speak to students of the formation of their character. But have you not found, with me, that this is a delicate and difficult task requiring much spiritual preparedness, a wise and sympathetic touch, and complete freedom from all feeling that obscures or gives bias to judgment ? ' Restless,' in the sense of fidgety or feverish, I do not think you consider me to be. You have come to me too often when there has been cause of excitement to think that. ' Autocratic ' I do not wish to be ; I pray not to be. And I have considered what I have ever done that was not required or expected of me by the committee. But I know that a man in earnest about any work does sometimes, and not quite rightly, appear to be both of these to others.

" But it is very hard to keep to the narrow way, not swerving to either hand, following the Master nearly, and I feel for both of us, situated where our life, our words, our example, our hourly conduct moulds and colours and inspires or deadens the many men called to the Highest Ministry in the universe, the ministry of redemption, there is but one thing to do : to seek for the most perfect consecration and concentration of spirit in our Master's service, and to help one another to do our utmost and to be our best, forbearing one another, and by influence of character rather perhaps than by open words, encouraging, exhorting, and even, it might be, admonishing one another. Few men have such a responsibility, such a mission as we. Let us try to fulfil it, and help one another to fulfil it, as *He* would have us do, and as we would wish when we look back at the end, which is not far off."

Attracted by the fame of the Nottingham Sermon Class, many inquirers have asked as to the method adopted. It is not hard to give an account of the method, but when that has been fully set forth, the Sermon Class itself remains still unexplained. The method was the man. What made the Sermon Class was his strong personality, his living faith, his glowing love recharged from the unfailing source of supply. His business was to train ministers, and a minister, to him, was an ambassador. The ambassador's business was to have a message, to know that message, and to urge it. It was this sense of urgency which was often so sadly lacking in its delivery ; the sermon had become a pillow for somnolent heads, or a whetstone for critical minds, something in short to be endured. There is no urgency without the feeling of reality. " How is it," asked a clergyman of Sheridan, " that preachers so often send their hearers to sleep, while actors can always keep theirs awake ? " " Simply," said Sheridan, " because the parsons preach fact as though it were fiction, and actors preach fiction as though it were fact." The first thing Paton insisted on was that the word was fact, and, being fact, should be brought home to the hearers as real living fact having a vital bearing on the life of to-day—the personal life of the individual, the business life, the social relationships of men, and public questions of policy. And, because it was a message of life and death, there must be the fire of intense earnestness in the delivery of it. The lips must be touched with the live coal from off the altar. No amount of learning could compensate for the lack of that altar-fire. A grate may be crammed with wood and coal and paper, but unless there be the spark, there will be no fire. He would never allow that zeal was a special gift of the few ; zeal was the heightening and intensifying of any ordinary man's power which resulted from the application of the spark. " Nothing will ignite the dead indifference of the masses," he said, " but the fire of holy fervour. Nothing will quicken fervour but the vital breath, the inspiration of a soul full of faith and of the Holy Ghost."

He knew that his men would work much alone, whether at home or in the foreign mission-field ; they would not have the incentives or the safeguards of other Christian ministers ; they would walk in dark places, where Atheism was writ large on the faces of their fellow-men and on their surroundings ; they would breathe a deadly, sin-stifled atmosphere, they would sink in deep waters. Only the daily baptism of the Spirit could bear them up, and the sound of the Voice within, the same Voice which woke them first with the " one clear call," and drove them with a power they could not withstand into the work.

" Let the memory of those awful moments," he said to his students, " when the voice of God summoning you to this mission sounded so clear in your hearts, awake again now. And now let your prayer rise up to Heaven that, through weakness or strength, hunger or fulness, loss or gain, good report or evil report, life or death, you may be faithful to Him who hath called you, and to His Son, whose friends and chosen servants you are. You have come to the Institute to be trained for your divine calling, to acquire knowledge, faculty, habits that may arm and strengthen you for nobler and more effective labours than you were competent for without. May these be yours, earned and won by faithful toil! But you know—and let the thought now bend you in prayer—the secret, the source of all power, the life of all life in your ministry, is not of man but of God. You will be mighty, successful, honoured in God's work, only as you are ' good men, full of the Holy Ghost and of faith.' "

There was one sacred season every week when he was among his men no longer as Principal, or even as Tutor, but as scholar with them in the School of Christ. On Monday afternoon, when all had reassembled after their Sunday work, they met together for prayer, and once a month they celebrated together in simple fashion the breaking of the bread. There was no special chapel set apart for the purpose, they met in the ordinary class-room where they met every day, for it was the hallowing of that place and the work done in it which they sought. The common meal was the seal and sanction of their common brotherhood with one another, and their common life in Him who was their Elder Brother. It was the renewed pledge that He who in history came down from heaven and gave His life upon the cross for mankind, still bids men come, each by each, to be partakers of the sacrifice once made, to receive anew the pardon of sin, the new creation, the nourishing of faith. It was to each one of the fellowship the visible sign that He, who had been to him the Author of life, would also more and more continually be the Finisher of the life He had given; that He would enter into him that believed and make His abode with him. When all were seated in their places, the Doctor would come in from his house " with a solemn, radiant expression of countenance, like a saint coming forth from his devotions." " He appeared to me," says one of his earliest students, " as a Moses who had been in the Mount of God and had seen God face to face, and his face shone with a

divine glory ; but ' he wist not ' that his face shone."
An hour would pass in prayer, one student succeeding
another in turn, each rising as the Spirit of God moved him.
Then the Doctor would fill the central portion of the day's
exercises with a Bible-reading, or an exposition of a passage
of the Greek Testament, or occasionally with an address.
He was always at his best on these occasions, giving out
of the overflowing riches of his mental and spiritual resources to his students. " I have often been caught up
in a divine rapture while the Doctor was unfolding divine
truths in his talk," writes another student. " The Spirit
took the things of Christ and showed them unto us. The
atmosphere was full of God." Then followed his own
prayer of thanksgiving and consecration, after which the
senior student passed round the bread and wine to all
present. Finally, there came the hymn of worship to
the Lord, and fellowship with each other, and then the
closing prayer and benediction.

At these services of consecration Paton would speak
of the need of the quiet hour, "the cloister in the
heart." The increase of knowledge, the growing stir
and strain of life, made this less easy, but more important than ever before. The steamer which did not
have its compass constantly rectified would soon get out
of its course. He delighted to speak of " the Father's
business," the pre-eminent " business " of our life, and
of the method, organisation, and eagerness which the
word " business " suggested (he never forgave the revisers
for omitting that word) ; and in this " business " of
the Father, the minister was not a servant only of the
Father, but a partner. He spoke of the greatness of the
redemption which it was the Father's business to fulfil—
how it extended to the whole man, his body and mind,
his pleasures and his surroundings, and all that apper-
tained to his daily life ; how manifold and how practical,
therefore, was the function of that redeeming process.
" How shall the prodigal know that the Father loves him ?
How can he believe there is love in God if I, who speak
for God, show him no sympathy, no helping hand ? "
But the Gospel of Jesus was not a mere matter of loaves
and fishes ; the deep roots of sin and evil could not be
reached by distributing a few material things ; it must
go right down to the unseen cause of all disease, physical

and moral ; it must convince and convert. The keynote of the minister's message and the burden of his heart must be, as it was with the apostles, Christ and Him crucified ; in Him was the power to convert the world ; in His death He took upon Himself the chains and power of sin, that He might break them asunder ; in that sign the Gospel conquered, evil passions were subdued, and the Christ was formed within the man renewed unto knowledge " after the image of Him that created him." Not only in word must the Cross be held up. The Cross must be embodied in the life ; every life must be a cruci- fix. The soldiers of the Cross did not wear the sacred emblem painted on the breast, but they wore it in their face, with " all the light of the sacred story " shining there, and all the compelling power of it pulsing through their hearts. " Soldiers of the Cross," but not soldiers of the barracks and the parade-ground, pranking it in proud uniform at home, rather soldiers on campaign, rough- ing it in the bivouac, hazarding life and limb upon the battle-field. " The bugle note " which he so constantly demanded from the students, was never wanting in his own words to them.

Constantly he would restate and emphasise the inward meaning of the sacred rite, which was at the same time a memorial of the past—" in remembrance of Me," and a prophecy of the future—" till He come."

The abiding impression which he made as teacher and leader of his students' thought may well be gathered up in some verses written by one of his most loyal sons according to the Spirit, the Rev. A. J. Owens, of Droitwich :

> The slow-evolving thought that burst at length
> In passion, or in smiling found its strength :
> The far-off, mystic look, so set and rapt,
> With quick return and application apt :
>
> The declamation fierce, that frighted men,
> That struck straight home, and palsied heart and pen ;
> Like lion roused, and growling for the spring,
> Or great archangel on puissant wing :
>
> The tide of feeling, full and deep and strong,
> That rose, o'erwhelming, at the tale of wrong ;
> The keen and eager welcome of the fight—
> Sublimely confident in God and Right :

9

The statesman's vision, purged by Christly love,
That saw his country's needs, and rose above
The lines of sect and party ; brain that wrought
The comprehensive scheme to fit the thought :

The holy hush that filled the wonted place,
When high communion lit the uplifted face,
The weakness and the love with tears confessed—
Deep-graven memories of the sacred Feast.

CHAPTER IX

CIVIC WORK AT NOTTINGHAM—THE OLD CATHOLIC MOVEMENT

" Thou shalt be called, The repairer of the breach, The restorer of path to dwell in."—ISAIAH.

THE condition of Nottingham in 1863 gave plenty of scope for all manner of political and social work. The growth of the town had been phenomenal. The common lands which hemmed in the town on three sides had greatly restricted building operations hitherto. Consequently the central town had been sadly congested and insanitary, while outside the belt of common lands there had sprung up large manufacturing and mining villages without adequate spiritual provision, without the steadying responsibilities of civic self-government, and without the salt of civic corporate spirit. The Inclosure Act had been passed in 1845, but it was not until 1850 that it began to have any substantial effect. The land to the north, east, and south was then opened out for building purposes, and the result was that in the next ten years the population increased by leaps and bounds. In 1851 the population was 58,419 ; in 1861 it was 75,765, showing an increase of no less than 30 per cent.

With towns, as with boys and girls, a period of abnormal growth brings with it special problems and risks. Nottingham was no longer the sedate, self-contained township which John Wesley describes in his Journal.

The rioters who burned the Castle in 1831 had earned for the town an unenviable notoriety for ruffianism, and the fact that Sir Robert Clifton was one of the members for the borough went far to justify the reputation. The opportunity to challenge this spirit of club-law was not long in presenting itself. The election of 1865, in which Samuel Morley stood against Sir Robert Clifton, was a

spectacle of national interest. It was an historic contest.
The magistrates sat ensconced in the Exchange buildings
guarded by the whole body of the borough police, while
outside, under their very eyes, the yelling mobs engaged
in their infuriate play with stones and bludgeons and
faggots. These excesses roused the moral sense of the
community ; many, who had taken little interest in
politics before, resolved that violence of this sort should
be mastered by law and the instigator of it branded with
a just opprobrium. Mr. Morley was returned at the top
of the poll, and his victory marked an era in the political
life of the borough. Mr. Morley took his seat, made his
maiden speech on the second reading of the Church Rates
Abolition Bill, and in the following year was unseated on
petition for illegal practices on the part of false and
foolish friends.

It was the first election after Paton's coming to Nottingham, and he had built much on it. Samuel Morley was
his personal friend, for whose " loving gentleness, combined with wisdom and strength," he had unstinted
admiration. He was confident in his hope that Nottingham was not only going to retrieve its bad name, but to
be the first of the big boroughs to sound the note of war
for the coming election. The unseating of Mr. Morley
was a great blow to him. He did his utmost to get
Mr. Morley to stand again in 1868, but the appeal of
the Liberal party in Nottingham, which he drafted, came
too late. Mr. Morley had already promised to stand for
Bristol, and he continued to represent Bristol till he
died. But it was not that he had shaken off the dust
from off his feet in disgust.

" The grace which is recognised to be the peculiar and
richest fruit of Christian culture," wrote Paton, " shone
radiantly in his conduct. The revenge wherewith he
sought to comfort himself and repay the wrong done to
him was this : he asked Canon Morse, of Nottingham, and
another to confer with him and advise him in what ways
he could do most for the good of a town where this great
wrong had been done him." [1]

The " other " whom Mr. Morley consulted was Paton

[1] " Contemporary Review."

himself, and nobly did he and the Canon give themselves, not only to advising Mr. Morley, but to carrying out the advice they gave. From henceforth they were sworn friends and fellow-workers in everything that concerned the spiritual life of the Churches and the betterment of the people's life. Never again did Paton take any prominent part in the party politics of the town; he was too much absorbed in other works which lie for the most part outside the party programmes and bear a closer relation to the moral welfare of the common folk. The friendship between the Vicar of St. Mary's, the leading Churchman of the city, and the Principal of the Congregational Institute was one of the leading facts of the town's life. It was more than a mere personal attachment. It stood for nobler manners, purer laws; it infected the whole spiritual life of the Churches with a spirit of brotherliness; it directed the attention of the Churches to works of healing and social righteousness. The two friends stood together in resisting the proposal of the Government to plant military barracks in the town—a proposal specially noxious in a town where there was so much employment for women attracting a large number of young girls from the surrounding country districts, and where the girls lived to so great an extent in lodgings, deprived of the ordinary protection of home and friends. They stood together in opposing the extension, and demanding the repeal of the Contagious Diseases Act— " this Continental system," Paton calls it, " of legislating on behalf of vice and against women "; they united to urge on the Christian Churches the duty that lies upon them " of purifying legislation from this pestiferous sanction of sin." They worked together in their advocacy of temperance and keeping the Watch Committee up to its duty in the enforcement of the existing laws. There were (and still are) two great market-days in Nottingham, when the open market-place, said to be the largest in England, is filled with booths, with country folk and cheapjacks of all kinds. When Paton found that there was no place within easy reach where any of these country folk could get refreshment except in licensed premises, he set up a stall of his own in the market, with a man to look after it, and supply tea, coffee, and cocoa, and simple refreshments; and he was very particular to see that the coffee should be something more nearly resembling what he found in France than was usually supplied in English hostelries. That coffee-stall was the father of all the cafés which now abound in the city. As soon as Paton proved " there was money in it," it was not hard to find a successor, who would put capital into the business and carry it on on a large scale. Some people thought it was a queer thing for a minister to run a coffee-stall. What did they think when the same minister got a mayor to call a meeting in order to discuss setting up a Glaciarium, or cold meat-store, in the town in order to make provision for frozen meat and to save the waste which was going on through meat and fish going bad ? Many a business man has envied this minister his gift for seeing a likely opening for business.

He kept up his habit of spending a part at least of every summer holiday on the Continent. He was frequently in Paris, where he was instrumental in starting a new mission Church ; but, after meeting Dr. Wichern, he was drawn more and more to Germany. He studied the method of the Raue Haus at Hamburg, and the Diakonissin-institut at Kaiserwerth. He found his way again and again to Halle, where he had converse with the great theologian Tholuck. It was joy in Halle to live as a student with the younger men in Dr. Tholuck's Convikt, sharing their simple quarters and Spartan diet, attending lectures, joining in discussions, and swinging out on the summer afternoons for a walk in the forest. Many a young theological student from England was received at his recommendation into Dr. Tholuck's hostel at Halle, gaining thereby not only insight into German university life, but personal contact with one of the leading German teachers. When Dr. Tholuck retired, Paton was eager in collecting a sum of money which should be some recognition of Tholuck's unwearying kindness to his English visitors.[1] He also met Dorner, Lotze, Ritschl, Harnack, Wellhausen, and J. Müller.

In the summer of 1871 he visited France, saw the scenes over which had swept the red storm of war, and conversed with men who had mingled in the mêlée, and were repairing the ruins. The impression of Paris was one of inexpressible dolour.

[1] Dr. Archibald Duff, of the United College, Bradford, was in residence at the hostel in 1863, and acted as my father's guide. This was the beginning of a happy friendship.

" I have never seen a Parisienne but she was in full mourning or half mourning. The attendants in shops were all dressed in black, and no working woman passing hurriedly in the street but wore some ribbon or article of dress to show that she shared in the universal sorrow."

He was struck by the fact that in the Versailles Assembly there were sixty-three Protestant deputies, a larger proportion than had ever been known in a French representative body since the Revocation of the Edict of Nantes. Also, in the last Paris elections a fourth of the twenty-one members elected were Protestant.

" It is well known that the Commune discriminated in all its proceedings the Protestant pastors of Paris from the priests. None denounced their crimes so boldly as these pastors; but their former fidelity to the cause of liberty, their respect for individual consciences, for the privacy of home, and the authority of the husband and father in his own house, was remembered, and their rebukes were allowed."

How was this to be explained ? At the beginning of the war Protestants were viewed with suspicion, and in the eastern provinces to be a Protestant was, in the popular mind, to be a Prussian. Undoubtedly, the Roman priests had represented the war as a war of religion to establish the supremacy of an Infallible Pope through the strong arm of the Church's " eldest son." The disasters of the war had opened the eyes of the people. The splendid devotion of the Protestants on the battle-field, in the hospitals, and among the suffering poor had given the lie to the accusation of treachery. The liberality of Protestant England and the reception given to Bourbaki's army in Protestant Switzerland had counted for much. But what counted for most was the widespread feeling that the failure of the nation was at bottom a moral failure, and the first need of the war a moral regeneration, impossible without religion.

" The moral regeneration of France is impossible without religion," he writes. " For this object Romanism

is futile, and worse. Romanism has, by its specific perversion of religious principle and duty, induced the moral
weakness and degradation which is deplored. In consequence of this conviction, Protestantism is becoming more
usually understood and appreciated by thoughtful men
who, in their divorce from Rome, had been alienated from
religion altogether.

" Romanism, it is seen, gives a spectacular, sensational,
sacerdotal religion, which gratifies, and even excites,
religious sensibilities, but which destroys the sense of
individual responsibility, and consequently the moral independence of men, and which does not train the conscience
by bringing all the powers of religious emotion to quicken
and sustain its authority, and to strengthen the will in
the performance of duty. By stimulating the emotions,
weakening the will, submitting the entire control of the
inward life to a spiritual director, and drugging the conscience by deceptive indulgences, it trains a people who are
prone to outward despotic authority in political life, and
who willingly accept a vicarious functionary system in it
as in the religious life. The contrast of Protestantism
in these vital regards has been brought prominently into
notice."

" Do you wish," exclaims Pressensé, " to reawaken moral
life ? Take away that which suffocates it, the cushion of
official religions. Appeal, in order to sustain your worship,
to personal faith and the spirit of sacrifice."

He sees a great opening for Protestant missionary work,
but the methods of these mission workers must be different
from those adopted in ordinary revival services.

" Such revival services seem adapted for populations that
are nominally Christian. They awaken dormant conviction. They quicken dead but accredited opinions into
living faith. But in Paris the population is not nominally
Christian, it is almost universally infidel.

" Like Paul in the school of Tyrannus, they must go out
to meet these masses of disbelieving men, ' disputing and
persuading those things concerning the kingdom of God.'
A Christianity which solves the social problems that agitate
their workshops and clubs, that gives the only sanction

and solid ground of human rights, that alone has power to deliver them from pressing evils, and crowns them with the blessings of freedom, concord, and peace in every sphere, whether within or without, in the soul or in society ; an agonistic religion, a religion that is eager for serious controversy, that mixes itself with the business, the speculations, the passionate strivings of the men of to-day ; that throws light on their vexed questionings, and gives rocky foundation and framework to their ideal doctrines ; which shows itself to be not only a religion, but the absolute religion, because compassing, illumining, purifying, and ennobling, like the heavens, the two hemispheres of life— viz. the human soul and human society,—such is the Christianity to which Evangelical Churches must challenge the attention and win the faith of the working men and the educated classes in Paris.

" Ere leaving Paris I went over to Versailles to attend the meeting of the Assembly there. The session was an important one: it was the famous discussion on the ' Provincial Councils.' And though I have seen our House of Commons in some of the most exciting and tumultuous scenes that have been witnessed in it of late years, I must confess amazement at the scene in the Versailles Assembly. It was not ' the noise,' for no noise can exceed the roaring storm that bellows in our Parliament on a furious night of battle, but the disloyalty to the chair. One speaker spoke thrice, and then again from his seat, against the protestation of the chairman, and amidst the outcries of the House, he ejaculated another oration, which was, of course, inaudible. Meanwhile the President —M. Grévy—rattled his paper-cutter, rang and rerang his bell, but all in vain. No authority seemed capable of quelling the riotous self-will of the Assembly. Flying sentences whizzed through the air, thick with confusion, like rifle-bullets ; men started from their seats and looked daggers at their opponents ; and only as storms rave themselves to rest did the Assembly gradually sink back to quietude. I could not but contrast the volatile feverishness of this Assembly with the grave bearing of the Italian Parliament."

As he travelled from Paris to Metz, he was struck with the wonderful resurgence of agriculture, and the ocular demonstration of what could be accomplished by *la petite culture* left an impression on his mind which was never effaced.

"War may devastate the surface of the country, but its agricultural riches cannot be lost. The wakening breath of spring and the refining heat of summer clothe France again with abundance. It were otherwise if her wealth, like ours, were mainly drawn from industrial interests. Foreign aggression would strike a deadlier blow in England than in France.

"Gravelotte is a battle-field never to be forgotten. The day I went over it was breezy and bright, yet all along the horizon a dark-blue bank of cloud hung, and against that cloud, far as the eye could reach, there *shone* like stars myriads of white crosses, mostly in groups, like constellations. These crosses were fixed at the heads of mounds, in which the fallen were buried. On walking over the turf, I found the ground pock-pitted with holes from one to five feet deep. These were the holes where the flaming *obuses* fell, burying and shattering themselves in the earth. The extemporaneous forts of turf, into which cannon were rolled and placed as soon as a position was gained, were still standing. The trees along the road were pierced, and in some places flayed by the bullet-shots.

"On one of the mounds lay prostrate the form of the lady who had driven past me, her body convulsed with grief, and her sobs filling that awful solitude of graves and crosses with a voice of solemn lamentations—heartbreaking voice it seemed to me as I hurried on, but the only language that could speak the sorrow of the place."

At Elberfeld he studied the system of poor relief which was beginning at that time to attract the attention of thinking people in England. That very year Mr. Goschen had sent out a commissioner to make inquiries.

"In Germany, as in parts of England and Scotland, the family feeling and the feeling of neighbourhood are very strong, and consequently the weak and aged are cared for by those to whom they are related. Besides, the old Saxon habit of mutual *Bürgschaft* holds strongly in Germany. The people of a town or district feel a mutual responsibility, and become a sort of security, for each other. Hence the care of the poor, as at Elberfeld, is assumed as a duty by the townsfolk themselves. And they subdivide the labour among themselves, that it may be efficiently done."

This study of the Elberfeld system was destined to bear a rich harvest later on.

He finished his tour with a longer stay at the Rigi Scheideck. There was a large company at the hotel. Most of the guests were German, some of whom were recovering from wounds received in the war. Among the Germans were two eminent University men.. There was Professor Huber, Professor of Philosophy at Munich, famous for his disquisitions on the deeper questions of spiritual philosophy—God, Man, and Immortality; a man of ample sweep of mind and eager enthusiasm. A Roman Catholic by religious profession, he had taken the lead of his fellow-professors at Munich in protesting against the recent Vatican decrees by which the Pope had claimed for himself infallibility and immediate universal episcopate over the entire Church. He had, in conjunction with Döllinger, written a series of letters to the " Augsburg Gazette " denouncing the hollowness and infamy of the procedure which converted the whole Roman Catholic Church into an exact counterpart of the Jesuit order, with the Pope for its General. These letters, republished in book form under the name of " Janus," had at once been translated into the chief languages of Europe, and had done much to make thinking men see the real significance and tendency of the Vatican decrees.

Professor Nasse also was there, the great political economist from Bonn, a leader of the National Liberal Party in the Reichstag, and also a leading officer in the Evangelical Church of the Rhine provinces. There were also representatives of Britain—a chatty, fiery High Church clergyman from Carnarvon, and a sober-minded, learned Anglican of the old Andrewes type, who had won a reputation as a High Church Canonist in the Lower House of Convocation. Acquaintance first sprang up between Paton and Professor Nasse, and, church questions being uppermost in the minds of both, they discussed the latest ecclesiastical movements in England and Germany. In these conversations Huber joined, making known who he was, and very soon the Anglican clergy were taking eager part in the discussion. The Anglican clergymen upheld stoutly the doctrine of the Apostolical Succession as being, if not the sole, at any rate the " regular " channel of God's grace to His Church. The Nonconformist professed himself to be a Churchman, as strict and as high as any of them ; he insisted that his doctrine of the Church was the doctrine declared in the creeds which all the others held and recited, viz. that the Holy Catholic Church consists in the communion of saints—the fellowship of those who are one in Christ, who are associated for the purposes of that faith, whose system of government is the instrument authenticated by them, the efficient defence and diffusion of their faith. So far from its rights being conferred by any hierarchy, he maintained that it alone, the *congregatio fidelium*, could originate and sustain the hierarchy, and indeed determine whether its government should take the form of a hierarchy or some other. Professor Nasse held to the doctrine of a State Church, as the spiritual organ of the Empire ; but, foreseeing that the time was not far distant when the Church would be separated from the State, he listened with special interest to the exposition of the Catholic principles that constitute the Independent or Congregational Church—principles which took him back to the history of the first three centuries.

Huber had come direct from the Congress at Munich, where the Old Catholics had declared themselves bound to a revival of the old Catholic principles of the Christian Church and to the formation of the Catholic Church on those principles. He listened not only with keen interest, but with some degree of amazement to the views expounded by the English Congregationalist, which repudiated so uncompromisingly the sacerdotal system of Rome and based the Church on a spiritual membership which was Catholic in the true sense of the word. The hope of those who rejected the Vatican decrees had been centred at first on a new reformation to be accomplished *within* the Roman Catholic Church. But the congress at Munich had made it clear that some provision must be made for communities of Old Catholics, excommunicated by the Vatican ; pastors must be chosen, and some system of oversight must be put into execution. The reconstitution of the Old Catholic Church as a branch of the Catholic

Church was, therefore, at the time, the most pressing of questions to himself and to other leaders of the movement.

The little band spent several days on the mountain-height in this happy interchange of inmost thought, and, before parting, by way of realising their unity of spirit, on the Sunday morning, in the quaint wooden chapel opening from the long terrace of their hostelry, they broke the bread and drank the wine in remembrance of Him whom they loved and owned as their common Master. The canonist rector presided and the Congregational minister officiated as an extempore deacon. And so the little company of friends broke up.

Returning to England, Paton grew more and more impressed with the conviction that some action—public and sympathetic—ought to be taken by those in this country who were interested, or ought to be interested, in the Old Catholic movement. He knew that, if only its aims and spirit were understood, it would command the cordial sympathy of English Nonconformists ; but he felt that, if this expression of sympathy came from the Nonconformist Churches alone, it would be less helpful to the Old Catholics and tend to compromise them in the eyes of Europe with ultra-Protestant tendencies. The thing to aim at was to have a joint expression of brotherly sympathy from the Anglicans and Nonconformists, from the laity as well as the clergy.

He wrote accordingly to the Bishop of the diocese, Dr. Wordsworth, Bishop of Lincoln, told him all that was in his heart, and proposed that some organised effort should be made to secure an expression of public sympathy in England with the efforts and the aspirations of those Old Catholics who were " uprising from beneath the usurped dominion of Rome," to secure also that public sympathy should be made intelligent and maintained in continuance by being supplied with information and kept in touch with what was happening. He urged that in this way attention would be called to the aims and spirit of the Ultramontane party, who found it easy to carry on their insidious propaganda among an insular nation, unsuspicious because it was ignorant.

" By creating sympathy with, and obtaining help for, the Old Catholic Church, you would, I believe, put

Englishmen on their guard against Ultramontane policy, counteract the tendencies to perversion Romewards, and foil the efforts made, at such expense and with such craft, to resubjugate our people to Rome."

Moreover, this was an opportunity for united action by Churchmen and Nonconformists, and such united action on behalf of Christian truth and true Church principles, so far as they were held in common, would furnish the best *apologia* against Romanism on the one hand and Rationalism on the other.

"I am assured," he writes, "that Nonconformists would rejoice to join with you and other English Churchmen in a national movement to co-operate in the new and glorious appearing of God's own delivering grace on the Continent."

The Bishop took the matter up sympathetically, and much friendly correspondence passed, through Paton, between Professor Huber and Dr. Reinkens on the one hand, and Dr. Wordsworth with Dr. Harold Browne, the Bishop of Ely, later of Winchester, on the other. The result was that the Bishop of Lincoln, presiding over the Church Congress at Nottingham in 1872, read a paper on the Old Catholic movement, told the Congress how he had summoned a synod of the clergy of his diocese, laid the whole matter before them, and obtained their concurrence in transmitting to Munich a document formally and heartily expressing their sympathy. The Bishop succeeded in arousing the enthusiasm and awaking the sympathies of his vast audience, and made frank and graceful acknowledgment of the influences which had led him to take action in the matter.

All this, it will be noted, was before Mr. Gladstone took the field. How it cheered the leaders of the new movement in Germany may be gathered by a letter written by Bishop Reinkens :

"It is a matter of great regret to our friends here that there has been in England such lack of knowledge and understanding of our cause, a lack which is painfully evident in the most important journals, *e.g.* the "Times." Our regret is the greater because we thought, and would continue to think so still, that the noble English nation was called to march with us at the head of the great religious movement of the present time. It is unfortunate also that the old Catholic families of England show such apathy and indifference to the moral corruption of the Roman *curia*, in which ambition and avarice are the chief motives of all action. . . . They do not even know what it is we are fighting for."

In the November of the same autumn, 1872, the second congress of Old Catholics was held at Cologne. Paton was present. He describes the great scenes at the reception in the Gartensaal of the Wienerhof, the meetings of the Congress in the Gurzenich, in which 400 delegates, for the most part laymen, and 100 representatives from other Churches took part. He describes also the great leader, Döllinger, the greatest Catholic theologian in Europe, Van Schulle, the greatest Catholic jurist, Professor Huber and Professor Friedrichs, who had just published his "Tagebuch," *i.e.* his Diary of the Vatican Council, and two volumes of documents "which serve to illustrate the Vatican Council." Professor Knoodt, of Bonn, "the Erasmus of this reformation," Abbé Michaud, and, greatest of all in the height of oratoric power and high Christian enthusiasm and mastery over men, Dr. Reinkens of Breslau. "One felt that, under the leadership of such men, the movement is not likely to run into the sand." Again and again did the cry go forth from the Congress " of the true Catholic, not Roman Catholic doctrine of the Church." " The Church," they ingeminated, " is not the Pope, the Bishops, or the priests : the Church is the fellowship of all believers. The Church does not save men, it itself is saved and is made up of the saved. Christ alone can save."

" There may indeed be hope for Catholic Europe," he writes, " if any religious movement that laid hold of the powerful Catholic sentiment of the people, and restored it to its original and proper significance, as a universal fellowship in Christ, instead of being a universal submission to the Pope, should, working thus from within the Catholic nations, lift them up to the moral independence, the freedom of conscience, and the spirituality of worship which the Gospel of Christ alone can secure."

Again, in August 1875 he was present by special invitation at the " Unions Conferenz " in Bonn, where the representatives of the Eastern Church met the Old Catholics to discuss the basis of a common union.   The occasion and the scene alike were historic and memorable.

" Never since the Council of Florence (1439) had so many Greek ecclesiastics been assembled together in any part of Western Christendom.   Their mission now was the same as then, but the venue, as the French say, had changed.   Then they came, cowed by the terrific onset of Turkish Mohammedanism, submitting to a union with the Papacy, if it did not outrage the orthodox faith of their Church, that they might obtain succour from the Christian nations of the West.   Then they met only representatives of the Papacy, who urged them by threats or deceived them by forgeries, to acknowledge the primacy of the Pope.   Now they came with the strength of the Czardom at their back, and they came to meet representatives of so-called Catholic Churches in Europe, that equally with them repudiated the insolent pretensions of the Pope, and desired union with the Eastern Churches, that they might together combat the more powerfully the flagitious claim he had just announced to universal dictatorship over all Christian men and Christian States."

Paton was deeply impressed, not only by the spectacle but by the erudition and historic judgment evinced by the representatives of the Russo-Greek Church and the Old Catholics ; he was painfully impressed also by the lack of these qualities in their Anglican confrères.

" One result of the Bonn Conference ought to be the formation of a school of scientific theology in the Anglican Church."

The Bonn Conference was a tentative effort.   The reunion at which it aimed was not accomplished ; the larger synthesis is still to come.   But the Conference proved that doctrinal differences, even serious differences, are no bar to religious communion and the charities of intercourse, the interplay of argument, above all the influence of the Holy Spirit prepare men for the synthesis that is to be.

J. B. PATON, ÆT. 40.

CHAPTER X

THE EXPANSION OF EDUCATION

"The University is a place where the professor is a missionary and a preacher, displaying his science in its most complete and winning form, pouring it forth with the zeal of enthusiasm, and lighting up his own love of it in the breasts of his hearers."—NEWMAN.

MEANWHILE, urgent problems presented themselves. The Government was attacking the question of national education. Ten years before, Paton had been averse to the intervention of the State in education. He shared the general feeling of Nonconformists, to whom education was a matter inextricably bound up with religion, and therefore not safely to be entrusted to the Secular Leviathan. The example of Scotland made him hopeful that, if England could only catch the true spirit of the thing, it might become an educated nation without compulsion. But the victory of the North in the American War, and the victories of the Prussians, had made a great impression on his mind. In both cases success seemed attributable in no small measure to systematic provision of universal education. The extension of the franchise enforced the same lesson. To place the sovereign power in the hands of uneducated people was worse than folly; it was suicide. New conditions were teaching new duties, and the path of progress lay clearly along the lines of organised education.

So far there was fairly general agreement. But, directly the Government proposals took practical shape, serious lines of cleavage presented themselves. One party held that the only logical line of solution was to set up a national system which should, sooner or later, eat up all the voluntary schools in connection with the various Churches, and should be strictly secular. Dr. Dale and the Birmingham School followed the lead of Fawcett and Mill, and threw in their lot with this school of thought.

10   145

Their reasoning seemed irresistible.   But Paton saw deeper
into the realities of the situation.   To him, education was
something larger than any mere training for vocation,
even the vocation of earthly citizenship : it was to him
a training for life, a life which was not limited to this
earthly span ; it was a great social force—

> A lever to uplift the earth
> And roll it on another course.

To fulfil this supreme function, it must do something more
than instruct the mind ; it must touch the springs of
character, it must build up an ideal of life, it must (in
Plato's phrase) " turn the soul towards the light."   The
school was not a mere knowledge-shop, it was a living
society with a life of its own which was inevitably colouring the moral life of every individual who belonged to it.
If Christian teaching, therefore, were eliminated from the
schools, the result would be either a blank negation or
some invertebrate moral and humanitarian teaching which
would never rise above the level of an enlightened selfishness, which would never generate the spiritual power that
lifts a nation's life.   His opponents said it was the duty
of the home to give religious instruction.   Paton did not
deny it ; but he saw how rare was the home that gave
it, and how many children would be disfranchised from
the kingdom of heaven if their chance of religion was
limited in this way.   Nor did he think it right to set up
a bar between the home and the school.   The home was
the first society into which a child came, the school was
the next.   In both he should be able to find scope for all
his being ; in both he should realise all relationships of
life, toward his Maker as well as towards the natural world
and his fellow beings.

Again, Paton refused to believe that it was impossible
for Christian teaching to be given upon lines on which all
could join in common, whatever their denomination.   His
prayer was always that " we may be one," and he believed the more men's minds were fixed upon the highest
things, the more they would find it possible to act heartily
in concert, in school teaching as in other matters.   This
was one of the cardinal points of his faith.   And he
thought it was a thing worth struggling for, and worth
failing for, to demonstrate that beneath all " these mon-

strous, Christ-denying, help-Satan separations," there was
a unity which bound together all the clashing creeds, a
unity strong enough and real enough to furnish a basis
of common action in the first and happiest duty of the
Church—the nurture and admonition of the child.

He threw himself, therefore, at this critical moment
into the gap, and battled with all his might against the
tendency towards Secularism, a tendency which was all
the stronger because it was so vigorously advocated by
men of the highest Christian principle. On May 16th,
1870, he, acting in conjunction with Canon Morse, called
a meeting in Nottingham of clergymen and ministers.
Finding at this meeting that it was not difficult to formu-
late a policy in which all could agree, they set to work to
hold similar conferences and public meetings in the large
towns which would be chiefly affected by the Bill. Encouraged by the result of these conferences, the two
friends got up a Memorial to the Government, setting
forth suggestions with a view to a settlement.

*" Memorial to Her Majesty's Government on the ' Religious
Difficulty,' in connection with the ' Elementary Education
Bill '*

" WE, the undersigned Ministers of Religion and Laymen
specially interested in Education, resident in the Borough
of Leicester, beg most respectfully to offer the following
suggestions to the consideration of Her Majesty's Government, with a view to a satisfactory solution of that Religious
Difficulty, which is felt at the present moment to be the
principal obstacle in the way of the immediate establishment of a general scheme of Primary Education in England.

" While venturing to offer suggestions with a view to the
solution of this difficult problem, we cannot refrain from
expressing our profound and grateful sense of the statesmanlike breadth and thoroughness by which the ' Elementary Education Bill ' of Her Majesty's Government is
characterised ; and our conviction that it furnishes a
satisfactory basis for the settlement of the pressing questions of National Education in England.

" The suggestions which we wish to offer are these :

" I. (a). That all existing Schools shall continue to
receive aid, as at present, from the Consolidated Fund ;

but without religious inspection by a Government Inspector, and subject to a Time-table Conscience Clause.

" (b). That all Schools, supported wholly or in part by local rates, shall be strictly *undenominational*; religious instruction being given solely out of the Bible, and by the regular School Teacher,—such Schools being subject, like the preceding, to a Time-table Conscience Clause.

" II. By a Time-table Conscience Clause we understand a regulation fixing a definite period, to be determined by the Managers, during school hours, in which the religious instruction shall be given, and during which any Child, whose Parents or Guardians desire it, and express the desire personally or in writing, shall receive other instruction instead.

" In making these suggestions we are well aware that they can only be considered as tracing the bare outline of a settlement of the question, and that it is quite possible to raise objections to them. But a very careful consideration of the subject has satisfied us that much more serious objections can be urged against any other conceivable solution of the difficulty, and that the plan proposed is a really practicable one. Experience, we are convinced, will show that it is quite possible to give such undenominational religious instruction as our suggestions propose out of the Holy Scriptures,—more particularly, out of the historical books of the Old Testament and out of the Gospels of the New ; and that it is, in fact, just the kind of religious instruction which parents among the educated classes are in the habit of giving to their children. The more distinctive religious teaching which, most unhappily (as some of us think), divides the various Christian bodies from one another, ought in our opinion to be given in the Sunday School, in Church, or in Chapel, or elsewhere, but certainly not in Schools supported, either wholly or in part, by local rates, which have been levied, without respect to creed or denomination, upon the entire community.

" We will only add that a very considerable acquaintance with the feelings of the Teachers in elementary Schools, and of the working classes generally, has brought us to the conclusion that such a settlement of the religious difficulty as we suggest would entirely meet the wishes of an immense majority both of Teachers and of Parents.

We think that if *they*, who are obviously most interested in the matter, are satisfied, the rest of the community may well be satisfied also.   Above all we deprecate, more earnestly than words can express, any such supposed settlement of the question as shall revive the bitter conflicts of past years (now happily terminated by the abolition of compulsory Church Rates) ; the revival of which would, we believe, lead to consequences in the immediate future, which would prove most disastrous to the best interests of religion and morality."

The Memorial was accompanied by the following letter. It received 5,173 signatures of clergymen and ministers.

" REV. SIR,
    " Allow me to state briefly the reasons that have induced me, along with other Nonconformist Ministers, to join the Rev. F. Morse in an important movement which he has initiated in several Midland Towns, and to concur substantially in the propositions which have been accepted by Representative Conferences in these towns as a satisfactory solution of the so-called Religious Difficulty.
    " These or similar reasons may, I hope, induce you to act with us, and to sign the Petition and Memorial which are enclosed.
    " 1. We have ascertained, from the Conferences that have been held, that many Clergymen are prepared to assent with us to the proposition that all rate-supported schools shall be undenominational.   To secure their concurrence in the assertion of this principle is most important.   Nothing will so surely influence the Government to alter that part of their Bill which authorises School Boards to make their schools denominational as the alliance of Clergymen with ourselves on the basis of this proposition.
    " 2. The country is plainly resolved that the Bible shall not be excluded from Elementary Schools.   No influential party or organ of opinion now insists upon its exclusion. If, then, a section of Nonconformists demand the exclusion of the Bible from public primary schools, which the country will not tolerate, they simply weaken their own friends who are fighting against the imposition of Denominationalism on these schools, and may thus, in their purpose to exclude

the Bible, cause that not only the Bible, but that the doctrinal formularies and special dogmas of one section of the Church, shall be taught in these schools. To assert Secularism just now as the only alternative to Denominationalism is to secure the certain triumph of Denominationalism.

" 3. We insist, in the alliance which we have formed in this and other Midland towns, upon the principle which is embodied in the petition signed by 5,173 Nonconformist Ministers, and likewise in the petition just issued by the Nonconformist Committee in Birmingham, viz. that all rate-supported schools shall be unsectarian. The accompanying Petition and Memorial are wholly in the sense of our previous united action as Nonconformists. Though agreeing with the Petition issued last week by the Nonconformist Committee in Birmingham, we differ in one particular from the Resolutions which that Committee has just published. These Resolutions urge that religious instruction be confined to the mere reading of the Bible. To insist on this point will raise needless difference of opinion between Nonconformists themselves, as well as between Episcopalians and Nonconformists. Let the unsectarian character of the School Board schools be secured, and all that Nonconformists desire is gained. To prevent a teacher from explaining the meaning of a Bible word, or from giving a lesson even on its history, geography, or morality, would, I conceive, stultify the teacher and degrade his office. Further, Bible reading would then generally be either an idle ceremonial—useless, if not injurious ; or a superstitious, because unintelligent, religious exercise. The Bible would be either a cypher or a fetich.

" 4. Our British Schools have shown that it is quite practicable, and even easy, to give Scriptural instruction that shall be strictly undenominational. Though, therefore, theoretically, it may seem difficult, practically it is not so.

" 5. The propositions embodied in our Petition and Memorial may be said to deal unjustly with two classes : (1) Those who do not believe in the authoritative teaching of the Bible, or who, on other grounds, prefer a purely secular education in Day Schools ; and (2) the Roman Catholics.

" With regard to the first class, I reply : These propositions require precisely what such persons prefer and want, viz. that public rates are to provide for them in every case, during the whole period of school hours, secular education, unmixed with Bible teaching. With regard to the second class, I reply : Churchmen and Nonconformists unite to demand for Roman Catholics what they ask for themselves—no more and no less, viz. that the Bible teaching shall be as undenominational with respect to the one as to the other ; that common schools shall teach what is common to all ; and that in districts where Roman Catholics are numerous, the Douay version may be used.

" I am, Rev. Sir,
" Yours faithfully,
" J. B. PATON."

He pressed home the argument unweariedly with his pen as well as with his voice. The following letter to the " Nottingham Daily Express " is dated June 20th, 1870. It was reprinted and widely circulated.

" Leaving out the scheme proposed by ' the Committee of the Congregational Union,' which is likely to fall still-born on the world, being the most unlikely scheme divulged, there are three alternatives before us if, as all Nonconformists insist, the School Board schools are to be undenominational : (1) That scriptural instruction may be given in them that shall be unsectarian. (2) That the Bible may be read in them without note or comment. (3) That the Bible shall be excluded from them by law, and that only secular instruction shall be given in them.

" I hold that our British School system and the Irish national system, under the administration of its founders, show that the proposal to give scriptural unsectarian instruction is quite practicable, and on many grounds I regard that alternative as much the preferable.

" I beg, however, in this letter to state some reasons which prevent me, though a Nonconformist and a voluntary, from insisting on pure secularism in School Board schools, and requiring the exclusion from them of the Bible.

" (1) For a quarter of a century and more, Independents generally maintained that Christian Churches ought, by purely voluntary effort, to provide the means of education for the people, and that the State ought not to interfere in this sacred work. National opinion grew more and more emphatic in its opposition to our Utopian doctrine, and at last, after years of noble resistance—which, however, in the opinion of many, have greatly weakened Independency—we have succumbed to its overwhelming voice, that the State shall secure the sound elementary education of all English children. Let us not raise another Utopia, which we again delusively cherish, and must again, after needless antagonism to the ' common sense ' of the people, abandon. It has been said that Independents, by their opposition to any State interference with education, have aided to establish and prolong the existing system of Denominationalism. This may be questioned, but I hold it to be unquestionable that, if Independents now combine to demand Secularism in our schools, the inevitable result will be that Secularism, being in the present mood of our country distinctly impossible, we shall rivet Denominationalism on all our national schools. If we divide and weaken the strength of those that plead for unsectarian national schools, we simply give the battle to the zeal of Romanists and Anglicans, who will struggle with unmeasured force to make all our national schools denominational.

" (2) The previous argument may be accused of a savour of policy. I grant it. But in questions of national interest we must not be impolitic and impracticable. I have wished to point the moral of our experience during the last twenty-five years, and to express the hope that the errors of which we are self-convicted may not be repeated. But now I leave the quicksands of policy for firmer ground ; and I say it would be a serious injury to the moral life of the English people if open discredit were put on the Bible in our national schools by its compulsory exclusion from them. Strange and sad, I think, if for our English schools an Index Expurgatorius were instituted, and only one book banned by it—the Bible. I do not enlarge upon this theme, as some have done, by speaking of the triumph that would be given to infidelity, and of the terrible reproach contained in the taunt that religious animosities have compelled such public rejection of the one book all Christians honour. These statements have an inflammatory complexion. I merely reaffirm that the moral and religious feeling of the country would be lowered and degraded by the public rejection from our national schools of the book that has made England's greatness.

" (3) I repeat a common argument which is not dulled by use : The English Bible is our great English classic. Its ' English ' is the canon of clear, bold, harmonious English writing. It is the well-head of our literature, holding in our language the place of ' Homer ' among the Greeks. Who has read Rogers's essay, ' The Blank Bible,' and can forget how the golden threads of Bible language have shot through the texture of all modern literature— especially of English. All Bible phrases being, in his dream, expunged, the author of the ' Eclipse of Faith ' writes : ' Never before had I an adequate idea of the extent to which the Bible had moulded the intellectual and moral life of the last eighteen centuries, nor how intimately it had interfused itself with habits of thought and modes of expression, nor how naturally and extensively its comprehensive imagery and language had been introduced into human writings, and, most of all, when there had been most of genius. . . . Many of the sweetest passages of Shakespeare were converted into unmeaning nonsense from the absence of those words which his own all but divine genius had appropriated from a still diviner source. As to Milton, he was nearly ruined, as might naturally be supposed. . . . Some of the most beautiful and comprehensive of Bacon's apophthegms were reduced to enigmatical nonsense.' Because of its relation to our literature, the Bible has a just title to a place in our day-schools.

" (4) What does secular instruction really mean ? Does it exclude information upon facts of history which have a religious interest and significance, either from their originating in earnest religious faith, or their producing changes in the religious faith of men ? If so, then there will be *hiatus valde deflendi* in the historical lessons of our schools. This question is large, and covers many subordinate questions, the tenor of which I indicate in four questions : May the history of Mohammedanism, or Parseeism, or Mormonism be taught, but no Christian history ? May the origin and history of the ' Reformation of religion ' in Europe be taught or not ? May Smith's ' Student's History of Greece and Rome ' be taught, but not his ' Student's Old Testament History ' and ' New

Testament History ' ?   May the history of Cæsar be taught,
but not the history of Christ ?   Each of these four questions
presents a separate aspect of one question, which cannot
be summarily settled by using such a phrase as ' secular
instruction.'   The history of mankind cannot be taught
without giving information concerning the religious history
of mankind.   The Bible has a just title to a place in our
schools, because it gives a history of a nation most remarkable in its religious character and influence, and of
the origin of the most momentous religious movement in
the world's history.

" (5) Does secular instruction include or exclude all
information concerning religious opinions, and the faiths
of mankind, or may information be given concerning all
religions but one ?   I know that here I tread on the white
ashes that cover red embers.   Yet the question needs to
be put and fully answered.   I am not satisfied with the
easy way in which the word ' secularism ' is used, as though
it solved the religious difficulty by professing to exclude
in every form religious phenomena.   Can the facts and
faiths of the religious history of men be thus easily ex-
scinded from any course of instruction in schools ?   As
Nonconformist voluntaries, our attitude in regard to the
State has been broadly defined in the words, ' separation of
Church and State.'   I would remind my fellow voluntaries
that it is a more complicated problem, and one in which
the use of hard, dogmatic propositions will only confound
us, to disintricate and annul all religious facts and influences from the civil constitution and ordinances of
society, or to harmonise them in accordance with the laws
of equity.   Practical problems now lie before us as Nonconformists, and we shall be forced to recognise the
supreme necessity of facts, which do not always square
nicely with doctrinaire theories.   Put briefly and
broadly, may the religious opinions and practices of the
Greek be taught and the list of Olympic gods, but not the
religious opinions and practices of the Jews and their
monotheistic faith ?   I know a limit must be put somewhere on the teaching of religious opinions.   But this is
just what I insist upon ; it is a question of limits, not of
absolute exclusion.

" (6) Morality is to be taught in national schools.   What
morality ?   Christian morality, of course ;   because it

presents the moral code generally accepted by modern society ?   Where shall we find Christian morality if not in the Bible ?   If even you exclude the Bible, you must bring it back in another and not a better form.   *Naturam expellas furcâ, tamen usque recurret*, is an old proverb, which may, with the alteration of a word, be applied to express my meaning.   Teach Paley, teach Wayland, teach orally, and you will have Bible words, and Bible passages, deformed probably, but yet distinctly Biblical.   Again, to raise a graver question of the sort I indicated under my last reason, may not the teacher enforce moral precepts by any allusion to God's authority, to conscience, to retribution ?   Is secular instruction to ignore these facts ?   And what if a child asks a question concerning them ?   Are they to be denied, or is the teacher to say, ' I dare not answer ' ?

" (7) Secular teaching, in the sense in which it is understood when it excludes the Bible and all religious truths or phenomena, is a simple impossibility.   To secure it a large proportion of the words in our spelling-books must be erased.   And then our children will grow up in ignorance of the most vital words in our current speech.   More, our school literature must all be revised.   Our most famous speeches, with their appeals to God and eternity, and our noblest poetry, with their thrilling lines which fire our highest religious sensibilities, must be expunged from our present school-books.   Sheer Secularism is impossible in a world in which God and the human spirit exist, and around which eternity lowers.

" But, further, a two-horned dilemma proves this impossibility.   Take three most frequent words of our language—Soul, Christianity, Heaven.   What is soul ? A personal entity—different from body.   That is a religious truth, the foundation of all religious faith.   The materialist objects to the statement ; will secular teaching, therefore, disallow it ?   Be it so.   Then the soul is not different from body ; it is the product of one or of many of its structural functions.   Be it so.   That is a dogmatic denial of a religious truth, and is itself religious teaching —destructive teaching upon a religious subject.   It is the materialist's religion.   In similar manner consider the word Christianity, or the word Heaven.   Look down the lists in ' Butter's Spelling-book,' and see in how many words religious ideas are necessarily expressed or implied, negatively or positively.

" If secular teaching is to ignore or deny all religious ideas, it will be a cunning and mischievous ignorance. I press the matter to this conclusion, because I notice that the word ' secular instruction ' is used somewhat flippantly by men who think that those who plead for Bible unsectarian instruction are compromising principles which they maintain intact."

A great effort was made to prevent a contested election for the first Nottingham School Board. Paton maintained that religious liberty and justice would be best secured by a fair representation of all classes and parties on the Board, that political controversy was altogether out of place. When the contest proved inevitable, he drafted the first election address of the unsectarian " team " of candidates. Two passages from that draft are worth quoting as showing that he had too generous a conception of education to limit it, as so many did, to acquiring the mere instruments of knowledge, " the three R's " as they began to be called, or to think that Englishmen could work out their new system satisfactorily without intelligent study of what was being done abroad. They show, also, his belief that education was not less educative because it had a bearing on the practical business of every-day life and made a man more intelligent in following his vocation :

" We believe that in all Elementary Schools the secular instruction needs to be improved and carried beyond the limits to which it has been usually confined. Especially in an industrial town like Nottingham, it is important that the elements of technical knowledge be imparted, and that the children be well prepared for the actual business of life. The prosperity of British manufactures of the future will depend on the careful instruction of our children.

" The School Board ought, further, to seek out and apply the results of the best experience in our own and in other countries, throwing light on efficient organisation and conduct of Elementary Public Schools."

But he was not built on controversial lines.

The year 1873 saw his thoughts and activities turned in two other directions which, while the natural outcome of what preceded, determined the two chief channels of his life-work from this time forth. He had heard of the lectures which had been given to the railwaymen at Crewe and co-operators at Rochdale by Mr. James Stuart, Fellow of Trinity College, Cambridge (afterwards Professor of Mechanical Engineering at Cambridge and member of the Privy Council), and in several ways, formal and informal, he and his friend, Mr. Richard Enfield, had been sounding the working men of Nottingham to see if there existed among them the same desire for higher education. The first outcome of these inquiries was a resolution passed at the Annual Meeting of the Mechanics' Institution, January 30th, 1871, a resolution which shows that the Mechanics' Institution, in Nottingham at least, had not outlived its title :

" That it is desirable the committee should establish classes at which the working men of Nottingham may have opportunities offered to them for being instructed in those subjects which are most important to them as workmen, as fathers of families, and as sharers in the political power of the country."

A large meeting of representative working men was held on April 9th of the same year in furtherance of this resolution to learn what subjects would be most likely to attract and interest working men. At this meeting the idea was mooted of applying to the Universities for assistance in providing teachers.

A beginning was made with lectures by Dr. Lankester on the science of health, which were attended by 1,000 people. Classes for oral instruction were held in connection with the lectures, and were attended by from 250 to 500, principally of the industrial class. Such results were encouraging. It showed that the working classes were not content to struggle only for the bread that perishes—that they claimed an opportunity to share in the progress of knowledge—that, given such opportunity, they meant to achieve in their day an ideal higher than the ideal of yesterday.

Thus the scheme began to take definite shape. At the annual meeting of the Mechanics' Institution, held on June 27th, 1873, the lines of future development were more fully considered. There were between forty and fifty representative working men present, who set forth very fully and frankly what subjects they felt to be specially needed for their higher education, and how they might be assisted in the study of them. At the end of the meeting, Paton summed up the whole discussion. The question was so large and so important, he said, that no other agency than the national Universities was competent to make the necessary provision. Oxford and Cambridge were the Universities of the nation, and, as such, had a responsibility to fulfil to the nation ; they held the treasuries of knowledge and the traditions of learning ; it was their duty to teach more widely than they had hitherto attempted. The meeting concurred and unanimously drew up a Memorial suggesting, first, that university lecturers might conduct evening classes for the working classes, and at other times of the day give lectures to people who had more leisure and more education ; secondly, that the various towns desiring such university tuition might be grouped together in circuits so as to engage the lecturer's full time and secure him adequate remuneration. The Memorial also suggested that such work might be recognised by the colleges by admitting the extension lecturers " to share the titles and privileges of fellows equally with those who teach in the University."

At the request of the meeting Paton undertook to go up to London on the following day to consult friends as to how the Universities could be approached and induced to consider this new form of National University teaching.

"When in London I met Sir Edward Baines, who told me, to my surprise and delight, that Mr. James Stuart, Fellow of Trinity College, had, the week before, delivered a lecture in Leeds in which he had specially urged the duty of the great National Universities to undertake some extension work amongst the people of England for Higher Education. Within an hour of learning this glad news I wrote to Mr. Stuart, and then the association was formed between Nottingham and the University of Cambridge. A strong committee was formed in Nottingham to develop the movement, which was approved by Mr. Stuart and by other leading men in the University of Cambridge. When the matter was brought definitely before the Senate of the

University, a representative working man appointed by the Trades Councils of Nottingham accompanied other members of the Nottingham Committee to lay the needs and the desires of the working men of Nottingham before the Senate."

The Syndicate appointed by Cambridge on February 27th had to consider other applications of a similar nature which had been sent up from other places, one of them as early as November 1871. But, as Professor Henry Sidgwick said at the Inaugural Meeting at Nottingham, it was the definite, well-thought-out character and practicality of the scheme presented by the Nottingham delegates, and their urgency, which decided the Syndicate to take the matter up. "They had not only zeal," he said, "but, what is rarer, clearness of view. The idea had existed for some time, but it would have remained an idea, but for the action taken by Nottingham."

Next autumn, as soon as Goose Fair was over in October 1873, a beginning was made. Nottingham was grouped together in one circuit with Derby and Leicester. The necessary guarantees were raised in each town to meet expenses. Three courses of lectures were held with classes. Mr. Stuart came down to the Inaugural Meeting, which launched the new venture in Nottingham. Lord Belper was in the chair; Lord Carnarvon and Professor Henry Sidgwick were among the speakers.

The whole story of the beginnings of this movement is charmingly told by the founder himself in his "Reminiscences." He acknowledges ungrudgingly the debt he owes to Nottingham and Nottingham men in getting the scheme started.

"My principal help in bringing the matter before the University came from the town of Nottingham, where a committee was formed connected with the Mechanics' Institution, of which the principal moving spirits were Mr. Richard Enfield, Dr. J. B. Paton, and Canon Morse. These gentlemen were not only amongst those who memorialised the University, but they cordially accepted the system proposed, and, after the Syndicate was appointed, they gave evidence before it in which they stated that they were prepared to organise classes for the various branches of the community, and to guarantee the funds necessary for the experiment. They were also indefatigable in assisting in securing the co-operation of Derby and Leicester. . . . There were no people connected with the University Extension movement, outside the University itself, who seized more fully its leading ideas, and entered more completely into its spirit, than did Mr. Enfield and Dr. Paton. Especially did they recognise a point which was very uppermost in my mind, namely, the great advantage that might accrue to the nation through the education of all classes being carried on by the same agency." [1]

"Nottingham is the heart of the matter," he writes to his friend on October 22nd, 1874. "Your meeting has truly national significance, and I have always regarded it as such. The one thing which is, to a certain extent, satisfactory to me is that I am so completely unable to come that I am left in no doubt about it, and have no alternative. But I should not say so; there are many other points of satisfaction. There is the fact that you, my dear friend, are there, and I regard you as another self in this matter."

The movement, once launched, never looked back so far as Nottingham was concerned. Paton was "visible secretary" for a short time at the beginning, but long after he had resigned that office Mr. Richard Enfield and he were "doing the work of the propeller." In January 1875 Mr. Richard Enfield was empowered by a friend whose name has not been divulged to lay before the Town Council an offer of £10,000 with a view to putting the work on a permanent basis.[2]   Under such golden sunshine the work grew rapidly, and plans were made for establishing a fully equipped University College. Mr. Gladstone spoke at the stone-laying, September 1877, and the completed building was opened by H.R.H. Prince Leopold, in June 1881.

The "work of the propeller" was of various kinds. That Nottingham was more successful than any of the

---

[1] "Reminiscences," by James Stuart, pp. 168, 169 (pp. 171-2, in the privately printed edition).
[2] For full details see "The Calendar of Cambridge Local Lectures," including the years 1875-9, pp. 80-1.

early centres in keeping touch with the working classes was due to the way in which Mr. Enfield and Paton kept alive the interest of the Trade organisations and encouraged their leaders. The different Trades Unions made donations to the funds, and received in return tickets for distribution at the rate of 1s. 6d. per course of lectures. All societies contributing 30s. or upwards had representation on the committee.

The missionary spirit which founded the movement did not die when it was founded. A report presented to the University of Cambridge by Mr. Moore Ede (now Dean of Worcester), in 1875 records :

" Shortly after the beginning of term, the Rev. J. B. Paton, one of the Nottingham Committee, succeeded in interesting some of the leading inhabitants of Lincoln in the University Extension Scheme. A Guarantee Fund was at once raised and a public meeting called. . . . This was one of the most successful meetings ever held in connection with University Extension ; about 2,000 people were present, and resolutions in support of the movement were carried unanimously."

This beginning developed into a North Midland Association for the promotion of University Extension for the people in Notts, Derbyshire, North Staffs and Lincolnshire. Nottingham University College was the hub of this Association, and Paton was indefatigable in getting Courses started in different mining and industrial villages, and thus linking them up with the new college. He was also instrumental in getting financial aid from the Gilchrist Trustees.

Another object for which he was quietly working for six years was affiliation.

" I look forward," says Mr. Stuart, in the letter already quoted, " to the time when the lectures shall be permanent institutions in large towns, involving a three years' course or curriculum, and when attendance at such a curriculum and the passing of some specified examinations shall be accepted by the University in lieu of the first year's attendance at Cambridge. The success of the scheme educationally is that which will bring the University to

11

do this, and everything is on the right train. *But it is still a year too soon to broach this idea publicly.* We have to nurse the University ! "

This also was carried through to a successful issue. A Memorial was presented to the University in this sense on June 1st, 1878, before the building of the college was completed, and on May 15th, 1879, Mr. Enfield wrote : " You will rejoice to learn that the affiliation scheme has passed the senate to-day." Under this affiliation scheme any person who had completed a three years' course at the college and obtained Honours in the final examination connected with that course was entitled to be excused the previous examination, and, on commencing residence at Cambridge, to proceed to his B.A. degree in honours after two years' residence instead of three. The advantage of this affiliation has been two-fold. It has helped to give vigour, elevation, and comprehensiveness to the work of the local colleges which have been affiliated, and it has benefited the University itself by associating it closely with the more active, stirring communities in commercial and manufacturing towns. The young student, on passing forward, has settled down in Cambridge, not as a stranger, but as a son, taking his place as a student in the second year.

But the privileges of affiliation represent only an in-finitesimal part of what the University movement has meant to the country. It has brought the ancient Univer-sities into touch with the living forces of society, and thereby not only re-established their hold upon the feelings of the people, but, as Mr. Sadler says, it has been " one, and not the least important, of the causes which have produced in England a changed attitude of mind towards university work, and a new sense of its value as an element in national life."

It has helped the Universities themselves by giving employment and experience in teaching to some of their ablest young men, and has trained them in this way for higher educational positions. But it has done more than that. It has brought the Universities back to their own best traditions, and enabled them to dig again the old wells. The Endowment Deed of Clare College, which dates back to 1341, expresses the prayer that the number of students may increase " to the end that knowledge, a pearl of great price, when they have found it and made it their own in the aforesaid University, may not be hidden under a bushel, but be spread abroad beyond the University and thereby give light to them that walk in the dark byways of ignorance." In the great movements of learning, knowledge has never been an end in itself ; it has been a sacred trust, held, like every good gift of God, in stewardship for mankind. The University Extension marked out the lines for establishing a wide system of higher education, spreading downwards from the fountain-head through a thousand fertilising channels till no corner of the land was left untouched. It was no small honour to have been one of the pioneers who did the spade-work in digging the first channel.

The following is an extract from a letter to Lord Edmond Fitzmaurice, October 13th, 1879, with a view to his forthcoming visit to Nottingham to distribute the certificates.

" The glory of our Nottingham system of extension is that it occupies a circuit including Derbyshire, Notts, and Lincolnshire ; and we propose, with our two sub-centres—Derby and Lincoln—to arrange so that every town of 5,000 inhabitants and upwards shall have university lectures and classes of a popular kind. We shall thus receive these three great benefits :

" (a) That university training and culture shall permeate the whole community.

" (b) That we receive a larger staff for our central college in the circuit than would otherwise be possible. Say that we have four resident Professors in Nottingham. They will organise and assist in the circuit work ; but they will, in return, be assisted by four teachers engaged in circuit work, who will be rotary and changeable every year. During three years, therefore, we shall have the assistance of twelve men at Nottingham, and, if these are selected wisely by the University, we shall have men strong in special subjects, say Literature, History, Law, Economy, or Science, who will enable us to furnish the full curriculum with a splendid staff of specially competent men.

" (c) We shall draw, as by a large net, the best scholars of all sections of the community in the district into our college for higher training ; the best of them again to be drafted off, if possible, to Oxford or Cambridge, so that

we shall provide the parent Universities with the ablest
young men and women of our whole district, having discovered and prepared them for the Universities."

Mr. A. J. Mundella, in a letter dated April 4th, 1911,
refers to—

" The invaluable but unobtrusive part he (*i.e.* Paton)
played between 1873 and 1880 in developing the University
Extension movement (in Nottingham) into the University
College. I have no material in the form of letters or records,
and it is possible that none exist, but it was a very vivid
period of my life, and I, probably more than any one,
knew all that his unbounded courage and optimism and
human sympathy and inspiring enthusiasm did at that
time. The Extension movement, after its first year or
two, was dying out, and the dream of something bigger
seemed quite impossible, and it was marvellous how he
and Mr. Enfield, kept the little feeble flame alive as
a nucleus and object-lesson, whilst the bigger idea gradually
took shape and was practically realised through untold
difficulties.

" This was probably such a small incident amongst
his many and great works, and was all so informal and
unofficial that it is possible it might be overlooked altogether in making a record of his life. But it was a great
thing, and due almost entirely to more special personal
qualities which made him such a power in the land."

Rev. Professor V. H. Stanton (one of the first lecturers),
writes (November 1911) :

" . . . In addition to his energy and enthusiasm, his
determination to bring all interests, religious and political
and social, to unite, told very much. The fact, too, that
there was a large-minded Vicar of St. Mary's, Nottingham—
Canon Morse—helped ; but he did not take such an active
part. This union of interests in the town especially
impressed me as one of the chief causes of success."

Interest in local matters was not confined to education.
A corner site of great importance fell vacant in the centre
of the town at the junction of Shakespeare Street and
Mansfield Road, opposite the present Victoria Station.
" A shudder came over me," he said, " when I thought

this plot of ground, so near our great educational centre, might be occupied with a flaunting gin-palace." He stole a march on the brewers, and, with the aid of a few friends, purchased the property. The question then came how to make use of it. The following letter to Mr. Samuel Morley shows the origin of the scheme to which Nottingham owes her present Y.M.C.A. building.

" Now we must decide what to do with it. It contains 380 square yards, and every inch can be built upon. Now I have drawn out a scheme which commends itself to the judgment of the business men I have consulted : Mr. Wells, Mr. Enfield, and others. We pay £2,200 for this land, of which £1,000 will be placed on mortgage. There are three institutions of the town now wanting accommodation, and which cannot have any other site or portion so central and convenient. There are the Sunday School Union, the Young Men's Christian Association, and the Samuel Morley Club. The gentlemen who joined me in the purchase did so in order to secure a café at the corner. All the institutions I name, especially the Young Men's Christian Association and the Samuel Morley Club, ought to be in connection with a café, in order to have refreshments easily. Well, let us, I say, ask each of these institutions to raise £500 in shares for a company to buy the land and build a noble structure which will accommodate them all. The gentlemen also have given £1,200 to let that money be part of the share capital of this company.

" There will be then £1,500
1,200
i.e. 2,700

Borrow on mortgage £1,000 on land
2,000 on building
3,000

There is room for five shops in addition to a café on the ground-floor, and the shops under Mr. Sylverton's adjoining chapel, which are not so central, let for £40 a year

each. The five shops will then certainly pay rent enough
to pay 4 per cent. interest on the mortgage, or £120—
leaving £2,700 of share capital on which the four institutions must pay an interest as a rent of 5 per cent., or
about £34 each, because we should arrange beforehand
that for such objects not more than 5 per cent. will be
taken as profit from these institutions ; but on the condition, clearly expressed, that, if any of them fail to pay its
proper rent so as to yield this interest, then its rooms
may be diverted to business purposes, for which they
would at once, in such a corner, command very much more.

" Now I have seen the representatives of the Young
Men's Christian Association and the Sunday School Union,
and they will, I believe, most enthusiastically concur in this
proposal. To get so easily rooms perfectly adequate and
unequalled for situation at such a small rental, and with
such little present effort, attracts them.

" But I am at a loss in reference to the Samuel Morley
Club. I have attended two or three meetings within the
last few months in order to keep it going. It cannot
thrive, or even live, unless it has suitable accommodation.
I remembered what you told me when you first asked me
to take some interest in it for its own, and for your sake,
that you would gladly help to give it a fair position in
the town. The object of the Club is certainly most worthy,
viz. to provide working men and all respectable citizens
with a Club without the temptations of drink. It would
be very popular if only it were known, and were convenient and comfortable. At present, it is none of these
things.

" Well, if you so wished, and it seemed to you right,
you could do everything that your promise covered (which
the members of the Club appreciated) by investing some
money (without giving a pound) in a building which must
by its position be a safe investment. You would further
unite with the Sunday School Union and the Young
Men's Christian Association to provide for them in this
building accommodation which they could not obtain
elsewhere, and in a corner which faces proudly the world,
and commands it.

" The fact is, the land was purchased from philanthropic motives, and I don't want an inch of it to go to
secular purposes that can be otherwise utilised. I want

it, from base to top, to be an Institution for the public good, vigorously at work night and day in fulfilling a Christian work.

"Oh, to think I should talk business in this way, and show that good can be done, great good, and yet the money given be invested in a good security and yield a good interest. Well, don't think the less of me because I believe that can often be done and that *wise methods* can save and make money whilst doing immense and direct good with it."

The temperance question was much in his mind at this time, and he gave considerable attention to the Gothenburg system, which was being advocated by Mr. Joseph Chamberlain. He enlisted the interest of the town clerk, Mr. (afterwards Sir) S. G. Johnson, and the Corporation agreed to take over the management of some smaller licensed houses which were thrown on their hands and to run them on Gothenburg lines. Before many years there were five such houses in Nottingham.

The opening of the Castle as an art-gallery raised two questions which agitated the minds of the townspeople and produced a sharp division of opinion. The first was whether the refreshment-room should be licensed for the sale of intoxicants ; the second was the question of Sunday opening. Both these proposals he strenuously resisted.

Letter to an Alderman

"I sympathise with many of the views urged by those who desire the Castle Museum to be opened, and at one time would have abetted its opening. I have, however, of late years considered the question more fully. I have considered it in relation to the extreme value, and indeed the necessity, of our English Rest-day—with its peculiar safeguards, protecting it against the exorbitance of eager traders and eager pleasure-mongers—to our English people, who owe more to it, in its quietude and leisure, physically, socially, and morally, than to almost any other single cause. I now very clearly and firmly oppose the project of opening our public Museums.

"I write, however, to ask you to read the enclosed

pamphlet,[1] which led me to take what I think larger and
wider views upon this subject. I respectfully beg you
before you give your vote, which may have great, and it
may be unexpected and irreversible influence, to read
this pamphlet carefully."

Literary work was going forward at the same time.
He was writing to the " Christian Spectator " (September 1867), rebutting Renan's argument that
Monotheism was the peculiar doctrine of Semitic
races, and expounding Pictet's demonstration, on
philological grounds, that the Aryan were also originally monotheistic. In the " London Quarterly Review "
(October 1869), he reviews Professor Huxley's famous
lecture on Protoplasm, and joins issue with him in a close-
reasoned dialectic. If, as Huxley asserted, when carbonic
acid, water, and ammonia " are brought together under
certain conditions," they give rise to protoplasm, and
" this protoplasm exhibits the phenomena of life," why
is it, he asks, that dead matter presents exactly the same
chemical combinations, and, so far as the most subtle
chemical microscopical analysis has penetrated, no difference can be detected in the disposition of the molecules
in a living tissue or vessel and in that tissue or vessel when
it ceases to live ? The whole fallacy of Huxley's argument
lies in the words " under certain conditions." It is only
a living being which can produce protoplasm. *Omne
vivum ex vivo.* Life is the condition of the existence of
protoplasm ; how, then, can protoplasm be " the cause of
life " ? Huxley instances the case of the watch.

" We live," he says, " in the faith and hope that, by the
advance of molecular physics, we shall be able by and by
to see our way as clearly from the constituents of water
to the properties of water as we are now able to deduce
the operations of a watch from the form of its parts and
the manner in which they are put together."

Huxley's own illustration is made to serve the purpose
of his opponent's argument.

" Here is a watch : it goes : what is the cause of the
special arrangement which makes it keep time ? By
every line and word of his reasoning Mr. Huxley is bound

[1] By the Rev. W. Arthur.

to say the properties of the component elements of the
watch are the cause of the watch and all its movements.
We press the analogy, for Mr. Huxley has cited it, and
we shall use it. It is true that we know that a mechanic
arranged the parts of the watch, so that it has its specific
time-keeping properties ; and that steel and brass, its
component elements, have never been known to arrange
themselves into such a complex body without a mechanic's
skill. We know, in M. Bertrand's language, that, the
' mechanic ' being suppressed, no watch will make its
appearance.   And, therefore, by right of his logical canon
and of common sense which it formulates, we pronounce
the mechanic to be the immediate cause—the producer
of the watch. But we know, with equal absoluteness of
certainty, every one of these facts likewise concerning
protoplasm ; that the peculiar arrangement of its elements is caused by a living organism, and that these parts
never arrange themselves into this complex body without
a living organism. We know that, if life be suppressed,
no protoplasm will make its appearance. What, then,
shall we pronounce to be its cause ? The molecules that
form it ? Then brass and steel make the watch ! Cannot Mr. Huxley see that, as he deduces the operations of
a watch, not from the matter of its several parts, ' but
from the form of its parts, and the manner in which they
are put together,' that the operations or phenomena of
protoplasm are to be deduced from the same source ?
And that, as the watchmaker is the producer of the
watch, because he gives its parts the needful form and
the needful arrangement, so that produces protoplasm
which gives its parts their form and arrangement ? A
skilful man makes a watch—a living body makes protoplasm. This analogy goes further. The watchmaker
brings the different parts together in order to form and
arrange them. So does the living body. These elements
that have been named are not brought in definite amounts
and due proportions to it. It seeks and selects them
separately or unitedly, and then forms and combines them,
by an inscrutable chemistry, into protoplasm. Therefore, again, and *a fortiori*, the living body is the cause of
its formation.

    " Huxley's statement of the case begins at the wrong
end. According to him, the three given elements are

brought together, or chance to co-exist, and then externally to them a certain condition arises and a certain influence is exerted, and, as a result, protoplasm makes its appearance and life begins. The real fact is, that a living organism exists, and it seeks out and assimilates from its environment the several elements it needs to build up its living protoplasm. Protoplasm does not explain life ; it is life which explains protoplasm, and no chemical skill has yet got behind the conclusion of M. Bertrand : ' If it were necessary to define life in a single word, I should say *life is creation.*' "

It was, in essence, the same controversy of Spirit *versus* Matter which he carried forward into higher spheres in two papers afterwards published in fuller form under the title " The Twofold Alternative," and dedicated to his old students. The first of these seeks to answer the question—as old as the " Phædo " and as modern as Robert Blatchford—Is man the accidental, or, if necessary, yet the transitory, composite of atoms whose only law is that imposed on his nature by the aggregate atoms which momentarily compose him ; or is he a personal being, the origin, law, and end of whose existence are found in a personal and righteous God ? Paton argued that matter is inert, and bound by necessary law ; the origination of movement, the production of endless variety, are only possible to a being who is self-acting and free, and such a being is spirit. The order and processes of the sensible world are luminous with thought. Thought must be conscious ; we cannot imagine thought which is unthinking. If there be freedom and thought in the First Cause of the material universe, then the First Cause of things must be a person.

The second part of the book deals with the question : " Is the Church constituted by a select priesthood created by an outward ceremony of initiation, and conveying the saving grace of Christ to other men by material ordinances which are not mere signs, but vehicles and true causes of spiritual life and nourishment, or is it constituted by an open fellowship of all who, having come into living touch with Jesus, profess a living faith in Him as their living Saviour and Lord, and who enter into this Catholic communion with each other in order that in it

they may nurture and discipline their faith into a perfect
habit of life, and fulfil the redemptive service to the world
which their faith enjoins ?   The discussion of this second
alternative is the clearest and fullest account of his conception of the Church.   " I am a Nonconformist," he
used to say, " because I am a Churchman " ; and no Churchman, however high, had a more definite and hallowing
conception of the Church.   It was the Master's creation, it
was his Master's Body, its life was to do the Master's work,
to proclaim the good news, to do the work of healing, to
take upon itself, as He did, the sins and sorrows of humanity,
to draw its life and sustenance from unceasing communion
with the Father through His Son, to foster that life and
organise it for redeeming work in unceasing communion
with all fellow followers of Christ.   Is the Church a
brotherhood, or is it a priesthood ?   That is the question,
put in the simplest form.   The Apostles' Creed defines it
as " a Communion of Saints " : it asserts the principle of
brotherhood to be the true formative principle of the
Christian Church.

   " It is a mistake to divide the one article of this Creed,
' I believe in the Holy Catholic Church, the Communion
of Saints,' into two separate and unrelated sentences, and
thus to mutilate the definition given by the Catholic Church
of her own essential nature.   Even the Catechism of the
Council of Trent says : ' This article [i.e. ' the Communion
of Saints '] is, as it were, a sort of explanation of the
preceding one.'   As is well known, the second epexegetical
clause was not added to the Creed till the fourth or fifth
century."

   Error has power to deceive mainly as it counterfeits
truth.   The best way, therefore, of exposing error is to
show clearly the greater glory of the truth it delusively
simulates.   First, we have a clear, concise statement of
what the Church is, for what it exists, and how it dis-
charges its functions.   Then, step by step, we see how the
spiritual becomes replaced by the mechanical.   First, the
Church of the saved becomes the Church of the baptized.
Then, because the inward principle of cohesion exists no
more, the outward coercive authority takes its place.
The Church ceases to be a living organism, and is changed

into a mechanical structure. Apostolic Succession, power of absolution, the sorcery of the sacraments, the concentration of all power and grace in the person of the Pontiff—all these are the inevitable outcome of that law by which every system must press forward to the fulfilment of its own idea. It is this pretension of the priest which creates schism, and the whole guilt of schism lies with the Church which imposes sinful terms of communion. He who refuses to communicate with her is not a schismatic: he does not commit evil ; he suffers it.

But no error is fully computed unless its origin is laid bare and its growth explained, and the history of the perversion of the *congregatio fidelium* into the Sacerdotal Church was worked out fully in " The Origin of the Priesthood," published in 1876. The argument shows in chronological sequence how the minister of the Church became gradually the minister *to* the Church, and the Holy Spirit was thought of no longer as the universal spirit of the Church, but as communicating His gracious powers through the Bishop ; how the Bishop in course of time took upon himself to pose, in a distinctive and pre-eminent sense, as the organ of the Divine Spirit whereby the Church lives. Paton is strong on the fact that it is the Church of Christ which creates and authenticates the several orders of the ministry, not these orders which create and authenticate the Church, deriving their validity by transmission, or from any other source. He quotes Cardinal Newman in support of this position, but turns upon the authority he has quoted with the question :

" When during long centuries has the Church, the *communio sanctorum, congregatio fidelium,* by word or notion given sign of its existence ? When was it convened or in any other way recognised and addressed as a living community ? When has its authority been either solicited or given to appoint any minister, institute any office, or ratify any Act in the Papal or Anglican communion ? No, the hierarchy of the priesthood stands isolated and apart from the body of the faithful that constitutes the Church . . . a co-optative, self-engendered, and self-sustaining *collegium,* whose mysterious and awful powers are rigidly enclosed within its own membership, whose authority professes to be derived directly from the

Lord Christ and therefore to demand the complete submission of all baptized Christians, which owns no acknowledgment (save by way of a rhetorical and misleading
gloss) and accredits no tittle of its warrant or power to
any body on earth—much less to that indiscriminate crowd
to whom it measures out in sacerdotal portions its supposi-
titious grace."

This was his last controversial writing. Other claims
grew too numerous and absorbing ; but he never lost his
interest in the question, and was always keen to hear of
any scholar who had been working on the first two centuries : in these, as he felt, lay the final settlement of the
great outstanding questions of the Church. In later years
he founded a prize, open to ministers of the Free Churches
and students in the Free Church Training Colleges, for
Essays dealing with some historical aspect of the doctrine
of the Church.
His note-books of this period are full of signs of many-
sided reading and intenser study, especially of Hellenistic
Greek and Patristic literature. He was still finding time for
the quiet studies which, as he said in a letter, " are the
Artesian wells struck down through the thick-ribbed crust
of this common life." But he had much trouble with his
eyesight, and the claims of practical redemptive work
became more and more insistent. There was no room for
controversy. Now that life had reached its meridian,
though the fire burnt as keenly as ever, he was no longer
Boanerges, but the Apostle of Love. Again and again,
even till the end, his joy was to reintegrate the great
principle of the Church. If that principle were set up
clear and radiant before the eyes of men, the counterfeit
corruption, he felt, was bound to stand self-convicted in the
light of its glory, and as men entered into the power of
that great Christ-idea, measureless Divine power and grace
would be liberated and set in operation for the redemption
of the world. But he is not found any more in the lists.
He had longed, in the struggle of his youth, to meet the foe
in the shock of encounter ; he had challenged some doughty
combatants—Renan, Huxley, Newman, Herbert Spencer
—and he had not been thrown. But now he bade farewell to
the tourney and the jousts. Henceforth he sought the Grail.
And therewith came a change in his style. Free, fear-

less, even defiant he had always been. There was still the same directness, the same courage, the same animation, the same robust and sinewy vigour, the same endeavour to get back to the first principles and work from them forward to the conclusion ; there was still the same power of formularising in a single sentence a large region of thought.[1] But the dialectic is now that of the later books of the " Republic," and not that of the preliminary boxing-match with Thrasymachus. We see no more the glitter of the steel, but the kindly badge of the Red Cross. The style is eminently persuasive. Its characteristic is grace rather than vigour ; its thought is constructive ; the adversary is no longer a person or a school of thought, but the all too patent evils which vex our human shores and stand between man and God.

It was in the year 1876 that he became interested in the " Contemporary Review." The Review had been founded by Dean Alford in 1866 to serve as an organ of educated opinion in England and among English-speaking people, in the same way as the " Revue des deux Mondes " had formed and expressed educated opinion in France. It had aimed at furnishing an arena for the earnest and thorough discussion of the great questions of modern controversy in the realms of science, philosophy, and religion. It had secured the co-operation of the most eminent writers in Europe and America. Whilst written in English, it was international and universal in the method and range of its discussions. The names of Gladstone, Herbert Spencer, E. A. Freeman, Lotze, Dorner, Janet, von Schulte, Döllinger, Renan, Taine, Monod, Ribot, and others among its contributors had secured it a foremost place among the literary periodicals of Europe. It was, in fact, a meeting-place and forum of exchange for the foremost thinkers of the world.

This success was due in large measure to the keen foresight and energy of Mr. Alexander Strahan, the publisher. Mr. Strahan was a friend of Mr. James Stuart, and had taken a great interest in the Inner Mission. His idea had always been that the Review should stand for the Christian doctrine of God and humanity. At the same time he made

[1] As an example of what I mean I take the following : "Wherever order is, reason is, for order is the universal signature and speech of reason."

it his practice to open its pages freely to serious and high-minded opponents of these doctrines, believing that it was only by open and honourable controversy that truth can be discovered, vindicated, and harmonised. But there were partners who did not share Mr. Strahan's Christian faith, and through their influence a bias began to appear which was distinctly hostile to the defence and uplifting of Christian truth. In 1876 Mr. Strahan— a most reserved man—paid several visits to Nottingham and unburdened his mind to Paton. The partners were willing to retire if the capital they originally invested were repaid. It was a question of raising £20,000 to form a company and save the Review from becoming definitely anti-Christian. Mr. Francis Peek and Mr. Muir had already promised to help. Paton places the whole matter before his friend Mr. Samuel Morley.

" I have been pleading with my friend to use the splendid unrivalled power he wields in the ' Contemporary Review ' and his other magazines more emphatically for Christ and the cause of Christianity. He has been fettered by his surroundings which are not Christian. At last his conscience is aroused, and he has decided to free himself from these, by either giving up all to his partners, or by getting them to give up their share to those that are more in sympathy with him. I cannot endure the thought of the ' Contemporary Review ' becoming, like the ' Fortnightly,' another and the ablest organ for distributing infidelity among our cultured people—all our own sons and daughters. Now his partners, who know that without him they are not likely to keep up the value of their property, have expressed their willingness to retire if they can get the money they invested in the business, and thus the opportunity is presented of securing the highest literary force and guide in this country for the highest Christian and social ends by a small expenditure of money, which will at the same time yield a very good interest. . . .

" I invest part of my little ' all ' in this undertaking, not indeed that I wish an investment in a business company, but because I cannot spare myself any sacrifice to save and use this foremost and mightiest engine of usefulness for the Great King and Captain of Salvation among men."

The affairs of Strahan & Co. had a long and troublous
history, and were a great tax on the time and temper
of all responsible for their management; but the Review
emerged into smoother waters when Mr. (afterwards Sir)
Percy W. Bunting was appointed Editor in December 1882,
with J. B. Paton as Consulting Editor. The friendship
between the two Editors, originating in their common interest in the Review, and cemented more closely by all
the anxieties of the recent years, was one of the greatest
blessings and happiest possessions of the latter half of
my father's life. Mr. Bunting's house in Endsleigh
Gardens became almost his London residence. No grass
was allowed to grow on the path of friendship; there
were no reserves. The old philosopher says, " Friendship
is when one soul dwells in two bodies." Such friendship
was theirs in the fullest, deepest sense. As Consulting
Editor, Paton was instrumental in securing the articles on
Supernatural Religion by his friend Professor (afterwards
Bishop) Lightfoot, and articles on the Eastern Question by
Rustem Pasha, whom he had met on his journeys. He
managed most of the negotiation with German contributors.
His connection with the Review lasted till April 1887.
He brought to it the interest of such friends as Professor
Henry Sidgwick, Professor Goldwin Smith, Professor
Tyndall, Dr. Martineau, Dr. Conder, Dr. Dale, Dr. Fair-
bairn, Mrs. Josephine Butler, Mr. F. W. Newman, and
Dr. Pressensé, and it brought to him the friendship of
Professor Laveleye, Mr. Richard Heath, Mr. Sheldon Amos,
Mr. Frederick Harrison, Rev. Edwin Hatch. The new
editors introduced a series of monthly papers picturing
contemporary life and thought in the leading countries of
the world, and monthly reviews of the work done in
Theology, Philosophy, History, Science, and Literature.
" Fulness of detail and description," says their new
prospectus, " cannot be given save in journals devoted to
specific studies, but the commerce of intelligent men requires a prompt and authenticated acquaintance with the
latest results of research and productions of genius." He
always looked back with pleasure on these five years with
" the commerce of intelligent men."

Other literary work of this period calls for briefer
mention. He wrote an article on " Organisation and
Life " in the " London Quarterly Review " for January,

1873, and two elaborate articles on " Offerings " and " Sacrifice " for the enlarged edition of Kitto's " Bible Encyclopædia " (published 1874). In the " Fortnightly Review " for February 1875 appeared a review of " Supernatural Religion," chiefly remarkable for its examination of the treatment of Marcion's Gospel by the author of that book.

Regularly year by year he went over to the Continent, usually to Germany, where his children were at school. It was with their father as guide that they gained their first notions of the wider world over-seas, of foreign lands and foreign ways. I shall never forget how, when my turn came to have my year in Germany, as a boy of eleven, he made me lean out of the train, and, miles ahead of us rising out of the level stretch of plain, I saw the Minster of Cologne, and learned then for the first time, and for all time, how the whole life of a medieval city was built round the church and centred in it. Nor shall I forget how we visited the Wartburg, saw the streets of Eisenach, where Luther sang with the " Singing Boys " ; how at Halle I sat under the arbour in the garden while the great Tholuck talked about things too high for me to understand. Many were the friendships he formed in such travel, and notable among them the friendship with Professor John Tyndall, whom he met at Bellalp, and with the Rev. John Percival, now Bishop of Hereford, the head master of Clifton College— a friendship which was soon followed by a visit to Clifton and ripened into a close-knit union of fellowship in thought and work.

Wherever he went he got into touch with Christian men and women labouring with high faith amid great difficulties for the furtherance of the Gospel. He kept constant touch with the Old Catholics, especially in Germany and Switzerland, where the movement kept itself untainted by Rationalism and worked out for itself a church doctrine and practice which he felt to be full of significance for our English Protestants. He studied the Falk laws and expounded in several articles the causes which prompted them, and the issues of the great conflict between the Vatican and the new German Empire. He was writing at the same time on the reorganisation of the Evangelical Church in Prussia. The feature which saddened him most about the newer developments of the Roman Catholic

12

Church was the loss of Catholicity and the suppression of
all liberty. Everywhere he saw the conflict resolving
itself more and more into a conflict between Liberals and
Catholics, the Liberals fighting for freedom without religion, and the Catholics fighting against freedom in the
name of religion.

" The Roman Church," he writes, " —one of Pharaoh's
lean kine—has devoured the Catholic Church ; and of this
Church the Pope says, as Louis XIV said of the State, ' It
is I.' He now concentrates in one solitary person the
authority, grace, truth, and honour which the Lord gave
His universal Church. Accordingly, the very antagonistic
pole of true Catholicity has been reached. Its most
schismatic denial has now been reached. The ' All ' is
now merged in one. Against the universal has been raised
the unit."

In happy contrast to this desolating blight stood out
two features full of hope. First, there was the disappearance of that mystic Rationalism which sought, after the
manner of Strauss, to reconcile the natural and supernatural, " by compromises hung, like Mahomet's coffin,
'twixt heaven and earth, resting on nothing." He rejoiced to see the Christian faith stripping itself at last of
rationalistic glosses and reformulating her creeds to testify
to a grace and a truth that are supernatural and divine.
Secondly, there were wonderful revivals of evangelical
religion in different places, some of them the most unlikely
and unexpected. He was specially interested in Mr.
McAll's Mission in Paris, and was instrumental in getting
a new mission station started there in connection with it.
He was present when Mr. Reginald Radcliffe spoke to a
large meeting of Parisian *ouvriers*, always supposed to
be the stubbornest of unbelievers, when the story of the
Prodigal Son, though it had to be interpreted into their
own language, broke down the old barriers, and woke again
the deep heart-hunger of their souls. He spoke much on
these themes in England, and it was on hearing one of
these addresses that Mr. Gray and his young wife formed
the resolution to give themselves to missionary work in
France.

In the autumn of 1876 came an invitation to become
Principal of Airedale College, Bradford, with some prospect

of fusion with Rotherham.   He thought it over carefully.
" My answer will be, I clearly see, the turning-point of my
whole life, and every aim and resolve needs now to be
solemnly scrutinised."   He wished " to be guided not by
circumstances, but by principles," and principles decided
him to stay where he was, to the great relief of the Institute's
Committee.

There were many other ties which would have been hard
to sunder.   What they were the following note from his
friend Mr. Frederic Harrison, will show :

" I greatly enjoyed my visit to Nottingham, and have
learned much in every way.   Not the least of what I have
learned is to understand how an earnest worker like yourself can infuse a spirit of social union and moral enthusiasm
into a great industrial city.   It gives me new visions of
what lies before our new industrial world to come."

It was at this time he lost his youngest sister and mother,
who were now resident at Great Crosby, near Liverpool.
Not long after he was summoned to the death-bed of his
father.   There was an anxious consultation with the
doctors, who said that life was ebbing fast and the time
was short.   As eldest son, it lay with him to tell his father.
He broke the news to him in prayer, and the old man's
last action was to raise his hand removing the nightcap and
baring his head as he entered into the Holy Presence.   The
father was bowed in prayer when his eldest son was born
into the world ; the last words that fell upon his ears in
this life were the prayer of that same son commending his
soul to Him that gave it.

The University Extension movement had owed much in
its origin to the demand of the working men for access to
the higher learning ; but for the working men it would
never have been launched, at any rate in Nottingham.   But
it had two defects.   The tendency of the movement was
to fall more and more into the hands of the leisured classes.
It could do but little to meet the growing need for technical
and commercial education.   Peripatetic lecturers from
academic groves teaching in public halls could not, from
the nature of the case, be expected to meet the need of the
operative who wanted to get some understanding of the
machinery at which he worked and the processes in which
he was engaged.   In his German travels, although his

interests had been mainly theological, Paton had not failed
to notice the rise of the large, well-equipped technical
schools and the sacrifices which even poor communities
were making to provide the best vocational training for
those engaged in the staple trades of the town.   His
friend, Mr. H. M. Felkin, showed him how Chemnitz had,
by virtue of its technical education, taken away the whole
of the glove trade from Nottingham.   Significant also
was the fact that the same year 1880 saw the first lace-
machine sent out from Nottingham to Plauen in Saxony ;
1880 was also the year that saw the appointment of a
Royal Commission to inquire into the question of technical
instruction.   As soon, therefore, as the University College
was established—indeed, three years before it was opened
—he began to get together some of the leading men in the
Trades Unions and urge upon them the necessity of
securing through the new college an adequate provision
of technical classes with instruction bearing directly on
the staple trades of the town.   " Whatever it be in which
we are called to act, that we are also called upon to study,"
he said.

The subjoined appeal to working men was issued in the
September before the opening of the first session of the
college :

" The COLLEGE standing in the centre of our town,
has been erected and has been provided with able teachers
and all educational apparatus, very largely for your benefit.
Do not despise and refuse the great advantages which have
been thus with much pains and expense brought to your
very door.

" WORKING MEN ought to rejoice in the opportunity of
getting a higher education, which has hitherto been limited
to the so-called upper and middle classes.   That education
will strengthen and enlighten the mind ; it will give knowledge of the great world of nature with its wonders, and of
the history of men—their homes, trades, laws, governments ; and it will show the cause of national progress
and prosperity, or of national decay and ruin.   Such an
education not only helps men to a higher enjoyment of
life, it trains and fits them for their important duties as
members of society—AS CITIZENS OF A FREE COUNTRY.

" In addition, however, the demands of modern industry

require that the workman be intelligent and skilful—a man with an able mind, as well as a clever hand. In all trades competition will take the work to the best-trained workmen. On the Continent, especially in our staple trades, viz. lace and hosiery, the most careful instruction is being given to workmen and foremen in everything that is likely to make them excel. The working men in Nottingham must not be left behind in this race. Let them set an example to the working men in other towns. They have done so by encouraging and aiding the erection of a College which they can proudly call their own. Now LET THEM USE THEIR OWN COLLEGE. *Special Classes* for young men engaged in lace and hosiery factories, in engineering works, or in joinery and other building trades have now been formed : and so far as possible the college professors and teachers will do their utmost to adapt their teaching to the needs of the working men of our town.

" Many working men are reluctant to attend classes or lectures, because they have forgotten much of what they learnt at school and they have lost their faculty and taste for book-learning. But at the College there are POPULAR COURSES of lectures on all sorts of subjects *intended for such persons*, where they will get information, and the healthy training of mind which comes from the exercise of thought, without more attention or labour than they give in listening to a good political speech ; and after these lectures full and *free discussion* of all points that have not been understood is encouraged. Everything has been done to provide a higher education for our working men, that will fit them for the duties and higher pleasures of life, and that will increase their skill and power, and therefore their wages, as workmen. Let them then come IN HUN-DREDS this winter to lay hold of this great boon."

The result was the formation of a " Trades Council of Learning," composed mainly of representatives of the Trades Unions with members of the School Board, the Chamber of Commerce, and the University Management Committee. The object was to obtain and distribute information respecting Technical Education in other countries and in other towns of Great Britain ; to co-operate with the School Board and the University College in promoting technical classes and stimulating public

interest therein—special attention was to be given to the
Evening Schools established by the School Board ; to
supplement these classes with other classes as might
prove necessary, and to induce employers and trade bodies
in Nottingham to interest themselves in this new line of
education. It was through him that Mr. H. M. Felkin
drew up a report on the educational equipment of Chemnitz
which was published for the City and Guild of London
Institute in 1881.[1]
One important feature was not taken by the commissioners of 1880 into their purview. They did not
touch on Commercial Education. Paton put this matter
before Mr. Samuel Morley, and, as the result, Mr. Morley
requested him, together with Dr. Percival (then President
of Trinity College, Oxford), Mr. Felkin, and Mr. W. Summers,
to prepare a report upon the Commercial Education given
on the Continent and in the United States, promising to
lay the report before the Associated Chambers of Commerce.
The report was not completed till 1887. Before that date
Mr. Samuel Morley was no more. Mr. Charles Morley, in
his father's place, laid it before the meeting of the Associated Chambers at Exeter in that year. It gives
a systematic report on the provision for commercial
instruction in the various States of Germany, in Austria,
France, Belgium, Holland, Italy, Switzerland, and the
United States. It calls attention to the almost total lack
of such instruction in England, and the loss sustained by
English commerce in consequence. It makes suggestions
as to the way in which existing educational instruction
in England might be adapted so as to give commercial
education most efficiently to scholars of every grade. It
insists that such instruction should be conceived and
imparted with that wider outlook which entitles it to be
called " liberal."

" Only an education that is in the true sense of the word
liberal can eminently fit a man for practical work, giving
him largeness of outlook, precision in aim, fertility of
resources, alertness and certitude in action. ' Bread-and-
butter science,' as it has been ignominiously called, is at
any rate better than bread-and-butter ignorance. . . . The

[1] " Technical Education in a Saxon Town," by H. M. Felkin. (Kegan
Paul.)

object of commercial education is not merely to make thoroughly capable, clear-eyed, and enterprising business men, but to *lift commerce to the rank of a profession,* and to give to those who enter upon it the habit and tone of mind which liberal studies, whether they be in history, law, physical science, or language, will impart. For our country, in which leading commercial men have so much influence upon municipal administration, social manners, and public policy, there will be many indirect advantages in each domain of our national life, when a commercial career ranks with a professional, and the training for it is equally ample, exact, and generous with that required for other professions."

Such was the first document which gave to English readers information as to what was being done by their commercial rivals to equip their young men of commerce. The lesson of the report, enforced by subsequent experience, is even now being brought home but slowly to the consciousness of the English public. But the Nottingham Chamber of Commerce took up the matter warmly, and a beginning was made in connection with the Evening Schools and the High School. Nottingham led the way in realising what may be called the municipal side of technical education.

The problem of national education is not solved by simply securing the elementary instruction of all the children of the nation. Most people, after 1871, were inclined to be content and rest on their oars for a while. That was just what was to be expected from an uneducated nation ; they could not be expected to realise either the preciousness or the full scope of what they had never experienced. But, to Paton, universal elementary instruction was only the spring-board for further education. We have seen how he strove to secure for the humblest and poorest an opportunity of continuing their studies and entering into the inheritance of intellectual wealth in the great national storehouses of Oxford and Cambridge. We have seen how he was endeavouring, through commercial and technical education, to bring into the ordinary life of the clerk and the operative that higher knowledge and skill which make work intelligent and therefore happier, which draw out the inventiveness of the operative and enable him to conform to the law of progress.

The other classes of the community were not neglected. As President of the Literary and Philosophical Society in 1874, he formed a new section for literature and social service, and organised a scheme of lectures which dealt with social subjects and the local history of Nottingham. He followed up the interest thus stimulated with a prize scheme for which Mr. Samuel Morley provided the powder and shot, and widely extended the influence and usefulness of the society by bringing into association with it a large number of persons outside the pale of its own members. The whole motive of the new movement was the same as with University Extension, viz. to broaden the basis of culture.

" Science and literature," he says, in the circular giving particulars of the new scheme, " belong to the republic of letters where all are welcome, and all can cordially join together to help one another and to promote the increase of knowledge, irrespective of social distinctions."

Another matter engaged his attention at the same time. There was no provision in the town for the secondary education of girls of the middle class beyond a few private schools. The education in these schools, even if good, was costly, and imposed a heavy burden on the less wealthy middle classes, who contributed largely to the Board Schools, but themselves derived no benefit from them. He felt there should be in the town a public school analogous to the high school for boys, and offering educational facilities in no way inferior. He therefore approached the Girls' Public Day-school Company, which had been formed two years before, and had already opened three schools in London. He got his friend, Canon Morse, to join him, formed a small committee, conducted the preliminary negotiations, got by his own solicitations a large portion of the money required, and in September 1875 the school was started, the first Girls' High School, after Norwich, to be started in the provinces. He kept up his interest in the school, and his connection with it. When in 1880 they moved to larger and better premises overlooking the Arboretum, he used all his influence with the members of the Town Council to secure them a private entrance through the Arboretum, so as to avoid any risk of jostling against the High School boys on the way to and from school. And later, when

Miss M. E. Skeel formed the Old Girls' Association in 1888, he gave the address at their Inaugural Meeting.

" Education does not cease, does it, with your school years ? Is it not the best part of the training which school gives, that it fits us for an education beyond—an education that is never to cease so long as life lasts ? But in the learning that follows school, we are all of us helped by fellowship, and by the sympathy and inspiration which it gives. We work better when we work together. Self-culture is not best achieved in isolation and solitude. Trees grow straight and in noble symmetry when they grow together. Minds grow in like manner, healthily and in order, when they grow together."

CHAPTER XI

THE INNER MISSION

" If you can say a man lived and never lifted a stone against his neighbour, it is a fine thing.   But it is finer far if you can also say, he took out of the path the stones that have caught his neighbour's feet."—M. SAILER.

THE corporate feeling of the Institute had soon led to the formation of the Association of the Old Students. They were called " old," but the name was as yet a misnomer, and they were never younger than when they met at one of their annual reunions.   Their meeting in September 1873 was in many ways the most memorable of them all.   For two days they conferred together about their common life in Christ and their common work for Christ.   The latter half of the week was given up to a public conference summoned by a circular headed, " Christianity and the Well-being of the People," and signed jointly by the Vicar of St. Mary's and the Principal of the Congregational Institute.   The circular was an appeal to Christian men and women to study the grave social evils of the time, and to labour earnestly and unitedly for their alleviation and removal.   Christianity, it said, was the true Social Science.   Christianity was the one power sufficient to heal.   In this work of healing and redemption every Christ-follower must bear his part ; by his own redemption he was pledged to be a fellow-worker with Christ in the redemption of his fellow-men.   As Christ, when on earth, proved His divine mission by works of mercy, so by works of mercy the Church, " His living Body " on earth, must make men know the fulness of His compassion and His saving health.

Papers were read on the care of discharged prisoners by Mrs. Lawson of Leeds, on the nursing of the sick poor by Miss Merryweather of Liverpool.   Mrs. Hind Smith spoke on the supplanting of the public-house, and Miss Mathews of Birmingham pleaded for the boarding out of

186

workhouse children. Mr. Bowman Stephenson and Dr. Barnardo spoke of their work for the street arabs. Paton himself read a paper on "The Inner Mission of Germany and its Lessons to us." The idea of the Inner Mission provided a comprehensive framework which gave unity to all the different branches of Christian social work which had been discussed, and all the other redemptive agencies carried on in connection with the Church. It supplied a platform broad enough for all Christians of whatever denomination to work in united effort. The spirit of Christ which had founded the Inner Mission furnished the supply of its power and the pledge of its continuance and its growth. The Conference felt this and expressed its feeling at the end by carrying unanimously a Resolution—

"That a union be formed in the town, consisting of the representatives of all existing Christian charities and Christian societies working for social ends, and of the representatives of the Church of Christ in this town. Its objects shall be—first, to strengthen by such union these several Christian societies and charities, to make them acquainted with each other's work, and to manifest the unity of the Christian spirit that inspires them all ; secondly, to collate and study facts connected with the physical, moral, and social condition of the town, and to impress on the public mind the practical relation and duty of the Christian Church with respect to these facts ; thirdly, to take counsel and action with the civil agencies of the town on matters with which they are connected, and which affect the social well-being of the people ; fourthly, to incite and direct individual and church labours, so as to relieve distress and save from vice, and to inspire and regulate all social institutions with a Christian spirit ; fifthly, where existing agencies and individual or separate church action do not meet any special and urgent wants of the town, to institute and conduct such agencies as shall ; and sixthly and lastly, to exhibit by such combined action for the well-being of the people the reality of Christian unity, and the social redemption that is effected by Christian love."

This Resolution may be called the agenda paper of Paton's subsequent life. The lack of unity among the

followers of Christ, the failure of the Churches to cope in
a practical way with the harassing social evils of the
world around them—these things had lain heavy on his
heart.   The work of Theodore Fliedner at Kaiserwerth
and of Immanuel Wichern at Hamburg had shown him
the one cure which availed for both these great defects of
English Christianity.   That there is a living unity in the
Christian Church, that we live in one another because we
are all rooted and centred in Christ, that we are adapted
both by the gifts of nature and by the gifts of grace to
supplement and complement one another, was clear to
any one who could stand outside his own denomination and
take a large and statesmanlike view.   That no union was
possible on the basis of doctrine or uniformity of ecclesiastical government was equally clear, it was demonstrated
by the tragic failures of the past.   Yet face to face with the
sick child, or the homeless outcast of the streets, all Christians were at one with another in their impulse to help and
heal and at one in the motive and spirit of their action.   In
practical, redemptive work, therefore, lay the formula of
unity ; in united work, and in that alone could the spirit
of unity take definite shape, and grow from strength to
strength.   By doing the will, the Churches would learn
thus the true doctrine of unity.   In the theology of the
heart there were no heretics.

One other truth stood out clear and beyond dispute.
There was no solution for all the problems of the age and
its deadly corruptions except the solution of Christ.
Officialism failed.   " Out of a single workhouse in London," said Miss Mathews, " inquiry was instituted two
years ago concerning girls who had left it and gone to
service.   *It was found that every one of them was on the
streets.*"   Science was impotent.   The religion of humanity
was incapable of raising man above himself.   Philosophy
philosophised, either with laughter or with tears.   The
Church alone, the living body of Christ, had the eye to
pierce with keen search to the secret places of human
need, the heart to seek and save, the hand to help, the
living power to endure unto the end.

The moment was opportune.   Never in the history of
England was there such an evident breach between the
Christian religion and the evils of society.   Christianity
was not a vital, social force.   Thoughtful men began to

ask if it was really anything more than a mere tradition
of a system once effectual, now effete ; whether it had not
served its purpose in the history of mankind. Culture in
the person of Matthew Arnold was wearied with—

> The sick hurry, the divided aims,
> The heads o'ertax'd, the palsied hearts—

of a generation staggering under the too great load of its
fate. Science, in the person of Professor Tyndall, was
defying the Church to prove by scientific tests that prayer
had any real value for the sufficing of human wants.
Common folk were indifferent, not through intellectual
superiority or scientific presumption, still less because they
were morally insensible, but from a blank conviction that,
outside the barren region of dogmatic assertion, Christianity had no power. If the Christian Churches could
cease to be great in petty things, and petty in great
things ; if they could sink their speculative differences and
address themselves efficiently and unitedly to the practical
needs of society blasted with pauperism, ignorance, disease,
perverted pleasures, crime and despair ; if, instead of
" dreams of good vainly grand " about another better
world they knew not where, they would grapple with this
world as it is, and make it sweeter, purer, better, and more
brotherly,—there would be the answer to the Agnostics
and the indifferentists, there would be the vindication of
Jesus Christ.

Nottingham had the honour of being the first town in
England where all sections of the Christian Church pledged
themselves to unite in work that should probe and heal
the festering vices of soicety, and reveal in living acts the
" reality of Christian unity and the social redemption that
is effected by Christian love."

These principles were not new ; they are as old as the
four Gospels. They are simple and self-evident, as all
great principles are. But are not all great discoveries in
religion really rediscoveries ? Are they not on a larger
scale what conversion has been said to be for the individual,
" the effective realisation of admitted truth " ?

For the " effective realisation " of the Inner Mission we
still wait. We have not yet seen all the Churches joining
together to work out any piece of social salvation. Here
and there has been joint action for some distinct agita-

tion, as, for instance, in matters connected with temperance and the Contagious Diseases Act. But, for the
purposes of organised social reform, co-operation has been
rather on the lines of political party than of Christian
confession ; it has been civic rather than religious. Still,
though the Churches as a whole have not seen their way
to any scheme of federation for fighting the common foe,
the movement has been in that direction. Federation is
coming. The formation of the Free Church Union was a
step in that direction. It was probably inevitable that
the Free Churches should unite among themselves before
they could expect to co-operate with the Established
Church. The circular which initiated the Free Church
Council was drawn up by the English Apostle of the Inner
Mission.[1] The Students' Christian Union is full of promise for what a new generation may bring forth. Men
who have worked heartily side by side in the common
cause at college are not likely to set up barriers between
one another in after life. The Christian Social Union, the
National Union for Social Service in England and the
Scottish Christian Social Union—all indicate that, if not
Churches, at any rate individuals of widely different
schools of thought, are ready to act in concert in practical
Christian redemptive work ; and every single agency which
Paton started yielded a proof of the same willingness on
the part of leading men in all political parties and religious
denominations to work loyally together in educational
and philanthropic work.

It was round the thought of the Inner Mission that all
his subsequent activities were built up, and, though he
never lived to see the federation of the Churches for redemptive work actually accomplished, he did begin to
see the central idea brought home at last to the consciousness of all followers of Christ. This central idea he had
to reiterate again and again ; he died like Falkland,
" ingeminating peace " ; but he learned to know that
only by much persistence are new ideas driven home into
the minds of Englishmen. " You have to say a thing
five or six times over before some people know you are
talking," he would say. At a second conference in Nottingham in 1875, at the Jubilee of the Institute in 1884,

---

[1] It was issued in 1891, and the main object proposed is social redemptive work ; the main directions of such work are indicated, see p. 491 ff.

in the last paper he wrote, indeed in all his addresses on
modern church questions, he goes back to the Inner
Mission as the corner-stone on which to build.

Its main principles may be stated in brief summary :

(i) Christ's command to His disciples was " Preach *and*
heal." This is still His command to His disciples of to-
day. Protestant Churches, in particular, have omitted
the second half. There is the *word* of love, but where
are the *works* of love ?

(ii) Christ not only gives the command, but he gives
the power to fulfil it. Nay, " *Greater* works than these
shall ye do." These endless potentialities are yet not
only latent, but undiscovered and even unsuspected.

(iii) The kingdom of heaven Christ came to establish
is not in the clouds, but here on earth. It exists wherever
and whenever God's will is done upon earth as it is done
in heaven. We have thought of the New Jerusalem as
" stored up perhaps in heaven," like Plato's ideal city ;
but the apostle saw it " coming down from God out of
heaven." There is to be a new earth, " wherein dwelleth
righteousness," as well as a new heaven.

(iv) To establish this kingdom is the great *business* of the
Church ; needing, like all human business, only in higher
degree, " rigorous method, indomitable persistency, and
wise application of means to ends." " Charity," as we see
it, is often foolish ; though she " thinketh no evil," she does
evil galore. " Christ had no money to give, and the Church
has not much. The Church may not bribe, as it cannot
bless, men with money." Silver and gold may be wanting,
but heart-service, pity, willing personal help—these things,
which the Lord freely gives, men should freely give. And
no redemptive impulse must be stifled, or allowed to
remain unused. Each varied gift, whatever it be, must be
trained and used and disciplined " under wise and definite
direction " in the work of the Church, which work is the
establishing of the kingdom of God on earth.

Not only his active work, but his prayer too, centred
round this central and unifying principle of the Inner
Mission. In 1875 he was at the house of Mr. James
Stuart, in Higher Broughton, Manchester, conferring and
praying with a few friends, among them Mr. Fleming
Stevenson, who, in his book called " Praying and Working,"
had written the story of Wichern and Fliedner's work.

Stevenson was soon taken from his side, but he founded a
Ministers' Bible-reading and Prayer Union which quickly
extended its membership to America. In this " covenant
of prayer " each member bound himself to pray :

" That all members of Christ's Church, and those
preparing for membership, may realise the privilege and
duty of membership in Christ's Church, ' which is His
Body,' in regard to their worship of the Father *through*
Christ, their fellowship with one another *in* Christ, their
working together *with* Christ in the redeeming of the world.
. . . That the prayer of our Lord may be fulfilled, which He
offered on the night in which he was betrayed : ' That all
who believe in Me may be one, as Thou, Father, art in Me,
and I in Thee, that they also may be one in Us ; that the
world may know that Thou hast sent Me.' "

How he carried the spirit of oneness even into controversy may be inferred from the following letter. Canon
Wilberforce had preached in a Congregational pulpit and
had been reprimanded by his Bishop. The letter was
written when he was away from home, when he had no
opportunity of referring to books.

" Torquay,
" January 5th, 1887.

" Dear Canon Wilberforce,
    " Allow me to indicate certain points which occur
to me after perusing carefully the Bishop's letter.
    " 1. Does preaching in a Congregational pulpit carry
with it the approval of Congregational doctrines, and
the repudiation of any special doctrine, or privilege, or
' prerogative ' position of the Anglican Church ? If I
preach in a Wesleyan or Presbyterian pulpit, I do not
thus signify my approval of their polity or repudiate my
own Church and its faith, though truly I recognise their
evangelic and Catholic faith, and their rights to fraternal
fellowship in it.
    " As an Anglican, I should feel that preaching in a
chapel belonging to Congregationalists was no more than
speaking in any unlicensed mission-room. To celebrate
with them in their place of worship the Holy Communion,
and to preside over that service of highest worship might,
according to some teachers of Anglican doctrine, be a

schismatical act ; but to preach, which is not a priestly or official act, is different. A Bishop of the English Church preaches regularly in Presbyterian churches in Scotland, nor is he rebuked for so doing.

" 2. The proposition maintained in the Bishop's letter— that there has been one National Church in this country from the apostolic, or post-apostolic age, which abides the same, though it has undergone reforming process—is not quite verified by history. The old British Church, so far as its history has been explored, was different in its constitution and ritual from the Church introduced by Augustine, the Roman missionary. The idea of one Church in a country was a late medieval conception. There was one Church in each city, town, or village, of which for centuries the Bishop was the representative, the symbol of its unity, and its authorised ruler. Afterwards the diocese was the one Church.

" Thus, there was the Church at Jerusalem, Antioch, Corinth, etc. And still we speak of the Roman Church, not the Italian ; whilst in England, as in all parts of Europe, the different missals and regulations or offices of worship—such as the ' Sarum ' use—show the diverse usages and authorities of the several diocesan Churches.

" Granted that these Churches, in their councils, spoke on behalf of the Catholic Church in that country, and that thus the Church in England did have, in a sense, a representative unity. This unity exists equally in the Churches of Sweden, Norway, Germany, Denmark, Scotland. These Churches underwent reformation, as the English Church did, and in ways as honourable ; but I fear the Bishop would not allow his argument to hold for them and maintain that any other Church—e.g., an Episcopal Church after the usage and law of the English Church—was in those countries a schismatic institution.

" 3. I have no doubt that the Bishop really considers the ' catholic ' authority and the identity of the English Church to be maintained because of the apostolic succession in the order of her priesthood. Now, upon that I may say—

" (a) That the English Church nowhere teaches and enjoins the doctrine of Apostolic Succession as the ground of the validity of her ' orders.' It is claimed for her that

13

she has it, but it is nowhere taught as part of her authoritative creed. She teaches that there are three offices of
ministry (wrongly calling the Episcopate a distinct ' order ')
—viz. bishop, priest or presbyter, and deacon. And in
this I may say most Congregational Churches agree, only
insisting that the Bishop is but the president of the presbyters—one of the presbyters—in this conforming to the
old usage and doctrine of the post-apostolic age. But that
the priest has his authority solely from the grace flowing
through episcopal hands down from the apostles, and that,
if this channel were broken, the grace of our Lord Jesus
Christ and the benefits of His salvation would be wholly
and irrevocably lost to mankind, the English Church has
not taught.

" (b) Now, in regard to this sacerdotal doctrine, which
is, notwithstanding, vaguely and very generally held, I
would remind the Bishop that the Roman and the Greek
Churches deny the validity of Anglican orders, believing
the mystic succession to have been broken. (I was present
at the Bonn Conference, when representatives of the
Old Catholic Church, the Russo-Greek Church, and the
Anglican Church discussed this question.)

" (c) It seems impossible to believe that the existence of
the Church of God should depend upon this accident of
accidents. Canon Mason, in his volume on the Diocletian
persecution, positively considers it a subject of wondering
praise that God blinded the eyes of the Emperor against
a simple and most efficacious method of at once and absolutely and for ever abolishing the Church of God and
shutting up the human race in the blackness of darkness
for ever—viz. that he had merely to behead all the Bishops
of the Church, and thus stop the Apostolic Succession.

" (d) Cardinal Newman, with many great Roman divines,
ridicules the notion of ' orders ' giving existence and validity
to the living Church. He says the living Church gives its
validity to ' orders.' It is not the fact of Apostolic Succession that gives them their authority and worth, but the
sanction of the living and abiding Church.

" (e) The old primitive doctrine of succession was that
the Bishops of certain sees—e.g. Jerusalem, Antioch,
Alexandria, Rome, etc.—were in the line of a succession of
Bishops who had occupied the sees of those Churches since
the apostolic time. And thus they were in themselves

conspicuous evidence that the chain of apostolic testimony and authority and grace *in those Churches* was unbroken.

" (*f*) It is terrible to think that the worst men in the world's history, men like Pope John XXII, should be able to communicate all the powers of sacramental grace— *i.e.* the full benefits of salvation, to others as bad as themselves, whilst according to this theory the holiest and most Christlike men—the most obedient in spirit to Christ—summoned to church office, as the first Bishops and elders were, by the suffrage of the whole body of believing disciples over whom they bear rule, have no power to speak truth with spiritual authority, or to communicate spiritual grace by prayer, and by expressing the sympathy and faith of the fellowship of that Church.

" (*g*) The old Catholic doctrine which still lingers in so many usages, and which the Old Catholic Church in Germany has so powerfully enforced, is that the Bishop must be chosen by the Church, and thus is invested with the spiritual power and authority of the whole Church, whose officer and representative he is—that he is thus the *persona ecclesiæ*, and not, as this exaggerated theory of apostolic succession perversely says, that the Church is the *persona episcopi*.

" (*h*) Does not the Bishop see that this theory expressly permits what he so righteously denounces ? It is not possible, he says, ' for a single man or body of men in recent times to constitute a new Church at their own pleasure.' Yet that is exactly what, according to this theory, a Bishop who happens to have been consecrated in ways acknowledged by the Roman or the Anglican Church can do. Nay ; it is what a priest can do in baptizing any number of people, be they whosoever they may, for they really, according to High Church views, are by him constituted a Church—a part of the Catholic Church.

" 4. The reason why many of us think the English Church is in a favourable position to effect a reunion of Christendom is because she has apostolic orders according to the judgment of, and in the sense understood and believed by, many members of the Greek and Roman Communion, whilst, on the other hand, she is a Protestant Church, not teaching or enforcing these ' orders ' as the ground of qualification and authority in her priests or as the cause of grace in her sacraments. If she abandon this middle position and take up the strictly sacerdotal position of the Roman Church, then she forfeits all her advantages in the future as a possible medium and advocate of such reunion.

" 5. ' The Church is from above.' Here is the doctrine which I, with other Nonconformists, hold. It is the creation of the living, ever-working Spirit of the Lord. He is the ever-present Head of the Church. His Spirit is the only power that renews its membership and so fashions the Body of the Lord, prepares for Him His Bride. That is our doctrine. But may I venture to say that the Bishop interprets his own phrase otherwise, and really means (a) that the derivation of the Church is from the past, the ' above ' in former times—i.e. it is derived from apostolic power, devolved officially and mechanically upon the apostles from our Lord—and by them upon certain successors ; and (b) that thus the Church lives in and by its Bishops, who create its membership through the priests whom they ordain to administer its sacraments, and by the act of Confirmation. Against this doctrine I would uphold the old Catholic faith and doctrine that Christ's Spirit bloweth as He listeth, that He accompanies and quickens the truth of Christ, especially when spoken by His spiritual servants ; that He, the Eternal Spirit, thus forms the membership of Christ's Church by quickening living faith in the souls of men, and drawing those who are thus quickened into fellowship with each other, in order that they may fulfil together, by the Spirit, in each other, and with each other, the great obligations and promises of their faith ; that the presbyters and Bishops are to be chosen, for government, for teaching, for the direction and training of each member of the Church in his or her ministry, by the whole Church, so that they may act in its name and be living exponents and agents of its spirit and mission.

" 6. Thus the Bishop will see how impossible we deem it that ' any single man or body of men in recent times may constitute a new Church at their own pleasure.' There is no new Church. There is one only Catholic and Apostolic Church, which is ' the Communion of Saints,' i.e. of believers consecrated unto God by their faith in Christ. The Spirit of Christ alone can form His Church, by the quickening of the souls of men, to receive and obey His truth. No men, be they Roman priests or Congregational preachers, can form a Church. We altogether repudiate, as very blasphemy, the notion that the Church of Christ is formed by men. Further, the unity of the Church is given by the one Spirit, in the one faith in the one Lord. We cannot create that unity, but, by every obligation of faith and every inspiration of love, we are compelled to manifest it, to cherish it, to seal and keep it as a most precious and a wholly inestimable blessing. Hence I long and strive for every possible means of showing the unity of the Spirit, and pray with most earnest prayer for the time when continually it may be seen by the world that all true Christians are one, and when the *one* body of Christ which exists now as always shall be fully disclosed.

" 7. Thus the two principles which the Bishop thinks to be principles of the Church of England are principles which I hold with all Evangelical Nonconformists and Protestants : (1) That the Church as a visible, living organism, has lived in an unbroken continuity from the days of our Lord's bodily presence to this day ; and that organism has been the true body of Christ *just in the measure in which it has permitted and enabled spiritually quickened souls* to hold communion with each other, to edify one another, and thus edify the body of Christ ; (2) and in which it has been able to reveal Christ to the world and to accomplish His redeeming work in the world.

" The ideal of the Church has not been realised in the actual organism which wears its name. So far it has not been the true body of Christ, for, as the Bishop says in the statement of his second principle : ' Though the Church is Divine ' (which surely means in its ideal and the Spirit of Christ which animates it), ' it has human elements, and so may require pruning—prudent and careful pruning—if it runs into excessive or unhealthy growths.' We say, like the Bishop, that the actual historical Church did overlay, and darken, and degrade the spiritual life and truth and grace of the true Church by these human, corrupting ' elements,' and that these ' elements ' should be wisely removed. But we consider that the Church of England was not in the wisest way reformed, and that some corrupting Roman elements remain, and thus, while we say, with the Bishop, ' The Church of to-day is to be regarded as one with the Church of the New Testament and the primitive ages,' we nevertheless think that the Church of England, as reformed, is not ' on the exact model of the primitive body.' We think the first English Reformers were nearer the spirit of the primitive Church than the Reformers of the Laudian age. We think the English Church has modelled herself upon the lines of the fourth century rather than of the first ; that the spirit and the agents of the Reformation were not the wisest or most prudent ; that, accordingly, the prayer and aim of all of us should be to secure what the Bishop desires—viz. that ' the Church be reformed on the exact model of the primitive body ' ; and that, when it is in any sense reformed to be like that model, Nonconformity should and will cease to be.

" 8. At the same time, few of us claim that our Churches are altogether fashioned on that model ; we only claim them to be what even Bishop Andrewes, the High Church and holy Bishop of the Reformation age, conceded all non-Episcopal Protestant Churches to be, viz. ' imperfect Churches.' We consider our Churches to be thus what we also think the Church of England to be, in its present state, ' imperfect ' as Churches. In many things could I point out such imperfection. But we do think we hold a vital church principle in holding the Headship of Christ over His own Church, not allowing that Headship to be usurped by pope, priest, or king ; and we rejoice in that ' Catholic faith and spirit ' which seeks fellowship and holds intercommunion with all Christian men and Christian Churches that hold the Catholic Evangelic faith.

" There was a canon of the Nicene Council which forbade any other test of communion in the Catholic Church than the declaration of Christian verities which it adopted, and denounced any further tests as schismatic. Bishop Wordsworth, in his able vindication of the English Church against Rome, insists that the Roman Church is the cause of schism in imposing tests of communion which are not apostolic or primitive. That exactly is our vindication as against the Anglican Church. In the law of uniformity, by the doctrine of the Establishment, which surrender spiritual authority and the appointment of spiritual officers to the Queen and her advisers, or to the purchasers of advowsons and owners of patronage ; and, above all, by the doctrine which teaches salvation to be by priestly ordinances, and which makes Episcopal orders to be

the only title for spiritual office, we consider she has imposed tests of communion which are not to be found in
the Apostolic Church, or even in the Nicene Creed. I do
not now complain of these doctrines being held by individual persons or Churches, but I do complain that they
are made tests of communion between Churches as
branches of the one Catholic Church or of admission
through them into the one Church of Christ. That is
hard, and I think schismatical. I believe that, as in the
Roman Church, we must have many orders of denominations in the one Church, in order to give expression and
actuality to diverse operations and gifts, and to ritual
and doctrinal and ministerial differences which will
always be found in the living Church ; and I hope that
ere long we may arrive at some principle and basis of
Catholic inter-communion which will recognise such
glorious variety as an evidence of fulness of life, and
which, having a breadth like that of the primitive Church,
will give opportunity for us all to honour and love one
another as brethren—servants of one Lord, quickened by
one Spirit, and heirs of one salvation.

" May that time soon come. Quickly, Lord, come in
that brightness of Thy coming, so that we who love Thee,
and love one another in Thee, may reveal Thee in the
oneness of our faith in Thee, which jealously forbids any
other faith to hide and weaken that Supreme Faith which
alone is the bond and the seal of an eternal unity."

CHAPTER XII

THE BUILDING OF THE EDUCATIONAL BRIDGE

"Qui tient l' école, tient l'avenir."

THE primary aim of University Extension, in the minds of its founders, was the popularisation of knowledge. Experience soon showed that the great body of working men, through the insufficiency of their education, were unable to avail themselves of the opportunities offered. Many a working man, honestly desirous of knowledge, came away from the lectures thoroughly bewildered ; the last state of the man was worse than the first. " I'm all in a fog like," one of them said ; " I don't know where I am, and I don't know what he's talking about." The result was, many working men were discouraged, and not a few of the promoters, losing their faith in the proposed desire of the operative class for higher culture, developed the University Extension movement on the line of least resistance among the leisured middle class.

The same thing was true with the Science and Art Classes of South Kensington, and the technical classes held by the City Guilds. Not many working-class youths were capable of profiting by the instructions they gave.

But that was not what happened in Nottingham. Paton saw that it was not enough to let down the ladder from above, unless one also built up from below, so that the ladder was within reach. Even when the Board Schools were established, and the standard of efficiency was raised, there remained a gap to be bridged over. And the only chance of bridging over the gap was the night-school. A beginning was made in the autumn of 1876 with three schools on different sides of the town. It may be interesting to reproduce the jelly-graphed circular which was the harbinger of one of the most fruitful movements of popular education in the nineteenth century.

"ELEMENTARY TRADE AND SCIENCE SCHOOLS

"The first term of these schools will commence on Tuesday, October 6th, 1876, in All Saints Upper School, Forest Road; Trinity School, and the Board School, Bath Street.

"These schools will give a special education, fitting boys for the business of life, particularly for the trades they are learning, so that they shall become educated and skilful workers.

"The schools will be open on *Tuesday* and *Thursday*, from 7.30 *to* 9 *p.m.*

"*Subjects taught:*

"Tuesday evenings:
"1. Industrial history and biography, history of trades, traders and inventors.
"2. Practical lessons in English.
"3. Applied arithmetic and measurement of surfaces and solids.
"Thursday evenings:
"1. Commercial and industrial geography; or places where products of trades are grown, manufactured or exchanged.
"2. Drawing adapted to the workshop.
"3. Elementary science applied to Nottingham trades.
"Half an hour devoted to each subject.

"Terms 2s. 6d. a quarter for all under sixteen years of age, 5s. for all over sixteen years of age, or 3d. and 6d. a week.

"Any youths debarred by poverty from the great advantages of these schools may apply for a free scholarship to the superintendent teacher of each school.

"These schools are opened for the following purposes:
"1. To continue the education of boys who have left school and gone to work.
"2. To give a special education fitting these boys for the business of life, particularly for the trades they are learning, so that they shall become thoroughly educated and skilful workmen.
"3. To prepare them for the School of Science and for

the Popular University Classes which they may enter
when about seventeen or eighteen years of age.

"These schools will thus serve as a bridge between the
public elementary schools and the university and science
classes ; it is also a technical school, training boys in
scientific and technical knowledge required in their several
trades.

"A Preparatory School

"Serving the purposes of an ordinary night-school to
prepare boys who are not qualified to enter this technical
school, will be held in another room of Trinity Schools, on
the same evenings, and at the same hours.

"Terms of the preparatory school 2s. 6d. per quarter, or
3d. per week."

The appeal of this circular is to the practical instinct
of the working lad, who wishes to become " a thoroughly
educated and skilful workman." But, as the experiment
went on, it became clear that, in order to catch the great
bulk of the working lads, the appeal must be wider and
more human. The lad who had been working in the
factory since six o'clock in the morning was not fit for
much in the way of industrial history and commercial
geography. All day long he had been under restraint ;
he wanted free play for his muscles. He had been sitting
in a cramped position ; he wanted to stretch hi slimbs.
His work had been monotonous ; he wanted recreation,
colour, joy. They were not all self-help heroes à la
Samuel Smiles, and, if the classes were to attract the
average, happy-hearted, boisterous, irresponsible lad,
they would have to cater for other sides of his nature
beside the pragmatic instincts and the desire to get on.
Accordingly, Paton set himself to work with the teachers
and his working-men friends to see what could be done by
way of making the schools more attractive. The schools
were thrown open half an hour before the classes and
simple games were provided ; one of the teachers was
there, and, as the lads strolled in to have a talk or a game,
teachers and pupils together found that night school was
becoming something of a club as well as a school. Physical
exercises were introduced and went with more go when
the teacher, or one of the class, strummed on the piano

by way of accompaniment. The piano (which figured very prominently at the School Board elections) gave the chance of starting singing-lessons, and the chance was not missed. David Livingstone had used the magic-lantern to bring home the lessons of the gospel story in pictorial form to the savages of Central Africa; why should not the lantern be used for the purpose of illustrating history, travel, science, and even literature? It was an evil-smelling oil-lantern which acted as pioneer, and it burned many fingers; but "it builded better than it knew." Tired eyes were refreshed with the glow of colour. Lessons became interesting. School lost its stiffness and the pedantry of the "standard" drill. In fact, it was "school" no more. To go to "school" like a "kid" was *infra dignitatem* to a lad who was earning five shillings a week, and "tipping up" four-and-sixpence of it towards his keep at home. They were called "classes" now, and the change of name meant much.

So much for the boys. Girls were not forgotten. Nottingham industries attracted a large number of young girls from the country. They lived in lodgings, dingy, bare, and often dilapidated; they had none of the comforts of home-life, none of its safeguards. The free hours of the evening had nothing to offer them except the music-hall, the dancing-saloon, the public-house; and the public-house would offer its beer free to a girl who was attractive and gaily dressed. Compared with these, mission-rooms were cold and repellent. "The last and worst thing that can be said of a nation is that it has made its young girls sad and weary," says John Ruskin. Sadness and weariness were not the worst things that happened to girls in Nottingham.

The first Evening Home for Working Girls was opened by Miss Annie M. Lewis, Miss M. Oliver, and Miss Caroline M. Paton (now Mrs. Figgis), in January 1879, and the movement rapidly extended. The Girls' Evening Homes were not, in the strict sense of the term, educational, but many a hint for making evening classes attractive and recreative was borrowed from them when classes came to be formed for working girls. The worker in the homes knew exactly how to teach cookery, dress-making, crewel-work, drawing, singing, and disguised arithmetic in such a way as to "strike on the box."

To both new movements one principle was common.
Both needed voluntary helpers. To secure these voluntary helpers, and to give them the training they needed
to take classes in musical drill, wood-carving, leather
repoussé, and various kinds of art-handwork, an association was formed in 1883 called " The Recreative Evening
Schools Association for Nottingham and Notts." The
Association affiliated two institutes already existing in the
town, the St. James's Institute and the Social Guild Institute, and, in its fourth year, reports no less than sixty-
eight voluntary teachers, some of whom take the musical
drill for girls, others the physical drill for boys, others
again take the singing, drawing, wood-carving, or work
the magic-lantern. The numbers in the schools show a
gratifying increase. From 244, when the Association began its work, they have risen to 1,712. This result was
due mainly to the efforts of the working-men managers.
Seven working men were appointed for each set of schools,
forty-nine in all. These managers appealed to employers,
ministers, and superintendents of Sunday-schools, and
visited each child leaving the day-school to urge in the
name of the School Board the claims of the Continuation
Classes. Every week each group of managers met at the
school to receive lists of absentees. Each absentee was
promptly visited. One working man spent sixty hours
one month in visiting absentee children and persuading
their parents to encourage their regular attendance. To
them also was entrusted the duty of paying the fees for
children who would otherwise be debarred by poverty
from attending.

But, though evening classes in Nottingham were showing such healthy signs of expression, in the rest of the
country they were fast dwindling to extinction. The
figures must have been distressing for those who had eyes
to see the things that belonged to the peace of Jerusalem.

The attendance was steadily declining, as the following figures show :

				Average No in attendance.
1870	.	.	.	. 73,375
1874	.	.	.	. 48,690
1876	.	.	.	. 49,868
1885	.	.	.	. 24,233

Excluding those over eighteen, it may be said that not one in a hundred children leaving school continued their education in evening schools.   It was only too evident that the old type of night-school, with its teaching of the three R's, was becoming rapidly extinct, and with its disappearance it became more and more apparent that between the time of leaving school and the age of sixteen or seventeen there yawned an ominous hiatus.   In those unguarded years the knowledge gained in the elementary schools was rapidly lost, for there is no ratchet on the wheel of the mind.   Also, the children lost those habits of steadied attention which alone enable them to learn anything.   With such a state of things, what prospect was there for technical instruction, University Extension, or, indeed any form of higher education to establish its footing ?   Perhaps the saddest feature of the whole case was the case of the lad entering on manhood who woke up to his need of further knowledge, enrolled himself in the technical classes, made heroic efforts to retrieve his footing, but sank back again into the lower levels with the common ruck of his less earnest fellows.

" The lack of an effective system of evening-schools to carry on and crown the work of day-schools is the most glaring defect in our national arrangements for elementary education," wrote one of the chief inspectors in his report for 1886.

The very efficiency of the elementary teaching was widening the gap.   The Act of 1870 assumed that the school age of a child was from five to thirteen, and an amendment to the Act allowed the term " child " to be extended for certain purposes to fourteen years of age. But it left with School Boards almost unlimited power to fix the conditions of exemption.   Most unfortunately, the attainment of a certain standard of proficiency, and not the attainment of a certain age, was made the basis of exemption from school attendance.   In many areas the standard fixed was deplorably low ; in 1,417 of these the standard for total exemption was the fourth ; in 249 the standard for partial exemption was as low as the second.

Two great evils resulted.

Inasmuch as grants were made to depend upon results, the teachers were forced to cram the children's heads with such knowledge as went to earn money payments.   School

became a place of mere mental drudgery, the " dry drudgery
of the desk's dead wood." The school teacher became a
hustler ; there was no freedom, no training of the hand,
no spontaneity, no joy. The child's first idea was to
escape at the first opportunity from this tread-mill grind.
The parents were eager to turn his labour to account. It
naturally followed that, as soon as the minimum standard
was passed, the child left school, flung up his hat, and
thanked his stars that he was done with that obnoxious
grinding process called education. This repugnance to
school was the first pernicious result.

Again, standard exemption worked badly. In practice it
made the attainment by the child of a certain degree of
knowledge a signal for its being deprived of all further
chance of school teaching. The clever child, having
attained to this modicum not infrequently by ten years
of age, was forthwith removed from school and penalised
for its cleverness. Instead of the leaving age being
thirteen, as the law intended, it was in many cases ten. At
Wolverhampton, for instance, where the standard of exemption was Standard V, the *average* age for passing that
Standard was eleven, and less that 3 per cent. of the
children remained on at school after the standard was
passed. In that town over 97 per cent. of the children
were leaving school at eleven years of age, and yet were
debarred by the Factory Acts from going to regular work
before the age of thirteen. The second result, therefore,
was that children of ten, and those precisely the most
promising children in the country,[1] were leaving school
with a rooted distaste for all things connected with education, were living for two or three years in idleness, under
no control or salutary influence, and in the school of the
streets were learning to be shiftless, ignorant, vicious, and
unclean.

Our whole educational system was turned into a labour
of the Danaides. Physically, mentally, morally, and
financially, the waste of it was appalling.

The first necessity was to make the evening-school
attractive. It could not compel attendance. Musical

[1] No provision was made in the Evening School code for anything
higher than Standard VII, so that there was no place at all in the Evening School for children who had passed Standard VII and were anxious
to continue their education in the evening.

drill and gymnastics, choral singing, lantern pictures in connection with history, travel, English literature, and science made the classes bright and recreative instead of repellent. Boys and girls who found it dry to read Shakespeare's plays found it was the best of fun to act them. The next thing was to evoke the artistic instinct which was smothered in the mechanical, and, for the most part, monotonous occupation of the day. Drawing, modelling, wood-carving, leather repoussé, gave scope to these artistic potentialities. Mr. C. G. Leland's work among the street arabs in New York had been a revelation of latent and unsuspected powers. Lastly, the evening-school had to show its pupils that it had a vital bearing on their daily occupations, for young folk of this age are all protensive in their outlook. The arithmetic had to emancipate itself from the current text-books and seek its application and illustrations in the workshop; drawing had to lead up to design and mechanical draftsmanship; science had to show a practical co-ordination with the industries of the locality. There had to be cooking, making and mending of garments, house management for the girls. And everywhere public opinion had to be awakened to see the shortcomings and failures of things as they were, and the glorious possibilities of things as they might be.

It was with these objects in view that the Recreative Evening Schools Association was organised on a larger scale. The beginning of the movement in London was a meeting of representatives from fifty-seven large trade societies held on May 14th, 1885. Mr. G. W. Taylor, Secretary of the Nottingham Trades Council of Learning, Mr. Thomas Smith, who had presided over the Trades Union Congress, attended with my father as a deputation to explain what had been done at Nottingham, and set forth how hopefully the experiment worked there. After several evenings spent in careful consideration, they resolved to forward a memorial to the London School Board. The School Board heard their petition and granted it. The question assumed national importance, and in January 1885 a large meeting was held in the Mansion House to launch the Association. H.R.H. the Princess Louise became President and took an active interest in its work. She headed in person the deputation which presented the

petition of the Trades Council, and attended a great
meeting at Nottingham on December 12th, 1885. In
April of the same year a Conference on " Education under
Healthy Conditions " was called at Manchester, and a
paper which Paton read at that Conference had a wide
influence in the country. Local Associations were formed ;
classes sprang up to train the voluntary teachers ; propaganda was carried on vigorously. The Trades Councils of
other towns were stirred up to appeal to their several School
Boards as the London Council had done. Public meetings
were held. Articles were published in the working men's
organs and religious journals. Sunday-school workers
and co-operators were appealed to in their conferences all
over the country. Employers of labour were canvassed,
and in many cases helped the movement by paying the
class-fees of young folk in their employment. Letters and
leaflets were sent out by the thousand to clergy and
ministers, rural and oppidan. Bills in Parliament were
promulgated by Mr. Samuel Smith (1888), and later by
the Bishop of Hereford. The question was raised from
time to time on the Education Vote.

In season and out of season, with pen and with tongue,
in private and in public, the founder of the movement
pressed it home upon the conscience of his countrymen.
His evidence given before the Royal Commission on
Primary Education in 1887 was widely circulated, and
produced such an impression that, when the report appeared in the following year, and the programme of the
Association was commended only by a minority of the
Commissioners,[1] disappointment at the result was generally
expressed in the Press. Statistics soon showed that the
tide had turned. The year 1885, in which the Association
began its work, marked the nadir; from that date the
curve rose steadily, and the crowning-point of all was
reached when Mr. A. H. D. Acland, in his Code of 1893,
adopted the main " planks " of the Association, added the
subject of Civics, and established once for all the principles
of the reform. The Code of 1893 may be called, not in-
appropriately, the Magna Charta of English Schools. It
swept away the requirement that every pupil should take

[1] The names of the signatories were the Hon. L. Stanley (now Lord
Sheffield of Roscommon), Dr. R. W. Dale, Mr. T. E. Heller, Mr. Henry
Richard, and Mr. George Shipton.

one or more of the three R's, it abolished the twenty-one year limit of age; it substituted considerate class inspection for individual examination; it made the curriculum elastic, and specially encouraged recreative and practical subjects and methods.

Year.	Evening Schools under Inspection.	Pupils on Register.	Average Attendance.
1885	839	40,854	24,233
1886	841	42,423	26,089
1887	917	49,128	30,584
1888	980	51,338	33,300
1889	1,043	56,525	37,118
1890	1,173	64,810	43,347
1891	1,388	76,915	51,974
1892	1,604	96,142	65,561
1893	1,977	115,582	81,068
1894	3,742	266,683	No Data
1895	3,947	270,285	,,
1896	4,347	298,724	,,
1897	4,980	358,628	,,

The results in London, where alone the Association was responsible for actually organising the classes, were even more satisfactory. The number of schools aided by the Association rose from 29 in 1886 to 232 in 1892, and the average attendance at these schools from 4,350 in 1887 to 12,500 in 1892.

The whole movement was characteristically English in its genesis and its growth. It took its rise, not in any Government department, not in the wisdom of the expert, but in the mind of one who stood outside the machinery of education, a mind quickened, sensitised, and illumined with the love of Christ for the perishing. It made its headway against the public apathy and departmental immobility by the help of volunteers who gave their services for the love of their fellow-men. The Association raised its own revenue as it went along. Organised voluntary helpers co-operated with the paid officials of the State—a novel thing in our country. And the principle for which the Association stood was even more novel. Hitherto the evening-school had been regarded as a mere accident and excrescence of the day-school system, supplementing the education of those whose instruction had been defective or forgotten. Henceforward it was to be recon-

14

structed so as to be an integral part of the system and carry
forward systematically, on practical lines, the education
of those who had completed the day-school course. It
was to be a *Fortbildungschule*, or " further-progress school,"
the secondary school of the industrial classes. The whole
popular conception of education began to be widened
and deepened. The day-school, instead of being the
end, became the beginning of a process continuous with
adolescence, and indeed with life. Hitherto the protecting
hand of the school had been withdrawn at the most critical
period of the child's life, when its nature was most readily
responsive to the influences, whether for better or worse,
which played upon it. Henceforward, in what now began
to be called a " Continuation School," that influence was
continued and corroborated ; scope was given for that
instinct for colour, freedom, movement, and actuality which
is in all young adolescents, and the idea of education in
their minds became associated, not with painful repression,
but the joy of self-realisation and corporate activities.
It is on these lines that future progress must be made.

Many to whom the educational side did not appeal were
drawn into the movement by the power of its moral
significance. More and more all social and religious
workers, from whatever side they attacked the social
problem, began to realise that the breeding-ground of
trouble lay in the years of early adolescence. Deterioration of physique, crime, irreligion, hooliganism, sexual
laxity, the failure of higher education—the germ and
genesis of all these evils, when scientifically investigated,
was found to lie in the neglect of the fateful years thirteen
to seventeen. More and more, ameliorative efforts have
begun to converge on the safeguarding of youth, for to it
belong the issues of life and of death.

A layman in one of the Midland villages wrote :

" Our ministers have relied too much on preaching,
and I think if they were to urge the importance of initiating
night-schools, workmen's clubs, and the like, great good
might result. My wife and I have worked on these lines
in this village for twenty years with success—that is to
say, the moral and spiritual tone of the place has been
raised, and its material prosperity consequently increased.
Here we have no resident minister of any kind."

The Rev. W. A. Coote, Secretary of the National Vigilance Association, wrote :

"*December* 31*st*, 1885.

"You will be pleased to hear that the idea of the night-school is being taken up by some of our Vigilance Committee. At Richmond they were very slow to move. I went to a drawing-room meeting. The ordinary phases of vigilance work had failed to arouse their enthusiasm. I then spoke to them about the failure of our night-school to lay hold of the boyhood and girlhood of England, and the danger arising therefrom to the boys and girls. Then I unfolded to them your scheme of musical drill, carving, moulding, and singing, and told them that, by thus engaging their attention at a time when they were most susceptible of devilish influences, they were doing the *prevention* work most effectually. They caught at this idea, and started the Association at once, with the idea of making the night-school work a branch of Vigilance Work. I went to West Hartlepool. I there put the idea before them, and so taken were they with it that a deputation from the Vigilance Committee is about to interview the School Board authorities with a view to its being introduced in the West Hartlepool schools. The more I think about this subject the more I am convinced that it will become a most important part of Vigilance Work. When Christian people become fully alive to the great inducements held out by the world and the devil to the boy and girl to be merry and jolly at the expense of their virtue, and the slight, very slight, efforts made by the Church and Christian people to break the monotony and dulness of their ordinary life, they will surely see in this system of education a means of making the boys and girls truly happy, and at the same time training and developing their highest and best faculties and thus lead them to prefer the good and avoid the evil."

CHAPTER XIII

SOCIAL INSTITUTES AND SOCIAL HOLIDAYS

" A healthy manner of play is necessary in order to a healthy manner
of work ; and therefore the choice of our recreation is, in most cases,
left to ourselves, while the nature of our work is as generally fixed by
necessity or authority. It may well be doubted whether more distressful
consequences may not have resulted from mistaken choice in play than
from mistaken direction in labour."—RUSKIN, *Stones of Venice*, vol. iii.

THE more closely Paton grappled with the problem of popular education, the wider grew its scope. Mere instruction was not adequate to its solution. Instruction, as
such, appealed to a small minority. A system of schools,
classes, and lectures did not touch the springs of conduct
or meet the forces of evil on the plane where they were
most operative. It was in the hour of recreation, when the
young man was master of his own actions, that the mischief
began. At work he was under control, and conformed
more or less to type ; but, when the hour struck for leaving
off, he was free to choose, and, considering how omnipresent
were the choices of evil, and how seductive, especially to
a pleasure-loving temperament, it was not wonderful that
so frequently he chose wrong. " The pestilence that walketh
at noonday," Paton would say, " is a direct allusion
to the dinner-hour ; and modern civilisation has added a
whole army corps of pestilences which walk the streets in
the evening and flare out their wreckers' lights at the
street corners." The publication of " All Sorts and
Conditions of Men," by his friend Sir Walter Besant,
strengthened in him this sense of the importance of the
leisure-time to the moral well-being of the people.

Leisure was a new feature in the working man's life.
Formerly he had worked from six in the morning, or even
earlier, up to eight o'clock in the evening, or even later.
He had only time, after his work, to get some supper and

212

go to bed, and had not much energy for anything beyond. There were no half-holidays, and no bank-holidays. But things had changed. Work was finished at five or six. There was a regular half-holiday on Saturday, and bank-holidays from time to time, with extra days at Christmas and Easter. The rise in wages and the fall in prices gave him, at the same time, a larger sum for what working folk call " spends." Every evening, from six o'clock till midnight, was his own to do what he liked with. Small wonder if new-found freedom was often abused.

Concurrently with the appearance of leisure, there was the disappearance of home. Home, in the true sense of the word, implies the possibility of quiet and comfort, and some resource in the way of books, or music, or recreation. The sanctities and decencies of home postulate a dwelling self-contained and inhabited by one family. But, for the poor in our big cities, who most need home, a home in the real sense of the word is not possible. Bare rooms, used as sleeping and dining-places, greasy, and dirty, and noisy, as they almost inevitably are, cannot be made places of comfort and refreshment at the close of the day's work, even if mothers do not go out to work. Just over the way is the smart bar-parlour, brightly illuminated, where mates are talking and laughing, and singing and drinking. Small blame to the man if the thought of it is more attractive than the free library, where " all talking is forbidden." " The fatal facility of the public-house " is easily intelligible to any one who has sufficient imagination to put himself in the working man's place.

The public-house had become the regular centre of the trade society and many a friendly society. Meetings were held there, for there was practically no other choice ; sick benefits, with out-of-work allowances, were disbursed there, and most recipients thought it a point of honour to spend something " for the good of the house " before they went away.

Temperance agencies were doing much to press the argument for teetotalism and its appeal, but they did very little to provide any substitute for the part which the public-house played in the social life of the people.

These thoughts burned themselves into Paton's head and bestirred him to act. " It is little use taking pledges,"

he said, " if we cannot help men to keep them." He felt
that human nature needed joy as much as it needed work,
that games, music, sing-songs, neighbourliness, and healthy
social merriment were strong enough to counteract the
perverted pleasures of drink and gambling, if only opportunity for them could be provided ; that Ruskin was
wholly right when he wrote strongly about the need for
wholesome " sensation." He writes to Archdeacon Wilberforce :

" The more I think of the Drink Traffic of our time,
the more convinced I am that very much of our other
temperance effort is not only handicapped, but to a large
extent ineffective and abortive, because all the time the
publican is catering for and exploiting what is a true
and most vital human need—the need of social fellowship and pleasant recreation, after the weariness and
monotony of the daily work.

" We had a conference of a few temperance workers in
connection with the National Temperance League on
Saturday week, and one young man there spoke of the
absolute cruelty of getting young fellows to sign the pledge,
and then leaving them with their mates to all the temptations of the public-house in their leisure evening hours,
when they have no other place to go to, but the public-
house, to meet their companions."

Here and there experiments had been made on these
lines, and with similar motives. A Select Committee of
the House of Lords in 1879 had discussed " Counter Attractions to the Public-house," and had commended
certain efforts, especially in London and Liverpool, " to
provide on a scale more extensive, and in a form more
attractive than hitherto, for the physical refreshment
and rational recreation of the working classes." But the
enormous expense involved in providing people's palaces
in all the crowded districts of all our big towns was sufficient to prevent any rapid progress on these lines.

And yet there were the public school buildings, built
at the people's expense, the people's own property standing just where such recreation centres were most needed,
standing for the most part dark and untenanted in the
evening hours with their fine assembly-halls, their plen-

teous class-rooms, and all the accommodation needed for a palace of delight. Why should they not be full of light and jubilant with song ? Why should not the various benefit, thrift, and friendly societies hold their meetings here ? Why should not the social life of the people find its centre here ? Here was a line of action which promised at last something commensurate with the need.

Accordingly, he urged the Recreative Evening Schools Association to take steps. The first thing was to appoint a committee with the Duchess of Bedford as Chairwoman, to establish evening homes for working girls in London, and the School Board provided suitable rooms in school buildings practically rent-free for the purpose. There were ten such homes in London. Shortly after, another committee was appointed to devise measures for providing similar social centres in Board School buildings for the lads and young men. The Charity Commissioners were at this time preparing a scheme for the administration of city parochial charities, and proposed to devote the money chiefly to the establishment of five or six Polytechnic Institutions in different districts of London, providing technical instruction with healthful recreation and facilities for social intercourse. The proposal of the R.E.S.A. Committee was to set up Social Institutes in Board School buildings, and group them in each district round a central Polytechnic Institute. The Social Institute was to provide for clubs, social meetings, and entertainments, and to combine with these recreative and technical classes of a more popular and elementary kind, sending on more advanced pupils to the higher classes at the Central Polytechnic.

" The Social Institutes grouped around the Central Polytechnic in each division of London will thus form a complete and organised system for promoting the higher education, the physical training, and social well-being of the people."

The Charity Commissioners approved the idea and made a grant of £300 towards carrying it out.

With the friendly co-operation of the School Board and the trustees of the City Parochial Charities, a beginning was made. In February 1894 the first Social Institute was opened in Dunscombe Road School, Islington. The central hall was used partly as a gymnasium and partly for games and other social purposes. The class-rooms were used for popular and useful classes likely to attract and retain lads of the working class. On Saturday evenings entertainments were provided in another of the large halls. Mr. T. A. Leonard, an old Nottingham student, was in charge, and in the following year five similar Institutes in different districts were opened, each under the direction of a local committee composed of voluntary helpers, representative working men, and local friends of education. The Social Institute was to be a centre of neighbourliness.

" The work of this committee will be to adapt each Institute to the needs of the locality, to surround it with the living sympathy of the community in which it is placed, and secure in its administration the co-operation and support of those for whose benefit especially it is opened. The school buildings belong in a true sense to the people. They are now, through the wise generosity of the School Board, available for the use of the people under salutary conditions which only safeguard that use. May they be now used by the people for the advancement of their own best interests—the production of their health, thrift, knowledge, industrial skill, and social enjoyment. That is the object of the Social Institutes." [1]

Thus was launched a movement which has in it the germ of a people's public-house, a people's drawing-room, a people's music-hall, a people's theatre, and a people's college—a movement which has in it still undeveloped possibilities unlimited for social improvement. The two Institutes where the experiment was carried through most successfully were Camden Street Board School in Camden Town, and Thomas Street Board School in Limehouse. In both these cases the Institute was opened six nights a week all the year round, with the exception of the summer holidays. Refreshments were introduced, and Paton was specially careful that working folk should have the best of coffee. " Let there be some froth on the top," he said ; " it is comforting to the lips." Billiard-tables were pur-

[1] Extract from the first circular written by Paton in 1895.

chased and other apparatus for games ; there were ambulance classes, swimming clubs, violin classes, and all the signs of vigorous social life.

In some cases old scholars' associations were formed which gave school-fellows the chance of carrying forward into later life their school-day friendships. The fact that every meeting of the Institute called for a certain amount of voluntary work in setting out the furniture and apparatus of the Institute, and putting it away, called out the right spirit of service, and, this spirit once evoked, found a new channel of activity. Ever since 1885 Paton had been urging on the School Board that the playgrounds should be thrown open on the light evenings of the summer time, on Saturdays, and in the holiday time, and the School Board had given permission subject to there being a sufficient number of helpers provided to supervise the play and see that no harm was done to the school property. The Social Institutes provided some of the best workers for this purpose.

As the movement spread to the provinces different towns adopted different methods. Some, like Nottingham and Glasgow, followed on the London lines. Glasgow, in 1904, had twelve Institutes in Board Schools, with 1,500 men in regular attendance,[1] and, though these Institutes were indebted to private generosity for initial expenses, the current expenses were met by current income. The school laundry was converted into a smoking-room, the kitchen into a billiard-room, and all manner of club activities for open-air pursuits, like rambling and football, grew up rapidly.

In Birmingham the Social Institutes Committee gained the consent of the civic authorities to use four public baths in return for the nominal cost of lighting and heating. In Leicester, again, and in other places the Institutes sprang up in connection with the early Morning Schools, the P.S.A.'s and Brotherhoods.

One point clearly showed itself as the result of experience. Churches and missions constantly find it difficult to attract into their buildings the people they most desire to reach. The poorest are shy about entering any private building. But a public school or a public bath is different ; it is in a sense their own, and they feel they have a right

[1] See Report of Scottish Christian Social Union, 1904.

to be in it. " The dread these fellows have that we are
trying to entrap thcm for the Church shows that we are
getting hold of the folks we desire from outside the pale,"
writes one of the workers.

The Social Institutes Union has now been united with
the Federation of Working Men's Clubs, with headquarters
in the W. H. Smith Memorial Building, Portugal Street,
W.C. No account of the work would be complete or
just which did not mention the great services rendered
by Archdeacon Sinclair, the Chairman, Mr. A. H. Rodway, Mr. J. Saxon Mills, Mr. Fleetwood H. Williams, and
Mr. Pearce.

" The dominant factor of the problem," Paton said at a
Birmingham Conference, " is that throughout our country
there is a vast industrial population who, tired with the
day's work, need and demand recreation, refreshment,
and social fellowship. It is a natural, vital, human, social
need which has to be met. The publican meets it and
caters for it in a double sense. He satisfies it in attractive, alluring, and effective ways ; and so long as we leave
the publican alone to satisfy and cater for that need, we
may talk temperance till the crack of doom, and he will
laugh at us."

*Letter to a Friend who is planning to establish a Temper-
ance Public-house in Nottingham*

" These reasons seem to me to compel us to provide
purer and nobler opportunities for social life of working
men and women.

" *First.*—The necessity to conserve and make really
effective for life among the people the best influences
engendered in our elementary schools, day and evening.
We must make these influences richer, nobler, and more
potent, and there are one or two movements on foot for
this end. But when the best and most have been done
at school, let us remember that we have awakened tastes,
created appetites, and formed faculties which require
development, nurture, guidance, and help. I almost pity
the working man in our large towns, living in a tenement
house, with no opportunities of higher social life and of
purer recreation The public-house and the music-hall

are open to him, but what else ?   A responsibility rests upon us to preserve and nourish the better germinant life which begins to open at school—to give it soil and sunshine, stimulus and environment.

" *Secondly.*—Let us remember that it is the evening, social, leisure life of the people which is the most important in forming moral habit and character.   When at work the mind is occupied.   After work, when effort is relaxed, the mind hangs loose, ready to be played on.   It is then open and receptive to all the influences that pour upon it from associates and surroundings.   We have not yet realised the importance of these social hours, the necessity of filling them brightly and recreatively, so as to quicken intelligence and elevate taste.

" *Thirdly.*—The demand for shorter hours of labour, which has already produced such great changes in the day's work, and increased the leisure time of our people, together with the higher wages which have given them more money to spend, has created at once a great peril and a great opportunity.   Doubtless these two causes explain the fact that our Drink Bill mounts up yearly, despite all efforts for the promotion of temperance.

" Having these views, you can well imagine with what deep interest I follow your scheme, which is really a development and expansion of our Social Institutes.   Of course, in a public-house you will have to meet all the various demands of the people in a place of public entertainment, not only in the evening, but throughout the day—catering for their needs in a rational and wholesome way, and seeking to promote the highest kind of social pleasure by music and other entertainments, as well as by the ordinary accompaniments of games, newspapers, etc.   You know, as well as I know, the tendency there is to swift degeneracy when mere pleasure is sought for, and it will therefore be necessary for those who conduct this public-house, as it is for those who conduct Social Institutes, to keep well in view the higher interests of life, and to seek to win those whom they influence to nobler forms of social enjoyment, and to the pursuit of the pleasures connected with some of the highest civic and moral interests of life.

" Keep, as I am sure that you will, this in view.   Then I can only bless your scheme, and plead not only with all

our Christian Churches, but with all right-minded people
in the city to assist you in carrying it out."

To the Rev. Thomas Towers, of Moseley, Birmingham

"*May 6th*, 1905.

" I am specially glad you have written me on the subject which now concerns you.   May I say it very greatly
concerns me, because I have always foreseen a great peril
with regard even to our Social Institutes.   Working Men's
Clubs have, by the hundred, succumbed to the peril which
besets them, and even Temperance Clubs have often
become merely pot-houses without the beer, with no uplifting influences in them.   We have always wished to
discriminate Social Institutes from ordinary Working
Men's Clubs.   I enclose you a letter from Mr. ——.   When
I knew afterwards of the manner in which he was running these social clubs, I told him that they were doomed
to failure, and so it proved.   The letter which I enclose
must be a danger-signal to you and to me.   I send you
that first leaflet, and also my pamphlet on counter-
attractions to the public-house.

" And now let me say—*First*, with regard to Social
Institutes apart from the Church, I hope you will not call
what we designate as a Social Institute a ' Working Men's
Club.'   The idea of mere ' club ' life is not elevating in
England to-day, but rather the opposite.   The phrase
' Social Institute ' means that there is something higher
intended, some educational influence and interest that is
to pervade the whole place.   With regard to such Institutes
when apart from the Church, however, you will see what I
have said in my letter to Bradford, and also in the little
slip in which I contrast Institutes with Clubs.   What I
have said there I think to be exceedingly important, and
I hope you will speak of it very freely and earnestly in
Birmingham, with regard to Social Institutes that are
formed independent of Churches, but which will certainly
lead to no good, and may even prove injurious, unless they
are conducted on the lines laid down in that letter to
Bradford, and in the little slip.

" *Secondly*, when you come to the Church, I think the
matter assumes a different aspect.   I could not but plead

with Mr. Holmes, of Whitefield's Tabernacle, that he must
not allow the Institute to be merely a place of comfort
and pleasure and games ; if so, it will prove a hindrance
to the Church, and will not be helpful, but harmful to the
young men and young women who attend it. I think
I would almost make it a condition, with regard to
every Institute that is connected with a Church, that
every young man and every young woman entering
it and enjoying its privileges should be willing to do
something unselfishly for the good of others. You may
not ask much at first, but I think you ought to insist that
they are to receive these helps and comforts which you
provide on the understanding that they are desirous of
coming under Christian influence and being helped in the
Christian life, and that cannot be unless they are willing
to do something for the good of others unselfishly. It is
for this purpose that I have formed a Young Men's Brigade
of Service, and a Young Women's Brigade of Service. I
send you the enclosed card, which I think will please you,
and I hope you may be able to enrol your young men and
women in corps or companies of this Brigade. We must
keep alive the true ideal of the Christian life as one of
service. It will be a horrible thing if that ideal is degraded
and sinks down into plans of mere recreation and idle
pleasure.

" With regard to billiards, and even card-playing : I
can give no definite opinion. Circumstances must decide.
When I started practically an Institute in Sheffield, at the
beginning of my ministry, the one game I had to forbid
was dominoes, because that was the game associated with
gambling in all the public-houses round about. I think
the rule ought to be to allow no game which is in the
public-houses, and generally in the neighbourhood, associated with gambling. If cards are so associated, I would
not have them ; if they are not—though I never play myself—it seems to me that card-playing is quite as innocent
a game as any other. So with billiards, which I think
is an admirable game, healthy and social ; but here again,
if gambling is associated with it, it must be sternly tabooed.
Surely, however, in an Institute young people should be
discouraged from spending too much time or money at the
billiard-table ; and with regard to all games, they must be
advised and encouraged not to spend too much time on

them so as to neglect higher interests which are both recreative and educative.

" The great matter, however, is that in every Institute associated with the Church there be a fine moral and Christian influence sweeping through the whole place and quickening every one who enters it. If the Church is not prepared to pray for the Institute earnestly in every prayer-meeting, and if some of her members are not prepared to go and mix with the men and bring to them their personal and friendly sympathy, and the contagion of an earnest Christian purpose which is full of loving-kindness, and brings with it glad sunshine, it would be better to close the Institute at once. I know the swift deterioration that comes to mere pleasure-seeking. Let the Institute be associated with the Church, but let that not be a formal association, but a living bond, and let the Church pour into the Institute the pureness and brightness of the saving health of God.

" Let me hear from you again, as to how you proceed in this matter, because I feel that this new activity of our Churches, as institutional Churches, needs to be most carefully guarded, and definitely inspired, or the Church may be dragged down to the world instead of lifting the world to God.

" Ever yours affectionately,
                                        " J. B. Paton."

                                   " March 10th, 1905.

" Dear Mr. Bush,
       " I wish I could be with you at the opening of the Institute. I hope it will be the first of many such Institutes in Wales. The need for them is most clamant, and at the present moment is imperative and urgent. Where are the converts—especially the younger ones—to have social fellowship and intercourse, and the recreation necessary after a heavy day's work, with the opportunities of social reading and bright, attractive, educational classes ? I pray you, as soon as you have started this Institute, to make an appeal far and wide throughout Wales for the formation of Institutes, large and small, throughout the country. The enclosed letter from Mr. Gilbert shows you how they can be established everywhere ; disused and discarded workshops and halls, or disused

haylofts and stables, can be made, by means of some bright drapery, pictures, flags and mottoes, and with splendid illumination of gas or lamps, most attractive Social Institutes.

" There are four things which distinguish the Institute like yours from the ordinary Club, and I hope they will be insisted on everywhere in Wales :

" 1. That not only there be rules against gambling and bad language, but that there be a strong Executive Committee, composed largely of the members themselves, but also of others interested in the social well-being of the neighbourhood and of the Institutes.

" 2. That the Institute shall be somewhat of a neighbourhood guild, in which representatives of all classes may mix on a basis of perfect brotherhood and good fellowship.

" 3. That in every Institute there be some educational influences and interests, popular lectures, classes in recreative and practical subjects. It is a profound mistake and a great evil to think that an Institute is to exist only for games. In every Institute there should be a desire to promote the higher interests of life (as is set forth in the leaflet on Social Institutes which we distribute everywhere), and so tend to brighten and ennoble life, in its personal, social, and civic aspects.

" 4. I hope the Institute will not only provide this social and educational Home for the people, but that it will also evoke and organise a spirit of service on the part of all its members. I hope all the young men and women associated with it will join the Young Men's Brigade of Service and the Young Women's Brigade of Service. I hope you will enrol them at once ; the only condition being that they shall be willing to give one hour a week in unselfish service to others, the kinds of service to be such as they would like to do, and are able to do, and have the opportunity of doing.

" In the hope that your Institute will fulfil this ideal, and that it will be the mother of hundreds of Institutes in Wales, I congratulate you, and pray for the benediction of God upon your Institute."

Extract from Letter

" I am very anxious to secure your co-operation in utilising the playgrounds of the London Board Schools during the summer evenings. The Board has granted the Recreative Evening School Association the use of these play-grounds under certain conditions, as you will see from the enclosed, and we are most anxious now to secure this great boon for the good especially of youths from thirteen or fourteen years of age to eighteen or nineteen in all parts of London. The conditions that will be necessary in order to utilise these play-grounds wisely and healthily for our youths are the following :

" 1. That their play should be somehow organised. It will never do to let them into the play-grounds just to rampage. We must see that they engage in play that requires certain order and discipline, and in which also the enthusiasm and healthy competition of rivalry are brought out. For such purpose, tennis, rounders, tug-of-war, prisoners' base, are good games ; also all forms of drill, whether musical drill (with a drum-and-fife band or cornet), marching-drill, fencing-drill, or club-and-wand drill, or such physical drill as they give volunteers or recruits in the Army to improve their physique and carriage.

" 2. There must be some one associated with the games able to superintend and direct, and by that very association give higher tone to the play of the lads, and to ensure that good order shall be maintained.

" 3. That the youths be encouraged during the summer months to attend the evening-schools or Social Institute in the following winter.

" If you could in any way assist us to get boys' clubs or the upper classes of Sunday-schools into these playgrounds instead of the streets for play of this kind, and if you could assist us in getting such superintendence, we should be delighted to apply for play-grounds and get them for the use of such clubs and schools. May I add that I think it would be well if one room in the school were occasionally used for training the drum-and-fife band, or for song, or for some illustrated lecture upon some subject interesting to boys, *e.g.* ' What may be seen on a Summer Holiday in Epping Forest,' or any talk, in fact, which would prepare for a Saturday half-holiday ramble. Summer-time is now close upon us, and if you could assist in this matter at once I should be greatly obliged to you.

" I think each youth should pay some small charge, weekly or otherwise, for his right to enter the play-ground and take part in the play organised there. This would cover the expenses involved, and will ensure the right sort of young people making use of the play-ground. A very small charge would suffice, if there were a good number in attendance."

But Paton held that there were many different lines on which the problem of the public-house should be attacked. He was himself in favour of the Local Veto plan, but, pending the passing of any measure of reform, he felt that much could be done by securing the vigilant and vigorous administration of the licensing laws as they stood.

" This should appeal to the very instinct of the English people," he urged; " they are surely a law-abiding folk. No laws on the statute-book affect so intimately and deeply the welfare of the community as do the liquor laws—physically, economically, and morally—and no laws are administered with such laxity, indifference, and feebleness. If these laws were administered with scrupulous fidelity and with thorough efficiency, a large proportion, perhaps half, the evils which devastate the country arising from the abuse of alcoholic drinks would at once be swept away. I don't blame those who hold office for the laxity of administration; I blame myself. I blame the high-minded men of the community for not giving to those called to undertake such responsible office the public support by which alone the laws can be effectively administered."

It was this feeling which led to the formation, in April 1896, of the Licensing Laws Information Bureau, of which Paton was the first President, and Mr. Chas. L. Rothera, the Borough Coroner of Nottingham, was Secretary and Solicitor. The national conscience had been deeply stirred on the question of the drink traffic. The continued introduction into Parliament of new measures for its regulation and control during the preceding five years proved that a strong determination had grown up in the public mind to find some relief from the incubus of the excessive number of licensed premises and the perpetual trouble that arose therefrom. This trouble was considerably enhanced by the conversion of many of the

15

leading breweries into limited companies, and the growth
of the " tied-house " system, under which a large number
of licensed premises were accumulated in the hands of
one business firm whose sole object was to manufacture
and sell strong drink.   The decision of the House of
Lords and other judicial authorities in such leading cases
as Sharpe *v.* Wakefield, Regina *v.* Justices of Miskin Higher,
Regina *v.* Rymer, had demonstrated the true position of
the justices towards the licence-holder, and of the licence-
holder towards the general public; but experience proved
that the attention of the licensing justices needed constantly to be recalled to these guiding principles.   The
licensing laws were technical and complicated, and the
licensing justices themselves, as well as social workers
in general, needed information and advice.   The result
of ignorance, apathy, and lack of organisation was that
the licensing laws, designed to promote public welfare,
were being largely converted into instruments for
promoting private profit and corresponding public injury.
     Paton felt that if the existing licensing laws could be
firmly and honestly enforced, if the true purpose of a
licence, viz. to enable the holder to supply the reasonable
needs of a district in such a way as to inflict the least
possible evil upon the community, rather than to sell as
much beer as he could for the benefit of the brewery
company who owned the house, could be strongly impressed
on the licensing justices; if the power possessed by the
justices to refuse a licence could be so used as to enable
them to insist on such structural arrangements in licensed
property as would ensure complete police supervision and
prevent secrecy; if they could be brought to consider
the needs of the locality as the first question in determining the grant and renewal of licences; if they would
rigorously refuse to renew licences to houses with a bad
record; if they would seriously consider the malpractices
connected with the tied-house system which was working
so disastrously; then, even under the existing licensing
laws, great social improvement could be effected at once.
In many places up and down the country citizens were
banding themselves together to this end, nowhere more
successfully than in Liverpool.   In order that such work
might be thoroughly effective, it needed to be systematised,
to be conducted intelligently, persistently, and with exact

knowledge of the law. The Licensing Laws Information Bureau was formed at a Conference held in Nottingham on April 9th and 10th, 1896. Its object was to collect and disseminate information by means of pamphlets, leaflets, and letters to the press, to give advice to persons or societies seeking to secure the effective administration of the licensing laws in their own localities, and to arouse and inform public opinion throughout the country by means of Conferences.

For five years Paton remained the President of the Bureau. Working in close association with Mr. Rothera, he did much to stir up feeling throughout the country, and Mr. Rothera's evidence before the Royal Commission on Licensing, on November 4th, 1896, led to increased vigilance on the part of Nottingham citizens as to the administration of the laws in their own borough, and a corresponding increase of strictness on the part of the Watch Committee and licensing justices.

Extract from a letter to Mr. W. S. Caine, M.P.

" I have taken for some years a great interest in the Gothenburg plan. Mr. Chamberlain's method of adapting that plan to this country by making the municipalities themselves the owners and managers of public-houses I thought extremely faulty, and opposed to the spirit of the plan in Sweden, and still more in Norway. On the other hand, the benefits of this method are most striking and indeed incalculable, for in some few years, I believe from five to seventeen, drunkenness in Sweden, the most drunken country in the world, has been reduced one-half. As a great object-lesson, that commands our serious attention. What I have ventured to suggest to my temperance friends, and have talked over in conference with my friend Mr. Bunting, editor of the " Contemporary," is this : that we should have three planks in the Local Option platform—I. As to whether there be any public-houses or not in a district. II. If there be any public-houses what shall be the number—a limit having been fixed by statute. III. Whether, if public-houses in any number are allowed, whether (a) they shall be conducted on the present plan by which a huge monopoly is given

without any counterbalancing good to a few private individuals, who, by the very circumstances of their position,
are tempted in every way to encourage the drinking
habits of the people, to ensure as large a consumption of
alcoholic drinks as possible without any regard to the
public good, and also, it may be, to adulterate their drinks
or to use kinds of drinks that are most deleterious ; or (b)
whether the houses allowed shall be given over to the
management of a company that will work them on the
Gothenburg plan.   The principles of this plan are doubtless well known to you, but I enclose a restatement of
them by me when we formed here a little Gothenburg
Company to manage the refreshment-rooms connected
with the Castle Museum.   In this case the result been has
admirable ; cases of drunkenness that had not been
uncommon before are never heard of now.   I am perfectly
confident that if this other third clause was added to the
Local Option Bill it would win the greatest favour
for it in many places where it is now somewhat distrusted
on even opposed, and that in the working of the Act—if the
Bill were carried—a result as beneficial to this country as
the results have proved in Sweden would be ensured."

    Mr. T. A. Leonard, the old student who ran the first
Social Institute, had taken a pastorate at Colne, a manufacturing town on the borders of Lancashire and Yorkshire.
There he came into contact with the same problem of
recreation under another form.   Every year there were the
holiday " Wakes " : the mills shut down, all business was
suspended, and the operatives, who had been saving up
their money in holiday clubs, drew out their savings and
went off for a week's enjoyment.   But in all too many
cases the holiday week did more harm than good.   They
joined the crowds of Blackpool or " the island," for the
difference between the rich man and the poor in the matter
of holidays is that the rich man seeks the solitude and
avoids his species, while the poor man seems to gravitate
by choice to the most crowded place he can find.   The
thoughtless spending of money, the unspeakable inanity
of the amusements, the unhealthy overcrowding in lodging-
houses, the utter unrestraint of gaiety, all tended to produce
deteriorative effects on character.   The whole influence of

a year's pastoral work was not infrequently blotted out by a week of " holiday," falsely so called.

Mr. Leonard set himself to show a more excellent way. It was clear that few of the young folk had a rational idea of enjoyment or knew how to get the best out of a holiday. He started a rambling-club, and took his lads and lasses out on long tramps on Saturday afternoons. The next thing was to take his young fellows out for the holiday week, first to Lakeland, then to North Wales. There, in long day-tramps over the hills and moors many a young fellow learned for the first time the real wholesome pleasure of a mountain holiday, and found that such a holiday was not only healthier, but less expensive than the usual " Black-pool bust." There were quiet services, too, on Sunday afternoons amid the heather under the clear sky. Some-how religion there had a different " feel " about it, full of the freshness of joy and fellowship, far more gladsome than that of the heavy, stagnant atmosphere of church.

It was not long before Mr. Leonard's old Principal got to hear of the new move, for old students always knew it would gladden his heart to hear of a new channel that had opened for the grace of Christ. At once he saw a new potentiality. " Why not do this for thousands ? " he said, and at once he set Mr. Leonard to work out a larger scheme which should open up holidays of this kind to the P.S.A.s and Working Men's Bible Classes throughout the North of England.

" We have gone infinitely wrong," he said, " in thinking that the devil has all the bright things in the world. The whole lives of men must be redeemed. We will give them such a holiday as they never dreamed of."

The National Home Reading Union was called in to give its name and its help, and it was arranged to open two holiday centres during the month of August 1892, one at Ambleside and the other at Keswick. There were four parties of men and women, each staying a week. Half of the party started the week at Ambleside and the other half at Keswick, with long walks and climbs daily over the fells. On the Wednesday both parties climbed Hel-vellyn and met on the summit. Then the Keswick party descended to occupy the quarters at Ambleside, and the

Ambleside party went down to Keswick, so that each saw
something of both ends of the Lake district.   The luggage
was sent round on a cart.   With each party there was a
Host and Hostess and a lecturer, usually some University
or professional man, who was able to chat on the
literary associations of the country, or interest folk in
the wayside flowers and rocks.   The idea from the first
was not to run the holidays for one social class only, but
that all should meet on the wide basis of the holiday
comradeship, Churchmen and Nonconformists, socialists
and individualists, mill-hands and mill-owners, those who
had graduated in the University and those who had
graduated in the office or the shop, joining in the same
games and the same songs, sharing the same joys and
lessons in " God's great out-of-doors."   It was to be a
Toynbee Hall in the Open.   From the first no distinction
was made between the sexes.

The cordial welcome and assistance of local friends
contributed in no small measure to the initial success of
the holidays.   Canon Rawnsley, at Crosthwaite, gave each
party week by week a talk on the literary and historical
associations of Lakeland, which set many a young fellow
on to reading Ruskin and Wordsworth.   The Rector of
Grasmere was no less hospitable, and local friends at both
centres provided a gentleman to act as guide for each
mountain expedition.

From the first, too, there was the thought of others.

> " The best things which any mortal hath
> Are those which every mortal shares."

It was on the Co-operative Holidays that we first learned
and loved Miss Lucy Larcom's hymn, and from the first
Sunday afternoon onwards at every service there has been
a collection to enable those to share in the holiday who
otherwise would have had none.   At first the money was
all given to the Children's Holidays Funds in the large
industrial cities, but later on, as the Association acquired
Guest-houses of its own, it sought out those who lay outside
the beat of ordinary philanthropies and were not provided
for by any existing agency—tired mothers, convalescent
workmen, washerwomen and weary women-workers of
many sorts.   These were entertained by the Association
under its own roof free.

A Co-operative Holiday Association was formed with Paton for President and Mr. T. A. Leonard as Secretary. It grew rapidly from the first. Its rapid development gave its President and Secretary many difficult problems to solve, and no precedent was to be found in the experience of other societies. But the vitality of the movement brought it through triumphantly. It is now a registered Company, and caters for upwards of twenty thousand guests every year. The able administration of Mr. Drummond Fraser, its Honorary Treasurer, has so firmly established its financial basis that it has, every year, over half a dozen centres in England, one or more in Wales, Scotland, and Ireland, and another in the Isle of Man. It has extended its operations to foreign parts, and provides cheap educational holidays in Switzerland, Brittany, and Germany. In Germany especially it has initiated a work of international significance. At a time when there have been many conferences deploring the unfriendly relations between the two countries, it has been at work solving the problem of Brotherhood on the only practicable lines, and the genial friends who did so much for the English parties at Frankfort-on-the-Main have caught the " holiday spirit," and initiated a Co-operative Holiday movement of their own.

No better instance than this could be given to exemplify Paton's rare gift of discovering the potentialities of both men and movements. He laid his hand upon his old student and said :

" God has shown you this line of work for Him ; He has specially fitted you with the gift to fulfil it. It is the redeeming of the people's holiday from all that makes for sin and degradation of life. Go in and do it in His Name who called you to it."

There was one hallowed experience which gave the Co-operative Holidays a place very near his heart. In August 1894, the third holiday season, his third son, William P. Paton, had given a week of his short holiday to act as companion-guide to the party at Barmouth, along with Percival Gray, son of Dr. Gray, of Oxford, an old Rugby boy, who was in his first year at New College, Oxford. The two young guides took a boating-party up

the Mawddach estuary on the evening of August 1st, 1894.
On returning, the larger boat was swamped by a huge
tidal wave, and both the leaders were drowned in their
efforts to save life.   It was the first break in the happy
family circle at Nottingham.   " Willy " Paton, as he was
called on the Liverpool flags, was one whose pure chivalrous
character and gentle unselfishness impressed even those
who thought little of anything except the price of cotton.
Though he was only a salesman in a cotton firm, and
twenty-seven years of age, he had for years made a practice
of bringing out slum children from Liverpool, three at a
time, to stay with him in his lodgings at the seaside.   It
was what one friend called " Christ's hospitality," not done
by deputy, or by means of an institution.   Every Wednesday morning in summer-time he was up at six, and went
off on his bicycle to gather wild-flowers to send in to the
old women in the sewing-room at the workhouse.   These
things were typical of a life full of thoughtfulness for others
and the spirit of service.   " His unselfish love and fear-
lessness," writes one who knew him well, " will be ever
the one bright spot in the remembrance of as black
a hell of suffering as can well come to a human home."
The loss of such a life so suddenly cut off was hard to
bear, but it seemed to bring with it a call to a higher,
holier consecration, to a new and gracious service.   The
insurance money, which amounted to £1,000, was offered
to the Convalescent Home at West Kirby, and accepted
by the committee, who gave to their new extension the
name of the " W. P. Paton Wing."   Other money which
was given by the family and relatives as a token of
thanksgiving to God for His great and precious gift, was
devoted to the erection of a new building on the Lingfield
Colony.

A LETTER OF SYMPATHY
To Mrs. Golightly

"*August 9th*, 1894.

   " I feel that, before returning to my ordinary life and
duties, after the dark and awful experience of the last
few days, I must beg you to let me breathe into your
heart some of the great and exceeding comfort that God
has poured into our broken hearts.   The mystery indeed
of that dreadful night remains inscrutable, so bright and

harmonious a party swept from us in a great darkness ; but our God is in the darkness as in the light, and if He called His own thus suddenly and together to Himself, let us not mourn, for we are confident our Father loveth His own with a love infinitely greater than even that of the parent's heart which He has given us.

" I like to think that they entered the calm, pure brightness of the eternal home together. They had formed happy associations with each other during the last week, and in death they were not divided. It may touch your heart with some sacred joy to know that Mr. Gray, who was with my son and your daughter that week, was one of the noblest, most chivalrous young men of our time, whose young life had been consecrated to most unselfish labour among the young and the poor ; and my son, too, has a beautiful record of a pure, devoted life, living much for others, especially the young, and sick and poor. Thus our children went home to the Father's House with brave and knightly companions, servants of Christ. Had not the Father a right to their young lives ? Had He not a Father's love for them, of which our longing is a poor, faint echo ? He wished His children home that night, and their lives will now bloom and fruiten in a purer, happier atmosphere than this. Our Father's service there will be to them perfect freedom and delight. Not for them, then, let us mourn.

" They have made it easier, too, for us to die now. I think to go and meet again my boy will be no hard thing, but to be worthy of our own beloved when we meet them, to be faithful unto death, so that they may give us blessing and glad welcome with their Lord—that, surely, shall be now our constant prayer and our unfailing purpose We have been baptized in our great common sorrow; shall we not also now be helpers of each other's joy in serving our Lord, and blessing the lives of others for His sake ? If I can at any time be your companion in the kingdom and patience of the Lord, as I am now your companion in tribulation, let me, by the memory of that night in which our children went home together, ask you to say so to me, and believe me,

" Ever with tender and heartfelt sympathy, yours."

Every year in January a Conference was held at which

representatives appointed officers and discussed the affairs of the Association. The President's Annual messages set the note high and kept the workers in good heart. They made all feel that the work was worth doing and claimed the best one had to give. One such message sent to a Conference he could not attend is appended :

" It has been pleasant to read the report which you are to present to the Conference, to mark the steady progress of the C.H.A. in every department, and the vigilant care with which its high aims and wise methods are sedulously maintained.

" I have been specially gratified to observe that, whilst our guests enjoy on their holiday healthy physical exercise, vivid intellectual interests, and a happy social fellowship, they also receive encouragement and help to continue throughout the year the same pleasures which brightened their holiday.

" In proof of this I note the numerous Rambling Clubs and the Social Reunions of our members, and also the new journal, with its attractive title, ' Comradeship,' which embodies the very soul of our movement, and which enables our members to talk in their Social Reading Circles on the social questions of our time, and on the beauties of nature and literature, just as they did in their holiday excursions or their social readings in our Holiday Homes.

" Thus the holiday spirit, with its mental uplift and refreshment, is made luminously to pervade the whole year, and our national life is being enriched thereby.

" Being so honoured by you in holding the office of your President, I must not only congratulate but thank you for the splendid work that has been achieved, and the glowing prospects that shine on us in the future. But again I must exhort you to remember the high price that will need to be paid for our success in the future, as in the past. I know no movement in our time fraught with nobler possibilities, but also I know of none that may more swiftly degenerate. The very height and splendour of our aims impose upon all of us the greater responsibility in securing their fulfilment. I know that you all realise this with me, and therefore I would in one final word pledge you all, as I pledge myself, that we will do our utmost, with wise and zealous vigilance, to make the C.H.A. more than ever a joy and an inspiration to all its members."

CHAPTER XIV

THE LAND PROBLEM

"Much food is in the tillage of the poor, but there is that is destroyed for want of judgment."—*Proverbs.*

"Though the plough has a silver share, the spade has a golden edge."—*Italian Proverb.*

"The wealth of a country does not consist in the number or exchangeable value of its agricultural or manufactured or artistic products, so much as in the strength and intelligence and virtue of the men and women whom it rears."—JOHN BROWN PATON.

THE summers of 1886 and 1887 he spent at Newtonmore, in Strathspey. There he had much loving intercourse with Dr. MacLaren, of Manchester, and Dr. Martineau, who spent a large portion of the summer every year at Aviemore, on the borders of Rothiemurchus' "forest primeval." In companionship with such congenial spirits he found a quickening of spirit, which made these holidays in the Eastern Highlands memorable seasons of refreshing from the presence of the Lord. But he was saddened by what he saw of the Highland crofters. Their condition seemed to be gravitating steadily to the worse, and the country-side, which had reared some of Britain's best soldiers, was gradually becoming a desert. Emigration seemed to be the only remedy of which any one thought, and emigration seemed to him to be a confession of failure and a counsel of despair. His whole soul revolted against such a lame and impotent conclusion.

He went much among the people and talked with them. As the result of his inquiries, he found that the old cottage industries had been gradually ousted by the cheap manufactured articles, and no other form of remunerative occupation had taken their place. Life had thus lost the happiness and hopefulness that come from useful occupation, and the margin of subsistence was growing steadily more slender. He found, too, that no crofter had any

chance of getting a piece of land for his own and working
his way upwards to a position of independence. The lad
who carried a marshal's baton in his knapsack flung out
into the new countries over-seas in order to find his career.
Those who remained behind were growing listless and
losing hope.

Sooner or later every reformer, at whatever point of the
compass he starts, is driven back upon the central problems
of education and the land. The question of the land forces
itself upon the attention of every thinking man who cares
for his country's welfare ; it forced itself more especially
on Paton's attention because his old students in the
village Churches were constantly confronted with the
evils consequent on the decay of our rural population, because everywhere on continental travel he had seen such
a different and more hopeful state of things, because his
friends, Professor Nasse, of Bonn, Professor Emile de
Laveleye, and Richard Heath had given special study to
this question and had written about it, because the grim
spectre of unemployment was making him ask, " What is
the cause of this evil, and where must we look for a cure ? "
because, finally, through his own veins there flowed the
peasant blood.

Before leaving Scotland in 1886 he visited the International Exhibition at Edinburgh, and through the Irish
stall got into touch with the Countess of Aberdeen, Mrs.
Ernest Hart, and others who were fostering home industries
among the cottagers of Donegal and other parts of Ireland.
This work was confined to the women, but the Hon. Horace
Plunkett was working at the same problem from the men's
side, and laying the foundation of the Agricultural Organisation Society, which was to do so much for the economic
regeneration of rural Ireland. Paton was also in touch
with Mr. Alfred Harris, of Kirby Lonsdale, and Mr. James
Baker, of Clifton, who had made special study of village
industries and technical training in Würtemberg, Switzerland, Bohemia, and other foreign countries. He was
convinced that the problem of Ireland was at bottom
economic rather than political, and that the problem of the
Highland crofters was very similar to it. He set to work,
therefore, to bring the light of foreign experience to bear
upon these questions. By means of the " Contemporary
Review " and the leading Scottish newspapers he was

LINGFIELD: THE FARM, AND THE COLONISTS AT WORK.

informing the public mind, and at the same time, with the
help specially of Mr. Alfred Harris, he was pressing the
matter upon the Royal Commission on Technical Education, and drawing up a lengthy Memorandum [1] to Government, showing in detail how the requisite training might
be given by means of village schools and peripatetic
teachers, and how the industries might be set on foot.

In 1886 and the two following years his letters to various
friends show that he was turning this subject over in his
mind, reading about it, and making many inquiries, especially about the experiences of Danish cultivators, who
had to contend with climatic and agricultural conditions
very similar to our own.   The English yeomen, the men
who won Agincourt and repelled the Armada, had practically become extinct.   The agricultural labourers had
declined from 1,253,800 in 1851 to 780,700 in 1891.   During
that period of forty years the urban population had increased by one-half, the agricultural population had de-
creased by one-third.   The robust, sturdy stock of the
country-side was becoming less and less ; a neurotic and
decadent and unstable generation was being reared in the
unhealthy slums of the great cities, and the fibre of the
race seemed to be doomed unless some measures were
taken to turn the tide of townward migration which de-
pleted the country-side.   Slumdom and the decay of
agriculture were only two different aspects of the same fact.

What made the outlook more depressing was the fact that
the town seemed to attract all the more vigorous and
capable of the youth.   " It is now common," said Mr.
Rider Haggard, " for only the dullards, the vicious or the
wastrels to stay upon the land, because they are unfitted
for any other life."   The country afforded no prospect for
a lad of parts who had laudable ambition to get on.   In the
town there was a chance of rising.   In the country, there
was no upward opening for ability and vigour.   The
outlook of the farm labourer was utterly blank—drudgery
and dependence till the end of his working days, and,
after that, the workhouse.   True, the new County Councils
were providing chances for learning, but what was the
use ?   Why take the trouble ?   There was no incentive for
improvement to the man who had no land of his own, and
no chance of getting any.   He had no stake in the country.

[1] Reprinted in Inner Mission Pamphlets, First Series, No. 11.

But Paton saw that, if the need was great, so also was the opportunity. Land was cheap. Large farms did not pay, but the evidence given before the Royal Commissioners pointed unerringly to the conclusion that the small cultivators could succeed where large cultivators failed. Intensive cultivation showed that a family could earn a comfortable livelihood on a holding of from six to ten acres. Denmark showed that even dairy-farming could be carried on to a large extent from the products of arable land on a small holding. Co-operation was in the air; co-operative purchasing, co-operative production, co-operative insurance, co-operative marketing made possible for the small man what hitherto had been possible only for the capitalist. Education of a practical kind opened the door for new development. Subsidiary industries like poultry-keeping, bee-keeping and pig-feeding were best carried on by the small holder whose wife and children gave the necessary personal supervision. Cottage industries must be revived.

" It is computed that a man can only work upon the land some 240 days in the year, and there are long winter evenings when he is perforce idle. It is, therefore, a great advantage to have an industry that will occupy those vacant days and hours. These industries further unite together the whole family, as all are able to take part in them."

Such home industries must perforce be art industries. The cottage cannot compete with the steam-loom in the production of large quantities. But therein lay an advantage. Artistic work would call out the higher gift, confer on the workers a certain refinement and sense of beauty, it would give them that joy in the work of their hands which the factory could not give. Was it not absurd that the English manufacturer should be sending his linen and calico goods, his muslin and lawn, over to Switzerland to be embroidered by Swiss peasants in their mountain-chalets, and paying the import duty upon the goods as they entered Switzerland, when all the while there were idle fingers at home itching for work ?

" Hear this, ye crones of Connaught, sitting in the ingle

with folded arms, and think what a ha'porth of iron between your fingers might do for the family, and ' caleying ' going on all the same."

The result was that in August 1893 he founded the English Land Colonisation Society. Several open-minded landowners had tried the experiment of breaking up large estates into small holdings, one of the most successful of these being that of Major R. Poore at Winterslow. Why should not many landowners do the same as Major Poore ? Or, supposing landowners were not forthcoming, why should not enterprising land-labourers club together for the same purpose and work out their own salvation ? What was wanted was a central organisation to investigate the causes of the evil, to show by means of broadcast information how the number of people earning their living by means of agriculture might be multiplied, to organise the various departments of co-operative work necessary for the success of small holdings, to provide help and advice to landowners, Boards of Guardians, and others in the formation of Colonies and Training-farms, to give all assistance to any groups of suitable persons who came forward to form a colony, and place the best experience available at the disposal of all. Rural industries were not forgotten, and every effort was to be made in connection with the County Council Technical Classes to foster minor arts and cottage industries.

The aims and methods of the Society were set forth at a Conference of the Poor Law Guardians of East Anglia in March 1894, and a " ticket system " for tramps was introduced throughout the eastern counties as the first step towards the introduction of farm-labour colonies on the German model.

The Local Government Board was approached and gave their consent to Boards of Guardians sending able-bodied paupers to be employed on farms, the Guardians paying a grant towards maintenance for each man. Under this sanction the Camberwell and West Ham Guardians began drafting men to the Salvation Army Colony at Hadleigh, and the Whitechapel Board sent men to the training colony established by Mr. Walter Hazell, M.P. The Society was much in request to give advice in the formation of such colonies and training-farms, also as to market gardening, intensive cultivation, and spade husbandry.

The basis of the policy advocated was co-operation. Small cultivators had failed in the past because they had worked in isolation, but if they would combine in small groups, purchasing their seeds, manure, and other requisites in common, consuming the main part of their produce themselves, and disposing of the remainder collectively, there was good hope of success. But the unit of responsibility was to be small. The large group did away with the free exercise of the mind and the judgment; it abolished that sense of mutual responsibility which is the life of all healthy communities. The principle of the old Anglo-Saxon frank-pledge was the principle by which the Society sought to bring new hope to the English agricultural labourer. Given the smaller unit with the spirit of co-operation and inter-responsibility, the upward grouping of the smaller units into larger ones was safe and hopeful. On this basis model rules were drawn up and published. The system was put into operation at Moat Farm, Alburgh, in Norfolk, which was offered for the purpose by Mr. Foard Harris. The farm was of the average value of £20 per acre. It was offered to a committee of small occupiers at an annual rental of 40s. per acre, payable for a term of thirteen years, or 32s. per acre payable for a term of eighteen years. At the end of such term, payment was to cease entirely, and the co-operative society of occupiers received the conveyance of the freehold by copyright. Any surplus left in the hands of the committee after meeting all costs was to belong to the general body of tenants and to be dealt with as they decided. There was security of tenure (which was copyhold) and every incentive to the occupier to spend his capital upon his holding, both in building and in improving the land, for he had secured a claim to the title and had the certainty that he would in no case be deprived of the value of these improvements. Had he found the whole of the purchase-money to begin with, he would have had far less capital to expend in this way. Had he left part of the purchase-money on mortgage, any failure to pay the principal and interest due on call would have led to the forfeiture of the holding and all he had put into it.

There were two lions in the way—one was want of

LINGFIELD: A GROUP OF COLONISTS, WITH THE HOUSE FATHER AND MOTHER.

capital, the other lack of skill. The question of capital led Paton to a study of the system of agricultural banks on the Continent, and particularly the Luzzati banks of Italy and the Wollamberg and the Raffeisen banks of Germany, with their unlimited liability. Here, adapted to modern economic conditions, was the old system of mutual frank-pledge, working with the most evident beneficial results to personal character. "The co-operative bank," said a German pastor to him, "has had more influence on the moral life of this village community than all the Church can do." This led to the foundation in 1899 of the Agricultural Banks Association, which worked from the first in closest alliance with the English Land Colonisation Society, after seven years had the same secretary, the late Mr. Henry C. Devine, and was ultimately merged in it.

The aim of these banks was, by means of combination, to secure to poorer folk the benefits of credit which rich people enjoy ; by means of credit they would be enabled to take up land of their own, and by spade-culture secure the benefits of their own industry. By participating from the first in the management of these banks, and learning how to handle affairs by joint co-operation and fend for themselves, it was hoped that the English country-side would work out its own economic salvation, and, what was even more important, restore that sturdy independence of character which has meant so much to the religion and history of the English people in the past.

When the Bank Association started its work it was soon found that there was as much need and scope for its work in the towns as in the country. The unconscionable usury of the money-lender had not at that time been checked by law. The banks offered means of counteracting the money-lender and financing small industries. This led to close co-operation with the Toynbee Bank Association. A joint meeting was held at the Westminster Palace Hotel on July 18th, 1899. Ultimately the secretary, Mr. H. C. Devine, was appointed as assistant to Mr. Nugent Harris, of the Agricultural Organisation Society, and the rural side of his work was merged in that of the Society, which, in its turn, was in 1912 merged in the Development Commission and became part of the Government administrative work.

16

" What struck me about the Doctor," says Mr. Devine,
" was his knowledge of economics, and his knowledge of
human nature. He knew exactly how far to trust the
good-will, the perseverance, the capacity of each individual, and he knew how to get full measure out of each."

The second lion in the way was the lack of skill. The
man who had fallen out of employment in industry could
not at once be drafted on to the land ; if that were done,
failure was inevitable. And yet the obvious line of
solution lay in putting the unemployed workman on the
unemployed land. How was it to be done ? The answer
was, the land colony.

No feature of the unemployed problem distressed him
so much as the swift deterioration of character in the
man who fell out of work. The workhouse treatment of
such men, instead of helping them seemed to help to drag
them down. There was the corrupting companionship of
the casual ward ; there was the demoralising test-work
of oakum-picking and stone-breaking. How much better
in every way was work on the soil ! It was productive,
it was health-giving ; it afforded scope for all kinds of
labour, skilled and unskilled ; it was not over-stocked like
other industries ; it did not put a man in competition
with others ; it was as full of interest to the spirit as of
healthfulness to the body.

" It is a sad thing that there are men who want work
and cannot get it, but it is a greater evil when men like
our able-bodied out-of-works, who have some honourable
feeling of independence, and some desire to work, should
be put to a kind of work that kills all such desire, that
makes work loathsome, and dulls and degrades the spirit
of the worker. We should rather seek to provide them
with work that will invigorate and interest them, and
give them a genuine love of work. Now, labour on the
land will do this. It is full of variety. It thus contrasts
agreeably with the picking of oakum or the breaking of
stones—the labour now frequently enforced as a test of
destitution. It awakens and stimulates the faculties of
the mind and exercises all the powers of the body, while
the very changes from day to day required in the treatment of the soil, and observed in the growth of plants,

give pleasure and inspire interest. Accordingly, labour of this kind may be attractive instead of repellent, and may be useful in rousing dormant or laggard energies in the labourer."

The only question was how to get this demonstrated in such a practical way that Boards of Guardians would be willing to take up the idea and apply it on a national scale. "The things that are for thee gravitate towards thee," said Emerson; and the thing that came to him at this time, by this law of spiritual gravitation, was a copy of Miss Julie Sutter's book, "A Colony of Mercy." This remarkable book gives an account of the colony for epileptics and unemployed established by Pastor von Bodelschwingh at Bielefeld, in Westphalia. It is a simple and straightforward narrative, but it was instinct with a Gospel message for the precise problem which confronted Great Britain at that time. The thing had been done in Germany ; therefore the thing could be done in England ; therefore it must be done. This was the irresistible logic of the book to one who had taken on his heart the burden of his workless countrymen.

Most opportune for the same purpose was Mr. Harold E. Moore's book on "Back to the Land," which discussed the training necessary for men unskilled in rural work and the conditions necessary for success in settlement on the land. This book attracted a great deal of attention in the Press and brought prominently before the mind of the public the idea of home colonisation and its feasibility.

To Mr. Alfred Harris

"1887.

" The three principal points are :

" 1. That labourers should be planted in colonies, so that the social life shall be cultivated amongst them, and that educational advantages, with some finer elements of recreation, may be possible to them. Also that they may be taught and helped to co-operate wherever co-operation will make their work more effectual.

" 2. That there shall be persons interested in them who shall give them all kinds of help apart from almsgiving— that will inform their industry with practical intelligence and aid them in their combinations and in every other way. I don't think it can be of much good, or is right, simply to settle the agricultural labourer on a piece of land without surrounding him by such practical sympathy and help.

" 3. To give the hope of ownership so as to incite to industry, and give the sense of security and permanence in their home, and the conditions for development of family life and all the higher, purer morale that grows with it. This advantage would be partly assured under a system of tenancy, if there was security of tenure, and if incentive to industry were given by assuring to tenants that the full value of all improvements would be given to them.

" These three principles being fixed, the greatest amount of elasticity will be allowed in the application, e.g. in some districts a twenty-acre farm will be better in poorer soil and a house might be used by two small farmers in common—we shall train them as far as possible to combine —and with poorer soil the carriage of manure is an all-important matter. In other districts a four-acre farm for market gardening will be best. In others a ten-acre with a certain proportion for grass and the rest to be worked by the spade. You will see, too, that we look much to the minor industries and to the house industries of the family. . . .

" We can do little till we have given greater educational advantages of a practical and sensible kind to our agricultural labourers. At present their children leave school at ten, or soon after, and the little they learnt—having no relevancy to their life-work—is soon forgotten, or gives a distaste for rough farmwork, which sends them (other causes combining) into our towns. Yet they must begin their work when young in order to earn a little, and to be initiated early in farm-work. At present the half-time system is quite inapplicable to such children, because, when employed, they must be out for the whole day ; but there are months in the year when many of them are not required. They can do little, or nothing, and so, having left school, loaf idly about at that early age, to their great hurt and to the vexation of their parents and others. Well, I venture to suggest that we adopt a half-time system which prevails in America and Switzerland, and formerly was universal in Scotland, viz. a half-year instead of a half-day system—a five months' attendance would suffice to give the number of attendances required.

LINGFIELD : AT WORK IN THE FIELDS.

244]

If, then, the child was thus a half-timer from ten till thirteen or fourteen, he would be ready to enter and profit by the Continuation School, in which the subjects taught would chiefly bear upon his life-work, giving him intelligence and the higher interest in his work that can only come from such intelligence."

To Mr. Harold Moore

" I read Lady Verney's pamphlets, and, when one of the editors of the ' Contemporary,' I had the pleasure of meeting her, and of publishing her articles on the ' French Peasant.' Like you, I abhor the thought of establishing a peasantry of that order in England. But will you kindly read carefully what I send you, and you will see that we have no Freeholders, that there is communal ownership, and that ownership is only a copyhold ownership—an ownership which gives security and united permanence of tenure, but prevents subdivision and insists upon the co-operation not only in the purchase and sale of commodities, etc., but also in the social life of the colony, or commune ?

To me there are three factors that will alone solve the problem which so deeply concerns us both, namely, security of tenure, with land sufficient to give a comfortable living ; co-operation of every kind ; and education. Simply to put people on the land to dig and starve and die after a sordid existence, is a pitiful thought, but to settle people on the land under the most healthy, economic, and social conditions, where they will have all the intelligence, stimulus, and the recreations of the best town-life, with the simplicity and healthy conditions of their country-life, and with organised home industries, which we must organise in the same way as they have been organised in Würtemberg—will restore to us again what will be the noblest type of family life and of English manhood that I can well conceive of. With this communal ownership, I should not at all object to the State being the landlord, under whom the copyhold and the tenure is held, but a State landlord, who should deal directly, might be the very hardest of all landlords, and would increase a bureaucratic administration, which I do not think the best. I want a decentralised, communal life, with its own local administration."

CHAPTER XV

THE COLONY OF MERCY

" Can I see another's woe
  And not be in sorrow too ?
Can I see another's grief
  And not seek for kind relief ? "

W. BLAKE.

" Christ hath fenced in this piece of ground,
  And made a garden there for those
Who want herbs for their wound."

GEORGE HERBERT.

" Love is the one motive power. The question is, Have you a sufficiency of it ? "

PASTOR V. BODELSCHWINGH.

THE stirring pages of " A Colony of Mercy, or Social Christianity at Work," by Julie Sutter, published in the spring of 1893 ; in other words, the account of the great work carried on at Bethel in Westphalia, proved the spirit-force which led to the formation of the National Union of Christian Social Service and Lingfield Colony. It came about in this wise : The Rev. J. F. B. Tinling, M.A., then Minister of the City Road Congregational Church, and some few kindred spirits, who were waiting like Simeon for the consolation of Israel, had made a habit of meeting together for prayer from time to time. " A Colony of Mercy " came to them as a guiding light in answer to their prayer. Their eyes were opened. Their hearts were humbled to think of Christian England being so far behind the sister country as revealed by that book. Mr. Tinling with his friend, the Rev. F. B. Meyer, went to see Miss Sutter, and got her consent to come and address a conference of Free Church ministers. In answer to a widespread invitation a large company of ministers met at Christ Church, Westminster Bridge Road, on February 27th, 1894. Miss Sutter urged two principles upon the

246

meeting: first, that if this thing were taken in hand, it must not be the Free Churches, but Christian England as a whole that should undertake it; secondly, if there was to be success, they must at once seek to raise a " Service of Mercy "—Brothers and Sisters like the " Deacons " and " Deaconesses " at work at Bethel, for these were the strength of the " Inner Mission." These two principles have been adopted by the Christian Social Service Union, which owes its origin to that meeting. A committee was appointed then and there, with Rev. F. B. Meyer as chairman, Rev. J. F. B. Tinling as Hon. Secretary, Dr. Munro Gibson, Rev. Tolefree Parr, Mr. Walter Hazell and others. This committee was commissioned by the meeting to seek a way for carrying out in England the great aims of Pastor v. Bodelschwingh's " Colony of Mercy " at Bielefeld.

It was to one of the early meetings of this committee that Paton was summoned. He was delayed in his arrival, and found the proceedings nearly at an end. The attendance was small, and there was a note of discouragement. It was six months since the appeal had gone out, and no response had been received. Some one had just proposed to adjourn *sine die*. But the entrance of the new member changed all that. " No," he said, " we've got to do this thing, and do it we will." Three things he urged on them : that the work should go forward on the broadest lines of Christian fellowship, all Christian Churches being asked to unite in the endeavour; that Boards of Guardians should be urged to provide maintenance for the men received in training, that there should be small holdings in the neighbourhood of the Colony in order to plant out men who had been trained in the Colony and help them with advice. These principles were very fully discussed, and, on their being adopted, Paton joined the committee. He at once enlisted the adhesion of friends in the Church of England : the Bishop of Hereford, Archdeacon Sinclair, from the south, Dean Kitchin and Dean Maclure in the north. Soon afterwards he called on Miss Sutter at Hampstead. " You must go stumping the country with me," he said. " Yours is a mighty mission ; the power is given you to rouse men ; you must come with me. We must have a Colony of Mercy in every county." " No, Doctor," was the reply, " you have just said that the power to rouse men is my mission ! You are roused ; Mr. Tinling is roused ; quite

a number are roused ; let me see a Colony of Mercy
growing up here ! I have given you a book, showing the
way ; go and do likewise ! "

It was in the next year, 1895, that Mr. Harold Moore
discovered a suitable farm of 268 acres at Lingfield on the
borders of Surrey. Paton got three other gentlemen to
join him in guaranteeing the purchase-money, and then
personally and alone purchased the Colony, taking the
whole responsibility on himself, and undertaking that the
farm should be transferred to the committee, when it was
able to accept it and nominate trustees.

Thus the first Colony of Mercy was started in England.
The Rev. J. L. Brooks, an old Nottingham Institute student
of the seventies, who had a Church at Hammersmith, and
had joined the Council of the Society, was made Director,
and a House-father with House-brothers was placed in
charge. The original farm-house gave accommodation for
the House-father and his family, for two of the Christian
Brothers, and a dozen men. A new iron building was
added, with a dining-room, lavatory, kitchen, and dormitory for other twenty men.

The object was to take able-bodied men and train them
for employment on the land. The great majority of the
men were sent by the Poor Law Guardians, who paid 5s.
a week towards the expense of their maintenance. For
the purposes of training, the men were grouped into small
gangs of six or seven, and with each gang was a Christian
Brother, who would work alongside his men in the field, and
teach them the beauty of work and the use of the tools,
sit alongside his men at meals, and share in the social life
of the evenings. The duty of the House-brother is to
help his men upward, not so much by direct preachment
as by the quiet, indirect influence of daily companionship ;
" not to talk religion, but to act religion." Though he
is to train others, he is himself in training ; for, after the
year or two which he spends at Lingfield, he passes on to
become a warder in a prison or a lunatic asylum. He is
to carry the redemptive spirit of Lingfield, with its sweetness and light, into those austere institutions of the State.

Very soon Mr. Brooks and his wife came into permanent
residence, and a new home was built for epileptic children.
The first idea had been to take cripple children during the
summer months, when there were not likely to be so many

of the unemployed; but the necessity of the epileptic
children was greater than the necessity of the cripples.
There are probably sixty to seventy thousand epileptic
children in England, and very few of them, even under
the most favourable circumstances, have much chance of
recovery. A large number of these children were under
the Poor Law Authorities. No special provision was
made for them. It was not safe to put them with the
healthy children, because a healthy child is liable to
become epileptic itself by the mere sight of another child
in fits. Besides, the disease irritates the brain, and is
apt to cause violence of temper and conduct which looks
like extreme naughtiness. For the epileptic child, too, the
companionship of healthy children is not the best, because
it is at once too exciting and too depressing, for he sees the
others doing many things which he cannot. Apart from
one Home in the North of England, there was no place
for these children to go except the Workhouse Infirmary,
and there they were herded together with the imbecile or
the aged—many of them half-crazed, unhappy creatures,
with painful records of failure and foulness in the past.
From such dismal companionship, from this semi-prison
existence, not brightened by any romps or lessons, and
enlivened only by occasional quarrels, Lingfield provided
a deliverance.

Lingfield lies twenty-six miles south-east from London.
If there were fir-trees in the background, the scene might
be Canadian, with that touch of hopefulness which be-
speaks the building up of a new homestead. But the wood
that shelters it from the northern blast, with its oaks and
elm and beech, stamps the scene as English. Outwardly,
there is nothing to distinguish the Lingfield fields from
an ordinary farm, unless it be the greater variety of crops,
the excellent trimness and order that prevail, with other
signs of plenteous labour. Also there is less grass land than
one is accustomed to see. There is a market-garden of
some five acres, and a large fruit-farm well stocked with
plums and currants. There is an orchard with hens cluck-
ing in the long grass under the whitewashed apple-trees
where the daffodils were blooming in the spring. There
is a patch of wood which supplies material for the wood-
chopping shed, and, tucked away under the lee of the
spinney, half buried in bracken and blue-bells, there are

the murmurous bee-hives. The cow-house and the various farm offices are models of their kind, well ventilated and fragrant ; as for the piggery, it might vie with the dairy itself in sweetness and cleanliness.

" What of the soil ? " you ask.

" Well," says the Director, " it is a clay loam, poorish stuff ; but it responds to treatment."

" And the colonists ? "

" Poorish stuff, too," is his reply ; " but also responsive to treatment. Don't forget that all the work on this farm is done practically by workhouse labour. That lawn in front of my house, the pond and the roads have all been made by workhouse labour. We have only one regular skilled farm-hand in our employ. Some of the men are of very little service to us when they come. Take a compositor who came to us last month, thrown out of work by the linotype machine, rather a shrimp of a man at the best of times, and pulled down by prolonged semi-starvation. He was no more fit for work in the fields when he came than he was fit to fly. We put him on to the poultry, and he did about two hours a day at first in relays. That was as much as he could manage. But he is coming on well There are others who are strong enough when they come, but no more use than he was, some of them, because they are so clumsy. Some of them, again, are unwilling ; they seem to need an electric shock to put some life into them, just dead-alive specimens of the routine workhouse life. Others are bone-lazy. For these lazy men I have a system of piece-work, and their diet both in quantity and quality, not to mention tobacco, is in proportion to the work they do. That touches them on the spot, and serves to give a motive for exertion, so they begin to get on. It is hard work, trying to one's patience ; but there is always some upward movement going on, always enough good result evident to keep one hopeful and cheery."

" What about the Brothers ? "

" They come to us usually with a strong recommendation from their Church and minister. Some of them, too, have what you call ' a history ' ; one or two of them have been workhouse lads, but they are really in earnest and as fond of singing as Billy Bray. There's no stopping them. They are the backbone of the Colony, the men who do the

lifting and the saving. We have other men, too, who
help us in the evening and on Sundays. They go up to
town every day to business, but live amongst us, and find
out one way or another, according to their bent, of helping
the life of the place. There's a young artist on the staff
of the ' Graphic.' I will show you indoors a picture he
painted of a spray of apple-blossom. He is teaching some
of these fellows to draw and paint, and when I see him at
it, I think of John Ruskin at the Working Men's College.
That's the sort of Socialism that helps to sweeten the
world."

" Does the farm pay ? "

" Yes, I knew that was coming. The Englishman's first
question. If it pays, it's a business proposition. If it
doesn't pay, it's a fad. I know. Well, you don't expect
farming to pay in England, and it doesn't pay with us. We
reckon that the cost works out at about £20 per head per
annum on each of the colonists, and of course that does
not take account of the buildings which are given us. But
put it another way. Which pays the country better, to
keep these men in the workhouse or to train them here ?
Then there is no hesitation about the answer. Independence, health, moral character, steadiness and ability
to earn one's own footing in the world—these are some of
the products of this farm, and though you can't put them
down in your balance-sheet, they are worth paying for.
And we have some striking instances. We have all sorts.
Here is one with the build of a giant, an ex-soldier who
has seen service abroad. You think he would make a
model policeman, but he goes down like a ninepin before a
pint of beer. Here's another lad, young and bright; he
can't read or write, but he plays football with the dash
and the nerve of an international. There is the lad who
never had a chance, and the lad who never cared whether
he had a chance or no. There is the man who has had
misfortune ; there is the man whose misfortune was his
father. But there is no turning down the thumb on
any one here. There's gold in each one of them. And to
each of them the Colony holds out the helping hand of
Christ."

" What happens to them ? "

" There are some failures, of course. Sometimes, but
rarely, we have to send a man back as unsuitable. He is

either mentally or physically unfit, or he is insubordinate. Sometimes—and this also rarely—a man absconds. That is only another way of saying that the discipline is real discipline. Some of them leave to seek work. But more than half of them we place successfully in situations either in England or the Colonies. Here's one man, a bad drink case, discovered by a Baptist minister and sent along to us. He became reformed, and returned to his ordinary employment. I regard that drink craving as a kind of disease, and, after all, there's nothing like health to drive out disease. Here's another case : a young clerk in a position of trust, led astray by gay city life. He misappropriated money and narrowly escaped imprisonment. He came to us, was trained for farm-work, and now holds a good position in Canada. Here is a workhouse lad, a regular problem to the Guardians, a case of 'chronic inertia.' He was placed in one situation after another, and made a mess of each. Finally, they sent him to Lingfield, and, after a year's training, we sent him out to Canada, where he is doing well. Then there's another workhouse boy whom they call 'Ikie.' He was trained in a poor-law school, but he was badly defective, and promised to become a chronic pauper. After two years' patient training the lights began to burn more brightly, his mental powers developed, and now he's out in Canada, earning his nine dollars a week with free board. I could go on long enough telling you of one case after another— this young fellow who came to us broken down with the drink habit ; this man, again, was a clerk in an important Government department, with a sad record for drink, delirium, and attempted suicide. He was suspended from his work, and came to us for six months, and now he is back again as a Civil Servant. You may say that, on an average, over 50 per cent. of those who come to us cease to be dependent."

" And you couldn't do this in the town ? "

" Never. The earth loves her foster-children ; they suck new health and new life from the breast of Nature. It makes them strong in will and in limb ; it makes them men."

" And when they are not at work, what do they do ? "

" There are special recreation-rooms and workshops. We abhor a vacuum. A man may choose what he likes

best.   There's a flourishing Good Templar's Lodge, there's
a Reading Circle, there's a Bible-class.   There's music,
and there are classes where a man can learn how to mend
boots, make baskets, read, write, reckon, render first aid
in case of accident, and do all sorts of handyman jobs
that will fit him for a pioneer life on the prairie.   There
are games clubs, too ; we put a couple of football-teams
in the field, and there's a fire-brigade, which gives us
plenty of fun.   Then, at nine o'clock, we all meet in the
hall, and I read a passage of the Bible with them, say a
word or two about its message, and we close the day with
prayer." [1]

But twelve has struck and the school is scaling.   Our
little sisters and brothers are coming out, two by two,
hand in hand.   They are a motley little group of all ages,
with strange, unchildlike faces many of them, and many
forms ungainly, with queer, spasmodic movements.   But
they are all happy, talking eagerly about the fruit, for
they are off with baskets to the orchard to gather currants
and raspberries for the market, and the payment of their
labour is to be in kind.

" Yes," said the Director, " we have sixty children now,
nearly all of them from London.   A sad little company
when they first came, and what else can you expect when
they have been scattered about in ones and twos among
aged paupers whose lamp is burning low ?   They were
made to feel, all along, that they were not like other chil-

[1] The following statistics are taken from the report.

Year.	Total left during year.	Withdrawn.	Left to seek work.	Absconded.	Mentally or physically unfit.	Insubordinate.	Successfully placed in situations in England or Colonies.
1903	54	..	6	12	10	2	24
1904	56	..	4	5	11	13	23
1905	58	..	2	6	13	4	33
1906	60	4	9	12	2	2	31
1907	62	10	..	9	4	3	36
1908	59	9	..	..	10	8	32
1909	57	2	7	10	8	2	28
	406	25	28	54	58	34	207

dren, and never would be like other folk, or good for
anything in the world. Here, at any rate, they are all
children together, and, though they are all ill, they are
all ill in the same way, and can share their childish duties
and pleasures. We give them all possible freedom, as
you see. There is no fence to divide them from the
garden. The whole place is open, and they see all the
coming and going. They run up to old friends and new
friends both alike in the same confiding way, just as they
ran up to you and wanted to shake your hand directly
you smiled at them. You can't show them too much
affection; pass your fingers through their hair, stroke
their cheek, take them in your arms ; if they can understand nothing else, they can understand love, and their
little hearts feed on it. It is beautiful to see the Doctor
among his little ones, as he calls them. They all know
the Doctor, and so do the men. Whenever there has been
any trouble in the Colony—and we have had some hard
rubs from time to time—I bring him away to this end of
the building, and they are all round him in a minute. I
have often seen the tear stand in his eye as they recited
to him their little piece or showed him the flowers they
had been plucking. You see I always let the grass grow
long round those evergreen clumps, so that those who
can't get far afield may have plenty of wild-flowers to
pluck and to play with. They love to send him a copy
of their concert programme, and some of their designs are
quite pretty and tasteful. Their latent gift for colour and
form has been quite a revelation to us. We are training
one or two as sign-writers."

"And you give them regular school, do you ?"

"Yes, indeed, though perhaps it would not be school
according to your notions. Will you step in and see ?
Mrs. Brooks is in command this end of the building, and
she will be there with some of the wee dots and the helpless cases. We arrange them in classes according to what
they can do, not in ages. We haven't any of the regular
standards here. You will see quite big girls slowly learning to prick on paper, or to do wool-work which might be
given to a child of three. We have to teach them largely
by touch. But the upper classes, boys and girls together,
can read and write and do sums in their heads. The
periods are very short, and we have songs every now and

again, especially if the day is wet and the sun refuses to shine. But we have as much of the school as possible in the open air. That would please Ruskin, and it is the best medicine for them.[1]

" As to mental training, the first thing we seek to awaken is the faculty of usefulness. Those who are strong enough make their own beds, while the bigger boys and girls help in dressing the smaller ones. We teach them knitting, basket-making, fretwork, needlework; the girls, and many of the boys too, do their own mending and darning; some of the boys get as far as carpentry. Then, as you saw just now, they can help a bit gathering the fruit, and their little fingers are better at that job than the men's. It's good for the men to have the little ones; it adds a touch of homeliness and tenderness to the life. And it's good for the children to have the men and to have the animals, and something going on every day on the farm. From seed-time to harvest, there is planting and haymaking, and marketing, and dairying, and hatching out the chicks, and lambing, and hiving the bee-swarms; something fresh is always happening."

" Do they get cured ? "

" I must be careful not to overstate the case, but the results, in many of our cases, surpass our wildest anticipations. We have one lad of seventeen now working on the farm. Five years ago he had fits almost daily, and sometimes several in one day—his health-chart recorded 133 in a single month. For full three years he has had none, and is now an active and apparently healthy young workman. In several other cases fits have disappeared. In nearly every case the seizures have been less frequent. The Guardians now send children at an earlier age, and already the records show improvement."

" And they are not upset when one of them is taken

[1] The subjoined figures from the report of 1909 look hopeful. Nine, no fits for three years; 11, no fits for two years; 17, no fits for one year. Of the remaining 199, 83 are improving, 20 are stationary, 16 deteriorating. One hundred and fifty-six altogether in the Home.

At Starnthwaite, the physician, Dr. A. J. McCallum, has made special experiments with the bromide treatment, a report of which was printed in the " British Medical Journal," March 14th, 1908. The children used to be sent by the Board of Guardians, but now the local Education Authorities are responsible for the epileptics and feeble-minded within their area until they are sixteen years old, and therefore the main supply comes now through them.

ill ? You must have some cases of seizure every
day."

"Yes, every day, but they take these things quite
calmly ; they are not alarmed. Out there on the verandah
you see the little mattress and pillow ready ; we have the
same in every room. We have our own House of God,
built by the colonists themselves. There the little ones
who could go nowhere else can join in public worship.
Their religious faith is very touching. When one of them
dies, they take it just as part of the heavenly Father's
good pleasure. ' She has gone to Jesus,' they say ; ' Jesus
has taken her.' He loves them, and that satisfies."

Lingfield is a scene on which one fain would linger, for
here one sees redemption at work, and the secret of redemption is love. " Are they kind to you ? " asked a
father of a poor little fellow who had to be removed to an
asylum. " Yes, dada," he said, " all of them. Everybody is, and I love them for it."

Here applied Christianity is on trial, proving its reality
and its worth. It recognises that it is not sufficient to
feed and clothe a man. A man's greatest strength is from
within ; if he is to recover himself he must learn the law of
serviceable work, the law which governs man's tenure
of the earth ; he must learn, too, the law of order which
is heaven's first law. Learning these twin obediences in
the atmosphere of human fellowship, he can build up a
new and permanent and honourable manhood. Even
from the broken earthenware can be made the vessel of
honour.

The workhouse was originally devised for a particular
purpose—to put an end to a wasteful and pernicious
system of doles in relief of wages. This purpose it has
achieved. We now expect it, under quite different circumstances, to succeed in answering quite different purposes. If this expectation is disappointed, we must not
be surprised. The workhouse treatment of able-bodied
unemployed is not calculated to keep up a man's spirit,
his efficiency and self-respect. To its deadening, depressing influence the Lingfield Colony opposes the hopeful
policy of living, active fellowship and healthful, happy
occupation with the prospect of a new start in a new
country with a new-earned capacity and self-confidence

to look forward to in the future.   If the State is to save
the human waste material of our social life, to make it
self-supporting, and give it an honourable place in the
world's work, Lingfield has shown the lines on which the
State must work.   The essential element is personal influence.   If sixty such inefficients are merely herded together, it makes little difference whether it be on a farm
or in a workhouse, they will sink to the level of the lowest.
No redemption is wrought unless they are grouped in
small companies with Christian men who share their work,
their recreation, their dormitory, and their whole life.
This is the pivot on which the whole work turns.   This
distinguishes Lingfield from any similar work in this
direction, and accounts for its larger measure of success.

Social service of the academic kind has no place in the
life of the Colony.   The social worker there is no mere
student of sociological research ; he is a man who is
willing to take off his coat, turn up his shirt-sleeves, and
work alongside the fallen brother whom he wishes to help.
He must handle the plough, rub shoulders with the pig
in the sty, and see Christianity in stubbing up ice-cold
cabbages on a frosty morning in December before it is
light.   In training the House-brothers Lingfield has re-
discovered what Dr. Wichern spoke of as a forgotten
text : "I was in prison, and ye visited Me."   One of the
objects for which they are trained is to act as warders in
prisons and asylums.   These are the men who will carry
on the work of John Howard and reform the prisons of
the twentieth century.   "The importance of selecting
good men for prison duties cannot be over-estimated,"
says General Sir E. F. Du Cane.   " The officer who is in
charge of prisoners has such power for good or for evil
over his fellow-men that I do not think there are many
positions more responsible than that which he occupies."
The governor of a jail has to trust almost wholly to the
wardens.   With many of the prisoners he never speaks
from the time they enter till the time they leave the
prison.   Indeed, the great object of "reclaiming the
prisoners" concerning which the Home Office so solemnly
warns all prison officers, is left almost entirely to the
wardens to carry out.

"No reform in our prisons or asylums," wrote Paton,

17

" would equal that which would follow the ministry of men who have some of Christ's spirit and would carry His healing grace to those now beaten down by the struggle and fever and sins of our age."

The first extension of the work of the Christian Social Service Union came in 1900. An estate of 143 acres at Starnthwaite in Cumberland, half-way between Kendal and Windermere, was, through Paton's instrumentality, offered to the Union in trust for the development of its work. It came as a generous gift from previous experimenters in social service. Mr. Tomlinson was distressed at the loss of money incurred in the Colony which he had practically founded for his friend, the Rev. Herbert Mills. He went to Lingfield, saw the work there, and induced the trustees of Starnthwaite to transfer the trust to some of the Lingfield Committee, so that the two estates might come under the same control. The stock and furniture Paton purchased on his own responsibility. The larger portion of the estate at Browhead, containing 125 acres, was suited to the work of a training colony and one of the Lingfield men was put in charge as House-father. The smaller portion of the estate at Starnthwaite, less than two miles distant, was to be set apart for the epileptic homes. But the pressing need of the time was that of the wounded soldiers returning in hundreds from the war. Many of them were disabled for all ordinary manual work of any kind. The presence of large glass conservatories at Starnthwaite suggested tomato-culture and other forms of nursery gardening, and for the first two or three years, with the help of the War Office, wounded soldiers were received at Starnthwaite. They were unfit to engage in ordinary farm work, they could not do the spade-digging of the ordinary market-gardeners; but there were many occupations such as weeding, planting out of seedlings, raking, pruning, watering, and manuring which a man with one leg or one arm could do quite well. There were poultry-keeping, agriculture, and mushroom-growing, and there were other simple indoor industries which afforded scope for all sorts of gifts. They learned at Starnthwaite how to supplement their pension with useful service, so that they were saved from sinking to the level of hangers-on at the public-house or any other form of pauperism. Since then, the whole building has

been used for epileptic boys sent by the various Local
Education Authorities in Northern England, and most
satisfactory results have accrued from the treatment there
pursued under Dr. McCallum. The boys took up the
scout movement, and were proud to be the first, if not
the only, epileptic scout-troop in the history of the world.

Letter to Mr. Arthur Sherwell

"*June 12th*, 1900.

" It was an interesting coincidence that Mr. Foljambe,
the Chairman of our Notts Committee, should have
spoken to me yesterday morning on the great responsibility that will be thrown upon us when our brave soldiers
return from the war—many of them seriously maimed
and disabled—unfit for the usual kinds of labour in which
they were formerly employed.

" The problem you have set before me, and which is
pressing upon the mind of your correspondent, is a difficult one—but I do not think it insoluble. I indicate
briefly, and in a tentative way, what I think will be found
the best practicable solution of the problem—but in the
carrying out of it in detail we should have, and we could
have, the guidance and counsel of the most skilful experts
in the various departments of the work.

" You are proposing to deal with the soldiers who are
seriously maimed in arm or limb, and with men of every
description of character, not only with those who are of
exceptionally good character, and who may be at once
recommended to situations of trust, *e.g.* as commissionaires,
gate-house keepers, time-keepers in workshops, etc.

" Now for this large and mixed class of men disabled
from ordinary manual work there can only be a suitable
opening in some occupation on the land which could *at
once* engage a number of men without displacing others,
and *at once* enable them to maintain themselves and so
preserve their self-respect and keep them from sinking into
pauperism or into crime, as otherwise multitudes of them
infallibly will.

" But on the land they could not engage in the ordinary
labours of the field, and could not do the spade-digging
of the ordinary market-gardener. There are, however,
in connection with the large and growing industries carried

on in cheaply built green-houses or in nursery gardening, many occupations of weeding, planting out of seedlings, raking, pruning, watering, manuring, in which hundreds could be employed—if they had only an arm, or if they had only one limb, or even none, moving themselves on movable seats. Mushroom-growing, tomato-growing, and the culture of many kinds of vegetables, such as early potatoes, sea-kale, etc., open now a great field of various industries. And then, in connection with these, you can have bee-keeping, poultry-keeping, rabbit-warrens and large piggeries, which are all profitable if conducted with thorough intelligence. And in all these industries unskilled work suffices, if it is under skilful direction and control.

" In any such colony—where all these industries were carried on, there would need to be indoor industries for bad weather and during winter-nights, and there is an infinite field for all sorts of gift or for men who have no special gift of any kind—industries, too, that can be adapted for every kind of disability—e.g. rough or fine basket-making, mat-making, rough boot-and-shoe mending and sandal-making, book-binding, carpet and rug-making, metal-repoussée work, and wood and iron work, and so on."

All through these years careful experimentation was going on at Lingfield. Brick-making, jam-making, cream-potting, and other ancillary industries were started, some of which succeeded, while some had to be written off as failures. Two small-holders' cottages were built by the generosity of Mr. William Morton, himself a Newmilns lad in the early days. An up-to-date laundry and Home for older Epileptic Girls was given by the Whitley family in memory of their sister, Miss Ada Whitley, who was from the first a very kind personal friend to the Colony. A Brothers' Institute was built by the late Mr. John Cory. A splendid school was built by the late Mr. J. P. Thomasson. The accommodation for epileptic boys was doubled by the erection of a new wing through the generosity of Mr. John Carter. A home for older male epileptics was built by moneys left for the purpose by the late George and Fanny Tucker, old friends of the Wicker in Sheffield, supplemented by the late Mr. Andrew B. Paton, of Liverpool. Adequate water-supply was provided and a new sewage system. Nor must we forget to mention what is commemorated by a tablet on the water-tower unveiled by Miss Sutter at the annual meeting, 1904, that she had been enabled to hand over £600 for freeing the water-supply from debt. This was part of a thousand-pound cheque sent her by a reader of her " Britain's Next Campaign," to enable her to rouse the country to the call of the Elberfeld system. The capital value of the estate grew from £8,000 to £22,000, the number of the population to over 300. Not the least interesting or valuable feature of development was the founding and maintenance of a magazine, " Social Service," edited by the Rev. J. F. B. Tinling. And last of all, in 1912, came the transplantation of the whole Farm Training Colony to a more spacious estate at Wallingford.

In 1909 a new Colony was established for thirty men on the Lingfield lines at Marple Dale, and a Manchester Committee was formed for its support.

Thus the little seed sown by God's hand fell into good ground and brought forth more than a hundredfold. The seed was Miss Sutter's book. The planters were the committee who were inspired to realise in England the ideal of that book. There were those that watered, but, chief among them, Mr. and Mrs. J. L. Brooks, who for twelve years gave their life to the nurture of the growing seedling, being father and mother to the epileptic children and the poor " left-behinds " who came as colonists.

To a Friend

" I have been permitted to take part in many kinds of Christian work, but in none of them have I felt in such close fellowship with our redeeming Lord, and certainly in none have I seen more wonderfully manifest His healing and saving grace, than in the Training Colony which was founded some four years ago at Lingfield in Surrey, and which has been called a ' Colony of Mercy.' I have been acquainted for a few years with the work of the Labour Colonies of Germany and Holland, and I have often thought that we ought, as they do, to use wisely the remedial and health-giving influences of labour on the land, and of simple country life, to restore men who have fallen out of work, and who consequently drift into our workhouses, where they rapidly sink into indolent and pauper habits of life. All this has been done at the Training Colony formed five years ago at Lingfield, and it has been wonderfully blessed in respect to such men. In all that we have done there we have received the cordial support of the Local Government Board. Indeed I have found no fuller Christian sympathy in this movement than has been given to us in that Government office.

" I cannot forget what I felt some years ago when I first heard from a lady, who was a Poor Law Guardian, of the sad lot of epileptic children who were sent to our workhouses. They cannot, of course, mix with other children, and, as there are not many of them, Guardians were not justified in providing them with separate rooms and special attendants. I was horrified when I learnt that these poor innocent children, many of them very bright, were placed in the workhouse infirmary along with adult imbeciles, many of whom are depraved in speech and conduct. There these children have generally grown up into hopeless idiocy, and have been a life-long burden to the State. I could not but feel that this is an evil that must cease in our Christian land. We have now sixty of these children in our Home at Lingfield, and it is delightful to see the improvement they soon show in many ways, and how quickly they take to the little industries of which they are capable. In both these departments we are overcrowded at Lingfield, and I therefore felt it to be a providential opening when an estate at Starnthwaite, near Kendal, was offered to the Christian Union for Social Service that we might form a colony in the north of England similar to that at Lingfield. I felt that this was an offer we ought not to refuse.

" At the very time this offer was made, a lady wrote to me describing the condition of soldiers who return from the war maimed and disabled, and who seem almost doomed to pauperism. Their little pension is not sufficient to keep them, though it is just sufficient to provide them with a drinking bout at the times it is paid, and they are not fit for ordinary employments. I could not but recognise the urgency of the appeal to consider what could possibly be done for these men, and the opening at Starnthwaite seemed to provide an answer, because one of the buildings already on the estate could be easily adapted to receive these men, and to form workshops for various industries in which they could be trained."

" In the little volume ' The Inner Mission,' which I published twenty-five years ago, I spoke (pp. 12–15) of the need of such a ministry in our prisons, etc. The late Mr. Samuel Morley greatly desired at that time to establish a Training Home for men who should thus enter into service in our prisons and asylums, and he invited two pastors from Germany to confer with him about the matter. It seemed impracticable then. Now it can be done "

To Mr. R. Dangerfield

"July 20th, 1906.

" . . . I was at Lingfield yesterday. I could have wished that you and Mrs. Dangerfield had been there to see one of the most beautiful sights you could see in this world. We have 130 epileptic children there—all happily engaged. It was our Annual Festival, when some of the children gave delightful recitations ; there were also beautiful gymnastic exercises performed by the girls and boys, who were very nicely yet simply dressed ; it was a charming spectacle, lasting for an hour and a half. We also saw the simple hand-work which they had done, and in which some of them are becoming expert. Think of these children, so happy and so improved in health—all of them from the workhouses, where they were immured in the lunatic or senile wards, not mixing with any children, and only rarely able to get out even into the workhouse yard. Surely that was a horrible thing for children in a Christian country—many of them bright and bonny. We are now hoping to have 200 children almost immediately sent to us from the London County Council."

" February 24th, 1906.

" DEAR MR. BURNS,

" I have written much in favour of Labour Colonies on the land ; you will therefore be surprised to hear that I said to many people that I was delighted you had spoken strongly in an adverse sense about them, because, though I am in favour of Labour Colonies adapted to special classes

and needs, and wisely conducted, I am amazed and even
alarmed at the glib and idle way in which people now talk
of Labour Colonies as being a very simple matter, and as
being a panacea—I might almost say a nostrum—for social
maladies.   Now, on the contrary, I have always insisted—

" 1. That Labour Colonies must be of various kinds,
wisely planned and adapted to meet the needs of various
classes.

" 2. That in every kind of Labour Colony there must be
a wise and effective administration, inspired too by the
highest moral influences—and I know you will understand
me when I say, Christian influences, for in their management we must get something of the high purpose and the
devotion which the Christian faith, if it be sincerely held,
will inspire.

" Enclosed I send you two copies of my pamphlet, as
you desired, on the ' Unemployable and Unemployed,' and
you will there see how I distinguish the different kinds of
colonies that are needed :

" 1. Colonies for epileptic and defective children and
adults.

" 2. Colonies for slum-born and slum-bred youths who
now potter away an idle and sordid existence in our
workhouses, but who, under the treatment which we give
them at Lingfield and at Starnthwaite for a year, or
more frequently two years, of country life and labour, with
a happy, moral, social environment, are perfectly transformed so that they are able to earn an honest livelihood.
Last year we sent out 25 such lads to America, and at one
time we sent out six to be labourers on the L. and N.W.
Railway ; others are sent to be farm-labourers in this
country.

" 3. The large and growing class, for whom I am more
concerned than any other, namely, the class of lads in
our big cities whom I there describe, who are there
engaged in many kinds of casual and irregular employment,
and are not trained to the habit and love of regular work.
For them I think you must have Industrial Training
Colonies, and some means must be adopted by which they
can be indentured in such Training-schools or Colonies.

" 4. The able-bodied men in our workhouses, who
might be received either in such colonies as the Poplar
Colony, and Hollesley, or I think preferably in such a

EPILEPTIC COLONY, STARNTHWAITE, NEAR KENDAL.

colony as Lingfield.   These colonies will be of great service, but only if these two conditions are secured, namely :

" *a.* The effective management by men of a high moral purpose and of true devotion.   I believe that this will generally, though not always, be found in connection with earnest religious faith. I have spoken of this class in the address (enclosed) which I gave at Gateshead, at a conference of Guardians, and which may interest you.

" *b.* That in every Colony of this kind you give the men the prospect of settling on the land, so that they may have the prospect of lifting themselves up out of their present pauper condition.

" 5. Free Labour Colonies for men out of work who are seeking work but cannot find it, and who ought therefore to have a place where at once they can find labour until an opportunity be given them, or their health be sufficiently recruited, to get labour suited to them in the ordinary labour market.   This was the purpose of the formation of the German Labour Colonies, viz. to provide for the great numbers of men out of work after the Franco-German War, when the roads of the country were infested with tramps.   In this Colony, as in ' No. 4,' there ought to be a training given to all who seem suitable for it, that will enable them to settle upon a colony as free cottage farmers, like the Colony at Fredericksoord in Holland, of which I speak next.

" 6. A colony of the type of Fredericksoord.   This I consider to be by far the most important kind of colony for England at the present time.   I have described it on p. 39 of the enclosed, and in the Appendix, No. 3. You will see that in this Colony families are established on the land, and single men are also received, either in a special home, or as lodgers with the small holders in their cottages.   I am glad to say that this kind of colony is now being formed in connection with the Free Labour Colonies in Germany.   They call them ' Heimath-Colonien,' or ' Home Colonies,' and men who show themselves fitted for agricultural work are specially encouraged to settle in these Home Colonies, where, however, they undergo a special probation of two years before they are accepted as small holders under what is practically a form of permanent tenure.

" I earnestly ask you, Mr. Burns, to consider this type
of colony, because here you have the means by which you
can restore to the land, under healthy conditions, multitudes
of the unemployed in our big cities.   In this way you can
again restore the balance between our rural and urban
population, and give to England a vigorous and independent peasantry.   I would almost plead with you to
look at this problem from the point of view of Fredericksoord.   And in this Colony, as you see, there is no danger
of the kind which you suggested to me as to colonies
becoming nests of (sexual) vice.

" 7. The colony which I have for twenty years been
earnestly pleading for, and which I set forth in a pamphlet
entitled, ' How to restore the Yeoman-peasantry,' and
also in other pamphlets.   The one enclosed sets forth
the whole case as I conceive it, and I think, if you glance
over it, you will find that, when we speak of Co-operative
Colonies on the land, we are speaking of another kind of
colony from those which you have had chiefly in your
mind.

" 8. Colonies for the occasionally and temporarily
unemployed, especially in our winter season ; and here I
venture to send you a letter which I wrote to the Local
Government Journals last summer, and which appeared
in one or two other papers, *e.g.* the ' Speaker,' etc.   I
should like you also to look at this because I think I have
there dealt with the problem in a way which you would
approve, or which at any rate you will think is not badly
conceived.

" 9. Vagrant Colonies.   I think that when you spoke
to me of a Labour Colony in the lobby of the House, you
referred to the great Vagrant Colonies in Merx-plas in
Belgium and elsewhere.   I have said all that I can say
upon this subject in my evidence before the Vagrancy
Committee, which Mr. Davy can show you. I supplemented
the evidence which my friend, Mr. Brooks, gave, so that
some of my evidence is included in the evidence given
under his name.   There I confess to you the peril of which
you have so wisely and earnestly spoken in private, is
likely to occur unless there is a wise subdivision and
classification of inmates, and unless there be commingling,
with the men in these institutions, of other men of the
highest type of moral character and influence.

"May I say, in one final sentence, that all this great movement for the rescue and redeeming of fallen men, and the restoring of many of them to self-respect and self-support, needs, above all, the out-breathing of a great moral and—I will use the word in the largest sense—redemptive purpose ; our hearts must be filled with one thought—how we can uplift, and help, and save ?

" May I add that I am getting out an estimate of the cost per man in every colony to which we can get access ? I should specially like you to consult the evidence of Mr. Thomas, who visited that Labour Colony at Neuchatel, which is self-supporting. I know that there too, lately, they have allowed a special agency to be introduced into the Colony to bring a healthier moral influence to bear upon the men whilst in it.

" And now let me add—you may command me in any way you think well to advance the good cause which is on your heart, namely, to do more and better for the suffering and neglected poor of our country."

To the Duchess of Sutherland

"April 28th, 1909.

" There is at the present time a farm offered [1] which seems to be, from all I can gather, wonderfully suited to the present need of our Union. It will be quite necessary that the department of work for our workhouse boys and men should be removed from Lingfield, and that Lingfield be wholly devoted to children and adults under medical supervision. The work for epileptics is growing so much, and is being so greatly appreciated, that the whole Colony must be devoted to it. The work, too, for workhouse boys and broken-down men is growing more important. The workhouse is seen to be, not only a failure, but a disaster for boys and men of that type. They can only be redeemed by healthy labour and surroundings on the land.

" In addition, we should like to ask the Government to form a Vagrant Colony, where we should have the right of detention and of training the vagrants to industrial work, and especially to work on the land.

" We also desire to show how unemployed men, selected,

[1] Turner's Court at Wallingford.

and who are willing and fitted for labour on the land,
should be settled on the land on conditions that would
be honourable to them, and involving no expense to the
State.   I have ventured to send your Grace a statement
with regard to the Fredericksoord Colony, of which I have
spoken for some years ; it seemed to me to give a model
which could be so easily followed by us, and from which
results could be secured even better than have been secured
in Holland, because the results achieved by the thorough
and intensive cultivation of the land are so much better
known now.   I have ventured to say that selected men, of
the unemployed, who are vigorous, and who wish to settle
on the land, should be tested by one month's earnest
work with the spade and hoe, and should then be settled
on a small colony for two years under the most careful
training by an able and experienced manager.   They
should cultivate every inch of their small holding to the
very best advantage, having their hedges, espaliers for
the growing of fruit, and having the roads lined with
fruit-trees, having poultry-runs, etc., wisely arranged,
and stocked with the best breeds of fowl, both for the
production of eggs and for table use.

" Now the principle at Fredericksoord, and the principle
which must be adopted in England, is that such able-
bodied men shall have an advance made to them by the
State and by Raffeissen Banks, as on the Continent, but
shall repay in instalments everything that is thus advanced, and so work out their own salvation honourably
without any sense of pauper degradation."

To Mr. Hunt

" *October* 27*th*, 1903.

" . . . You, of course, are not aware that it has been a
fundamental principle of this movement from the beginning, that, when the generous public provide the capital
of the estate, we are not to appeal to charity for the support of those who really are under the direction and charge
of the State, and must be supported by the State.   What
we have offered to the State is that we will give service
in the most economical and yet efficient way, because of
our desire to promote the moral and religious well-being
of those whom they entrust to us.   This principle must

not be on any account violated.   All the money that has
been given to us has been given on that understanding.
It has been again and again reiterated, that our colonies
shall never become charities.   On the other hand, as the
estate is not clear, we have a right to ask interest, and
we have no right to charge a colony with the expense of
the general director of the movement, and of yourself,
so far as you give half your time to be his secretary ; also,
the expense of training of the House-brothers must not
in any way come out of the colony funds.   On the contrary, I think we have a right to contribute to the Colony,
as we do now, a part of the money that we expect to
receive for the training of each brother, as their labour
is partly devoted to the assistance and care of the men.
In my own mind, I think that the work of every House-
brother on the Colony ought to pay for his board and
lodging, and the difference between the £13 and £20
which we expect to receive for him may be regarded as
payment for the time he gave to the care of our men
during his training.

" We have shown, so far as regards epileptic children,
the money is quite sufficient, and I am quite sure that,
with intelligence and thorough organisation, and with
House-brothers who will direct and energise the labour
of the men, each House-brother being the ' stroke oar '
of each gang with which he is associated, the work of
the men will suffice, with the 7s. that is given us, to pay
not only their board and lodging, and clothing, but the
administrative cost of the Colony."

CHAPTER XVI

NATIONAL HOME READING

" To make boys learn to read, and then place no good books within their reach, is to give men an appetite and leave nothing in the pantry save unwholesome and poisonous food, which, depend upon it, they will eat rather than starve."—SIR W. SCOTT.

" The first use of education is to enable us to consult with the wisest and the gentlest men on all points of earnest difficulty. To use books rightly is to go to them for help."—J. RUSKIN.

" If he shall not lose his reward, who gives a cup of cold water to his thirsty neighbour, what will not be the reward of those who, by putting good books into the hands of those neighbours, open to them the fountains of eternal life ? "—THOMAS À KEMPIS.

BY the Act of 1870 the State brought the opportunity of self-education within the reach of every member of the community. Rightly considered, this Act was nothing more than the first step towards a national system of education, but the tendency for many years was to regard it, not as a first step, but as a final act. A kind of superstitious regard was attached to the mere acquisition of the three R's. The results of that acquisition, the purposes to which these tools of knowledge were applied, were, generally speaking, a matter of indifference. Even in the schools, reading was regarded as a mere exercise in mechanical elocution, a mere interpretation of printed symbols. It was divorced from thought, it was not associated with joy or interest in the subject-matter. The reading-books of the standards were as full of useful information as Magnall, but made absolutely no appeal to the imagination or the higher feeling.

The result was a generation which had acquired the ability to read and the reading habit, but had as little sense of duty in the use it made of the gift as it had of the glorious treasuries to which it had acquired the key. With the cheapening of the printing process an enormous stimulus was given to the democratisation of printed matter. Public libraries sprang up broadcast. Reading became, as Mr. Balfour put it, " more universal than any other form of human activity." But both periodicals and libraries had to accommodate themselves to the public taste, which was superficial and low. The problem was no longer one of gaining access to books. What was needed was some guiding hand to show folk what to read, some enthusiasm for higher things, some taste in choosing the better, and refusing the worse, some help in overcoming the difficulties which attend always upon the higher choice.

The danger was twofold : on the one hand to the people at large, on the other hand to our national literature. We are all, as some one has said, " prisoners of our ideas." The danger was that the youth of England should grow up to be the prisoners of ideas that were coarse, narrow, unhealthy, unenlightened. The danger to literature was that it might go on increasing indefinitely in bulk and quantity, but lose all the saving qualities which make literature worth while ; it looked as if it might gain the whole world, but lose its soul.

For three years these thoughts had been simmering in Paton's mind. At St. Cergues, on the Dole Mountain, above the lake of Geneva, he had met two American ministers who had told him about the wonderful development of the Chautauqua movement on the other side of the Atlantic. In 1873 Lewis Miller and Bishop J. H. Vincent had pitched on Fairpoint, Chautauqua, for the meeting of a summer assembly, which was to provide Sunday-school teachers during their holidays with training for improved methods of Biblical instruction. Out of this scheme for a summer holiday course of instruction had grown up a system of literary and scientific circles with organised courses of home-reading which comprised some 150,000 people. The tent which sufficed for the lectures and meetings of 1874 had grown into a group of twenty-nine handsome buildings which were crowded during the summer months with visitors who came to seek not only health and pleasure, but enlightenment of mind and soul. The American ministers who first told the story of Chautauqua to their British friend were not allowed to leave the Observatoire at St. Cergues till they had told him all they knew. " I felt at once," he wrote, " that this was a very important enterprise, and that we should do well to have something of the same sort in our country."

And so it came about that, in the early spring of 1887, Bishop J. H. Vincent paid a visit to Paton at Nottingham and kindled his soul with the recital of what was being done in America. The idea of an English Chautauqua had been in solution in his mind ; the Bishop's visit was the crystallising touch. He determined to gather together a few like-minded persons, and get some kindred organisation started for England, and, with a view to preparing the way for such a movement, he induced Bishop Vincent then and there to write an article for the " Contemporary," describing the spread of the Chautauqua movement in America.[1] A circular was drawn up by Paton and signed by Dr. J. Percival and Mr. A. H. D. Acland, M.P., with himself, convening a small conference at the London School Board offices on July 15th, 1887. Mr. H. R. Rawson was in the chair. The conference decided " that it was desirable in this country to devise and adopt a plan similar to that adopted by the Chautauqua Reading Circles in America, in order to direct and assist in a systematic and practical way home-reading among the people, and to quicken and sustain the interest of such home-reading by means of local circles and the influence of a central national organisation."

To draw up such a plan a small committee was appointed consisting of Dr. Percival, who acted as chairman, Mr. Acland, Mr. J. E. Flower, Mr. Joseph King, the late Dr. Richard Roberts, Mr. Charles Rowley, and Mr. M. E. Sadler. Mr. King and Mr. Rowley agreed to act as secretaries. This committee held various meetings through the winter. The outcome of its work was that it was decided to hold a Summer Assembly in the month of August at Oxford. The original suggestion of this came from Mr. Charles Rowley, and Mr. W. A. S. Hewins was appointed to carry out the organisation of details. Before the Assembly, schemes of reading were to be drawn up for the systematic study of selected subjects, and every endeavour was to be made, both before the meeting and during the course of it, to organise reading circles and secure capable leaders for them.

[1] Chautauqua, a Popular University by J. H. Vincent, " Contemporary Review " (May 1887).

The Assembly was held and passed off successfully, but there arose, unfortunately, a difference of opinion as to the best policy for further development. The representatives of University Extension, who had from the first given heartiest support to the movement, thought the best line was to take, as a basis, the University Extension already in existence and widen out the movement in connection with their lectures. For instance, when lectures were discontinued for any reason at a centre, or the subject of the lectures was changed, a reading circle could be formed to carry on the work which had been begun. The lecturer's class would form the core of such a circle, and the extension authorities could advise as to books for further study and provide help by correspondence and by occasional visits or lectures for carrying forward the work. Mr. Hudson Shaw had already organised reading circles in connection with his lectures at Huddersfield, and other lecturers were not slow to see the advantages of the system.

Paton was anxious in every way to work together with the University Extension, but the proposed line of development seemed to him too narrow. He was convinced that the movement for a revival of reading should be national in its scope, and that the time was ripe to begin on a national scale.

Letter to Dr. Richard Roberts

"1887.

" I am glad that we are agreed as to the objects, because I consider that they practically determine the methods we must adopt.

" Dr. Vincent has shown how a widespread system of reading circles may be established, in an easy and practical manner, and without great delay, so that the plan suggested is not untried. It is necessary that we should have a definite method of action laid down. Nothing can be done otherwise. It is quite true that a merely paper scheme does not work; but a man must put his working scheme on paper before he carries it out. At the commencement of the University Extension movement the method was drawn out quite as definitely and precisely before a single lecturer left the University as it is to-day; and, so far as I know, nothing has been added since. And,

18

had it not been so, there would not have been the success which has attended this movement. Our proposals to the University sent up from Nottingham were precise, clear, and workable, and hence Professor Sidgwick said, at the first great meeting held in connection with this movement, that, if we had not framed such a practical scheme in Nottingham, the aims and hopes of University Extension would have continued for some time a dream.

" You would see from the report which I drew up how anxious I am that this movement should be closely associated with the Extension movement and should also become a means of greatly developing it.

" When Dr. Vincent was with me, and when he undertook to promote the two movements for recreative evening schools and University Extension in America, and when I (after three years' conference with friends and earnest consideration) undertook to promote the true ' Reading Circles ' movement in this country, I pointed out to him how the University Extension movement was the most powerful ally of, and should give continual stimulus and guidance to, this movement for Home Reading. And we must endeavour to keep them in close connection. But I do not think that we should make it simply an annexe or supplement to the Extension lectures, because—

" 1. The places are but few in which these lectures are held, and even in these places there are comparatively few persons reached by them, whereas there are multitudes everywhere who want guidance and help in their reading.

" 2. There are great bodies which should furnish us with readers, and that need the help of this home reading educational movement. I refer to Sunday-schools (teachers and scholars), Young Men's and Young Women's Christian Associations, Co-operative Societies, Trade Unions, Science and Art and Technical Schools, Mutual Improvement Societies, etc., etc.

" 3. It is necessary to provide this help in reading to young people (boys and girls) and to working men, whom at present the Extension movement is not touching, and some of whom it is not likely to reach *at present*, if it ever does.

" On the other hand, I believe that by forming circles of reading we shall gradually provoke the desire for personal teaching, and thus prepare for the extension of University Teaching by means of lectures, etc.

" I hope, on reflection, you will agree with me that it is not advisable to limit, as you suggest, the means of education which we hope to provide in our Reading Circles. This movement will ally itself with University Extension Lectures, and with all other kinds of teaching, but reaches further than any of them.

" You know that it is no easy matter to start local societies, and keep them going.   Hence, though I see the great value of such societies as that in Huddersfield, I do not think that this movement should depend upon them. It has been shown in America, and I am persuaded that it will be so here, that a central body alone can direct this movement.

" We will, wherever it is possible, and when we have a man of Mr. Learoyd's zeal, start local societies to co-operate with it and be its local organs ; but it of itself will never give the help required to the numerous persons, scattered all over the country, that desire to engage in systematic reading so as to make it educative.

" I shall be sorry if you do not see your way to join us in this work, which somehow or other must, I am assured, be done."

In the summer of 1888 Dr. (afterwards Sir) Joshua G. Fitch, the celebrated Inspector of Schools, went over to America.   Paton told him of Chautauqua, armed him with a letter of introduction to Bishop Vincent, and begged him to find out all he could about the movement. Dr. Fitch accordingly paid a visit to Chautauqua, saw the Summer Assembly in full swing, and himself delivered a memorable address in the Hall of Philosophy on August 8th, 1888, on the subject of Reading :

" If you let the whole contents of a book pass at once from your thoughts, your reading has done little for you. It is in the subsequent reflection, in putting to yourself the question, ' Have I comprehended that author's meaning ?   Do I agree with his conclusions ?   If not, why not ? ' that the whole value of the book, so far as it is a help to your mental development, consists.   The practice of writing down something about a book which has interested you—not a summary merely, not a number of extracts, but an epitome of the facts which have struck you most, and perhaps a criticism of its argument—is a very valuable one, because it forces you to turn over the whole subject in your mind again, to ruminate upon it, and so to make what is in it a part of your permanent possession for life. It is from this point of view that I feel your Chautauqua reading circles to be of special value. They will, I hope, encourage each of their members, when he has read a new book—say, of poetry, history, or philosophy—to write a paper or to give an account of its contents, and, if possible, to associate himself with those who have read it to discuss its merits. In this way you will not only provide every member with a new motive for reading, but will also give to your own studies a coherence and permanence which else might, in the midst of the many intellectual distractions of a busy life, be wholly wanting."

On his return home Dr. Fitch was full of Chautauqua. In the " Contemporary Review " he pressed home on the British thinking public the lesson of what he had seen and heard. In season and out of season he joined with Paton in preaching a national revival of reading. Their advocacy stirred the minds of many thinking men to see the great need and the great opportunity of the moment. But Paton felt, from the first, that our English movement must be organised on more democratic lines than the parent movement in the States. The American Scientific and Literary Association was confined to those already well educated and relatively in comfortable circumstances ; it was, in fact, if not bourgeois, at any rate suburban. The needs of this class in England were to some extent supplied already by the University Extension lectures and classes. The net must be flung more widely. The children in the Elementary Schools, the lads and lasses who went daily forth to their work until the evening, the plain, russet-coated labourer who did the world's dirty work—all these must be swept into a movement which was to be, in the real sense, a national movement, a national revival of letters.

" We were specially anxious to interest the young people

in the senior classes of our day-schools, and those who had just left the day-school; but we wished also to include the working men and women of England and others who had little time, whose reading should be on subjects that were popular and of immediate and practical bearing."

On this wider basis the work of the Union was now planned out. Schemes of reading were to be drawn up for four different classes of readers: for the young people who had passed through the elementary schools, who had been taught to read and needed some guidance and help so as to make their reading educative and useful; for working men and women; for general readers who, amid the rush of life, have little leisure; and for a fourth class consisting of those who had enjoyed some educational advantages, had leisure for reading, and desired to make that reading effective for purposes of culture. The books recommended in each section were grouped under three heads: books required, books recommended, books of reference. Wherever possible, readers were to be associated in circles under a leader, portfolios of pictures and other illustrative material were to be circulated from circle to circle, and it was hoped that there might be some experimental and object-teaching in the circle; occasional lectures were to be given which might serve to kindle interest and widen the area of the work; rambles might be arranged to do field-work in botany or geology, or to visit some historic mansion, some museum, or battle-field in the neighbourhood. The Young People's Circles were to be associated, if possible, with a particular school, to become the basis of Old Scholars' Associations, cherishing the spirit of loyalty to their old school and continuing the friendships of school-days, as the old boys of Winchester and Eton and other public schools do. There were to be certificates for those who carried out the prescribed course of reading, but there was to be no examination for these certificates. All books were to be bound in a special cover (registered as the property of the Union), and supplied from headquarters at reduced prices. The courses of reading were to be drawn up by the best authorities in the country; this reading was to be as real and human, " as full of living and practical interest as possible. May I use the word 'genial' to express my meaning ?"

Lastly, there was to be a Summer Assembly every year in some holiday centre. This Assembly was to bring the readers into touch not only with each other, but with some of the ablest living exponents of literature, history, and science ; it was to recharge the enthusiasm of members for the work of the ensuing winter, and to popularise the movement among the holiday crowds. " These assemblies will be dynamos by which we shall generate the electricity."

The new National Home Reading Union was definitely launched at a meeting held at the house of the Earl of Aberdeen in Grosvenor Square, on April 13th, 1889. The Bishop of London (Dr. Temple), the late Dean Farrar, Dr. J. Percival, now Bishop of Hereford, Canon Barker (now Dean of Carlisle), the late Rev. Hugh Price Hughes, the late Sir Joshua Fitch, and Mr. George Howell, M.P., were present at the meeting. Mr. T. E. Heller represented the National Union of Teachers, and Mr. B. Jones the Co-operative Wholesale Society. Mr. George Howell, M.P., and the Rev. J. T. Lawrence, M.A., of Cambridge, were appointed as secretaries. It was decided to hold the first Summer Assembly at Blackpool.

The choice of Blackpool was a bold *coup* ; so bold that even the best friends of the movement on the spot, like the late Rev. J. Wayman, were at first opposed to it. But the very arguments they urged against Blackpool were turned against themselves. Blackpool swarmed with visitors : that was just the reason why the Union should go there ; these hard-headed folk of the northern manufacturing districts were the very people the Union was out to lay hold of ; it was the best pulpit for preaching the new crusade. Blackpool was given up to pleasure ; therefore, it had plenty of large halls and assembly-rooms for lectures, concerts, and social gatherings. It was a higher pleasure which the Union brought with it to—

" Poison all meaner choice for evermore."

The proposal was taken up eagerly by the Mayor of Blackpool, who summoned an influential meeting at the Court-house. Paton addressed this meeting, and won it over unanimously to his proposal. Fortune favoured the bold. What was described at the time by meticulous persons as " a leap in the dark " proved, in the event, to be a leap in the light. The gayest, idlest, and inanest of watering-places found itself transformed in a few hours, as though by magic, into a Summer University. " Bewildered visitors and inhabitants," said Mr. Churton Collins, " gazed in wonder at theatres and concert-halls placarded with names which they had never seen anywhere but on the title-pages of books and in the columns of literary and scientific reviews. For the old programmes, gaudy with the attractions of melodrama and *opéra bouffe*, had been substituted programmes grave with the syllabuses of academic professors. Winter gardens, pier-head, assembly-rooms—all had been subsidised for addresses and lectures. Every morning and afternoon audiences, numbering in some cases upwards of 500, assembled in the Opera-house and the theatres, not for the ordinary amusements of such places, but to hear teachers like the Master of Downing expounding the mysteries of physiology, or Professor Rhys Davids the origin of fables."

The key-note of the whole meeting, and in a sense of the whole movement thus inaugurated, was struck in an inspiring address by Professor James Stuart, M.P., on February 16th, 1888. Going back to the Act of 1870, he spoke of " the new wants, new desires, new capabilities which crowd upon us, and the new prospect of hope." The immediate aim of the Union was " to assist the reading of the people," its ultimate purpose " that we should be part of the means by which Higher Education is brought to the people's homes. The object of all education," he said, " is to help people to think for themselves. . . . The man who does not think sees and hears a thousand things which make no impression on him, whereas all nature is an open book to the man who thinks."

" Whenever new schemes, new ideas, are brought forward —new plans for the amelioration of the lot of mankind— there is one thing from which they suffer quite as much as from the opposition of their enemies, and that is from too much being expected of them. Because they are capable of doing something they are expected to do everything, and, because they do not succeed in fulfilling so great an expectation, there sets in a reaction against them. Let us not fall into this fault by expecting too much either from this particular movement for education, or from the education movement itself. Boundless as our hopes from these may be, and may justly be, I am not one of those who look for the regeneration of the world to arise from education alone, although I am very confident that that is one of the means towards it, inasmuch as it develops one portion of that many-sided thing, human nature. To have secure national progress, it must be made along all lines simultaneously, intellectual, material, and moral. What is the good of preaching of intellectual culture to the man who is cold and hungry? And if the world gains its longed-for wealth and leisure without having attained also to some measure of moral as well as intellectual cultivation, *its wealth will chiefly increase its cares, its leisure will increase its crimes*. It is only when we join, as part of an universal advance of the whole host, that we can carry forward the cause of human progress, that we can run and not be weary, walk and not be faint."

Archdeacon Farrar preached a great sermon on the ensuing Sunday in Christchurch. Dr. Percival, Dean W. Moore Ede, Dean Barker, Prebendary Harry Jones, the late Dr. J. A. Macfadyen, the late Dr. J. Guinness Rogers, the Rev. Dr. Scott Lidgett, the late Sir Joshua Fitch, Sir M. White Ridley, M.P., Sir Henry Roscoe, M.P., Mr. R. Yerburgh, M.P., Professor G. F. Browne (now Bishop of Bristol), Dr. Courtney, S. Kenny, Professor W. F. Barrett, Dr. J. H. (now Sir J. H.) Murray, the Rev. H. R. Haweis, Professor Baldwin Brown, Professor Milnes Marshall, Miss Jane Harrison, Sir Robert Ball, Professor J. S. Symes, the late Mr. Churton Collins, Mr. W. E. A. Axon, Dr. Kimmins, the late Dr. R. D. Roberts, Mr. J. A. R. Marriott, and many others took part in this historic assembly. Small wonder that the forts of folly were stormed by the legions of sweetness and light. The presence and assistance also of the Secretary of both the Cambridge Syndicate for University Extension and of the Secretary of the London Joint Board was proof positive that University Extension Authorities, so far from regarding the Union with disfavour, welcomed it most cordially as an ally.

The striking success of the Blackpool Assembly made clear beyond all controversy three distinct propositions: first, that there existed deep-seated and widespread, among all classes of people—adult and young alike—a readiness

to avail themselves of the guidance and assistance offered
by the Union ; that the scheme of the Union, as it was
proposed to organise and carry it out, had the full approval
of men of the highest authority in learning and education,
and could rely on their support ; and that such assemblies
as that just terminated would, if arranged annually, be
as great a success in England as in America, and even wider
in the range of their usefulness.

Next began the spade-work. Many influential persons
gave the help of their names as Vice-presidents ; many
others formed the Council and took active part in shaping
out the work. Dr. Percival became Chairman of the
Council ; Dr. Alex Hill, Master of Downing College, Chairman of the Executive Committee ; Mr. T. F. Hobson was
appointed General Secretary, and Miss M. C. Mondy as
his assistant, with special charge of the Young People's
section ; Sir Owen Roberts was Treasurer, and Paton
Honorary Secretary. Six thousand, three hundred and
forty-three members were enrolled in the first year. At
first the attempt was made to keep intimate touch with
the reading of all these members. During the first reading
season memoranda sheets were sent out each month to
every member. On this sheet each member was required
to state definitely the reading which he had done in the
course of the previous month, to answer certain questions
set in the magazine, to submit his difficulties, and the
points on which he required further information. These
sheets were stored and indexed under an elaborate system
which soon necessitated an accessory office in Cambridge
fitted with innumerable pigeon-holes. But such detailed
control proved both too onerous for the staff and too
exacting for the victims : it had to be given up after the
first year. Still it was a great good fortune to the new-
born Union that Dr. Alex Hill and the Rev. T. J. Lawrence
happened to be in residence at the same college at Cambridge. The careful collaboration of these two gentlemen
in devising the methods and formulating the rules of the
Union resulted in a scheme of operations which has stood
practically unchanged from the beginning. That there
were two men so able and so willing to do this work, and
to supervise the working of the machinery, was all the
more important because in the autumn the founder of
the Union was laid aside with a bad attack of congestion

of the brain, and was unable to give any attention to the
work for practically a whole year.

" In no other work to which I have set my hand," said
Paton, " have I found so many spontaneous offers of help,
nor have I ever had fellow-workers so devoted and disinterested, so loyal in co-operation with each other, so
unstinting in the time and trouble they gave to the common
cause."

Foremost among these helpers, next to Dr. Alex Hill,
must be named Miss M. C. Mondy, who became General
Secretary in the third year, and now, after retiring from
the more arduous office, still continues the " Young People's
Magazine." Miss Annie E. F. Barlow undertook the
General Readers' Section and its magazine. In that work
and in the collection of illustrative material for the cir-
culating portfolios, in the propagation and advocacy of
the work, she has been untiring. She gave most liberally
towards the funds, and was for long years the only effective
connecting link between the Home Reading Union and
the Co-operative Holidays Association. Miss M. R.
Pridham, who kindly undertook the Secretaryship of the
Union pending the appointment of a successor to Miss
Mondy, and who followed Dr. Hill as editor of the " Special
Course Magazine," and Miss Ada M. Read, who succeeded
Miss Mondy as General Secretary, deserve special mention
for work ungrudged and unceasing, not done in the lime-
light, but " as ever in the great Taskmaster's eye."
Without such trusty helpers the good ship would have
foundered. As it was, there was no smooth pilotage for
her. It was comparatively easy to draw up on paper a
scheme of reading and an organisation of Reading Circles ;
it was no easy matter, after the first excitement, to
awaken interest, to compel an inert, ignorant, apathetic
set of people to believe that they would be genuinely
interested in the contents of a book. " People in general,"
said Dr. Johnson, " do not willingly read if they can
have anything else to amuse them." As always in
educational matters in our country, the supply preceded
and outran the demand. It was not the help of the
highly placed which had been wanting. H.R.H. the
Princess Louise, Marchioness of Lorne, consented to

become President in 1895. The Bishops, the most celebrated Professors, and other men and women of eminence have not been slow to give their support and help. But the man in the street has not been responsive, or, having once responded, he has shown himself lacking in what the Calvinistic theology calls " final perseverance." The fees were fixed so low that, without large numbers, the Union could not pay its way. It was sheer financial pressure which led to the ultimate abandonment of the Summer Assembly. But, in spite of that, the Union has, thanks to the generosity of its friends and the enthusiasm of faithful circle-leaders and members, kept its head above water, and grown in dimensions, till, at the present day, it numbers 6,500 members, whilst there are some 70,000 schoolchildren in Reading Circles under the direct guidance of the Union.

The educational authorities were prompt to recognise the Union as a serious educational factor in the life of the country. In the volume of instructions issued to H.M. Inspectors of Schools in 1890, the Educational Department called special attention to the advantage of the circles. The London School Board, in answer to a memorial in the same year, issued a special circular to the head masters, teachers, and managing committees of all their schools, setting forth the desirability of using the machinery of the circles in connection with the Union so as to keep the past and present scholars in the common pursuit of reading. The United Education Committee of the Co-operators issued a circular to all co-operative societies urging them to form circles. The Gilchrist Trustees urged that Reading Circles under the Union should be formed after the delivery of a course of their lectures. The Working Men's Club and Institute Union helped things on in a similar way. Ministers of Education, Sir John Gorst, the late Sir William Anson, Mr. Augustine Birrell, high-placed officials like Dr. M. E. Sadler, Sir Robert Morant, Sir George Kekewich, Sir Joshua Fitch, Dr. W. Garnett, Dr. C. W. Kimmins, Professor J. W. Mackail, and Mr. A. P. Graves, the author of " Father O'Flynn," have helped the cause by public advocacy, private advice, and steadfast friendship ; eminent librarians like Dr. Richard Garnett of the British Museum, Mr. L. Stanley Jast of Croydon, Mr. Potter Briscoe of Nottingham, Mr.

Pacy of Westminster, Mr. C. W. Sutton of Manchester, have linked up the movement with the free libraries. Branches and Circles have been formed over-sea in Canada, Jamaica, Egypt, the Gold Coast, South Africa, New Zealand, and Australia, the last of which has set up as an independent Union working in friendly alliance with the parent Union. The Co-operative Holiday Association has ultimately taken the place of the Summer Assemblies ; its organ, "Comradeship," runs a course of reading (including "open-air" books) largely selected from the Union's programme. The idea of the Union has been adopted by the Diocesan Reading Circles and the Wesley Reading Guild. The Universities, both ancient and modern, have done all in their power to help.

"We are most anxious," said Paton, before ever the Union was launched, "that the whole plan should build itself up into those great Universities which I regard as treasuries that have been gathering up for us, not only the knowledge, but the grace and culture of the ages. And I wish this movement to be one of the channels through which that knowledge, that grace and culture, will be distributed broadcast among the people at large."

All manner of experiments have been tried to meet every form of demand. An introductory section of a simpler and shorter type was started to catch the average working man who did not deal much in books. For this section, and its magazine, Paton bore the whole of the expense. Commercial Supplements for business youths, Browning Supplements, Dante Supplements, Music Supplements, Welsh Supplements, have been issued, if by any means they might catch some. Efforts were made to start work among the sailors and the soldiers.

And yet, in spite of all that has been done, the national standard of reading is low, the national taste still inclines toward the worse. To thousands of boys and girls "the fateful gift of reading" is a curse, not a blessing. The devil, as Charles Kingsley would say, seems to be gaining on the parsons. His Satanic Majesty has not been slow to avail himself of all the new chances of temptation afforded by ignorance that has learned to read. Gutter literature grows apace. There seems to be an ever-

increasing flood of publications. Some of it is mere
trash ; some of it is silly puff advertisement of drugs and
beautifiers ; but much of it is filth. It is filth of the per-
fumed sort, which throws a glamour over vice and makes
lust appear as manly. It appeals to low instincts and
awakens the lowest passions. In his later years the
problem of this garbage literature touched Paton deeply
and moved him to new effort. School teachers, school
inspectors, and social workers like Mr. R. P. Corfe and
the Rev. F. C. Spurr opened his eyes to what was going
on, and his whole soul rose in flaming revolt against these
new triumphs of the Evil One.

" We must save our children, if possible," he wrote,
" from the malarious infection of this pestiferous literature, trashy and often most injurious, which is poured out.
We must strain every nerve to save the tastes of the
young from early corruption."

Our schools seem to have called into existence new
agencies and furnished new opportunities for evil and
vulgar suggestions to be poured through open channels
into the minds of our youth.

" The evidence that has been laid before the Joint
Committee on ' Lotteries and Indecent Advertisements,'
which has just issued its report, together with the fact
that one of our most respectable publishing firms, when
summoned before the Police Court in Bow Street, surren-
dered 40,000 of an annual magazine tainted with obscenity,
which they had purchased for sale on their bookstalls,
has startled many, like myself. We have now learnt that
there is an ' impure literature industry ' in our country
which has immensely increased of late years, and which,
in the opinion of those who know most of the youth of
our time, is doing more to corrupt them, and to undo the
moral influences of our day and Sunday schools, and of
our brigades and clubs, than anything else."

" I am assured if this truth were fully realised there
would arise at once a new censorship in an aroused and
vigilant public opinion that would quickly denounce and
arrest this evil. In day-schools and in Sunday-schools

much might be done at once by our teachers if they spoke
earnestly to their scholars of the immense influence on
their life and character of their reading, so giving them
warning and counsel. Also, if the working men of England were made to understand, as they easily could be,
how this evil is embruting the life of their children, sap-
ping their strength, and corrupting their minds, I am
certain that the associations in which the working men
of England have now organised themselves for social,
economic, and political objects would promptly and
mightily intervene to save their homes and their children
from the moral contamination which now blights the
hope and joy of their home life, and imperils the future
well-being of the people."

When such evil was rampant in the land, he could not
stand by and remain idle, even in the weakness of extreme old age. It roused him to new fire in his seventy-
seventh year, and Mr. James Marchant's volume, " The
Cleansing of a City," contained two papers on " The Moral
Training of our Youth " and " The Reading of our Youth "
which were as full of fire and force as anything Paton ever
wrote. Against this combination of the powers of wicked-
ness must be set the greater power, if only it could be
realised, of the communion of the saints. He called
on them to come to the help of the Lord against the
mighty. Culture, like every Christian grace, must be used
not for self, but in the service of others. The readers of
the community must recognise their duty to the non-
readers. Those who have freely received must be ready
to give freely to those whose need is greatest. The passion
for worse must be overcome by the dynamic, expulsive
power of a new passionate affection for the highest.
Above all, he appealed to the teachers.

" The Home Reading Union was chiefly formed in order
that it might, before children left school, train them to the
right use, the healthful use, of the gift of reading, so fateful, so perilous, and thus train them in the beauty of our
literature, so that they may be elevated beyond the reach
of pernicious writings."

But the teacher cannot do all. If he give the hunger for

the mental food that is wholesome, there must be provision for after-school years. If children were left to struggle singly, the survivors would be few, *rari nantes in gurgite vasto* ; but in association enthusiasm could be maintained, hitherto gain could be consolidated and built up, extravagances and errors could be corrected, and the right taste, the right habitude securely established. The Circle is the Union's central idea, and all that stands between it and the realisation of all its beneficent possibilities for England, is the lack of Circle leaders.

The central idea, however, and the governing policy of the N.H.R.U. was not destructive but constructive. The gift of reading had been universally bestowed by the State, but it was, as Paton used to say, " a perilous gift, which may be the source of highest good, but also of direst evil. In bestowing this gift we have given something like Pandora's box to every child, and opened it, so that from it winged powers fly forth to brighten and to bless or to darken and destroy." The nation, as a whole, had not waked up to see the moral issues of the Act of 1870, the influence of reading upon character.

" We need to realise the subtle, infectious, and most penetrative influence that steals silently into our whole being from the books we read. Each book steeps the mind in its own atmosphere, which slowly impregnates the imagination and feeling, and breathes upon us its own quality, good or evil. We say that a man is known by his friends with whom he consorts. It is equally, if not more, true that we know a man by the books he reads, not only because his choice of books reveals his inner taste, but because, whatever he may be, the books he reads will gradually, but most surely, form his taste, sway his judgment, and fashion his conduct. Some who lament the malign influence which they see exerted by this fateful gift of reading, which may be so potent for evil, regret its bestowment upon the people. To withdraw that gift, however, is impossible ; and to desire to withdraw it is a vain and impious wish, for this gift of reading, with its marvellous influence, is as potent for good as for evil. It is well that we cannot thrust back the shadow on the sun-dial and rob the people of this gift, which may be used for their highest good. But, having bestowed this gift upon our

people, and bestowed it upon them in their childhood,
when life is young and all its possibilities are before them,
how unspeakably great is the responsibility which rests
upon us in bestowing this gift upon our children to train
them in its right use !   That was, indeed, in a pre-eminent
sense, the object for which the N.H.R.U. was formed.
The elementary schools teach our children how to read;
the object of our movement is to teach them what to
read."

A great American preacher, who used to be a Yorkshire
blacksmith, tells how, as a mere lad, he gathered a few
friends around him, lads who cared for books as he did,
and together they used to read and help each other.   "We
became companions, and gave the roughs a wide berth.
The books did their work, too, and fought the devil with
a finer fire than his."   This was the principle of the
Reading Circle.   It is a means of realising the companionship of the greatest minds of the past by means of
companionship with one another.   George Grote, John
Stuart Mill, and William Ellis discovered the virtue of the
same method in the early days of the nineteenth century,
and traced back to its influence some of the most helpful
formative influences in their own intellectual life.   Paton
called it "Associative Reading," and believed that a
great book never yielded up its full virtue except to such
associated readers.

"Converse upon a subject that has been read at home
will increase the interest in that subject, and infix on the
mind the memory of what is read.   Also the variety, and,
it may be, antagonism, of opinion that are expressed
upon the various topics that are dealt with in the book,
and the criticism by others of the various arguments or
statements contained in it, must open the mind to a
larger range of thought and to a wider and fairer judgment.
"We all know how words become very much more
effective when they are spoken, even though they have
never been read before.   In this way, for example, poetry
becomes much more impressive, and the emotion which
it portrays is conveyed with much more effect, to the
hearer than to the reader.   Mr. Yeats has truly said that

the finest poetry is meant to be spoken—it is designed to give pleasure through the medium of sound appealing to the ear. He therefore says how desirable it is that those who would foster the spirit of poetry should take it into their social lives—friends reading to friends, or one member of a family to others. There is no doubt that poetry would be much more appreciated, and more widely enjoyed, if it were thus made more of a social delight. Also every one knows that reading a play never evokes the same keen interest, or reveals to the mind so clearly the interplay and development of the varied characters, with their subtle affinities and contrasts, as does the reading of a play by a Circle when each one takes the part of one of the characters in the play. When thus read, there is a reality and vividness in the personages of the drama, and in its evolution as it develops from act to act, as is seldom the case when the play is merely read.

" All of us know how social sympathy gives a genial brightness to humour, a keen edge to wit, and a solemn tenderness to pathos. We know this in daily life. And it is remarkably evidenced in social reading. I have little time for reading, but a friend of mine has read me more than once some passages of Mr. Dooley's fantastic and piquant pages from the ' Westminster Review.' I know that we both have laughed at his droll caricatures of the political and social world of the time, as we never could have done if we had read them privately for ourselves. Let then this magnificent power of social sympathy, this reverberation of feeling when we have social reading, be more cultivated, that the enjoyment of life may be fuller.

" More, however, than this. Associative reading will lead to tolerance of judgment, clearness of thinking, and also accuracy in expression, as each one in a social Reading Circle seeks to give his view upon the subject read. We need to encourage one another in the reading of the best books, and then to help one another in the discussion of these books, so as to get the very pith and marrow of them into our thought, whilst we also inhale the delight and inspiration they give. All this can be assured by associative reading."

Lastly, the Home Reading Union was, as he used to say, the People's University, which threw open its doors

19

to everybody in the land and made the humblest man sharer in the highest joys and the best culture of all times and all peoples. " You must see," he wrote, " as I have clearly seen, that the widest and most universal, the most varied and in many senses the most effective agency for culture and education must be the reading of the people." The hope of an educated democracy lay in giving definiteness, continuity, and system to the home-reading of the working man, and that is what the Union set itself to do. In so doing, it brought the highest minds into personal touch with the humblest.

" There is a kind of Socialism which pervades the N.H.R.U. in which I delight. Socialism has become a chameleonic word, having many aspects and colours ; but the Socialism which is found here is one in which all of us must rejoice. A child in one of our Reading Circles was taking the history course in our young people's magazine. There was something in the book which she could not understand, and which the magazine did not explain. Mr. York Powell, the eminent Professor of History in the University of Oxford, was the leader of that course, and wrote the articles in the magazine. The child's letter, putting in simple words her difficulty, was sent from the office of the Union to Professor York Powell, and he himself, with his own hand, wrote a letter to the child explaining her difficulty, and giving her even greater pleasure than his explanation gave by the kindly words he used. Here, verily, we have the true Socialism which should pervade all life—the highest stooping to the humblest ; the strong giving of their strength to the feeble ; the wise giving of their knowledge to the ignorant."

In spite of such shining potentialities, and the splendid help he received from so many quarters, the progress of the work was slow. Perhaps no other work to which he set his hand taxed so much his powers of endurance and of optimism. Results were slow to accrue, and took much pains in the getting. The water was there, the steed was brought down to the very bank, but it took much persuasion to make him drink. The financial difficulty was always with them. Though many friends and relatives gave nobly, notably Mr. R. Yerburgh, Mr. and Mrs. J. P. Thomasson, the Misses A. and S. Peckover, the

Bishop of Hereford (Dr. Percival), Mr. J. R. Barlow and Miss A. E. F. Barlow, Mrs. Greg, Mr. W. Morton, Mr. Alex Hill, the late Mr. A. B. Paton and the late Mr. J. R. Paton, not to mention many others, the Union was forced to live from hand to mouth, and never had a margin available for vigorous progaganda. When the time of the majority celebration drew near, Paton felt, with others, that the best way of signalising its coming of age was to raise an endowment fund of £10,000, and he himself gave £400 to launch the fund. The scheme was to be inaugurated at a meeting at the Mansion House, at which H.R.H. the Princess Louise had promised to attend, but the death of King Edward VII made it impossible to hold the meeting. A most successful garden-party, however, was held in the Botanical Gardens, Regent's Park, on June 18th, 1910, attended by thousands of school-children, and from that garden-party a hearty message of greeting was sent to the founder, who was at that time already in his eightieth year, and laid aside from active life.

It would not be possible to make a selection from his correspondence which would be representative of all the various ramifications of the work done by the honorary Secretary of the Union. There were negotiations with publishers for securing cheap editions ; there were letters to the press ; there were appeals to School Boards and educational authorities all over the country ; there were arrangements for meetings and Summer Assemblies ; there was correspondence with editors and printers of the magazine ; there was the attempt to stir up Sunday-school teachers, club and institute workers, leaders of P.S.A.'s and men's Brotherhoods, to avail themselves of the facilities provided by the Union ; there was much correspondence with librarians, culminating in a paper which he read at the Glasgow Conference of the Library Association in 1908; there were letters to H.M. Inspectors whom he was allowed by the Board of Education to circularise; there were, finally, the numberless letters appealing for money to meet the " everlasting lack of pence." The extracts below are given as samples :

To the Secretary of Education in one of the Colonies

" May we venture to quote from a letter written by a gifted writer who was for some years resident in one of

our Colonies.   In a letter which was addressed to editors
of several papers in the Colony, where she resided, she says:

" The loneliest reader, buried in the bush, will be kept in
touch with the reading life of thousands of companions,
through his monthly magazine—his course marked out, his
difficulties met, and his progress tested.   It is, however,
most desirable that Circles should be formed wherever at
least four readers can be gathered under a leader.   This
will prove a great stimulus to study, and, where necessary,
may lessen the expense, since the members can arrange
among themselves each to buy two or three of the books
required, and pass them round.

" One of the privations which educated colonists often
feel most is the absence of intellectual conversation for
their children to hear.   Yet there must be few colonial
townships, if any, without men and women of intelligence
and cultivation who can talk well, if anything occurs to
draw them out and draw them together.   The Home
Reading Union aims at helping two classes of people—
those who have so much leisure that Satan finds mischief
for their idle hands to do, and those who have so little that
they want a powerful motive to save them from complete
absorption in each day's grind of toil—these last being in
an overwhelming majority among you.   May we urge
that, wherever Young People's Circles are formed, parents
should join as honorary members, and make an effort to
read (or hear) some of the books.   Numbers of excellent
parents in the Colonies have never in their lives—or, at
any rate, in their colonial lives—had time to read.   Their
children are often less clever, but more educated, than
themselves.   Few things could give more pleasure to the
promoters of this Union than for it to become a means of
bringing such parents more abreast with their children's
mental life, able to give them the benefit of their own
shrewd, intelligent judgment on some of the books they read.

" It is hoped that the Union will also prove a pleasant
link with friends and relatives in the dear old country.
Young cousins on opposite sides of the world, following
the same course of reading, would find they had topics
in common when they sat down to the difficult task of
corresponding with relatives whom they had never seen.

" We need to draw closer together, individually and

nationally.   Even now the mass of the English people are but slowly waking up to realise the wealth of affection of young, energetic life and national vigour which the young nations born of her are ready to pour back into the old country's heart.   We should indeed be glad to think that, by the simple methods of this friendly Union, we may learn, on both sides of the sea, to know one another better."

To Miss Mondy

" There is very much in your proposal that I greatly like.   May I ask you, in reference to ' dancing,' to consider the following points :

" 1. Our Young People's Circles are often mixed.

" 2. We expect them to be in these Circles till eighteen years of age.

" 3. The dancing which is general now is not of the old sort—square dances—but round dancing, in which Byron's judgment remains, I think, unchallenged.

" 4. Dancing saloons are, as all know, the cause of more moral mischief and ruin to young people than anything else, and it is important not to form tastes that will lead them there.

" 5. So closely is dancing associated with moral peril in some places that I know respectable working people, not religious, would not allow their children to go where it is practised.

" 6. In my daughter's Girls' Homes, though all are of one sex, some parents would not allow their children to go there, if dancing was allowed.

" 7. We must look to Sunday-schools for a large clientèle ; they would mostly be repelled from us if they saw such encouragement given to it.

" Of course, if a leader of his own accord invites his young people whom he knows to a party where there is dancing, that is a different thing.   A public recommendation sent out by us generally and indiscriminately, would be judged by many adversely."

To Dr. C. W. Kimmins

"*June 7th*, 1907.

" We are on the right track, and will succeed in what will be a great national, educational, and moral enterprise. It is the moral life of our people that chiefly concerns me."

To Mr. Fred Marquis

"*October 2nd*, 1908.

" Your letter has uplifted me. I have had many cheering letters of late, from many quarters, and in reference to many causes ; but your letter, I think, has brimmed a full cup to overflowing.

" I am seeing now, with definite clearness and certainty, that two things are necessary :

" 1. That we bring the school into closer touch with the home life, and make the influence of the school somehow to pervade the home ; and

" 2. That we conserve the best educational influences and elements of the school in the after-life of our boys and girls. See also what I have said in the enclosed on ' What Boys Read.' We must thunder this message right and left wherever we can. I shall endeavour to make the Board of Education make it almost a duty in every school to have a Reading Circle for the objects named, otherwise the literature by which our boys and girls are now debauched (for I can use no other word) is undermining and destroying the good done in our schools.

" You cannot imagine how grateful I am for the splendid sympathy and support that younger men like yourself are giving to me, and oh, how much it is needed ! I want you also to delight with me in the work that is being done in Scotland by Mr. W. Temple, the son of the late Archbishop. The enclosed letter has been sent to every minister there, and you will see how Mr. Temple spoke twice every day and preached thrice on Sundays during the fortnight. This campaign has lifted up thousands of people in Scotland to a nobler vision of the Church and of her social redemptive work. You may well imagine how greatly this delights me, for here we are on common ground with all the highest and best thought of the world."

To Mr. Fred Marquis

"*November 17th*, 1909.

" We must not allow the teachers of England to fall away from the great responsibility which is theirs—to train the children in the right use of that fateful and perilous gift of reading.

" . . . If we cannot show them that we are bringing great advantages to them in giving them the very best form of self-education and of social fellowship, we might close our work."

" March 12th, 1909.

" I feel myself that the N.H.R.U. is only at the beginning of its great educational work for the people."

Letter to H.M. Inspectors in England

" February 6th, 1909.

" In a letter which I wrote some ten years ago, of which many issues in leaflet form have been published, I said : ' Much evil arises from the worthless, and sometimes immoral, literature which children read out of school. I am, therefore, intensely desirous that the reading-lesson of the school should become a central and directing influence in the reading of the elder children at home.' Since this was written, the Board of Education has authorised the reading-class of senior standards in all schools to be, if desired, converted into a Reading Circle associated with the N.H.R.U.—these Reading Circles being formed specially to direct, encourage, and in a sense supervise the home-reading of the children during the last two years of their school-life. They thus train the children ere they leave school in the right use of the gift of reading which is now universally bestowed upon them. A pamphlet has just been issued on the ' Reading of our Youth,' of which I send you a copy. May I ask you to glance over its pages, and also to read a Memorial which was addressed to directors of education and to H.M. Inspectors and teachers ? I hope that after reading these you may be willing to ask the teachers in your district to consider the advantages of the Reading Circle for their elder scholars, so that the influence of the school may pass on to the home of the scholar, and also may abide when the school is left. For it may be hoped that the habit of reading bright and inspiring books at home may be so formed during those two years as to continue in after-years ; especially if, as the Board of Education has recommended, the younger teachers, or the managers of schools or other friends, will form Reading Circles for scholars who have left school, who will meet in some cheerful room of the school buildings."

Letter to Inspectors

"*June 30th*, 1910.

"My friend, Canon Rawnsley, has taken great interest in the moral life of our people, and has been led to see how profoundly it has been affected by the reading of the people, and especially by the reading of our young people. I send you an extract from a sermon which he preached, which I think cannot but impress you as seriously as it impresses me. The statement made by a judge some few years ago was alarming when he made it, and Canon Rawnsley is quite right when he says that the number of these journals which the judge denounced is now greatly increased. It was the thought of all this unspeakable evil which is being wrought by the fateful gift of reading —in itself a gift which can and ought to be productive of the highest good—that led the N.H.R.U., which was formed chiefly for this object, to get the reading-class of the day and evening schools converted into a Home-reading Circle, and to plead that the last two years of every child's life in the school should be devoted to training that child to use the gift of reading in the happiest and most profitable way. By doing so it was hoped also to bring the home into closer relations with the school, and, which is of even greater importance, to prepare the children when they leave school to carry on Reading Circles in the same bright and social and inspiring manner.

"I need not tell you how the Board of Education has supported us. I enclose you two letters which they sent out two or three years ago, and I also enclose a letter which Sir Robert Morant has written in support of the endowment fund which we are raising, to make the N.H.R.U. permanent, and to make its influence and methods more widely extended and effective.

"And now I write to you because we have found that the one thing that is needful, and which, if possible, we must endeavour to attain, is to induce the teachers to adopt our simple but most effective methods of achieving this end, which is, as I think you will recognise, so momentous. Unfortunately, the teachers of England have not seemed universally to recognise the simplicity and efficiency, and the unspeakable value of this method of the Reading Circle in the school which takes the place of the Reading Class. I write, therefore, with a certain diffidence and reserve, but urged by the extreme importance of the matter, to entreat you to use your great influence, for there is no other way in which we can reach and arouse the teachers universally, and secure their adoption of this method which is earnestly commended by the Board of Education.

" If you will do this, you will, I am confident, have conferred an inestimable boon upon our country, and will have made the education given in the schools of our country a blessing instead of its being really harmful, as it is unfortunately in many cases."

Note.—The present address of the Union is 12, York Buildings, Adelphi, W.C.

CHAPTER XVII

THE SUNDAY-SCHOOL

" All thy children shall be taught of the Lord, and great shall be the peace of thy children."—*Isaiah* liv. 13.

THE Sunday-school has played a conspicuous part in the history of English education. Up to the middle of the last century it was occupied mainly, though not exclusively, with the teaching of young children, and up till a much later date the instruction, though spiritual in motive, was mainly secular, and consisted in teaching children to read. With the development of national education, the Sunday-school had to adjust itself to new conditions and new needs. When all the children were taught to read in the day-school, the Sunday-school curriculum and method had to be entirely remodelled, and the Sunday-school teacher, in order to maintain himself on any sort of parity with the day-school, had to aim at a far higher standard of efficiency. Moreover, the Sunday-school had to play its part in the great work of safeguarding the years of adolescence to which Paton had addressed himself in his reform of the Evening-school system. In regard to these years from fourteen to seventeen the Sunday-school had a special responsibility to fulfil towards the Church. In theory, the function of the school was to prepare the child for church membership ; the door that led out of the Sunday-school was meant to lead straight into the Church. But the Sunday-school, like the day-school, failed in continuity. As a matter of fact, 80 per cent. of the scholars were leaving before the age of fifteen, and only a small number of these were attaching themselves to the Church. It is a significant fact that the working men and working women who now stand outside the Church once sat in the Sunday-school. Closely associated with this aspect of the problem was the relation of the Sunday-school to the home.

These were the three problems which the Sunday-schools had to face in the latter part of the nineteenth century.

Paton did not hesitate to assume that the child belonged to the Church. If baptism meant anything, it meant that the minister, as the Church's representative, claimed the child for a Christian Church ; the parent, on his part, undertook to do his part in carrying out the nurture and admonition of the Lord. The failure to retain the Sunday-school scholars was an open mark of failure on the part of both Church and Home.

" The leakage and waste of our Sunday-schools," he said, " is more lamentable than even of our day-schools. It appals me to think that we should lose 80 per cent. of the young people we have had in our Sunday-schools. To retain them, and safeguard them, to ensphere them in healthful influences, and to mould their life by Christian principles and win them into the fellowship of the Church and its ministers seems to me to be the very first and foremost concern and duty of the Church at the present time."

The basis of all reform, he felt, must be found in a proper insight into the nature and needs of adolescence.

" We must clearly understand the nature of the material that we have to handle. This means a psychological basis for all our teaching—in other words, pedagogy must be built on psychology.

" We must have sympathy with that material. This is necessary at all times, but especially so at the adolescent stage. New interests are awakened with the coming of adolescence ; light and guidance must be given to these new interests. New instincts and emotions come into play ; scope must be given for development. In the Sunday-school itself the scholar at the age of fourteen must be separated off from the younger ones, whom he regards as ' kids.' The change, in most cases, is best marked by a change of name. ' School ' implies authority; ' guild ' implies membership of a society in whose activities each member has a voice. With the instinct of comradeship goes that of leadership. The Sunday-school should recognise this instinct, as Dr. Arnold has done, and adapt to its own conditions the system of prefect government. There must be more regard paid to the psychological truth that there is no lasting impression without expression. Greater care must be exercised in dealing with emotion. Butler's great law has to be remembered : all emotion must become motion. All teaching, therefore, must have training associated with it. Christianity is essentially life and action. Its deep secrets are learned through service. In addition to better teaching, we must have, from the earliest stage, training, practice of the Christian life. Doing is not a deadly thing. To young people, as to old, it is the highway of revelation.

" Where the home is not in living co-operation with the Sunday-school, the Sunday-school itself must seek to give opportunities of practice in Christ's Name and open avenues of service. Our Sunday-schools have taught about Christ ; they must now begin to train in the practice of the Christian life."

Such, briefly stated, were the principles of Sunday-school advance as he saw them. They were not new, they were not original, they were not his special monopoly. No one ever more readily acknowledged his debts to others. No one was more ready to co-operate or avail himself of co-operation, and, full as he was of schemes of his own, he often astonished others by his willingness to help on their projects to wider recognition and application.

The winter of 1891–2 he was compelled to spend abroad. Most of the time he was in Florence. There he met with Dr. Duncan, of Syracuse, U.S.A., and heard from him with great interest of the work of the Home Department of the Sunday-school in America. The opportunity of adapting his system to the needs of our English Churches was no sooner seen than grasped, and no sooner was he back again in England than he talked the whole question over with the late Rev. W. Crosbie, his pastor at Park Hill Church. Mr. Crosbie took up the idea eagerly. There were many parents who sent their children to the school, but never attended the church themselves. The Home Department seemed to open up a way of reaching them, and Mr. Crosbie at once organised his districts and undertook to act as visitor himself for one of them. At the same time he approached the Sunday-school Union, the Church of

England Sunday-school Institute and the Wesleyan Sunday-school Union, giving them full particulars of the American movement, and suggesting certain modifications of method which would make the scheme more suitable to English conditions.

Letter to Miss Hearn

" When in Florence I had the great pleasure of forming the friendship of Dr. Duncan of Syracuse, New York State, and he very greatly interested me in the new movement which he has initiated called the Home Department of the Sunday-school.

" I think there are great possibilities connected with this movement in our country. I send you some papers which he has given me, and will be glad to supply you with more. In our country I think the movement must be somewhat associated with the Church as well as the Sunday-school, because the Sunday-school in this country is almost wholly adapted to children and young people. In America they have large numbers of adult scholars.

" Now as we desire especially to draw older people into fellowship with us in Bible-reading, I think it is well not to make it so prominently an extension of the Sunday school, but an extension, through the school, of the Church, which invites others to join them in this pleasant weekly Bible-reading. I send you two cards which we have issued from our own Church and School at Park Hill. Let me, in a word or two, indicate what seem to me the objects to be secured by this very simple method.

" 1. There are great multitudes who cannot come to church: invalids, mothers chained by family duties, etc., and there are others who have fallen into the habit of non-attendance at church, many of whom might yet, I think, be induced to engage in this simple exercise of reading a small portion of God's Word every Sabbath. In this way we should increase very largely the numbers of those who read at least a small portion of the Bible weekly.

" 2. By getting them to do this, which is all we ask them to do, they will be encouraged and may be induced to read a small portion of the Bible every day. For this object I think it very desirable to give the enclosed leaflets to every one who engages with us in this Bible-reading.

This leaflet gives, as you see, a portion of reading for every day in the week, and gives also a verse of a hymn which sets forth the spiritual truth of the lesson in an emotional form likely to be remembered, and also gives a golden text, as a text to be specially cherished and thought about.

" Thirdly and chiefly, in this way I think a number of people who are quite out of the way and unattached to any religious body or place of worship will be led to feel that they belong to somebody, and in any case of sickness or other trial, they will know to whom they can refer for spiritual comfort and counsel ; there will be some Church with which they have at least this connection, and in this way I think many may be brought into closer sympathy and fellowship with our Churches.

" 4. As the cards will have to be distributed every quarter, the visitor who distributes these cards will have an admirable occasion for speaking about the portions of Scripture read, and of introducing religious conversation in a natural way ; the visit will not be objectless, as too often the district visitor's is.

" 5. You will see that in America all the readers are arranged in classes. I think our people would not like to be considered members of a class, as though they were children, so we have on our cards simply arranged them in districts ; but each district will be under a special super-intendent, who will thus have the pastoral charge of all in the district who are engaged in this fellowship."

The movement has not found any wide acceptance in this country, but, where it has been tried, it has done much to restore the habit of systematic Bible-reading, and many folk who were out of the way, without any religious attachment, have been led to feel they belonged to some religious body ; in case of sickness or trial they have known where to turn for comfort and counsel ; and, best of all, a bond has been established uniting together the Home and the Sunday-school.

But this scheme was only accessory to a much larger scheme which had been for years in his mind and linked itself on to the larger question of the whole week-day life, and specially the leisure hours of the young adolescent life of the Church. The short hour of class on Sunday afternoon, he felt, was quite insufficient to counteract the evil influences of street-life and companionship during the week. He wanted to see a continuity of influence between Sunday and week-day. Clubs which catered merely for amusement, he thought, were not much help. "Just public-houses without the beer," he used to say. He wanted to see the week-evening and the Saturday afternoon brought under influences that were in the widest sense of the term educational, and under the term "educational" he included all that belonged to healthful recreation and sport. The following letter contains the germs of what afterwards shaped itself out into the Home Reading Union, the Sunday-school Institute, the Boys' Life Brigade, the Girls' Life Brigade, and the League of Honour. It shows how, in his mind, all these various institutions were really concerned with the same central problem. It shows, too, how quickly, with him, the inspiration of the prayer-meeting translated itself into a plan of campaign.

To Bishop Vincent

"*March 25th*, 1887.

"Yesterday was an all-day Convention among our Wesleyan friends here, and such a day they have not known for a quarter of a century. Mark Guy Pearse, Hugh Price Hughes and Mr. Chapman were here. I spent the day with this branch of the Catholic Church. I have seldom felt more the inspiration of our common faith—the joy of communion in the presence of our Lord, and the thrillings of His redeeming love.

"I am prepared the better to write you and to tell you of the good news which open for us a marvellous opportunity, and which I communicate to you at once, that now even amid your revellings in Ancient Art and the new world of a glorious Italian spring, you may give us some consecrated thoughts in the very beginning of our united work on both continents.

"I saw the two secretaries of the Sunday-school Union. The Wesleyan Sunday-school Union, through its Secretary, said that they would also join most earnestly with us in the proposed Conference. I placed before the Secretaries of both these Unions the great problem which underlies all other social problems, and which, if solved, carries with it their solution too, viz. how the Church can give nurture, protection, wise guidance during those perilous years from thirteen to eighteen when character and destiny are formed, to the children whom they have in their Sunday-schools. These children, now, alas, during those years desert Sunday-school as they have left the day-school.

"On Monday last I lunched with the Archbishop of Canterbury. The Archbishop took up the matter very earnestly, and at my request asked one of his leading clergymen in London, the Rector of Spitalfields, to co-operate with me in inviting six or seven of the ablest men of the English Church to meet six or seven of the Nonconformist Churches in a private preliminary Conference next month, so as to look at the whole question and draw up a body of well-considered suggestions to be submitted and commended to the larger and public Conference which we will, I hope, hold in May.

"This is admirable, and is the right way of going to work. Now I will put the problem in a larger and fuller form, viz. how to continue the educational and inspiring and protective work of the Church over those whom she has in her Sunday-school up to thirteen or fourteen, but whom she then to a large extent loses, and whom, even if she does retain, she does not influence mentally and ethically as she ought. In this larger sense the problem will divide itself into—

"(a) The requirements of the age, which may be said to be an advanced school age, up to seventeen or eighteen; and then

"(b) Of the age of young manhood and womanhood which lies beyond eighteen.

"Dividing the problem into these two divisions:

"1. Our children go to work at thirteen. Then the young soul first begins to be conscious of its individual personality and to feel the stirrings of independent life and the desire of freedom, and soon after there is the dawning of the social instincts. How are these young people, as they begin to regard themselves, to be treated (a) on the Sunday, (b) on the week-evening?

"(a) I have the idea that our scholars should pass at that age into a new rank or standard. I think even the name 'School' ought to be dropped. They should be enrolled then as members of the Church 'Institute,' be handled in a different spirit, be called to take some share in the responsibilities and government of the Institute, be invited to take active part in the class exercises, have the practical and ethical teaching of our faith impressed on them, be associated in Guilds for separate religious objects, especially objects that require and call out their activity, for it is through their active energies rather than their intellect or even their emotions, that they will be saved to us, kept in sympathy and living connection with the Church, and grow up to confess the Lord of Life.

" (b) In the winter evenings, in the leisure time, must not the Church care for the recreation—the physical, industrial, mental training, and the social life of these young people? Now, for this end, should not the Church adopt, take up, and use Recreative and Practical Classes of our Evening-schools, provide them with Christian teachers who will meet and look after the children of the Church in these schools, show their sympathy with them in their recreations, and practical classes there, e.g. in the making and mending classes, or cookery classes for the girls, and handwork classes for the boys. And then, in addition to these educational classes which the State supports but which the Church utilises and blesses, should not the Church have special social classes ?—a Guild for entertainments of a very high kind full of Christian spirit, for direct religious work (of a kind suited to the active and sympathetic natures of young people—therefore largely practical and humane), for Christian teaching illuminative and ethical, and for prayer.

" Thus the Church will encompass with her guardian wing and her brightening influence the opening life of all our youth—boys and girls.

" In this age, too, we can, and should, adopt the principles and methods of your Young Folks' Reading Union.

" 2. Then, for the later years of young manhood or young womanhood, I think in the same way the Church can, on the Sundays, have special classes and services for them. Many of them should now be able to become teachers, and take part in definite church work of a religious and especially of a practical kind ; others should be associated in district catechumen classes, more like Methodist class or band meetings. And, for the week evenings, should not the Church still go on to adopt and utilise the Technical Classes of all kinds—the Science and Art Classes, the

20

University Extension Classes that are being formed or that the Churches could always obtain in their neighbourhoods ? And then, for others who may not care for such higher instruction, such institutions as the Evening Homes for working women and girls, Clubs and Institutes for working men and youths. Especially for this class let us use your mighty agency, and have Circles for Home-reading directed by some of its abler members, and catching the inspiration of the great movement of which they are a part ; let us unite with it what you are doing—reading and instruction in art and art work, and in Natural History, which will quicken and elevate their sense of beauty, lead to the adornment of home and of home life, and make their holidays enjoyable and useful ; let us do what you are also beginning to do, viz. give instruction and association in the highest kinds of practical redemptive work.

" I have very roughly sketched what is in my mind—always remembering that for both periods, but especially for the first (a) instruction of all kinds must be very bright, interesting, and real (i.e. dealing with real things—the facts, the business, the actual enjoyments of life), and that (b) the principle of association, with its fellowship and leadership, is infinitely powerful, and (c) that life is doing, not knowing, and that young lives must have all their powers exercised in doing.

" This is our question—answer it for us, by the gracious help of the redeeming God, and let us unite in the first task which is given to us—this work of considering the problem and devising so far as we can the best means of solving it."

The immediate result of this letter was a small conference of Churchmen and Nonconformists held at Sion College in April 1887, which appointed a Committee " to consider how far the recreative and practical classes in the Evening-school might be made to have, directly and indirectly, an influence in promoting the moral and spiritual welfare of young people between the ages of twelve and eighteen. In a letter asking Dr. Hannay to attend this conference he writes :

" To me it is becoming almost unbearable that the Church from her Sunday-schools, like the State from its day-schools, should shoot into the great abyss the young committed to her care, just at the age when life becomes perilous, and the great testing and formative period begins, and when, therefore, the care and sympathy and help of the Church are especially necessary. I would have the whole Church to face this problem, to devise the best means available for its solution, and then, under the guidance of its leaders, gird itself to attempt at least this great redeeming work which is to hand. Let us make a great crusade of it, a ' business ' of God and of His Christ. It would gloriously crown all your life-work, for to hold and train these young people for Christ is to save England."

Mr. Acland's Evening School Code of 1893 opened up new possibilities. There was no reason why every Sunday-school should not start week-evening classes, and earn, with the help of grants from the County Council as well as Government, sufficient money to pay for all expenses of heating, lighting, and cleaning, and to provide all needful apparatus. All that was wanted was some person with the ability to organise and teachers willing and able to help. From that time the message which he pressed home with constant iteration upon Sunday-schools, was the Week-evening Institute.

" The years from twelve to eighteen," he would say, " are the neglected years of life. Our younger children are cared for—for them we provide schools. After nineteen our young men and young women have clubs of many kinds, and they are old enough to form associations of their own and thus to care for themselves. But the intermediate years, though in a real sense the most important, are the neglected years. They are the years which, on every ground, need most a wise and vigilant guidance and appropriate training, but they receive the least. This neglect is chargeable not only upon the State, which has the first responsibility in this matter, because it is vital to the well-being of the State, but also upon the Churches, who have had nearly all the children of the country entrusted to them in the Sunday-schools, but who, somehow or other, lose their hold upon the children and cease their care for them just when they enter these adolescent years of terrible peril.

" How are the Church and State to be aroused as,
they must be, to fulfil their responsibility ? We have
seen that in those years there is a wonderful and subtle
change of temperament, the awakening of new desires and
aspirations, the birth in a sense of a new nature, with new
impulses, new faculties and new powers. Surely, then,
what is required is that we respond to the appeal dumbly
made to us by this awakening life— the nature and meaning
of which are little understood by those who feel it surging
within them ; that the needs of this new nature shall be
recognised and realised, and its wayward forces rightly
directed ; that the new instincts and impulses, the new
faculties and powers, of this adolescent life shall be rightly
exercised and trained, and that protection shall be given
as far as possible, against the temptations to which it is
exposed. In a word, that there shall be a suitable education given to the new life that begins and asserts itself at
this adolescent stage, and that thus the higher and more
' completely human traits,' that are born in this stage
shall be developed and fashioned so as to give a true and
healthful manhood and womanhood."

With regard to the reform of the Sunday-school itself,
he took his stand in the same way on a study of the nature
of the boys and girls whom it was so important to retain.

" We must follow the law of human nature in all this
great redemptive work. What are the natural instincts
of a youth at the age of fourteen or fifteen ? First and
foremost, an intense desire *not to go to school*, to be emancipated and recognised as an independent and self-acting
person, to be distinguished from ' the kids.' It follows
that the boy of fifteen should be taken out of school and
put into something different, which we call an Institute.
Of this Institute, he is not a scholar, but a member. Extend the Sunday-school idea, not so as to drop Bible-
teaching and religious influence, but so as to make them
the heart and centre of a comprehensive training of the
young life, body, mind, and spirit. The teaching must
bear more directly upon conduct in life and the dangers
and temptations to which young people are specially
exposed. It must be Christianity applied to common
life."

He did not escape criticism. The frank claim to use such profane things as football, tents, hunting-songs, and horizontal bars for the purpose of spiritual education shocked the sensibilities of many. " If you had preached the forgotten Gospel of the Holy Ghost to the teachers assembled," writes a well-meaning straitlacer, " I think you would have got nearer the mark." His answer was thoroughly genial :

" Let us not forget that the Holy Spirit means the Spirit of Holiness, and holiness is a large term, and means the health of our whole being consecrated to God. Some think of the Holy Spirit as a mere emotional power associated with worship and the contemplation of God. He is much more than this. The Holy Spirit is the principle that gives health and harmony to our whole being, which can only be secured when all our powers are bounden unto and are regulated by the will of God. That will is to be obeyed in the care and treatment of the body, in the conduct of business, in companionships, and in every other part of our lives. What I deplore is that we have too much separated religion from the conduct of life. Do not let us think of prayer to the Holy Spirit as a sort of incantation."

To another critic he writes :

" The boy is at work now and must have recreation. He needs it, and has a right to it, and it is only a question whether the devil is to provide it, or whether the boy is to find his recreation under the sheltering, healing wings of the Church. Do I despair of religion ? No; every boy is at heart a hero-worshipper, and the Hero of all heroes will not appeal to him in vain."

Others asked : " Where are the workers to come from ? "

" The answer is being given in many Churches to-day," he replied, " where young men who had no gift or calling for any other service of the Church have found here a service to which they have given themselves with full delight, and in which they have been able not only to show their loyalty to our Divine Lord by engaging in service for Him, but also to exercise unused gifts, and to find new joys in the companionship and leadership of their boys."

It was an axiom with him that, if God had work to do,
He would always find the workers to do it.   When he was
asked, how the workers were to be found, he would say,
" They are waiting round the corner."

His full ideas as to the teaching in the Sunday Institute
and the various activities of the week-evening Institute,
which should work in conjunction with the Sunday Institute, and under the same teachers, were fully developed
in an appeal which he prepared for the Sunday-school
Union in 1905, and a pamphlet which was circulated at the
same time, called " What are the Sunday Institute and
Week-evening Institute of the Sunday-school ? " [1]

The Week-evening Institute was an adaptation of the
Recreative Evening-school to the requirements of the
Sunday-school, and earned grants under the same Evening-
school Code.   In the same way he sought to link up the
work of the Sunday-school with that of the Home-reading
Union.   In 1894 the Victoria Reading Circle of the Sunday-
school Union was definitely associated with the Young
People's section of the Union, and courses of reading were
planned in the senior magazines specially to meet the
needs of Sunday-school teachers.   He prepared a paper
for the World's Convention of Sunday-school teachers
in 1889, urging them to give more attention to providing
guidance in the choice and reading of literature.   He spoke
of a recent murder committed by two lads of Tunbridge
Wells, both under seventeen years of age.

" From the day these two lads left school they had
excited and drugged their imagination by the cheap,
maddening literature which abounds for such as they were.
The influence struck home ; no poison could work more
fatally.   They believed the true heroism, the real worth
of life was to pluck off your victim as coolly as you would
a bird, and then to die game.   And they fulfilled, with
absolute and villainous accuracy, the part they had been
educated by their home-reading to think so splendid. . . .
The case is exceptional, but only in the rapidity with
which the mental poison worked, and in the sombre tragedy
which filled the public stage for a while.   The same deadly
influences are working everywhere."

[1] Reprinted in " Inner Mission Pamphlets," Second Series, Nos. 4 and 5.
(J. Clarke & Co.)

CHAPTER XVIII

TO SAVE LIFE

"If you are going to do anything permanent for the average man,
you have got to begin before he is a man. The chance of success lies in
working with the boy."—ROOSEVELT.

"Along our front no sabres shine,
No blood-red pennons wave ;
The banners bear the single line,
'Our duty is to save.'"

O. W. HOLMES.

CLASSES and Clubs were not sufficient by themselves to
solve the problem and stop the leakage of the Sunday-
school. Classes, however recreative, did not appeal to
lads whose muscles were restive and finger-tips itching for
something to do. "Clubs are a failure for boys of fourteen
to sixteen. There is no discipline in clubs. If a boy can
please himself whether he goes or stays away, whether
he breaks a rule or keeps it, very little good is done. The
mere club, when all is said and done, is only a form of
indoor loafing." The line of real solution for the problem
had been shown by the late Sir W. A. Smith in founding
the Boys' Brigade. In the Brigade it is a question not of
"may," but of "must": instead of aimless fooling about,
a boy's path is marked out for him clearly for months
ahead. He learns the meaning of *esprit de corps*, his militant instincts are brought under control and diverted into
wholesome channels. He is trained now to work with
others for a common end, to respect authority, and to
obey ; he has a prospect of regular graded promotion by
which he can climb to a position of authority himself.
The man in control finds that, as soon as he puts a
soldier-cap on the boy's head and becomes his officer, his
strength is as the strength of ten. Orders are carried out
promptly, discipline is established, and, whether it is a
football team or an arithmetic class, the management is
tenfold easier.

Paton realised this. He had taken a great interest in

311

the Boys' Brigade work in Nottingham under Captain J. A. Dixon, the famous cricketer, and in the first company which was formed at Rugby. But, when he began to ask why Sunday-schools did not take up the Boys' Brigade, he found teachers and deacons, more especially deacons, very shy of what they thought to be the military spirit of the Boys' Brigade. In particular, they disliked the dummy rifles and the shooting drill. Their shyness was increased by the jingo mania which possessed the country, like an evil spirit, at the time of the Boer War. Even before the Boer War, when Mr. W. T. Stead organised his Peace Campaign, " War against War," many speeches of the peace advocates showed how suspicious they were of the Boys' Brigade. It was regarded as a sort of Kindergarten for the Army. The Brigades were inspected and reviewed from time to time by eminent officers of the Army, and the officers, in their addresses to the boys, not infrequently spoke of the advantages of the Army as affording a career to a lad of mettle. It was quite natural that they should do so, and there was no tittle of evidence to show that any boys were lured into the Army through the Brigade ; indeed, probably there was more evidence in the opposite direction, for the boy who had served a few years in the Brigade had had his fill of military drill and was immune to the fascinations of an elegant uniform. But, nevertheless, there was the familiarisation of boys with the idea of firearms, and the tacit acceptance of war as a commonplace of life. The fact remained that the great majority of Churches held aloof from the Brigade movement, and some Churches which took it up found strenuous opposition among their own members from old ladies who had never been boys themselves. They feared that the military methods would generate the soldier spirit. In any case, the field was not covered. There were still a million and a quarter of English lads who were untouched by Brigades. Clearly, therefore, there was room for a new movement, which would not clash with the sensibilities of pious folk, who were well-meaning, even though they were mistaken.

This was the thought which he turned over in his mind for two or three years, and which led to the founding of the Boys' Life Brigade. The first person to translate the idea into practice was his old student, the Rev. T. A.

Leonard, of Colne, who had already done pioneer work in the Social Institutes and the Co-operative Holidays. In 1897 he started a corps of Boys' Life-guards in connection with his Sunday-school. It was a Boys' Brigade on non-military lines. It had drill, but it was ambulance-drill, fire-drill, and life-saving drill for the rescue of the drowning. Its work was " to honour life, to help life, to save life." It had a uniform, consisting of cap and belt, each bearing the symbol of the red cross.

The Boys' Life-guards were so successful that in the very next year, on September 15th, 1898, a similar movement was started by some Quakers in Liverpool, Mr. Thomas D. Lawrance, J.P., acting as President of the new movement, and Mr. George M. Benington as Secretary. The officers of the Brigade bore the titles of Captain, Instructors, Inspectors, and Monitors.

These preliminary experiments showed the lines on which the new venture might be successfully carried out. In the autumn of 1899 it was launched. Military foot-drill was retained, so were the military titles for officers. The Liverpool experience went to show that it was a mistake to do away with them ; also, the Salvation Army had used these titles and had found them effective, yet no one dreamed of accusing the Salvation Army of fostering the military spirit. But all the drill bore upon the idea of saving life.

" We shall have," Paton said, " many of the features which make military drill attractive. We shall have companies and officers, with a sense of difference in ranks. We shall have uniform with stripes for non-commissioned officers. There must be imperative obedience and alert attention. I believe in the quick reactions of drill. The great word ' —shon,' we shall not give that up." (And as that word shot from his lips one heard an echo of the old Covenanting Captain that would have been very disconcerting to many pacificist old ladies.) " We mean to have bands, drum-and-fife, or, if possible, brass bands. We believe in marching. Nothing helps so much the spirit of solidarity. Besides, there is nothing like a parade through the streets to bring in the recruits.

" The drill will be concerned with saving life and enlarging its capacities in the widest sense. In addition to the ordinary physical exercises we shall have stretcher-drill, a course of first-aid lessons dealing with accidents of all kinds, and a course of hygiene dealing with the conditions for ensuring a healthy life. These, with the physical exercises, will be arranged in a two or three years' course to enable the Brigade to earn the Government grant under the provisions of the new code. There will be life-saving drill in rescuing from fire and water. The first thing will be to teach swimming. We shall make a special point of this. The first swimming exercises will be given on land as part of the physical drill. The Life-saving Society are allowing us to reprint in our Manual their rescue-drill, release-drill, and resuscitation-drill, with all the diagrams.

"Then there will be fire-drill. This will be a novel feature. It will deal with three conditions:—fire in the house: how to enter a house on fire—to cover the face with a wet handkerchief or a worsted stocking, to crawl on hands and knees; the way to help others to escape—tying of nautical knots; the art of holding a sheet on which persons can jump; how to handle a person partially suffocated with smoke, and how to carry a body down a ladder, ' the fireman's clutch,' as it is called. Then, how to put out fire, the use of earth, sand, or ashes. For instance, if you fling water on flaming paraffin, it only spreads the fire all over the place; sand puts it out. I learned this from my friend Sir Edmund Verney, who put me up to several wrinkles in connection with the fire-drill. We shall have bonfires which will be extinguished in this way as proof of the efficacy of this plan. Then fire in the streets : the boys will be taught how to hold a mob back and clear a street, by forming up as they do for a Rugby scrimmage. It is wonderful how a few who act together in this way can control a whole crowd of people and resist their impact. There will be hints as to how to act when fire is detected; and don't forget that the boys, with their sharp eyes, are usually the first to notice an outbreak. Commander Wells, of the London C.C. Fire Brigade, tells me they have never had a false alarm given by a boy. Commander Wells is taking a great interest in our project and giving us considerable help. The third part of the fire-drill deals with the prevention of panic in public buildings in case of fire.

" You can see how all this appeals to the heroic spirit implanted in the heart of every boy. It gives him something to fight that is worthy of his steel.

"We do not intend our Brigade in any sense to be a rival to the Boys' Brigade. I would rather call it a complement to it—in this sense, that while the Boys' Brigade is hindered by the objection which many people take to its military organisation and associations, the new Brigade will meet those who desire to have boys secure the advantages of the discipline and so on of the Boys' Brigade, free from the objections I have named. Personally, I do not object to the military form of the Boys' Brigade, but it is useless to ignore the fact that many people do. Also, we hope to retain the lads for a longer period than they do. Our physical drill and education course will occupy longer time and will, therefore, compel the lads who want to be efficient to stay longer with us.

"We want to associate Christianity with all that is most manly and noble in a boy's sight. If we do this, we shall be going a long way towards disabusing his mind of the idea that there is something essentially effeminate about Christianity ; that, while it is the right sort of thing for girls, it is something alien from the nature of high-spirited boys. Every company of the Brigade will be associated with a Christian Church or Mission, or some religious organisation."

The new Life Brigade was launched under the auspices of the Sunday-school Union, which appointed Mr. H. E. Norton as Brigade Secretary, and a special delegation from their own Council to act with the Executive of the Brigade. The headquarters were at the S.S.U. Offices in Old Bailey. Paton was chosen President. In addition to the Code of Rules and Regulations, they published a Manual of Drill for Marching, for Gymnastics, for Ambulance, for Semaphore Signalling, for Life-saving from Water, and from Fire. There were also manuals for Physical Exercise and pamphlets on Board of Education grants, on the Duties of Officers, Company Discipline, and Section Competition. There was also a hymn-book, with careful omission of the " tender lamb " element ; and a health-manual entitled, " How to be Well and Strong," was written by Mr. W. N. Edwards, F.C.S., the well-known Band of Hope lecturer. All these, if not actually initiated by the President, passed through his hands. He worked hard to get a penny song-book published. In this he was helped by the Rev. A. Norman Rowland, M.A. (then of Putney, now of Manchester). He gave £50 to the Sunday-school Union to help in defraying the initial expenses.

Two Companies in his own immediate neighbourhood helped to lead the way. Major C. R. Woodward formed the first Company in Nottingham, and called it the " Paton Company," after the founder of the Brigade. He was more than a mere name to them. From time to time, on Bank Holidays, or on a march out, they would draw up in front of his house, and, if he was at home, he would go out and say a few words to them ; occasionally he would entertain them to tea. With Major Woodward he was constantly in conference, and no new step of any importance was taken without consulting him. Near to Nottingham is the mining village of Eastwood. It is not too much to say that the whole life of that village was changed by the advent of the Boys' Life Brigade. In Captain F. D. Chambers it found an ideal leader of boys. The ambulance-van is only too well known in the streets of Eastwood, and the lads were not slow to see the practical value of the first aid to the injured and the fire-drill which were taught in the Brigade. The value of the water-rescue drill was soon demonstrated when one of the Brigade boys succeeded in rescuing two lads who were drowning in a lock on the canal. The local corps of the St. John Ambulance Association recognised at once what a valuable feeder the Brigade would be, and gave most valuable assistance. The local colliery proprietors made themselves responsible for the rent and rates of the premises occupied. Evening-classes, which were very thinly attended before, became a great success, and earned grants from the Government and the County Council which proved of material assistance to the funds. The annual camp initiated the lads into the pure and manly pleasures of God's out-of-doors and the comradeship of mutual service. Every lad had to attend Sunday-school ; failing that, he was disqualified for prizes, for promotion, and all other privileges of the Brigade.

" It's a revolution on a small scale," said one who knew

the village well, " and if you want to know the difference
that this Brigade has made, go and see the Brigade boys
play football; then go and see a match between young
colliers not in the Brigade. You will see then how much
it means. Many a time I have seen the Brigade play an
exciting game, and never a squabble or a wry face—no
officers in charge either; then is the time to see what the
influence of the Brigade means."

Every good seed is bound to grow. There is an inward
urge that forces it upwards, and the B.L.B. at Eastwood
has developed into a Senior Club, with a large Cadet Corps.

Eastwood does not stand alone. The growth of the
Brigade as a whole was very rapid. Before the founder
died there were 14,531 boys in the ranks, and 1,805 officers.[1]

Has it stopped the leakage of the Sunday-school ? The
above figures are an answer to the question. Whatever
the boy's previous record may have been, the Brigade
rule is that, after joining the Brigade, a lad must attend
regularly either at Sunday-school or his Company Bible-
class. Many boys attend both. One Sunday-school in
the North of England was accustomed to lose practically
all its scholars as soon as they had turned twelve years of
age. The average attendance of boys above that age for
many years was five. A Company of the B.L.B. was
formed. After two years the average attendance was
between fifty and sixty. The Superintendent assures us
that the Brigade has awakened general interest in the
Sunday-school, and at the last Anniversary (when the
B.L.B. boys attended in uniform), the sum collected at the
service was four times as much as had ever been collected
on previous occasions. The Cardiff Sunday-school Union,
seeing there was a wide difference of opinion as to the
character and value of the Brigade movement, appointed
a Committee of Inquiry. After taking evidence, the Committee reported in these words :

" It was shown, both as to the Life Brigade and the
Boys' Brigade, that the effect upon the boys has been of
a *distinctly religious character*. Those who have experience
of their working, although they may have been at first
suspicious, even antagonistic, to the idea, have been driven

[1] There are now 405 companies, 1,497 officers, and 15,589 boys.

to the conclusion that the Brigades are *essentially a spiritual force.* At the initiatory stage they attract to the Sunday-school (and other church organisations such as the Band of Hope) boys who might have otherwise remained outside the circle of church influence ; and, once these have been brought in, their personal association with the officers, and the effect of the discipline, drill, and camp-life, give them spiritual and moral, as well as physical, training which otherwise they would not obtain."

The practical value of the instruction in life-saving was constantly receiving illustration. Numerous cases have been recorded where first-aid was administered by B.L.B. boys in public accidents, and lives have actually been saved. The effect of the teaching was not restricted to the letter of the Manual ; the spirit of it entered into the lads and made them quick to observe an opportunity of service and seize it. One of the last smiles which over-spread the founder's face was the smile of joy when he was told of an incident which took place shortly before he died, on January 22nd, 1911, in Burlington Street, Man-chester. The 2nd Manchester Battalion of the B.L.B. was marching down the street, headed by the band, to the annual inspection and display in the drill-hall. A pair of horses attached to a carriage conveying some of the guests to the hall took fright, broke away, and dashed madly down the street. Rearing on to the pavement, the horses were making straight in the direction of a nurse in charge of two little children, when Sergeant Neaves, of the Belle Vue Company, a lad of seventeen, ran out from the ranks and seized the horses' heads. He succeeded in pulling the horses off the pavement when they were within a yard of the frightened children. Neaves was dragged along the street a considerable distance past the drill-hall, where a policeman came to his assistance, and brought the runaway horses to a standstill.

To see that smile on the founder's face was to know something of the measure of the joy which was his exceed-ing great reward.

So much for the influence of the Brigade upon the boys. That is the main thing, but it is not all. It is not the Brigade as such which does the work. The Brigade is not a machine of which you work the handle, and turn out manly, God-fearing boys. It is the personal character of the officers that tells. The Brigade has brought into the active service of Christ hundreds of young men who had in them the willingness to serve, but for whom the ordinary devotional activities of the old-fashioned Church offered no appropriate sphere of service.

There has been also the reflex influence on the Churches themselves. Many of them have had the feeling that, if a man cannot be saved by preaching and praying, he is hopelessly lost. If there have been week-night meetings, they have been of such a kind as demanded quiet premises, and were incompatible with the presence of noisy boys in the same building. Yet these racketing lads are the sheep which the Master gave the Church to feed and tend ; these are the souls which the Master will require at her hand. How the due regulation of our lower life may help the full development of life on its higher and nobler plane, is a lesson the Church has been slow to learn. It is all-important in dealing with the young. "Keep fit, and keep good," was the motto of "Loony" Balfour, the well-known Scottish athlete. There is a vital relation between the two things.

The B.L.B. has opened the eyes of the Church to another important but neglected truth. It is not enough to preach the duty of service. Young folk must be taught how to serve in a practical way. If they do not know how, they cannot act. If they do not act, the spirit of service within them dies of atrophy. The Good Samaritan knew the principles of first aid, that enabled him to be a neighbour to him who fell among thieves.

Relations with the Boys' Brigade have been friendly throughout. The two Brigades often go to camp together, and the B.L.B. has often taken part with their comrades in a sham fight, only the B.L.B. boys have simply followed behind and picked up the dead. Each Brigade has learned from the other.

But there are girls as well as boys in the Sunday-schools, and girls, too, have their difficult adolescent period. The girls were not forgotten. Ever since he was at Kaiserwerth and came into touch with Fliedner, Paton had thought and written much on Women's Work in the Church. To women's share falls the care of the home, the rearing of

the children, the nursing of the sick and injured. The
girl's opportunities for service are even more numerous
than the boy's. The conditions of life in large cities
weigh more heavily on girls than on boys. The need for
self-control seemed to be even greater in her case, for with
the girl independence was a comparatively new thing.
Outward control had been rejected, but there had not
come any compensating control from within. Any street-
scene on a general holiday, or at any public rejoicing during
the course of the war was sufficient to demonstrate the
need of some organisation for girls similar to that for the
boys. Physical training and instruction in elementary
hygiene were just as important for them as for boys. Presence of mind was wanted just as much by girls working
in factories as it is by men, in case of any outbreak of
fire, or other panic.

Accordingly, in 1902 an organisation was started for
girls, called The Girls' Life Brigade. It was also under
the Sunday-school Union.   Mrs. William Garnett was
the President, and Mrs. Cadbury took much interest in it.
Miss Alice E. Towers and Miss Frances Dawbarn (now Mrs.
Towers), were Hon. Secretaries, and the book of Physical
Exercises was prepared by Miss Therese Stempel. Miss
M. E. Hudson of Nottingham and Miss Ormiston Chant
(now Mrs. Burtt) did yeoman's service in the preparatory
stages. The programme of its activities was similar in
most respects to that of the boys, with the addition of
sick nursing and various forms of musical drill. In
1908–9 there were 267 officers and 2,703 girls enrolled ;
in the present year there are 182 companies, 424 officers, and
4,074 girls.

One other scheme was being hatched in his mind. It was
crowded out by the multitudinous claims of other activities,
and never came to the birth. No tree can ripen all its
fruit. But it lay very near to his heart, and he devoted
much time and thought to it. The Children's National
Guild of Courtesy had been in existence since 1889. Its
progress had been very slow at first, but, after some six
or seven years of struggling, it began to get a strong
footing in the elementary schools, and numbered some
300 branches in Great Britain and the Colonies. But
its work was confined to the schools, and its influence
ceased when the scholars left. There was, therefore, in

its work the same lack of continuity as in the Sunday-school and the elementary school: there was the same waste of effort, for what teacher has not had to deplore the rapid deterioration in a scholar which takes place on leaving school? In 1895 Paton began to give his attention to this matter, and in 1898 he was corresponding with Mr. H. E. Norton, head master of New Ferry Boys' School, Birkenhead, the Hon. Secretary of the Guild of Courtesy. His plan was to form what first he proposed to call a Legion of Honour, then a Guild of Honour; but ultimately the name he adopted was " The League of Honour."

The aim of the League was to foster and inspire that sentiment of honour which is so marked a characteristic of the adolescent age. The elements of honour he defined in the case of boys as: (1) courage; (2) truth in word and deed; (3) self-command; (4) generous fair-play in games, competitions, etc.; (5) chivalry under three aspects: (a) help to the weak, (b) rescue of those in danger, (c) deliverance of those in any way oppressed.

In the case of girls he felt that, though in essence honour meant the same thing, the terms into which it was trans-lated would be somewhat different. With boys, courage was the first thing, the basis of all; with girls, courage was a later acquisition. After careful correspondence with Mrs. Higgs, Mrs. Price Hughes, and Miss L. Corry, the needful modifications were made. Self-command was thought to be too militant a word, and was softened into self-control. Chivalry, again, was too masculine, and was replaced by " Guardian care of self, helpful care of others, service with sacrifice in order to succour the needy, raise the fallen, and save the lost."

The unit of the organisation was to be the Court, with a Warden at the head of it, a Secretary, a Chaplain, Com-panions, and Initiates. The officer in charge of the door was to be known by the Old English title of Tyler. Regalia were to be worn by all the officials during the sitting of the Court, and regular forms of address were to be ob-served. Due ceremony was to be maintained also by the adoption of a simple ritual for the opening and closing of the Court and the admission of new members. Each Court was to take the name of some honourable knight without fear and without reproach, such as Bayard, or Livingstone,

21

or Gordon, or Sir Philip Sydney. At each meeting a roll
of honour was to be hung up, on which was to be inscribed
the name of any boy who was acknowledged by the Court
to have done a brave and noble and beautiful action. At
the meeting of the Court any member was to be encouraged
to give, either in writing or in speech, a report or a description of some noble deed which he had either seen, or heard,
or read of during the month.

The boys incorporated in the Court of Honour were also
to undertake special duties, that would enable them to
exercise and fulfil the ideals in which they encourage one
another. Among themselves there was to be a confederacy
of honour, binding them to stand by one another honourably
in times of sickness or difficulty of any kind. It was to be
understood that any boy proposing or seconding a new
member was to some extent responsible for him, and, in
case that new member at any time brought disgrace upon
the Court, his sponsors would be required to state what
they had done by example and by precept to keep the
errant straight, and what they intended to do to help him
to recover his position in the Court. Opportunities were
to be sought out to help and cheer other boys of their
own age, or younger, who were in special need. For example, it was suggested that boys might provide flowers
for sick children in their neighbourhood ; they might care
in some special and brotherly way for cripple and blind
youths and children in their neighbourhood, perhaps by
taking them out into the open air, aiding and guiding them
in their walks, reading to them, or otherwise brightening
them in their affliction. They might help to organise
the games of those younger than themselves. Paton felt
keenly that the open spaces provided for play in London
by the agency of Lord Meath were too little used, and the
offer of the Educational Authority to give the use of their
play-grounds in evening hours was never properly taken up.

Other elements were added later. He drew up and
printed a weekly Calendar of Boys' Heroes which gave a
guiding motto for each week of the year—" some brief
sentence," he said, " which will sting his soul keenly and
move it upward." Illustrating each motto there was a
short life of some hero, or heroine, which illustrated it.
He was eager, too, that his Courts of Honour should follow
the example of the " Beautiful Oldham " society by taking

up some vacant plot of ground in their town and making it beautiful by tillage.

The idea of the League of Honour was to meet the lack of effective moral training in our schools. He wished to utilise the adolescent's instinct for association to secure, in the first place, that there should be an inspiring ideal set before the youth of both sexes, and, in the second place, that there should be expression for enthusiasm in action.

" All who know boys and girls in the adolescent period of life, know that the sentiment of honour is that which most strongly appeals to them. All the five elements of honour which have been set forth as the most noble qualities of character appeal at once to the boy's inmost soul, and he gives a ready response to them. What, therefore, we have to do is to cultivate and train these finer impulses of his nature; to quicken and strengthen them by those indirect influences of which he is eagerly receptive and by which he is most powerfully affected; and to give scope and opportunity for the exercise of those elements of conduct which he admires, so that they may guide and shape his actions, and gradually form the habits which will make the character of his future life. For we must never forget the truth which Bishop Butler so wisely enforced, that idle fancy and passive sentiment avail nothing to form character, and may even weaken and degrade it. The desire needs to be transmuted into the deed : for action alone builds up and strengthens character and makes it durable and perfect.

.   .   .   .   .

" The public mind of our country was greatly impressed by the high sentiment of honour which was exhibited by the Japanese nation in its conflict with Russia. The spirit of ' Bushido,' as it is called, was seen to possess and inspire the nation and the army of Japan in a way that had rarely been witnessed in the history of the world. It was *this high sense of honour*, which had been *ingrained* into the *thought* and *conduct of the people*, which made the Japanese nation great and victorious, inspiring its soldiers with indomitable courage in the field of battle, with valorous fidelity to one another, and with courtesy and magnanimity in the treatment of their adversary. It was also this spirit of honour which gave the self-command of the

Japanese nation that was shown in their moderation and
generosity, as they concluded an honourable peace when
sweeping forward in a full tide of victory.   That soul of
honour has been inbred into the Japanese nation from
their patriotism, from the respect they cherish for their
ancestors, and from their devotion to their ruler—the
Mikado.   And the thought has come to many, as to
myself, that *every British boy might be uplifted and inspired*
in like manner, by his love of country and by the splendid
record of the men and achievements that have made his
country great.   In addition, however, to these patriotic
sentiments, which may well animate the youth of Britain
as they have imbued the youth of Japan, surely a higher
inspiration should come to every British boy from his
faith in God, and in Him, the Eternal Son of God, who
came with incomparable heroism to subdue the powers of
evil in this world, and lift men everywhere up to the
freedom and joy of the service of God."

To Mrs. Mary Higgs, of Oldham

" Now we want to have a Guild of Honour for Girls.   I
am thinking of the ordinary working girl who goes out to
the factory or workshop, about thirteen years of age.   We
have the Snowdrop Band, and one or two other beautiful
societies or unions, but they are for a somewhat better
and more refined class.   We want something that will
attract the ordinary girl exposed as she is to such great
perils in her daily work, and in her companionships.   The
Girls' Life Brigade promises to be one of the most helpful
things that has been started for girls.   You will see what
I have said to Mrs. Price Hughes about the Girls' Guild
of Honour.   I know boys, but I do not know how to deal
with girls ; still, I have thought we might set forth to them
some of the things that we are setting before boys, and
other matters which I suggest to Mrs. Price Hughes, such
as healthful guardian care of their own person, and helpful
care of others, and loving service, and even sacrifice, for
those in need."

The League of Honour was never tried in practice,
whether for boys or girls, except by Mr. Frank C. Heley,
of Dalston, N.E., who formed a " Charles George Gordon
Court " in January 1909.   He writes as follows :

" The League of Honour seems destined to remain an
idea, a good seed which never struck root.   Probably it
was crowded out by the wonderfully rapid growth of the
Scout movement, and to some extent by his own Boys'
Life Brigade.   There were also many who feared that the
ritual would lend itself to ridicule owing to the proneness
of youth to see the comic side of things and get as much
fun as possible out of it.   Whether that would be so or
not could only be ascertained by actual experiment.
One thing is certain : the youth who can join a club or a
society when the only ritual is the payment of a subscription, is apt to rate the club at its own valuation ; he can
hardly feel its obligations.   The League of Honour avoided
this weakness.   Whenever a boy or girl is admitted to
a new society, that new society should not forego, as the
Lads' Club usually does, the opportunity of stating clearly
what the admission should mean, and what standard of
conduct is expected, if that admission is not to be revoked.
The occasion is one from which he expects a certain degree
of solemnity, and that expectation ought not to be fobbed
off with a payment of copper."

" The great object," Paton wrote, " is by every possible
means to awaken in the boys a noble conception of life, and
band them together in comradeship to strive after it."

For the actual League of Honour the way never seemed
to open.   No fruit-bearing tree succeeds in ripening all
its fruit.   But there was a twofold principle embodied in
the idea of the League, and that principle found free course.
It was constantly in his mind, and he was constantly urging
it upon Sunday-schools and Christian Endeavourers. It was
in essence the principle of the old chivalry, and it had two
sides, the conception of the ideal and the effort after it.
Chivalry held up to the eyes of the young aspirant during
his most impressionable years the picture of true honour,
fed his mind with the stories of it, and filled his imagination
with the love of it.   Chivalry also trained him in honourable deeds ; it did not allow the youth's feeling to evaporate
in empty and ineffectual dreaming.   The League of
Honour was to do the same, not for a few favoured and
well-born youths alone, but on the widest scale ; it was
to foster the idea of true honour, " the honour which
cometh from God only," to encourage lads and lasses to

fix their thoughts on it, and not only to seek it out and recognise it in the behaviour of common life, but to practise it themselves.

The weakness of the Sunday-school on the side of training in actual practice had already been seen by the Countess of Meath, who had started the Ministering Children's League. The rule of the League was that every member must try to do at least one kind deed every day, and be loving, kind, and useful to others. The League's object was to show that holiness, instead of being a remote ideal, scarcely compatible with our every-day drudgery, is, in fact, something practical, and the most fruitful field for its exercise lies in the common path of a working life. Paton heard of this League with joy; it seemed to him to supply exactly what was needed. With Lady Meath's heartiest concurrence he induced the S.S.U. to institute a special branch of the League for their own schools, and, in order to make the teaching as specific as possible, he drew up some simple and practical suggestions as to how the principles of the League might be applied in the ordinary life of the home and the school, in visiting and cheering the sick, blind, or infirm in the neighbourhood, in helping to beautify the street by keeping front gardens pretty and neat, or growing a few flowering plants in a window-box, in helping children in other countries, especially heathen countries.

" I can see," he wrote, " that by this card and the lessons it inculcates we may make the Sunday-schools of our country and of other countries training-schools of Christian conduct, as our children are taught to exercise themselves in the service of love, which is the service of Christ."

How far was his preaching justified by results ? Were the Sunday-schools which adopted the Brigade and the Week-evening Institute able to retain their scholars after the age of fifteen ? When so much depends on the personal equation and special circumstances, it is very fallacious to lay too much stress on cumulative statistical results. But an investigation which was carried out in Nottingham by a Science Lecturer at the University College, yielded some startling results. The investigations fully bore out

Paton's contention that, where nothing is done for the week-evening, the Sunday-school loses fully 80 per cent. of the scholars; it also showed that the success of the Sunday-school in retaining her scholars is in exact proportion to the amount of care which it gives to the week-evening leisure of her scholars. One of the diagrams prepared by this gentleman sums up in itself the results of the whole investigation. It relates to seven Sunday-schools of the city. The black columns represent the number of scholars below fifteen years of age; the shaded columns the number

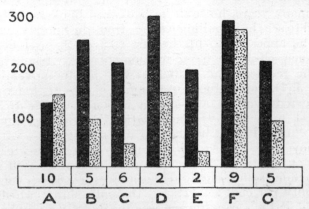

No. 3.—COMPARISON BETWEEN LOSS OR RETENTION OF SCHOLARS ON SUNDAY, AND WORK DONE FOR THEM DURING THE WEEK.

This diagram gives the figures of seven Sunday-schools in Nottingham. The height of the black columns represents the number of scholars below fifteen years of age; that of the dotted columns the number above fifteen. The figures below represent the number of events organised for the scholars during the week. These include Wesley Guild, Band of Hope, Evenings for Games, Gymnasium, Boys' Life Brigades, Football, Cricket, and Swimming Clubs, etc. Two schools, viz., A and F, have practically the same number of scholars above as below fifteen. These two are the schools which do most for the scholars during the week.

above fifteen. The figures below represent the number of events organised for the scholars during the week. These include the Wesley Guild, Band of Hope, Evenings for Games, Gymnasium, Boys' Life Brigades, Football, Cricket, and Swimming Clubs. Two schools, A and F, have practically the same number of scholars above as below fifteen; these schools are those which do most for their scholars during the week. E does very little for its older scholars during the week, and consequently loses nearly all its older scholars. C has six items, but fails to keep its scholars, because those in authority " don't believe in this sort of thing," and apply the cold-water blanket. D does no better for its scholars, but reaps the advantage of a splendid unsectarian Institute for Boys and Girls which is run in the district. The Institute keeps alive the taste for better things, and preserves the girls and boys from " flying the kite " in the streets.

One picture may fitly close this chapter. It gives one happy incident of a long campaign. Paton was the guest of the Free Church Council at Bournemouth, and in the Landsdowne Baptist Church he gave an address on the responsibility of the Church for the training of youth. For many years, he said, he had worn blinkers. He had failed to see the appalling leakage from the Sunday-schools, and he appealed to his hearers to free themselves from any such self-delusion—to see things as they are and hasten to the rescue. The audience was deeply moved. The Rev. J. D. Jones stood up to move a vote of thanks, and whispered over his audience a winsome tribute to " the biggest man in my denomination." " No speech," he said, " that I have listened to in the last nine years has so moved me as has Dr. Paton's to-night. How can we show our gratitude to the old man eloquent ? Will it not be by doing something to reduce that tragic 80 per cent. ? " " Eighty per cent ! " It was the only phrase which had caught Paton's ear, for age was by that time muffling his hearing. Mr. Jones stood just a pace in front of him. Without rising from his chair, he stooped forward and caught the younger man's hand. With tear-filled eyes he besought his friend to urge a crusade for the rescuing of those 80 per cent. who were as sheep going astray. A strange wave of feeling swept across the audience. One young man near the platform rose to his feet. It was a tribute of respect for age and eloquence that would not cease from strife until it had " planted the New Jerusalem in England's pleasant land." " We all wanted to do the same," said one who was there, " but conventionality held back impulse."

THE MORAL VALUE OF GAMES
From a Presidential letter to the B.L.B., 1904

" For active boys whose ' mischief ' is but wholesome energy that has not been used and directed in right ways, there must be physical exercise ; and here nothing can excel the out-door games in which they delight.   These games can be made the means of splendid discipline in courage and endurance, in obedience to command, in loyalty to one another, and in fair play ; whilst they induce what may be called a healthy habit of body, which is of the highest moral value.   It is in such games that the young men who are the officers of the B.L.B. will find opportunity of pleasant comradeship with their boys, and also for training them to a perfect sense of honour and fair play in every detail of the game, which will lay the basis of justice and right conduct in their future life. But out-door games cannot in English weather always be played ; and hence the need for indoor physical exercises which also can be used not only to promote health of body but to give precision and accuracy to eye and limb, and to form an erect and manly gait, which helps to form a frank and manly temper.

" Of all physical exercises that can be used to allure and capture boys, to hold them fast and make them amenable to the finest discipline and some of the finest influences that can mould their character, the best are found in the Boys' Brigades, which have happily now come into vogue. It is not merely the charm of the uniform or the blast of the bugle that stirs the boys' hearts ; everything else appeals to the boy, and, in appealing to him, calls out the best that is in him, and trains him for far better things. The erect attitude, the regular march, the quick command and the prompt reply, the companionship and officership of the brigade—all these act like a spell upon him, and train not only his body, but his whole nature for higher service. And now, in the Boys' Life Brigade, all these attractions and all that discipline are given without the least tincture of militarism ; whilst, on the contrary, special instruction and drill are given in exercises adapted to save life from the dangers of fire, or water, or accident.

" Thus the moral training of the Life Brigade aims at and prepares for the highest duty of life, namely, to help and save others, and imbues the boy with the conception of a redemptive purpose in life, and leads him in real ways to understand the spirit and the salvation of his redeeming Lord."

To Miss Rose Moore

"*August* 18*th*, 1909.

" I feel that, in addition to physical exercises and games such as are specially recommended by me in the pamphlet on the Sunday and Week-evening Institute, there ought to be more distinct and impressive teaching on the true honour and noble worth of life. We appeal also to what is in a peculiar sense the boy's instinct, and at that age, fourteen to fifteen and onward, specially attracts and captivates him, namely, what is brave and heroic. Let us cultivate that sense, and show how it ennobles ordinary life at home, in the workshop, in companionship, and in all civic life. Do you not agree with me in this ? If so, I shall be so glad if you will help me to work out this problem, because I feel that the management of the Court of Honour must be specially arranged for this object."

To Mr. C. E. B. Russell

"*December* 6*th*, 1909.

" There are certain instincts native to the boy which ought to be awakened and nurtured and strengthened, and which will form the very elements of a noble manhood. He loves what is heroic, he admires everything that shows courage and loyalty which is the element of truth, and fine self-command and chivalry in its different elements. Now these are the very finest instincts possible, and, if we laid hold of them and developed them wisely, and showed how they could all be carried out and exemplified and realised in daily life, we should, I think, create a new standard of moral conduct for our boys—one which they would thoroughly appreciate and grasp.

" There are two or three principles that need to be remembered in dealing with our boys in this League of Honour :

" 1. The elements of honour shall be such as appeal to the boy's inmost soul. We must adopt the very best methods of eliciting and strengthening these instincts which are rooted in his nature. I think that boys appreciate belonging to a set, being a member of a Court. The Club instinct is strong in boys, and we must utilise this and give them rank in the Court, and positions in which they will take interest and a certain pride. Even the fact of the Court being strictly private, and that admission to its meetings is carefully guarded, is, I think, an attraction to boys.

" 2. Then I am sure boys love to have certain regalia. I know the ceremonial must be very simple and have in it nothing that lends itself to ridicule. But something of this kind is often very attractive—I think they have found it so in the Juvenile Courts of the Good Templars.

" I feel that something of this sort may be very useful to boys, giving them a nobler conception of life, and yet will be one that harmonises with their own ideals, which, however, because these ideals are not developed and shown to be realisable in daily life, are sadly broken and trampled underfoot."

To an Officer of the Brigade

" Find out the boy's hobbies ; they are an index to his character, and they are handles that he holds out to you by which you can catch him. Form rambling, cycling, camera clubs. Don't forget the wonderful influence of song—the camp sing-song. If we leave the boy to be trained by the devil, all his best instincts are dragged in the mud. A boy's religion is hero-worship. Christ should be presented to him as the Hero of heroes. A boy feels the danger of having to face the powers of evil alone, and he feels the need of a hero—a Christ—who will be his helper and guide. Handle him rightly at this age (i.e. thirteen to sixteen) and he can be brought, as never again at any later time, into the spirit of love and trust."

Letter from the Rev. W. B. Fitzgerald

" January 16th, 1906.

" I often look back to that very interesting talk I had with you at Harrogate. In those days the Guild idea was in its infancy, and you may remember that I consulted you about the Guild I was forming in connection with my own Church. That scheme was the foundation of the Wesley Guild Constitution, and in all essential points is the same to-day. You have had something to do with the early stages of a great many important movements, and the Wesley Guild promises to be one of the most helpful."

CHAPTER XIX

RETIRING FROM THE PRINCIPALSHIP

AMID the multifarious social activities, it is hard to realise that Dr. Paton's work at the Institute was going on day by day, and that this work meant not only teaching and pastoral supervision, but also responsibility for raising year by year the sustentation income for an Institution which started without a penny of endowment and gave instruction, board, and lodging free to practically all its students.

Yet the work of the Institute was steadily progressing. There was no shortage of men ; the money was always forthcoming. The work of the class-room continued with unabated force. Many country Churches were rescued from decay. Many important missions in the great centres of population were developed into self-sustaining Churches. In Nottingham itself the Churches in Queen's Walk and St. Ann's Well Road owed their existence to the Institute ; missions were established at Old Radford, at Carrington, at Thorneywood Lane. Outside the town Churches were founded and built up into vigorous life at Burton Joyce, Hucknall, Westwood, Arnold, Long Eaton, and Carrington.

In 1876 he was invited to become Principal of Airedale College, Bradford.

To Mr. Samuel Morley, M.P.

" I have been asked to take the office of Principal in the new Airedale College at Bradford, and during the last ten days my mind has been full of perplexity (not anxiety) as to my duty. Nor do I as yet see my way clearly, though I have the assurance that ere I act my Lord will make His will known to me without a doubt shadowing my mind. The facts that combine to make this problem difficult lie in my relation to Nottingham and the Institute here, and likewise in the peculiar position of the Yorkshire Colleges and my relation to Yorkshire.

" 1. So far as regards ease, comfort, money considerations (the same salary is offered at either place), perfectly and supremely happy relations in this town, with my large body of students, with my committee, and with many men engaged in philanthropic enterprises—all weighs on one side in favour of my present home and sphere. And, were I to be guided by these considerations of happiness which appeal to one's heart, the decision would be easy. But when I seek to discover my duty by the only sure test, viz. how I may make my life, be it long or short, most largely useful, most economically, widely effective, then the answer is not so clear, nay, seems to me to be in the opposite direction.

" 2. You know my connection with the Institute, and how much the Institute has had a personal relationship to me—more than I could have wished—so much so that when unwell last winter, I could not but ask myself with some concern—if I die, what of the Institute ? Will it not collapse ? You are aware of the jealousy and even vehement opposition which the Institute has encountered from the other higher colleges. I know that I have been greatly favoured by many who have trusted me whilst they would not see the paramount importance of the Institute to our denomination (*i.e.* the larger communion of our Churches). Now I cannot but feel that, if I were at the head of one of the other Colleges, I could at once vindicate the position and necessity of the Institute from a much better, less interested (as it would seem) platform. During the last two years I have been obliged to give up the direct work of canvassing for subscriptions, and what I now do—by way of testimony and earnest support by word of mouth and by pen—for the Institute, I could do not only as well, but better, at the head of another College. I must, as long as I live, live for the Institute ; but I wish to live to nurse it into a state of independence apart from a personal relation to myself, and having an organised proper footing of its own in the midst of our Churches.

" I, however, pleaded with you to be at the head of the Institute,[1] and you generously and most kindly consented.

[1] Mr. Morley became Chairman in 1873.

If you, with your great influence, would allow me, being at the head of one of the other Colleges (from which most needless jealousy has been poured out on us here) to work with you, I could, from a position that was disinterested, find scope to speak of the Institute, as I most profoundly believe, and without the suspicion that I was pleading for myself, or for my hobby. We could, thus together, most powerfully and adequately sustain the Institute, gathering round it the men of the country who should be its supporters. On the other hand, I feel that, if I did not receive your consent and blessing on the step, I could not with perfect satisfaction go elsewhere. When I speak of my labouring with you, I do not mean that you should do more for the Institute : your name is a tower of strength. And if, as years ripen, you feel a desire to be more entirely associated with Christian work which fitly belongs to the Sabbath of years, there is no institution through which greater blessings can be diffused over this country than the Institute. If, however, as you thought you possibly could, you gave one day or so in the year, we could then concert measures and awaken influences that would ensure not only the continuing, but the increasing power and usefulness of the Institute. I do want to see the Institute in a more independent, I would say, safer position than it is in at present. I even fear lest my present connection with it may hinder to some extent it being thus taken up by others and sustained as a Denominational Institution, whilst, if I were outside, and especially as Principal of another College, I could stimulate, especially with your guidance and help, many County Associations, leading laymen, etc., to take this direct responsibility in regard to it.

" 3. In Yorkshire, as you are aware, a great schismatic evil has been wrought. Two new colleges have been built. Much discord and division have ensued in the county. If the supply and training of an earnest, able ministry should fail our Churches in the north, then they lose their main element of power and vitality, and will suffer unspeakably. That these two divisive Colleges should suffer, or even be extinguished, would not pain me. But that, through this schismatic evil, the Churches of Christ should be weakened, and gravely imperilled, is a matter of deepest concern to me. Now it is urged on me that I could do something—much, it is even said—to harmonise these two institutions, to make them work together as two parts of one system of training, and rally the support of the Yorkshire Churches to the great cause of securing a zealous, effective ministry for themselves and for all aggressive work. Yorkshire is a noble county. Independency should be nobly maintained in it. Through its collegiate system it can, and must, either upbuild and extend itself, or dwindle into feebleness. I cannot but recognise the great importance of these considerations.

" 4. All the work which I have taken in hand here of a special kind may be carried out before Christmas. The People's Café Company—the Company for the purchase and utilisation of the corner of land on Mansfield Road and Shakespeare Street, the Handel-Schule, the Elementary Trade and Science School, and the Working Women's Institute, are all in a position that warrants their successful start before Christmas.

" 5. As for that great special work which apart from, and subordinate to my own immediate work, the training of men for Christ's service in His Church, is the work to which I wish to devote my life—' The Inner Mission,' that divinest work in which I trust, so long as life is given to both of us, we may be permitted to work together—it might be as well (perhaps better), assisted, so far as I have to take part in it, from Bradford as from Nottingham.

" I have enumerated all the points that weigh on my mind. I wish to have your judgment. If you were to ask me to come to you—wished to talk more fully with me—I would even run down to Skye, for I do wish, whatever I do, to have your sanction, and more. I recognise this as the great crisis, turning, and deciding point of my life, and I must now scrutinize most deeply and clearly every aim and motive of my life before my God and Redeemer, that my decision may evoke no thought in my mind in after-years of any bias, that was not given directly by God Himself.

" I think of going to Tunbridge Wells on Wednesday for two quiet days, that I may give myself there to meditation and prayer ere I resolve.

" . . . I have not spoken articulately of the immense attractions of Nottingham. These are so close to me, and weigh so powerfully. They are so patent to everybody, that I have not mentioned them. But do not think that one of them is overlooked—or can be. The joy of training fifty men is incalculable. There are only fourteen at Airedale now."

The pull of Nottingham was stronger than the pull of Airedale, and he resolved to stay.

" Yes," he wrote, to Mr. Farrar, an old student, " I was greatly perplexed about Yorkshire. My heart is much in such work as I could have done there. But I was compelled to remain here till I saw my work consolidated and preserved against future contingencies."

Again, to another friend he writes :

" Nothing short of the plainest and resistless leadings of providence should remove me from a sphere where I believe I am useful, and where I know I am happy."

But he took the occasion to start a Students' Trust Fund of £10,000. He calculated that the average cost per student worked out at £60 per annum, half of which was needed towards the expenses of board and lodging. The income of the Trust Fund was to be used for this latter purpose only.

In 1884 the Institute reached its majority. During the twenty-one years of its existence, the Institute had received over 450 students. About 100 of these had been prepared for, and sent forward to other Colleges for a more complete course of education. Two hundred had gone out as fully accredited students, and with very few exceptions—chiefly caused by early death—were working in different parts of the world, though chiefly in England. Some fifty other men had been received as private students for shorter courses of study ; many of these had been already engaged in the ministry, but, feeling their need of education, had contrived, not without difficulty, to procure the means of residing for one or two years at Nottingham, and attending the classes. Only three of the 450 were not engaged in the public service of the Church. " There is not one student," said the Principal, " but has honourably fulfilled the purpose of the Institute and the

conditions laid upon him when he left it." The number
under training had risen to nearly seventy. Something
substantial had been, therefore, achieved towards meeting
the need of the Churches for a supply of trained and
approved men for the ministry.

The Bishop of Lincoln (Dr. Wordsworth), had made a
careful study of the method and curriculum, and adopted
much of what he found in successful operation in Nottingham for a new Theological Institute in his own diocese.
The Baptists had established an Institute of their own on
the same lines at Bury, in Lancashire. The Bibliotheca
Sacra had recommended the Nottingham plan to the
Congregationalists of U.S.A. Each successive yearly report
accumulated evidence of the good work done by the old
Nottingham men. One such testimony must suffice : it
comes from the Secretary of the Norfolk Congregational
Union.

" Good service has been done in the county by your men.
The truth is, the men mean business. They seeem to
have invoked the help of God ; they are good men and
carry weight. This, with prayerful, painstaking, per-
sistent labour, has yielded spiritual prosperity. They
brought to us fresh air and inspiration. I find the county
has never been so quickened and revived. Your men,
by the blessing of God, have had much to do with it."

" All the men who have left the Institute," wrote the
Principal, " have entered upon those spheres of service for
which the Institute specially trained them, and the great
majority have remained pastors of country and mission
Churches ; not, indeed, because none of them had an
opportunity of going to pastorates of higher social importance and richer income, or had the ability needful for
such a position, but from a reason which was well stated
in the answer given two months ago by one of them to a
unanimous invitation from a wealthy Church, when he
said, referring to his present Church : ' Their claims are the
claims of the weak ; yours are the claims of the strong.
I have listened to the voice of conscience and to their
appeal, and therefore beg most kindly to decline your
invitation.' "

The chivalry of this answer showed the spirit of the

22

Nottingham men. It was worth more than the most brilliant academic successes to the heart of their old teacher.

" May the earnest spirit of self-sacrifice continually lead our students, in the future as the past, to follow Christ into the most difficult spheres of service both at home and abroad. For, where the need is greatest, and the work is hardest, His joy will abound unfailingly until the daybreak of the eternal glory."

The Coming of Age was celebrated on November 23rd, 24th, and 25th, 1884. The main object of the celebration was to magnify the great missionary idea of the Church which the Institute was founded to promote. Dr. Fairbairn, Chairman of the Congregational Union for the year, preached in Castlegate Church, and a two days' conference was held at the Institute, at which Paton read a paper on " the Home Mission of the Church," and Drs. Hannay and Clemance introduced the subject " Independency, its power and aptitudes for the work of the Lord in our time." Dr. Percival, the President of Trinity College, Oxford, sent a brotherly letter speaking of his friend's " irrepressible enthusiasm, inspiriting ardour, tenderness, and self-devotion." " I know," he said, " that your one thought and prayer is for the realisation among all Christians of the life of Christ and the union of all men in Him." Special missions were held in most of the Congregational places of worship in Nottingham and the county. By way of preparing the way for this simultaneous mission Paton wrote a leaflet " Read and ask, ' Are these things so ? ' " which was widely distributed. The leaflet was reprinted in " Inner Mission Leaflets," vol. i., leaflet 1, and has been used in many special missions. It states simply and clearly the great truths of the Gospel, and its power to lift men from a state of degradation and misery into " newness of life."

This was the first occasion on which the Principal met his old students as Doctor. In 1882 the University of Glasgow had conferred on him the Doctorate of Divinity in acknowledgment of the work he had done as a writer and a teacher.

The life of a regular teaching institution from year to year is much like that of a river. Though in each the component parts are continually changing, yet both river and institution acquire a definite character, and, as the record of change in the river is secular rather than annual, so with an institution; the real movements of growth are spread over long periods, and do not adapt themselves to detailed narrative year by year. The definite character of the Institute had been now well established. The next period in its development brings us to the year of Paton's retirement in 1898, after thirty-five years of service. By this time the building had been enlarged to accommodate 100 men by the addition of the Morley Hall. The new wing had been opened, like the original building, without "a single particle of the dust of debt upon it." The Endowment Fund had mounted up steadily to over £22,000.

It was a memorable scene in the large hall of the Institute, on June 27th, 1898, when the old students who had gathered together filled the hall. They had conspired together beforehand to mark, not so much the occasion, as their own generous feeling of loyalty, with two munificent presents. First, there was a pony carriage which was meant to show that they wished Mrs. Paton and the invalid daughter to share in their gift; and then there was a handsome library bureau with ample accommodation of pigeon-holes and drawers and cupboards for the papers and letters which kept multiplying indefinitely in connection with their old tutor's various causes. The bureau bore the inscription:

PRESENTED TO THE REV. JOHN BROWN PATON, D.D., M.A.,
PRINCIPAL OF THE CONGREGATIONAL INSTITUTE,
BY HIS PAST AND PRESENT STUDENTS,
IN TOKEN OF THEIR LOVE AND REVERENCE FOR HIM
AS THEIR MASTER,
WHOSE INSPIRING TEACHING ANCHORED THEM TO THE
DEEP THINGS OF GOD,
AND AS THEIR FRIEND,
WHO ALWAYS FELT FOR THEM MORE THAN THEY FELT FOR
THEMSELVES.

July 1898.

The whole assembly rose to their feet and cheered

when their revered teacher stood up to express his gratitude and to say a last word of God-speed to those who
had been his students, and to those who were going to
carry forward his work.

"My brethren, dearly beloved and longed for, my joy
and crown," he said, "I give thanks unto God always for
your fellowship in the Gospel, from the first day even until
now."

He was glad that the gifts to be presented to him were
gifts in which his true and beloved wife could share. Her
sweet, and sacred, and unfailing sympathy had upborne
him in every undertaking of his life, and to her loving care
alone, under God, he owed it that he was there. He
thought, too, that, if they had seen, as he saw yesterday,
the outshining eyes and radiant face of his dear, dumb,
invalid daughter as he told her of the pleasure and honour
which his beloved students were giving to her mother and
to him, and in which she would also share, they would
have seen a tribute of praise and thanks which they would
not easily forget. For himself, he felt as if his heart were
filled with a strange, glad paradox. When he thought of
the little that had been done to deserve so much, and
that little had been so happily done, done under the
inspiration of love which had never ceased throughout all
those years—the love of his students, which had no
measure—he was abashed and humbled ; and then, on the
other hand, he could not but confess that he was uplifted
and enriched when he thought of those overflowing streams
of love that had been poured upon him and around him.
After long and arduous toil—and he would confess it
had been long, strenuous, and arduous—he seemed to
stand that evening on the very roof of time, like the
warrior troop, following their leader up the rugged
heights of Darien, who, when they reached the summit,
saw, to their amazement and delight, glowing under the
western skies, the wide, bright seas of the Pacific; so
now, having climbed through long years his Darien peak,
he stood there, and lo ! there shone below him the calm
western sea in which the sun of his life would shortly sink
—that sea whose farther waters washed the shore of
eternity, the land of the blessed.

That evening, however, he had a record and testimony
to give, and it was fitting that he should make it there,

for it was a record and testimony, so marvellous, of the faithfulness and the loving-kindness of God, that might breathe courage and hope into every true child of God. He thought of the long, long past, and the daring (should he say) with which that Institute was founded. He knew of no other Institute that had been founded under similar circumstances, without a penny of endowment; there was nothing but faith, a faith which laid hold on God. He thought of the multitudes of students that had been trained there, many of whom passed, after short probation, out again into business life, there, however, to do their work for God with quickened power which they had received at the Institute : others pressing forward into the open fields of service to occupy the hottest and hardest posts with heroic devotion. And he thought of the wonderful generosity by which that Institute, through all those years, had been maintained. For many years they had not a single penny of endowment; yet that great and beautiful building was erected after four years had been spent in Nottingham, and opened without a grain of the dust of debt upon it. Extensions were made in the same way, not only without incurring debt, but always leaving a little surplus in hand; and never—a wonderful record— had the door of the Institute been closed upon a man sent from God because funds were wanting. If a man was sent from God, he must enter in. The funds had never failed, for in their work they were serving Him who could not fail; and so it came about that, after those long years, when called upon to retire into service of an- other kind, that noble building stood there so splendidly and perfectly equipped that it could hardly be improved for the work it had to do, and there was a balance in hand on the revenue account.

Without any doubt that was a great record and testi- mony; but he had a more wonderful record and testimony to give than that. It seemed scarcely credible, but it was true. During those thirty-five years in Nottingham the whole history of the Institute had not been disturbed or jarred by one serious cause of anxiety. He looked back on those thirty-five years, during which there had been scarce a ripple of trouble. Difficulties, great difficulties, there had been, but they are a healthy stimulant and a delight to earnest workers. And, looking back, it

seemed to him as if the light of God's favour and love
had fallen upon that long track of years like the light of
a long, refreshing summer day. It was most beautiful
and wonderful. Should they not magnify together the
goodness and grace, the faithfulness and loving-kindness,
of God ? To what was all that owing ? It was owing
primarily to that of which they had such witness this
evening—the love and loyalty of these men — " *my
students* "—every generation of them. Love and loyalty
made the joyful music to which they had marched
all those years, music that made a toilsome journey pleasurable and a heavy burden light. And then the wonderful good fortune—no, it was something far richer than
that—that had befallen him in the blessed fellowship and
comradeship of colleagues. What men to have been
associated with ! No wonder there had been such harmony and delight in the work of the Institute. And then
the splendid generosity of those men who were the first
to support the Institute, and who continued to support
it—men who were, as he might say, princes in Israel, with
a large, clear vision of the interests of the Church, with
strong, faithful purpose, and with generous heart and
generous purse. How splendidly they upheld the Institute throughout those years ! There was one thing he
might say there for the encouragement—nay, more, the
inspiration and education—of every one present. Venerable and saintly men—he saw present the daughter of
one and the son of another—trusted him. He marvelled
at it at the time. They put loving, perfect trust in him,
and he seemed so unworthy of it. But was there ever
any human power so potent to touch the deepest springs
of energy in a man and thus to make him what those men
believed him to be ? And he learned the best lesson in
his life-work from these first, truest friends of the Institute and himself, for he learned that he should evoke,
through like trust to that given to him, the best that
is to be found in every man who came there.

The crowning joy of all was that, when he retired from
the Principalship and its great responsibilities, the office
would rest upon a man eminently qualified by splendid endowments, faculty, and experience [here the whole gathering
rose], having rare practical gifts and that uncommon grace,
the grace of common sense, and, above all (should he say ?),

devoted with a whole-hearted devotion to the great objects of the Institute and the evangelic faith which had been the theme of all their teaching and the inspiration of all their work there.

He had spoken of the objects of the Institute; perhaps it was fitting that he should specify what those two objects were, and again in their presence lift high that banner of evangelic faith which had ever waved so gloriously over their Institute. The first was to give training to men who enter our ministry. According to our church doctrine only men who are manifestly called of God should enter the ministry. And this implies the corollary that all who are so called should receive the necessary training and provision from the Church for the sacred duties of the ministry. Now, plainly, many men are called to this work who, by their age and past experiences, and their temperament, are wholly unable to undergo a classical and mathematical training, and who would simply waste their time if such training were forced on them; yet these men are capable of receiving a training that will be suitable to them, and at the same time be most practical and effective. The other was to raise a mission ministry. This motive moved him most. He could not bear the thought that Independency should be a sect fitted only for one section or class of the community. Independency was to embody and proclaim the divine and true doctrine of the Church; therefore it must show itself able to fulfil all the responsibilities and meet all the needs of the Church of Christ. And, to do this, it must pre-eminently show itself able to reach the masses of the people and train them in the methods of a free and well-ordered government and in all the ministries of the Church. But such a mission ministry must be filled with a deep, fervent, exultant faith in the Gospel of the grace of God. To them, as to the Apostle Paul, it must be the *glorious* Gospel—revealing the highest glory of God, and bringing the highest good to men. Hence the supreme and constant aim of the Institute has been and will be to witness, and teach, and magnify the evangelic faith. What, then, is the essence of that evangelic faith when liberated from conventional formulæ, the casement and sheathing of dogma? Surely it is this—that the Eternal Love, in infinite com-

passion, has stooped down to this world of ours, filled with
sin and sorrow, in order by sympathy and service and
sacrifice, in righteous ways which magnify the law of God,
to restore man individually and socially to righteousness,
to that perfect state, full of blessed health and harmony,
which is conformed to the will of God. He confessed that
the evangelic faith had been obscured and even narrowed
by limitations in some quarters. What are they ? Religion had been too much an individual interest, each
thinking of himself and his own salvation. But to be
saved is to receive the life of Christ, to enter into the
obedience and fellowship of His life, and so to be filled
with a love for God and men in which selfishness is lost.
And what was the other limitation ? He had held, and
taught with all the power that was in him, that religion
was not only for the individual but for society, that,
where the Gospel was preached and Christianity was
established, there must go forth an influence that should
purify the customs of the people, that should inspire and
regulate all the institutions of the people.

He must add a few words to his dear old students ere
concluding. This was a dark and troubled time in which
their lot was cast. Whirling controversies seemed to be
shaking the very foundations of the faith. He wanted
them to see with him the vision of the Apocalypse—to
see Him who stood at the end of this century in white,
with eyes terrible as a flame of fire, with a fan in His hand
—standing upon the great harvest-floor to winnow the
chaff and the dust from the wheat ; and so to remove
" the things that may be shaken in order that the things
that cannot be shaken shall abide " in eternal peace and
security for ever. May the peace of God which passeth
all understanding, in the midst of those dark and whirling controversies, keep—keep securely as behind bastion
ramparts—their heart and mind through Jesus Christ.
They were entering upon a new century, and he asked them
to read again the address of his sainted and beloved friend
Dr. Reynolds, and the letter which he himself wrote
accompanying that appeal, to prepare them for the century which now loomed so close at hand. It was to be
a great century in the history of mankind. Great issues
were to be determined in it, and they were going forth
as soldiers of the Cross, believers in the kingdom of God,

into that century, to bring into it the glory of the Latter Day.

He had one word to say to them, which he had said to one of the most distinguished men of our time, with whom he had conferred in respect to the great social work that he as well as himself wished to accomplish. He said to him, and he said to those present, there were three great powers, which were the inspiration of the Church, giving to her ardour and abiding strength, and without which their labours would be in vain. They could be spoken in three words. The first was the Divine Law, the sovereign will of God ; the law of the Kingdom of their Father, which will be fulfilled in that new order of the social world which would come through the salvation that was in Christ. The second was Love—such love as was only kindled in us by the love that burnt in the heart of Christ ; such love as His when He looked upon the sin and death of the world, and bore it and vanquished it through love infinite, eternal. And the third—oh, the joy of it !—was their Leader.

Before he sat down, let him ask them to support his beloved friend Mr. Mitchell as they had supported him. The work was to be far greater at the Institute than it had been. The capacious and nobly equipped building was there, the man was there, and the work had to be done, for the need was greater than ever. He had pledged himself to do what he could, and he pledged those present also. In conclusion, Dr. Paton said that he retired, not to seek rest, but he turned now to service which would not be so exhausting physically, but which would be, he trusted, fruitful to the glory of Christ. The first service he put before himself was that he might seek in their time, and especially in their Churches, to revive and reinforce the divine doctrine of the Church to fulfil her mission in the world. This service would be undertaken with failing strength of body, but he prayed for the renewing strength of the Spirit. Would they not lend him the support of their sympathy and the benediction, sought for, longed for, of all their prayers ?

. . . . .

This is the occasion which, for want of a better term, is spoken of as his retirement. But it did not mean actually retiring even from work in connection with the

Institute. For the next year he remained as Associate-
Principal, to share the direction of things with his successor, the Rev. J. A. Mitchell, M.A., and after 1899 he
still continued to live in his old house in the Institute
building, and bore the title Principal Emeritus. " I
desired, while still living," he said, " to see the Institute
fulfilling its mission apart from myself." Mr. Mitchell's
long and intimate association with the Institute, when
he was minister of Friar Lane Church, had demonstrated
his special fitness for the work, and given him a thorough
insight into the aims and methods of the Institute. He
knew the men and had won their hearts.

But still less did it mean retirement from other work.
" When I retire," he used to say, " I shall retire to heaven."
Other projects which were dear to his heart were sufficient in themselves to tax the whole time and energy even
of a man in the heyday of his strength. Nor was there
any break in continuity. " My hope for the evening
of life," he said, " is the hope of life's morning : what was
the morning star is now the evening star, shining the same
amid ever-changing lights." Though he was no longer
teaching, he was to the end a working minister of the
Gospel.

Before we pass on to the other activities which come
flooding up like a tide into every creek and cranny of his
life, we will take one more look at him among his students
in these later days.

The monthly Communion Service remained the Pentecostal time.

" Perhaps the most enthralling, inspiring, and lasting of
the great days of the Doctor," says the Rev. W. H. Towers,
" were the times we had at the Communion Services,
regularly held once a month during the college session.
The rapture that possessed our Principal, the glowing
thought that possessed him as he spoke of the ever-present
Lord in the fulness of the Christian redemption, the voice
modulated in tone, the countenance tender unto tears
and ever and anon shining, as though a sunbeam had
broken through upon it, and the eye lighted as with living
fire, his whole soul seemed to go forth with such holy
ardour that every man must have felt the power of God
in the life of him whom it was our great privilege to hail

as teacher and master. What would one not give to have a repetition of those Tuesdays when we had the ordinance at College ? . . . I can see now the sunshine that seemed to play on the Doctor's face as he examined our Mission Book on the Monday afternoon. We had as many as 200 hearers in the open air, and, through the good Doctor's influence, the old iron chapel that had done service at Hucknall Torkard was erected on the site where our preaching services had been held at Bulwell. Quite a number of colliers and others became members of the Church, and it was my great joy to be present when Mr. Mitchell and Mr. Kidd (a deacon of Friar Lane) visited the candidates. In this way I became closely associated with the Rev. James Mitchell, M.A., whom to know was to love. Thus the Doctor's policy of interesting the city Churches in evangelistic work bore most precious fruit."

" The Doctor used to say, ' A man who cannot keep a congregation in the open-air on a fine day has no right to impose himself upon a congregation in a Church, where, if he fails to grip them, they cannot go away.' "

The Rev. J. W. Dickson, St. Helens, writes :

" It was not my privilege to enter the Institute before the first year of the last decade of the nineteenth century. Dr. Paton had not yet returned from abroad after one of his physical breakdowns. As a junior student, the occasions of sitting under him on his return were the monthly Communion Service, the weekly Prayer-meeting, and the weekly Sermon-class. At one of the Communion Services I saw him for the first time. And the mere looking at him did one good. If this was the ' good old Doctor,' as the senior students called him, in his age and in his weakness, what must he have been in his youth and manhood and strength ? Surely there never was a nobler-looking man ! How good, how great, how strong, how kind he looked ! As time went on, it often occurred to one that in him there were all the majesty and the meekness, the virtues and the graces, of such men as Abraham, Moses, Samuel, Elijah, John, and Paul. Which of the patriarchs, prophets, or apostles was he most like ? That we could not decide as to his appearance, but we were sure that in his mental and spiritual make-up he had something of all of them.

" To see him was an inspiration. To hear him was to be enriched and ennobled. Ours was a priceless privilege. To be in his presence was to enter into a new world—we were transformed by beholding him, and strengthened and purified by listening to him. Who could look at Dr. Paton without feeling that he was a saint and a seer, a scholar and a sympathising friend ? Nay, a saviour of men ! He was what he told his students to be—' Do not be Christians,' he said, ' be Christs. Let there be in you this divine passion for sacrifice to win men to your Lord. Give to Christ the full cup of life, and your full life He will fill with His own Spirit. This poor human instrument may thus be filled with His power.' His very face showed that Dr. Paton had this divine passion—that his life Christ had filled with Himself. His face ! Words cannot adequately describe it. That look—that glow in the eye— the ecstasy of it, the invincible strength of it, the holy and tranquil calm of it ! One of his maxims on sermon delivery was that ' Oratory is spoken thought, not by the mouth only, but also by the face, eyes, lips, hands, and body.' And of himself it could be said that rhetoric shone in his face. The kingliest and the kindliest of men— his mind, his heart, his will beamed in his eyes. He used to tell us that ' a good sermon has heaven for its father and earth for its mother,' and if it is permissible to adapt that statement to his own countenance we would say it portrayed both the human and the heavenly spirit that was in him. He was a good man, with a great soul. He was incapable of doing a mean or unworthy action, and he would not do a trivial thing. His own nobility came out in his words : ' Do not select a trivial part,' he said. ' Toil nobly ; toil bravely ; toil greatly ; and toil terribly.'

" It may not be absolutely and always true that ' a great man cannot do a little deed,' but it is true of Dr. Paton. He could not do a little deed. He turned trifles into deeds of perfection, because of the greatness of soul he put into the humblest tasks. Charles Lamb was a favourite writer of his, and he quoted from him, ' No deed of mine shall shame thee,' and, after dealing very charitably with him as ' the brave, gentle, Christlike hero he was,' he would say for our good, ' Let no deed of yours bring shame upon your sacred office ; let your deeds bring delight and triumph to your Lord.'

" In a thousand ways he tried to infuse us with his own nobleness and greatness. If we had become half as good men and half as good preachers as he tried to make us, we should be no ordinary men and far above the average of preachers. ' Oh, you must be a preacher, Mr. —— ; you must be a preacher, you must,' said he one day after a sermon in class of an average sort, but not as good as the man was capable of giving. The Principal saw undeveloped powers, probably unknown to the preacher, and wished to give the necessary encouragement and stimulus for the exercise of that unused force. And when another student, returning home after preaching one Sunday, said he had made up his mind to settle down as ' an ordinary preacher,' he had escaped for the time being from the Doctor's inspiration. It was impossible to listen to him without determining to be ' a great preacher '— or, at least, much better than you were then. ' It is only the adjective " good " that will decline into " best," ' he would say ; ' but " bad " never, that declines into " worst." The French have a motto, " The good is the enemy of the best," and so it is sometimes. It kills the best. But no ! not with you. Let your good be better, and then make better into best. Never be content with less than the best. Remember, every one of you—the best, the best, the best—every one of you ! " Why will ye live and not be glorious ? " ' '

" On another occasion he said, ' Be men who have a great business in hand. Each of you be a man standing four-square on a firm basis. Do not under-strike your ministry by some laxity, some slippings away. Never let it be said of you, as it is said of some ministers who are indiscreet, unstable, and soft, that " He is a man—but a man spoiled." ' '

" How pathetic, but how powerful for inspiration was his personal appeal, when once in these later years, in his tenderness trembling on to tears, he said, ' Men of the Institute, my only hope of living is to live through you.'

" He was as practical as he was good. ' What the world wants is reality,' he would say. In Sermon-class, during my four years alone, he said things that would fill a good-sized book worth reading the world over. Great truths, mighty inspirations, glorious unfoldings of God's Word, and gracious revelations of the Spirit of Christ in him—

there are hundreds of these which could be reproduced.
What wealth of practical help in sermon-building he
bestowed upon us! 'The introduction is that by which
you hook on the interest of the congregation. It sets
the tone, creates the atmosphere, in which the subject can
be well received. It ought to lead up to the subject of
the text.'

" 'Have a definite object—a definite thesis. There is a
subject, and there is an object, of a sermon. Never divorce
the two. Without an object it is no sermon, but a very
poor essay.' In my hearing he startled a student one day
when he said : 'Mr. ——, your plan is like one of the shows
at the Goose Fair. It is one of the greatest wonders of
the world. It is a headless object. You have no subject.
That is a marvellous thing. A sermon without a head.
But it is better than a preacher without a head. Do not
forget it again.'

" 'Let there be faithful exegesis. Keep within the four
corners of the text. Explicate—unfold the text. There
must be specific teaching and sequency of thought ; good
arguments, coherences and harmonies of reasoning. Exegesis is the expression of the soul and spirit and savour
of the thought and feeling of the text. Try to realise
the feeling of the speaker of it, and of the one to whom it
applies, and his position.

" ' The divisions of your sermon ought to be propositions.
In the plan, heads must come from the subject, and be
rhythmical. Reason first, rhythm after. Have a unity—
one topic, not many, which are confusing. A sermon is
a tree that grows up from its root. One trunk stem,
with limbs or branches. The text is the root, the sermon
is the stem. Subdivisions are the branches, and these
must be logical and orderly. All art must have unity
in it, and conspire to one end. The elements and basis
of a sound philosophy must be in each plan and sermon.
At the same time, the pulpit must not be the rostrum of
the school ; it is not to teach philosophy and science.
Science is powerless as ever to allay the troubles of the
soul.' 'Limit your theme. Have a small field, but dig
deep—trench it—get out of it all you can.' 'Define your
aim, and stick to it. Put the mint press upon it—a
definite stamp—stamp of brain. Be definite. Indefiniteness is the blight of good preaching.'

" ' In the conclusion there must be relevance. Yes, and there must be point, edge, bite in it. Let everything work to a point ; focus to one point ; marshal to the point of attack. Make people feel the bite of your flame. Your sword must have brightness and edge, so that it will shine and cut.'

" At another time he said : ' The angler needs a crooked pin, with barbs, to hold and stick. So with speech. It must strike, interest, seize and hold. A straight pin will go in and come out again easily. So will a hookless sermon.'

" Again : ' The pulpit is the boat, the congregation is the whale—send out your harpoon, and catch them. We want a little more harpooning, Mr. ——. Strike with a hook that is barbed—that will stick so that they can't get away from it.'

" He would quote the Roman phrase, *Totus in illo.* ' Work up to a climax. Only at the end let your congregation see fully what you are after. Let the sermon grow in vigour toward the end. It must be full and resonant in the body, like the thong of a whip, and put the lash— the knots—at the end.'

" Good rules for composition were given to the students, but in addition to these Dr. Paton was constantly emphasising essential points. ' Put energy and strength into your sentences. Beauty and tenderness as well. The first essential to good composition is perspicuity—then strength—then beauty. There must be validity, force, and grace. Let there be mass and velocity, with faith behind it.'

" ' Get the phrase that is inevitable—the very thought you intend—is this *the* one phrase ? Never be in the air, but always on the ground—real, actual, familiar. Let there be sweat of brow ; put substance into it ; let there be no want of brain-stuff ! '

" ' Let there be directness, brevity, and vigour. You must have persuasion, severity, gentleness, and cheerfulness. See that it interests, for that is one of the first elements of good composition and of a good sermon. Mind your p's and q's—your pauses and questions ! You must have interrogative, invective, and invitation. And no great excrescence or bulging protuberance ! Let there be soundness of argument, arguments bolted and chained together.'

" ' Be epigrammatical, logical, and metaphorical. Strong words are always metaphorical words. Passion creates metaphor ; passion creates the flowers and the figures.'

" As to the delivery of a sermon, Dr. Paton was the master of masters. He gave us theory, and he gave practice. As an orator, I never heard his equal. He was the most gifted and eloquent speaker it has been my good fortune to hear. To sit at the feet of such a master was a priceless boon. Nature, culture, and grace combined to make him a prince among preachers. More than that, he was a maker of preachers. He said, ' Give me the men, and, God helping me, I'll make them the men they ought to be.' In standing firm, in gesture graceful and effective, in feature flexible, in voice well-modulated and of great range, in sympathy and purpose most powerful—in everything, in short, he was a good model of what a good and great preacher should be.

" How he used to reproduce for our examples the great orators and preachers of the ages ! We could see them live before us—in him. He told us of Chalmers, in his intense passion and earnestness, perspiring so profusely that he was ' like a watering-can,' and men said, ' It's fell preaching yon.' He liked to see ' holy sweat on preachers.' Quoting Aristotle, ' The passion is dyed in all colours,' he would say : ' To be vigorous and vivid, you need not be loud and strident. There must be sympathy between voice and subject. Aristotle had that sincerity which is the most powerful element of a man's speech. A man's words have just the weight of what he himself is. Words without sincerity are simply the froth of language.'

" ' It is not hypothesis, but the very truth of God you are to speak. Then speak as strongly as He would speak, and speak as gently as He would speak. Where there is more voice, more emphasis, or more gesture than there is feeling, there is waste—and worse. Powder beyond the shot is disastrous.'

" ' Identify yourself with your subject. Have the magnetism of moral sympathy. Authority comes out of character. The prophet who has seen God is prepared with a revelation of the Being whom he proclaims. Speak with obedience, and faith, and courage, and God will clothe you with words and power. If the intellect is charged with the mighty emotions of the heart, your words will have immense weight with those who hear you. To be a great teacher there must be great sympathy. You must have that if you would approach, impress, and win men. The whole man uttered Himself when Jesus spoke. And your speech will have weight only when it is backed by yourself.'

" Dr. Paton liked a man to be himself. A student was preaching a sermon in class which was ' a grand patchwork quilt.' The purple patches were beautiful and bountiful ! The diction was exquisite, and the continual flashes of brilliant colour were startling surprises even to the men. They felt that it was too grand to be his own. But the Doctor—he watched and waited ! Those tell-tale lips of his quivered with self-control and self-denial. How he wanted to be at him ! But not yet ! Give him a chance to preach something of his own. The observant students watched and wondered. Would the Doctor put the snuffers on before the sermon burnt itself out ? No ; he watched and waited to the end. The preacher had been too engrossed with his own borrowed brilliance to see the Principal's face. When the preacher had resumed his seat, the Doctor, as if in imitation of the eloquent oration, said with vehemence : ' Splendid ! Splendid ! '—then, after a pause, and in much lower tones, he added, ' rags ! ' Such was his hatred of pretence that he had lifted the culprit up to Paradise only to fling him down to perdition. But it was done to make an honester man of him.

" To another parader of purple patches he said : ' Too many bangles ! There is more grace in a nicely formed arm than in all the bracelets and jewels you ever saw. Put off all these false adornments, if you would not cloy the taste of your hearers.' He could not bear cant, and he could be severe in his condemnation of it.

" He was always ready to encourage a man who had done a poor best, if it was with his own abilities. After a moderate sermon, with that tenderness of sympathy he encouraged so much in his men, he said, ' Mr. ——, you haven't hit the mark to-day ; indeed, you are rather a bad shot at present. But keep on practising, and you'll be a good shot yet.'

" If he liked a man to be himself, he liked him to be himself on fire. He often advised us to—' Begin low, proceed slow, rise higher, infuse fire.' On one occasion

23

he said : ' Dig down into the depths of that text, and there would have been a little more enthusiasm—of Vesuvius —at the top. We wanted a little more soul-fire ! ' He wished us to be good builders—good creators—of sermons ; but this he reckoned as next to nothing if we could not deliver them well. ' Essays are like go-carts, where babies have no weight on their own legs. Your MS. should not be a go-cart. When you preach, stand on your own legs, and put your whole soul into your words. Remember the text, " I am come to bring fire on the earth." Every preacher should be included in that other Scripture— " Who maketh . . . His ministers a flame of fire." Burn with holy passion, and get your congregation on fire too. They are cold enough as a rule ; inspire them with love and enthusiasm.'

" Our Principal was always a good friend to us, and delighted in us. He praised our good points and showed us our weak ones—that he might make us truer and mightier. This time it was not the go-cart, but the donkey-cart that was made to pay tribute to the sermon class. What we students needed was more holy ambition, and this was how he got stimulus for it. ' Don't buy a donkey-cart. Buy four good blood-horses—full-bred ! And drive them ; mount them ! But it takes a clear head, a bright eye, and a strong heart to drive blood-horses. Still, that is what you must do ; you can if you will. And don't let them run away with you. It is not fanaticism we want, but well-controlled enthusiasm.'

" It was marvellous with what variety and aptitude these similes came from him. Until he heard it, he was ignorant of what the text was to be, or of the kind of sermon the preacher would give, but there came out of that rich storehouse of his heart and mind something appropriate and helpful every time. To a man lacking in zest he said, " You have seen a blacksmith's forge, when the coal seems all black. But with one or two blasts all becomes aglow and burning—all in a moment. So is it with enthusiasm. It transfigures what is otherwise a black, cold, almost lifeless thing.' Another time, it was the potter and his wheel : ' You have got the clay and the wheel. But you must make the wheel spin— make it spin ! Make the clay a thing of beauty. You are the potter. And you must do more than mould the clay—you must fire it, and decorate it. Make it ready for use—make your sermon a thing of beauty that will be to your congregation a joy for ever.'

" Demosthenes was more than once held up to us for inspiration and imitation. ' He revealed to us the characteristic of true eloquence ! Δεινότης τις, " a certain terribleness " in the orator—it flames out of him. When the famous Greek addressed the Athenians, no sooner had he ended his oration than the people cried, as with one voice, " Let us arise and attack Philip ! " So with you. Let the people so feel the bite of your flame—the truth and urgency of your Gospel—that they will at once rise up and cry, ' To the help of the Lord against the mighty ! '

" ' A man who is going to take hold of his fellows must have a soul-stirring conviction and awakening of heart and conscience. Men are blinded and drugged by habit. To quicken their dormant faculties—to make them conscious of sin and of the possibilities of good in them—the preacher must be on fire. Plough deeply enough into the sinner's nature, and there will be discovered powers that have not yet broken their way up to the surface— to the light of day. To do this needs all the brain-stuff you can put into it ; but it is soul-stuff that is needed most. The sermon may be the wood, the altar, the sacrifice ; but it is the fire that is wanted—one great flame ! ' This same great essential was wanting when he applied that very caustic criticism : ' All very nice ; but nobody can be saved by a bit of candy-rock ! '

" So we might continue on and on the record of his loving and masterly help. ' The preacher is the man who has the greatest power in the world.' 'Though the Gospel is simple, it is not childish.' ' Ignorance is the curse of God.'

" ' You should always assume something in a sermon. There is no need to explain " the Gospel " always. Deal with one great theme or thesis, and not with each word in a text separately—as in John iii. 16—God, loved, world, Son, whosoever, believeth, perish, everlasting life.

" ' It is a bad plan always to wind up a sermon with heaven. The Gospel is not a remedy for that world alone, but for this world as well—for all eternity. As heirs of God, we shall have unlimited glory ; but we are to serve Him here below as a condition of entering into our inheritance above.

" ' Never have the division of saints and sinners in your sermons. Some of the saints are sinners, and some of the sinners are nearer saints than the saints imagine.

" ' Never use the word " felicity " about a fellow-man. It is a word used by weak clergymen and men-servants. You can use " felicity " about pigs.

" ' Never call a man " blessed " till he's dead.' "

" Dr. Paton was mighty in prayer. But, though a master in the spirit and science and art of prayer, he always claimed that in this he was only a scholar in the school of Christ. He had learned much in that school. He was on very intimate terms with his Master. And he taught his men the gracious lessons he had gained in fellowship with his Lord. I think he could almost forgive anything in a student rather than a disinclination to pray. We dare not attempt to reproduce the words of his prayers ; our memories are not trustworthy enough to do him justice. But one or two things he said about prayer can be recalled :

" The Christian by prayer lays hold of the arm of God ; the child draws his Father to his help.

" Prayer—the communion of the human spirit with the divine—is the proper food of the spiritual life. Who can renew my soul ? I need some one to do it for me : a Hand on the other side of the wall continually pouring the oil that keeps the flame continually burning. I can't do without it. It would go out.

" Restraining prayer, we cease to fight. What miraculous power prayer gives us ! Effluence will do more than effort. A mere outbreaking of an influence wrought more than all the preaching of Peter.

" Intellectual as well as emotional faculties should be employed in prayer. There must, however, be glow and warmth of spirit in addition to reason and intellect. The light of religion is not that of the stove—heat without much light ; neither is it that of the moon—light without much heat ; but it is like the sun—both much light and much heat. The soul must have both light and warmth in prayer.

" Give more time to prayer and less to mere enjoyment. Novel-reading, party-going, pleasure-seeking, theatre-going, leave the heart as empty as a dream. They are nothing as compared with spiritual fellowship. Prayer fills with lasting love and strength. A life of faith and love is a joyous life. This is a glorious world when it is lived in the light and atmosphere of heaven. The Christian life is sphered on earth, but atmosphered in heaven. As Schiller tells us, ' Seek God upon thy way, and He will come to thee.' "

Speaking of intercessory prayer on one occasion, and referring to his own enforced inactivity when in search of renewed health, he said with true pathos and appeal : " Even then, doing nothing, I was perhaps doing most for the great Master."

It was the same with praise as with prayer. Because he prayed much, he praised much. " Praise," he said, " is every feeling of my heart that leads me to extol the love, the glory, the power, and all the admirable character and matchless grace that are in Christ."

" Song will always accompany and follow sacrifice, when it is a whole offering. The miserable men are those who put snippets on the altar. A truly forgiven sinner cannot keep his joy to himself—he must sing the song of the Lord. The unforgiven sinner may pipe a little song, but it chokes in his throat."

There were always wise counsels from the Principal when he was sending his students out on mission work, visiting and preaching ; or when several men had completed their training at the Institute and were leaving for the pastorate :

" Live to make heaven around you wherever you are. Be a friend of all, but a partisan of none. Remember that a spirit which gives rise to schism generally remains in the schism. The condition of Christian fellowship is love. A Church without love is a fiction. Comradeship in the midst of real difficulty binds members together. They bivouac together ; they face the foe together. Each member will say, ' My safety depends upon my next neighbour being faithful to me, and therefore I'll be true to him ! '

" Christian people and Christian ministers fail because

they do not allow Christ's love to constrain them, and to bring them into sympathy with His methods and aims in the world. He died for me, for men, for the world. He died because He loved me. The effect of Christ's love in our hearts and minds 'adds a precious seeing to the eye,' makes us thoughtful, brings us into sympathy with Christ, and with what is dear to His heart. Where genuine love is, it will constrain to energy, service, and self-sacrifice. Get springs of feeling wakened in your soul, and the wrestling power for victory will come.

" Close sympathy with every instinct and need of man is the Christianity that will bless. But let your help be of the right kind. Helping the poor, is giving him a start to help himself. A wise, brotherly help to overcome his weaknesses is worth more than doles of money. The word ' charity ' is used in a poor, degraded sense when limited to ' alms.' It is more than that. It is love in life and conduct. So-called charity is pauperising England and modern Europe. It is creating a pauper class. Give personal, redemptive sympathy ; give Christlike service ; and, wherever you go, carry Christ to the people. Expect help in money from those who have money ; but expect something better from those who have what is better—love, sympathy, and service. Do not make your appeals exclusively to the rich, who are few, and who do not come to your chapels. Get the means of helping the poor and perishing people from all classes in your Church—but in men as well as in money. Do not denounce the poor millionaires ; show that every one can be a helper of men—can serve them in love. Have the tender note, the appealing note, the sympathetic note—with these you vindicate the word ' charity.' Nothing good is ever in vain.

" We are saved that we may serve. But, unfortunately, some Churches are more like social loitering-places than a busy vineyard. There are people who have a church connection which is very unreal. They have a single eye to Christ's glory only in the sense that they have a double eye to their own. Those who have the most doubt have the least work. Constant service is the highest form of service. ' I have no time for doubts and fears.' If there is not vigilance, there is fatal treachery. I hate sluggards, and God hates sluggards.

" There is a religion of service, of valour, as well as for sadness and suffering. We have degraded our religion by pandering to the appetite for comfort. There is a selfish, indulgent form of religion. We must be warriors —we must be wounded in the fight. All religion is not a tender kind of sick-nursing. Comfort is not lullaby and opiate, but to be strong together with God. Men have had a very wrong standard of manliness. We are to make great sacrifices—to face great wrongs—to face the dragon in his den—to face death. We are to have the martyr spirit in us—to forget self and our own sufferings. The martyr did more by dying than by living. The measureless, unspeakable love of God calls you to valiant service. There are gems amongst the rubbish of humanity which need to be brought out and fashioned for the Saviour's crown.

" On your mission and in your ministry, throw your heart into your work, and do not be anxious about it. You are an ambassador. You need not fear. Do work for God, and the whole weight of heaven is behind you— on your side.

" Bring outsiders into the services. Take no food till you have brought some passer-by to your meeting. Even the publican can teach us in this. He gets his living by intercepting the loiterers. If no one came in ' to be eaten,' he himself would have nothing to eat. The footballer had to deny himself to win his goal. So must the Christian minister. Do not eat food unless you have brought some one into the presence of the Saviour.

" Make the discipline of your Church honourable. Too often the bankrupt is hardly dealt with, whilst a mean, covetous man is condoned or overlooked. Pride is a sin, too. It is the first to enter our nature and the last to come out. Do not judge as the world judges. You cannot coerce belief or exact belief. A clergyman treated Bradlaugh like an atheist, and he became one. The building up of Christian character is the great work of the Church, and the one thing that will bring about the kingdom of God is a true brotherhood among men.

" A minister needs time to take heed to himself. Many ministers need to be evangelised. There is no place so difficult to begin work for Jesus as the home. Said a servant-girl of her master, a Wesleyan minister : ' Many

conversions at chapel, but never a word for poor Polly ;
I do wish I could find Jesus.' We think of congregations,
of young men, of the outsider ; but we need to think of
home and of ourselves. Men tend to take care of others
in spiritual things, and not to take heed to themselves in
spiritual things. We must keep near to the Fountain of
all life if we are to keep fresh. And whilst the highest
thought in the Christian minister is not to save himself,
but to save others, it can only be maintained by personal
fellowship with the Redeemer. Do the strenuous, hard
duties of life with delight and obedience, but cultivate
the beauty of holiness by ever living in the Father's presence. Great will be the joys which come to the devoted
and self-sacrificing.

"Live a life that has rest-periods in itself. Refresh
yourselves in fellowship with spiritual persons. Disen-
gage yourself from worldly interests and affairs. Spiritual
retirement is so to refresh yourselves in communion with
God and with Christian people that your bodily and
spiritual health is promoted. Your rest-periods are to
prepare you for the active periods of life. Encourage
this in your ministry. Not in the ascetic spirit—nothing
mawkish, but purity, simplicity, openness, freshness, and
brightness.

"Take bodily exercise. But nothing feverish, morbid,
or of the nature of spiritual priggery ; not being better
than others, but manly. Take moderate and healthful
food. Be full of life and delight. And with freshness
and brightness deal with grave and solemn interests."

A few of the *obiter dicta* of the class-room are also supplied
by the Rev. J. W. Dickson, of St. Helens :

Dr. Martineau.— ' Many modern Unitarians are mere
rationalists. They deny the supernatural altogether.
Dr. Martineau cannot worship with them. He protests
against them. He believes in Christ's personality as
supernatural, but not in miracle. Yet how can a person
be supernatural, and yet do no supernatural thing ? How
could he say to the manacled, ' Rise up and walk '; how
could he say, ' Be ye perfect,' or ' Be ye condemned,'
without its being done ? But we have a revelation as to
how He can do this. He who has redeemed us, He upon
whom the Church and the individual soul has to rest,

He is divine, He is God ; He to whom we give ourselves
in submission, homage, worship, and trust—must be God.
This is the sheet-anchor of our faith."

Calvin.—" By magnifying God you make great men,
and magnify men. Calvinism—what men it made ! What
mighty tempering of men ! Like steel ! Faith tempered
them." Speaking of Geneva, he said : " Calvin knew more
of theology than of human nature, and tried to make
the same clothes fit every person ; but this they would
not do."

Herbert Spencer.—" The highest mental faculty of our
time. He dealt with the great objects of human society.
Towards the close of his great work he rises up to a more
definite faith in the divine than he seemed to have at the
beginning. He was so absorbed in his work that he was
not able to give himself to the question of ontology. This
is the science of being in itself, whilst the science of
phenomena deals with apparent being, or manifestations
of being. The greatest disciple of Spencer was John
Fiske, who wrote on ' Cosmic Theism,' ' The Destiny of
Man,' and ' The Idea of God.' These were doctrines of
highest scientific teaching leading on to evolution. Fiske,
in Spencer's presence, committed him to the doctrine of
immortality. And Spencer certainly did approximate to
this doctrine. The Unknowable is moral, says Spencer
And that is the highest result of philosophy, of all ages, and
of every school, in this country.

" *Dwight L. Moody* was almost drowned on one occasion,
and he said, ' All life, in one vast picture, seemed to live
and move and have its being before me.' We ourselves
may be a book of remembrance, and our whole life may
be opened up to ourselves, as well as from God's own
book. As in the phonograph, by indentations on the coil,
the instrument, as it turns round, transmits the recorded
sounds, so in some crisis, or even by some little incident,
the whole of your life is brought before you. It is said
that an instrument was once invented to make men, by
electricity, forget what they desired. No. There is no
true river of Lethe. Memory will be the chief torment in
hell. There are many in hell here on earth, through
remorse and anguish because of the memory of evil. ' Unfit for earth, undoomed for heaven.' As Byron has it,
' The mind that broods o'er guilty woes is like a scorpion.' "

Charles Lamb.—" Books were his midnight darlings. He loved to linger in quiet thought over the quiet page. And a brave, gentle, Christlike hero he was ! " Then, with reference to Lamb's failing, Dr. Paton said : " Drunkenness is sinful, but so is pride, so is malice. Don't condemn a man because of one sin."

Charles Macready.—In announcing to the students that he intended to dictate to them some practical rules for the mechanical portion of the art of elocution which Macready had given to him, Dr. Paton said : " Charles Macready was a Christian, a worthy man. He lost two fortunes in trying to reform the stage. He never would allow his own children to go to the theatre. He died blessedly poor."

Baxter.—" When Baxter was told that he would have a glorious reward because he had suffered so much in the cause of Christ, he replied that he didn't want any reward other than a little more persecution. He was not weary, but willing to have more of it, if God willed it. He gloried in tribulation, like Paul, and panted for more of it, resolutely assured that no foe could work anything upon him other than the will of God desired and permitted.

" *Martin Luther* tried to be perfect. But the devil said to him, ' Martin, you'll be a sinner as long as you live.' That led him to the necessity of going somewhere where he would find it easier to keep out of sin's way. But even the cloister can be the devil's roosting-place. Martin found there was no refuge but Christ. ' The just shall live by faith.' Luther was greatly overburdened before he found peace. He sought it in legalism, as the Jews did. The hot-press of life weighed him down with its burden, like a poor camel. But while under this burden he was called to conflict and to greater service. His cross became an easy yoke—great wings of help. Christ converted his burden into a splendid auxiliary and help to him. He was overdone, yet helped. From worried toil and antagonism he was carried to victory and peace.

" *Maclaren and Spurgeon* are living inculcations of the text, ' Bear fruit, and your fruit will remain.'

" *Judas*, like many others who are unworthy and unprepared, answered the call of Christ. If he had been faithful in the opportunities and services he had, he would have risen to the highest and best service and discipleship and faithfulness. Unfaithfulness to-day makes us more unfaithful to-morrow.

"*Scott, of Demerara,* tells the story of an old Indian who was learning to read with difficulty. He was advised to give it up. 'Give it up!' he replied, 'not till me die. It is worth all the trouble to read that one verse, " God so loved the world that He gave His only-begotten Son." ' "

Edmund Burke.—" Burke was tall and noble and pre-possessing; amiable in private life; a man of much vigour in public life, but few smiles. He was great, but not like a meek or gentle man. De Quincey said of him that ' he was the supreme writer of the century; but vehement rather than earnest.' Carlyle said Burke was ' of the highest genius, taking rank with Shakespeare or Bacon.' He had immense resource of information, illustration, and persuasiveness. But he was a rhetorician, and not an analyst. He was saturated with ideas, but polemical. He had sagacity; but no wise politician predicts. There was inability to look with the eyes of other men, and that marred his work in Parliament. Burke's vocabulary was rich, multiform, repetitious. There was a varied presentation of the same subject-matter. His language was appropriate and beautiful. He had the eloquence of classical diction, with the nerve of strong Saxon speech, which had point, persuasion, invective, and gentleness in it."

Channing.—" Differing as I do from Channing, and pro-testing as I do against him, I can never cease to honour and admire him for this—he always wrote and preached on those things which he considered the great things. The democracy must be reached. People must be made to feel that the heart of the minister is with them. Common people require this; the age requires it; young men require it. It is a shame for a minister not to be familiar with the deep needs of the people."

Canon Knox Little said: " Dr. Paton is the highest Churchman outside the Church," to which Dr. Paton replied: " Yes, or inside the Church either."

The High Church Party.—" The High Church party seek separation of Church and State because they seek to have entire dominion over society without hindrance by the State. The laity have control of the State, and there-fore have control of the Church. Ritualists desire a priest-

hood like the Roman Church, so that they may control all
men—have complete dominion over men. Disestablish-
ment would at present advance Ritualism, no doubt. We
must not hand over the Church to a hierarchy."

The Jews.—"The Jews are among all peoples but of
none. This is a miracle of God. They remain one
people. They have survived persecution through all the
Christian era. Many of them are Unitarians. The Jews
are mostly believers in rationalistic naturalism. They
are abandoning all faith in God and in their own faith
and people. They are undergoing a trial never experienced
before. The solvent of sceptical criticism is being applied
to them now as it has never before been applied. But
no solvent will take their unity away, until the day their
eyes are open to see the glorious revelation of Christ.
How does the wealth of the world get into the hands of
the Jews ? They are a big-brained race. The Stock
Exchange and the newspapers are mainly in their hands.
There is one kind of stock which no brain but the Jewish
brain is able to manipulate. He will buy at the click in
one market at $\frac{1}{128}$ less and sell in another immediately,
and get the advantage of his alertness. The Jews are
the great usurers and liquor-sellers. You know the saying, ' Trinkery, drinkery, and chinkery,' applied to them.
They are pedlars, wine-sellers, and usurers. That is the
reason of the frequent anti-Semitic agitations. Pride is
the root of their unbelief. But their unity they will never
lose ; and their present apostasy is but superficial and
temporary. They will get back to their old position.
Immovable as a rock, a great centre of the world, with in-
expugnable faith in God. They will be able to say, ' We're
here and in God, notwithstanding the inroads of ages.'
Scattered everywhere, missionaries of the world, having
the gift of ascendancy, with unwavering faith. Their
love of money is a grand lacquer on them. It is a great
veneer, a great armour-plating, if but of gold. It will
take a big jemmy to wrench it away, but at the heart of him
you will find he is related to God. Get through the brass,
and you have the real Jew, in strong, unchanging faith."

" To be a *Comtist* you need to be a Christian. You live
for men when you live for Christ's sake. What is done
for Christ's sake enriches, fulfils, and gives the glory of
heaven to it.

"*Monism* is impossible where there is movement, activity, variety, change."

Ritual and Puritans.—" Outward acts have great influence on internal life and character. It is important to have right habits and customs. The outward habit has much to do with training the inner life. The force that gives life to ritual is the deep, deep need men feel for these props, these helps to the inner life. The Puritans had a strict, noble ritual of their own. Who so careful as they about the Sabbath, family prayer, and solemnities— a ritual belonging to personal character and life ? By doing without these religious observances you are leaving the poor, helpless soul without helps and supports. The great thing is the relation of that soul to God, and not the ritual itself. Encouragements, incitements, and helps to worship and devotion quicken the devout spirit. If we have not the Puritan ritual, we shall have that worse ritual of Rome and Puseyism. If there be not strict attention to outward act, the soul will suffer ; but mere outward act will not do."

Apostolic Succession.—" The apostles had no successors in a sense. There was no lineal descent. But there is a sense in which every worker for Christ is in succession to the apostles. The preacher is not to be judged as an individual, but as an ambassador for Christ."

Despotic Government.—" Unlimited power is the ideal thing when it is in safe hands. The despotism of heaven is the one absolutely safe government. An earthly despotism would be the absolutely perfect earthly government if the conditions were the same, namely, the despot the perfectest individual of the human race, and his lease of life perpetual. But as a perishable perfect man must die, and leave his despotism in the hands of an imperfect successor, an earthly despotism is not merely a bad form of government—it is the worst form that is possible. Corruption of the best thing is the worst corruption.

" Knowledge of God is gained chiefly by love. Affection lifts up and enlightens the mind, and knowledge purifies and increases love. When love to God possesses us through and through, revelation grows clearer and clearer. Life sustained by love reveals love. In love we have all : richer, deeper, fuller life and knowledge. We talk of ' a cold hand and a warm heart,' but a Christian cannot have a clear head and a cold heart. Divine love is always transcending, yet always inviting. Love begets in the lover the character of the object loved. Religion does for us all we are capable of. Inwardly possessing and outwardly realising this love of God, we become full of it. A child is full of joy, and the angel is only full; a flower is full of colour, and the canopy is only full. The more we love, the more we draw from Him the vital powers of life, until His life fills our being. Love is the life-force and guiding principle of man: God's royal law of love. And we have the capacity for and destination to glorious knowledge of God in His holiness and love. Love perfects faith. It perfects righteousness. It perfects the law. It perfects everything good and great. Love makes life to burst forth in the beauty and song of a glorious spring-time. By loving and intimate communion we know and rejoice in the Lord.

" The world is a blank without a human mind. Matter is only a dustbin, however big. But the soul knows what it is and what it does.

" Death is the vestry through which we pass into eternity.

" Death is the point and hinge of existence.

" All men are building for eternity, whether they know it or not.

" God does not see fit to do the work of redeeming the world alone, and man cannot do the work alone.

" We have given up all we are called upon to give up for Christ when we have given up sin.

" Not to oppose material evil by spiritual forces is to dishonour God.

" Thinking of sin creates sin ; fill your soul with good, and you will thus overcome sin.

" To discuss football from Saturday to Monday is not to exercise a faculty, but to indulge a passion.

" The heart has reasons which the reason cannot understand or explain.

" Satan knows men are his when he sees their hands continually in their pockets.

" Light in its effulgence covers up the substance from which it glows.

" Facts make sad work of weak men's dreams.

" The religion that will not suffice to govern a man, will not suffice to save him.

" There is no virtue in redemption if we minimise guilt or sin.

" Make your work a cross—a burden. If life is too easy, then ask God ' Why hast Thou dealt differently with me from Thine own Son, from the apostles and martyrs ? ' Make a trouble, if you haven't got one, or else the devil will find you one for himself.

" Why are men content with getting a beggarly 5 per cent. dividend, when they can get 10,000 per cent. in the kingdom of God ? Onefold is 100 per cent. And a hundredfold is promised. Why, the $2\frac{1}{2}d.$ they spend in half an ounce of tobacco would, if given to a poor widow, dry her tears.

" No man, not even the sinner of the deepest dye, says that sin is the true law of his being. He knows that it has put him out of joint.

" Gratitude is the memory of the heart.

" Indifference is to deal with vital things ' like a swallow touching the water and skimming away.'

" God is metaphysically free ; but morally He has the compulsion of love, which is His own nature.

" Grace reigns because grace suffers.

" Christianity does not mean uniformity of expression, but it does mean unity of spirit.

" Repentance is the tear-drop in the eye of faith—the evidence of faith.

" Environment determines the character of that it surrounds. The whole moral being is conditioned by its influence. When we are in Christ, we are atmosphered by His matchless love.

" Bear the cross ! You must be prepared for a self-denial and sacrifice for others ! Is the cross too heavy ? Is the burden too great ? Then live with the world, live for yourself ; let not the woes of others appeal to you— but know this : you will not know either the travail or the true, eternal life. You will not have the glory of joyful fruition. Yours will be a barren life.

" The marks of Christ. These marks were some of the proofs of Paul's apostleship. His was a love born of piety, and not of mere pity. His was not a religion that evaporated in mere words. These scars and marks were the marks of Christ's proprietorship. There was the mark of Christ which was written on his forehead. But there are other marks approving our relationship to Christ more distinctly than marks of the body. The certainty of conviction a believer has that he himself owns and possesses the truth is one mark. The very vision a man has of the eternal clothes him with the power of the truth. This is the authority of eternal wisdom, and this is effective and absolutely conclusive. What are the sources of authority ? Direct communion with Christ, and the shining mark of Christ—the indwelling Spirit. The true worker for Christ need not be ashamed of his authority : it comes from Christ.

" Heaven. Fellowship with God—that is heaven. The full consummation of what we know of heaven will be in heaven only ; but heaven is not to be limited to the future life. Heaven is the perfect development and fulness of what we have the beginning of here. The fulness of joy and service and blessedness of what is in heaven, I know here and now in some measure. In part, but it is a part only. If we haven't heaven here, we shall not have heaven yonder. Christ is now at the right hand of God, and I am walking in fellowship with Him here now. And He has called me, by faith, up into fellowship with Him yonder. I see only darkly, but then I shall see fully and unveiled. The veil gets thinner and thinner day by day. Heaven is simply the perfection and fulness of what I have here Heaven can give me no more, and I don't want heaven to give me more. It has been a great mistake of evangelical preaching to put all joy in the future world. It is not so. It is not ' the sacrifice of this world to the next.' It is the opposite. It is the great heaven—the eternal world— that has come down to us. Heaven has sacrificed itself for this world. Heaven was in Calvary, or it was nowhere. Suffer with Christ now, and you reign with Him now. The more I suffer, the more I reign with Him now. We are born here into life eternal—and thus into that promised heaven. But heaven is not our due because we suffer : it is a gracious gift of God. Rise up, my soul, and enter into the risen life of thy Lord. That life is yours. Thy Brother sitteth on the throne—then share the great life of love and truth which are His. If we do not know the joy of that life here, we shall not know it hereafter. The infinite delight of this life within me—that is heaven O soul, thy pencil only pictures what thine eyes have seen.

Life is the prelude to a song, the vestibule to eternity, the beach of the great ocean of immortality! God and eternity are the only realities. The light of the other life breaks in upon our darkened sight. Think much of heaven, which is so bright and fair, and you yourself will become bright and fair. He who could give us life on this side of the grave can surely give us life after death, beyond the grave.

" Cut my head from my heart, and my head would be the greatest rationalist that ever lived. I have never met a greater rationalist than it."

Speaking of Schiller's " History of the Thirty Years' War," when Gustavus Adolphus and Wallenstein, the two most eminent commanders of their time, and both hitherto unconquered, met on the plain of Lützen, on November 16th, 1632, he said : " One of my ancestors was at Lützen, when the unconquered met the unconquerable— the unbeaten met the unbeatable. You may have a fine woven embroidery covering Scottish granite or Sheffield steel. A good man may be as tender as he is strong. He may be simply indomitable—a man who doesn't know how to be beaten, but who knows how to beat. The living God can make us unconquerable. He could have made Wallenstein unconquerable.

" Christ says He is the Door to the kingdom of heaven and the Church of the redeemed. What the door is to the building He is to the kingdom. Man closed the door by his sin, and God opened it again. Christ is the great embodiment of life, therefore life-giving. It is at the Cross that heaven and earth meet ; Christ by one hand takes men, and with the other His Father. Christ not only takes us into the kingdom, but He keeps us in safety. He is the way to God the Father, and there is no other possible way. Through Him we enter into the Father's forgiveness, and family, and likeness, and business, and home.

" The call of Christ. Think who it is that calls you to follow Him—to be near to Him in this service. To be uncalled of Him is to be unblest of Him. The call comes to every Christian to do work for Him. There is a moral ' mustness ' in it. But notwithstanding the moral urgency and necessity of it, there is in man the terrible prerogative of disobeying and shrinking from His call. I refuse, and

24

I have the sense of arrant cowardice all life long : shrinking from noblest duty. It is a difficulty of human life, of the deep human heart, this trial of ascending to the highest and best, or of sinking to the lowest and worst. Only use the light of to-day, and you will get more light to-morrow. Earnest effort is ever the present duty of the Christian.

" By his conception of God man is exalted and inspired more than by ought else. All greatest thought deals with the highest—with God. The Gospel gave such a glorious revelation of God that it magnified our conception of God. It not only meets our deepest need, but shows us the holiness of God. It gave men a new faith in the Father.

" Grace reigns through righteousness unto eternal life. Righteousness is the great end of Christ's sacrifice. Through righteousness alone we get eternal life. It is more difficult to live a healthy life and be a Christian than to be a Christian in affliction. Grace begins by an inward renewal followed by an outward change.

" Sacrifice is the measure of love. There can be no love without self-sacrifice. Coldness of heart causes a denial in the heart. To lose love is death ; declension of love causes sin to break out again. Love is the one arresting power of evil. The barrier removed, old habits and sins come back. When love declines, fidelity decays. Life is love—love to God and His Christ and His world. And loss of love is loss of life ; it is opening the gates of death, and leads to outer denial. There is a vital relation between feeling and conduct. Love is measured by self-sacrifice, and not by self-satisfaction.

" True freedom. The law of God and the law of nature are one. Everything is truly free when it is fulfilling the true law of its being delightfully. Man is free when he is enabled to fulfil and honour the true laws of his being. He is free when he is possessed and impelled by the glory and beauty of right. Then physical health, mental health, and spiritual health will be his. Each part of his being will be properly energised, and with ease and freedom he will fulfil all relations. He will be freed from outward restraint and internal weakness, and able to fulfil that which belongs to his proper nature. Moral freedom is the highest and most real necessity. It is an internal and not an external necessity. It is not opposed to law ; but our love of right enables us to fulfil the true moral law.

Just as political freedom, the freedom of the city, freedom of thought, freedom of life are not opposed to law, but in conformity to it. When the whole being is possessed by the desire of doing right, everything else comes into its right place. When this truth comes into my nature, the true king reigns, and all is peace and order and health. The wrong is subdued and the right is exalted.

" The Gospel is a lever to uplift a ruined and depraved world. It is Christianising and civilising. A reforming and transforming power to all who believe, but a dead letter to men until they believe it. The Gospel is the sunlight of life, operating upon the lives of men omnipotently and graciously. Rome's hotbed of corruption grew sweet and verdant under its power.

" The House of God. What constitutes it God's House ? The presence of God. Wherever God meets His people— that is Bethel. Assemblies of God's people make a place His Sanctuary.

" Hope. Hope is being filled with great expectancy— which lifts you from the past and above the present, and gives you all the splendid energies that come out of the soul. Christian preaching of the Lord to-day is not glorious enough—not jubilant enough. If a man has a great hope, he makes ready for the thing that he hopes for and glories in it. His life and service shine from it. Christians live down in their boots too much ; instead of with the ceaseless and tireless purpose and activities of men with hope before them, and life in them, and rock beneath them. Activity is the outcome of aim and hope. Preaching to-day is not inspiring enough, not full enough of great thoughts.

" Election. It has been thought of as an election to mere favour. Men were called, they thought, to mere bliss, pleasure, security, delight. That is a travesty of the doctrine of election. There would be no grumbling at election if they knew what election means. Is it not an election into the life of Christ, into the purity, the cross-bearing, the great redemptive service of Christ ? The elect of God are an army, a body of men, and Christ is the great Captain of that body. He has got a difficult position of the enemy to take—he has to redeem a lost world— God sent His Son to be Captain of the Lord's host, that body of men and women, and the devil's citadel He has to take, and the elect are they who are called to join a forlorn hope, to go and storm a Redan. Yet it isn't a forlorn hope—there is victory ! But it is an election to the cross.

" Law is the expression of the feeling that, when wrong is done, it must be punished. The law of the land takes no cognisance of a man's own private and personal conduct, only of such acts as trespass on the rights of others. God's law deals with the conduct of a man's inward life, for what a man is in himself, the way he deals with himself, will in the long run determine how he will act toward others.

" Sin in its essence is the tearing down of the moral law of the universe. Its action is both horizontal and vertical ; it acts on our contemporaries, it acts on us from those who have preceded us, and it acts from us on those who will follow after us. We communicate not only what we have received, but also what we do—as a living power to the ages that follow. It goes on through every child of mine and through all I have influenced, and through them to their children and posterity. But the same principle applies to goodness.

" Sin acts more upon me than it acts upon any one else. It is my act that works greater evil on me though I intended the evil for another. The murderer is his own worst murderer.

" Love has only one measure—its willingness to sacrifice itself. Love's general law is to seek to do good to others, by service, toil, suffering, both passively and actively. What does a mother endure for her child ? Sleepless nights, without food, as she soothes the suffering of her little one and wins back life and health to the child by the offering and sacrifice of her own health and life. What of Father Damien, and others like him, who became lepers to save lepers ? Sister Kate Marsden, too. They give themselves to remove the curse of leprosy, or at least to remove the darker curse of leprosy. It is love undertaking on another's behalf, by means of sacrifice, to win for them some good. There is nothing great and noble and praiseworthy in the world, but this principle of love is at the root of it. Has this principle been applied to punishment—bearing it for another and winning of favour ? In Anglo-Saxon law all penalties could be expiated by fines, i.e. by the sacrifice of another. Men were bound and suffered for one another, with and for one another. An exile was accompanied by others into exile, and thus they shared his exile and did him service. That was voluntary exile to bless another. Then there were hostages for cities or nations. The closer the relationship the more the right of those who suffer to suffer for the other. A member of the family, or a representative citizen, the head of the family, or the chief citizen, standing in place of the family, or city, is substitute. The principle of mediation and love for another pervades all human law, jurisdiction, and equity. Christ is the second head of the human family. Heads of nations act on behalf of nations. Christ is the new head of humanity. We are His in creation. He made us in His own likeness. We are brethren of His. He has a right to stand for us, to plead our cause, to suffer for us, because of the near relation in which He stands to us, the second Adam, the federal head of the race. He has a right to stand on our behalf. Our interests are bound up in Him so closely. He stands nearest to us. His act has a value added because of this right. These things give us a clue to the rationale of the Atonement, and show it to be reasonable and right."

As the number of Old Students grew, Paton increased the library of the Institute and so organised it that each Old Student who applied could have a monthly box of books sent to him. He devoted to this purpose the testimonial with which he was presented by his students past and present on the occasion of his silver wedding in 1884. This was a great boon to many a minister in an out-of-the-way country district where there was little intellectual society. And many a letter passing to and fro helped to corroborate the bond which bound the old students to their *alma mater*. " It has been a pleasure," he would say, " to be associated in the work of the Institute. Let us be united evermore in the sacred fellowship of divine truth and life."

" I always feel happy when I have my ' old men '—if I may so call them—with me," he writes to Rev. L. Beaumont. " They are near my heart, and I feel as if they understood the message that, with great humility and with much prayer, I feel called upon to give to this generation."

Constantly he would impress on his Old Students that they were not to do all the work themselves. He thought that Independency was apt to throw too much upon its ministers. He rejoiced in the Revised Version of Ephesians iv. 12 : " He gave . . . some pastors and teachers, for the perfecting of the saints unto the work of the ministry, unto the building up of the body of Christ." It was the saints who were to do the work of the ministry, the pastors and teachers were to make the saints fit for that work.

" You are quite right," he writes Mr. Dickson, " in doing everything you can to get people to work. Your ministry must be preparing them and helping them in their ministry, as it is only in and through their ministering that they can become strong and wise and helpful in their Christian life."

The Institute was his child, and was always very near to his heart. It was his first-begotten, and though his other works were more in the public eye and of a wider scope, though they yielded more imposing results, no other ever even challenged the first place which the Institute held in his affections. That for which one does most is that which one loves most. His parting gift was the foundation of two scholarships, which bear respectively his wife's name and his own. But the great gift which he gave to it was himself, and that gift of sympathetic help and thought and prayer he went on giving to the end. As long as the building on Forest Road rears its gables to the sky, it stands as a memorial to the founder, but more lasting and more real is the living impress of his personality stamped on the lives of the 600 men who have gone out from it, and the new inspiration which has sent them forth to do the Master's work, to build up His kingdom in the world and extend its borders.

CHAPTER XX

A MINISTER AT LARGE—THE PRAYER UNION

" I considered of the reason why God helped me to pray and yet did not answer me, yea, things did not stir or move, but rather things in Church and elsewhere in men's spirits went worse and worse. So I saw hereby what need I had of all the prayers of others. . . . And I saw also that all prayers of faith are heard instantly in heaven, but many times they are not heard from heaven, until many shoulders are set to the work."
THOMAS SHEPHARD.

BUT his retirement from the work of the Institute was an occasion which aroused a wider circle of interest. Many others outside the circle of the Old Students wished to mark in some tangible way their appreciation of his personal character and the creative and inspiring force which he had brought to bear in so many departments of social and philanthropic work. A committee was appointed which comprised the Archbishop of Canterbury, the Bishops of Durham, Hereford, Ripon, and Southwell, Lord Battersea, Dr. Robert Bruce, Principal Cave, Dr. Fairbairn, Dr. Forsyth, Dr. Monro Gibson, Dr. Martineau, Dr. Alexander Hill (the Vice-Chancellor of Cambridge), and many other friends representing all branches of religious and social life. Mr. Bunting and the Rev. J. E. Flower acted as Secretaries. Mr. Evan Spicer acted as Treasurer. No public appeal was made.

The outcome of this movement was a meeting at the Nottingham Exchange Hall on the evening of October 26th, 1899, when his old friend the Bishop of Hereford, on behalf of the subscribers, presented to the City of Nottingham a full-length portrait, painted by Mr. Arnesby Brown, an artist whom Nottingham claims as her own. A replica of the portrait was at the same time presented to Mrs. Paton. The balance of the fund, amounting to £150, which was presented at the same time, was given to the furnishing of the new Epileptic

Home at Lingfield. The Bishop, in making the presentation, spoke of his long and intimate friendship.

" It is thirty-five years since I had the good fortune to meet Dr. Paton in the Alps and to walk for a whole day down a beautiful Alpine valley, drinking in some of the inspiration which he carried with him wherever he went in those days, and which he carries with him still. I confess that of the many friends of the past there is not one to whom I owe so much for inspiration to good works, so much suggestion, so much encouragement to persevere in the face of difficulties. To have had a share in so many different movements is in itself much for one man, but Dr. Paton has not only been connected with these movements, he has been the heart and soul of them, the inspirer, the initiator, and the suggester of methods, a supporter in times of discouragement, and a uniter at all times. . . . The spirit which has animated him we may describe as the spirit of the Inner Mission of Christ. If there is one idea that has inspired him it has been that all who bear the name of Christ should realise that they are engaged in the Inner Mission of purifying the whole life of the community, that they are doing the work, however humble it may be, in Christ's name and in response to His call, to be at their posts as His servants and soldiers."

After acknowledging gratefully the honour conferred on him, Dr. Paton said :

" There is one thing which almost compensates me for the ordeal through which I am now passing, and that is that men and women of many Christian communities and of many parties have united in the preparing and presentation of this gift. I confess that, throughout my life, I have greatly desired that Christian men of all communities should be drawn more closely together, that they might know one another better and love and honour one another more. My prayer has been that they should find the centre and bond of their unity in their common reverence and obedient love for their one redeeming Lord. As I look out upon the evils of the world, I have thought and prayed earnestly that Christians of every name, thinking less of their differences, touched by the fire and passion of their redeeming Master, should unite their labour in such a way as will more wisely, immediately, and effectively assuage the bitter sorrow of our times and lessen the threatening evils which curse so many parts of the world."

It was to the furtherance of this spirit of unity that he gave himself as soon as he was more free.

In a journey to Egypt in 1889 he had become interested in the Christians of the ancient Coptic Church, and this interest had brought him into very intimate relations with a fellow traveller, the Rev. George Greenwood, M.A., Warden of the Guild of St. Luke's. In point of theological doctrine the two were very far apart, but, in their desire for a better understanding between the different bodies of Christians and a closer fellowship of work for the furtherance of Christ's Kingdom and overcoming the works of darkness, they were at one. " That they may be one," had been with both the constant burden of their daily prayer. Mr. Greenwood was actively interested in the Home Reunion Society of which Lord Nelson was President, and on returning to England he made it his endeavour to get together a Conference between representatives of the Anglican Church and representatives of Nonconformity. Lord Nelson eagerly seconded his efforts, and in March 1888 a small Conference was formed consisting of twelve members. Six of these were of the Anglican Church : the Rev. Dr. Gott, the Dean of Worcester, Canon Westcott, the Rev. Chas. Gore, then Head of Pusey House, Canon Medd of Cirencester, and Mr. John Shelly, who had been originally a Congregationalist. The Free Church representatives were all Congregationalists : Dr. Allon of Highbury, Dr. Reynolds of Cheshunt, Dr. Paton, the Rev. R. A. Redford, M.A. (Emeritus Professor of New College, London), and Dr. Barrett of Norwich. Lord Nelson was appointed as permanent Chairman and the Rev. J. Radford Thomson, M.A., Professor of Philosophy at New College, London, was asked to act as joint-secretary with Mr. Greenwood himself. The meetings were held at Mr. Greenwood's residence, No. 10, Langham Street, and the Conference was named the Langham Street Conference in acknowledgment of his hospitality. All the members were strongly impressed with the feeling that the present state of disunion among the Christian Churches was opposed to the intention and the teaching of the Divine Head of the Church. There was not much argumentation at these meetings; there was certainly no disputation, but there were on both sides frank statements of conviction and of the grounds on which these convictions were based. The whole spirit was fraternal, and much was done at any rate towards a mutual understanding of each other's position and the corroboration of mutual regard. The report which was issued in 1889 by the Home Reunion Society brought into prominence the great amount of agreement subsisting among all the members. There was a general acceptance of the teaching of the Apostles' and Nicene Creeds, including of necessity the great doctrines of the Trinity, the Incarnation, and the Atonement. They agreed that it was desirable to encourage Christian discipline by the exercise of greater care in receiving converts from one Christian body into another, especially of those seeking admission to the ministry. They agreed in their desire for a larger measure of united action in furthering Christian efforts for the welfare of humanity and the extension of Christ's kingdom. They agreed as to the principles of importance for the conducting of common worship, Congregationalists accepting the treasuries of devotion—hymns, collects, liturgies— accumulated by the Church; the Churchmen accepting the use of extempore prayer. They were at one in the conviction that belief in the Incarnation of the Son of God was the special bond of union which drew together most powerfully all those who heartily held that belief. If the Langham Street Conference did not solve the problem, at any rate it brought it one stage nearer to solution; it showed the lines on which it is possible for the different Confessions to be one in their worship and their work.

" That they may be one in us." In a special way Paton made the Master's prayer the burden of his heart, and he knew that, if all followers of Christ would join in that prayer, the day of unity would not be so far off. " A united Christendom," he used to say, " that would be the real apologetic." As the new century drew near it seemed to sound the call to all Christian Churches everywhere to agonise together in earnest, united, and importunate prayer for the coming of the kingdom. The hour seemed to have come when all Christendom should rise

up as one man, and, in the power of Christ, fill up what
was lacking in what Christ did for a perishing world.
In the union of prayer, the differences of doctrine would
almost disappear. Before the mercy-seat all are one.

> The saints in prayer appear as one
> In word and deed and mind.

The first idea of a prayer-union had come to him in a
very simple way. He proposed it, in the first instance,
when he was laid aside from work for a twelvemonth.
Unable to take his part in the active work, he strongly
desired not to lose touch altogether with his men, and all
his students, both those already settled in the ministry
as well as those at the college, agreed to join with him
at stated times in fellowship of prayer. This fellowship
was still continued when he returned to work. In 1887 the
Rev. W. Crosbie had come to Nottingham as pastor of
the Park Hill Congregational Church, where Paton and
his family worshipped. Mr. Crosbie, whom he had known
as a student at Rotherham, had written a book called,
" Is the Spirit of the Lord straitened ? " in which he
had given an account of the movement for united prayer
which originated with the Scottish ministers in 1744, and
awoke a friendly response in the heart of Jonathan Edwards in America, who wrote " A Humble Attempt to
promote Explicit Agreement and Visible Union of God's
People in Extraordinary Prayer." Mr. Crosbie showed
how, through this treatise, many had been led to join in a
concert of prayer and to meet periodically in their several
neighbourhoods for this purpose. To this preparation of
prayer he traced the great spiritual revival of the eigh-
teenth century, and the impetus of the missionary spirit
which founded the great missionary societies and made
itself felt throughout the Christian world. Paton had
also much converse on the subject with his friend, Dr.
H. R. Reynolds, of Cheshunt. The result was that in
1895 Dr. Reynolds wrote an earnest letter of appeal
addressed to the ministers and officers of Congregational
Churches, putting before them the special difficulties of
the time, and the corresponding difficulties and responsibilities of the ministry, and urging that they should agree
together in prayer for special light and special power
from on high.

" The mutual interchange of affection, the reciprocal recognition of the deep inner life—the more than electric current of common prayer—may and will bring us into closer and more direct communion with our Lord. . . . As we pray together, we shall rise up from our personal preferences to the purposes of our Master, we shall ask according to His will, we may touch the springs which will open the flood-gates of the divine love, and which will pour out in blessing greater than it is possible to receive."

It was the last message of Dr. Reynolds to his brethren, and it bore much fruit. To this new movement Paton linked up the Prayer Union of his own students, and with the help of a few friends gathered in some fellow ministers into the fellowship. Though there was as little publicity as possible, and no machinery, there were soon 700 ministers banded together. Every Saturday evening and Sunday morning they prayed for each other, and for the Church of Christ.

At the close of the century Paton felt the time had come for a new and wider expansion of the movement. On May 30th, 1900, he addressed the annual general meeting of the Ministers' Prayer Union of the Free Church of Scotland. Speaking of the effect of the theory of evolution on modern thought, he says :

" The belief that sin is not wholly evil, but is a necessary product, probably a temporary product, of the process by which man passes from lower to higher stages of development ; and that redemption is but the final achievement of that process, when man shall have sloughed off from his nature the tiger and the ape, and shall be liberated from the evil that has beset his earlier growth,—such a belief, which is widely, though it may be vaguely held, cannot prepare the mind to receive the Christian doctrine of sin and of salvation, but rather, like an opiate, its influence dulls and deadens the hearts of men as we preach to them that which is the very essence of our Gospel. We say to them that man's nature is akin to God's, and can find its only satisfaction and rest in the fellowship and service of God ; but that an alien and malign power has beset and enslaved his nature, dragging it darkly down

away from God, and so working its ruin and death.   Or
we speak to them of the marvellous grace of God in Christ ;
we proclaim the yearning compassion and pity of the
Father's heart over His lost and wandering children, and
show how these have broken down the mystic barrier
between eternity and time, and have intervened in the
sad drama of human history in order that here, in the very
prison-house of our captivity, in this death-shadowed
world, He might seek and save and bless His own, who are
infinitely dear to Him.   Are not these two truths the very
sum and essence of our Gospel—the two central columns
of the fabric of our Faith—which we must preach because
necessity is laid upon us ?   Yea ! woe is unto us if we do
not preach them.   And they are truths, too, which in the
last issue and final court of appeal, find their most certain
witness and authentication in the heart of man.   But
how shall we speak these truths convincingly in this world
of modern unbelief, so dead and unresponsive, drugged
by the subtle opiate of our time ?   How shall we gain the
clear vision, the fervency of faith, the force of conviction,
the fire and unction of the Holy One, whereby we can make
these great truths of the Gospel burn and shine again in
the souls of men ?   How, indeed, unless with humble and
continuous and importunate prayer we pierce into the
Eternal Light, and feel in our own hearts the beating of
the Eternal Love—the pulsing of those infinite compassions
which broke upon our world in the breaking heart of the
Beloved Son ?   How, unless we are able to see sin as it is
seen by the holy eyes of God, and long with the longing
of God to redeem men from its curse ?

" Secondly, there has dawned upon our age a new vision
and conception of the Church of Christ.   Many of you, I
think, will have felt with me how imperfect is the definition
and idea of the Church expressed in a number of our
Protestant Standards and Confessions.   And herein, perhaps, may be found one of the causes of the weakness of
our Protestant Churches.   You know how, in these
Confessions, the Church is spoken of as the assembly where
the Word of God is duly preached, and the Sacraments
are rightly administered.   These are the two notes of the
Church which alone are expressed or emphasised.   How
meagre is that conception of the Church compared with
the glowing figures of the Church presented to us in the

apostolic writings, especially with that figure, so often repeated, of the Church as the Body of Christ, the immortal Body in which He ever lives upon earth to fulfil His Father's will, and to finish His work! Surely, then, if the Church be the Body of the Lord, it will have some likeness to that mortal body in which He tabernacled with us, not only proclaiming the holy love of the Father here among men, but revealing and commending that love, and making it known and felt by men, through the mighty works—all of them wonderful works of love—by which He healed their diseases and comforted their sorrows. Must not the Church of Christ now, in like manner, not only proclaim and reveal in faithful speech and testimony the righteous love of God among men, but also interpret and commend and enforce that love, making it intelligible and real to them, bringing it home to them and making it true, by those ' greater works ' which our Lord promised that His Church, being endued with power from on high, should do in the world ? By these works the Lord in His Church would now, as of old, undo the cruel and heavy bonds under which sin has bound our fellow-men, and assuage their bitter sorrows. As upon Christ Himself, so the Spirit of the Lord comes upon His Church, in gracious baptism, and clothes her with the lustrous evidences of her divine mission, as she now, like Him, heals the broken-hearted, preaches deliverance to the captives, and recovering of sight to the blind, and sets at liberty them that are bruised.

" But if this be the mission and ministry of the Church of Christ upon earth, how glorious, and yet how responsible and arduous, must be the duties of her ministers, those who are not only to teach and preach the doctrine of the Church, but are to be its leaders and inspirers! Who, we may well ask, is sufficient for these things ? The burden of these great responsibilities may well bend and bow us down in abiding and earnest prayer, so that in our weakness and our great need we may find our sufficiency of God, and that we, ' having always all sufficiency in all things, may abound unto every good work.'

" Thirdly, we are standing on the threshold of a new century. It looms before us with strange and awful portents. Men feel that it will be a fateful century in the history of mankind, in which momentous issues will be

decided. The vast industrial masses of the people are
now emancipated from political vassalage, and hold in
their hands political power, giving them all the forces
which government can create and wield. They are also
being loosened and liberated in all civilised countries from
ancient customs and traditions which have hitherto held
and trained them. There is among them the stir and
unrest of new ambitions and new desires and new ideals.
We seem even now to stand amid the rush of mighty
forces pouring into the new century to determine there
the destinies of our race.

"Amid the tumult of present controversy there are
seen to be two great forces arraying themselves for strenuous and it may be final conflict. On the one hand there
is materialistic Socialism, which ignores or denies the
highest sanctions and aspirations of the human spirit ;
which is ready to sacrifice both the independence and
freedom of the individual, and the sanctity or even the
existence of the family, in order that it may construct
a human society in which, as they conceive it, the material
advantages and comforts of life may be more equally
distributed. On the other hand, we see the Church of
Christ, with that old Gospel which was heard first on the
hills of Galilee, reborn upon her heart and lips, 'The
kingdom of heaven is come nigh unto you.' The Church,
which also seeks to reconstruct human society, but according
to the pattern which was shown her on the mount ; and
for her the mount is Calvary. The Church, which would
reform and transform human society into one holy brotherhood, the family of the one Father in heaven, so that His
will may be done here upon earth as it is done in heaven.

"Which of these forces shall prevail in the coming
conflict, the day of the Lord which is at hand ? Will
not this depend in large measure upon the fidelity and
devotion and unconquerable courage of the ministers, the
leaders of the Church, the captains of the Lord's hosts ?
Surely, then, as we listen to the cries of these mighty forces
uplifted against each other, we may hear sounding above
them all the trumpet voice of our Lord calling to us, that
we humbly and fervently unite together in continuous
prayer, and that in this prayer we link ourselves, in the
closest and most blessed fellowship, with Him from whom
alone come the wisdom and the conquering grace needful

for this solemn hour of awful perils and glorious opportunities. So may we who are ministers of the Church enter into, and abide faithfully in, this covenant of prayer with one another and with Him till our warfare be accomplished, and over this dark world, amid opening heavens, the angel's song again be heard proclaiming, ' Glory to God in the highest, peace on earth, good-will among men.' ''

A resolution was passed expressing a general desire that, on the eve of the new century and in view of the solemn and ever-growing responsibilities devolving on the ministers of all Evangelical Churches, all ministers in the United Kingdom, in the Colonies and in America, might be led to form a Covenant or Concert of Prayer. The resolution authorised Paton to take what steps he might think best in the way of approaching the leaders of the Evangelical Churches referred to.

The first step was to approach the National Free Church Council of England and Wales, which had been formed to bring together in one common fellowship all the Evangelical Free Churches of England and Wales. Paton called together all the Free Church ministers in Nottingham, opened up his mind to them, and, at his instance, a letter was drawn up and signed appealing to the National Free Church Council to knit together in a "covenant and concert of prayer," not only all the ministers of the Free Churches in England, but the ministers in all Evangelical Churches throughout the English-speaking world :

" The reasons which induce us to lay before you this request are these :

" *First.* We bear upon our hearts continually our Lord's last prayer ere He went to His cross, ' That all who believe in Me may be one ; as Thou, Father, art in Me, and I in Thee, that they also may be one in Us.' Many signs of the times show that Christian men feel, as never before, the longing for such oneness in the Father and His beloved Son, and we believe that few things would tend more to deepen this longing throughout Christendom, and would accordingly work with more powerful and growing influence towards the fulfilment of our Lord's prayer, than the communion in prayer of ministers in many lands, pleading earnestly for their own enduement with spiritual power, and for a true revival of the Church.

" *Second.* Further, the times seem to call with special urgency for closer fellowship of all ministers of Free Churches with one another and their Lord, so that they may uphold and encourage one another amid the difficulties and perils of our time. We briefly indicate some of those difficulties and perils which seem to draw ministers into profounder sympathy with each other, and to lead them to more fervent and united prayer for one another.

" 1. There is a new and subtle form of unbelief that besets and hinders all of us in our foremost duty, that, namely, of preaching the Gospel of the grace of God, and of winning men to repentance and faith. This arises from the widespread unsettlement of opinion with respect to the composition and the inspiration of the Holy Scripture, and also as to the sinful nature of man, and his need of redemption.

" 2. There is the new warfare being waged in all English-speaking countries against the claims of an Anglican and a Romish priesthood, which arrogates to itself the name of Catholic, and denies the true Catholic doctrine of the universal priesthood of believers.

" 3. On the other hand, there is the new and larger conception of the Church of Christ, and of its redemptive social mission. It is a thought that fills our age, that the Church must not only proclaim the love of God in Christ, but must exemplify and commend and make real to men the divine compassion by undoing the heavy bonds, and lessening the sorrows, of men.

" These conditions of our time lay new and solemn responsibilities upon the ministers of our Churches, who not only have to preach and to teach the Church's doctrine, but are to be its inspirers and leaders. To fulfil these high and onerous duties how profound is their need of closest fellowship with one another, and of the abounding grace of their Lord, that, ' having always all sufficiency in all things, they may abound in every good work ' !

" *Third.* Lastly, we are on the threshold of a new century. It will be a fateful century in the history of mankind. The Church stands now face to face with mighty revolutionary forces, which must be subdued to the obedience of Christ, or they will reconstruct human society on a materialistic basis. On the fidelity of our ministers the life, the devotion, the triumph of the Church (humanly

25

speaking) depend, and with the Church are bound up vitally the highest interests and issues of humanity. Surely, then, at such a time, this ' burden of the Lord,' which is laid upon us collectively, should bind us in united prayer for ourselves and for one another, that we may be faithful in the great Day of the Lord which is at hand.

" In view, too, of the Simultaneous Mission which it has been resolved to hold in all parts of the land, what more blessed preparation could there be than for the ministers of our Free Churches to gather together with one accord and at one time in prayer around the throne of the Heavenly Grace, ' watching thereunto with all perseverance with all saints ' ?

" These are some of the reasons that lead us to think the time most opportune, and the call most urgent, for such a Concert and Union of Prayer.   The times of prayer, and all other arrangements, may be fitly decided by you if you accede to our request."

The Council responded readily to the suggestion, but it was felt that it should not be a matter of circulars issued in an official way by the Secretary as part of the ordinary office routine.   A small committee was accordingly formed representative of the various denominations, and Paton became the Honorary Secretary of the movement.   There were soon 1,000 members who bound themselves to consecrate one hour each week, preferably on Saturday evening, and one day at the beginning of each quarter to pray for one another, and for the Church of Christ.

" They thus seek to realise more fully the solemn and momentous duties of their high office—being called not only to preach the glorious Gospel of the blessed God, but also to teach, nurture, and train the members of the Church and to equip them for faithful and holy service to one another and to the world."

Members of the Union were further urged to meet together from time to time for combined prayer, and, especially before entering upon their winter's work, to set apart one quiet day of prayer and conference waiting upon God, and seeking His guidance and inspiration by the outpouring of His Spirit.   From time to time occasional papers written by one or other among the leaders were sent out, and for each New Year a card of Bible-reading was prepared and sent out by the secretary. This entailed much work, and the work was hard, but nothing gave him more delight. It seemed to make real what he had always prayed for—a Catholic Evangelical Church. He knew the fascination which the Romish Church exercised over multitudes by the claim she made of being a catholic and universal Church. Over against this false claim he longed to set up the one holy Evangelical and Catholic Church. By witnessing unitedly n this public way to their common faith, by upholding each other thus in common prayer, the ministers of this Church were not only witnessing to their oneness in Christ, but magnifying the true catholic faith of the Church. The formation of a Bible-reading and Prayer Union in America, which adopted the same scheme of Bible-reading, and agreed to plead the same petitions at the throne of grace, went far to establish such a catholic spirit. It helped also to create that spirit of enlarged expectation and earnest looking forward that prepares the way for spiritual revival.

The new century was ushered in with a Simultaneous Mission organised by all the Free Churches. He was very anxious that the converts gathered in by this mission should not be left to sink or survive without a helping hand. "The work must begin when the mission ceases," he urged.

To the Rev. C. H. Kelly

"*Oct. 27th*, 1900.

" I think you will agree with me that it is most important that, in connection with the Simultaneous Mission to be held in England at the beginning of the century, there should be some not only earnest preparation for the mission, but there should be the wisest and most loving care taken of the converts who are brought to the knowledge of Christ and to decision for Him during the mission. I have known so many cases where it seemed as though the soul had been awakened to the true life of God, and yet, because of the lack of shepherding and instruction and wise training, especially in some suitable service for Christ, in which the love and enthusiasm of the convert could express itself and so strengthen and confirm itself, that love was quenched.   We all know that it is a perilous thing to have emotion of any kind, but specially spiritual emotion, aroused, unless it is at once connected with the conduct of life, and becomes the energy to form noble and Christlike habit.   I therefore would like to suggest that an occasional paper be prepared to be sent to every minister taking part in the mission either as a missioner or pastor, setting forth what seems to be the wisest way in which our Churches can nurture and protect and educate and train the life of the young believer."

To the Rev. R. J. Campbell

"*Jan.* 31*st*, 1901.

" Many souls doubtless will be touched and thrilled with new emotion, and, we hope, led to decision for Christ. These souls, new born to the Church, by the Spirit of God, will need to be very specially shepherded and cared for, otherwise a terrible calamity will befall them, and the Church ; the emotions that have been awakened may die away and the last state of many of them may even be worse than their former state. . . . This shepherding and care and training and discipline of our young converts will involve not only direct teaching and fellowship, and the nourishing of the soul through divine worship and the fellowship of the Church in loving mutual service and in the sacraments, but also the training of young life in service—service such as may be suitable to the faculties and circumstances of the young converts—service in which they will at once, before the world, make known their obedient faith in Christ and their desire to do something for Him in healing the sorrow and helping the need of others.   In this way Christian character, too, will be formed in the healthiest way, through emotion of love for Christ, leading to some form of active service by which a practical Christian habit of life will be formed, and our young converts will be yoked at once unto the active ministries of the Church."

CHAPTER XXI

THE EDUCATION QUESTION

" The good or ill bringing up of children doth as much serve to the good or ill service of God and our whole countrie as doth any one thing beside."
                                                                ROGER ASCHAM.

" Every science is prejudicial, injurious to him who has not got the science of Goodness."—MONTAIGNE.

THERE is nothing so inimical to unity among Christians of our country as the question of the schools. The Education Bill of 1902 reopened the flood-gates of controversy. As in 1870, the driving force of public opinion, which was needed to shape out an educational system on a scale commensurate with the national need, frittered itself away in sectarian conflict. On both sides there were leaders who deplored this misunderstanding, and endeavoured to find a path of solution which should be satisfactory to both parties concerned. It was in this spirit that a large number of Churchmen and Nonconformists met together in a united prayer-meeting in the month of June, and at the end of that meeting the Bishop of London, Dr. Wynnington Ingram, invited a few leading Nonconformists to meet some leading Churchmen in conference at Fulham Palace. He wished to see if some arrangement could be suggested, acceptable to both sides, which would allay the controversy then raging, and prevent the rankling discord and continuous strife sure to ensue if the Bill became law in the form in which it stood. Paton was invited to the meetings of this Conference. He had already been in conference with the Bishops of Carlisle and Ripon on the matter, and had made suggestions to them which seemed to secure what fair-minded Churchmen would desire and reasonable Nonconformists would accept. These proposals formed the basis of the discussions at Fulham Palace. They were, in brief, as follows :

389

" (i) That there should be in every voluntary, or non-provided school, Bible-teaching, with a simple hymn and the Lord's Prayer, three or four days in the week, according to the wish of the managers, and that on the other one or two days an hour should be given in the school for teaching of the Church Catechism, and other distinctive Church formularies, and that during those hours in which the Church teaching was given, opportunity should be given for Nonconformist children, probably in their own school, to have similar teaching in their distinctive Church doctrine ; also that the regular hour of the school-teaching for that day should begin after such distinctive and separate teaching had been given. A suggestion was afterwards made that the Nonconformists might also use a part of the Church school for that hour, on the payment of rent : this as an alternative.

" (ii) That in such a school the head master should be an Anglican Churchman, but that the other master or masters might be Nonconformists, and it was suggested that, if there were Nonconformist children in the school, it would be right that the second master should be a Nonconformist.

" (iii) That a majority, if only a bare majority, of the Board of Management should be popularly elected, leaving thus to the Church a portion of the Board of Management to be nominated as representatives of the Church. It is felt that, where the State contributes practically the whole support of the school, apart from the upkeep of the building, public control to this extent must follow the gift of public money.

" There would seem to be gain both to the Church and to Nonconformists," he wrote, " in some such concordat.

" (a) *To the Church :*

" (1) That they secure definitely the right of giving Church teaching on one or two days in the week to their own children.

" (2) That they secure the headmastership of the schools over which they have hitherto had control.

" (3) That they themselves appoint directly Churchmen on the board in considerable proportion, so that, with the number of Churchmen who are certain to be popularly elected, they are absolutely certain to have a majority of Churchmen in every parish of the land.

" (4) That they will have the continual use of their own schools for Sunday-schools.

" These advantages will surely fairly compensate Churchmen for the money they have expended on the schools, and for the cost of the maintenance of the fabric. At the same time they secure what I know Churchmen consider to be essential—the right to teach their own catechism, and to have the head master one of their own communion, to whom they could entrust such teaching.

" (b) The gain to Nonconformists consists in :

" (1) The privilege—which many Nonconformists consider to be a priceless privilege—of having the children of the school taught all together their Bible-lessons, and joining in the Lord's Prayer, and it may be in some very simple hymns adapted to children. This, in itself, it seems to me, would symbolise the common Christian faith of our land, and teach it in a way wholly delightful, and would secure us against the dreadful alternative to which we shall be driven, unless some such arrangement is made, of universal secular schools.

" (2) That Nonconformist teachers will have a right to a place in all parish schools as assistant teachers.

" (3) That an opportunity will be given to Nonconformists, during one or two hours in the week, to give teaching in their doctrine of the Church, to their children, and so carry out what Lord Hugh Cecil desired, that the children should be taught in the faith of their parents. There can be no doubt that, in our time, the idea of the Church, and the value of its associative and collective life, is much more appreciated than it was ; and that the individualism of our Protestant faith is being complemented by this larger and nobler sense of the collective church life, and of the powers and promises which Christ has given to His Church. As Nonconformists realise this, with members of the Church of England, they will better understand one another, and will, I believe, be drawn into fuller sympathy with one another.

" (4) That we shall be saved not only from the terrible conflict which now rages, and which will continue to be waged, about this Bill, but from the bitterness of feeling created by a sense of cruel injustice which will continue, and I fear grow, during the coming years.

" (5) If such an arrangement is made, the religious ques-

tion will not embroil the popular elections for the Parish
Council and County Council, seeing Churchmen will have
secured what they desire by legal enactment.

" (6) That the way will thus be open for immediate co-
operation in dealing with the terrible social evils of our
time, which I know can only be dealt with by the earnest
sympathy and the combined service of all Christian
people, who can co-operate at once in this service, without
any compromise or prejudice, and act together, so that
what they do shall not overlap or collide, but shall be co-
operative to the common end which they all seek.

" Many of these advantages I have named that will be
secured to Nonconformists, will, of course, be equally
secured for Churchmen, who have the desire to live in
peace and good-will with their Christian brethren."

Unfortunately, peaceable counsels were frustrated by
partisan spirits on both sides. The injustices of the Bill
remained unredressed in the Act. The Government, with
its khaki majority behind it, dared, as Cromwell once said,
" to decree injustice by law," and the only course for
those whose conscientious scruples were roughly over-
ridden was to offer passive resistance. Though he loved
his country, though he respected its law, Paton's feeling
was clear that there was a part of his nature the State
could not bind, and there was a higher duty which trans-
cended all political obligation. He refused to pay the
education rate, and his goods were distrained on; but he
did not join any league of passive resisters. He felt it
was one thing to resist himself, and another thing to
conspire with others in resisting.

Certainly, when the Act was once passed, he endeavoured to make the best of it : there was no trace of
sulkiness in his nature. At the same time that he was
refusing to pay the rate, he was spending many times
the amount of the rate in getting up a circular to the
new Local Education Authorities, urging upon them
that, in shaping out their new schemes for educational
advancement, the supreme object of all education—the
formation of character, should be the dominating consideration. The circular, which was signed by leading
men and women of all creeds, urged that Bible teaching, fitly graded, should be continued in the schools,

but pointed out that religious teaching is not sufficient, unless supported by influences inspired by the spirit of that teaching : principles must be translated into living example, and be maintained by forming habits of self-restraint, true conscientiousness, fidelity, honour, and kindness. " From these habits springs character, the best asset, it has been said, of a nation's wealth, the best guarantee of its industrial energy, and the strongest bulwark of its security."

The right sort of reading should be encouraged, and good songs, ennobling pictures should be hung on school walls ; instruction should be given in the laws of health and Christian conduct ; the evils of intemperance, gambling, and other vices should be pointed out ; by organising and superintending games, teachers could promote manliness, self-control, and a love of fair play ; the formation of Old Scholars' Associations would help to perpetuate the good influence of the school.

A permanent committee was formed to co-operate with the local authorities in furthering the objects of this appeal. The object of the committee was to indicate methods by which moral training could be promoted, to get books and literature bearing on the subject more widely circulated, to promote conferences for securing efficiency in moral training in the same way as conferences were promoted for securing efficiency in intellectual and technical training, and, above all, to inspire the profession at the fountain-head by influencing all normal and training colleges. " This must be taken up with persistency of effort," he said, and it was largely due to his persistency of effort that Dr. Michael Sadler undertook his historic inquiry into moral training in 1907. It was his tact which saved that inquiry from falling into the hands of those who ruled out all religion from the sphere of moral training.

Mr. Birrell's Bill of 1906 he welcomed as a deliverance from the injustice of 1902. He thought it showed consideration amounting to generosity towards the Church schools, but, in view of the opposition excited, he toiled hard to meet the conscientious objections of the Bill's opponents. Indeed, though he was seventy-six years of age, and had so many irons already in the fire, he worked far harder in 1906 to remove what gave offence to the

Churchmen than he had worked in 1902 to remove what gave offence to himself and his own friends. He felt that the fresh outbreak of sectarian controversy was leading straight to the elimination of all religious instruction. " We are bringing on ourselves, and almost inviting, the appalling evil of Secularism in our national schools.

" Reverent Bible-teaching, by competent persons, in all schools, and denominational teaching for the children whose parents desire it, to be given by the Church to which the school belongs "—that, in a word, summed up his position, and that position he maintained against the secularisers, who at this time cropped up from many un-expected quarters, both among convinced High Churchmen and convinced Nonconformists, among the organised Labour Unions as well as among the materialistic Socialists.

The weak point of Mr. Birrell's Bill, he felt, was that religious instruction was treated as an extra, an outside and optional subject, whereas it ought to be an integral part of the curriculum, and the opening service of the school should give the note of all the school work.

" I deeply regret that the religious teaching of the school is to be separated by such a cleavage from the ordinary instruction of the school. I wholly sympathise with Mr. Birrell in his desire that there be no obloquy attached to the child whose parents withdraw him from religious instruction ; the conscience clause at present makes that child an *object of obloquy*. Now, however, as he confesses, he is making the child who is absent for half an hour from school *an object of envy*, and that is, I think, a great misfortune and a great wrong. For what will ensue ? If the child is even desired by the parents to attend religious instruction, the child may stop on the way to school to play, and so may not receive religious instruction ; and yet no action can be taken, the school attendance officer cannot take action against the parent who has desired the child to go, and no action can be taken against the child. Again, many parents will find it convenient to keep the child away for half an hour from school for some duty at home, or some employment. I believe even at present children are sometimes sent to school without sufficient food, because the mothers have not risen early enough to provide the food ; but now mothers of that sort will be tempted to be lazy, and keep the child till twenty minutes to ten, when the ordinary secular instruction of the school begins. All this, I think, will work very injuriously upon our schools, and upon the training of our children. I would therefore entreat Mr. Birrell to allow the regular instruction to begin at 9 o'clock, let the school register be filled up during the first ten minutes, and let the religious instruction be given at the close of school, say from 11.30 to 12, when those children whose parents had sent a special request that the child should not attend the religious instruction should be allowed to go home. In this way the attendance officer can ensure that the child is in attendance at the time the school begins, and only those children whose parents have sent a special request that they do not attend religious instruction shall be allowed to leave the school at 11.30."

Not for one minute would he allow it to be said either that undenominational instruction according to the Cowper-Temple clause constituted the Nonconformist religion, or, on the other hand, that the logical outcome of Free Church principles was the secularisation of the National Schools. To maintain the position of Christian teaching in the National Schools he thought far more important than the prickings of any individual conscience. As in 1870 he had organised the Nottingham League to support Mr. Forster's Bill, to secure Bible-teaching in the Board Schools, and so defeat the purposes of the Birmingham League which aimed at secularisation, so now he sought the help of the Bishop of Southwell and large-minded men on both sides to secure the same end by preventing the religious instruction being either a detachable extra (as it was likely to become under the Bill), or being ousted altogether by the jangling of the sects. In the hottest of the fray he believed steadfastly there existed an elemental unity " below the tides of war."

" I must say that I sometimes thought it was a great compliment to Nonconformity to affirm that its religion was the religion of the Bible. That used to be considered the distinction of the Protestant religion. Chillingworth claimed this great honour for the Protestant faith—that it was the faith of the Bible. Chillingworth's famous phrase must not be forgotten : ' The Bible, the whole Bible, and nothing but the Bible, is the religion of Protestants.' I cannot, therefore, claim this great distinction and honour for Nonconformity alone. Nonconformity has distinctive doctrines of the Church and of the Sacraments. I have throughout my public life continually said that the only reason I am a Nonconformist is because of the doctrine of the Church which I hold. Nonconformists have separated themselves from the Church of England simply because they hold what they conceive to be the apostolic doctrine of the Church, and must realise that in every way that is possible to them. We have given evidence of the intensity of our conviction with regard to the doctrine of the Church that we hold by the sacrifice we make in our Nonconformity. It is not a matter of pleasure or of convenience to be in any way separated from those who are members of the Church of England, many of whom are our dearest friends. Now in the National School we Nonconformists insist that this doctrine of the Church, which we prize so much and for which we have suffered so much, *shall not be taught ;*— and for one only reason—because it is distinctive of Nonconformity. We insist that the Bible shall be taught under the Cowper-Temple clause, so that nothing that might be to our advantage, or that is, in any specific sense, denominational, shall be for one moment taught in the National Schools. We wish these schools to teach that which is the common and general faith of Christendom, and which therefore represents the common Christian faith of members of the Church of England as much as of Nonconformists.

" 2. The second error is that the principle of Nonconformity logically involves the secularising of the National Schools. It is continually being said that that is the logical outcome of our Nonconformist doctrine.

" During my student life and at the beginning of my ministry, when national education was becoming a prominent subject of discussion, it was asserted by our Nonconformist leaders, of whom Sir Edward Baines, of Leeds, was perhaps the chief, that *education was so essentially a religious matter* that it could not possibly be given save on a religious basis and under religious inspiration, and that therefore the Churches must alone undertake the national work of education. When, however, it was found that the Churches could not possibly undertake this burden ; and when more and more it was realised that the State must, for its own sake and for the good of the people, secure for all the benefits of education, then Nonconformist opinion was divided into two sections : (1) Some said, if the State can alone bear this great burden, and alone ensure the education of all children, then the schools must be secular, because the State has no concern in religion and no power to teach it.   (2) The other section, which comprised by far the largest number of Nonconformists, maintained, on the contrary, that *secular education was impossible because religion was the greatest factor in human life*—in history and literature and conduct ; that you could not teach history or literature apart from religion, and that you could not influence human conduct aright, especially in children, unless the great sanctions and inspirations of religion imbued the mind and quickened the feeling of the scholars of the school.

" Further, the great bulk of Nonconformists, though they have to a large extent advocated the separation of Church and State, because they could not allow the State to dominate and direct the Church in her great ministries of worship and redemptive service in the world, have yet *repudiated with their whole heart the doctrine that the State was itself irreligious or non-religious ;* and that, therefore, it had no concern in religion.   The State is an institution, like the family, founded of God ; and the very object of the Church is, by all her ministries of teaching and worship and sacrifice, to make the State more and more full of God and of His righteousness, and so to promote peace and good-will amongst all citizens who, whilst members of the State, are a great brotherhood, united by their common bond of allegiance to the one Father of all.   There never has been a State known in the world without a religion. It has been more than any other the great uniting force and principle in every State.   *Pro aris et focis* (For the altars and the hearths of the country) has been the watch-word and the war-cry of every nation.   In America, whilst the Church and the State are separated from each other, the State is not irreligious ; God is honoured and worshipped in the great representative assemblies of the State, and God is honoured by national festivals of thanksgiving to Him.   Woe be to the State which seeks to dethrone God !

"This being the principle of the great majority of Nonconformists, they cannot allow it to be said that the principles of Nonconformity require the schools to be secular, that our teachers are to ignore the existence of God, or to fail to impress upon the children the highest conceptions of God which have been accepted and are reverently honoured by the people of the land. Now these highest conceptions of God in our time and country are those which are revealed in the Bible, and have been specially and gloriously manifested in the life, and teaching, and sacrifice of Christ. We want, therefore, this Bible-teaching in the schools, because it gives us at once THE HIGHEST IDEA OF GOD that the world has known, and also THE HIGHEST IDEAL OF LIFE which has ever been conceived. To expel that teaching from our schools is to veil the finest light that shines upon human life in order to illumine and ennoble it. And Nonconformity, by its great doctrine that the Church lives in order to serve and save the State and to fill it with religion, is bound to insist that the schools of the State shall train the children in the knowledge and love and service of God."

To the Bishop of Ripon

"*July 27th,* 1906.

"I state very briefly what has been in my mind, namely, that there should be, at 9 o'clock, a brief devotional service, with a hymn and brief prayer, which would give the key-note to the whole of the morning's work, and would give the right tone to the minds of both scholars and teacher. I believe that very few parents would object to a simple service in which their children were taught reverence. Most Agnostics desire this as an element of character, and few parents would be tempted to withdraw their children from this service, which would be very short, in order to get work done by them, as they would if they were able to withdraw them for half an hour or more from Bible or religious teaching in the morning; also, lazy mothers would not be tempted to keep their children away from school till 9.30 because they had not got breakfast ready in time for the children to make an earlier attendance. Thus the school attendance officer would secure that all the children were present at the beginning of school, and that the school thus began in good order. I cannot but think that, to allow a number of children to come in half an hour or forty minutes later than the others, avoiding the religious lesson, would very seriously affect the order and discipline of the school.

"The further suggestion is, then, that the Bible or religious lesson shall be given at the close of the morning, for twenty minutes. There will then be much less temptation to parents to engage the children in any kind of work ; there will be no encouragement to lazy parents by their children leaving school twenty minutes earlier if they wish them not to have religious teaching, and parents will therefore be much less likely to object to their children having the religious lesson when they can get no advantage thereby from the work of their children, or for themselves. In most cases, I believe, if a parent did object to the Bible and religious teaching, he would yet desire that his children should have instruction in some other subject, it may be some moral lessons, instead of withdrawing his children altogether from the school.

"The great advantage, to my mind, is the advantage of securing compulsory attendance of every child at the beginning of the school, and also that there shall be a proper tone in a brief devotional service at the beginning of the school, in which practically I believe all will unite.

"The Methodist Conference being in session in this city, I have conferred with two or three very leading men amongst them, and I find that the following statement which I drew up has been very much approved by them, and states what they think to be the general view of Nonconformists, and which they think will be willingly signed by leading and representative Nonconformists. May I say that I find considerable objection to the use of the phrase ' Apostles' Creed,' in any such statement ? First, because, as you know, Nonconformists—especially Congregationalists, both Baptists and Pædo-Baptists— dislike a subscription to any form of creed, but also and chiefly because it is felt that Scripture is the true canon, the ' regula fidei,' that creeds are to be tested by it, and that it is not to be tested by creeds ; that creeds have not the definite authority that Scripture has ; also that Scripture sets forth Evangelic truth in a fuller and yet simpler manner than even the Apostles' Creed. The great vital elements of our faith, the redeeming love of God in

Christ, the compassion and healing grace of our Lord—these elements which touch the child's nature and move the child's heart, and the heart of all of us, are more powerfully set forth in Scripture than in the Creed. In addition, however, it is felt that if the Apostles' Creed were desired to be enforced in our schools by Nonconformists, even by those who profoundly believe in the Apostles' Creed, there would be an immediate outcry on the part of other Nonconformists who, though they may not be numerous, are yet vigorous and eager combatants, and who, too, influence the Press, because they are accustomed to public agitation and controversy, so that any manifesto signed by Nonconformists with such phraseology would do perhaps more harm than good, as it would appear to show a certain division among Nonconformists much greater than really exists.

" I now send you the statement which I drew up, which I should delight to sign, and which I think the greater number of Nonconformists would approve and sign, and which would awaken much less antagonism than a form which specified and enforced the Apostles' Creed as the canon of Bible teaching :

" 'We desire that the Bible-teaching in our elementary schools should give the meaning of the Bible which is generally understood and accepted by the English people, and which represents the common faith of all the larger Christian communions in this country. We hold that the religious education given in our schools should be truly Christian, and we trust to the Christian sense of the whole community, which it is the duty of the Churches to illumine and inform, to see that the Education Authorities appointed by them provide the most effective moral training, inspired of Christian principles, to the children of the nation. We, moreover, desire that no child shall receive this religious education which we deem so important for the well-being of the nation, if his parents object, and that his absence from such instruction should neither cause any disadvantage to the child, nor interfere with the good order and discipline of the school.' "

To Mr. M. E. Sadler "1906.

" I have never met a teacher who did not assure me that his influence and the enforcement of moral lessons would be weakened if he were not able to bring the sanctions and motives of religious faith to bear upon the mind and heart of the children.

" The child, in a remarkable way, manifests faculties that indicate its spiritual nature, and which cannot be trained healthily apart from religious faith. The child is instinct with curiosity, with wonder, with strong impulses to fear and to faith, and the child's imagination naturally soars at once beyond the present and material world that is seen and felt. It believes in the unseen ; it questions wonderingly the origin of things and must have an answer. If no answer is given, it will create its own imaginings as to the unseen. Surely it is of infinite importance that the child should know of God—who is the perfectly Good One, the Origin, the Sustainer, the Ruler of all persons and things ; who favours and blesses the good and who opposes the evil. How that thought, which the child willingly accepts because it is accordant with its nature, illumines the imagination, delights the soul and at once inspires and reinforces the will of the child ! The child cannot possibly be trained for life by mere negations with regard to the unseen world. The child resents such vacuity ; and, on the other hand, what cosmological or ontological doctrine can you teach that will be so easily apprehended by the child, or can so awaken delight, and inspire and sustain and ennoble the moral life of the child as that primary and all-embracing doctrine of our Father —God, the Being from whom all are derived and to whom all are continually related, who is perfect Goodness, the Ideal, the Source, and the Upholder of Justice and Love.

" In all honourable life there must be reverence. How can reverence possess and imbue the soul apart from the thought of God ? The greatest peril in our age is the down-draught to materialism, which makes life vulgar and sordid, without high aspirations, without serious thought or any sweet odour of sanctity. To exile God from the schools is to exile the child into a far country to feed on swines' husks. I know that for many refined natures, poetry and the arts supply some ideal elements that nourish a higher life. But for the mass of the people it is religion alone that can supply these elements, and to extinguish this is to debase and destroy the true life of the child."

26

Before closing this chapter it may be fitting to attempt a summary of what Paton did for national education.

He realised the growing importance of the public elementary school in the life of the people, and saw that it must be the basis of all further development. He saw that many influences were at work, fostering the ' informational ' side of education, and therewith obscuring and weakening the moral elements of the training. He believed in an education which was wider and richer and deeper in its scope—not merely filling what he called " this poor knob at the top," but training in all noble exercise the body, the imagination, the feelings, and the spirit.

He saw how the growing organisation of industrial life increased enormously the moral dangers for both boys and girls, and he strove to use the very instincts for play, music, and colour, which enticed children from the school, to entice them to it.

He fought to uphold the Christian character of our educational system. But he wished to make religious teaching and all the school life far more effective than it had hitherto been for the formation of moral principle and conduct. He saw that in the great public schools the moral tone was fostered by the corporate life, the organised team-games, the personal influence of masters, the continued attachment of the scholars after they had left. These same elements of moral health he wished to see in the schools of the poorest.

He realised the educational needs of adolescence, and laboured with unceasing devotion on behalf of a generous ideal of further education. By the help of song, art, rhythmic movement, and every means of healthy self-expression, he sought to make this further education attractive and joyous by making it practical, recreative, social. The paramount importance of this further education he impressed on Sunday-schools as well as upon the public authorities, and he sought to establish what he called a " Concordat " between the Church and State by virtue of which they should mutually support each other in safeguarding the unguarded years of youth.

He saw the weak point of educational efforts in England was their discontinuity. The work of the elementary school carried forward in evening-classes, brigades, and other institutions for adolescence, was to lead up to still higher educational achievement. He revived the Evening School, humanised it and assigned to it its true place in a national system as a Continuation School. Though he did not first conceive the idea of university extension, he first embodied it in a practical working scheme. Always quick to seize on a good idea wherever he found it, he was the first to realise the educational significance of the American Chautauqua, to adapt it to English conditions on more democratic lines, and to organise guidance in the choice of books for private and social reading. He saw the problem of education as a whole *uno intuitu*, its interlacing factors of intellect, physical need, social instincts and character. He allowed for the great subconscious hinterland which governs so large a portion of human conduct. He believed steadfastly that the strongest appeal was the appeal to the highest part of man's nature. " There is a hero in the heart of every boy," he would say, " and we must make that hero act and rule his life."

The epileptic children and the feeble-minded were very near to his heart. He rescued them from the degrading associations of the workhouse, he brought scientific treatment and Christian influence to bear on their special needs.

He had uncommon power of initiative and energy of attack, with a quick sense of the lines on which attack was possible. His mind was constructive rather than critical. He had the gift of organisation and direction, more especially the latter. He believed in doing things and setting others to do them.

Finally and chiefly, though he held no definite assigned position, he was one of the greatest inspirational forces in English education. He was a general who not only planned the campaign, but organised the expeditionary forces, reheartened the wavering, re-established the ranks, reconciled the quarrellers, and infected each fighter with something of his own joy in the service and assurance of victory. " I wish you a glorious New Year," he wrote to one of his helpers ; " from glory to glory."

CHAPTER XXII

THE INSTITUTE OF SOCIAL SERVICE

"The experience of all for the benefit of each."—DR. JOSIAH STRONG.

THERE were several contributory streams which converged in the formation of the British Institute of Social Service. But all these streams had the same source in the League of Social Service which was founded in America in 1898 by Dr. Josiah Strong. Few men have made their influence more deeply felt than he. Few men's work has matured so rapidly. The results achieved by the League of Social Service were so conspicuously useful in many directions and attracted the attention and sympathy of so many eminent people that, after five years, in 1903, the American Institute of Social Service was formed in order to carry on in a more thorough and extensive manner all the varied departments of its work. The income of the new Institute amounted to £3,000 per annum, and the U.S.A. President, Mr. Theodore Roosevelt, wrote a letter to be read at the opening, in which he said :

"This Institute is fitted to render a great and peculiar service, not merely to this country but to all countries. Apparently it is proving to be the beginning of a world-movement, and is being recognised by the best men of many different countries as a necessity in each and all of these countries in order to facilitate the readjustment of social relations to the new conditions created by the modern industrial revolution."

Among the men who in different countries were following this new move in the advance of Social Progress was Dr. Strong's friend, Paton of Nottingham. In the year before his installation, as first President of the new Institute, Dr. Strong came over to England in the month of

April 1902, and spent two days in earnest conference with Paton. Their talk centred mainly on the new development which Dr. Strong was projecting. How thoroughly Paton entered into that project, and how that project dovetailed into the modes and shapes of his own thought, is shown by a letter which he wrote to Miss Helen Jay Gould, dated June 1902.

To Miss Jay Gould

" *June*, 1902.

" Dr. Josiah Strong has informed me of the desire to establish in New York a Sociological Museum and Institute, which shall be the centre and mainspring of careful studies and inquiries into the laws which have governed and do govern social life, and the development of mankind in all their social, tribal, and national relations, and which shall be the central source for the diffusion of knowledge thus carefully acquired and accumulated, scientifically classified and co-ordinated, and directed to present practical uses and the solution of pressing social problems. Dr. Strong has also expressed to me the hope that you may be interested in the formation of such an important institution, which will not only be national, but will have the greatest possible value for all other countries, and will have a supreme directing agency and influence for all those in every country that are seeking to promote the well-being of the people. I have told him that I would venture, under the cover of his introduction, to submit to you the reasons which, to my mind, make the establishment of such a Museum and Institute a matter of profound significance and value at the present time, especially in its relation to the Christian Church, and the great mission which the Church has to fulfil in the world. During the whole of my life as a Christian minister, I have been impressed with one idea, that the great doctrine of redeeming love, which is the central doctrine of our faith, needs to be manifested and realised in other ways and larger senses than we have hitherto conceived and desired. The redeeming of humanity is not only the conversion of individual souls, and the training of individual lives, but it is also the forming of new and healthy conditions of life for men, and the inspiring of all human law and custom with a regular and definite Christian idea

and spirit. The conviction which I have thus expressed
has been the inspiration of my whole life. Early in my
ministry I went to Germany, to study especially the
methods of the Inner Mission, as it was called, founded
by the great Dr. Wichern, under the auspices then of
King Frederick of Prussia, who was the intimate friend
and ally of Dr. Wichern. The central idea and purpose of
the Inner Mission are set forth in a booklet which was
published many years ago, of which the first section is an
address which I delivered on the Inner Mission of Germany, and its lessons to us. The whole of the booklet
sets forth the meaning and method of the Inner Mission
of the Church, by which is meant the mission of the Church
within the land in which it is planted, so as to make the
country which it thus occupies a truly Christian country,
in which the laws and life of the people, its institutions
and usages, shall harmonise with the righteous will of
God. May I be permitted to give you a copy of that
booklet, and also the set of a first series of Inner Mission
leaflets, which have been published this year, and which
will be followed by a second series, both series covering
much of the ground which I feel the Church in this country
and in America needs to occupy, if it fulfil what I have
thus called its Inner Mission. The whole object, to my
mind, of the Sociological Museum and Institute, which it
is hoped may be founded in New York, is to study most
wisely and reverently and earnestly the great and complicated problems of social life with the true and exact
analytic and synthetical method of scientific inquiry, so
as to learn what is in truth the will and law of God manifested in and through these social phenomena of the past
and of the present, and so to give sure and effective
guidance to all who are inspired by a philanthropic and
redemptive purpose, especially therefore to the leaders
and members of the Church of Christ in making the
righteous law and will of God to predominate and rule
throughout the whole community in all the relationships
and conduct of life.

" It seems to me that New York would be a fitting site
for such an Institute and Museum, which would serve its
high, and, in a true sense, redemptive purpose for all the
leading civilised nations of the world. It seems to me
that the English-speaking nations of the world hold the

foremost place, having thus an immense and sacred responsibility devolving upon them to guide other nations,
it may be, in the establishment of the kingdom of God
and of His righteousness, and among the English-speaking
peoples, to whom have been specially entrusted the
principles of liberty and good government, of individual
responsibility and of collective action, organisation, and
these principles of what may be called Western civilisation, have found, I think, their fullest expression, and
seem to be pressing towards a fuller co-ordination and
realisation on the large continent of America than anywhere else. It is there that all the problems of modern
life, especially in the English-speaking world, and also in
the modern civilised world, are presented in the largest
and most insistent form, and it is there that the solution
of them in harmony with the will of God will, I trust, be
most clearly and definitely secured.

" I cannot but hope that this Sociological Museum and
Institute will bear upon it in its forefront the title Christian, and this without any disparagement or clouding of
its truly historic and scientific character, and for these
reasons :

" 1. There must be certain pre-suppositions in every
science, such as are the mathematical axioms that underlie
all mathematical and physical science, and the logical laws
that underlie all philosophic reasoning. Now in the moral
world, even among agnostics, the life and teaching of our
Lord is confessed to reveal the supreme moral law for the
guidance of both individual and social life, and all social
problems are fundamentally moral problems in regard to
which we need the clear and certain guidance of an authoritative moral law.

" 2. The Christian Church has always recognised, but
in our time more than ever, the great truth enunciated by
Paul, that, as Adam was the natural head of humanity,
Christ is the Second Adam, the Head of the new humanity,
in which all collective life, as well as individual life, is
fashioned and ruled by the righteous will of God.

" 3. The great doctrine of the Christian faith is the
doctrine of Redemption; in which we see our Divine Lord
Himself magnifying the holy law of God and making it
honourable, and in which we know that He is inspired to
this by the passion of an infinite love so as to save men

from the curse of disobedience, and bring them with Himself to obey perfectly the will of God, the will of our Heavenly Father, and so to obtain the perfection of their being, the perfect health and harmony of individual and social life, which is the end and fulfilment of God's law. It is the love that inspired Christ to this great redemptive service which He pours into the heart of his servants, so that they co-operate with Him towards the redeeming of the world from evil, and the establishment everywhere of God's Kingdom, in which His law is honoured, obeyed; and fulfilled. It is love alone, inspired of the Cross, that will avail to inspire men to seek perfectly to know the will of God in all human life, and to search out the deeply rooted causes of evil in man's nature, which is at once the cause and fruit of disobedience, and that will enable them; by alliance with the sovereign love and grace of God, to uproot and remove these evils. For these reasons I do earnestly hope that a Sociological Institute and Museum, founded in the heart of the English-speaking and Christian world, may thus bear on its forefront the shining glory of the name of Christ.

" There are three great functions which, it seems to me; such a Museum and Institute will fulfil, if properly equipped and administered.

" I. (a) To collect and collate all information with regard to the past history of mankind, in all the varied and contrasted forms of their social life that appear in every stage in that history. The existing forms of civilisation are the product of an evolution that has progressed through former centuries, and; to its understanding, the whole of that process of evolution needs to be most carefully studied. The roots of the present lie thus deep in the past, and it is by the study of the genesis and growth of the present civilisation in the past that we can not only understand it, but can also forecast and prepare its further developments in the future. In such a Museum historic records of the past, so far as they describe and illustrate the varied organisation and usages and multiform influences of human society under all kinds of conditions, would be gathered together. In this way potent influences of climate; soil, geologic and geographic phenomena, the causes which determine military instinct and organisation, or; on the contrary; which induce peaceful industries, the effects of government; and the results which are influenced by government, art, literature, social and industrial activities and commerce will be stated, as they appear in every stage of human social development. These records of the past would be contained not only in books and monographs, but be illustrated by charts of historical, statistical, geologic, geographic, in short, every method in which information can be graphically tabulated and represented, also by photographs and other pictorial illustrations, as well as by exhibits, which may reproduce and represent the varied elements of the social structure and of social life, in each period of human history and of social development. The great object of all this study of the past will be to show what elements and influences have tended to the well-being of men and of society, or have tended to their deterioration, and how far they may have enhanced or degraded special powers in individuals or in races, and have thus exalted or trodden down and enfeebled certain races.

" (b) With regard to the present, such a Museum and Institute would set forth the immensely varied and complex elements of modern civilisation, and show the great tendencies which are at work in modern civilisation, whether for good or for evil. It would thus represent not only the great factors of religion and government and art and literature and industrial and commercial activity and social recreation, which are the formal elements in every social State, but the interaction of these under the new conditions which the spread of education, the marvellous industrial change wrought by the introduction of steam and electricity, and intercommunication, especially through the Press, creating a public opinion which hitherto has been unknown. All these in like manner would be set forth not only in books but in charts, pictorial illustrations; and other exhibits. Here also the great object will be to show what there is in every one of these elements that is working towards the higher good of mankind, and what is working injuriously, so that the purpose in all these inquiries shall be to learn the righteous will of God, which seeks the full well-being of individual men and of society, and that righteous law which is the norm of individual and of social perfection, for the righteousness of God surely consists in men holding right relations to one another and to God, and in being enabled in these relations to achieve the most healthful development of all their powers.

" II. The second object of such an Institute will be to pursue such studies scientifically, and; to accumulate and systematise the knowledge which is necessary. To this end there must be an endowment of research, so that in the great domains, many of them unexplored, of what is the greatest science in the universe, the science of humanity, not only individual men but all men, as they are knit together in one great social organism, the great facts and factors may be registered and classified.

" III. Such an Institute and Museum, to fulfil its highest function, must not only gather such knowledge and classify it, and make it so as to illuminate the one social problem, the highest good of man, in relation to God and humanity, but it must be the fountain-head from which such knowledge will be sent forth as the very truth and light of the sanctuary of God, to give guidance to all those, especially in the Churches of Christ, who are seeking to promote the highest good of men, and to establish everywhere the kingdom of God and His righteousness. To this end the curators of the Museum must not be merely custodians, but must be men and women inspired with the central thought and supreme object of the Museum, so as to reveal and to impress upon all who come the significance and value, and the inward soul of meaning which is set forth in all that they thus exhibit. The Museum will be itself a dead thing unless it be filled by the living soul of men thus possessed with the great end of such a Museum, to show what is the true good of man, and how that good is to be wisely and effectively shown. Also lecturers should go forth in order to convey the great lessons taught by the science of the Museum, that is by the whole of the knowledge which is organised in its bearing upon definite, and intricate and most pressing social problems of the present time : how men everywhere and most wisely can not only fulfil their own, but the good of others, and how all of them, as one great brotherhood, will obey and honour the one holy Father of all, and thus fulfil His will, and show forth His glory."

About the same time or even earlier, certain persons who

desire to remain anonymous, having heard of the League for Social Service in America, asked Mr. Budgett Meakin, the great traveller and the well-known authority on Morocco, if he would undertake to organise a similar League in England, and to deliver lectures like those of Dr. Tolman with that end in view. Mr. Meakin, accordingly, set about the organisation of a similar movement in February 1902. But, learning from Dr. Strong that the American League was being reconstituted and starting again under a new name, it was decided for the time being to proceed with the lectures alone till the American movement had crystallised out into definite shape. Thus the Shaftesbury Lectures came into being, Mr. Budgett Meakin doing the brunt of the work. In March 1903 the guarantors of these lectures placed at Mr. Budgett Meakin's disposal a special fund to enable him to go to America and learn what he could of the working of the new Institute there.

Meanwhile, Mr. F. Herbert Stead, of the Robert Browning Settlement, Walworth, had written on February 9th, 1903, to a number of leading Christian sociologists, suggesting the idea of a week's devotional conference. " Let us wait on God," he said, " endeavour to find out His mind, and what step He means us to take next." He wrote to Dr. Josiah Strong among others. On February 24th Dr. Strong replied, heartily approving the idea of the sociological retreat, and proceeding :

" There are coming in Christian countries organisations bearing more or less resemblance to the Musée Social of Paris. We have recently organised in New York the American Institute of Social Service. I have written to Dr. John B. Paton, Dr. John Watson, Mr. Samuel Smith, M.P., and the Rev. J. F. B. Tinling, suggesting that they move in the matter of a British Institute of Social Service along the lines of our organisation. I have heard from all these gentlemen except Mr. Smith, expressing their sympathy with the idea. It strikes me that such a gathering as you have intimated might facilitate such an organisation."

On March 18th Mr. Budgett Meakin wrote to Mr. Stead telling him of the progress and success of the Shaftesbury Industrial Betterment lectures. He went on to speak of

his own projected tour to the States and Dr. Tolman's
proposed visit to England. He proposed that before Dr.
Tolman returned a few prominent social workers should be
invited to confer with him with a view to establishing an
Institute in England on the lines of the American Institute
and the Musée Social in Paris.

The result was that, as soon as Mr. Budgett Meakin
returned on July 8th, 1903, a provisional committee meeting
was held at the Browning Club on Mr. Stead's invitation.
Paton was present. Professor Geddes and Mr. V. V.
Branford represented the Sociological Society, Mr. Budgett Meakin represented the Shaftesbury Lectures, Mr.
Frederick Rogers represented the National Committee of
organised labour. They agreed, if practicable, to form a
British Institute of Social Service, and that this new
Institute should co-operate in every way with the newly
formed Sociological Society, thus wedding " thought and
action, science and practice, interpretation and ideal,"
as Professor Geddes put it.

" I think it should not be at all impossible to use this
simultaneous development of Sociological Society and
Institute of Social Service for the good of both, and to
link them vitally instead of allowing them to diverge; as
philosopher and philanthropist are so apt to do. I am
convinced that the note of synthesis will now increasingly
characterise the opening age, and that the association of
theory and practice, survey and service, fact and ideal,
will be easier and clearer for the rising generation than it
has been for us and ours ; it will be, in short, *synthesis* and
synergy upon the widest basis of *sympathy*."

The most energetic members of this committee were
Mr. Stead, Paton, and Mr. George F. Warden (Hon. Sec.),
who attended every meeting. Dr. Tolman, when he was
over, spent some days at Hareshawmuir and had conference
there with Paton. Mr. Rolland Ramsay and his Scottish
friends, though willing to co-operate with the British
Institute, felt that Scottish problems were so different
from English that Scotland would require a separate
organisation of her own.

The Constitutive Meeting was held on Monday, March
28th, 1904. The Earl of Lytton presided, and a pro-

visional committee was appointed to prepare a draft constitution, and to see what financial support would be forthcoming. The meeting was adjourned to the Whitehall rooms, July 8th, 1904, when, under the Presidency of the Earl of Meath, the Constitution was finally adopted, and President, Vice-President, and twelve members of Council were elected ; twelve societies of a national character, dealing with social questions in general, were invited to nominate representatives to the Council. At both these meetings Paton was the spokesman of the new idea.

" This is not the place or the hour for any vapourings of foolish, extravagant pretence or promise. The objects we seek are not to be achieved at one bound, but they are to be achieved by wise, earnest, painstaking effort. I have heard one and another say our objects are nebulous and vague. It is my task to expose and dispel that illusion, to show that our objects are definite, clear, and attainable, and that our methods are business-like, sensible, and effective. Our objects are two : first, to collect and focus information about all social effort, both successful and the reverse ; secondly, to make that information available for all social workers to whom it can be of service.

" In every civilised country there is a general desire for social amelioration. The finest element in the spirit of our age is a new-born enthusiasm of humanity. The relation and duty of the individual to the social organism of which he is a member, and the influence of environment upon the character and destiny of men, are truths which are powerfully enforced by all teachers of Social Science, and the most eminent leaders of public opinion. ' Association ' is felt to be a watchword of the future. Unions are organised by all the various classes of the community to protect and promote their interests ; societies are formed in endless number to promote various forms of public good ; municipalities assume more and more functions that enable them to further the social well-being of the communities which they represent ; and legislatures in every civilised land discuss measures and frame laws to advance the economic and social interests of the people.

" Alongside of this general movement in every civilised country, the zeal of the Christian Church is being re-

tempered in the fount of its origins : the life and teaching
and example of Christ Himself illumine and interpret the
doctrines of the Church, and inspire its activities. The
brotherhood of man is seen to be rooted in the great
doctrine of the Fatherhood of God, and the doctrine of
human redemption is seen to mean the redeeming of the
individual and of the race from the evils that beset them.
And so it is felt that the abounding charities of the Church
must now be regulated and ordered by scientific method,
so as to avoid the evils they have hitherto unwittingly
caused, and to ensure the good which they have always
contemplated.

" At the same time, whilst this good omen shines upon
us at the beginning of this century, great and alarming
evils overshadow it.   The industrial revolution of the last
century has wrought results which stand out in lurid
contrasts. Wealth has been enormously increased, knowledge has been widely spread, the comforts of life have been
multiplied, and luxury abounds as never before in the
world's history.   At the same time the population is being
massed together in large industrial towns and cities, where
multitudes live in congested districts full of insanitary
homes ; our work-people are crowded together in large
factories where work is monotonous and spiritless, and so
the love of garish excitement, of gambling, and of intoxicants, grows appallingly ; the apprenticeship and
personal care of our youth in workshops is almost abolished ;
the old personal and friendly relations between the employer
and his employed have become impossible ; the wealthy
and the poor are now sundered and removed from each
other, living apart in widely separated districts ; the
immense accumulations of wealth by a few, and the
gorgeousness of modern luxury, confront and affront the
terrible poverty and squalor of the large numbers of the
very poor, who are the wreckage of modern civilisation.
Meantime, amid these startling contrasts, the spread of
education, and the democratic spirit of freedom which
has given political power to the people, have awakened in
all civilised countries a spirit of restless discontent, which
creates anxiety and forebodes peril.   It has seemed to me
that, in the evolution of human society, much of the
anguish and the bitter cries of our time which perplex and
sadden are the birth-throes of a new birth.

" The spirit of humanity and of religion, awakening zeal and enterprise in every land, stands now in the face of these evils, and strives in numberless and varied ways to cope with them.

" In every civilised country efforts are being made by individuals and societies, by civic authorities and the State, to abate these evils and to discover the causes that produce them.   These efforts are necessarily more or less in the nature of experiments, and these inquiries are being conducted more or less according to scientific methods. And so a new spirit of scientific exactitude and order is introduced into all departments of social inquiry and reform.   It is therefore wise, and even necessary, that the countless experiments which are now being made in all parts of the civilised world in connection with varied forms of social wrong and evil, should be collated, as it is through them that social theories are being tested, and the laws and tendencies of social well-being are being verified. It is in them, and through them, that we see how the desire for the public good, that animates them all, succeeds or fails.   If the vast and varied experience which is thus being given to us is focussed—if it is classified and illustrated—it will pour searching light upon the social problems of our time in our own country, and it will give sure guidance, warning, and encouragement to all workers in every department of Social Service.

" This then is the object and mission of the British Institute of Social Service—namely, to collect, codify, and index information respecting the numberless forms of social effort, that are of the nature of experiment, throughout the civilised nations of the world, and to make that information available to all persons, societies, and corporations, that are interested in, or engaged in, varied forms of service for the well-being of people."

Between the meeting in March and the meeting in July Dr. Strong paid another visit to this country, Paton making himself responsible for all expenses. Dr. Strong spoke at Dr. Horton's Church in Hampstead, at Garden City, Letchworth, at Liverpool, at Glasgow, and the English International Peace Congress. He saw many of our leading men, and the success of the new venture was in large measure due to the effect produced by his visit.

The initial success of the Institute was largely due to Mr. R. Dangerfield, who not only gave his services as Honorary Director, but gave also of his means and made several journeys of investigation for its benefit. The difficulties of the work were great, and there was perpetually need of what Paton called " the oil of sympathy and good sense."

" There is endless promise for us in the immediate future," he writes playfully to Mr. Dangerfield, " but what shall we do if the founder and father of it all hands us over without further help to a future in which we must struggle for ourselves or die ? I somehow or other do not think you will let such a calamity befall us. God has blessed you with this child, and though you have had some difficulty in its upbringing, as most parents have with their children, let it be an Isaac and not an Ishmael to you."

In these juvenile ailments of the new Institute, Paton bore a large share of the nursing. A volume could easily be filled with his letters alone, if all the details were gone into. In spite of all ailments, the Institute grew and developed. It moved into more spacious accommodation, first in Southampton Row and then in Tavistock Square. It answers every year thousands of inquiries on all manner of subjects from all countries. It gives introductions to foreigners who come to England to study social activities, it organises conferences and lectures which shape and guide public opinion. Its library is classified and catalogued in exactly the same way as the sister Institute at New York, and, spite of the insufficient finances, is the most complete and efficient for its special purposes in the North of Europe. Its magazine; " Progress : Civic, Social, Industrial," keeps students of social work *au courant* with the latest developments of their work ; it saves them from repeating the blunders of the past, it suggests hopeful methods, it knocks windows into their minds in all directions. To the late Mr. A. Holden Byles, who was for so many years the editor, Paton wrote " God has been training you all these years for this work."

Some men of prescience have suggested that the twentieth century may show a progress in the human sciences which will be as wonderful as the progress made in the nineteenth century by the natural sciences. If that is to be so, such a central clearing-house of ideas and experiences as the Institute provides is the first requisite. The very multiplicity of our endeavours necessitates the creation of a body to do on behalf of all, what lies beyond the scope of any existing body. What the army of social workers need more than anything is a Headquarter Staff, some central organising body, whose business it is to survey the whole field of social service, direct operations from the centre, and concentrate the available forces in the most profitable direction. Before the Institute came into being, human experience was either filed or forgotten. Now it is stored and used, if those who might use it are awake to their opportunity ; at any rate, it is available. The Institute represents an alliance between Science and Philanthropy. Philanthropy deals with symptoms and effects ; she is the hospital nurse. Science finds out the causes and discovers the means of prevention and cure ; she is the research professor in the laboratory. Philanthropy has the practical gift, and deals with present evils. Science has the prevision born of insight and study of conditions both past and present. In the association of these two lies the hope of future progress, civic, social, and industrial.

The two movements, so diverse in origin, the scientific and religious, need each other. Social survey and social service must go hand in hand.

To Professor Patrick Geddes

"1903.

" This has been the central thought of all my life, namely, that Christ has shown to us what I feel is in itself eternally true—the love of the Eternal Father spending itself in sympathy and service and sacrifice to redeem His children, the race of man, from the evil that does most sorely beset it, howsoever that evil has arisen. In this great ministry and process of Redeeming Love I think every true Christian should engage, and we must lay hold of all the forces and influences of nature which science and art reveal to man. You see, therefore, how interested I shall be in your teaching and outlook as a man devoted to both science and art, and yet having always before

27

you the great inspiration of a world's education and redemption."

To Mr. C. S. Loch

"March 5th, 1904.

"I have been much interested in the proposal to form a British Social Service Institute, as I have been also in the Sociological Society. These two seem to me, along with the Charity Organisation Society, almost complements of one another. At first I was reluctant because my strength is limited, and I have so much in hand, even to contemplate the formation of such an Institute in this country; but the more I looked into the matter, and saw the possibilities of great and immediate service being rendered in many directions for the good of the people and at little cost, I have been constrained to do what I possibly can to establish in this country, as in America and in France and Sweden and in Italy, and as I have reason to believe in every other European country, an Institute for the objects set forth in the Constitution of the American Institute.

"I understand that you have had some hesitation in supporting this proposal. I should hate the idea of starting what would be thought a new society. It seems to me to be rather a clearing-house and meeting-ground of other societies working for the public good, not only in this country, but in all civilised countries working for the public good, so that they may make each other acquainted with what is being done, with the good results achieved in some directions, and the failures in others.

"I have read with great interest the recent numbers of the monthly magazine and also the weekly letters published by the American Institute, and I have been amazed at the practical value of the information given, and the help that is so manifestly offered in them, not only to individuals, but to societies, institutions, and municipalities seeking in different ways to promote the public good. The chief recommendation, to my mind, in establishing a British Social Service Institute, is the fact that so much can be done at such little cost, as all the information that is obtained by the other Institutes, say, for example, the American Institute, will be available to us with practically no cost, and we can make use of such of it as seems to be most required and likely to be helpful in this country. However, I greatly value your judgment, and I should like, when I am next in London, to have a brief conference with you on this matter. I feel that this British Institute of Social Service ought to be closely associated with the C.O.S. and also with the Sociological Society, and it will be, to my mind, a misfortune if this triple alliance is not carried out."

To Canon Barnett

" March 5th, 1904.

" ... All the information that is collected by the American Institute, and by the Musée Social, and by other Institutions, will be at our disposal practically without cost, and I have been delighted to find in how many ways the information given and the suggestions made, promoted and in a sense ensured endless good being done, not only by private persons or by associations, but by municipalities, and even in some cases by state legislation. Take as an example, the Museum of Security which they have established, in which models and descriptions of all kinds of appliances for the saving of life in dangerous trades are collected. Dr. Strong believes, and I am sure he is right, that this Museum will be the means of saving thousands of lives throughout America, and the same result will attend the formation of a similar Museum, which will cost very little, in this country."

To Mr. Budgett Meakin

"July 1st, 1904.

" I shall meet the Scottish friends on Tuesday. What I think all must feel is that the work of this Institute can only be done in one great, strong, central Institution. If we triturate and divide the work, nothing effective can be done. The whole conception of the Institute is a strong, central bureau of information, with a social museum, and a museum of security, and a vast amount of tabulated and indexed information available, and with an expert staff of two or three able men and women directing the investigations, answering inquiries, etc. There are, in addition, several international aspects of the work which

make it still more important that there should be such a
central Institution. I am sure, therefore, that if sections
be formed, with central committees and officers, we shall
lose altogether the commanding and central interest and
support of the one great Institute. Local Institutes, of
the kind you name, it seems to me will have no efficiency,
and can have very little special work."

To Mrs. Moser, of Bradford

"*May 7th*, 1907.

" . . . I have given much thought and energy to the
British Institute, as has also our dear friend Mr. Byles.
I have done so because I think in it there are enormous
possibilities and opportunities of most valuable and
necessary service in regard to all social work in our time.
There are now institutions established not only in America,
but in Germany and France, Italy and Holland, having
the same aims as the British Institute, with which we
are in correspondence, so that we can obtain information
of all that is being done in various parts of the world in
connection with social service ; and, on the other hand, we
give them information of what is being done in this country.
I believe that shortly there will be an Institute established
in every civilised country, with precisely the same aims
as the British Institute, and all these will then be in
correspondence with each other, so that the results of all
kinds of social work, and of legislation in regard to social
well-being, will be thus transmitted to and from these
Institutes, and made available for social workers in all
countries. How often failure would have been avoided,
and what guidance and stimulus and help can be obtained
in countless ways from the experience already gained in
other countries ! Think, for example, of the methods of
planning the new districts and suburbs of towns and cities
adopted in Germany, and which we are only beginning to
understand here. . . . You can at once see what a boon to
all social workers, and what a stimulus will be given to
wise social activities, by social workers in one country
being thus brought into touch with social workers in every
part of the world."

CHAPTER XXIII

THE YOUNG MEN'S BRIGADE OF SERVICE

" Dost thou need salvation ?   Arise, and become a saviour."—MAETER·
LINCK.

IT was in the Rev. R. J. Campbell's house at Enfield that
the Brigade of Service first took shape.   The old warrior
was paying a visit to the young minister who had just been
called to succeed Dr. Joseph Parker at the City Temple.
A large number of young men had been received into the
fellowship of the Church.   How was their Christian profession to be made real ?   How was their faith in a Saviour
to find expression in daily doing and by such expression to
grow strong and effective for the saving of the world ?
That was the question.   Both the young man and the
old felt that the modern Church had failed as yet in giving
the answer to that question.   The sort of work that it
offered to the young convert was nearly all of a pietistic
kind : " Attend the prayer-meeting, speak at the mission
service, distribute tracts, take a Sunday-school class."
There arc some whose gifts lie in this direction ; for them
such forms of service are appropriate.   There are more
whose gifts lie in quite different directions.   The deeper
their convictions, the charier are they in speaking about
them.   Yet they, too, have gift for service, and they have
willingness as well.   But their service must be something
real, something they can do with hands and limbs.   The
Church of Chivalry would have found work in plenty for
such willing hands and strong arms.   The modern Church
has not found out yet how to use the spirit of chivalry
in her young men and women.   Right up to her very
walls the great Adversary plunders and lays waste the land,
but the Church has not yet organised either her fighting
forces or her ambulance train.   Isolated sallies are made,
but there is no combined movement, no marshalling of the
host, no plan of campaign.   Here were the young recruits

offering for active service, eager for the fray; what lead
was the Church to give them ?

A literary and debating society had been suggested ;
it was to hold its first constitutive meeting next Thursday,
September 22nd, 1904. But neither the ardour of youth
nor the ardour of age could feel satisfied that a literary
and debating society was any adequate answer to this need.
It meant more speechifying ; how was speechifying to
satisfy the young men in whom Carlyle's call to " Be
real," had found a ready response ? It meant self-
cultivation. How was self-cultivation to satisfy the
young soul which meant in earnest to deny self, take up
its cross daily, and follow Christ ?

The inaugural meeting of the Literary and Debating
Society was held, but literary matters and debating were
hardly so much as mentioned. The note of the meeting,
first and last, was service. " Why stand ye all the day
idle ? " was the question that came home to each soul. It
was real work that Paton called upon the young Templars
to do, work for the crushed, the stunted, the starved, the
suffering, the crippled, the wayward, the ignorant, the
fallen. Outside the walls of the Temple lay the pagan
city of the twentieth century, with its abyss, and the
perishing souls that moved in the abyss and stretched lame
hands for help. Many would gladly be up and doing, if
they only knew just what to do. Let those who were thus
minded come together, group themselves into small corps,
and pledge themselves to give at least one hour a week to
some unselfish service for their fellow-men. There was
young life running to waste on all hands in the city—lads
and lasses whose leisure hours were leading them fast into
ruin for lack of leaders ; other lads and lasses, again, who
were making havoc of their lives for lack of friendly counsel
as to employment. There were clubs and institutes ham-
pered in every direction and giving up for lack of helpers.
There were crippled children and blind folk whose lives
wanted a touch of brightness. One corps might take a
particular street or slum in hand, and see what they could
do to lift it and humanise it ; another might run the
public-house off its legs by running a Social Institute,
and getting up a regular Saturday " pop." Some might go
in for public work on a local Board or Council—that,
too, was Christian work, when the motive was love of

Christ.   But all service ranked the same with God,
whether high or low, and sometimes the big results
came out of the small beginnings.   The Polytechnic
began with Mr. Quintin Hogg teaching two boys to read
under a railway-arch by the light of a halfpenny candle.
But, though the service was to the lowly, there was to be
nothing desultory about it.   Every man must be faithful.

"We'll have no casuals," he said ; "we'll drum every
such man out of the Brigade.   There are a lot of casuals
beside those who enter the casual ward of the workhouse.
There are a lot of casuals in the Christian Church, who like
to do a little sometimes, irregularly.   We will have no
such men in our Brigade."

At the end of the meeting, slips were filled in by those
willing to sign on for service.   A committee was appointed,
and the Young Men's Brigade of Service came into existence.   The bond of union was to be, not a statement of
doctrinal opinion, but of willingness to do good.   The
confession of Christ was to be made, not in phrases, but in
deeds.   Service was to be wholly spontaneous, and as
varied as human need, but it was to be regular and disciplined.   The only expense was to be 1d. per annum for
the card of membership, and on the card were to be set
forth the different kinds of service in which members
might engage according to their several gift, taste, or
opportunity.   Corps meetings were to be held in private
houses, or in buildings connected with Churches and
Sunday-schools, so that there should be no expense.
Among the first volunteers were Mr. Albert Dawson, Editor
of the "Christian Commonwealth," who volunteered to
teach a Shorthand-class, and Mr. G. J. Heinz, the great
manufacturer of Pittsburgh, who was present at the
meeting, and signed on as the first Transatlantic member.

"The hope of the Christian Church," Paton said, "is
in its young life.   If only the young men of the country
can be roused to a sense of their responsibilities and
opportunities, a new era will dawn.   When I think of the
active energies of young people, I am quite sure it is only
as we train these energies in service for Christ, service
which is natural and unforced, that we shall attach them

in loyal bonds to Christ as the great Leader of their life, and enable them to understand more of His Spirit and His salvation."

The impulse of the inaugural meeting was not evanescent. More than two years after, in December 1907, a young man wrote :

" You will perhaps remember that I went with you to Farringdon Street Station and carried your bag for you. Ever since then I have been waiting for an opportunity of suggesting an organisation of a Brigade of Service at the Church with which I am connected. With the new pastor, the opportunity has come."

The Brigade was not confined to young men. From the first the idea of a Young Women's Brigade of Service was in the founder's mind ; the dangers of an emotional and pietistic form of Christianity were even more real for them than for the men. In 1906 the companion branch of the Brigade came into existence through the help of Mrs. Price Hughes and friends in connection with the West London Mission.

Scotland took up the idea. The first Brigade was formed at Galashiels in connection with the Church of the Rev. George Wyllie Howie, M.A., which became the headquarters of the movement in Scotland.

" One effect," wrote Mr. Howie, " for which our office-bearers are particularly grateful, is that we never lack for workers within the Church, and we find our young people ready for the most menial duty. New forms of service are constantly cropping up. One young man has found out a widow who keeps a small shop in the town and has a hard struggle of it ; he has taken charge of her accounts, and goes every week to see to them."

There were two extensions which Paton set himself specially to achieve. He felt that the Christian Endeavour movement would never realise its potentialities until it yoked itself to definite service, and acted the Christian life as well as talked about it. On Thursday, February 6th, 1908, he went down to address the Council meeting at

Portsmouth, and at their request reduced to writing the substance of what he said :

' You will remember I stated, what I am sure all of you approved, that the Christian life is eminently a life of service—unselfish, helpful, redemptive service to others. It is a life of fellowship with Christ, and of obedience to Him, following Him in His life and ministry in the world. If this be the Christian life, as I think we are all agreed, then it is our duty, and must be our supreme care, in dealing with the young, to train them in and for that life. I then said that there have been published in recent years very important studies on adolescent life. In the adolescent age great changes pass over the child-nature, and new powers awake which are necessary for the adult life, but which need in special ways to be trained for that life. Of the features of the adolescent life, two were specially to be observed, namely, the development of the emotional life, which is then fuller and more easily stimulated, and the increase of active powers, not only in the body but in the mind. Now, in the training of these powers in developing adolescent life, there is one law of paramount importance. The emotions are in themselves a source of pleasure, but they also incite to action and become a motive power. There is, however, a moral law according to which they alone can be healthily cultivated. Bishop Butler has enunciated this law. If emotions as passive impressions are freely indulged, they become gradually weaker and ebb away : or they may be continually stimulated ; but in that case they always need a stronger stimulus, and this terrible result follows— that they become inoperant, and lose their power to incite to appropriate action. On the other hand, if these emotions, according to their healthful law, lead to action, the acts which they induce are more readily done by repetition. They then form habits, and habits form character, and character forms destiny. Now this great law, which applies to the training of our youth in the adolescent age, bears specially and with profound significance upon the Christian life. Emotions awakened in the Christian life are full of delight and blessing, but if they are indulged selfishly, without leading, as they are intended, to healthful and appropriate action, they will either ebb away, as has been seen so sadly in the great Welsh Revival, or they may be repeatedly stimulated until they become morbid and inoperant, having no effect upon conduct and character. Our Lord gave to His disciples the rapture of the Mount of Transfiguration, but only for a short time. They had soon to follow Him to the bottom of the Mount, when the poor epileptic child sought for healing, and thence to follow Him, bearing their cross— in training for service.

" I ventured then to plead with you that, whilst the weekly devotional meeting of the Christian Endeavour Societies should be diligently observed, and thus the healthful emotion awakened in devotion should give joy and blessing to the young who gather in these meetings, we must sedulously guard against the peril attending even such meetings. For there is a peril lest religious emotions be indulged in a selfish manner for the mere delight of them, and that they be not directed and used, as they must be if they are to continue healthful, so as to incite to action—to lead to definite and faithful service, in order that the will of our Lord be actually done in respect to others as well as in respect to ourselves. If, as I said, the Christian life is pre-eminently a life of service, it is necessary that there be wise and constant training for it during the adolescent years ; and so I pleaded that every member of the C.E. Societies should be called to some form of unselfish and helpful service, regularly and continually, and that this active service should be conducted in such a way as to train and prepare them to regular and faithful Christian service throughout life.

" I then spoke of the Young Men's and the Young Women's Brigade of Service which we have formed, in which there are three principles :

" 1. That each one entering it shall at least undertake one hour a week of service to others ; but in many cases, if they undertake one hour they will gladly give a second.

" 2. That this service is to be of a kind that they are fitted for, for which they have liking, opportunity, and gift. We cannot force any service that is to be done for Christ. Young men and women can only give that with which our Lord has endowed and qualified them to give. For this reason, therefore, all kinds of helpful service should be available to them. And let us remember that,

as our blessed Lord Himself has taught us, love to our
fellow-men can be shown as much by giving a cup of cold
water, and helping others in simple, kindly ways as by
giving a scriptural lesson or taking part in a religious
service.

" 3. That the service must be such as will be super-
vised, and shall thus be made a real training in Practical
Service, and under proper regulation and control. For
this purpose it is proposed, as you will see in the enclosed
card, that those who engage in any service shall be
formed into small companies of twelve or a few more,
each company having a head officer and assistants, so
that they shall be knit together and give bond to one another for the doing of their work. If for any reason one
member fails in his weekly service, then one of the officers
in charge will see that the duty is done. There can be no
real training if any service be undertaken in a casual and
amateurish manner.

" Now, then, to apply all that I have ventured thus to
urge—and I urge it with much humility, but also with
great earnestness, because I know that what I say is not
only true but is of vital moment in the training of the
Christian life—I plead with you to consider whether each
C.E. Society might not become a Committee of Social
Service, every member of the Society being desired—and
I would say required—to give one hour a week of unselfish
service to others ; that this Committee of Social Service,
which would consist of every member of the C.E. Society, should provide the kind of service that is most
suitable and acceptable to each member, and organise
them in small groups or corps, under appropriate leadership, so that the work shall be done systematically and
under due supervision. The members of each Society
might unite in these groups or corps, according to the
work in which they engage, or the locality in which they
live. Further, being engaged in such varied service,
the members will find most real and immediate objects of
prayer in their devotional meetings—prayer for those
they serve, and for themselves, that they may be divinely
helped in their service.

" On the enclosed card I have indicated four divisions of
service ; but these are only typical—anything done in the
name of Christ, in service to others, and done regularly

and faithfully, will give the training desired. Each Society thus organised would become practically a company of the Young Men's and Young Women's Brigade of Service, and would, if desired, receive its cards and other literature, and lead the whole movement in this and other countries.

"And now I commend to you a suggestion that has been made to me. You have, I know, associate members, but I believe they are comparatively few. There are many young people who cannot as yet take the pledge which you rightly desire of your active members ; but the Spirit of Christ has touched them, and they desire to do some helpful thing for others. Will you not encourage and invite numbers of young men and young women to come as associates, and join you in the service which you are undertaking for others ? I believe you would thus multiply your numbers very greatly and possibly double your membership in a short time. You would also thus lead your associate members to know more of Christ, and more certainly to decide for Him, than by anything else you can do for them.

"In conclusion, let me say, as I said at the meeting, there are two reasons why I plead my cause with you. They are :

"1. There is such a need for service. I send you two pamphlets—The Appeal issued by the Sunday-school Union, and a pamphlet on the Sunday and Week Evening Institute. I send you also Mr. Spurr's two leaflets. There you see the need. The young people of England, under the new social and industrial conditions of our crowded towns and cities, are swiftly sinking down into perilous ways which lead to death. Oh ! let young Christians rejoice in the brave word 'endeavour' (for 'endeavour' means 'doing '), and form a Brigade of Service to help and save the youth of our land. I am told that there are 500,000 Christian Endeavourers in your Societies. There are five millions and more of the youth of England, for whom I plead ; let your members unite in a *mighty and holy endeavour* to safeguard them and win them to a better life.

"2. It is in training our young Christian people, and those who will associate with them, in and for faithful service, that we shall uplift and invigorate our Churches, by filling them with men and women who are trained and prepared for active service, and who are thus ready for all the redemptive ministries of the Christian Church —to which they are urgently summoned in our time."

The revival in Wales in 1905 he followed with the eager interest of one who is always waiting for the coming of his Lord. He was very anxious to secure in some permanent fashion the results of that wonderful outpouring of the Spirit, and to prevent any backwash from setting in as time went on. How was this to be done better than by brigading the young converts for active service ? He wrote many letters to friends and old students in Wales with a view to establishing institutes for senior scholars and safeguarding the leisure hours of the young folk during which the devil plies all his baits to seduce and corrupt. When the devil was so active, it would not do for the Church to be idle. In pursuance of the same object, he paid two visits to Wales himself, to which the following letters refer :

"April 17th, 1906.

" I cannot but hope," he writes to Mr. Liscombe, " that our meeting on Good Friday will bear very abounding fruit. It seems to me as if an opportunity were given to Wales now to realise the kingdom of God in that beautiful country such as perhaps has never been given to any Church in any country of the world before. The great religious movement ought to raise the level of life in all relationships, so that it shall be seen that the righteousness of God, and the peace that comes with it, fills the heart and rules the conduct of all men."

In the autumn of 1906 he paid a visit to Aberystwyth, where he met with a most cordial reception from Principal Roberts, Mrs. Tom Ellis, the late Mr. T. H. Darlington, H.M.I., and others. He spoke much, both in private and in public, about the different ways in which the Church might safeguard the life of its youth, the brigades for boys and girls, the League of Honour, the Home-reading Circles, and their adaptation to the Sunday-school ; and when people asked, " How are we to get all these undertakings properly manned ? " he pointed to the Brigade of Service and said :

" If the fine religious feeling that has been awakened in Wales is to be made vital and helpful to life, it must lead to definite and unselfish service to others. Here are the obvious things to be done. Here are the obvious people to do them, your young converts. Set them to work; in service they will know more of Christ and will be drawn closer to Him.

" I recall Plato's great word, that virtue is not a thing to be taught, but to be practised, and hence I feel that every young convert shall be given something to do for Christ that will fulfil the desire that has been awakened in his own heart, and that will train and discipline him in the service of Christ.

" One fears sometimes that Christ's service may be narrowed, as Ruskin said, into thinking of worship and religious concerns as the only ways in which we can honour our Father and His Christ, whereas it is through these that we can obtain the guidance and strength needful to accomplish the unselfish and redeeming service in the world to which they call us.

" May the love of Christ be seen in Wales, in all His Churches, spending itself in blessed sympathy and service and sacrifice by those who have His spirit and follow Him.

" Then, in truth, they will find, in Rutherford's beautiful words, that, whilst they bear the cross, lo ! it uplifts and bears them. It becomes no more a burden to them than are wings to a bird or sails to a boat.

" One final word. If there be no other service open to the young convert, no service appointed to him by the Church, let me plead with him or her at once to think of some lonely one, near at hand, some one afflicted and in need, and try to show the love of Christ to that one. Verily, I promise that he will find Christ Himself and be blessed of His Father, as these words thrill again in his spirit, ' Ye have done it unto Me.' "

To the Rev. R. J. Campbell

"*Sept. 27th,* 1904.

" Both Brigades must be natural, knowing and allowing no division on account of creed or religious association —uniting all who in the spirit of Christ are willing to serve those who are in need, and so aiding all Churches and beneficent societies in their various redemptive ministries. And therefore I was grateful for your suggestion that you should ask the Bishop of London to co-operate with you in the formation and conduct of both Brigades. We all know his intense sympathy with young men and women, and what he has already done for them. If he were willing thus to be associated with you, the truly *national* character of the work would be at once emphasised and declared, and these Brigades would be strong and effective agencies of nurturing a national and practical religious life, and of manifesting the unity of all who love and serve our one Redeeming Lord.

" Would it be possible for you and him to be associated in the presidency of the Brigades ? There might be two headquarters—one, say, in the Jerusalem Chamber or another chamber at Westminster Abbey, or at the Chapter House of St. Paul's, and the other at the City Temple—or, so long as the combination and union of the two great divisions of English Christianity was made clear and certain by the constitution of the Presidency and Council of the Brigades, there might be only one headquarters, either at Westminster or St. Paul's. The Dean, at the former, or the Archdeacon at the latter, might then be associated with you both along with another Nonconformist. At any rate, you will kindly impress upon the Bishop our great desire that he should co-operate with you in this most needful, hopeful movement, and that we should rejoice if he put himself at the head of it in ways that will be honourable to him in his high position and also honourable to our Christian Nonconformity.

" I have spoken to Archdeacon Sinclair on the matter, and you may probably have seen the Bishop of London. I gather from what the Archbishop tells me that it would not probably be very successful to attempt to unite Church and Nonconformity under the one leadership, and, therefore, I think it may be better to make the following suggestions—That the Young Men's Brigade of Service, National and Christian, shall have three divisions, according as it is associated with :

1. The Established Church,
2. The Free Churches of England,
3. The Roman Catholic Church.

There might be a presiding officer of each division and a council of each division, and the officers and councils of the three divisions might meet very occasionally, say, on some annual occasion, to let it be seen that, though they are divided in the fields of service, they are members of one Brigade of Service, all of them having one Christian principle and motive. This would give a certain unity to the movement, and would do what one longs to do, to represent, in every way we can, a union of the Christian forces of the country, and of all Christian Churches.

"We had agreed, I think, that each corps might be associated with a Church, or P.S.A., or a C.E. Society, or a Guild, or the Sunday Institute (*i.e.* the Senior Division of the Sunday-school), or other religious associations, and that each corps, if it were large enough, might be divided into sections, territorially according to the residence of its members, or according to the service that was being rendered by them. I was pleased to see the suggestion made by one of your friends that a corps might make itself responsible for a definite piece of work, or, in a similar way, a section of a corps might make itself responsible for an entire bit of work—not one member, but the members of that section, uniting, and taking the responsibility of the work. I had even in my mind the thought that a corps, or a section of corps, might take one particular street or alley in a slum district, and seek to bring various kinds of influences to bear upon it, sanitary and social and educational; so that a corps or section of a corps might find really a true mission-field, as dark as any in Africa or Asia, in which to labour at home, and to labour in it by means of social as well as distinctly religious service. Dr. George Newman, who had a mission in Drury Lane connected with the Friends, when he was head of the Friends' Settlement in Queen's Square, did an admirable bit of work of this kind, which might be repeated endlessly in our towns and cities."

To the Rev. R. J. Campbell

"You know, even better than I, that the young men are to be attracted, not by providing them with lounges and pleasant evenings of selfish enjoyment in comfortable rooms (although that is right, and even necessary in a way) but by invoking them to do something noble, and even it may be heroic : something that they can do with delight to themselves, whilst they are giving discipline and delight to others, and enjoying comradeship with them."

To the Rev. Dr. Watson

"Sept. 8th, 1909.

" I am profoundly impressed with two things : First, that it is only through young people a little older than the boys and girls whom we want to train that we shall be able to interest and protect and train them during those critical and important years from thirteen to seventeen. Second, that we have hitherto been going on a wrong track with regard to our young men and women, inasmuch as we have catered for them in numerous ways ; but we have failed, I think, to train them *in* service and *for* service. I think this failure has led to a certain deterioration in the character of our young men and women, making them perhaps think of their own interests selfishly, instead of the greater interests of the world, and of those whom they can help ; also we have in this way injured and weakened our Churches because our young men and women have not been trained for *service* which must be esteemed the very essential element of that Christian life which the Church has to nourish and develop and exercise."

To Dr. Scott Lidgett

"July 4th, 1910.

" Ask only an hour a week, and offer them something to do which they would like to do. In this way we shall give them another ideal of life from that which they get by mere recreation and pleasant social leisure in comfortable rooms. I think that it is a very vital matter.

" In regard to the Young Men's and Young Women's Brigade of Service, my idea has been that it should never become a separate organisation, but that the Committee that represents it, and the headquarters in which the literature is kept, should have as their object to encourage and form young men and women, wherever they are found, in groups for definite special service of various kinds.

28

Thus I would have Christian Endeavourers organised in service in the only way in which service can be rendered faithfully and regularly. Individual, casual, desultory service means little or nothing in the way of training, but grouping them in corps, under good leadership which they form for definite objects, you get what I desire. . . . Also I believe that elder scholars and young people such as those you will gather in your Young People's Institutes, can never be fitly trained for service unless they are thus formed into special groups under supervision and leadership for service of various kinds.

"I also desire the members of the Cadet Corps of the Boys' Life Brigade to be trained for service on the principles of the Brigade of Service. Also the elder boys and girls in Clubs and in the senior Bands of Hope. I hope that there will be, during the next fortnight, a special appeal made to young men and women in our Institutional Churches and to the young people in our great wholesale and retail establishments, to organise themselves for service and to give an hour a week for service. There is a great opportunity in the wonderful offer that is made by the L.C.C. in two directions, namely, with regard to their play-grounds, and also their school buildings.

"Lastly, I have carefully thought over what you have said about the word 'Brigade.' It commended itself to me, and I must say it still commends itself most strongly, because the word 'brigade' means a company—small or great—of those who unite in a close bond for some definite work in which they will uphold and assist one another. The essential meaning of the word is union for action. The Fire Brigade is an example, and it pledges those who enter it to steadfast co-operation in the work undertaken. Now that is the very idea that is in my mind, and which I must seek to impress upon those who desire service, and who desire our young men and women to be trained for service. The word 'League,' on the contrary, has a wider meaning. It associates people who have simply common ideas and interests, but who have no special service in which they are mutually pledged to one another. Thus we have International Leagues of various kinds ; also Leagues of Peace, Leagues of Mercy, etc., etc. Sometimes, of course, the word 'League' associates people in a common enterprise, like the Anti-Corn Law League, but then it was a large national movement and involved no personal service. The word ' Brigade ' exactly embodies my thought, and it seems to me to be a thought that is most vital and necessary. If we are ever to have young men and women trained for really effective service, they must understand the conditions and responsibilities of such service that is to be undertaken. We have had enough, and more than enough, of casual idle sentiment, and occasional desultory service which does not give effective training."

To Mrs. Price Hughes

" Christianity is the true social service. In this way our young people can make splendid personal experiments in the varied application of the law of Christ to social conditions. Every Christian is pledged, by his own redemption, to be a fellow-worker with Christ and his brethren in the holy work of rescuing his fellow-men and society from every form of evil."

CHAPTER XXIV

THE NEW GOSPEL IN SCOTLAND

" Lengthen thy cords and strengthen thy stakes."—*Isaiah* xiv. 2.

THE land of his birth became increasingly dear to Paton in his later years. Formerly his holiday thoughts had always turned to the South; for several years past, ever since his visit to Newtonmore in 1891, it was to Scotland that he looked for rest and recuperation. When his brother, the late Mr. A. B. Paton, of Liverpool, bought the estate of Hareshawmuir, on the moors above Kilmarnock, no summer holiday was complete without a long visit to Hareshaw. There he had the moorland air, which did him more good than any other; he was seven miles from the nearest railway-station, and he had the constant companionship of friends and relatives who came on the same health-seeking errand as himself to that hospitable home. Within half a mile was Meadowhead, the farm of his great covenanting ancestor, and far away at Lochgoin, on the sky-line of the moors, stood the obelisk which commemorated the sufferings and the triumphs of the men who made Scotland great. Away to the west, as the sun went down, the blue, misty peaks of Arran stood sentinel over an enchanted land. It was a place of peace—

> Where essential silence cheers and blesses,
> And for ever in the hill recesses
> Her more lovely music broods and dies.

Quite close were the homely folk of Newmilns and Galston and Darvel, with memories of lang syne, the moor of Eaglesham to which he had taken his youthful Rechabites on the summer outing, the parish church of Fenwick with its monument to the brave Captain, and all the countryside in which his boyish life struck root before the flaxen locks had turned to raven black. He was never tired of

436

Hareshaw.   Long days he would lie out in the open, communing with his Heavenly Father, drinking in the beauty of the scene and the freshness of the air, always at home with God, and always finding some new thing to enjoy. " I never saw such cloudscapes in my life as I do here," he said, the last time he was there.

But the still sad music of humanity was always with him.   Up on the moors all was beauty, all was harmony. But twenty miles away was the sorrow " barricado'ed evermore " in Glasgow slums, and his heart was filled with longing that the Church of Scotland should be up and doing, awake to the sense of the social sin that was perpetrated daily in her midst, and should buckle on her armour in her Lord's name and in His power for a glorious campaign of social redemption.

" During the whole of my life as a minister I have been impressed with the one idea that the great doctrine of redeeming love, which is the central doctrine of our faith, needs to be manifested and realised in other ways and larger senses than we have hitherto conceived and desired. The redeeming of humanity is not only the conversion of individual souls, and the training of individual lives, but it is also the forming of new and healthy conditions of life for men, and the inspiring of all human law and custom with a regulative and definite Christian idea and spirit."

So far Scotland had no Association corresponding to the Christian Social Union of England to gather up and focus the opinion of the Churches on Social Questions, and give to the efforts of each the wisdom and the power of all.

One day in the summer of 1900, Dr. James Paton, of St. Paul's, Glasgow, the brother and biographer of the famous missionary, was playing a round over the golf-course at Milngarvie, with Dr. David Watson, of St. Clement's in the same city.   Dr. James Paton happened to speak of his namesake of Nottingham, of his manifold social endeavours, and his great desire that there should be in Scotland a Union for social service like that in England. He found a ready response in Dr. Watson, and wrote to Nottingham an account of the conversation and the interest Dr. Watson had shown.   The result was a letter from Nottingham to Dr. Watson urging him to take up the matter, and the letter was followed by a visit.

" For an hour," says Dr. Watson, " he talked in the most fascinating way about the larger Gospel, the social mission of the Church, and the need for union in social redemptive work. I felt myself in the presence of an apostle. He was, without doubt, the most magnetic personality, the most inspirational force it was ever my lot to meet. Simply to be in his presence, to behold his grand head and beautiful mobile face and flashing eye, to hear his matchless voice, now pleading tremulously for the weak and wretched, now vibrating with divine passion at some wrong or injustice, now pouring forth stores of knowledge and gathered experience on social problems, or expounding with fine persuasiveness the principles of all social redemptive work—was an education in itself. That hour spent in my study proved one of the most momentous and fruitful in my whole life. From it sprang the Scottish Christian Social Union and nearly all the social work which I have been privileged to do."

A letter from Dr. Watson published in " Saint Andrew," February 14th, 1901, mooted the project. The response was immediate. Letters poured in supporting the proposal from leading ministers in all the Churches : Dr. George Matheson, Dr. George Reith, Dr. Alexander Whyte, Dr. McAdam Muir, Dr. Marshall Lang, Dr. Thomas Martin, Professor George Adam Smith, Professor James Orr, Professor Charteris, Professor Henry Jones, Rev. Andrew Miller, and Rev. C. Rolland Ramsay. It was clear that the Presbyterian leaders of every hue were not only alive to their social mission, but prepared to take united and effective action for putting into practice a programme of social Christianity. Things moved on rapidly, already by April 4th a constitution had been drafted, and the Union formally launched with Dr. David Watson as Chairman of Executive and the Rev. C. Rolland Ramsay, M.A., as Honorary Secretary. The basis of membership was wide enough to include all Christian Churches. It was, in fact, the basis of the Inner Mission.

Paton was unable to attend the inaugural meeting, but he sent a letter which struck the keynote and outlined the programme of campaign.

" Let my Scottish brethren," he says, " bring out into full light the guiding and inspiring influence of the two cardinal doctrines of our faith as applied to the social ministry and mission of the Church. I mean the doctrines of the Incarnation and of Redemption. What is involved in the doctrine of the Incarnation in regard to human relationships and the needs of human society has been most wisely and powerfully set forth by many members of the Christian Social Union of the Church of England. But it seems to me the great doctrine of Redemption needs also to be specially emphasised, and all that it involves brought home to the conscience of the Church. For is it not in that doctrine that we see holy love by labour and by sacrifice revealing and accomplishing the Father's will, and establishing the Father's righteousness in the world— a righteousness which brings men into right relations with one another and with God, and fulfils both the spirit and the duties of these relations ? Is not this love manifest in Christ, the burning heart of our Gospel and the glory which crowns our Divine Lord, making Him the peerless ideal and the inspiration of all Christian life ? And it is such love which redeems us and others from all evil, that is poured from the heart of Christ upon all His followers, so that they long to share something of His redeeming service and joy, and so to share with Him, however humbly, in the work the Father gave Him to do.

" It is in dealing with the sorrows and evils of the world that this redeeming spirit of love finds its opportunities of exercise, and it is in dealing with them that we learn also how the redemption of humanity, which is our Lord's business, and in which He calls us to serve Him, means not only the winning of individual men and women to the obedience and fellowship of Christ, but surrounding them with influences and forming an environment by which their lives may be healthily and nobly developed. The thought of our age has shown us how no individual can live by himself or for himself, and that human society must be charged with influences which will sustain and quicken the individual."

Then the letter goes on to outline specific lines of action which might be taken in hand at once by the Union.

Although so far away, the Scottish Christian Social Union was very near to his soul and to his prayers. He paid frequent visits to headquarters.

" If he ever found us flagging and discouraged (and he did more than once)," says Dr. Watson, " he always left us refreshed and charged with newborn zeal. The teeming brain was always suggesting to us new schemes of work, new forms of service."

It is heartsome to recall that the first paper published by the Union was on " Child-life in Cities," by Dr. David Watson, and most of the reforms advocated in that manifesto were embodied in the Children's Charter and are now part of the law of the land. Other subjects were taken up and prayerfully studied with a view to ascertaining the mind of the Master and formulating a plan of action—Sunday labour, Social Centres, the registration and inspection of working men's clubs. The work spread to Edinburgh, which took in hand the erection of a lodging-house for working lads, to Greenock, Helensburgh, Dunfermline, Clyde Bank, Rothesay, Craigmore and Aberdeen.

It was not long before Paton found practical work for the enthusiasm of the Union to take in hand. It was not his way to forge a tool and then leave it unused.

The fine Guest-house of the Co-operative Holidays Association was standing amidst its fair pleasaunce on the shores of the Gareloch. For the greater part of the year it was practically unused. Why, he asked himself, should not this building, with its first-rate accommodation, be turned to account for practical purposes ? His nature abhorred a vacuum. Accordingly, in the spring of 1906, a Holiday School of Social Study was held at Ardenconnel. He took the service on the Sunday afternoon, and spoke that same evening on " The Church and Social Problems."

In the following year he was busy preparing to open at Ardenconnel a school for farmers' sons, similar to the People's High Schools of Denmark. For his knowledge of these Danish High Schools, and the effect they have produced on the Danish national life and agricultural productivity, he was indebted, as all English-speaking people are, to the writing of Mr. J. S. Thornton.[1] The experience of these schools was, he saw, full of inspiration and hope for the revival of our decaying country-side. It

[1] See especially "Recent Educational Progress in Denmark," vol. i. of Special Reports, 1897. Also in Dr. M. E. Sadler's "Continuation Schools in England and Elsewhere," chap. xvii.

showed that such revival would not be accomplished by any mere technical instruction, however efficient and elaborate ; it must appeal to the heart, it must stir the patriotic feeling, it must enrich the mind and imagination with noble ideas. The Danish High Schools are almost wholly humanistic in their education. By history, literature, and song, by simple fellowship of life, pervaded by religion, they have, to use Bishop Grundtvig's phrase, " opened a well of healing in the land," and, by raising the character of the people, have raised the whole standard of life and work. The young men and women trained in the schools are live-minded, quick to grasp and carry out new ideas, efficient, ready to co-operate, honourable.

With the help of Mr. Rolland Ramsay, Secretary of the Scottish Christian Social Union, and Mr. R. Patrick Wright, Principal of the West of Scotland Agricultural College, arrangements were made for an experimental school on the Danish lines which was formally opened in the month of November 1907 by the Secretary for Scotland, the Right Hon. Mr. John Sinclair. The experiment was limited to young men in the first instance, and the course extended over four weeks. The teachers gave their help gratuitously. It was a new thing in Scotland to have all the students resident under the same roof, sharing the common meals and social life, and perhaps one of the happiest and most valued features of the education received was that wearing down of angularities, that breaking down of prejudices and broadening of ideas which come through the sharing of a common life. For the promotion of the spirit which makes co-operation possible, nothing could have been better.

Other practical work was taken in hand by the Union : social institutes for men, clubs for lads and girls, guilds of play for children, were started under Paton's guidance, and a commission was sent out to visit Elberfeld and report on the working of the poor-relief system in that city.

In 1908 he felt that the time was ripe for a big forward movement, and he put his hand on Mr. William Temple, M.A., Fellow of Queen's College, Oxford, whose recent speech at the Albert Hall had fired the hearts of the Pan-Anglican Congress and given the world assurance of a man commissioned by his Master for this very purpose. He bade Mr. Temple carry the fiery cross from town to town in Scotland. Mr. Temple generously gave his services and Paton gave generously towards the expenses of the campaign, full notice of which was sent out with papers announcing the meetings to every minister in Scotland.

" The widespread awakening of thought and activity in our Churches with regard to the social life of the people is a conspicuous and significant feature of our age. It has arisen from two facts which face and challenge one another.

" (a) The working people of our country, enlightened by education and possessed of political power, are calling out for better social conditions, and in some places are deserting the Church, whilst they reproach her for her indifference to their well-being.

" (b) On the other hand, the Church everywhere is beginning to apprehend her true social mission and to understand more fully the Gospel, which Christ preached and commanded her to preach, of the Kingdom of Heaven to be established upon earth, which is to bring righteousness and peace and joy in the Holy Ghost to men here and now. It is seen that the Church cannot exist merely to maintain and edify herself. She exists to fulfil, by the Gospel she preaches and by her great and gracious activities, the object for which she was founded, and for which she is continually upheld and inspired by the living Spirit of her Lord. This object is the same as that for which Christ came into this world, and which He proclaims in His Gospel of the Kingdom, namely, that the whole of our humanity be redeemed, and that the kingdoms of this world may become in truth the kingdom of God.

" Amidst the tumult of social controversy there are two phenomena that certainly give stimulus and encouragement to the Christian Church, as she now uprises with fresh and faithful devotion, to fulfil her divine mission. They show what is not only the world's need, but the world's longing for the Evangel which she alone bears to men, and which alone can satisfy the human heart and reform human society.

" 1. The wisest Socialist leaders of our time discern that
the problem of poverty cannot be solved by the mere distribution of wealth, that there can be no industrial peace
among men until there has been breathed into the heart of
men the spirit of brotherhood, and of mutual trust and
sympathy. The Socialist's dream can be fulfilled only
when men have formed a true ideal of life, and are prepared with one accord to help one another in fulfilling
that ideal. Accordingly, one of the ablest Socialist writers
of our time, in his last book, says : ' I recognise quite
clearly that with people just as they are, with their prejudices, ignorances, misapprehensions, their unchecked
vanities, and greeds, and jealousies, their crude and mis-
construed instincts, their irrational traditions, no socialist
state can exist,—no better state can exist than the one
we have now, with all its squalor and cruelty. Unless
you can change men's minds, you cannot effect socialism.'
In other words, he proclaims the Christian faith : let
men seek the love, and obey the law, of the righteous
God—their Father in Heaven, and let them serve one another as brethren, then His kingdom will have come
upon earth.

" 2. On the other hand, at the very time that Christian
men and women have been deploring the fact that the
great industrial classes of our country seemed to be falling
away from the Christian Church, a new and wonderful
thing has come to pass. Spontaneously in every part of
the country, thousands of the working men and women
of our country are found gathering themselves together
on a Sunday afternoon, seeking after the Christ of God,
and listening to the glorious Gospel of grace which He,
and He alone, proclaims to a sinful and sorrowing world.
Already there are more than half a million of working
men thus gathered into these brotherhoods, as they call
themselves, on the Sunday afternoon. And on the
Sunday morning, other 200,000 are meeting in Adult
Sunday Schools for worship and the study of God's Word.
In both these great communions it is Christ's own Gospel
in which they rejoice, the Gospel which sets forth the
grace and truth of God, which inspires with divine love
and righteousness all human life, both in individuals,
amid their varied relationships, and in the institutions of
human society."

The campaign was a great success. Mr. Temple's addresses made a deep and lasting impression, and the work of the Union has grown in compass, in power, and in that wisdom which comes to those who do the will. It has enlightened and focussed public opinion. It has made the social mission of the Church a conscious aim of Scottish Christian Churches. It has promoted many social reforms, notably in connection with child-life, such as the provision of open spaces, probation for first offenders, juvenile courts, and the restriction of child-labour. Best of all, it has furnished a common platform on which ministers and Christian workers of all denominations can realise their oneness in the Lord by becoming fellow-workers with Him in the fulfilment of redemptive love.

" . . . How delighted I am," Paton writes to Dr. Watson, " to think now of that first happy conference in your own home, and to think of this great flowing stream of blessing which took rise in your study that day."

To Dr. Watson

"*Dec.* 18*th*, 1907.

" . . . Of all of them, I think the one that most profoundly interests me is the one on Continuation Schools from a Higher Point of View. I see more and more clearly that, if we do not take far more care of our young people in connection with our Churches and Sunday-schools, we are losing the very foundation of all further progress. If our young people are lost to us, everything is lost for our country, and our Churches.

" . . . Above all, may I earnestly entreat you, in what you say, to awaken and deepen the purpose and passion of redemptive service on the part of Christian Churches and Christian men and women. It is the spirit of Christ which we seem so wholly to have misunderstood by thinking of individual salvation in a wrong sense—as though it meant our personal safety, instead of its being that we are to live in the Spirit of Christ, which is wholly unselfish and seeks only to have the will of God fulfilled in the world, in every relationship of life, both personal and social, civic and national.

" . . . It is only as we get our young men and women from eighteen to twenty-four, that we can do these two things, namely—guard, guide, and train our boys and girls from thirteen to seventeen (they will be led and helped by young men and women who are just a little older than themselves as by no others), and have an active, living membership in our Church prepared for service. Do, I pray you, plead for this as the very first necessity in our Churches."

To Dr. Watson

"*June 23rd*, 1908.

" It seems laid upon my heart to bring before every minister in Scotland a sense of the solemn responsibilities of the Church in dealing with the evils and sorrows of the world so as to bring the redeeming and healing grace of our Lord into the darkened and burdened lives of men."

To Dr. Watson

"*August*, 1908.

" I know that a letter and papers sent to all ministers will cost something, but how little in comparison with other expenditure and in comparison with the possible results, if we can awaken our Scottish Churches to a more clear and definite conception of the very meaning of the Church and of her redemptive mission. To do that will make any little sacrifice of money one of the highest joys of life, and it can be done, if we now realise and proclaim with the solemn powers of a deep conviction the truths you so ably set forth in your first letters in " St. Andrew." It does me good to read them.

" It must have surprised and delighted you to see how these first enthusiastic meetings of the Pan-Anglican Congress rang with the glorious testimony of the Church's social redemptive mission.

" I am not a Socialist. In fact, I oppose, and in a sense dread it. But it will spread and overcome, unless we show the nobler, truer faith of Christ's Gospel and of the Lord's Prayer, that the kingdom of God, *i.e.* the kingdom of righteousness, of love, of harmony, of brotherhood, will come into the world, and that it is the mission of the Church, as it is her prayer, to establish it in the world."

To Dr. Watson

"*November 5th*, 1909.

". . . There is no one I know who seems to me to have so fully understood the inmost spirit and objective aims of my life as yourself."

To Dr. Watson

"*Sept. 27th*, 1910.

". . . I lie on my couch very weak, being only able to walk totteringly from one room to another with a little support; but when I rest quietly, my mind is clear and active, and I am able to do a little by correspondence to support causes that are so dear to me. For my heart is much in Scotland, and I delight to think that you and Mr. Rolland Ramsay so earnestly and ably uphold the standard of the true Christian faith and the true church life."

CHAPTER XXV

MINISTERIAL JUBILEE

"Honour, reverence, and the good repute
That follow faithful service as its fruit
Be unto him whom living we salute."

THE first week of October 1905 my father spoke of as his
"martyrdom." From all over the country, and even
beyond its borders, old students and friends assembled to
celebrate "College Week" at Nottingham. A special
interest attached to college week in October 1905, because
it marked not only the thirty-eighth anniversary of the
Institute, but the fiftieth anniversary of its founder's work
as minister of Christ. Castlegate Church was crowded
with friends from far and near who had assembled to do
honour to one they had loved as friend, as leader, and
father in God. Principal Ritchie was in the chair. The
Rev. W. S. Houghton was the spokesman of the old
students, who presented an address charged to the full
with expressions of thanksgiving for the faithful and
fruitful many-sided service of the past, and of prayerfulness
for the future.

"We rejoice to think," he said, "that the fire has not
abated within you, that your enthusiasm still glows.
We thank you for your open-mindedness, for your friendliness to new schemes, for your encouragement to all earnest
workers, and for your benediction upon the work of young
men."

The late Rev. J. Brierley, better known as "J.B." of the
"Christian World," coupled the name of his friend and
teacher with that of another famous citizen of Nottingham,
General Booth.

"These two," he said, "are the youngest men in the

country. It is these youngsters of between seventy and eighty who are setting the pace to-day, and they are the most magnificent of all possible advocates for the virtues of the Christian Gospel."

The whole assembly rose to its feet when the address was presented.

" It is with a bowed, and almost breaking heart, and with faltering lip," he said in reply, " that I rise to receive, on behalf of my dear wife and myself, this address freighted so richly with affection and incensed with the odour of many prayers. Indeed the apples of gold have been brought to us in the baskets of silver. Who am I, to be dowered with such marvellous grace ? Ah ! as I look back on these fifty years, a moan of reproach breaks from my heart, in memory of the weakness, failure, and sin which blur the brightness of those years. I need and seek forgiveness from many of you who knew my failures, but have forgotten and buried them in the charity of your unfailing love. And yet, if there be truth in the words I have heard, if I have given the inspiration of faith to any man, if from the dark background of the Cross I have let the love of the Father shine upon any of His weary and wandering children on earth, if I have made the peerless ideals of Christ and His sacrifice to shine before men, if I have gathered Christian friends of many communions into closer fellowship of service, then may I not in humble ways rejoice with you, and join in the song and sacrifice of thanksgiving to my God, who has helped me so aboundingly with His grace ? "

He spoke of the Institute as " the central column " of all his work. What had sustained and constrained him through it all was his sense of the solemn responsibility that centred in the work of the ministry under the new conditions of industrial urbanised life. The Church, the Catholic Church, as he conceived it, was the burden of his speech. By magnifying the Church, both ministers and people would magnify the Lord and His energising power for the redemption of the world.

The week was taken up with conference and discussion. The Rev. R. J. Campbell preached in Castlegate. The central event was a paper by Paton on the Inner Mission of the Church. The subject which he had taken more than forty years before was the subject of his last address to " his men." It was the Inner Mission at which he had been working all his life, and more and more as he worked he had come to see its meaning and its potency for the healing of life. The Inner Mission was, in fact, " applied Christianity," and his paper which was published under that title, first of all asked—What, in the essence of it, is Christianity ? What are the chief facts and problems of our social life to-day which call for the Gospel of Christ ? What are the various ministries through which Christ's followers in His Church and His Omnipotent love, must solve these problems ?

" This is the mission of the Church in the world where God's laws have been ruthlessly ignored, defied, and broken by men, and where the endless miseries which afflict humanity have come, the sharp and dreadful penalty of their sin—to magnify these laws again, and make them honourable, to reveal, apply and incarnate them in human life, as can only be done by Christ's own Spirit in His Church ; and then, finally, by bearing all these sad and manifold evils of men, gradually to assuage and destroy them. In a world gangrened with the festering sores of human sin, nothing but the omnipotent power of a love in the Church of Christ can bring the healing that it needs, can reach and staunch the deep wounds of our social malady, and awaken the new powers of a healthful social life. Such love alone will win men to learn and do the will of God ;—and His kingdom comes only as His will is done.

" The Inner Mission of the Church roots itself, believe me, in the evangelic faith of the Church, and though it may seem formally distinct from, it is closely associated with the preaching of the Gospel, for it will make the good news of God's forgiving and healing love to sinful men, which seems so wonderful and almost impossible, it will make that love intelligible and credible, and real to them, as it shows the love of those whom he has so richly and wondrously blessed, spending itself in ways like God's own, though infinitely lower, in undoing wrong, assuaging sorrow, and bringing into this world righteousness and peace."

29

With that address the meeting came to a close, but, before separating, it was decided to inaugurate a Thanksgiving Fund and raise £50,000 for strengthening and extending the work of the Institute. The fund was to be an expression in tangible form of that deeper feeling of indebtedness which so many old students and other friends felt towards the Institute and its founder.

There were shoals of letters during that week and the week after. Though he had filled his life and thought with so many far-reaching schemes, the largeness of the schemes had never prevented him from entering with a wonderful intimacy and sympathy into the personal life of almost numberless individuals of all stations in life. The universal had not, as it does with so many, swamped the particular : interest in humanity had not swamped interest in the man.

" I must take the opportunity," writes one, " of stretching a hand from the back seat to the front man, the old man eloquent and irrepressible, and wishing him over again for myself all the good wishes showered on you."

" You are the best antidote to the pessimism of the age that I know," wrote Dr. Adeney.

" Since I have had the privilege of knowing you," wrote Dr. Alex. Hill, the Master of Downing College, " my conception of service has taken a new and a larger form."

" Monday is a desperately awkward day for me," wrote an old student, " but I'm going to be there unless all the winds and waves of circumstance beat me."

" Dr. Paton taught me," wrote another, " that easy things are not worth doing, and that preaching the Gospel was a passion born in the soul by having seen the Lord."

" Although it is considerably over twenty years since I left the Institute," wrote another, " yet in one's heart and in one's prayer grateful acknowledgments to Almighty God for the privilege of discipleship under your enthusing leadership have not ceased."

One more old student : " To see you and to hear you again was a recall to first principles and a baptism of encouragement."

The young men write to thank him for his benediction and encouragement. Older men trace to his inspiration the impulse of their subsequent work. Mr. W. A. Coote, the Secretary of the National Vigilance Society, wrote :

" I should like to see you again to tell you how much of what I have done, or, rather, what God has done through me, is largely owing to the glow and inspiration I caught from you over thirty years ago."

In speeches and letters, as in the address, his true yoke-fellow in Christ was not forgotten ; those who knew most of him knew best how much he had leaned on her, and how his life was rooted in the home with " its sevenfold cord " as he called it, of the family, and especially in the love of his little afflicted daughter.

" Well, father," said his eldest daughter to him with a playfulness allowed to the firstborn, " it is mother who has brought us up. You have been so busy that it all fell on her."

" My dear," he said, " you owe everything to me. I chose your mother."

Happy the workers who live to see some ingathering of the vintage God has granted to their planting.

" To the Pastor, Officers, and Members of the Park Hill Church

" MY DEAR BRETHREN IN CHRIST,

" I am deeply touched by your remembrance of the Jubilee of my entrance upon the public ministry of the Church, and I am most grateful to you for the loving message you have sent me.

" Living now in partial retirement, and separated from public activities in which I once delighted, I have spent this Jubilee season quietly, reviewing these fifty years with adoring and thankful praise to God for His upholding grace throughout them all, and with earnest prayer that His atoning love revealed in Christ may forgive their manifold shortcomings and sins. I have also sought to consecrate the remaining days of my life with a more childlike and perfect faith to the ministry of Christ's Church which I began fifty years ago, and which will only cease with my life.

" It has, however, been most pleasant during this quiet celebration of my ministerial jubilee to receive your gracious and affectionate letter.

" I have always loved and sought the fellowship of my

brethren in Christ, for such fellowship quickens and exalts every holy feeling and purpose. And so your loving sympathy and fellowship with me in this sacred season have humbled me before God, but have also greatly comforted and strengthened me.

" It is true that throughout my ministry I have seen that the glorious salvation of the grace of God for men has a wider meaning than has somehow been appreciated, and that in His Church, as His living and immortal Body on earth, our Lord would still reveal to men, as He did when dwelling with us in His mortal Body, the infinite compassions of the Father's love for them, and win them by this love, made real and credible to them amid their daily needs and sorrows, to know, and trust, and love Him. I have believed the redemption of Christ for the world was a redemption from the evils that actually beset men at the present time. I am thankful, therefore, that you have given me this encouragement in the service which I am still permitted to render in appealing to our Churches to understand and realise what I have called their Social and Redemptive Mission.

" It was a joy to Mrs. Paton and my family as well as myself to join the membership of St. James's Street Church when the Church was pressed with difficulties, and it has been a joy to abide in your fellowship. Now, under God, the Church is blessed with the instructive and inspiring spiritual ministry of Mr. Somervell. It is now situated in a locality which offers every opportunity for vigorous and effective service of every kind. New populations are growing thickly around us. I therefore earnestly hope and pray that these great blessings and opportunities which are given to us, and which impose equally great responsibilities, may inspire and summon us to wise and abounding labours ; and that especially the young men and women of the congregation may rally under the leadership of older members to faithful and grateful labours in our rapidly growing neighbourhood.

" Mrs. Paton unites with me in grateful acknowledgment of your affectionate greetings to us both, and we most warmly reciprocate them.

" I am, with loving regards,
    " Ever your affectionate friend and brother in Christ,
                    " J. B. PATON."

CHAPTER XXVI

CHINA

"They shall come from the land of Sinim."—Isaiah xlix. 12.

It was in 1905, at Sir Percy Bunting's house in Endsleigh Gardens, that Paton first met Dr. Timothy Richard, the eminent statesman-missionary from China, founder of the Christian Literature Society for China. At the end of the Boxer revolution, when the Chinese Government consulted him as to the compensation to be made for the loss of life and property sustained by the Missionary Societies established in China, he had disclaimed all compensation for martyred lives ; those lives, he said, had been offered willingly as a sacrifice to the Lord whose Gospel they had come out to proclaim. He could accept no compensation, but he suggested that the money might be spent by the Chinese Government in founding a university for the diffusion of Western knowledge and civilisation. His advice was taken ; the University was founded in Shansi, and Dr. Timothy Richard became its President. Within a short time of its foundation, the Dowager-Empress issued an edict directing that a university should be founded forthwith in each of the eighteen provinces of China. Hitherto the Dowager-Empress had been stiffneckedly opposed to all Western ideas ; suddenly she had awakened to see their importance, and not only ordered the foundation of new universities on Western lines, but contributed money towards their endowment. In this new educational movement Dr. Richard had played a leading part, and had received from the Chinese Government the high distinction of " Double Dragon," an honour never hitherto conferred on any other Englishman save Sir Robert Hart, the Imperial Commissioner of Customs.

In 1905 Dr. Richard came over on a visit to Great Britain and America with a view to laying before the

Churches at home the position created by the new turn of
affairs, impressing upon them its crucial significance and
appealing to them for help. It was inevitable that such
a man, with such a mission, should find his way to Sir
Percy Bunting's house in London ; it was more than
probable that there he would meet Sir Percy's greatest
friend, J. B. Paton.

" I was much struck with his remarkable greeting,"
writes Dr. Richard ; " it was not like that of a stranger, but
like one who had entered into my life : such was his
marvellous sympathy. When he heard that the keynote
of my missionary life was the establishment of the kingdom
of God, not merely for the comfort and salvation of individual souls, but for the uplift of humanity as a whole,
by having the principles of heaven embodied in the institutions of earth, he grasped my hand with eager appreciation, and said that was also the keynote of his own
life."

It was into willing ears that Dr. Richard poured his
tale of the revolution which was sweeping over China, the
great door and effectual which God had opened, and no
man could shut, for entering into and claiming for Christ
that great empire, with its four hundred millions of people.
Here was the biggest nation in the world awakening from
the slumber of three millenniums, throwing away her old
culture and civilisation, and turning to the Christian
missionaries, whom before she had loathed and persecuted,
for light and guidance in the shaping out of her future.
" When I think of the importance of this movement," he
said, " I feel appalled by its magnitude. Truly China is
preparing a highway for the Lord."

Here was a new problem of world-wide dimensions
which might well have staggered the faith of a man of
less than seventy-five years, who had not already on his
hands a score of other undertakings for the welfare of
his fellow-men. But, so far from being staggered, his
spirit rose at once to the sense of all that was involved and
the urgency of immediate action. Instead of saying, " I
am old and well stricken in years," he said : " The fewer
the years that remain, the more need for immediate
action." Instead of saying, " I have enough irons in the

fire already," he said, " God's fire is big enough to heat all the irons He needs for His own work." At the very first meeting with Dr. Richard he suggested that a China Emergency Committee should be formed, including representatives of all the Evangelical Churches, and that the work of the committee should be planned out on broader lines than could be possible for any missionary society acting singly. Already on the next day he was writing letters and arranging to see the Dean of Westminster, the secretaries of the Church Missionary Society, and representatives of the other great missionary societies. There was no time to waste. It was for the civilised nations of the West to pour into China, while she was in a mood to receive them, those Christian ideas and influences which would permeate and fashion the new civilisation of that country, and bring China into harmony with the civilisation of Europe and America, not only as regards the science which has created our military and industrial forces, but as regards our moral and Christian ideals which have created all that is best in our culture and our social life.

" There are new conditions in China, intellectual, moral, social, political; but at the present time education is paramount. One of the greatest viceroys, a man who helped to stem the tide of the Boxer rising, has written a book with the title ' Learn,' and has declared education to be China's only hope. The old system of imperial examinations and Confucian training has been swept away, so that millions of literati are cut off from old moorings and are seeking a new and safe course to a desired haven. The Imperial Government, for the very existence of China, because she cannot at present cope with foreign Powers, has determined on establishing schools of first, second, and third grades, and a University in each of the eighteen provincial capitals. It is the greatest educational step ever taken by the human race at one bound."

He succeeded in forming the committee. It consisted of fourteen Churchmen and an equal number of Free Churchmen. Bishop Welldon, who had just returned from a visit to China, and the Dean of Westminster were

of the number. They met regularly at the Deanery, Westminster. The Rev. W. Gilbert Walshe, Vicar of Pembury,
Kent, shared the duties of secretary with Paton. Already
in April of the following year Dr. Richard wrote from
America to say : " This Committee I commit to your safe
hands to act as soon as you can."

Action was prompt. The first thing was to send out a
commission to examine into the state of affairs in China
and report upon the line of action which should be taken
in this country. Five commissioners went out early in
1907—Lord William Cecil and his wife, Lady Florence
Cecil, Sir Alex. Simpson, Emeritus Professor of Edinburgh
University, Professor Alexander Macalister of Cambridge,
and Mr. Francis W. Fox, a leading Friend who had done
much, and has since done more, for the promotion of peace
and good-will among the nations of Europe. For their
guidance, Dr. Richard had suggested five separate lines
of inquiry: (1) the evangelistic (including theological);
(2) the educational (especially higher education); (3) the
literary (text-books and translation work); (4) the philanthropic (including medical work) ; (5) the organising department of mission work.

Keeping to these suggested lines, Paton set himself to
sketch out what is included under each of these headings :

" I have been asked if in any way I could define more
clearly what is included under these various objects. I
should prefer that a small committee should be appointed
for that purpose ; but briefly I can indicate several points
which were mentioned by Dr. Richard and which have
been stated to me by others.

" *Under the first department, the Evangelistic :*

" (*a*) To inquire whether the evangelistic work of
various societies might be so divided and arranged that
one society should occupy one district and that thus there
should be no overlapping.

" (*b*) That every means be taken to exhibit and impress
upon the Chinese mind the unity of the evangelic faith,
held and preached by all evangelic societies—*e.g.* by all
accepting and using the same translation of all parts of
the Bible ; by using the same Chinese terms in translat-
ing important theological words or phrases ; by the acceptance of a common symbol of the faith ; and by agreement

upon certain religious books which they commend to their Christian converts, etc., etc.

" (c) That as the evangelisation of China must be chiefly carried out by Chinese Christian teachers and preachers, it should be considered in what way these preachers and teachers can be most effectively trained ; if there should be the establishment of schools or seminaries for this purpose and how far these schools should be under the superintendence of British missionaries, and associated with them in evangelistic work.

" (d) How evangelistic mission centres may be most wisely placed, so as to command the attention and regard of the people of every class in each of the Chinese provinces, and how these mission centres can be most effectively organised.

" (e) How the newly formed Chinese Churches can be most wisely placed and trained under the supervision and direction of missionary superintendents, and led safely towards a position of freedom and independence.

Under the second department, the Educational :

" (1) There are now, I understand, eighteen universities placed in the capitals of eighteen provinces, and in these universities they are seeking, and are willing to support, professors from England and other Christian countries that will occupy chairs of science, literature, history, medicine, and engineering ; it is important, therefore, to consider how these positions of great influence may be filled by gifted and devoted Christian men, who, whilst teaching in the best manner their separate subjects, would also impress upon their students the Christian spirit, and thus influence them to think truly of the Christian faith. In these universities, all the future mandarins or governors of every part of China will be educated, and so these universities will really fashion the spirit and method of government throughout China.

" (2) Whether, in addition to these universities, there should be formed in China, as in India, Christian colleges of university rank that shall be wholly inspired and controlled by Christian men, and whose object shall be to instil into every student the vital elements of the Christian faith and life, and whether these colleges are necessary to give the training that will need to be given to Chinese preachers and pastors,

" (3) There is also an amazing development of high schools of various kinds in China, and in many of these it is believed that Christian teachers of different subjects would be welcomed, and adequately supported—that it is important to consider how this demand can be supplied, and how these Christian influences may be disseminated among the more educated Chinese classes.

" III. *Philanthropic, including the Medical:*

" (1) In connection with the educational department of this inquiry, it is specially considered how professors of medicine and surgery, who are earnest Christian men, can be appointed in these different branches in the universities, and in special medical schools that are likely to be established in China.

" (2) How medical missions can be most wisely associated with evangelistic missions—and how far medical missionaries may be able to instruct Chinese students in some simple forms of medical service.

" (3) How far the work of lady practitioners may be extended in China, as in the Zenana Mission in India.

" IV. *Literature:*

" As there is a great intellectual awakening throughout China, and multitudes are seeking the best books representing Western thought and culture, how this great demand may be most wisely and immediately met—in the selection, the printing, and circulation of books which shall convey to the educated Chinese the Christian inspirations of literature, art, and science.

" V. *Organisation:*

" I do not quite know what Dr. Richard intends ; but imagine that he desires some expert in organisation, especially from a business point of view, to advise and assist those who are inquiring into each of the other departments, how the various work in each department may be most wisely organised, so that each part shall be mutually helpful to the others ; and also that all these departments may be co-ordinated and regulated so that they may be effectively co-operant, and unite in furthering the one end—the winning of all classes in China to the knowledge and obedience and fellowship of our divine, Redeeming Lord, Jesus Christ."

The Commissioners were to attend the great Centenary

Conference of Missions at Shanghai, and the committee
formulated certain questions which they commended to
the earnest consideration of the Conference, so that every
aspect of the great problem might receive full attention.

Meanwhile, Paton was trying in various ways to bring
the challenge of China before the English universities,
which he always considered to hold in trust for the rest of
the world the highest elements of culture and civilisation.
He got into touch with the Student Volunteer movement,
and wrote an article for the " University Review," appealing for a Universities' Mission to China, as there was
already a Universities' Mission to Africa and a Universities'
Mission to India. Here was a vast empire which had for
thousands of years maintained a civilisation and well-
ordered government, with no barriers of caste or diverse
language,—homogeneous and cohesive, with a high ethical
code and an aristocracy of learning. She stood stretching out her hands for the literature, the science, the
spiritual forces that had built up and upheld Western
civilisation. The chance was such as had never occurred
before, and was never likely to recur in the history of
the world. Was not this an opening worthy of the best
intellect, the boldest spirit, the most statesmanlike mind,
the most unselfish chivalry of a great nation's youth ?
Five hundred men and women to go out from the universities of Great Britain and America as professors, teachers,
doctors—that was what he appealed for. If the men
and women were forthcoming, he had no fear about the
money.

" Dr. Richard specially says that the influence of such
a mission would immediately pervade, and move, and inspire in subtle and penetrative ways that are inconceiv-
able in other countries, the whole of this vast empire.
This people, throughout the length and breadth of the
land, have a *communis sensus*—a common atmosphere of
opinions, habits, laws, such as no other people have.
They are divided by no caste ; they speak one language ;
the governing bureaucracy which presides over every
province and section of the country is an educated class
that has one stamp of character and thought and
authority. Accordingly, the whole country vibrates to
the impact of a movement in any part of it, and seeds

of thought planted in a few minds germinate and are
quickly spread broadcast over the whole empire as in
no other country in the world.   No nation is so easily led
in the mass. . . . It may be that a whole nation shall be
born in a day.   This is not an impossible desire or dream,
or, if it be, it is one of Napoleon's ' impossibilities,' which
mean ' things that shall be done.' "

The Commissioners spent many busy months in China,
visiting every part of it.   They attended the Conference
at Shanghai, where the leading representatives of every
missionary society working in China assembled in order
to consider how all the societies might best work together
in the new birth of Chinese life and thought.   They had
personal intercourse with the chief men who were at that
Conference, and with leading statesmen and officials, both
Chinese and English.   On their return they prepared a
report, and Lord William Cecil also wrote five letters to
the " Times " which created great interest and impressed
public opinion.   In view of this report, the committee
felt that an organised effort must be made on a national
scale, to arouse the country to a sense of the momentous
responsibility laid upon her and the splendour of the
opportunity.   A special Appeal Committee was formed,
to which the Duke of Argyll, the Archbishop of Canterbury, the Bishop of Ripon, and Sir Robert Hart gave their
names.   The appeal itself was drafted by Dr. Boyd Carpenter, then Bishop of Ripon.   They appealed for £100,000,
of which £40,000 was to be allocated to medical colleges,
£40,000 to the establishment of normal schools and
divinity colleges for training Chinese teachers, pastors,
and evangelists, and the remaining £20,000 to assist in
the translation and distribution of the best Western
literature, including text-books, amongst the mandarins
and literary classes.

Now began the work of getting the money—work which
is less inspiring and needs more grace than any other.
But " the battle must not be lost for lack of powder and
shot," Paton would say.

" I have sometimes thought there was a providence
in the fact that, whilst such an appeal was being made to
us by China, God has at the same time poured out mea-

sureless wealth upon Christian men and women in England and America, so that they are able to respond to this appeal."

To Dr. Timothy Richard

"Jan. 23rd, 1908.

" You will see how in my own mind I have distinguished two departments of work in our China Missions Emergency Committee.

" The first is one in which we associate ourselves, so far as we may, with the different missionary societies, encouraging them to federal action in their educational, medical, and philanthropic work ; we also must co-operate with them in awakening a profounder interest in China in their various constituencies and so increase the support which they obtain from their constituencies for work in China.

" The second, as you will see, is that we appeal to Christian England and to Christian America—which is a wider constituency than that of the missionary societies, because our wealthier people in both countries are not, I think, specially interested in missions, but would be interested in a great public and national enterprise such as we propose in regard to two most important elements of Western civilisation which we would seek in an unselfish and generous manner to give to China.

" The first is what you have described and what I have been promoting, viz. the Universities' Mission. We should endeavour to raise funds—apart from missionary societies —through the Christian Students' Union, and, by appeal to the general public, to send out ten men of the kind that you have desired, to be statesmen, educational missionaries, who would co-operate with the civil authorities in China in every way in which they possibly can in their educational work, and in diffusing throughout China the best literature of the West in every department of knowledge.

" The second is to advise and to assist the Imperial and Viceregal Governments of China to train a native medical service, to found hospitals and medical schools, economically, in every province of China so as to give to the Chinese people everywhere the great benefits of our Western medical knowledge and experience. In this we must associate ourselves with leading medical men in England and America.

"In connection with this second object of our more public appeal, Mr. Fox, Sir Percy Bunting, and I visited the Chinese Ambassador, Prince Li, who was greatly interested in our proposal, and said that any memorial that we sent to him to be presented to the Imperial and Viceregal Governments in China, he would translate and forward at once, and he would also promote and assist our movement in every way he possibly could and make it known through China. He told us that at present they have only a trained medical service for the Navy and partly for the Army, and that it would be the one benefit of Western civilisation which would be appreciated throughout China, more than any other."

To Dr. Douglas McKenzie

"*March 20th*, 1908.

"There has sprung up in China everywhere throughout the whole of the empire an intense desire for Western education. They have suddenly discovered how obsolete and useless and obstructive is their system of education which has prevailed in China for millenniums, and which up till lately they considered superior to all other systems in the world. In this vast agitation and yearning after Western knowledge and culture and civilisation, they are very much under the influence of Japan, and they have seen in Japan what that Western knowledge and science have produced in the way of naval and military strength, and also of manufacturing industries and of commerce. But, unhappily, the example of Japan and the influence of Japanese education are infected with materialistic conceptions and aims. At the same time there is, in very wonderful ways in China, and also to some extent in Japan, a spiritual yearning, and the beginnings of an appreciation of Christianity in itself, and in its spiritual ideals, and also a growing apprehension of the fact that it is the spiritual faith of Christianity that lies at the root of our Western culture and civilisation. It is in the crisis of this great movement in China that Dr. Richard desires that the universities of England and America, and it may be of the Continent, should send out ten men—the ablest that these universities can provide—who shall give their whole life to one great object, namely, to promote in China the very best educational methods that the Western world has adopted, to be prepared thus to confer with the leading mandarins who are now organising everywhere universities, colleges, normal schools, and primary schools ; to give full information and the very best counsels that can be given to them in this great intellectual and educational Renaissance in China ; and also by their personal influence and by reasoned speech to impress upon all educational authorities the higher spiritual influences that must quicken and inspire true education. They will thus, in every way that is possible to them, seek to counteract the material influences and agencies that have spread already in that country, and by all means propagate and develop the higher spiritual influences of the Christian faith."

To the Rev. Tissington Tatlow

"*April 18th,* 1908.

" I feel that, somehow or other, for lack of strategical tactics, or, it may be, wise and practical enthusiasm, we are losing the great opportunity which God has given us— or at least, we are not making the most of it. We all know that the next two or three years will determine very much the whole future history of the East ; that this is a most critical time, pregnant with infinite possibilities for good, but also for evil ; that it is a time, therefore, which challenges and demands the utmost effort and the wisest deliberation, and, under wise guidance, a sort of intensity, and even daring in action. It is a time that calls for a certain magnificence of courage and devotion.

" I hope I am not wrong in writing you in this sense ; but when I think of the two great events—the marvellous opening of China, and at the very same time, in God's providence, the formation of the Christian Student Movement, calling hundreds of our educated and noblest young men to service for Christ (as you know, I consider that there is a great providence in the occurrence of these two momentous events at the same time, and that God created your movement in order that He might, at this opportune and critical time, supply the very men and women to China which she is needing and calling for) I feel I must ask you kindly to read this letter to your Executive, and if you like to send copies of it to your leading members I should be grateful. At any rate, I know that you have sympathy with all that is in my heart, and I pray that God may give us both wisdom and courage in this hour of trial for us, as well as for the Christian Student Movement, and for the world."

To the Rev. Dr. T. Richard [1]

"April 14th, 1906.

"I do not think that we shall be able, in the present condition of Europe, to do much in forming a League of Peace between the leading nations of Europe, by which they will mutually and respectively guarantee the territory occupied by each State. In France, in Austria, and in Turkey, things are in too unsettled a state to make that at all probable; but we can preach the doctrine of Peace, which, as you say, is a doctrine gradually entering the very conscience and living thought of all the peoples of the world. What I think we can do, as I have said before, is to form a League of Western nations with Eastern nations that will guarantee the territory of those Eastern nations, and will therefore disabuse the mind of Eastern nations as to the selfish and covetous spirit of Western nations wishing to exploit the East for their advantage. I am sure that it is only as we can remove that suspicion, and even hatred, which has naturally been aroused among the Chinese people by the aggressive policy of Western nations in the past, that we can open the way for the entrance and reception of the finest Christian thought, inspiring and moulding the best civilisation of the West, into China. They will naturally decline and refuse to accept the spirit and religious faith of Western nations as long as they associate these with the selfish and tyrannous and rapacious spirit which many of the nations have shown to China in the past. I am sure you will give the committee, when it is formed, a free hand in this matter, and that we make it our first object at any rate to form an *entente cordiale* between the Western nations grouped

---

[1] Dr. Richard at this time was in the United States. He had been advocating in writing and in speech a world-wide league of peace.

together and the Eastern nations grouped together. This very alliance of the Western nations in their relation and attitude and action to Eastern nations will help to promote the idea and spirit of unity amongst them, and thus bring nearer the time when they will be prepared to regard themselves as the United States of Europe, with some united, central, governing body, both legislative and administrative. That is a great object to aim at, and has been an inspiring thought with many of our best men for years. But, as you say, the times are now favourable to the fulfilment of ideas which hitherto have been deemed Utopian, and not within the realm of practical politics, and therefore we shall keep this idea always before us. But I am convinced that the first step to be taken is to have these nations united together in their relations to the East. That is practicable, and is a matter of immediate urgency, and one which will help forward the higher civilisation of the world and the coming of the kingdom of God more than anything else that can be at the present moment conceived or desired."

To Sir William Hartley

" The new events in China are not merely political, commercial, and literary. These more conspicuous changes are accompanied, and in some measure caused, by great social transformations. The Western knowledge is opening the minds of Chinese youth to think of all manner of reforms. But, of the improvements needed in Chinese life, nothing is probably so important for the immediate welfare of the people as a reform of medical practice. A large number of hospitals are maintained by Europeans in China, who draw aid from home, and they tend, more than any other means of intercourse, to promote good-will and friendliness between Western people and the masses of the Chinese. But the testimony of the medical men and women who give their lives to this service is that, great as are their efforts—scattered, of course, here and there, in only a few spots, amidst overwhelming masses of population—the need for medical provision and medical knowledge is appalling. The remedies of the native Chinese practitioners, beyond a very few who have had some scientific training, would be simply ludicrous, if they were not so

30

tragic. To some plain, and small European charitable hospital, poor women will trudge, with their bound-up feet, for miles over the mountains, in hopes of a little relief from their sufferings. No means are so effective for commending Western people, or the Western belief in the Fatherhood of God to the Chinese mind as this humble service of humanity. No means are so likely to break down the barriers of race, or to smooth away political dangers and make for friendship. Both on the ground of humanity and of political expediency, it would be well worth the while of the British people to make a great and united effort to extend their medical services to the Chinese people, and make them into a truly national offering of peace and good-will—as from one nation to another."

To Lord Winterstoke

"*August*, 1910.

"These four medical colleges, to cost £40,000, will be splendidly equipped with all that modern science and medical skill have devised, and they will be wholly supported by students that attend them. From them thousands of trained medical practitioners will go forth every year throughout China. And, to supplant the most barbarous and cruel medical practices that are now followed, other colleges equipped in the same complete manner will doubtless be established throughout China by the Chinese themselves, having seen the wonderful results obtained from the four colleges thus established.

"The present Chinese Ambassador to this country has said that no gift to China would so profoundly impress the Chinese people with not only the advantages of our Western civilisation, but also with other beneficent purposes of those who confer that gift.

"In like manner, normal schools to train teachers for the Chinese elementary and secondary schools which can be established in every part of China at little cost, will be supported by the students who receive training at them, and will set again the model for other normal seminaries as they are needed in China. So also the divinity schools for the training of Chinese pastors and evangelists will again be supported wholly by the Churches that require and call for these trained ministers, and doubtless be increased and extended as these Churches grow in number.

" And, lastly, the literature provided by the sum of £20,000 will be the best that Europe can provide, and will be inspired by the highest Christian ideals. For this literature the educated men and women of China are now beginning to seek, and it will abide as an eternal possession for the people of China.

" Thus £100,000 will be able to achieve results which are measureless and far-reaching in their scope, and will pervade and fill even that vast empire with the moral and spiritual influences of our Western faith and civilisation. What a result to follow such a comparatively small expenditure !

" Our appeal is to the British nation. The missionary societies, in order to meet the demand of this New Awakening in China, are straining themselves to the utmost. We cannot, therefore, appeal to them, but to the British nation, which of all Western countries is the most closely related to China in commerce, and which has a wrong to expiate in having forced upon China the noxious opium traffic. And our appeal is that it assist in the regeneration of this vast Eastern world which calls out for the help which we can give."

The story of this chapter remains necessarily incomplete. The wealthy men of England, who might have completed the story, missed the chance. The " magnificence of courage and devotion " was not forthcoming in measure adequate to the noble chance. Some were alarmed at the increased taxation of large incomes at home ; some were not anxious to see China manufacturing her own goods. But the movement in China goes forward. The great nation of the East is being reborn in a day, not without birth-pangs, and in its new birth it has turned to the Christian peoples of the West and asked for prayer—

" For so the whole round earth is every way
Bound by gold chains about the feet of God."

CHAPTER XXVII

THE PROBLEM OF THE CITY POOR

" Some day the individualist community on which we build our faith will find itself obliged, for its own sake, to take charge of the lives of those who, from whatever cause, are incapable of existence up to the required standard."—CHARLES BOOTH.

" Effectual sacrifice is not of money only. . . . The relief which can be given without the personal ministries of love is, at the best, destitute of moral value to the receiver, and, for the most part, to the giver also."—BISHOP WESTCOTT.

ALREADY in 1871, as we have seen, Paton had made a study of the Elberfeld system of Poor Relief. At that time Elberfeld was exceptional in Germany, but the system spread widely and rapidly through the German Empire. In some towns it was adapted rather than adopted. Everywhere, whether adapted or adopted, it influenced the methods of Poor Law relief.

There were many features in the Elberfeld system which specially attracted him. The English workhouse system was hard and inhuman ; it had accomplished the object for which it was called into existence, which was to make poverty deterrent, but it was not capable, he felt, of grappling hopefully with the problem of the poor, whether in the towns or in the country. At Elberfeld the duty of helping the poor was not devolved on paid officials : it was a civic or municipal undertaking manned by the citizens themselves, and to that combination of free civic spirit with the municipal authority it owed its success. It was regarded as a civic duty, a part of that mutual *Bürgeschaft*, that sense of responsibility for each other's welfare which belonged to the Anglo-Saxon tradition and even antedates the introduction of Christianity.

Again, the attitude of these voluntary helpers of the poor towards their work seemed to contrast favourably with the spasmodic and sporadic efforts of English charity, as wasteful and injurious as they were unscientific. In

468

Elberfeld there was no jealous isolation of Church from Church in the work among the poor. The town was treated as a whole. Districts were mapped out. Each visitor had a small number of families allocated to him as his share of the work. Visitors were not left without guidance ; they met in regular conference, they reported each case to the meeting of visitors in their own district. All actual money relief was paid, not through the regular visitor, but by a special district almoner.

" They are not mere amateurs," he said, " playing in an irregular and inefficient way with civic duty, but become trained and expert citizens who are guided by certain defined rules of procedure, and who act in concert, sustaining one another and carrying out one system throughout the whole town or city."

In England he knew it was not possible to devolve the whole of our outdoor relief on such private citizens, as would voluntarily accept this duty and train themselves for it. But he thought it possible to devise a system whereby private citizens might co-operate with the relieving officer, and he believed that such a system of " Associate Guardians," as he called them, would make the administration of outdoor relief at once more effective and more humane. *L'état doit avoir aussi des entrailles.* He proposed that these " Associate Guardians " should be authorised by the Guardians to act under their instructions. Their duty should be to assist the Relieving Officer of the district, making the needful scrutiny of each case which applied for relief, and giving such assistance as was required in a neighbourly way, which was not possible for an official dealing with so large a number all at one time.

" Those who seek relief," he wrote, " would often be assisted in a much better way than by receiving merely a weekly dole of alms. Many of the poor seek work, not alms, and, if wise arrangements were made and some special effort put forth by people qualified and authorised to do so, they would often obtain work and be restored to independence. In many other cases the Associate Guardians would evoke the sympathy and help of the relatives and friends of those they visit, and in this way the family spirit

would be cherished and a deeper note given to friendly
service. If relief is to be given to old and deserving people
in their own homes, as seems now to be generally desired,
it will be advisable, if not necessary, that these old and
deserving people should be handled and dealt with by
other than the merely official Relieving Officer. Public
Charity to them must be clothed in sympathy and minis-
tered with the respect due to age."

He insisted that such Associate Guardians must give
themselves a certain training for this service. Nothing
but evil would ensue if the work was done in an irregular,
impulsive, and ill-directed manner. He insisted also that
the Guardians should no longer be empowered to assess
the rating values of property, or make any contracts for
expenditure connected with the relief of the poor. These
duties should be entrusted to the Municipal Council, which
controls the financial and general interests of the community.

" The civic service to which the Guardians are appointed
requires special qualifications, and they should be chosen
only for their fitness for it. They should not be tempted
to seek the office from any other considerations, or to secure
civic influence by work of a wholly different kind from that
for which they are chosen. The office of Guardian should
be magnified as one that gives no place or opportunity
for any business but the diligent care of the poor ; and an
office thus magnified would attract the best men and
women of the town or city, because of its freedom from
business transactions of an alien nature."

When Miss Julie Sutter, in 1901, published her book,
" Britain's Next Campaign," a great impetus was given
to the Elberfeld idea. " Her voice," wrote Paton, " has
kindled a new world of sympathy and of service for the
neediest in our country." " The Daily News " followed
up the first edition of " Britain's Next Campaign " by re-
issuing in its columns the larger part of it in the form of
articles, and Miss Sutter subsequently distributed 10,000
free copies. Thus the good news of Elberfeld was carried
through the length and breadth of the land, rousing the
national conscience to the true state of our poor, and

creating the willingness to serve which blossomed forth in the Guilds of Help and in other undertakings.   Mr. and Mrs. Priestman, of Bradford, formed a committee with a view to adapting the system to the needs of their city.   This Bradford Guild of Help seems to have determined in the main the form which the movement has taken in England.

The Guild of Help was not the form of application of Elberfeld principles for which Paton had hoped.   It lacked two things which would have been secured by his scheme of Associate Guardians, viz. authority and the power of the purse.   This Miss Sutter herself has constantly pointed out.   But it incorporated the great Elberfeld principle of human neighbourliness to the poor, and it seemed to " catch on."   He was not the man to stickle for his own scheme if another scheme seemed more feasible of accomplishment.   He had a keen eye to see where the possibilities lay ; he was for doing what was doable, and he threw himself into the movement for the extension of the Civic Guild of Help.   Only what he advocated was something far wider and more constructive than the mere relief of poverty.   On November 21st, 1904, with his friend the Bishop of Hereford, he came to Manchester and addressed a large meeting of social workers, held at the Grammar School.   He thought the time had come when the men and women of the city who were inspired with enthusiasm for the service of their fellows might group together all the philanthropic societies of the City into one social and educational league, which would add an immense momentum to the work then being done in all the scattered agencies.

" I want you," he said, " seriously to consider whether you could not, by combined effort among the agencies for social service, create an environment which would incite every young man and woman to take their part in the service of their fellows.   There is need to combine the various social agencies and then to inspire them with this great national purpose of bringing to every man and woman in every class of the community the means of culture and nourishing the higher life. . . . Do you not feel that the breeze of the morning blows over our land, and men everywhere are turning to behold the splendid dawn of a new day ? "

A small committee was formed including Rev. Arnold Streuli and Mr. Frederick J. Marquis. The first work taken in hand was the formation of a Civic League of Help on the Bradford lines, but the special difficulties of organising the work of so huge and complex a population made progress slow, and it was not until 1906 when Paton opened a series of lectures at the Central Hall with an address on " A Civic League, social and educational, for Manchester and Salford," that the proposal took practical shape. Even then the organisation of the districts had to proceed gradually, Salford was not included, and the word " educational " had to be abandoned as being in those days of Mr. Birrell's Bill too explosive.[1] But the League was founded, and, under the able guidance of Alderman Fildes and the two first secretaries, Mr. W. R. J. Clarke and Mr. W. S. P. Grundy, the different districts of the city were mapped out and manned, a survey was made of the different charities and philanthropic agencies, the basis was laid for a new synthesis wider than any which had preceded, and new channels of definite work were opened for the spirit of altruism.

Long before Manchester got started, the Rev. J. Renshaw Bailey, of Eccles, had made a beginning with Swinton. The Vicar of Eccles, Canon F. D. Cremer, associated himself with Mr. Bailey. The Mayor was requisitioned to hold a town's meeting, the proposal to extend the system to the whole of Eccles was enthusiastically adopted, and was at once set on foot with Mr. Bailey as President and Canon Cremer as Vice-President. The case of Eccles was of special interest to Paton, because the initiative in that case came from the Churches, and the co-operation of Church with Chapel under broad-minded, large-hearted leaders showed that the idea of the Inner Mission is not Utopian, when there are men of feeling sufficiently brotherly to take the idea in hand. The consequent enlargement of sympathy among the Churches has been all to the good, and the instinct of human brotherhood which is found outside the pale of all Churches was given a sphere of definite service.

---

[1] This address was afterwards published under the title, " Social Questions of the Day. No. 2. Applied Christianity."

Letter to the Rev. Arnold Streuli

"*Nov. 26th*, 1904.

" . . . My idea is that these different agencies that I named to you—I think some ten of them—should join together in a social and educational league. They are working at present separately, and yet they form parts of a great whole. If united, they would be seen to meet the needs of every class of the community, and through them the environment and influence that I spoke of can be brought to every individual, however humble and poor, in the community. If they were thus united and co-ordinated in such a League, and inspired by a great purpose which animates the League and all the societies associated with it, it would impress the public mind and imagination and bring home to every person in the community what advantages and opportunities and influences are available and quite nigh at hand. Also, when thus united, it would be seen whether any one of these agencies was somewhat weak and defective, and the representatives of that agency in the united League would be encouraged to fulfil the mission for which they, in a sense, are responsible.

" There would practically be no expense in the League itself, save for the convening of meetings, and, it may be, an occasional memorandum or statement through the public press and through the pulpits of the city as to its aims and as to the methods in which these are being fulfilled by the different societies which it represents."

Letter to the Bishop of Manchester

"*May 14th*, 1906.

" I have reason to think that the controversy which has been raised about Mr. Birrell's Education Bill is leading you to suspend your interest and action in forming a Civic League for Manchester and Salford. I regret that it should be so. While not urging your Lordship to pursue the matter at present, if you have the least hesitancy or difficulty in regard to it, may I, however, submit the following considerations, which may lead you to feel that, however we may differ as Christian men upon the policy of Mr. Birrell's Bill, we need not, and ought not, either to lose our regard for one another as Christian men, or to cease to unite for great and urgent objects about which there is no difference, and in which we may show to the world that, despite our differences on one subject, there are great interests which we love to uphold in common, and in which we can manifest the reality of our Christian faith and the devotion of sacrificial service for the good of those who need us in our cities ?

" I was greatly pleased to know that the Archbishop convened a meeting at Caxton Hall in London, and invited members of all Christian Churches to support him there in the one great common purpose, namely, to secure the better observance of our Sabbath, which is being in so many ways desecrated. I also read with profound gratitude the appeal issued by Bishop Gore and Mr. Jowett, who are supported by all the leading representatives of the Christian Church in our country, that we should make the coming Whitsuntide a time in which earnestly to seek and pray for brotherly concord, and the inspiration of true fellowship in Christ, so that, though we differed, we might yet honour one another in these differences, and seek to understand one another, and, above all, to promote the religious well-being of our people. This appeal has, I know, gone home to all Christian people with whom I am acquainted, and Whitsuntide will be, I am sure, a time in which a Pentecostal blessing of love and peace will be earnestly sought.

" I am happy myself to be associated here with Bishop Baynes, the Vicar of St. Mary's, in inviting a number of Churchmen and Nonconformists to meet together before Whitsuntide, so that we may seek in love to honour one another, and seek above all to do nothing in our differences that will excite animosity and ill-will, or injure the cause of our holy religion in our country.

" With these precedents, I think that we might make this present occasion even the opportunity of showing to Manchester and Salford what would be really a glorious example, which would impress men everywhere, that in Christ's name we are willing to unite together and serve Him and our city in a matter in which we are all agreed, and which we feel to be of immense and immediate urgency, because it involves the well-being of the poor, the health of the city, and enables us to fulfil something of the redeeming compassion and service of Christ to those who suffer and are in need."

Letter to the Conference of the Charity Organisation Society
                                              "*Jan. 11th*, 1909.

"To aid in the discussion of this afternoon may I briefly
state the three essential principles of the Guild of Help
movement which determine everywhere its constitution and
methods of work ?

"1. It is a civic movement ; it has sprung from a new
spirit that pervades this age, the finest element of which
is a larger interest in the well-being of others. A social
conscience is awake. It is felt, as never before, that there
is a corporate life in our towns and cities, so that each
member is responsible in a sense for the health and welfare
of all its members. Wherever, therefore, a civic Guild of
Help is formed the public initiative has been taken by the
Mayor of the town or city, assisted by others of its leading
representatives. The preliminary committees have generally been instituted by public authority ; and, in every
case that I know of, the civic Guild has been inaugurated
at a public citizens' meeting, over which the Mayor, supported by leading members of the Corporation, presided.
It is thus an essential principle of the Guild of Help that
it shall be a citizens' Guild, fulfilling the duty of charity
as a public duty for which the citizens are responsible.
Accordingly, the Guild is necessarily always a lay movement—its officers and all associate helpers taking rank
and place in its service as citizens. Clergymen have
everywhere, I believe, greatly favoured and supported the
movement ; but they also, with the district visitors connected with their Churches, always take rank with other
citizens as fellow-helpers in the movement. Also in each
Guild of Help men and women join, with equal rights and
duties, in its service, and the most influential citizens are
associated on equal terms with intelligent and able working
men and women.

"2. The principle of the Guild is that every part of the
city shall be equally cared for. In some places, where it
is not possible to organise at once the whole town or city,
large districts are organised one after the other ; but the
object that is sought, and must be achieved, is that the
whole city shall be so divided and occupied by the helpers
of the Guild that every poor person in the town or city
shall be known and cared for. It is thus alone that the
civic responsibility for the poor of the town or city can be

fulfilled.   It is also thus alone that the city charities can be
rightly and equally administered ; and, above all, it is
in this way alone that casual alms-giving, which is so
injurious both to those who give and to those who receive
it, can be effectually stopped, for there is no need to give
alms when it is known that every case of extreme poverty
is being dealt with; and the charitable contributions of the
generous will be dispensed through the citizen-helpers of the
poor with wise sympathy, and after careful investigation of
the needs of the poor and of the causes of their poverty.

" 3. Then, the whole town or city is divided into districts,
and each district is again divided into sub-districts, in
which one helper is engaged and for which he in a sense is
responsible.   Such sub-district may include several streets
or only half a street, but is so arranged that the helper is
not expected to have more than one case usually in his
charge, and never more than four.   His interest accordingly
is focused upon that special district of his own, so that he
becomes acquainted through many channels (district
visitors, health visitors, school attendance officers, etc.)
with every poor person in that district, and has or can
obtain information which enables him, in visiting any case
of which he is informed, to appreciate the conditions with
which he has to deal.

" Further, the League of Help deals with every class
and description of the poor in the town or city.   So far
its operations extend beyond those of the C.O.S., but still
its object is that of the C.O.S. as it has been defined—
namely, the promotion of a method of organised local
charity.   The conditions of modern life make it necessary
that not only the well-deserving poor should be helped in
times of distress, but that also the ill-deserving shall be
thought of and cared for.   We are conscious that, as
things now stand, there have been social causes at work
which have weakened and degraded those whom we think
the less deserving.   The conditions of their birth and
breeding, or the vicissitudes of industrial life, have often
made them what they are.   Wrong has been done to
them, if they themselves are now wrong-doing, and all the
more, therefore, they now deserve whatever can be done
to uplift them from their low estate.   But in their case,
even more than in the case of the well-deserving, that
which has been the axiom of the C.O.S. from its forma-

tion must be strenuously insisted upon—namely, that whatever is done shall be done so as to strengthen character and to form a better habit of life. As Mr. Loch has said : ' We must think how to help men as completely as may be, so that their manhood may be strengthened.' Mr. Loch has himself pleaded for this class—whom he calls the ' downward marching '—to have exactly what the civic Guild of Help is formed to give, when he says, ' Why should there not be a much greater concentration of influence and effort to help those of that class whose lives are still unwrecked ? ' Accordingly, every helper is called to deal with every case of poverty, and to do whatever may be possible to reclaim from evil habit, to evoke new effort towards independence, to help in getting work, to solicit the succour of neighbours or of charitable institutions, and thus to give a friendly hand to uplift, and to abide in this service amid much discouragement and occasional defeat till the utmost has been done that can be done.

" The whole city being thus divided into districts, and these being the duties of the district visitors, it will be seen that there are two things necessary for the efficient working of every Guild of Help.

" 1. An adequate number of efficient helpers ; and it is wonderful to know that so widespread is this feeling of humane interest and of civic responsibility throughout the community that in every case where the duty is clearly set before the conscience of the people helpers in sufficient numbers are always forthcoming. In Sheffield, for instance, one thousand helpers at once offered themselves, and everywhere men are found in equal numbers with women willing for this public duty.

" 2. These helpers must be trained in the work for the work, and this in every Guild is being done in a remarkable manner. Full and minute instruction is provided for each helper with regard to the various kinds of cases with which he may have to deal. Further, the helpers in each district never of themselves determine the monetary relief that is to be given, but submit the case to the committee of twelve or fifteen other helpers associated in the district, and whose chairman is chosen by them as the best informed and ablest to advise them. All the helpers in each district associated in their respective committees are under the direction of the central body, which

has minute and exact knowledge of every case that is
dealt with by every helper, and which by conference and
special visits of trained officers gives needful direction
and counsel to all the helpers."

The idea of " Associate Guardians " formed the subject
of a Conference held with the Nottingham Board of
Guardians on July 2nd, 1903, and was worked out fully
in the evidence Paton gave before the Royal Commission
on the Poor Law, 1907.   Birmingham has carried the principle into practice,[1] but most other places have adopted
under one name or another the principle of the Civic
League of Help.

To Mrs. Moser

"*Jan. 21st*, 1910.

" Life is not with us to be selfish ; it is to be full of
unselfish thought and love.   This is the Christian, and it
is the true, law of humanity.   I am so afraid of the ministries of the community becoming official and bureaucratic."

"*Jan. 24th*, 1910.

" I agree with very much said by Mr. Sidney Webb in
the article in ' Progress,' but I have a real dread of
officialism, and greatly wish to cultivate the sympathetic,
humane, neighbourly spirit in the community, so that
the community will feel its responsibility, and exercise a
spirit of helpful and kindly care of its members.   That,
to me, will be worth everything."

To Mrs. Sidney Webb

"*Oct. 1st*, 1909.

" Will you allow me to send you the evidence which I
presented at the request of the Commission on the Poor
Law ?   You will see there how I have had specially on
my mind the need for more communal humane sympathy
and responsibility in each city, town, and village.   I think
this is a matter of supreme importance for the life of each
local community and of the State.   It was that feeling
which drew me, years ago, to study the Elberfeld system,
and I do earnestly hope that, in all you are now undertaking to study and organise in the life of the State, you
will not ignore this supreme concern."

[1] See " Progress," July 1911.

CHAPTER XXVIII

THE CHURCH

" That which gives value to temporal life is its convertibility into life eternal."

" To you and to me and men like ourselves is committed, in those anxious days, that which is at once an awful responsibility and a splendid destiny—to transform this modern world into a Christian society, to change the Socialism which is based on the assumption of clashing interests into the Socialism which is based on the sense of spiritual union, and to gather together the scattered forces of a divided Christendom into a confederation in which organisation will be of less account than fellowship with one Spirit, and faith in one Lord—into a communion wide as human life and deep as human need—into a Church which shall outshine even the golden glory of dawn by the splendour of its eternal noon."—EDWIN HATCH.

WHEN Paton began his ministry the conception of the Church had almost faded from the minds of English Non-conformists. The individualism of the prevalent school in politics and economics had infected the Christian thought of its day. Mazzini [1] openly proclaimed that Christianity was the religion of the individual, and knew nothing of association, which was the only method of progress. To rescue the jewels from the puddle one by one was the work of the Christian ministry. But Paton's English training had never effaced the strong conviction begotten of his Scottish ancestry as to the constitution and essential authority of the Church, and from the very first the Church was one of the great dominant notes in his ministry.

The doctrine of the Church he held in its primitive and simplest form. Wherever true believers met in Christ, drawn together by a common devotion to their Lord, seeking to have their life, both individual and corporate, fashioned by Him for the fulfilment of His purposes, there, nowadays, just as much as in the apostolic times, was a Church. He believed in the *ecclesia* before it became

[1] " The French Revolution of 1789." Translated by T. Okey, p. 187.

479

ecclesiastic, as a community of persons who had come into personal touch with Jesus, who had been by Him quickened into new life, in whom the Spirit was becoming incarnate, dwelling in them, energising in them and through them, perpetuating, replenishing, extending the life of the Church. Entering into communion with their Saviour, men entered into a new communion and fellowship with one another, and in this corporate life there was a new manifestation of God's grace and power, for in it every human relation was made sacred.

This fellowship brought each member into the immediate presence of the glory of God ; each member was a temple, a priest. And just as each member shared immediately in the life of the Lord, so each little body of God's company were sharers in the spiritual privileges and glory of the whole Church, and were a vital unit of the whole. No single Church could shut itself off from any other Church in Christendom. As all shared the same allegiance, so all shared the same life, and therefore all believers, whatever their denomination, were members of every Church, for they were members of the whole, which included every Church. They were " fellow-citizens with the saints, and of the household of God." Fellowship in Christ was a principle, not of exclusion, but of inclusion.

In a world where the word " Church " has come to be almost synonymous with the erection of barriers and the narrowing in of the Divine Grace, he set himself to restore its true significance to the word " Catholic."

" I am a Nonconformist," he said, " because I am a Catholic. I cannot belong to a Church that excludes any one who loves and serves my Lord. The Roman Church, though it calls itself Catholic, has the audacity, the childish audacity, I might almost call it the impertinence, to exclude two-thirds of Christendom. Still less can I believe in a Church which calls itself Catholic, whether it be Anglican or Roman, which limits the grace, the boundless grace of God that flows like a sea through the whole of the universal Church, which says the grace of God trickles down to me through the hands of a human priesthood in the line of an apostolic succession. To think that the grace of my God should come to me in such trickling driblets ! "

The word " Church " was one which to him had been soiled almost past recognition by erroneous and ignoble use. The only way to rehabilitate it was to get back to its first principle, and one of the great ideas of his life had been to work at the church history of the first two centuries. But it was not to be.

" My life has been ordered otherwise than I had dreamt and purposed, but how much better," he writes to Dr. Dale, in 1894. " To maintain the Institute through many years, with sixty students, and no endowments, needed all my energy, and the weakness of my eyes which fell upon me after coming here, showed me that the service of scholarship in the Church which I had hoped for, was not His appointment. I sought other work which was less exhausting to the brain, and more varied."

It was with him as with the scholar of whom Whittier sings :

> Forego thy dreams of lettered ease,
> Put thou the scholar's promise by ;
> The rights of man are more than these.
> He heard and answered, " Here am I."

What he could not achieve himself he sought to do through others, and in his later years he and his brother, Mr. Andrew B. Paton, set apart £500 in trust to provide prizes for essays to be written by ministers of one of the Evangelical Free Churches of the United Kingdom, or students of the Theological Colleges of those Churches.

" The general subject to be dealt with in these essays is the Primitive Apostolic Church, especially in relation to the Church of our own times ; but each essay should be confined to a discussion of it under one or other of the following aspects, viz :

" (a) The constitution, worship, and doctrines of the Primitive Apostolic Church ; the fellowship that existed in a local Church, and the inter-communion of the Churches ; the Church and its relation to the world and to the civil authority ; its influence upon social customs and its ministry to social needs ; its relation to the Jewish synagogue, to the ritual of the Jewish worship, and to Jewish policy, and also to the usages that prevailed in the con-

31

duct of assemblics, and in the regulation of societies throughout the Roman Empire.

" (b) The causes that led to corruption in the Church, whether in its constitution, worship, doctrine, or fellowship.

" (c) How the original principles of the Church can be restored and applied to the conditions of modern life."

That all who believed on Christ should be one in Him was the constant burden of his prayers. Uniformity of creed or of organisation was impossible, and, indeed, undesirable ; but unity of spirit could be based, not on the questioned variety of human belief, but the unquestioned realisation of the filial life towards God, and this he strove for. " It is not my unity or your unity that I want, but Christ's unity," he would say. The old theologians used to speak much of " the Church invisible." It is a term of which little is heard nowadays. To his consciousness the thought was always present, and it was that thought which made him see in their true perspective what are called " our unhappy divisions." To him they did not exist ; those who came into personal contact with him found them strangely disappear.

" I have felt as much at home in your study," wrote the Rev. H. Biddell, the Vicar of St. Paul's, Nottingham, " as an officer of the Black Watch might feel with an officer of the Grenadiers. We have our regimental traditions, but we fight for King and Kingdom side by side."

The basis of unity he sought not in any doctrinal compromise or concession. The Langham Street Conference made it clear that there was no hope of solution in that direction. But there was hope on the line of concerted action. Let but Christians of all regiments combine for the attainment of certain practical ends on which all were agreed, and for the Churches, as for individuals, the word would be true, " If any man will do the will he shall know of the doctrine." There was a saying of John Ruskin which pleased him :

" At every moment of our lives we should be trying to find out; not in what we differ from other people, but in what we agree with them. And the moment we agree as to anything that should be done, kind or good (and who but fools couldn't ?) then do it, push at it together. *You can't quarrel in a side-by-side push.* But the moment that even the best men stop pushing and begin talking, they mistake their pugnacity for piety, and it's all over."

This was the whole motive of his Inner Mission. " Here," he said, " is the beginning of a ' Catholic ' Church in the old primitive sense. All who have faith in, and therefore share, God's redemptive love, unite to show it in fields where our divisions only injure our work." The practical success of this concerted action of the Churches, first in the smaller field of the borough where he lived, then in the repeal of the Contagious Diseases Act in 1875, and in many other reforms municipal and national deepened the conviction in his mind that on this line lay the hope of concord. The China Emergency Committee was an attempt to extend the same spirit of oneness into the wider field of foreign missions. And, because it was so eminently worth doing, " the highest faculties, the fittest agencies, the most economic methods were needed in order to understand and vanquish the deep-rooted evils of human society, and to inweave the equities and charities of the divine righteousness into the divers relationships of human life." Because it was God's service, nothing but the love that was set on fire by God was equal to the doing of it, and the one certain measure and test of love was sacrifice.

" I know that you have realised, as few men have," he writes to the Rev. R. J. Campbell, " that to subdue sin and win this world to God will still call from us all the dropping of heavy sweats of blood in Gethsemane and the suffering even of the Cross on Calvary. And, strange to say, it is the splendour of this great conflict and sacrifice that rouses the courage of men, and makes them men."

It was his ideal of an aggressive Church—a Church militant, not comfortably lodged in barracks but vigorously campaigning in the field—which drew him to William Booth, the General of the Salvation Army. It was one of the most valued friendships of Paton's life. It dated back to the very beginning of his Sheffield ministry in the early fifties ; it was continued in Nottingham ; many a time Paton went with his friend through hooting mobs to preach in Sneinton market. Nottingham was the place of the General's second birth, and whenever he revisited it he would stay with his old friend. This intimate friendship has given rise to some loose assertions as to the Army's social work having been first suggested by Paton. The exact truth is best stated in his own words. The letter quoted is written to the Rev. Rolland Ramsay, and refers to a contribution which he had written to a book published in October 1909.[1]

"*Oct. 9th*, 1909.

" There is one sentence which I will ask you at once to correct. You have said that the social work of the Salvation Army was undertaken as the result of a conversation I had with General Booth many years ago. That cannot, with any truth, so far as I know, be said. You have been thinking of what I said in the address which I delivered to the Council and members of the Scottish Christian Social Union in October 1902, which was correctly reported by you, but what I said was wholly different. I there said what was wholly true, that years before I had had much conversation and frequent controversy with my dear and life-long friend, General Booth, of the Salvation Army, respecting the social redemptive work of the Church, which from the beginning of my ministry had engaged much of my thought. He then inveighed strongly against the expenditure of money and effort in the humane and social ministries of the Church by which, as I conceived, she was able to attest and prove her great message of divine and saving love to men. General Booth insisted that we needed only to bring the prodigal back to his Father, and then all would be well with him. He would soon be found fitly clothed and in his right mind. ' Yes,' I replied, ' how true it is ! but can the prodigal hear, or ever know that he has such a Father who will fold him, even when clothed in the rags of his shame and sin, in the embrace of His love, if those who are the children of the Father—who are His repre-

[1] " J. B. Paton, Social and Educational Pioneer," by James Marchant. (James Clarke & Co.)

sentatives and have His Spirit—have no thought or care
for him in the sore distress that now afflicts him—showing
him no sympathy and giving him no help ?   How can the
prodigal believe that God is in very truth his Father
and has the love for him of which Christians speak, if
they themselves show no such love ? '   I then said, ' I
need not tell you how wonderfully General Booth; in after-
years; changed his thoughts respecting the methods by
which Christ and His Church will bring about the salvation of the world.'

" That was what I said, but I have no reason to believe
that any conversation of mine so marvellously influenced
my dear friend General Booth, who has been so immediately
under the direct inspiration of God that I always believe
him to have been, in his great social redemptive work,
under the special direction of God and His Christ, and it
is as the revealer of God and His Christ that I welcome
and rejoice in the abounding and wonderful social redemptive work which he has been able, in all parts of the
world, through the Army, to accomplish; and most fervently I pray that every Church may catch his inspiration
and follow his example.

" I became intimately acquainted with General Booth
when he was an Evangelist in connection with the Methodist Church.   He then visited Sheffield, when I had just
settled as a pastor there, and I was profoundly impressed,
not only with his intense earnestness, but with the mighty
emphasis of his preaching to deliver men, not as was then
so frequently the burden of other evangelists, from the
awful condemnation and punishment of sin hereafter,
but from its malign power and curse here.   Salvation from
sin, which was in itself hell, was the doctrine he then
preached.   I soon also became acquainted with his dear
wife, who also most profoundly impressed me and won
my whole-hearted faith and friendship.   She was the
saintliest, wisest, and most tender and inspiring woman
I have ever known.   You may, therefore, understand
how earnestly, when he went to London and began the
Christian Mission, I did all I could to support him.   My
dear friend, Samuel Morley, used to call me ' Booth mad '
because of my devotion to him and his wife, and the
mission upon which they had so bravely, and at such
sacrifice, wholly cast themselves.   And now that the

work has spread as no other work throughout the long history of the Church has ever spread, I can only, with a joyful but humble heart, thank God with a measureless gratitude for His unspeakable grace in calling out General Booth and his sainted wife, and clothing him with the power and wisdom that have made him the burning leader in the advance of Christ's army against the sorrows and evils of time and the dark curse of human sin and guilt."

It was Paton's larger conception of the Church which made him lend such ready sympathy and support at the very outset to the P.S.A. movement, or, as it came later on to be called, to his great joy, the Brotherhood movement. Already, in November 1865, he was writing in the "Patriot" that Christianity had become the religion of a caste, and that it was this social exclusiveness, rather than the spread of Rationalism, which alienated the working folk from the Church. He frankly urged at that time that the Churches should confer with representative working men, and adapt Church methods to the needs of the workers instead of expecting the workers to adapt themselves to the methods of the Churches. The Brotherhood movement he hailed as a religious revival among the manhood of the nation, "a revival in our time of the spirit of the early Church." He was conscious that it was not perfect, but, as he said in a letter to one of his old students, "the Church of Christ has so long failed to exhibit the spirit of Brotherhood in a way to draw the people, we must now be content to gather the people first into Brotherhoods and Sisterhoods, and then later into that united Brotherhood and Sisterhood of the Church." He was constantly urging on his old students to throw themselves into the Brotherhood movement and combine with the Sunday services the week-evening Institute, and all manner of Helping-hand Societies and other practical work. But in his address at the National P.S.A. Conference, held in London, September 1906, it was the spiritual note which he emphasised, and as "the glowing heart of the Gospel which brings glad tidings of great joy to all men," he held up what he called "my three L.'s": "The Divine Law, the Divine Love, the Divine Leader."

His belief in the unity of all Christians in their Master

was not a mere aspiration, it was the working formula of
his life. The sacrament of the Lord's Supper which he
shared in the old shed on the Rigi with the Catholic
Huber, the Lutheran Nasse, and the Anglican rector was
typical of much in his life. At Jerusalem he experienced
much brotherly kindness at the hands of the Armenian
Patriarch and an Archimandrite of the Greek Church.
Before leaving he proposed that they should meet at
a lovefeast in remembrance of the Lord's death, and they
sat down, just twelve in number, men of different tongues
and differing creeds, but all one in their loyalty to the
same Lord. In 1873, when the clergy of the Episcopal
Church were preparing for a mission in Nottingham, he
called together his fellow-ministers and secured their
signatures for a letter which assured the clergy of their
prayerful sympathy.

" Our conceptions of the constitution and maintenance
of the Church of Christ, in which we differ from one
another, do not impair our sense of the supreme importance of our common faith in the perfect example, the
atoning sacrifice, the abiding help, the ceaseless intercession, the divine glory of our Lord Jesus Christ, which is
the foundation of all Christian Churches and which it is
their mission and privilege to proclaim to the world."

Any incorporating union he knew to be for the present,
at any rate, quite impracticable. What he deemed practicable, and found in experience to be practicable in no
small measure, was not incorporation but concorporation,
not fusion but confederation, not unity of government
but unity of spirit. Given that spirit of oneness, the outward forms of oneness would grow out of it in the fulness
of time.

But no unity would be worth having unless each group
of the Christian family held conscientiously to the truth
as it conceived it, as to personal salvation, as to the form
of Church government, and as to the ritual of worship.

" Many Congregationalists agree," he writes to an
Anglican friend, " that there should be only one Church
in one place, as was the case in the apostolic age, although
that one Church was subdivided into smaller congregations to which the name Church was also given. It is the

delegation of apostolic authority to deacons or bishops that will be found to be the main question in dispute. The Lord Christ, we say, abides and rules in His Church by His Spirit, that its members, inspired by His Spirit and subject to His written Word, are free in the government of the Church, and thus best express and fulfil His Spirit and Will—and that no men officially hold power over the Church because it is delegated or bequeathed to them by the apostles.

"However, this great crux of our controversy we will seek to consider in love and with due regard for each other's view, for we are brethren in Him, and not because of any view we hold of the source of authority in His Church."

In working towards a larger concorporation he felt the first necessary step must be union of the Free Churches among themselves. This idea had suggested itself to many other minds. John Angell James, of Birmingham, may perhaps be called the originator. Dr. Guthrie, in 1867, worked out an ideal scheme. These, and others, were the sowers of the seed. The National Free Church Union was the tree that sprang from the seed.

Already in 1874 the idea was germinating in his mind.

"Naturally in any work of union," he wrote, "they who stand the nearest to each other are likely first to cross their boundaries and honour the larger truth which they severally hold, though in differing form."

On April 22nd, 1891, he formulated the proposal in a letter to the Rev. J. A. Meeson, then Congregational minister at Harrogate.

"I was sorry that I could not write you last week. I now fulfil my promise. You will see that the first three general objects of the Union are to create (1) an organ through which the Christian Churches may unitedly influence public authorities and form public opinion. The latter could be done by public meeting, by lecture or conference, by the press and the placard. (2) To form an eye and ear for the Churches so that they may see and hear the evils that exist in the world around them. All our Churches become absorbed in their routine of work and in their local interests, and their members are often wholly unconscious of what is taking place in the world about them. How can they believe except they see and hear! Such a union as we are proposing would bring the fact of these evils and their extent vividly before the conscience of each member of the Church, and give direction and help as to the ways in which these evils can be met and subdued. (3) The Union would in many ways, by combining the agencies of the Churches in practical efforts, sustain them and inspire them and give effective counsel as to methods of action.

" All this is impossible unless the Churches have a union that will be a council of work and warfare in this matter.

" But it is the fourth general object that seems to me of greatest importance. Let me suppose that each Church has a special mission district allotted to it. At present, in our town—and I expect it is the same elsewhere—there are some of the poorest and neediest districts of the town that are not visited or cared for at all, whilst a few others are being visited by four or five Churches and in both cases alike great evil ensues ; in the one case from neglect and in the other from superabundance of almsgiving and a sort of rivalry which seems almost like canvassing. But if the Churches unite, and each Church had a district allotted to it, every district in the town would be equally cared for. Then in such district thus entrusted to one Church we should all agree that fervid gospel mission must be the centre and root of all that is done in the mission by that Church. It seems to me further that if entrusted with a small district, in this way, each Church could deal effectively with the evils which we wish to overcome.

" These evils may be arranged under four heads : Poverty, Ignorance, Sickness, Vice or Crime. Let us see how each evil may be dealt with. For the first the Church should, I think, put itself in connection with the state official who has to care for the poor. It is grievous to think how little the relieving officer is conferred with by either Churches or Charity Organisations. I think that it is most important that in this matter Church and State should be associated. Then the method which has been proved so useful in Elberfeld might be adopted : One person on behalf of the Church having the care, say, of four families, the object of such person being to serve

as a most helpful friend, not so much in the way of alms-
giving, which ought to be only rarely bestowed, and as
the last resort, and generally by some other person than
the visitor. But this friend should endeavour to secure
work for those that are out of work, and help, if no other
way is open, the poor to migrate to districts where work
can be found. (Probably the Union of Churches would
find it necessary to have some place available for the poor
of all districts, where temporary work is provided for
those that are out of work, similar to General Booth's
plan.) In the case of the poor that have to go to the
workhouse from this district, the Church, through its
visitors, should follow them there, and seek to brighten
and bless the life of the poor in the workhouse.

" 2. Ignorance : I know no other way of meeting this
than by promoting Continuation Schools of a most healthful and attractive kind for the young, to be followed by
social Institutes (see enclosed paper) for the young people
when they get older ; or Evening Homes for girls, and
by methods of influencing the reading of people in their
Homes, such as are adopted by the National Home-reading Union. In connection with this reading of the
people, I think that most interesting methods might be
adopted by means of popular lectures, illustrated by
the lantern, to awaken interest in the subjects which
then the people might be encouraged to read upon, and,
as you will see by the enclosed, they can be helped in their
reading by forming them into circles and meeting them
so as to explain and illustrate what they are reading.
Such circles form an admirable opportunity for coming
into pleasant relation with the poor who need this help.

" 3. With regard to sickness : It seems to me that
the Church in every such district should be the ally of
the sanitary officer, and call attention to any want of
sanitation in the district ; also by methods like those of
Miss Octavia Hill, in London, the people might be gradually taught the benefits of ventilation and of cleanliness as
bearing upon health. But, chiefly, surely it is in this
sphere that the Church can show the very love of Christ
to the poorest by helping them to nurse their sick, by
comforting the blind and deaf in Christ-like ways. I wrote
a paper some years ago on ' Woman's Work in the Church,'
in which this point is greatly urged.

" 4. With regard to vice and crime, the Church in each district should keep a watch upon public-houses and places of amusement to see that the law is kept. Remedial and preventive influences and methods are known to all of us, and are stated amongst special methods of work in the paper. I know nothing more effective than the ' Help One Another Society,' founded by Alderman Palmer, of Reading. I enclose a paper respecting its methods. Surely, too, the Churches of the town ought to have a Refuge open every night for the fallen who wish to turn from their sin, and should seek in the case of the first, especially juvenile, offenders, to save them from the contamination of prison, and, if they go to prison, surely the Church should meet at the prison gate those who leave the prison, having perhaps some desire to amend their life, but who can hardly hope to do so if they are met at the gate by their companions seeking to drag them down to their former ways.

" I only sketch here what is really a great subject, but I am quite sure that, if the work were divided, and if it were undertaken in each district under the direction of a Council chosen by the Churches, we should soon grapple most successfully with the evils that we now deplore, and thus the Church would show to the world the redeeming power of Christ's love."

Mr. Meeson took up the idea with so much warmth of conviction that in the following month the following circular was issued to all Free Church ministers in England, showing how the leaders were ready to lead as soon as the Churches were ready to follow :

" We respectfully ask your attention to the following proposal, which aims at the union of our Free Churches in the social redemptive work, which must, it is generally agreed, be thoroughly and systematically undertaken by them.

" We must all rejoice in the fact that our Churches are awaking to see that it is their duty to consider the grave evils that corrupt and darken modern society, to explore their causes, and work for their removal. They thus recognise the necessity of carrying out more earnestly and fully their great redemptive ministry in the world,

so that God's kingdom may come, and His will be done
on earth.   Our Churches are everywhere entering on this
glorious work, but through the indefiniteness and in-
adequacy of their methods, and, above all, because of their
want of that unity which is needful to give sustained
vigour, system, and precision to their action, they often
fail to accomplish the objects they have at heart.

" Accordingly we venture to suggest that it is desirable
to form a Union of Evangelical Churches in each town and
district for their mutual aid and encouragement, for the
guidance of united counsel, and for the co-operation and
power of united action, in their social ministries of redeeming love.   If such local Unions be formed it will be possible,
and certainly it will be most desirable, to form a Central
Representative Council, in which all the Free Evangelical
Churches would be united, and by which all Local Unions
and their branches would be largely directed and greatly
supported.

"We very earnestly invite you to submit this suggestion
and the plan of such a Union, which we subjoin, to the
Church of which you are pastor.   We hope that you will
agree with us that the formation of such a Union is, on
many grounds, eminently desirable and even necessary at
the present time ; and we trust that you will use your
influence to bring your Church into active co-operation
with other Churches in your town or district for the
objects contemplated.   A small committee might, in the
first instance, be appointed by your Church to confer with
other Churches in the matter.

"We are,
        "Yours faithfully,
                "Hugh Price Hughes (London).
                "John Clifford (London).
                "R. F. Horton (London).
                "J. Scott Lidgett (London).
                "G. Howard James (Nottingham).
                "H. T. Marshall (Ashton-under-Lyne).
                "H. T. Chapman (Leeds).
                "T. Guttery (Southport).
                "J. B. Paton (Nottingham).
                "R. Westrope (Leeds).
                "J. A. Meeson (Harrogate)."

Out of this circular grew the National Union of Free Churches. In the platform work Paton was not able to take any prominent part. His head could not stand it; he was too full of other work. But, as Sir Walter Besant said of him in connection with his educational work, he was the person who sat quietly in the corner, did the thinking, and wove the web.

This Union of the Free Churches marks one great forward step on the road towards the wider union of the future—the great Reformation which lies somewhere ahead of us.

" Perhaps the greatest reform of all is the faith which shall enable us all to say, ' Our Father.' This is the faith which both Dissenters and Churchmen have all along been aiming at. As it can no longer be reached through terror, may we not agree to proclaim it in love ? "

To catch glimpses of this all-embracing union of the future and greet it from afar, was one of the greatest pleasures of his life. But he could never conceive of it as an end in itself. The union of Christians, whether partial or complete, was to his mind always a means towards a practical end—the social redemptive ministry of the Church. Always before his eyes there gleamed the vision of the kingdom, proclaimed by his Saviour, the new order in which God was effectively sovereign, all men were obedient to His will, and all social relationships in harmony with His mind. The Church was the instrument by which God was seeking to accomplish on earth this kingdom of heaven. " As in heaven, so on earth." In heaven this kingdom existed already; to realise it here on earth was the function of the Church. In many individual hearts the kingdom has come, but for its full expansion, for its social realisation, it needs the social instrument of the Church.

This conception of the Church as the instrument through which God is working for the fulfilment of His kingdom, a conception which Paton expounds in his earliest public work, involves a change in the ordinary point of view which has several important consequences.

If no Church, however great, is in itself anything more than an instrument for building up something greater still, the kingdom of God, then sectarian asperities are alto-

gether out of place, because that "something greater" can
only be accomplished by a combination and co-operation
of all our fellow-men under the guidance and inspiration
of the same indwelling Spirit. If the rescue of individual
souls from hell be the one purpose to be fulfilled, then no
wonder that the several Churches which have found their
own way effective for this end (whether it be by means
of the penitent-form or by means of confession and absolution), regard their own methods as representing the
whole counsel of God. But if this need of personal salvation from the terrors after death is only part and parcel
of a much larger need, the need of the kingdom of God,
the " new earth wherein dwelleth righteousness," and if
the several Churches are to be valued according to their
several contributions to that great consummation, then
any sectarian conflict is absurd and insufferable ; all
strength is needed for fighting the common foe ; we cannot
afford to spend it in mutual antagonisms. Again, the
wider point of view eliminates the old danger, so difficult
to define, the danger of Erastianism, because it eliminates
the dividing-line between the secular and sacred. All
things are made sacred, because all things are summed up
in Christ. The State itself becomes sacred, because political measures become the methods through which Christ's
Church seeks the accomplishment of Christ's will.

Above all, the new conception of the Church means a
strong forward policy of action.

" In my opinion the Church has hitherto been regarded
too much as a passive assembly of people to receive a
certain amount of pulpit eloquence. We need the pulpit
to proclaim truth, but what I long to see is the minister
quickening the energies and directing the activities of the
Church for practical redemptive service. And in that
service all saints must share. I think the new version of
the passage in Ephesians iv. 11 and 12, is one of the most
important corrections in the revised text. It sets forth
what I hold to be the primary duty of the Christian minister,
and gives the key-note of what I think ought to be the
ministry of to-day. The old text runs : ' And He gave some,
apostles ; and some, prophets ; and some, pastors and
teachers ; for the perfecting of the saints, for the work of
the ministry.' Now the true rendering is ' for the perfect-

ing of the saints unto the work of the ministry—of their ministry.' The minister is to be the pastor, teacher, and evangelist. He has to teach from the Word of God, so that the great principles and motives of the Christian faith shall inspire and direct the saints (those who are consecrated in faith to Christ), in the work of their ministry, both in regard to the worship of God and the uplifting and strengthening of the brethren, and also with regard to the redeeming of the world. To this end there must be teaching, far more definite and practical than it is. There must be training ; the Church ought to be a training-school. There must be organisation. The minister should not be simply a pulpit exhorter. Though I believe the pulpit, properly used, can be made the greatest instrument for the inspiration and direction of the Church, I am convinced that the first duty of the minister is to brigade—if I may use the word in this connection—the members of the Church in the loving discharge of their great duties, the redemptive work of Christ which can be shared by all. We of the Free Churches have preached freedom, but we have not organised it. We must organise freedom so as to quicken and educate our members to fulfil the great responsibilities that devolve upon them.

"The function of the Church is to reveal Christ. If only men could see Christ and know Him ! And where should men see Him if not in ' the Church which is His Body ' ?

"The specific duties to which the Free Churches are called are three : (1) The study of Christ's teaching of the fundamental principles of the Christian faith in relation to the social problems of our time. (2) The upholding of Christ's authority as the Lord and Redeemer of human society, as well as of individuals. (3) The wise direction of Christian redemptive efforts so as to redeem and purify the customs, tastes, and habits of the people, to inspire and regulate their civic and social life, and so to abate and remedy the great social evils which degrade humanity."

This was the central purpose of his life. It fulfilled itself in many diverse ways, it expressed itself in all he spoke and wrote. It remained the joy and inspiration of all his labours. "I thank God for one gift more than another," he wrote to Dr. Horton some fifteen months before he died, "that, at the very beginning of my ministry, He showed me what I have seen with growing clearness ever since to be the true mission of the Church of Christ, the Church of His Son." The idea has won its way now to general acceptance. If it is not yet a positive actuating motive, at any rate it no longer provokes dissent. This general acceptance makes it hard to measure the vastness of the change that has come about since Lord Shaftesbury, in the midst of his agitation for reform of the factory system, exclaimed, " All the Churches are against me."

The vision of this Catholic Confederation of all Churches grew all the brighter and clearer and more glorious with the lapse of time. It was " the ocean to the river of his thoughts." The more his thought turned heavenwards, the more it saw laid up in the heavenly places the pattern of a regenerated society for the world. To him, as to Plato, the triumph of what is most divine in the world was also the triumph of what is most human.[1] In his eightieth year, from his sick-bed, he dictated a little pamphlet which sums up all the truth touching God and His Son, as it was given him to see, and on that truth he built up what he called a " Brotherhood of the Kingdom," a brotherhood based on community of prayer and community of service. The actual brotherhood never took the shape which he intended, though many men, members of all communions, consented to the spirit and the practice of it. But God fulfils Himself in many ways, and the seed which the gardener sows does not always spring up in strict accordance with the gardener's label.

" This is the last work of my life," runs a letter to Dr. Watson, dated March 10th, 1910; " it sums up what has really been the purpose of my whole life, which I hope may be continued in this larger and more effective way after I have gone."

In the " Collegium " which has arisen out of the work of the Student Christian Movement—" an experiment towards the corporate study of the will of God for modern life "—there has come to be, under another name, the beginning at any rate of the " larger and more effective way."

[1] Plato, "Republic," 589 c.

To the Rev. H. R. Williamson, of Hove, on his Ordination

" The life within is not a mere truth lodged in the under-standing. It is a habit, a temper, a spirit, which has to penetrate and subdue. Every member of the body and faculty of the mind has to be quickened and irradiated by that new life. Life is an energy. What is the Christian life ? Analyse every one of those ministries of which I spoke. Do you not see that every one of them is a love—love to the Father, love to the brethren, a holy and de-lightful sympathy, love to the lost, wandering children of God. It is not a mere custom, it is a great living principle which has to be trained, perfected, disciplined for service. The Lord formed His Church for the very purpose that it might become a school and place of training for His own children. Battles have to be won, work has to be done, and, if the world is to be redeemed from the tyrannous powers embattled against us, it cannot be done by casual and irregular service. The forces of Christ's Church must be trained and disciplined and directed by wise, I would even say by scientific, direction.

" It may be asked—Why is any one asked to enter the Church ? Why is any one born into a family ? For this one reason in both cases—that the life of that individual might be perfected, enriched, ennobled, and disciplined in a larger life. What a little thing is the one solitary indi-vidual life ! But when it becomes partaker of a larger life, and shares its vitality and power, what a life it be-comes ! It becomes perfected.

" In the visible world living things are all organic and dead things are inorganic. The principle of organic life is that every part of the body is sharing in the larger life of the whole body, is quickened and made vital and lives for the life of the whole body. That is why we become members of a Church : that we may share the large, full blessing and triumphant life of the whole body.

" The higher the life the higher the organism, and the highest life is that of the eternal Son of God, who has made the Church to be His body. An organism in which His own life fulfils its functions must be the most perfect in the universe—the body of the Lord. Let there be wise generalship, skilful combination, trained service, and so let there be splendid compact unity in the Church.

32

To Mrs. Mary Higgs

"HARESHAWMUIR,
"*August* 18*th*.

" Your letter strikes many chords in my heart. Your experience, in some respects, has been mine. I have had to fulfil myself and my ideas of Christian life and service out in the world, and, to a large extent, apart from the Church—without its sympathy or aid.

" But I have never lost my faith in the true Church of Christ, or my vision of her true mission in the world. Also I have understood how it is that, through centuries, the Church has been misled and falsely taught as to the very meaning—nature—objects of Church fellowship.

" Just think that in all great Protestant ' symbols ' or Confessions, the Church is defined as a place or institution in which the Gospel is duly preached and the sacraments are duly administered. That and that *alone* is the meaning, the object of the Church. Horrible !

" But after these centuries do you wonder that the Church has been so self-involved, so blind to the glory of the Redemptive Life, the true service of Christ ? The salvation of the soul has been wrongly and mischievously conceived. To rise into the fellowship of Christ, to be saved not only by Christ but into Christ, to rejoice in sharing His work, breathing His Spirit, being yoked with Him—has this been taught or realised ?

" But now what a change is passing over the Church ! Within these fifty years of my ministry a new world of thought and sympathy and desire has been created in the Church. See the Christian Social Union in England, the Scottish Christian Social Union in Scotland, the Union for Social Service in the Wesleyan and the New Methodist and the Primitive Methodist Church—read the enclosed, which we are issuing on behalf of the Social Questions Committee.

" I therefore greatly desire you to join with me and so many others in awakening and informing, marshalling and training the Churches of Christ in their true mission. Let them know and understand what is the true faith, the true life, the Spirit of Christ. What a mighty force will then be created in our land !

" And the Church itself will be saved in bringing salvation to the world."

CHAPTER XXIX

TWILIGHT AND EVENING BELL

" Till, slowly worn his earthly robe,
   His lavish mission richly wrought,
   Leaving great legacies of thought,
His spirit fail from off the globe."—TENNYSON.

"The evening of life brings with it its lamp."—JOUBERT.

OF John Brown Paton it could never be truly said that
he grew old. Years grew upon him, and his bodily powers
decayed. His sense of hearing in particular grew blunted
after he had passed the age of seventy ; the first symptoms
indeed were earlier. But the inward eye and the inward
ear were quicker than ever to catch the monitions of the
spirit ; languor was not in his heart, and weakness was not
on his brow ; his mind was fuller than ever of plannings
for the redemption of mankind. When, after founding the
British Institute of Social Service at the age of seventy-
three, he took up the great problem of Christianising the
millions of China, he seemed to have taken the whole
world for his parish and to have " specialised in the
universe."

Recognising that he no longer had much use for his
theological and philosophical books, he stripped his study
shelves and sent off half to Mansfield College Library at
Oxford, and half to Westminster College at Cambridge,
adding to the gift a cheque for the expenses of housing.
But his study became more a workshop than ever. The
vacant shelves were quickly filled with boxes containing
correspondence, pamphlets, blue-books, and other ammuni-
tion for the warfare of social redemption. Visitors usually
found it hard to find a chair that was not loaded, and, as
Charles Lamb would say, " every seat was booked." His
brain went on actively energising on behalf of the big
things. " If you saw my correspondence to-day," he
writes to Mr. Fred Marquis, " even you would be staggered,

and I am getting unfit for all this glorious service; therefore I entreat co-operation and bequeath great bequests of divine work and bliss." It was in vain that those who loved him best urged him to confine himself to the transactions of so much business as three strong men might be able to get through.

One of the last sermons he preached was in the Free Church Hall at Garden City, where all the Free Church denominations combined for common worship. He was then seventy-five years of age. The picture given of him in the local paper is singularly happy:

" The calendar tells us that Dr. Paton is becoming an old man. But no one can be in his presence without feeling that his spirit is yet in all the strength of its eternal youth. Looking into Dr. Paton's eyes no man can disbelieve in immortality: he has already triumphed over the grave; the sting of death is not for him; he is already in the heavenly places for which his soul longs. Yet Dr. Paton is by no means a shadowy presence: he has the majestic bearing of simplicity; he has the royal look; his step is firm and his eye bright. He has not lost the secret of this earth: he lives among us bearing the bloom of the celestial city. Unlike so many men, he is not sinking in years, but growing into eternal life. Unlike so many men of his years, he is not putting off the concerns of this world, but he is investing all our common works and ways with the glory of heaven.

" In the pulpit he is a man out of the body. We see none of the arts of the preacher. Bodily tricks and limitations there are none. It is the tried and tested spirit of a man appealing to the minds and consciences of men. The voice is like a bell, pure and clear as the speech of angels. There is no practised eloquence; all is natural and harmonious. The simplicity of his soul is revealed in the unadorned beauty of his speech. He preaches with smiles and tears. At times he can hardly speak for the ravishing splendour that is set before him, and again, his voice is choked with sobs. His smile is perhaps one of the most wonderful characteristics of the man. It springs from the overflowing joy of his soul. It radiates through his worn face and lightens it with a light from above. It was worth a pilgrimage to feel that smile."

A picture of his private life is given by Dr. Forbush. Writing in the " Congregationalist and Christian World " of March 1912, he says :

" Two years ago I took a journey across England on purpose to see him, acting on Emerson's idea that a man may prove as exciting as a cathedral. All I knew about him was gathered from some of his letters, written either in a feverish, illegible handwriting, or in a muddled, much corrected typewriting. Before I ever had time to execute any of his commissions, I had usually received another. Everything from him was marked urgent. I was prepared, therefore, to meet a somewhat strenuous personality. I had somehow expected to find him a young man, tall, wiry, and athletic; but in a moment there came bustling into the room a short, white-haired veteran of seventy-eight, with a thatch of grey beard on the sides of his rosy face, who literally fell upon my neck. He hurried me into his study, as if there were not a moment to spare, although I was to spend the night. We sat down knee to knee, and he handed me the larger end of a speaking-tube, for he was very deaf. But instead of my using it as a channel down which to pour the information which he had declared himself as most anxious to secure, it became indispensable rather for him to gesticulate with. At once it was manifest that nothing could be more fascinating than to listen while this extraordinary man should tell me the story of his prodigious activities. For he had evolved a chain of societies, most of them in a healthy condition, which dove-tailed into one harmonious scheme for the intellectual and moral uplift of the middle class of all England, and which extended from a National Home-reading course, to a Country Farm for epileptics, and from a boys' organisation which was the precursor of the Boy Scouts to a plan for putting reproductions of great paintings into the homes of the people.

" After I had listened to the full story, I sat back, breathless. I seemed to be in the ' Arabian Nights ' of goodness. He was Edward Everett Hale and Washington Gladden and Bishop Vincent in one. I could well believe that the Dean of Westminster had said of him once after leaving him, ' I have often read about the prophets to-day for the first time I have seen a prophet.' "

" He drives a whole row of horses abreast," said Canon
Scott Holland, " and he never doubts that he will keep
them all going." He would never consent to either im-
potence or inaction, or even mere defensive measures, in
the presence of evil. He was always for attack. One
day, in May 1904, he was speaking on the question of
small allotments at the Deanery of Westminster, to a
meeting of younger men, many of whom are now in Parliament. The feeling of that meeting was expressed by Miss
Jebb, who said :

" There is a proverb about rushing fools and fearsome
angels. Now in this matter, if each rushing fool would
take a timid angel by the hand and lead him into the arena
of active effort, and then leave him to work out his own
salvation in the agricultural sense, we should probably do
very well. Dr. Paton I should call a ' rushing angel,' and
under his leadership we shall do well."

The incessant multiplication of his enterprises, out of
all proportion to his strength, was the perpetual anxiety of
his wife. Constantly he was making promises to confine
himself for the future to some three or four of his many
schemes and devolve on others the care of the rest ; but the
keeping of the promises was always postponed, and anon
a new scheme came upon the scene and claimed a new
set of boxes on the study shelf.

'When the gods for one deed asked me, ever I gave them twain.'

In spite of the multiplicity of his own work he could
always find interest and joy and helpful suggestions in the
work of others. There were plenty ready to criticise, ready
to sniff at the day of small things, or at any rate not to
commit themselves till some degree of success was assured.
But he was constantly discovering the day of small things
and holding out a hand to help a fellow-worker for the
kingdom before he had won his way to recognition.
Joy in the work of others made his own cup of joy to run
over. As soon as he heard of the League of Ministering
Children, he recognised that Lady Meath had been working
out in that League an idea which was specially dear to
his own heart. He at once got into touch with Lady
Meath and did his best to get a branch of the League started
in each Sunday-school under the Sunday-school Union.

The Workers' Educational Association was not of his devising, but, as Mr. Albert Mansbridge says : "Before the W.E.A. was, he had been doing its work."

" I remember it so well—it was a busy morning at the Co-operative Building Society where I was employed. A man of noble presence came to the business counter. It was my lot to attend to him. ' Can you tell me how to find Mr. Mansbridge?' he asked; 'I am told he has to do with the Woolwich Co-operative Society.' When I told him that my name was Mansbridge, he lost no time, but at once enlisted me in the army of those who, led by him, strove to fight against ignorance and apathy, and taught purity and truth everywhere in the common life. His delight at the recent formation of the W.E.A. was boundless. It seemed to him to embody many of his ideals; he prophesied its power; he blessed it with double blessings. Just at the time it was struggling on—it had no money—but the Doctor on that very day said he had money placed in his hands to use, and he would place £50 at our disposal. I remember we purchased a type-writer and a copying machine—badly needed—and were so enabled to employ in the evenings our first typist, who still works for us.

" From that day onwards he felt our work was his. I do not remember one word of criticism. His great influence over us lay in his abounding confidence, his great belief in all that we did. Nothing in connection with us was too small. He took our families into the great expanding love which was peculiarly his. How could we flag or get depressed when the warrior with the heart of a little child was always cheering us on ?

" Sometimes he visited us in our homes. I remember how he came, at great expense of time, to Ilford, where we lived, and a number of us greeted him. He sat in an armchair, and told us of the essential spirit of the reformer. He brought all ideas to his service. To my wife he turned and said : ' When your husband comes home tired, make fun for him; ask him what sport he has had ; how many fish he has caught.' And all the time my little lad was on his knee. How he loved children, and how they loved him !

" Never in the most serious letter did he forget a message, and a few stamps to buy the little one ' some chocolate, to be administered in wise proportions by his mother.'

" He was indeed a ' father in God,' and we were of his family."

He was constantly seeing the good in others, and in each good trait the potentiality of its full development. The fact that Dr. Paton believed in him made many a young worker to believe more firmly in himself.

Very rarely has the pioneer the gift of the cultivator. He opens up new paths, but as a rule he is not fitted for spade-work and settled life. What amazed people in Paton was his combination of administrative ability with the power of vision and of initiative.

" In ability to grasp the situation and to keep in mind the details of many varied matters he excelled any business man I have ever met," writes Professor James C. Stuart. " If Dr. Paton had become a business man, he would have a position of the first rank in the business world. As it was (or is) no man has struck me as having less care to accumulate money, nor indeed for public purposes has he ever magnified the importance of money. To my knowledge he has before now returned part of the amount sent to him by a friend for one of his many enterprises."

Rarely, too, has the pioneer the gift of working with others. Paton did all his work with and through committees.

" London is so large, and in a sense impossible," he writes to Professor Patrick Geddes, " that, in order to accomplish anything definite and practical, it will be necessary to have a fervent and compact body of associates working with us to fulfil a definite programme. The Garden City is an example of what can be done if there be such a compact and earnest body of workers."

In these committees he was not always or often the Chairman, or even the Secretary, but he was the inspirer. His presence was always a clarion call to march, it always inspired fresh hope and vigour. " The gold is in sight," he would say, " and only needs working." That was why he never found committees, as so many ardent souls have done, more of a hindrance than a help He shared all the worries; he never built any barriers round his life to save himself from the niggling, irksome details of the actual. The working secretaries of the Home-reading Union, of the Co-operative Holdings, of the Christian Union for Social Service, of all his social schemes, were never met with " You mustn't bring these worrying things to me." He was always the big brother who helped. Though he was constantly seeing the golden gates gleam in the distance, he knew that there were long and weary marches before the crusading host could reach its goal. " You know I believe nothing in this world can be carried *per saltum*," he wrote to Mr. Isbister, " but, given wise methods and right aims, it's dogged that does it."

He had the great love which availed for the small things as well as the great, and through that love the impossible became the possible. In all the detail and the friction of the daily routine, as well as in the larger conceptions, he was the inspirer. He " did the work of the propeller," as he had urged his old student to do, out of sight for the most part, but, though out of sight, never out of harness.

" My colleagues and I," says one of his fellow-workers, " only blew the bellows, so to speak, while he in masterly fashion handled the keys ; yet he would never take the bow, and somehow managed to make us almost believe that the glory was ours."

But light has a double function, it is reflected by the bright surface, but it ruthlessly exposes any dark stain upon that surface, and it is the same with the light of a man's presence when it comes into contact with dishonour-able ways. Sometimes he found it necessary to speak straight words to a crooked person.

" Am I wrong in thinking that you have allowed your-self to be entangled in these strange mis-statements by attempting to evade the difficulties and complications which press upon you ? If this has been the case, let me entreat you to break from all such evil entanglements of every sort by the full and fearless confession of the truth. I have sought and laboured to help you from difficulties which pressed upon you. But honest and utter truthfulness alone will help you or any of us. Truth alone can make us free, and I would delight, if you were boldly and with perfect frankness to confess your error and fault in these mis-statements, to stand by you in the further hard work that lies before us. I know how difficult it will be for you—with your high temper and spirit—to do this, but do, by the love of our Lord and by the hope of His favour and of a true manhood, in His sight, make the one supreme and holy effort. Such humility will bring truth and love and peace with it—an evil pride will work evil. If you do not answer my last letter I shall judge that you prefer that all co-operation between us should cease—and perhaps that may be right. It cannot continue save, as I said, with the confidence and openness of truth."

There was wrath, deep, stern wrath, but it was selfless. As Dean Church said of Stanley: " His wrath reminds me of that wonderful phrase in Revelation, the 'wrath of the Lamb.'"

One of his most difficult achievements was to overcome that repugnance which Englishmen, and especially Free Church Englishmen, feel towards accepting the help of a government department.

" I quite agree," he wrote, " we must carry out the plan with the freedom of Christian love; but we must not reject the proffered hand of help, nor kick against any reasonable conditions as to inspection and control which are laid down for the expenditure of money which, after all, is not ours, but public money. We must readily submit to whatever orderly co-operation with both State and Church is not incompatible with freedom and with love."

And again to Mr. Simpkinson, he writes in December 1904:

" I have often said I have received more help from the Board of Education and the Local Government Board than, I think, from any one else in all the charitable work in which I have taken a part."

The chronic difficulty of most committees and most

philanthropies is money. Raising funds represents the prosaic side of humanitarian enthusiasm. Paton did not shirk it. His wife and children often complained that he had to write so many begging letters. If he did the work, we thought that others might supply the means; but he himself never uttered one word of complaint. He not only accepted the extra work, but rejoiced in it, as he rejoiced in all that belonged to the service of his heavenly Father. He would give money himself in royal fashion, for he was frugal in the small things so that he might be generous in the great things. "Money is no use to a sieve like you," said a rich man, "it all runs through." "Yes," was his reply, "it runs through, but not a penny runs to waste. Keep on pouring." He was called "the prince of purse-bleeders," and he revelled in the nickname. "Go to," he would say of a rich man who was hoarding, "we must bleed his purse for the good of his soul."

"I prayed the Lord to give me success," said a rich man in his company in June 1893. Paton seized the opening: "And He has given it to you. What a debt you owe to Him! How do you intend to repay it?"

Many stories could be told of his happy captures. Mr. Henry Harrison, of Prestons, Bow, tells the story of his setting out with a few friends to climb a mountain in Arran. They set out just after sunset; at midnight they knelt in prayer together upon the granite altar-steps; at dawn they watched the sunrise from the summit, "and before the sun was well up I found I had promised him £100 towards the Institute."

The Rev. J. Radford Thomson had a rich man in his congregation. He, too, had to bear his scot and lot. "Thomson," Paton would say, "use my authority with him."

If a thing was according to the need of man and the will of God, it had to be done, and Paton laughed at the idea that considerations of money should stand in the way of its accomplishment. "We must never lose the battle for lack of powder and shot," he would say.

But in itself money was nothing to him. It was kept in its proper place as means and not end. "Money I care not for," he writes to Mr. Henry Ollard, "save as all influence and all agencies it can bring are used unreservedly

and sacredly for the winning of the world to God and
holiness."

.   .   .   .   .

Travelling once in a train one of his friends happened
to mention Paton's name. "Oh, you know Dr. Paton,
do you?" said a fellow-traveller, " now he's a man with
a bee in his bonnet if you like." "A bee in his bonnet!"
was the reply, "he has a whole hive of them, and they're
all humming."

He could not have kept his hive full of workers unless
he had a wonderful faculty of enlisting new recruits for
new enterprises, and also of converting drones into
workers. Few men have had the gift of inspiration so
immediate and so complete. The very first meeting
served to establish a contact of soul with soul.

"I can never forget," writes the Rev. A. T. Saville,
"how you took me by the hand nearly fifty years ago
one Sunday evening at Archer Chapel, and how you and
your dear wife welcomed me to supper that evening. It
was an epoch-making hour for me. Humanly speaking,
on that memorable occasion the first link was made that
led me to the ministry."

All through his life he was constantly laying his hand
upon this or that person and saying, "Do this work—
not for me, but for your Father and mine. God has
specially gifted you, and God has been training you for
this very thing." He was always acting the recruiting-
sergeant, and pressing men and women into the service.

"Whenever he laid an egg," says Mr. Holden Byles,
" he immediately looked out for some hen to sit upon it,
and, having found her, he told her that she was the only
hen that could hatch that particular egg, and so the hen
felt constrained to sit. Like the centurion of the synagogue, he could say to one man " Go," and he went; to
another, "Do this," and he did it. And it was all because his own enthusiasms were so infectious that every
one with whom he came into contact seemed to catch
them."

Frequently the casual meeting in a train or restaurant
was enough. His personality was so diffusive and so

conciliating. In his presence no one could be cynical.
Again and again his very aspiration was an inspiration.
He made men realise in some inexplicable way the beauty
of goodness. And the humblest as well as the highest
shared in the glow of his diffusive happiness. The maid
who took up his breakfast to his room, the porter at the
club who helped him on with his greatcoat, felt, just as
much as the Earl and the Countess, that even to see him
made one better.

One single incident I must select among many. I
select it not only because it is typical, but because it
serves at least to mention one side-track of his activity
which has not found a place hitherto in this narrative.

" On a certain Saturday afternoon," writes Mr. Charles
E. Hecht, " just before Christmas, 1895, I happened to
be working late at my chambers in the Temple preparing for a lecture I had undertaken to give that evening.
I was feeling, I remember, somewhat down in the mouth
—weary of waiting for the chance of secretarial work that
would not come. Returning from an adjournment for
tea, I encountered on the stairs an old gentleman with a
manner as kindly as it was winning. ' Does Mr. Edward
Atkin live here ? ' he inquired. ' Yes,' I replied, ' on the
next floor, but I doubt if you will find him in. May I
run up and see ? ' I did so, only to find the stout outer
door closed. ' May I come into your room and write a
note to him ? ' he asked. The letter finished, his quick
eye discovered on my table some printed facts relating
to the temperance work of the London County Council,
with which I had been specially desired to deal in my
lecture that evening. We discussed the subject eagerly
for a few minutes, and then parted. Before doing so,
however, we had discovered—I forget how—a mutual
friend in the person of the Rev. J. D. Jones, then of
Lincoln and a lecturer at the Nottingham Institute, and
my old chum at the Victoria University. On the Monday
afternoon immediately following, two visitors were announced, who proved to be my newly made friend and
the late Mrs. Sheldon Amos. Without wasting time in
preliminaries, they explained they had come on a mission.
It was within a few weeks of those appalling massacres in
Armenia organised by the late Sultan with such cold-

blooded deliberation, and carried out by his underlings and the Mohammedan population at large with such fiendish barbarity and cruelty. 'We want,' they told me, 'to make known the terrible facts to the English people, with their peculiar political responsibility, and to Christian people everywhere. We want for this purpose to start a society,—no name or other details have as yet been determined,—and we have come to ask if you will consent to help us by acting as its Secretary.' This I agreed to do. After the lapse of years I cannot recall further details save the noble old man's fiery zeal and a sublime faith which would remove mountains. With enthusiasm such as my visitors and their little band of fellow-workers possessed in such a high degree, no difficulties were allowed to stand in the way ; and the day after Boxing Day we opened, in Arundel Street, Strand, the office of " The Information (Armenia) Bureau," as, after much discussion it was determined to call it. Canon Scott Holland was our Treasurer, and Mrs. (now Lady) Bunting and her sister, Miss Lidgett, were among its leading spirits.

" Our first piece of work was the circulation of a Call to Prayer, signed by a number of the Bishops and eminent Nonconformist ministers, and subsequently translated into French, German, Russian, Italian, and Arabic. The arduous task of despatching this and other papers to some ten thousand representative people was undertaken by as devoted a band of workers as it was ever my good fortune to meet. Many of them were teachers and social workers (Mrs. Pethwick Lawrence, then Miss Pethwick, was among the latter) giving up part of their hardly earned vacation to the work. In point of numbers the committee was the smallest I have ever known. It was, however, prolific of suggestions, and was by no means the least effective in its influence on public opinion. Dr. Paton's health at this time left much to be desired. Frequently his first request was for an improvised sofa, and in this recumbent attitude the brave old warrior would pour forth a torrent of suggestions. Like Napoleon, the word 'impossible' was not to be found in his vocabulary."

Some idea of the multiplicity of his latter-day activities may be gathered from his engagement-book. I select the list of engagements for a few days' visit in February 1908 to that meeting of the waters called London :

China Emergency Committee.
Home-reading Union.
Collection of Essays defining Evangelical position as to the Church, etc.   See Dr. Garvie and others.
Lingfield and Christian Social Service Union.
Brigade of Service.
Boys' and Girls' Life Brigades.
Social Questions Committee of Free Church Council.
Small Holdings.
Co-operative Banks.
Pictures for Schools ; appointments with Dr. R. P. Scott, H.M.I., and Educational Supply Association.
Christian Endeavour.
Social Institutes.
Moral Education—Mr. Clifford Barnes and Dr. M. E. Sadler's inquiry.

Sandwiched in with these, and almost smothered by the multitude and magnitude of its neighbours, is one personal matter, the drafting of his will.

And yet, with all these activities humming in his head, he was full of freshness and full of welcome for any old acquaintance and any new recruit. " How are you, Doctor ? " the friend would say as he met him in the thick of the Strand. " I am very old," he would say, " very deaf, and very happy."

" Well, Doctor, you don't look very old."

" You're quite right," he would say, " I'm eighty years young, not quite, but very nearly now." And then he would begin, how there was a hero at the heart of every boy, and it was our supreme business to find out that hero and give it scope and growth and authority.

" There has never been any one like him," writes Canon Scott Holland. " In a world of dire despair he never lets his hope flag or his light burn low. That is the wonder of the man. Age, far from dulling his outlook, seems to kindle new fires. Dauntlessly he pushes on, as I catch sight of him, amid a heedless crowd in Ludgate Hill, bearing his bag, stuffed full of his last suggestions, on

towards some far-seen vision of the end. Did any one
ever retain such unbroken confidence in the good that
is somehow going forward ? Always he is knocking at
one's door with a new Bill, drafted on measureless stores
of hope, in his pocket. Always, the post brings you
another large envelope, bursting with articles, calls, schemes,
and all of them are tingling with force and charged with
effective expression. Each paper is just what one wanted
to say, said as one never could say it. And the only
difficulty comes from the multitude of brimming ideas
which come hurrying along, each of which would take a
lifetime for its practical realisation. Dr. Paton means
them all to be travelling on at once. He drives a whole
row of horses abreast ; and he never doubts that he will
keep them all going. We, poor weaklings, are left far
behind, anxiously whacking our own poor lame cob
along. The old man beats the youngest of us. And his
faith in what he is doing ! What a reward it carries
with it ! "

Enthusiasm fires others, but it burns self. Ever since
his breakdown in 1863, he had been forced to put some curb
upon his ardour for work. Yet ever and anon he was
plunging into new work with the energy of a boy just set
free from school, and from time to time there was a breakdown. His nerves became very susceptible ; he could not
attend public meetings because he could not stand the
heat of the gas on his head ; the sun's heat affected him
in the same way ; sea air worked too strongly upon his
nerves, and any tea or coffee but the weakest and flimsiest
solution had the same effect. The worst of his breakdowns came immediately after the starting of the Home-
reading Union, but there were many other times when
he was quite laid aside, and unable to do any reading or
writing. He was a man without any recreations. All
attempts to entice him into playing croquet or any other
game, however gentle, were failures. His hobby was his
work. This would have made his case inconceivably
difficult for the doctors, had he not learned in a wonderful
way how to rest. A small shelter was put up in the
garden, and for long periods he would lie out in the open air
alone, always calm and always happy. " I have had a
glorious morning adoring God for all His goodness," he

would say, and his face would beam with joy as he said it. With him, as with Byron, it was in solitude that he was least alone.

" It is such hard work to do nothing," he said, when first the Doctor prescribed this entire cessation of mental work, and any physical exertion seemed to exhaust him quite as much as business. But he turned his necessity to glorious gain. His great friend, Mr. George E. Tucker, who had been one of his most vigorous helpers at Sheffield, had been by sudden illness disabled from all active work, and his old pastor suggested to him that, though the ministry of preaching and church work was no longer possible, there remained for him the ministry of intercession. The ministry he had suggested to his friend now became his own. His soul went out in silent prayer and communion, and in those long hours the fountains of his soul were replenished in a wonderful way.

> Love, to be Love, must walk Thy way
> And work Thy will.
> Or if Thou say, " Lie still,"
> Lie still and pray.

There is nothing the body suffers which the soul cannot turn to advantage, if it be in tune with the Infinite.

And so, while he was kept outside the fray, he was holding up his hands to bless. How closely he followed the fortunes of the field his lieutenants know full well. " Tell me exactly where you are with the book, and what you are engaged in now," he wrote to Dr. Josiah Strong; " I want to pray intelligently." " Which is to be the day ? " he wrote to a lady who was to be married, " I long to know it, that I may calendar it in my prayers and gild it with my hopes." In the same way he always wished to visualise the scenes in which his loved ones moved. It was part of the way he had of projecting his life into that of others. Whenever one of his children moved to new quarters he would always come to see them as soon as he possibly could, and, when his travelling days were over, he asked for as many photographs as possible, both interior and exterior, of a new house to which one of his sons had moved, that so he might have his mental picture set in the right framework of environment. It was in these pauses, too, that he learned, what so few even of the saints learn, to pray for the great causes, that men might

33

come to know God's mind and might be moved to do His will with regard to China, and with regard to all the great social questions in which his mind was perpetually engaged.

It was thus the Good Shepherd made him to lie down beside the quiet waters, and restored his soul. " Be still and know that I am God." In the stillness he came to know his Father with a closer intimacy than before. It was in stillness that God came very near to him, printed His will upon the mind, and His feeling on the heart, for it is in wise passivity a man learns what no books can teach—not only the truths he finds, but the truths which find him.

" I was thinking the other day," wrote Mrs. Josephine Butler to her friend Professor James Stuart, " what it is makes one like to have a man like Mr. Paton on one's side as a personal friend. It is, to my mind, because he lives near to God. This makes one turn to such men with confidence as one would to a person who had come from a recent conversation with Christ."

This was written in 1874, and it was what many people felt about him all through his life. He seemed to come straight from the Presence-chamber, nay, more, he brought the Presence-chamber with him. " That man does not need to go to heaven," said one who had met him for the first time; "he lives in heaven already." More and more, as he grew older, men were conscious of a radiance in his very face which seemed to be—which was—the spirit breaking through the flesh and irradiating it with the glories of the Eternal. This was the secret of his continual joy. No languor could touch it, no note of resentment or impatience ever jarred upon the eternal melodies within. His being was " rooted in sunlight." No outward happenings made any difference. He had the inviolable royalty of inward happiness.

    .   .   .   .   .

As age crept on, the growing deafness and the imperative need of rest kept him more at home than he had ever been before in the whole course of his working life. But the tide of correspondence never ceased. Twice a day it surged into his study and twice a day it poured out again upon the world. The lines of communication were never cut between the general and his operations along the extended front. "One never makes a little suggestion," wrote Canon Barnett in 1908, " but you have at once a plan ready for its execution."

His handwriting in earlier days had been a trial to many friends, and a constant source of merriment. "Chaotic unintelligibility," was Mr. Bachelor's description of it. One business man always kept his letters till Sunday, because he knew they were about something good, and there was more time on Sunday to make them out. Another friend said, "I do better still. I wait till he comes himself, and reads them to me." In his last years he had a typist, and his correspondents were saved from the solving of many curious puzzles. But what they gained in one way they had to pay for in another. It was quicker to dictate, and the type-writer made multiplication of copies fatally facile. Many of his letters missed fire because of a certain too-muchness which frightened busy people, and the mass of enclosures was apt to smother the real gist of the message. But some found the bulky envelopes full of powder and shot for the campaign; to others they were full of new inspiration and hope; to many like the touch of a brother's hand.

" He wrote me a very kind letter," says the Rev. Richard Roberts, " to say how much he appreciated certain work I was trying to do. I had no notion that he knew anything at all about it, and the letter was therefore wholly unexpected; but it was a real uplifting, and I remember it as a kind of outstanding point in the otherwise trivial record of my work. It chanced that I was interested in two of his main concerns—religious education and Christian social service, and, though knowing how preoccupied he must be, I refrained from writing to him save only on the most rare occasions, yet he frequently sent me a word to advise me of any new and important developments in these two directions, which he considered one should know about and watch."

He was, in fact, to the last a spontaneous intelligence department for all manner of social workers, keeping each in touch with the best that was being done by the others in widely sundered portions of the field.

Nor was the ministry of correspondence all one-sided. Many a letter told him how much help he had given, and was still giving. In serving mankind he had not forgotten to love man, and the love he had given was returned in rich measure. Never, till I read the letters my father received, did I realise how much one chance word or greeting may help a fellow-pilgrim on the way, or come as an angel at midnight to set free an imprisoned soul.

.   .   .   .   .

In his restful periods he was much with his little invalid daughter Muriel. The life of the family centred round her invalid couch, and she had always been specially beloved.

" I thought it better to-day to telegraph to you at once, so that you might have my address," he wrote from Halle in 1872, " that I might learn at once if our sweet Muriel were worse. It has come to me, as a revelation of her perfect sweetness, the thought—the fear of her loss. May God spare her dear life, even though it be the life of an invalid, for her bright and peaceful nature will shine with purity and tenderness upon us all, though it be through a darkened window.

" The other children are always in our minds," he would say ; " but it's Muriel, the afflicted one, who is always on our hearts."

It has been said that all happy families are alike, and each unhappy family is unhappy in its own way, and that is probably the reason why the history of the happy family is never written. In the happiness of the family at the Congregational Institute there was, in ways that cannot be told, that influence of sweet and sacred unifying love that surrounds the bed of constant suffering meekly borne.

In May 1909, after one day of painful suffering, quietly in her sleep, his loved Muriel breathed her last. God's finger touched her, and she slept.

" It is of God's grace," he writes to Sir Percy Bunting, " that dear Muriel has gone home before her parents, who cannot now long linger ; and for her the manifestation and joy of the perfect life in the Father's home must have brought unspeakable bliss. She was the brightest of all my children, incomparably sweet and loving ; she was the dearest bond of my family, and has drawn all our hearts to the place where now she knows the perfect life. She has gathered us all into the most blessed and loving sympathy with herself, and so with suffering childhood everywhere. It is just wonderful to think that a life so limited should have been a fount of such bright and holy influences."

It was a summer evening in June of the same year. I had come home, breaking my journey, as my wont was, at Nottingham, on the way up to committee-meetings in London. That evening there was to be a great display of physical exercises by the school-children. It was to be in the Forest, and after tea we wheeled my father out to the head of the slope from which he commanded a full view of the scene. He was bowed now, like an autumn tree that stoops with the weight of its fruit-laden boughs. Totteringly he could walk from his couch to the bath-chair, but through the noble face of the earthly tabernacle there shone the heavenly light which

> Seemed a thing that could not feel
> The touch of earthly years.

Below, the spacious fields were filled with thousands of school-children, the girls in white and the boys wearing bright scarves of red and yellow and green. At the sound of the bugle the movements and the marching began. The order, the rhythm, were perfect; the sight was one to gladden the soul of any man who thought of what England's children might accomplish for England's future, and this great spectacle seemed like the fulfilment of one of his own visions of thirty years ago. The light of joy was in his face, his every breathing was unworded praise, there was something in his look which spoke of—

> Solemn troops and sweet societies
> Which sing, and singing, in their glory move.

He needed no shepherd's glass to see the shining city, as he

> Stood on the heights of his life
> With the glimpse of the life that is higher.

There is one glory of the celestial and another glory of the terrestrial, but in my father's face one saw how the lower glory was ready to be clothed upon with the higher.

No wonder men asked for his benediction. " If N. had not been there, I would have knelt and asked for his blessing. But, even as it was, I knew that I was getting it all the time," writes Mr. Frank Lenwood. Many a Christian worker who saw him on his couch in the later days left him with new hope and heart for the conflict, and a newly sharpened sword.

To most people the radiance and peaceful joy of his old age seemed so natural that they thought it came by nature. That was not so. By nature he was active, and even restless; there was in him the spirit " that bids not sit nor stand, but go "; by nature he was tempted to impatience; by nature he found it the hardest task in the world to keep within the limits of his shortened tether; and now and again there would gleam out a flash of the will that must be about the Father's business, and forgot that the Father's business was for him not doing, but to be still and see the salvation of the Lord. It was by the grace of Christ, by much prayer and striving, that he became trustful, peaceful, content to lie and wait the good time of the Lord. In his private litany the first grace for which he prayed was meekness.

To Mrs. Higgs

"April 29th, 1909.

" L. has told you that I have now begun what he calls my Sabbatic year—the working years are ended; but in communion with my chosen friends and fellow-workers, and with Him we love and serve, my Sabbatic year will, I hope, be a very blessed, and it may be a very useful year. I am allowed to dictate a few letters, and so I may, by counsel, sympathy, and prayer, still give help."

"Oct. 29th, 1910.

" How can I thank you for that loving and most spiritual and soul-reaching letter which you have sent me ? I shall keep it by me, as I have two other of your letters, and read it often again, for I do wish to enter into your holy and happy faith, your perfect rest in the ever-watchful and gracious love of our Lord, and His sweet and abiding and blessed fellowship with you. How I delight to think of such an experience as God is giving you, and how I long to enter into that experience and abide in it! Your beautiful ' Song in Sickness,' too, I shall copy, and seek not only to repeat it for myself and to know its holy peace, but to give it, if I may, to others—weak, and it may be suffering, but who yet may have an ecstasy of joyful faith in the midst of it. How I do bless God for all that He has given to you, and even more that you are able to tell it to others like myself, and lift them up not only to see the vision which you see, but in some measure to win faith and peace which are given to you."

To George Tucker, whose ministry of intercession he was now sharing, he writes :

" You remember your mother's window above the door was always alit to welcome us when we came back from meetings. The window of heaven is now alit to welcome us."

. . . If old age had yet its work and its inward discipline of meekness, it had also its abundant honour. In October 1909 Mr. James Marchant published what he modestly spoke of as a short sketch of a great man's work, " J. B. Paton, Educational and Social Pioneer." [1] To that volume many friends contributed, and out of the fulness of their hearts spoke of what he had been to them.

" I am humbled to the very dust," he wrote, " and even awed, by the wonderful outpouring of love from those who have been associated with me in the fellowship of service. . . . I cannot understand how it is that they are led so to think thus of me, for I am conscious of much weakness, and have always seen so much more that might have been done. Yet I must rejoice that God has given me this great joy of the warm affection of those who have been associated with me."

What gladdened him more than any personal joy was that the vision of the Church which had been given him at the beginning of his ministry—a Church full of redeeming and practical sympathy, of effort and sacrifice as wide and as deep as humanity's utmost need, was gradually

[1] Published by James Clarke & Co.

filling the minds of all who took upon them the name of Jesus.

In September 1909 came the fiftieth anniversary of his wedding. By his own special desire, and that of his wife, the prospective event was kept as quiet as possible. The doctor, also, Dr. J. G. Johnston, thought it wiser. His children celebrated the occasion by installing a system of hot-water heating in the house, and building for him a little sunny shelter opening out from the room on the ground-floor in which he lay, so that he might lie out even in cold or wet weather with the windows open and enjoy the fresh air, the sight of green, growing things, the flight of the birds and their song, and, not least, the varied glories of the cloud-scape and the sky. It was a thank-offering for a home life, singularly blessed by God.

One day, two of the students had come to take his instructions about some business connected with the Institute library. When business was over, he said: "Will you open that door, and see what my children have done for me ? What do you think of that ? I call it my 'nook.' " Then, after a pause: " I wonder if the money might not have been put to better use; but I remember that our dear Lord allowed the box of ointment, very precious, to be broken over His feet."

In this bright chamber of peace he would lie, enjoying the flowers and the fresh air and the communion of spirit with his God and his friends. Beside him stood a Calendar of Cheer, prepared by Miss Annie Barlow, with a message of joy for each new day. Beside him, too, stood an illuminated copy of Canon Rawnsley's Sonnet on *Work and Make Music*, also the work of a dear friend, Miss Emily H. Smith. The morning's letters were under his pillow, and on a low table lay the letters he was to sign or to answer, the doctor sometimes insisting that all business letters should be removed out of sight for the time being. But always, whether he was allowed to dictate a letter or not, his thoughts were of the work and the triumphs of the future.

" He has made lovers," wrote Principal Forsyth in Mr. Marchant's volume. In the following year, November 1910, his lovers conspired together to dedicate to him

MRS. PATON.

the report of the proceedings of the Conference on Public Morals held at the Caxton Hall. A beautiful sonnet written by Canon Rawnsley [1] was printed in the centre of a large card, and round it were the autograph signatures of some forty men and women who took part in the conference, the leaders of the nation in the work of public morals. " Churchman of all Churches," Canon Rawnsley called him, and all Churches are represented in the signatures : Father Bernard Vaughan, the Bishops of Hereford and Durham, the Chaplain-General of the Forces (Bishop Taylor-Smith), Bishop William Barry, General Bramwell Booth, Dr. F. B. Meyer, the Chief Rabbi, Dr. R. F. Horton, Dr. A. E. Garvie, the Head Master of Eton (the Hon. E. Lyttelton), Mr. G. A. Aitken, Mr. Ramsay Macdonald, Mr. Charles Voysey, Lady McLaren, Mrs. Sidney Webb, Mrs. Booth, Mr. Alfred D. Acland, Mr. W. T. Stead, Mr. St. Loe Strachey, Mr. A. G. Gardiner, Mr. William Ward, Mr. Robert Donald, and others, including Mr. James Marchant, who was, one suspects, the contriver of the whole conspiracy.

Nothing ever gave him greater joy. The co-operation of so many men and women of widely differing creed in furtherance of the common cause and the common faith seemed to him a foretaste of the great fulfilling of all his highest hopes. " I feel it is the very greatest honour that has ever been conferred upon me," he wrote, and that dedication was the most valued heirloom he bequeathed to his posterity. The best was kept to the end.

. . . . .

Now that the Lord was letting His servant depart in peace, his thoughts dwelt much in memory; but it was the memory, not of all he had achieved, but of God's goodness ; not of what he had done for God, but of all God had done for him. The wonderful lyric of the Shepherd God which had comforted the death-bed of the old weaver in the Scottish village seventy-six years ago, the first psalm he ever learned by heart, was now the music which brightened his own death-bed. In times of wakefulness and physical helplessness he constantly repeated it very slowly to himself. Every day, too, he repeated C. E. Mudie's beautiful hymn :

[1] The sonnet is printed in full on p. 526.

I lift my heart to Thee,
  Saviour Divine,
For Thou art all to me,
  And I am Thine.
Is there on earth a closer bond than this,
That my Beloved's mine, and I am His ?

"It seems almost strange to me," he said, "looking back,
that I have always been called to take hold of new enterprises.   I went to a Mission Church in a new district of
Sheffield.   I came to a new and arduous enterprise at
Nottingham.   I have been called to many new enterprises
which seemed to me to help forward the kingdom of God
in the world.   But the wonderful thing is that in every
new enterprise I have been sustained and enriched by
the loving friendship and support of noble men and
women.   Oh ! the grace of God for crowning my life with
His loving-kindness.   God's goodness has followed me all
the way.

"I have had difficulties," he would say.   "What else
could I expect ?   But I have never had to cope with the
sort of difficulties which proceed from envy and spite and
malice.   Truly God has been good to me."

From time to time he was allowed to see friends, though
the time allowed for each visitor was carefully prescribed.

"Mr. Mansbridge kindly said he would come and see
me," he wrote to Mrs. Mansbridge.   "I shall be delighted
to see him, that I may speak to him, especially of the
higher and deeper things which I rejoice to know are now
possessing his heart.   He will do a great work in England,
especially among working men, by winning them to know
the joy of Christ's salvation."

"As I talked to him," Mr. Mansbridge said, "he might
have been a young man fronting the dawn."

Indeed, he was even in his last year projecting new
ventures of faith and reaching out in prayer to America,
to France, to China.   At the end of his life, as all through
it, he was always postulating eternity.   He lived again
in his friends and lieutenants.   "Here, or yonder," he
wrote to Mr. Marchant, "my spirit will be ever with
you."   He saw his great friend, Dr. F. B. Meyer, before
he set out for America in the autumn of 1910, and laid
upon his heart specially the care of the young folk in their
unguarded years.

" He looked worn and spent," said the Rev. J. G. Henderson, " when I saw him last. His strength was fast ebbing away.

" ' I can still do something,' he said, ' I'm spending all my time praying that the Church may reveal my Lord to men. I am afraid they do not see my Lord as He is, in all the wonder of His marvellous grace and redeeming love. If only in His Church they could see Him ! ' "

In the late summer of 1910 his beloved wife was laid low with painful illness. As the weeks went by, it became clear that there was no hope of recovery; but Paton himself had a severe attack of bronchitis, and not till the end was near was he strong enough to know what the doctors said. On Christmas morning, as the church bells were sounding to the Supper of the Lamb, with all her children near her, peacefully she fell asleep. It had always been the Christmas morning which brought round her once again the loved ones whom varied duties had sundered from the home. It was on Christmas morning she passed home from the loved ones who remained to the loved ones who had gone before. No truer helpmeet was ever given to an earthly saint. All that she was to her husband, and through him to others, all that she was in herself not even her husband could have told. She, too, gave her life a ransom for many. Her quiet peacefulness of nature, her deep, strong gentleness, first drew him to her, and in over half a century of closest wedded life he had never sounded the full depths of her self-giving, soul-poised nature. She stood between him and all the small worries of life. She sustained him in all his great endeavour. Her love of God's Word, her intimate knowledge of it, was constantly helping him. Her quietness of spirit and her love were a constant rest to his ardent, impetuous nature. " She was my wisest counsellor," he said. " She shared and enriched every part of my work ; she lightened every burden ; she consecrated every trouble in her utter loyalty to the Lord of her life." His letters to her are full of a wonderful tenderness.

" Bless thee," he writes from abroad on the anniversary of the wedding day, " for thy dear, sacred goodness to thy husband. Ever since that day more than all my heart had hoped for hast thou fulfilled, though sadly have I fulfilled what my heart desires towards thee. . . . I have wedded thee again to my soul before God and the Lamb."

And now the tired hands were folded on the breast, and she was making ready against his coming in the home above, as so often she had made ready for him in the home on earth.

"I have the saddest news to tell you," he writes: "My beloved wife was taken home on Christmas morning. I am now alone, and feel the loneliness. My strong boys have carried me upstairs to her room. I have been twice to see her face, the most beautiful in death that I have ever seen. The purity of it, the calmness and sweetness, are almost inexpressible. I am now alone, dear brother, but my heart is now more than ever in heaven."

The lines which follow were written by the Rev. Thomas Dunlop, of Bootle, for her memorial card:

> The helper's help, her task complete,
> Laid humbly at the Master's feet,
>   In peace has passed;
> Through scores of happy, strenuous years,
> Lit up with smiles, yet tinged with tears,
>   Rest comes at last.
>
> The tired hands folded on the breast;
> In new-born heavenly radiance drest
>   The tranquil face;
> Sweet sleep has closed the weary eyes,
> Tender the thoughts—where now she lies—
>   Haunting the place.
>
> Her task, not less intense and good
> Than his, with philanthropic mood
>   Full to the brim;
> To men he, with big, restless brain,
> A willing slave, with might and main,—
>   And she to him.

And so the link was formed in heaven which drew him to her side. For the time being he bore up beyond all expectation. Never did the light of his faith seem so triumphant. The doctor, who had feared a sudden failure at the end of long suspense, was specially pleased. "The heart seems stronger. We have found just how much work it can do, and it is doing it well." These were the doctor's last words to me before I went back to my work.

Then came a letter from my sister, who had nursed him and her mother devotedly through the long months : " Father is much weaker. There is a reaction. He has been doing too much. It is hard to keep him back." I went home. I found the table at his bedside full of affairs. To all the old activities he had added an interest in the prevention of that preventible blindness which arises from " ophthalmia neonatorum." He was engaged in collecting information for a State Commission recently appointed in New York to inquire and report upon the methods adopted in England for the distribution of congested city population in rural districts. The Home-reading Union, the Lingfield Colony, the League of Honour, were all in evidence.

Always before he had been full of talk about any new interests, or any new hope which had appeared in connection with the old interests, or some kind and helpful letter which had cheered his heart. But this time he said nothing of all these things. He asked me about the school, about the Old Boys' Association, about our Club for Working Lads. I told him how the Grammar School boys had done better than ever before for the club, and I found him rejoicing in all that I told him more than I had ever joyed myself. His eyes were homes of silent prayer, and he spoke, as he always did in the last days, but very quietly, about the goodness of the Lord which had followed him all the days of his life.

It was just a week later, on January 26th, 1911, that the doctor came in for his usual morning visit. " Nurse," he said, " the day looks brighter. When the sun comes out, you may take him into the garden." In the forenoon he was lying on his couch in the " nook," with his head propped upon pillows, when suddenly, without warning, his head fell forward on his breast, and " he was not, for God took him." The sun had come out, and he was taken into the Garden of the Lord where the trees of healing grow.

" So the trumpets sounded for him, and he passed over."

He was spared all pain, all struggle, all sadness of farewell. There was a great calm and fulness of joy.

.   .   .   .   .

The long line of carriages stretching down the road, the

rows of silent houses with drawn blinds, the hushed
assembly in the crowded Church at Castlegate, the last
words of touching tribute from two fellow-labourers who
were so near his heart, Dr. F. B. Meyer and Principal
Ritchie, the strong bass swing of the students' voices
lifting to heaven the hymn of praise—

For all the saints who from their labours rest,

the long, black column of the students, past and present,
old and young, who marched up the hill with their tutors
before the hearse, and said one to the other, " Our Master
is taken from our head to-day " ; the steady tramp of the
Life Brigade boys in uniform following behind ; the throng-
ing crowds in the street ; the man in corduroys at the
street corner with the lifted cap ; the mother from the
cottage home with her "bit of black" ; the hushed gathering
round the open grave ; the prayer of committal read by
the Dean of Norwich ; the parting word of benediction from
the generous friend of so many years, the saintly Bishop of
Hereford ; the long-drawn notes of the boy buglers as they
sounded the Last Post echoing over the valley to that
home upon the hill where for more than forty years he
lived and toiled and prayed ; and, crowning that hill, the
warm glow of a winter sunset, as though the dark hanging veils of the antechamber had been drawn aside and
men's eyes might see through to the glory of the Presence,
into which his soul had found abundant entrance,—such
were the last scenes of a life which had finished its course
with joy, and left its fibre inwoven for ever in the work
which is bringing Christ's kingdom upon earth.

To you, who underneath the weight of years
    Wear the young heart that Hope alone can feed,
    To you, who from the snare of party freed
Christ's will in all our wranglings still can hear,
Who still can see the Gospel vision clear,
    Gleam-follower, you who know the nation's need
    And Churchman of all Churches still must plead
For faith to fight and love to persevere.

To you, knights-errant of the Table Round
    We come with tidings of our perilous quest
        To hear your voice and see your eyes flash light,
    And though no more your lance is set in rest,
Unfaltering still your lips the call shall sound
        To send us back fresh-hearted to the fight.

                              H. D. RAWNSLEY.

1910

BIBLIOGRAPHY

Inspiration, " London Review," July, 1858.
A Review of Renan's " Life of Christ." 1864.
The Origin of the Priesthood in the Christian Church. 1877.
Papers in M. Buisson's " L'Education populaire des adultes en Angleterre," on " The Secondary Education of Working Men," and " The National Home-reading Union." 1896.
Criticisms and Essays. Vol. i. 1895 ; vol ii. 1897.
Church Questions of the Day, containing six Essays and four Appendices (reprinted from above). 1909.
Social Questions of the Day.   Six Booklets.
   1. The Unemployable and the Unemployed.   1904.
   2. Applied Christianity.   1905.
   3. Counter-attractions to the Public-house.   1904.
   4. Secondary Education for the Industrial Classes, etc.   1905.
   5. Continuation Schools from a Higher Point of View, etc. 1905.
   6. How to restore the Yeoman-peasantry of England.   1904.
A Twofold Alternative presented in our time.   1889.
   1. Materialism or Religion.
   2. The Church—a Priestly Caste or a Christian Brotherhood ? With many appendices and notes.
The Life, Faith, and Prayer of the Church.   Four sermons.   1909.
The Inner Mission.   1888.

Published separately.

   1. The Inner Mission of Germany and its Lessons to Us.   1873.
   2. The Inner Mission of the Church.   1884.
   3. The Present State of Europe in Relation to the Wide Spread of the Gospel.   1879.
   4. Woman's Great Work in the Church.   1875.
Inner Mission Pamphlets, two series in 2 vols.   1909.
Inner Mission Leaflets, two series in 1 vol.   1909.
The Moral Training of our Youth.   1908.
" The Social Redemptive Mission of the Free Churches," a manifesto published by the National Free Church Council.   1904.
Organised Independency.   1902.
The Boys' League of Honour.   1907.
Evidence presented to the Royal Commission on the Poor Law 1908.

Charity Organisation Societies and Guilds of Help. A letter addressed to the C.O.S. Annual Conference. 1908.
Present Remedies for Unemployment. 1909.

INNER MISSION PAMPHLETS

First Series

1. The Inner Mission of Great Britain, a paper read before a Congress of Christian Workers at the Chicago Exhibition in 1895.
2. An address on "The Church and her Mission," delivered to the Ministers' Prayer Union of the Free Church of Scotland. 1900.
3. The Origin, Aims, and Methods of the National Home-reading Union. 1888 and 1908.
4. The Home-reading of Senior Scholars. An address prepared for the World's Convention of Sunday-school Teachers. 1886.
5. Evening-schools under Healthy Conditions. A plea for Recreative Continuation Schools. 1885.
6. Recreative Instruction of Young People. 1886.
6a. Supplement to Nos. 5 and 6. "From 13 to 17" (Continuation Evening Classes, Recreative and Practical), by Sir Walter Besant, reprinted from the "Contemporary Review." 1893.
7. Secondary Education for the Industrial Classes. A Memorandum presented to the Royal Commission on Secondary Education. 1905.
7a. The National Home-reading Union and our Public Libraries. 1908.
8. Labour for the Unemployed on the Land. 1894.
9. Home Colonisation. A Plea for Co-operative Colonies of Small Holdings. 1893.
10. How to restore the Yeoman-peasantry of England. 1904.
11. Cottage Industries in Connection with Cottage Farms. A Memorandum to the Government respecting the establishment of Home and Village Industries in Ireland, based on recent experiences in the Kingdom of Würtemberg, etc., with letter from Prince Kropotkin in an Appendix. 1889.
12. How the Small Holdings and Allotments Act may benefit our Country, and our Churches. 1907.

Second Series

1. Applied Christianity. A Civic League (Social and Educational) for our Towns and Cities. 1905.
2. The Unemployable and the Unemployed. 1904.
3. Counter-attractions to the Public-house. How may the drinking habits of the people be changed ? 1904.
4. An Appeal to all Churches to form Sunday and Week-evening Institutes for their Young People. 1906.
5. What are the Sunday Institute and Week-evening Institute of the Sunday-school ? 1906.
6. "The Continuation Schools Bill" explained and commended. 1904.
7. Continuation Schools, from a Higher Point of View. 1905.

8. A Concordat between Church and State for the Guardianship and Training of our Youth. 1906.

8a. The Reading of our Youth. 1908.

9. The P.S.A. Brotherhoods: their Special Mission, and their Relation to our Churches. 1907.

10. The Christian Faith in Relation to Sociology and " Institutes of Social Service." 1902.

INNER MISSION LEAFLETS

First Series

1. The Good News of " The Kingdom." 1884.
2. Christianity and the Well-being of the People. 1873.
3. The Christian Social Union. 1901.
4. Home Reunion. 1887.
5. Social Redemptive Work. 1891.
6. A Message sent to an Assembly of Young Christian People. 1898.
7. The Home Department of the Sunday-school. 1892.
8. Moral Training in Day and Evening Schools. 1897.
9. The Social Institutes' Union. 1901.
10. How to save the Drunkard. 1896.
11. How to control the Drink Traffic. 1886.
12. Associate Guardians. 1901.
13. Juvenile Crime and Immorality in Europe. 1906.
14. The Social Mission of the Church. 1907.
15. The Christian Endeavour Union—a Brigade of Service. 1908.
16. A Letter on Religion in Schools. 1907.

Second Series

1. The Church and " The Kingdom." 1884.
2. Faith which worketh by Love. 1902.
3. Christian Service in Prisons. 1902.
4. Continuation Schools; what they should be, and why. 1888.
5. Pleasant and Useful Evening-schools and Classes Everywhere. 1905.
6. The National Home-reading Union—the People's University. 1904.
7. National Home-reading Union Reading Circles in Schools to encourage and direct Home-reading. 1908.

7a. The Advantages of National Home-reading Union Reading Circles. 1908.

8. Associative Reading—Social Reading Circles. 1908.
9. Suggestions for Reading Circles in Day and Sunday Schools. 1894.
10. The Boys' Life Brigade—its Objects and Methods. 1899.
11. The Boys' League of Honour. 1907.
12. The Young Men's and Young Women's Brigade of Service. 1904.
13. Shall there be Bible Instruction in the National Schools ? 1905.
14. Labour Colonies. 1897.
15. Co-operative Colonies of Small Holdings. 1904.

34

16. The Seasonably Unemployed. 1904.
17. Various kinds of Land and Labour Colonies : an Open Letter to the Right Honourable John Burns, M.P. 1904.
18. The British Institute for Social Service. A Prefatory Note. 1903.
19. Christian Social Programme for the Nation. 1901.
20. Social Work for Christian Women. 1904.
21. " Greater Works than these shall he do that believeth on Me."— John xiv. 12. 1895.
Christ's Miracles of To-day. 1905.
How Local Committees can most wisely and effectively help Cripple Children. 1907.
An Appeal for the Extension of the Scottish Christian Social Union to every District of Scotland. 1908.
The National Home-reading Union and its Work (reprinted from " School," October 1908). 1908.

INDEX

A

Aberdeen, Countess of, 236
Aberdeen, Earl of, 278
Acland, A. H. D., 208, 272, 307, 521
Adeney, Dr., 450
Adler, Dr., 521
Agricultural Banks Association, 241
Agricultural Organisation Society, 241
Airedale College, 178, 332–336
Aitken, Mr. G. A., 521
Albert, Prince, 40
Allon, Dr., 377
American Institute of Social Service, 404, 406–411, 412, 418, 419
American, War, 40
Amos, Mr. Sheldon, 176
Amos, Mrs. Sheldon, 509
Anson, Sir William, 283
Ardenconnel, 440, 441
Argyll, Duke of, 460
Armenia, 510
Associate Guardians, 469, 470, 478
Axon, Mr. W. E. A., 280

B

"Back to the Land," 243
Bailey, Rev. J. R., 472
Baines, Sir Edward, 158, 397
Baker, Mr. James, 236
Ball, Sir Robert, 280
Barker, Dean, 278, 280
Barker, Rev. Professor, 22, 34, 78
Barlow, Miss A. E. F., 282, 291, 520
Barlow, Mr. J. R., 291
Barnes, Mr. F., 68
Barnet, Canon, 419, 515
Barrett, Dr., 377
Barrett, Professor W. F., 280
Barry, Bishop William, 521
Batchelor, Mr., 54, 515
Battersea, Lord, 375
Baynes, Bishop, 474
Bedford, Duchess of, 215
Benham, Dr., 20
Benington, Mr. George M., 313
Benson, Archbishop, 304
Besant, Sir Walter, 212, 493

"Bible Encyclopædia," Kitto's, 176
Bibliotheca Sacra, 337
Bi-centenary of 1662, 40, 70, 83
Biddell, Rev. H., 482
Binney, Rev. Thomas, 23
Birmingham, 25, 26, 70, 217, 218, 220, 474, 478, 488
Birrell, Mr., 283, 393–395, 472, 473
Blackpool, 278–281
Blanc, Louis, 25
Bodelschwingh, Pastor von, 243, 246, 247
Bonn, Conference of Eastern Church and Old Catholics, 144
Booth, General, 447, 448, 483–486, 490
Booth, General Bramwell, 521
Booth, Mrs., 485, 521
Boys' Brigade, 311, 312
Boys' Life Brigade, 303, 312–320, 326–329, 331, 403, 429, 434, 501, 511, 526
Branford, Mr. V. V., 412
Bremer, Miss Frederika, 69
Brierley, Rev. J., 91, 447, 448
Bright, John, 25
Brine, Rev. T., 51
Briscoe, Mr. Potter, 283
Bristol, Bishop of, 280
"Britain's Next Campaign," 261, 470
British Institute for Social Service, 404–420, 499
Brooks, Rev. J. L., 248, 250–256, 261, 266
Brooks, Mrs., 248, 254, 261
Brooks, Shirley, 29
Brotherhood Movement, 217, 291, 486
Brown, Alexander, 5, 6, 13–15, 17
Brown, Dr. Andrew Morton, 6, 8, 13, 20, 21
Brown, Andrew, 17
Brown, Arnesby, 375
Brown, Dr. John, 12
Brown, Mary, 5, 6, 19, 179
Browne, Professor G. F., 280
Browne, Dr. Harold, 142
Bruce, Dr., 9, 13, 14, 16

Bruce, Dr. Robert, 375
Bunting, Sir Percy W., 176, 227, 375, 453, 454, 462, 516
Bunting, Lady, 510
Burns, John, 263–267
Burtt, Mrs. 320
Butler, Mrs. Josephine, 176, 514
Byles, Mr. Holden, 416, 420, 508

C

Cadbury, Mrs. George, 320
Caine, W. S., 227
Campbell, Rev. R. J., 388, 421, 429, 432, 448, 483
Canterbury, Archbishop of, 304, 375, 431, 460, 474
Carlisle, Bishop of, 329
Carpenter, Dr. Boyd, 375, 389, 398, 460
Carter, Mr. John, 360
Cave, Principal, 373
Cecil, Lady Florence, 456
Cecil, Lord William, 456, 460
Chalmers, Dr., 19
Chapman, Rev. H. T., 492
Charity Organisation Society, 418, 419, 475–478
Charteris, Professor, 438
Chautauqua, 271, 275, 276, 403
Cheltenham, 20, 21, 28
Children's Charter, 440
Children's National Guild of Courtesy, 320, 321
China, 453–467, 499
China Missions Emergency Committee, 455–467, 511
Christian Endeavour, 424–429, 433, 434, 511
Christian Social Union, 190, 498
"Christian Spectator," 168
Civic League of Help, Manchester, 472
Clemance, Dr., 338
Clifford, Dr., 492
Cobden, Richard, 25
Collier, Rev. Robert, 288
Collins, Professor Churton, 279, 280
Cologne, Congress of Old Catholics, 143
Colony of Mercy, 243, 246–269
"Colony of Mercy, A," 243, 246
Conder, Rev. J. W., 78
Congregational Union, Birmingham, 70
Contagious Diseases Act, 133, 483
"Contemporary Review," 174–176, 227, 236, 245, 272, 276

Continuation Schools, 210, 245, 370, 444, 490
Convalescent Home, West Kirby, 232
Co-operative Holdings, 505
Co-operative Holidays Association, 228–234, 282, 284, 313, 440
Coote, Rev. W. A., 211, 450
Corry, Miss L. M., 321
Cory, Mr. John, 260
Cremer, Rev. F. D., 472
Crosbie, Rev. W., 300, 379
Crossley, Mr. John, 68

D

Dale, Dr. R. W., 22, 23, 67, 68, 145, 176, 208 note, 481
Dangerfield, Mr. R., 263, 416
Danish High Schools, 440, 441
Darlington, Mr. T. H., 429
Darvel, 9, 10, 13, 436
Davidson, Archbishop, 431, 460, 474
Dawbarn, Miss Frances, 320
Dawson, Mr. Albert, 423
Dawson, George, 26
Devine, Mr. Henry C., 241, 242
Dickson, Rev. J. W., 108, 347–373, 374
Dixon, Captain J. A., 312
Dobell, Sidney, 28, 29, 69, 70
Döllinger, Dr., 139, 143, 174
Donald, Mr. Robert, 521
Dorner, 134, 174
Du Cane, General Sir, 257
Duff, Dr. Archibald, 134 note
Duncan, Dr., 300, 301
Dunlop, Rev. Thomas, 524
Durham, Bishop of, 375, 521

E

Eastwood Boys' Life Brigade, 316
"Eclectic Review, The," 45, 46, 59, 63, 67–71
Ede, Dr. Moore, Dean of Worcester, 161, 280, 377
Education, 20, 69, 83–87, 145–164, 179–185, 200–211, 270–297, 298–310, 389–403, 473
Education Act, 1870, 145–156, 270, 279, 285, 287; 1902, 389–392; 1906, 393–401, 473
Education, Commercial, 182, 183
Education, Technical, 179–183, 200–211
Edwards, Mr. W. N., 316
Egypt, 377

Elberfeld System, 138, 139, 261, 441, 468–478, 489
Elementary Trade and Science Schools, 201
Ellis, Mrs. Tom, 429
Emerson, R. W., 25
Enfield, Mr. Richard, 157, 159–162, 164, 165
English International Peace Congress, 1904, 415
English Land Colonisation Society, 237, 241
Ervine, Rev. T., 77

F

Fairbairn, Dr., 176, 338, 375
Fairbairns, Mrs., 44
Farrar, Dean, 278, 280
Federation of Working Men's Clubs, 218, 283
Felkin, Mr. H. M., 180, 182 note
Fenwick, 436
Ferrier, Dr., 16
Figgis, Rev. J., 78
Fildes, Alderman, 472
Fitch, Sir Joshua, 275, 276, 278, 280, 283
Fitzgerald, Rev. W. B., 331
Fitzmaurice, Lord Edmond, 163
Fliedner, Theodore, 188, 319
Flower, Rev. J. E., 272, 375
Forbush, Dr., 501
Forsyth, Dr., 375, 520
"Fortnightly Review," 177
Fraser, Mr. Drummond, 231
Fredericksoord, 265, 266, 268
Free Church Council, 190, 384, 386, 387
Free Church of Scotland, 17, 19, 380–384
Friedrichs, Professor, 143
Fulham Palace Conference, 389
Fulton, Dr., 16

G

Galston, 3, 5, 11, 13, 436
Garden City, Letchworth, 415, 500, 504
Gardiner, Mr. A. G., 521
Garnett, Dr. Richard, 283
Garnett, Dr. W., 283
Garnett, Mrs. W., 320
Garvie, Dr., 511, 521
Gavazzi, Friar, 25
Geddes, Professor, 412, 417, 504

Germany, 134, 138, 139, 143, 144, 177, 179, 187, 188, 319, 441, 468, 516
Gibson, Rev. A. G. E., 108, 109
Gibson, Dr. Monro, 247, 375
Girls' Evening Homes, 203, 293, 306, 490
Girls' Life Brigade, 303, 320, 324, 403, 429, 511
Girls' Public Day School Company, 184
Gittings, Rev. Enoch, 122
Gladstone, Mr. W. E., 160, 174
Glasgow, 54, 111, 217, 291, 338, 437
Gloucester, 20, 21
Gore, Bishop, 377, 474
Gorst, Sir John, 283
Gosse, P. H., 69
Gothenburg System, 167, 227, 228
Gott, Rev. Dr., 377
Gough, J. B., 25
Gould, Miss Jay, 405
Grant, Rev. James, 113
Graves, Mr. A. P., 283
Gray, Mr., 178
Gray, Percival, 231–233
Greenwood, Rev. George, 377
Greg, Mrs., 291
Grundy, Mr. W. S. P., 472
Guild of Courtesy, 320, 321
Guilds of Help, 471, 472, 475–478
Guthrie, Dr., 489
Guttery, Rev. T., 492

H

Haggard, Rider, 237
Hale, Edward Everett, 501
Halle, 134, 516
Hamburg, Raue Haus, 134
Hannay, Dr., 306, 338
Hareshawmuir, 412, 436, 437, 498
Harnack, Professor, 134
Harris, Mr. Alfred, 236, 237, 243
Harris, Mr. Nugent, 241
Harrison, Frederick, 176, 179
Harrison, Mr. Henry, 507
Harrison, Miss Jane, 280
Harrop, Rev. W., 98
Hart, Mrs. Ernest, 236
Hart, Sir Robert, 460
Hartland, Rev. E. J., 78
Hartley, Sir William, 465
Hatch, Rev. Edwin, 176
Haweis, Rev. H. R., 280
Hazell, Mr. Walter, 239, 247
Hearn, Miss, 301
Heath, Richard, 176, 236

Hecht, Charles E., 509
Ileley, Mr. Frank C., 324, 325
Heller, Mr. T. E. (N.U.T.), 278
Henderson, Rev. J. G., 523
Herbert, Rev. C., 91
Hewins, Mr. W. A. S., 272
Higgs, Mrs. Mary, 321, 324, 498, 518
High School for Girls, Nottingham, 184
Hilditch, Mr., 93
Hill, Dr. Alexander, 281, 282, 291, 375, 450
Hill, Miss Octavia, 490
Hobson, Mr. T. F., 281
Holden, Rev. J., 91
Holland, Canon Scott, 502, 510, 511, 512
Hollesley Colony, 264
Holmes, Rev. (Whitefields), 221
Home Reunion Society, 377, 378
Hood, Rev. E. Paxton, 71
Horton, Dr., 415, 492, 495, 521
Howell, Mr. George, 278
Howie, Rev. G. W., 424
Howitt, Mary, 69
Hüber, Professor, 139–141, 143, 487
Hudson, Miss M. E., 320
Hughes, Rev. H. Price, 278, 303, 492
Hughes, Mrs. H. Price, 321, 324, 424, 435
Hunt, Mr., 268, 269
Hunter, Dr. John, 91, 112
Huxley, Professor, 168–170, 173

I

Ingram, Bishop, 389
Inner Mission, 186–199, 263, 310, 335, 338, 376, 406, 438, 448, 449, 472
Institute, Nottingham Congregational, 75–93, 95–130, 332–374, 447–451, 522, 526; founding, 78, 79; new building, 92; majority, 336, 338–345; sermon-class, 98–106, 125–127, 348–360; communion service, 127–129, 346–348; Association of Old Students, 186; Students' Trust Fund, 336; Old Students' Library, 373; Morley Hall, 98, 339; Thanksgiving Fund, 450
Institute of Social Service, 404–420
Isbister, Mr., 505

J

Jackson, Rev. Robert, 115–118
James, John Angell, 26, 489

James, Rev. G. Howard, 492
Jast, Mr. L. Stanley, 283
Jebb, Miss, 502
Jerusalem, 487
Johnston, Dr. J. G., 520
Johnston, Sir S. G., 167
Jones, Mr. B. (C.W.S.), 278
Jones, Prebendary Harry, 280
Jones, Professor Henry, 438
Jones, Rev. J. D., 328
Jowett, Rev. J. H., 474

K

Kaiserwerth, Diakonissin-institut, 134, 188, 319
Kekewich, Sir George, 283
Kelly, Rev. C. H., 387
Kenny, Dr. Courtney S., 280
Kidd, Mr. G. B., 347
Kilmarnock, 1, 11, 13, 16, 18, 66, 436
"Kilmarnock Herald," 18
Kimmins, Dr., 280, 283, 291
King, Mr. Joseph, 272
Kitchin, Dean, 247
Knoodt, Professor, 143
Knox, Bishop, 473
Kossuth, Louis, 25

L

Labour Colonies, 239–245, 263–269
Land Question, 235–245, 263–269
Lang, Dr. Marshall, 438
Langham St. Conference, 377, 378, 482
Laveleye, Professor, 176, 236
Lawrence, Mrs. Pethick, 510
Lawrence, Rev. T. J., 278, 281
Lawrance, Thomas D., 313
League of Honour, 303, 321–325, 429, 525
League of Ministering Children, 326, 502
League of Social Service, 404, 411
Lee, Mr. Arthur, 44
Lenwood, Mr. Frank, 518
Leonard, Mr. T. A., 216, 228–231, 312, 313
Lewis, Miss Annie, 203
Li, Prince, 462, 466
Lidgett, Rev. Scott, 280, 433, 492
Lidgett, Miss, 510
Lightfoot, Bishop, 176
Lingfield Colony, 232, 246, 248–253, 260–269, 376, 501, 511, 525
Liscombe, Mr., 429

Liverpool, 226
Loch, Mr., 418, 477
"London Quarterly Review," 168, 176
London School Board, 207, 215–217, 223, 224
Lotze, Professor, 134
Loudoun, 1, 9
Louise, H.R.H. Princess, 207, 282, 291
Lyttleton, The Hon. Rev. E., 521
Lytton, Earl of, 412

M

Macalister, Professor Alexander, 456
Macdonald, Ramsay, 521
Macfadyen, Rev. J. A., 280
Mackail, Professor, J. W., 283
MacLaren, Dr., 235, 362
Maclure, Dean, 247
Manning, Miss Anne, 69
Mansbridge, Mr. Albert, 503, 504, 522
Mansfield College, 499
Marchant, James, 286, 484 note, 519, 520, 521
Marple Dale Colony, 261
Marquis, Mr. F., 294, 472, 479
Marshall, Professor Milnes, 280
Marshall, Rev. H. T., 492
McCall, Mr., 178
McCallum, Dr., 255 note, 259
McKenzie, Dr. Douglas, 462
McLaren, Lady, 521
McLeod, Dr. Norman, 6, 9, 10, 15, 19
McLeod, Donald, 9
Meadowhead, 4, 436
Meakin, Mr. Budgett, 411, 412, 419
Meath, Lord, 322
Meath, Lady, 326, 502
Medd, Canon, 377
Meeson, Rev. J. A., 488, 491–493
Memorial to Government on Religious Difficulty, 147–151
Memorial to University of Cambridge, 162
Meyer, Rev. F. B., 246, 247, 521, 522, 526
Miall, Edward, 25
Michaud, Abbé, 143
Miller, Dr. Andrew, 438
Miller, Lewis, 271
Miller, Mr., 111
Mills, Mr. J. Saxon, 218
Mills, Rev. Herbert, 258
Milne, Mr. S., 89, 90

Ministering Children's League, 326, 502
Ministers' Bible and Prayer Union, 192
Ministers' Prayer Union of Free Church of Scotland, 380–384
Mins, Rev. J. H., 32
Moat Farm, Aldborough, 240
Mondy, Miss M. C., 281, 282, 291
Moore, Mr. Harold, 243, 245, 248
Moore, Miss Rose, 330
Moorhouse, Bishop, 35, 36
Morant, Sir Robert, 283, 296
Morison, Rev. James, 11, 13, 19
Morley, Charles, 182
Morley, Samuel, 68, 75, 78, 79, 131–133, 165, 166, 182, 184, 263, 332, 333 and note, 485
Morley Hall, 339
Morse, Canon, 132, 133, 147, 159, 164, 186
Morton, Mr. William, 260, 291
Moser, Mrs., 420, 478
Muir, Dr. McAdam, 438
Müller, J., 134
Mundella, Mr. A. J., 164
Murray, Dr. J. H., 280
Musée Social of Paris, 411, 412, 419

N

Nasse, Professor, 139–141, 236, 487
National Free Church Council, 190, 384–386, 387, 505
National Home Reading Union, 229, 270–297, 303, 305, 306, 310, 429, 490, 501, 505, 511, 525, 572
National Union of Free Churches, 190, 488–493
National Union for Christian Social Service, 190, 246–269, 303, 505, 511
National Vigilance Association, 211, 450
Nelson, Lord, 377
Neuchatel Colony, 267
Newman, Professor Francis W., 24, 176
Newman, Sir George, 432
Newtonmore, 235, 436, 521
Nightingale, Florence, 40
Norton, Mr. H. E., 315, 321
Nottingham, 79, 86, 88, 131–134, 147, 151, 156–164, 167, 183, 184, 200–204, 207, 208, 216, 217, 225–228, 316, 326–328, 332–346, 375, 379, 395, 474, 478, 482, 517, 526; Addison Street Church, 124; Nottingham Board of Guardians,

478; Castle Museum, 167, 228; Castlegate Church, 338, 447, 448, 526; Chamber of Commerce, 183; Friar Lane Church, 89, 346, 347; High School for Girls, 184; League, 147, 397; Mechanics' Institution, 157; Park Hill Congregational Church, 300, 379, 451, 452; Recreative Evening Schools, 204; School Board Election Address, 156; University College, 160, 164, 180–182; University Extension, 156–164; Y.M.C.A., 165–167
Nottingham, Literary and Philosophical Society, 183

O

O'Connor, Feargus, 25
Old Catholic Movement, 140–144, 177, 195
Old Catholics' Conference with Eastern Church, 143
Oliver, Miss M., 203
Ollard, Rev. Henry, 79, 123, 124, 507
Orr, Professor James, 438
Oswestry, 29
Owens, Rev. A. J., 129, 130

P

Pacy, Mr., 283
Paris, 70, 72–74, 134–137, 178
Parker, Dr. Joseph, 41, 76, 85, 421
Parr, Rev. Tolefree, 247
Passive Resistance, 392
Paton, Alan (brother), 53
Paton, Alexander (father), 3, 4, 6, 7, 11–18, 54, 179
Paton, Andrew B. (brother), 14, 260, 291, 436, 481
Paton, Annie (sister), 179
Paton, Caroline M. (daughter, Mrs. Phillips Figgis), 203
Paton, James (brother), 53, 291
Paton, Dr. James, 437
Paton, Jessie (wife), 54–65, 72–74, 339, 340, 375, 448, 451, 452, 520, 524
Paton, Jessie Muriel (daughter), 339, 340, 451, 516, 517
Paton, John Brown, birth, Dec. 17th, 1830, 3; school, 7, 9, 10; Springhill, 1846–1853, 21–29; double M.A. London University, 1854, 29; Pastor of Sheffield Wicker Church, 1854–1863, 32–52; marriage, Sept.

14th, 1859, 63; tutor of Cavendish College, 76–79; editor of "Eclectic Review," 1856–1862, 66–78; Principal of Nottingham Congregational Institute, Sept. 10th, 1863, 79–94; declines invitation to Principalship of Airedale College, 178, 179, 332–336; retires from Principalship of Nottingham Congregational Institute, June, 1898, 332–346, 375–377; Hon. D.D. of Glasgow University, 338; Associate Principal, 346; Principal Emeritus, 1899, 346; Ministerial Jubilee, Oct., 1905, 447–452; golden wedding, Sept., 1909, 520; death, Jan. 26th, 1911, 525
Paton, Captain John, 4, 5, 436
Paton, Mary (sister), 53
Paton, William (uncle), 10, 11
Paton, William P. (father-in-law), 54
Paton, William P. (son), 231–233
"Patriot, The," 46, 70, 71, 486
Pearce, Mr., 218
Pearse, Mark Guy, 303
Peckover, the Misses, 290
People's Café Company, 335
Percival, Bishop J., 177, 182, 208, 247, 272, 278, 280, 281, 291, 338, 375, 376, 471, 521, 526
Perry, Mr., 68
Plunkett, The Hon. Horace, 236
Poole, 8, 9
Poor Law Commission (1907), 478
Poore, Major R., 237
Poplar Colony, 264
Powell, Professor York, 290
Prayer Union, 379–388
Pressensé, Dr., 136, 176
Pridham, Miss M. R., 282
Priestman, Mr. and Mrs., 471
"Progress," 416, 478
P.S.A. Movement, 229, 291, 432, 486

R

Radcliffe, Mr. Reginald, 178
Raffeisen Banks, 241, 268
Ramsay, Rev. Rolland, 412, 438, 440, 441, 446, 484
Rawnsley, Canon, 230, 296, 520, 521, 525
Rawson, Mr. H. R., 272
Read, Miss Ada M., 282
Recreative Evening Schools Association, 204–211, 215, 305, 306, 310

Redford, Rev. R. A., 377
Reid, Rev. Robert, 99–105
Reinkens, Bishop, 142, 143
Reith, Dr. George, 438
Renan, M., 71, 72, 168, 173, 174
Reynolds, Dr., 344, 377, 379, 380
Richard, Dr. Timothy, 453, 459, 461, 462, 464
Ridding, Bishop, 375, 395
Ridley, Sir Matthew White, 280
Rigi Scheideck, Conference at, 139–141, 487
Ritchie, Rev. D. L., 124, 447, 526
Ritschl, 134
Roberts, Principal, 429
Roberts, Sir Owen, 281
Roberts, Dr. Richard, 272, 273, 280
Roberts, Rev. Richard, 515
Robinson, Dr. Armitage, 455, 456, 501
Rodway, Mr. A. H., 218
Rogers, Mr. Frederick, 412
Rogers, Rev. Guinness, 78, 280
Rogers, Professor Henry, 21, 23–25, 66
Rooseveldt, Theodore, 404
Roscoe, Sir Henry, 280
Rothera, Mr. Charles L., 225
Rowland, Rev. A. Norman, 316
Rowley, Mr. Charles, 272
Russel, Alexander, 18, 19
Russell, Mr. C. E. B., 330
Russell, Rev. David, 13
Rustem Pasha, 176

S

Sadler, Dr. M. E., 272–283, 393, 400, 440, 511
Salvation Army Colony at Hadleigh, 239
Saville, Rev. A. T., 508
Scottish Christian Social Union, 190, 217 note, 437–446, 484, 498
Shaftesbury Lectures, 411
Shalders, William, 22
Shanghai Centenary Conference of Missions, 459, 460
Shaw, Rev. Hudson, 273
Sheffield, 30–52, 80–82, 260, 484, 485, 513, 522 ; Queen St. Church, 31, 32 ; Wicker Church, 31–47, 51, 52, 80–82, 260 ; Garden Street, 34, 51, 52
Shelly, Mr. John, 377
Sherwell, Mr. Arthur, 259
Sibbertoft, Rev. C., 88
Sidebottom, Mr. J. W., 78

Sidgwick, Professor Henry, 159, 176, 279
Simkinson, Mr., 506
Simpson, Sir Alexander, 456
Sinclair, Archdeacon, 218, 247, 431
Sinclair, Right Hon. John, 441
Smith, Alexander, 69
Smith, Professor George Adam, 438
Smith, Professor Goldwin, 176
Smith, Samuel, 208, 411
Smith, Mr. Thomas, 207
Smith, Sir W. A., 311
Social Institutes, 212–228, 313
Social Institute Union, 218
" Social Service," 261
Somervell, Rev. C., 451, 452
Spencer, Herbert, 173, 174, 361
Spicer, Sir Evan, 375
Springhill College, 21–25, 29
Spurr, Rev. F. C., 285, 428
Starnthwaite Colony, 258, 259
Stead, Mr. Herbert, 411, 412
Stead, Mr. W. T., 521
Stempel, Miss Therose, 320
Stevenson, Mr. Fleming, 191
Strahan, Mr. Alexander, 174, 175
Streuli, Rev. Arnold, 472, 473
Strong, Dr. Josiah, 404, 405, 410, 411, 415, 419, 513
Stuart, Mr. James, 191
Stuart, Professor James, 157–162 and note, 174, 279, 504, 514
Students' Christian Union, 190, 461, 463, 464, 496
Students' Trust Fund, 336
Sunday School, The, 38, 274, 291, 293, 298–310, 311–331, 402, 429, 432, 502
Sutherland, Duchess of, 267, 268
Sutter, Miss Julie, 243, 246–248, 260, 470, 471
Sutton, Mr. C. W., 284
Sutton, Mr. R. C., 92
Symes, Professor J. S., 280

T

Tatlow, Rev. Tissington, 463
Taylor, Mr. George, 96
Taylor, Mr. G. W., 207
Taylor-Smith, Bishop, 521
Technical Education, 179–183, 200–211
Temperance, 14, 15, 18, 25, 36, 133, 134, 167, 212–231, 335, 434, 491
Temple, Dr. F. (Archbishop), 278, 294, 375
Temple, Rev. William, 294, 441, 442, 444

Tholuck, Dr., 134, 177
Thomasson, Mr. J. P., 260, 290
Thomson, Rev. J. Radford, 76–78, 377, 507
Thornbury, Walter, 69
Thornton, Mr. J. S., 440 and note.
Tinling, Rev. J. F. B., 246, 247, 261, 411
Tolman, Dr., 412
Tomlinson, Mr., 258
Towers, Miss A. E., 320
Towers, Mrs., 320
Towers, Rev. T., 220
Towers, Rev. W. H., 91, 346
Toynbee Bank Association, 241
Tucker, Miss Fanny, 260
Tucker, Mr. George, 260, 513, 519
Tulloch, Principal, 69
Tyndall, Professor, 176, 177

U

University College, Nottingham, 160, 164, 180–182
University Extension, 156–164, 273–276, 280, 306, 403
Universities' Mission, 459, 461

V

Van Schulle, 143
Vaughan, Father Bernard, 521
Vaughan, Robert Alfred, 26–28 (and note 27), 54, 67, 70
Verney, Lady, 245
Village Preachers' Union, 46, 75
Vincent, Bishop, 271–276, 303
Voysey, Mr. Charles, 521

W

Wakefield, Bishop Russell, 526
Wallingford Colony, 261, 267 note
Walshe, Rev. Gilbert W., 456
Ward, Mr. William, 521

Warden, Mr. G. F., 412
Watson, Dr. David, 437, 438, 440, 444–446
Watson, Dr. John, 411, 433, 496
Webb, Mr. and Mrs. Sidney, 478
Weeks, Rev. F. W. B., 32
Week-evening Institute, 307–310, 326–328, 330, 428
Welldon, Bishop, 455
Wellhausen, 134
Wells, Commander, 314
Westcott, Bishop, 375, 521
Westminster College, 499
Westminster, Dean of (Dr. Armitage Robinson), 455, 456, 501
Westrope, Rev. Richard, 492
Wichern, Dr. I., 134, 188, 257
Wilberforce, Archdeacon, 192, 214
Williams, Rev. Charles, 88
Williams, Rev. F. S., 79, 117, 123, 124
Williams, Mr. Fleetwood H., 218
Williamson, Rev. H. R., 497
Wills, Alfred, 69
Winterstoke, Lord, 466
Woodall, Mr., 29
Woodward, Major R. C., 316
Wordsworth, Bishop, 141, 337
Workers' Educational Association, 503
Working Men's Club and Institute Union, 283
Working Women's Institute, 335
Wright, Mr. R. Patrick, 441

Y

Yerburgh, Mr. R., 280, 290
Y.M.C.A., Nottingham, 165–167, 335
Young Men's Brigade of Service, 221, 421–435, 511
Young Women's Brigade of Service, 221, 424–435, 511

Printed by Hazell, Watson & Viney, Ld., London and Aylesbury.